F6
TAXATION (UK)

STUDY TEXT

ACCA

Fourth edition October 2009

ISBN 978-1-84808-019-5

Published by

Get Through Guides Ltd.
Unit – 2, 308A Melton Road
Leicester LE47SL
United Kingdom

Website: www.GetThroughGuides.com

Email: info@GetThroughGuides.com

Student Support Forum: http://GetThroughGuides.co.uk/forum

Limit of liability / Disclaimer of warranty: While the publisher has used its best efforts in preparing this book, it makes no warranties or representations with respect to the accuracy or completeness of contents of this book and specifically disclaims any implied warranties of merchantability or fitness for any specific or general purpose. No warranty may be created or extended by sales or other representatives or written sales material. Each company is different and the suggestions made in this book may not suit a particular purpose. Companies/individuals should consult professionals where appropriate. The publisher shall not be liable for any loss of profit or other commercial damages including but not limited to special, incidental, consequential or other damages.

All rights reserved. No part of this publication may be reproduced, stored in a retrieval system or transmitted, in any form or by any means, electronic, mechanical, photocopying, scanning or otherwise, without the prior written permission of Get Through Guides Ltd.

The publisher has made every effort to contact the holders of copyright material. If any such material has been inadvertently overlooked the publishers will be pleased to make the necessary arrangements at the first opportunity.

No responsibility for any loss to anyone acting or refraining from action as a result of any material in this publication can be accepted by the author, editor or publisher.

Please check the back of this book for any updates / errata. Further live updates / errata may also be found online on the Get Through Guides Student Support Forum at: http://getthroughguides.co.uk/forum. Students are advised to check both of these locations.

© Get Through Guides 2009

STUDY CONTENTS

F6-TAXATION (UK)

About the paper   i - vi

Section A — The UK tax system

1. The overall function and purpose of taxation in a modern economy.   A1.1 - A1.4
2. Different types of taxes   A2.1 - A2.4
3. Principal sources of revenue law and practice   A3.1 - A3.4
4. Tax avoidance and tax evasion   A4.1 - A4.4

Section B — Income tax liabilities

1. The scope of income tax   B1.1 - B1.4
2. Income from employment   B2.1 - B2.44
3. Income from self – employment (Part 1)   B3.1 - B3.30
3. Income from self – employment (Part 2)   B3.31 - B3.64
3. Income from self – employment (Part 3)   B3.65 - B3.94
3. Income from self – employment (Part 4)   B3.95 - B3.110
4. Property and investment income   B4.1 - B4.18
5. The comprehensive computation of taxable income and income tax liability   B5.1 - B5.26
6. The use of exemptions and reliefs in deferring and minimising income tax liabilities   B6.1 - B6.14

Section C — Chargeable gains

1. The scope of the taxation of capital gains   C1.1 - C1.6
2. The basic principles of computing gains and losses   C2.1 - C2.20
3. Further principles of computing gains and losses   C3.1 - C3.12
4. Gains and losses on the disposal of movable and immovable property   C4.1 - C4.22
5. Gains and losses on the disposal of shares and securities   C5.1 - C5.24
6. The use of exemptions and reliefs in deferring and minimising tax liabilities arising on the disposal of capital assets   C6.1 - C6.24

Section D — Corporation tax liabilities

1. The scope of corporation tax   D1.1 - D1.8
2. Profits chargeable to corporation tax (Part 1)   D2.1 - D2.24
3. Profits chargeable to corporation tax (Part 2)   D2.25 - D2.52
4. The comprehensive computation of corporation tax liability   D3.1 - D3.16
5. The effect of a group corporate structure for corporation tax purposes   D4.1 - D4.22

Section E — National insurance contributions

1. National insurance: scope and class 1 and 1a contributions for employed persons   E1.1 - E1.10
2. Class 2 and Class 4 contributions for self- employed persons   E2.1 - E2.6

Section F — Value added tax

1. The scope of value added tax (VAT)   F1.1 - F1.8
2. The VAT registration requirements   F2.1 - F2.12
3. The computation of VAT liabilities   F3.1 - F3.30
4. The effect of special schemes   F4.1 - F4.6

STUDY CONTENTS

F6-TAXATION (UK)

Section G — The obligations of tax payers and /or their agents

1. The systems for self- assessment and the making of returns — G1.1 - G1.6
2. The time limits for the submission of information, claims and payment of tax, including payments on account — G2.1 - G2.14
3. The procedures relating to enquiries, appeals and disputes — G3.1 - G3.6
4. Penalties for non- compliance — G4.1 - G4.6

Index — 1 - 4

Total Page Count: 552

A government does not intend taxes to be neutral but to encourage or discourage certain activities. The objectives will change over time and successive governments. Increasingly the UK government tax policy is influenced by worldwide economic influences such as international defence policy and overseas aid.

1.2 Social purpose of taxation

Politicians use taxation policies to encourage social justice; however, there are many different ideas as to what constitutes social justice. The taxation system within the UK would suggest that it operates on an equitable basis. The taxation policies are intended to redistribute income and wealth. In a bid to direct funds away from the rich and towards the poor, the UK government adopts a process of redistributing wealth through its taxation policies. This is the Robin Hood Principle.

There are various principles to consider when debating the social justice of taxation:

1. **The progressive / regressive principle**

a) **Progressive:** a tax such as the income tax demonstrates the progressive principle. As income rises so does the proportion of tax i.e. the rate of tax rises as well as the amount of tax. This can be considered as just and fair, as the higher tax payments are made by those with higher incomes. Taxes which take a higher percentage of the incomes of higher income earners are said to be progressive.

b) **Regressive:** as income rises, the proportion of tax decreases, e.g. the tax on a packet of cigarettes remains the same, regardless of the income of the consumer. Regressive taxes can be justified in that smokers are likely to require additional hospital care, so only they should contribute towards the cost of it. Taxes which take a higher proportion of the incomes from lower income earners are said to be regressive.

2. **The income / capital / expenditure principle**

a) **Income:** tax on income is just, because it is only paid by people who have income. People who have very low incomes can be taken out of the tax net by the use of personal allowances and effective tax rates.

b) **Capital:** tax on capital is just, as it ensures that people are not avoiding tax by having no income and living off the disposal of capital assets.

c) **Expenditure:** tax on expenditure is just, because it is only incurred by those who spend, not those who save.

3. **The ability to pay / benefit principle**

a) **Ability to pay:** tax is only paid by people who have the income to pay.

b) **Benefit:** people should only contribute to those types of government expenditure from which they are going to benefit.

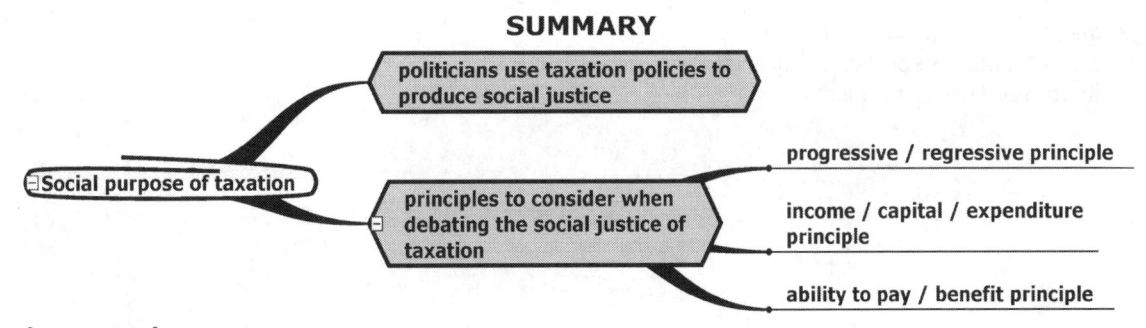

SUMMARY

Social purpose of taxation
- politicians use taxation policies to produce social justice
- principles to consider when debating the social justice of taxation
  - progressive / regressive principle
  - income / capital / expenditure principle
  - ability to pay / benefit principle

1.3 Environmental concerns

A specific use of taxation in influencing behaviour is in relation to the environment. These are commonly referred to as "Green Taxes". Currently there are environmental concerns about renewable and non-renewable energy and global warming.

It is considered unlikely that individuals will contribute voluntarily to protect the environment as they are unlikely to be affected in their lifetime by the changes taking place. As a result, the government aims to protect the environment through taxation and spending policies.

These policies include:

a) Taxation on vehicles and fuel provided by companies: taxable benefits are based on the CO_2 emission.
b) Climate change levy which relates to the proportion of energy consumed by businesses.
c) Landfill tax charged on operators of landfill sites to encourage recycling.

These taxes are part of the UK's Climate Change Programme published by the Government on 17 November 2000.

A1.4: The UK Tax System

Tax policies are formulated with an aim to increase government revenues. They are framed on the basis of clear principles such as:

a) savings and investments
b) fairness
c) equality
d) enhancing work efficiency

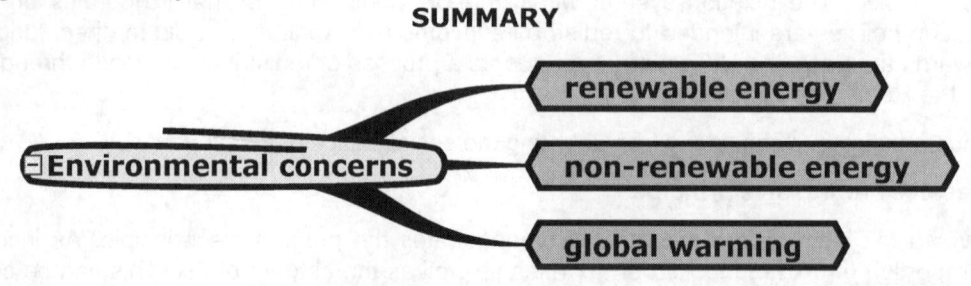

SUMMARY

Environmental concerns
- renewable energy
- non-renewable energy
- global warming

Quick Quiz

Fill in the blanks.

1. The UK tax system is managed by_____.

Answer to Quick Quiz

1. Her Majesty's Revenue and Customs (HMRC).

Self Examination Question

Question 1

What are the various principles to consider when debating the social justice of taxation?

Answer to Self Examination Question

Answer 1

The various principles to consider when debating the social justice of taxation are:

- the progressive / regressive principle
- the income / capital / expenditure principle
- the ability to pay / benefit principle

AIM

To develop knowledge and skills relating to the tax system as applicable to the individuals, single companies, and groups of companies.

APPROACH TO EXAMINING THE SYLLABUS

The syllabus is assessed by a three-hour paper-based examination.

Assessment: Taxation (UK)

The paper will be predominantly computational and will have five questions, all of which will be compulsory.

Question	Topic	Marks
1	Income Tax	55
2	Corporation Tax	
3	Chargeable gains	20
4	Any area of syllabus	15
5	Any area of syllabus	15

There will always be at a minimum of 10 marks on value added tax. These marks will normally be included within question one or question two, although there might be a separate question on value added tax.

National insurance contributions will not be examined as a separate question, but may be examined in any question involving income tax or corporation tax.

Groups and overseas aspects of corporation tax will only be examined in question two, and will account for no more than one third of the marks available for that question.

Questions one or two might include a small element of chargeable gains.

Any of the five questions might include the consideration of issues relating to the minimisation or deferral of tax liabilities.

There are various differences between the order of the syllabus published by the ACCA and the layout of the GTG study text. These differences are a result of changes which have been adopted to make the text easier to read and understand. These changes are as follows:

1. Sections C and D have been reversed and re-labelled accordingly.
2. The content of chapter C5 has been covered in various chapters throughout the same section (GTG Section D).
3. The order of chapters in Section D (GTG Section C) has been changed and can be mapped to the original ACCA syllabus as shown in the table below:

Section & chapter number	
ACCA	GTG
D1	C1
D2 Learning Outcome a,b,c	C2
D2 Learning Outcome d,e,f	C3
D3	C4
D4	C5
D5	C2
D6	C6
E2	E1
E3	E2

DETAILED SYLLABUS

A The UK TAX SYSTEM

1. The overall function and purpose of taxation in a modern economy
2. Different types of taxes
3. Principal sources of revenue law and practice
4. Tax avoidance and tax evasion

B Income tax liabilities

1. The scope of income tax
2. Income from employment
3. Income from self-employment
4. Property and investment income
5. The comprehensive computation of taxable income and income tax liability
6. The use of exemptions and reliefs in deferring and minimising income tax liabilities

C Corporation tax liabilities

1. The scope of corporation tax
2. Profits chargeable to corporation tax
3. The comprehensive computation of corporation tax liability
4. The effect of a group corporate structure for corporation tax purposes
5. The use of exemptions and reliefs in deferring and minimising corporation tax liabilities

D Chargeable gains

1. The scope of the taxation of capital gains
2. The basic principles of computing gains and losses.
3. Gains and losses on the disposal of movable and immovable property
4. Gains and losses on the disposal of shares and securities
5. The computation of capital gains tax payable by individuals
6. The use of exemptions and reliefs in deferring and minimising tax liabilities arising on the disposal of capital assets

E National insurance contributions

1. The scope of national insurance
2. Class 1 and Class 1A contributions for employed persons
3. Class 2 and Class 4 contributions for self-employed persons

F Value added tax

1. The scope of value added tax (VAT)
2. The VAT registration requirements
3. The computation of VAT liabilities
4. The effect of special schemes

G The obligations of tax payers and/or their agents

1. The system for self-assessment and the making of returns
2. The time limits for the submission of information, claims and payment of tax, including payments on account
3. The procedures relating to enquiries, appeals and disputes
4. Penalties for non-compliance

SECTION A

THE UK TAX SYSTEM

A1

STUDY GUIDE A1: THE OVERALL FUNCTION AND PURPOSE OF TAXATION IN A MODERN ECONOMY

■ Get Through Intro

Tax is a financial charge imposed by the government. The fundamental purpose of taxation is to finance government expenditure. Any money the government expends mostly comes from taxation.

You will agree that having to pay tax from you earnings is a painful experience. You must also have wondered why the government needs to collect taxes. What is the purpose behind collecting a part of our hard-earned money? Most of the tax payers feel that paying taxes is a waste of their money.

This Study Guide explains the various economic and social purposes of taxation. You are advised to understand the Study Guide thoroughly so that you can encourage your clients to pay taxes regularly and help your country to grow.

■ Learning Outcomes

a) Describe the purpose (economic, social etc) of taxation in a modern economy.

A1.2: The UK Tax System

Introduction

Case Study

This man is counting money. How happy he looks! If the income of this man is £100, some part of this £100 will go to the government in the form of tax on his income.

The fundamental purpose of taxation is to finance government expenditure. The tax system can be used for purposes other than revenue rising. In certain situations, imposing a tax may potentially increase efficiency if markets fail to price factors such as pollution or congestion, or the health costs of particular types of behaviour such as cigarette smoking. The government uses the process of taxation to encourage or discourage public activity in specific ways.

So, even if this man has to pay tax, i.e. money goes from his pocket, he should not feel bad because the government uses this tax money for the economic and social benefits of the country as a whole. Therefore, it is the taxpayer himself who ultimately enjoys the benefits of paying taxes.

(Source: http://comparativetaxation.treasury.gov.au/content/report/html copyright commonwealth of australia reproduced by permission)

1. Describe the purpose (economic, social etc) of taxation in a modern economy.[2]
[Learning outcome a]

General introduction

The UK tax system has developed over the years as each successive government makes changes to the legislation to reflect its political objectives. The UK tax system is managed by Her Majesty's Revenue and Customs (HMRC). These are appointed officers of the government to administer and collect taxes. They are charged with the responsibility of implementing and enforcing the legislation of the government.

The imposition of taxation by governments withdraws money from the economy, and their expenditure returns the money to the economy. The overall position of the UK economy is affected by the tax policies and in turn will influence the success or failure of the country's economy.

The level of economic activity in the UK is affected by:

- the government's net position regarding taxation and expenditure, and
- public sector borrowing policies

1.1 Economic purpose of taxation

The government used to change its taxation policies in response to short-term changes in, for e.g., levels of employment, imports and exports. This was not always effective, and the current government prefers to plan ahead over a longer term. It publishes a plan for its expenditure over the next three years. This plan shows the proportion of the economy's resources that will be left for the private sector to make decisions on after the government has fulfilled its spending plans.

The government's spending plans will influence the demand for health and education, the demand for consumer goods is influenced by private spending. Changing levels of demand will affect employment and profitability.

The government imposes taxation policies to:

1. **Encourage**

   a) saving by individuals
   b) taking risks in investments by entrepreneurs
   c) entrepreneurs building their own businesses
   d) donations to charities
   e) investment in industrial buildings (e.g. factories, warehouses)

2. **Discourage**

   a) motoring e.g. to minimise pollution
   b) smoking and alcohol
   c) office buildings

SECTION A: THE UK TAX SYSTEM

A2

STUDY GUIDE A2: DIFFERENT TYPES OF TAXES

■ Get Through Intro

In this Study Guide we will discuss the different types of taxes which are levied on the public. It is essential to have knowledge of the nature of taxes because the law provides various provisions relating to deductible expenses, exemptions and different rates of taxes etc.

This Study Guide introduces you to capital and revenue taxes so that the relevant provisions in other Study Guides are easily understood.

This Study Guide also introduces you to the core difference between direct and indirect taxation.

As a tax consultant you should have thorough knowledge of the types of taxes and also the difference between direct and indirect taxes so that the chargeability of tax can be calculated accordingly.

■ Learning Outcomes

a) Identify the different types of capital and revenue tax.
b) Explain the difference between direct and indirect taxation.

A2.2: The UK Tax System

Introduction

Case Study

Taxation is a mechanism used by the UK government to raise funds to pay for public spending in providing the basic functions of the UK, such as social welfare and health systems.

Taxation is a compulsory charge imposed by the government on income, expenditure or assets owned by individuals and companies. The method of raising tax is determined by statute and case law. It is administered by Her Majesty's Revenue and Custom's (HMRC).

The taxes of note can be split into two categories as follows:

Direct taxes: either deducted at source or paid directly to the tax authorities.

Examples of direct taxes are Income Tax, Capital Gains Tax and Inheritance Tax (all paid by **individuals**), and Corporation Tax (paid by **companies**).

Indirect taxes: charged when a taxpayer buys an item, and are paid to the vendor as part of the purchase price.

Examples of indirect taxes include VAT (value-added tax), stamp duty, customs duties and the excise duties levied on alcohol, tobacco and petrol.

1. Identify the different types of capital and revenue tax.[1]

[Learning outcome a]

The government raises revenue from many different types of taxes. The main taxes employed within the UK are as follows:

Tax	Suffered by
Revenue taxes	
Income tax	Individuals Partnerships
Corporation tax	Companies
National Insurance contributions	Individuals Partners Employers Self employed
VAT	Final consumer
Capital taxes	
Capital gains tax	Individuals Partnerships (Companies pay corporation tax on their gains)
Inheritance tax	Individuals

1.1 Revenue Tax

1. Income tax

It is a tax levied on the income of an individual.

Income can be from any sources such as:
a) income from earnings (e.g. employment income / trade profit)
b) income from pensions
c) income from other benefits (e.g. rental income)
d) income from savings (e.g. interest income)
e) income from investments (e.g. dividend income)

Income Tax is calculated on earned income, i.e. from employment, and unearned income, i.e. income from savings. Income from the various sources is pooled together and tax is charged on the aggregate income after deducting the relevant personal allowance. Taxpayers who are employed, pay income tax on their earnings under the statutory Pay As You Earn (PAYE) scheme.

2. Corporation tax

It is the tax payable by companies on their 'chargeable profits'. There are numerous provisions relating to corporation taxes which are dealt with at length in section D.

3. National insurance Contributions (NIC)

After the Second World War, National Insurance Contributions were introduced to fund the establishment of retirement pensions, sickness benefit and the National Health System. National Insurance Contributions are a system of taxes which are paid by employees and employers on the basis of their weekly earnings. The money generated is used to provide social security.

4. VAT

VAT is Value Added Tax. It is the tax which is paid on the value added. This tax is levied at each stage of production. VAT is a consumption tax paid by customers in addition to the price of the product.

1.2 Capital taxes

1. Capital Gains Tax

When a person is in possession of an asset which he then sells, the profit arising from this sale is chargeable to tax as capital gains.

Therefore, capital gains tax liability arises when a 'chargeable person' makes a chargeable disposal of a chargeable asset.

> **Example** Adam sells his business asset at a profit of £5,000. So, the amount of profit i.e. £5,000 is chargeable to capital gains tax.

2. Inheritance Tax

When a person is in possession of an asset and on his death the ownership of such an asset is transferred, the value of the transferred asset is chargeable to inheritance tax, subject to certain tax free thresholds.

Therefore, inheritance tax liability arises when the value of chargeable property is transferred by a chargeable person.

Such tax liability also arises when, during the lifetime of the owner, the asset is given as a gift to any other person unless the person holds the asset for a period of seven years or more, in which case it becomes an exempt transfer.

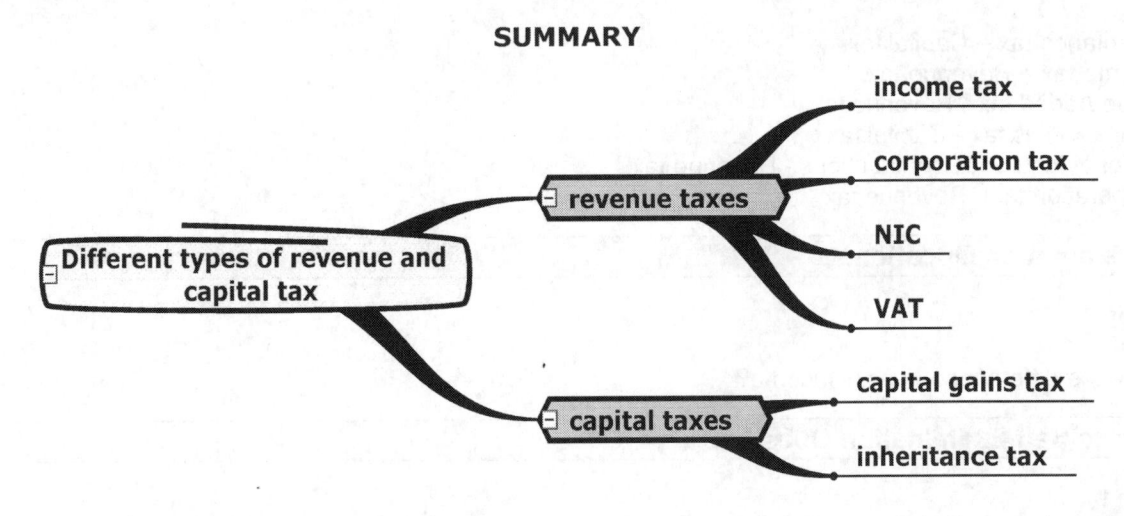

SUMMARY

Different types of revenue and capital tax
- revenue taxes
  - income tax
  - corporation tax
  - NIC
  - VAT
- capital taxes
  - capital gains tax
  - inheritance tax

2. Explain the difference between direct and indirect taxation.[2]

[Learning outcome b]

In order to function effectively, the tax system divides taxes into the following two types:

- Direct taxes
- Indirect taxes.

2.1 Direct Taxes are either deducted at source or paid directly to the tax authorities.

1. Tax on income or capital.
2. Tax imposed directly on taxpayers (individual / company).
3. Direct taxes can be progressive i.e. the more you earn, the higher rate you pay.
4. Examples
   - Income tax
   - Corporation tax
   - National insurance contributions

2.2 Indirect Taxes are charged when a taxpayer buys an item, and are paid to the vendor as part of the purchase price. The vendor in turn passes the tax element on to the government, acting as a collector of tax.

1. Tax on what people spend, rather than on what they earn.
2. People with low incomes pay a higher proportion of their income on indirect taxes than wealthier people.
3. Example: VAT, stamp duty, duties levied on tobacco, alcohol and petrol.

Quick Quiz

1. State whether the following are Capital or Revenue taxes

a) Inheritance tax
b) Income tax
c) Value Added tax
d) Capital Gains tax
e) National Insurance contributions
f) Corporation tax

Answer to Quick Quiz

1.
a) Inheritance tax – Capital tax
b) Income tax – Revenue tax
c) Value Added tax - Revenue tax
d) Capital Gains tax - Capital tax
e) National Insurance contributions - Revenue tax
f) Corporation tax - Revenue tax

Self Examination Question

Question 1

What are the different sources of income?

Answer to Self Examination Question

Answer 1

Income tax is levied on the income earned by an individual. The different sources of income are

a) Income from employment
b) Income from pensions
c) Income from trading
d) Income from other benefits
e) Income from savings Income from investments

SECTION A: THE UK TAX SYSTEM

A3

STUDY GUIDE A3: PRINCIPAL SOURCES OF REVENUE LAW AND PRACTICE

Get Through Intro

In this Study Guide we will discuss different sources of revenue law.

It is essential to have knowledge of the overall structure of the UK tax system because it is the government bodies that collect tax from the general public.

This Study Guide introduces you to how the UK tax system interacts with other tax jurisdictions.

As a tax consultant you should have a thorough knowledge of the overall structure of the UK tax system so that tax matters can be effectively handled with government authorities.

Learning Outcomes

a) Describe the overall structure of the UK tax system.
b) State the different sources of revenue law.
c) Appreciate the interaction of the UK tax system with that of other tax jurisdictions.

A3.2: The UK Tax System

Introduction

Tax law is the body of law that establishes how taxes are imposed and regulated by the government. Taxes are used to produce government revenue and support government programmes and initiatives. While a variety of taxes exist, the most significant taxes within tax law include income tax, social security tax, estate and gift taxes, property tax and value added tax.

In this Study Guide, we will study the overall structure of the UK tax system.

1. Describe the overall structure of the UK tax system.[1]

[Learning outcome a]

Diagram 1: Overall structure of the UK tax system

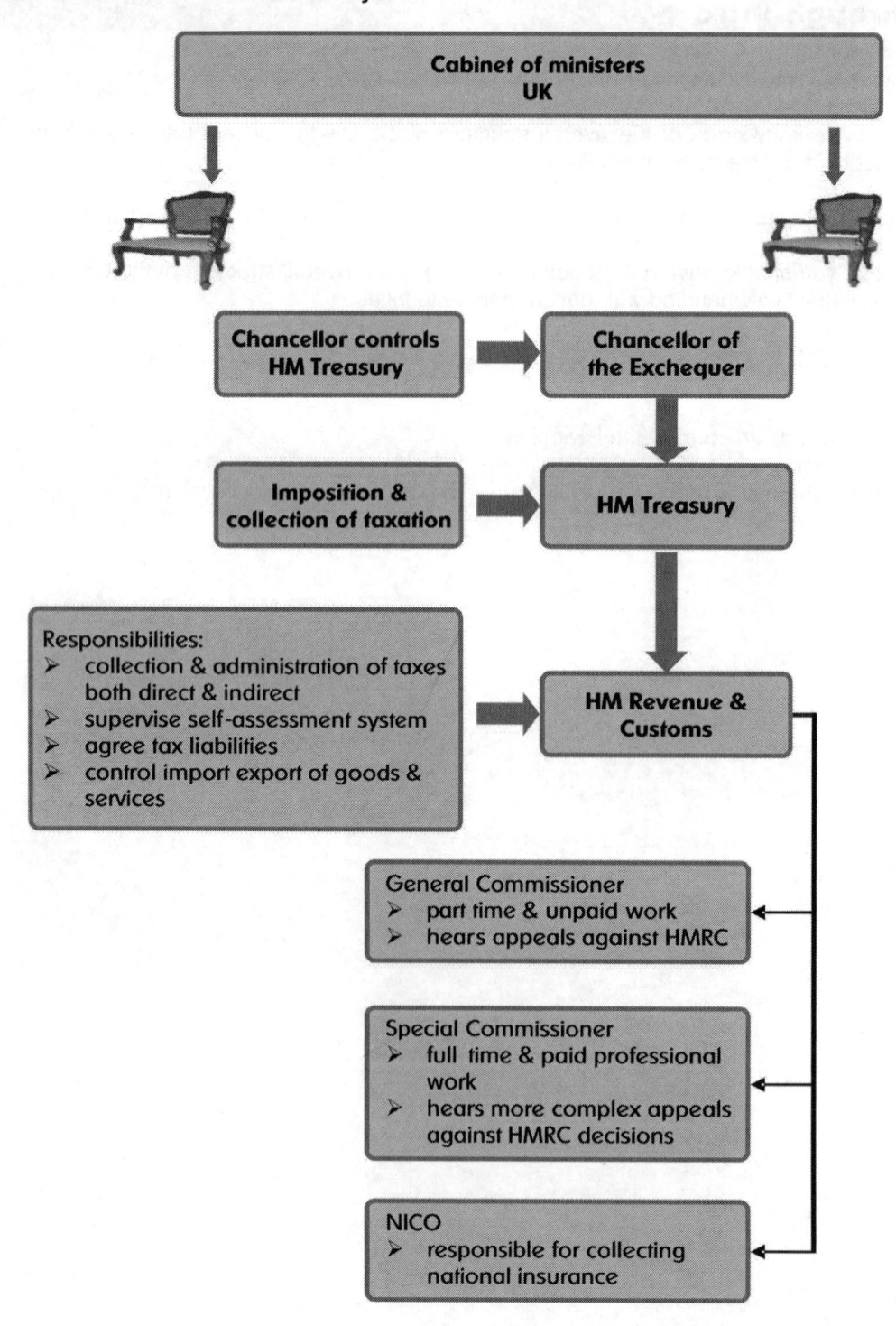

Cabinet of ministers UK

- Chancellor controls HM Treasury → **Chancellor of the Exchequer**
- Imposition & collection of taxation → **HM Treasury**

Responsibilities:
- collection & administration of taxes both direct & indirect
- supervise self-assessment system
- agree tax liabilities
- control import export of goods & services

→ **HM Revenue & Customs**

General Commissioner
- part time & unpaid work
- hears appeals against HMRC

Special Commissioner
- full time & paid professional work
- hears more complex appeals against HMRC decisions

NICO
- responsible for collecting national insurance

2. State the different sources of revenue law.[1]
[Learning outcome b]

The sources of revenue law are
1. Statute law
2. Case law
3. Statements and documents issued by HMRC

1. Statute law

a) Acts of parliament contain the basic rules of the UK taxation system.
b) This legislation is altered and added to by the Annual Finance Act and consolidating statutes.
c) Some detailed legislation is made by Statutory Instruments, which do not necessitate the parliamentary procedure required to pass an Act of Parliament.

2. Case law

Case law serves to interpret and clarify statute and is continually evolving.

3. Statements and documents issued by HMRC

HMRC issues the following documents to explain how the law is to be implemented in practice:

a) Statements of practice set out how the law will apply in practice.
b) Extra-statutory concessions detail circumstances under which the statute will not be applied or whether it would be unfair to do so.
c) Press releases and explanatory notes giving the views and interpretations of the inspectors.
d) Internal guidance manuals commonly known as the inspectors manuals.
e) Pamphlets.

> **Tip** A good source of up to date information can be found at www.HMRC.gov.uk. This is the website for HM Revenue and Customs.

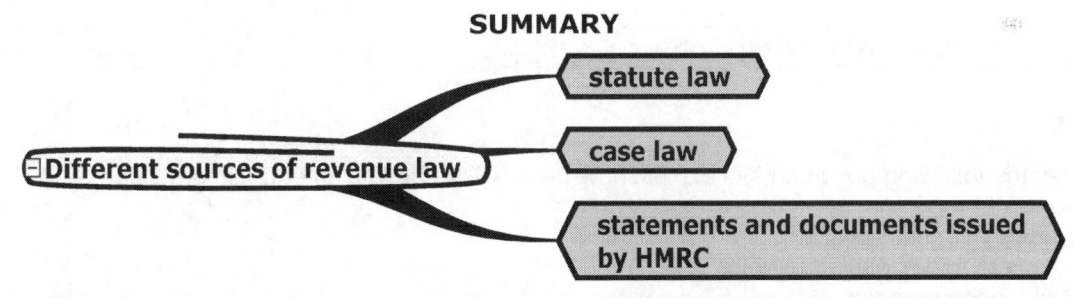

SUMMARY

Different sources of revenue law:
- statute law
- case law
- statements and documents issued by HMRC

3. Appreciate the interaction of the UK tax system with that of other tax jurisdictions.[2]
[Learning outcome c]

Parliamentary supremacy has been affected by membership of the European Union. In certain circumstances European law has supremacy over domestic law.

It is not intended that each member state has a common system of taxation, but states may agree to pass laws which provide a common code of taxation in a certain area of taxation, as they have done with VAT. These are known as Directives and set down a common approach to a specific area of taxation.

The UK must follow EU treaties which promise the freedom of movement of workers and capital and to establish business operations in the UK. The European Court of Justice has held that taxation provisions which show prejudice against non-residents are not allowed under European law. Information sharing between European Union revenue authorities takes place.

Double Tax Treaties

The UK has agreements with a number of countries which avoid income being taxed twice. For e.g., an individual earns income in France, and pays tax on the income under the local taxation rules. The individual returns the earned income to the UK where upon the double tax treaty prevents the income being taxed for a second time.

Quick Quiz

1. What are the different sources of revenue law?
2. What is the relevance of Case Law with regard to taxation practice?
3. Where would you look to find up to date press releases or publications relating to taxation?

Answers to Quick Quiz

1. The different sources of revenue law are
   a) Statute law
   b) Case law
   c) Statements and documents issued by HMRC.

2. The case law provides clarification of the statute and demonstrates the practical application of the legislation.

3. We can find up to date press releases or publications relating to taxation on the website www.HMRC.gov.uk

Self Examination Questions

Question 1

List the documents which are issued by HMRC to explain how the law is to be implemented in practice.

Question 2

What are the main responsibilities of HMRC?

Answers to Self Examination Questions

Answer 1

HMRC issues the following documents to explain how the law is to be implemented in practice:
a) Statements of practice
b) Extra-statutory concessions
c) Press releases and explanatory notes
d) Internal guidance manuals
e) Pamphlets

Answer 2

The main responsibilities of HMRC are:
a) collection & administration of taxes both direct & indirect
b) supervise self-assessment system
c) agree tax liabilities
d) control import export of goods & services

SECTION A: THE UK TAX SYSTEM

A4

STUDY GUIDE A4: TAX AVOIDANCE AND TAX EVASION

Get Through Intro

In this Study Guide we will discuss the meaning and difference between tax avoidance and tax evasion.

It is essential to know the difference between the two because whilst the law makes various provisions relating to the taxability of different types of income. You should be aware of the risk associated with tax evasion and avoidance. Committing either one of these is likely to have different consequences.

This Study Guide highlights the importance of understanding the difference between the two, because tax avoidance is permitted but tax evasion is illegal.

As a tax consultant, you should have thorough knowledge of the difference between them so that your client does not unwittingly commit tax evasion. In addition, you should advise your client on how to effectively and legally reduce the tax liability.

Learning Outcomes

a) Explain the difference between tax avoidance and tax evasion.
b) Explain the need for an ethical and professional approach.

Introduction

For many years individuals have found imaginative ways of avoiding a liability to tax. Large companies employ highly skilled tax planners in a bid to legally reduce their overall tax liability. There have been many instances of individuals' under-declaring their income to reduce their tax liability. The question is one of whether these activities constitute tax avoidance or tax evasion.

Tax evasion is a deliberate act by an individual or company to mislead, misinform or otherwise mis-state their tax position to HMRC in order to evade taxes. Tax evasion is illegal and is punishable by hefty fines and imprisonment.

Tax avoidance is legal. It involves the arrangement of individuals' or companies' tax affairs in a way which reduces the tax liability. For example, using incentivised tax savings schemes such as ISA's or Enterprise Investment Schemes. More complex tax avoidance examples would include establishing an offshore company in a tax haven or by forming a limited company to avail of more favourable tax deductions.

---

1. Explain the difference between tax avoidance and tax evasion.[1]
[Learning outcome a]

Tax avoidance is any **legal way** of reducing the amount of tax payable – involving a sensible arrangement of the taxpayers' affairs so as to minimise the liability to tax. All activities must remain legal at all times. It is the **utilisation of "tax loopholes"** within the legislation in an ingenious way, thereby affording the tax payer, legally, a favourable tax position.

Tax evasion is the intention **to deliberately mislead** HMRC and is illegal. It involves dishonest conduct or behaviour by the taxpayer.

It could consist of:
- providing HMRC with false information
- not giving HMRC information to which they are entitled.
- concealing a source of income

SUMMARY

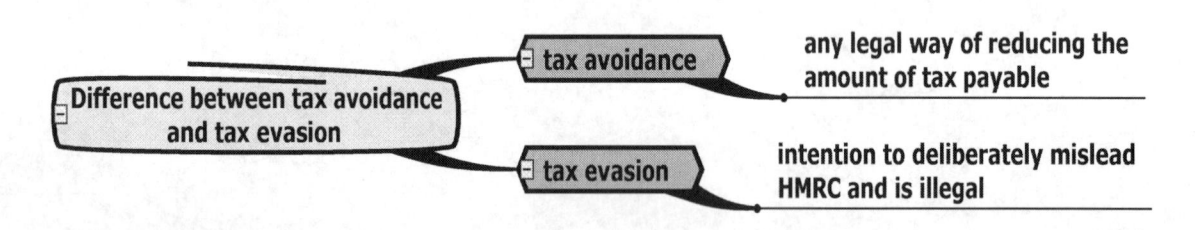

Difference between tax avoidance and tax evasion
- **tax avoidance**: any legal way of reducing the amount of tax payable
- **tax evasion**: intention to deliberately mislead HMRC and is illegal

---

2. Explain the need for an ethical and professional approach.[2]
[Learning outcome b]

An accountant has responsibilities to

1. Individual clients
2. Employer
3. HMRC

In addition he has a responsibility to act in the public interest.

From time to time these duties may conflict. Questions of judgement may be involved in resolving these conflicts. An accountant may suspect that a taxpayer, for whom he is acting, is not being honest in regard to declarations of income or in the provision of information. The accountant will have to act with integrity and uphold the following Code of Ethics and Conduct.

The Code of Ethics and Conduct provides a framework within which to make these judgements.

The Code requires **members to comply** with the following **principles**:

a) Integrity
b) Objectivity
c) Professional competence and due care
d) Confidentiality
e) Professional behaviour.

Quick Quiz

1. Which is legal and permitted, tax avoidance or tax evasion?

Answer to Quick Quiz

1. Tax avoidance is legal and permitted whereas tax evasion is illegal.

Self Examination Question

Question 1

What are the principles which a member has to comply with?

Answer to Self Examination Question

Answer 1

The Code of ethics requires members to comply with the following principles:

a) Integrity
b) Objectivity
c) Professional competence and due care
d) Confidentiality
e) Professional behaviour

SECTION B: INCOME TAX LIABILITIES

B1

STUDY GUIDE B1: THE SCOPE OF INCOME TAX

Get Through Intro

The **residence** of an individual is **very important** because it **determines the income chargeable to UK tax**.

An individual's **nationality makes no difference** when determining **his residential status in the UK.** This means that no matter which country a person is a citizen of, if the individual satisfies the conditions of being a resident of the UK, they have to pay UK tax for that year.

Individuals who are **resident in the UK** for any tax year are liable to **pay UK tax on their entire income** for that year i.e. on their UK income and also on their overseas income.

This Study Guide explains the basic conditions which determine the residential status of an individual and also the circumstances in which an individual is said to be ordinarily resident in the UK.

A tax payer should consider the effect of his residence and ordinary residence on his tax liability as this is a major factor in an individual's tax planning. You need to understand this concept thoroughly for success in the examination, and for success in your professional life after you become ACCA qualified.

Learning Outcomes

a) Explain how the residence of an individual is determined.

Introduction

Residence is a question of fact, and usually requires physical presence in a country. In today's increasingly global business environment, there are a considerable number of individuals who usually live in the UK but make frequent and regular business trips abroad which may affect their residence. It is possible that an individual is resident in more than one country for tax purposes.

Determining the residential status of individuals is very important to decide their tax liability. UK residents are liable to income tax on worldwide income, non-UK residents are liable to income tax only on the income generated in the UK.

This Study Guide explains the various conditions which determine whether a person is a resident of the UK.

1. Explain how the residence of an individual is determined.[1]
[Learning outcome a]

The basic conditions for residency are as follows:

1. An individual who is **physically present in the UK for at least 183 days or more (> half of 365 days)** during a **tax year** (excluding days of arrival and departure) is deemed to be resident in the UK **for the whole of that tax year**. This can be a single continuous period, or spread over a number of visits during the tax year.

2. An individual, who **is present in the UK for an average of 91 days or more in a year, for four or more consecutive tax years**, is deemed to be a resident in the UK from the earlier of:
   a) the start of the fifth tax year, or
   b) the start of a tax year where an intention to continue long-term visits is apparent.

An individual fulfilling **either of these conditions** is a **resident** of the UK for tax purposes.

> **Tip**
> A UK resident is liable to income tax on **worldwide income** and a **non-UK resident** is liable to income tax **only on his UK income.**

Test Yourself 1

Pearl, has lived in Germany her entire life, arrives in the UK on 15 April 2009 and stays there until 15 March 2010. On that date she goes back to live in Germany. What is her residential status for 2009-10?

It is important to note that the concept of **UK residence** normally applies **to a whole tax year**. In other words, an individual is deemed to be a UK resident for the whole tax year or none of it. It is usually **not possible to apportion a tax year** into periods of residence and non-residence.

> **Tip**
> Income tax is charged for a **tax year**. The tax year runs **from 6 April to the following 5 April**

SUMMARY

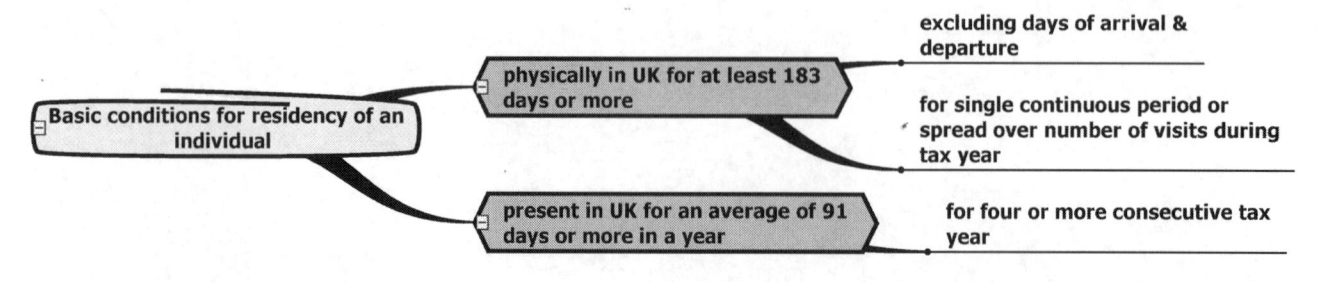

- **Basic conditions for residency of an individual**
  - **physically in UK for at least 183 days or more**
    - excluding days of arrival & departure
    - for single continuous period or spread over number of visits during tax year
  - **present in UK for an average of 91 days or more in a year**
    - for four or more consecutive tax year

Income tax is payable by an individual on his total income which comprises of income from different sources. In one tax year he may have, for e.g., employment income, property income and dividends – all these are chargeable to income tax.

In a nutshell, we can say that an individual's taxable income is the total of the different types of income. A personal tax computation of an individual's total income may be presented in the following format.

Computation of taxable income of an individual

	Non-saving Income	Saving Income (excluding dividends)	Dividend Income	Total
	£	£	£	£
Income from employment	X	-	-	X
Income from business	X	-	-	X
Income from UK dividends	-	-	X	X
Property income	X	-	-	X
Bank interest	-	X	-	X
Total income	**X**	**X**	**X**	**X**
Less: Loss relief and interest payments	(X)	-	-	(X)
Net income	**X**	**X**	**X**	**X**
Less: Personal allowance	(6,475)	-	-	(6,475)
Taxable income	**X**	**X**	**X**	**X**

Computation of income tax liability of an individual

	£
Tax borne (Using Tax Tables)	X
Add: Tax deducted from charge	X
Total tax liability	**X**
Less: Tax credit on dividends	(X)
Less: Tax deducted at source	(X)
Tax payable	**X**

In order to calculate an individual's income tax liability, we need to learn how each different type of income is taxed. Therefore, income of an individual includes various types of income which are covered in Section B of the Study Guide:

1. Income from employment: this source of income is explained in Study Guide B2.
2. Income from business: this source of income is explained in Study Guide B3.
3. Income from dividends: this source of income is explained in Study Guide B4.
4. Property income: this source of income is explained in Study Guide B4.

After aggregating all the income, the appropriate rate of tax is applied to calculate the final tax liability. The different sources of income may attract tax at different rates, which is why we show the income split into the three main sources. The calculation of income tax liability is explained in detail in Study Guide B5.

Section B deals with the calculation of an individual's tax liability for the year.

Answer to Test Yourself

Answer 1

Pearl is a **resident in the UK** for the tax year 2009-10 as she has spent more than 183 days in the UK during the year (15 April to 15 March = 11 months i.e. more than 183 days).

Quick Quiz

State in the following cases the residential status of an individual

1. Konjit, a resident of Kenya, arrives in the UK on 24 August 2009. She stays till 4 April 2010, and then returns to Kenya.

2. Gladius is a UK resident, but for the year 2009-10 she was in India.

Answers to Quick Quiz

1. **Konjit will be classified as a UK resident,** because an individual who is **physically present in the UK for at least 183 days** during a tax year (excluding days of arrival and departure) is deemed to be a resident of the UK **for the whole tax year**. Konjit is present in the UK for (24 August 09 to 4 April 10) 222 days i.e. more than 183 days.

2. **Gladius is a non-resident** because although she is ordinarily resident, she is absent from the UK for the whole of 2009-10, and therefore she is not resident for that year.

Self Examination Questions

Question 1

Why is residential status important?

Question 2

In what circumstances will an individual be treated as a UK resident for UK tax purposes?

Answers to Self Examination Questions

Answer 1

Liability to income tax depends on whether an individual is resident in the UK. An individual is broadly liable to income tax on worldwide income if he is a UK resident. On the other hand, he is liable to income tax only on his UK income if he is non-UK resident.

Answer 2

An individual will be treated as resident for a tax year if:
1. he is in the UK for 183 days or more in the tax year, **OR**
2. his visits to the UK average 91 days or more per tax year for four or more consecutive tax years.

SECTION B: INCOME TAX LIABILITIES

B2

STUDY GUIDE B2: INCOME FROM EMPLOYMENT

■ Get Through Intro

Employment income is an income in the form of salary or wages. Legislation allows an employee to make **various deductions** from the employment income when determining the amount subject to tax.

This Study Guide discusses how employment income is assessed to tax, the various deductions allowed by the legislation, the PAYE system and the rules relating to tax deducted under the PAYE system.

As an aspiring tax consultant, you are expected to understand all the employment income aspects thoroughly, as you will be required to advise your clients on their employees. Moreover, you will want to ensure that the tax charged on your salary is calculated correctly.

■ Learning Outcomes

a) Recognise the factors that determine whether an engagement is treated as employment or self-employment.
b) Recognise the basis of assessment for employment income.
c) Compute the income assessable.
d) Recognise the allowable deductions, including travelling expenses.
e) Discuss the use of the statutory approved mileage allowances.
f) Explain the PAYE system.
g) Identify P11D employees.
h) Compute the amount of benefits assessable.
i) Explain the purpose of a dispensation from HM Revenue & Customs.
j) Explain how charitable giving can be made through a payroll deduction scheme.

Introduction

Case Study

Cynthia is a fashion designer. During the year 2009-10, she started working for Beauty Designs Ltd. The terms of her contract include:

1. Beauty Designs Ltd will pay Cynthia a fixed fee of £20,000 for each contract she works on. She is under no obligation to accept all of the contracts offered. Cynthia reports directly to the MD of the company.

2. Cynthia will procure the equipment and materials required for her work; the company does not provide her with any such tools of the trade.

3. Cynthia will visit the company only when she has a meeting with Suzy, the MD of the company regarding the patterns and style of dresses; otherwise she works from home at her convenience.

Cynthia is unsure whether she will be treated as employed or self-employed.

This Study Guide explains the various factors that are considered in determining whether an individual, such as Cynthia, is employed or self-employed. It then goes on to explain how an employed person is taxed.

1. Recognise the factors that determine whether an engagement is treated as employment or self-employment.[2]

[Learning outcome a]

Usually it is very clear whether a particular person is employed or self-employed. However, sometimes there are borderline cases. For example, in the case of an employee with a number of part-time jobs it is difficult to decide whether he is employed or self-employed. He will usually prefer to be self-employed, because a self-employed person enjoys the followings tax advantages over an employed person:

➢ A much **wider range** of expenses are allowed against the income of self-employed people, than against the income of employees.

➢ Self-employed people pay their tax later, as they pay their income tax by **instalments.** However, in the case of employees, tax is **deducted at source** under the PAYE system. (This will be explained in more detail later in this Study Guide).

➢ An individual's employment status also affects his national insurance contribution. Self-employed people can pay **less** National Insurance contributions than employees.

One important test to be applied in deciding whether a person is employed or self-employed is the **nature of the contract** between the taxpayer and the person who is paying for the work done.

Employment involves a contract of service whereas self-employment involves a contract for services.

The **factors** that help to determine whether an engagement is treated as employment or self-employment are as below:

1. Control

The **degree of control** exercised over the person who is doing the work is an important factor to determine whether an engagement is employment or self-employment. Employees are under the control of the employer to a higher degree. They have to report to work on specific dates, given times having to obey the instructions of the employer.to deliver the result expected by the employer. In most instances specific work instructions are given by the employer though in technical fields such as information technology or taxation the employer demands the result and the employee can use their own methods.

Self-employed people have a greater degree of freedom to decide and plan their work, schedule their time and the manner in which they will work.

2. Financial risk involved

Employees do not normally risk their own capital in the business. They get their remuneration regularly without considering whether their employers earn any profits. Self-employed people may not be paid if the performance does not meet the expectation of their customer. They also run the risk of losing their capital if the business fails and can earn **profit from sound management** (work faster, earn more).

3. Equipment

Usually, the **employer provides the equipment** required for **the employee.** Self-employed people generally procure their own equipment.

4. Assistance

Employees are required to do their work themselves. Self-employed people are able to employ their own staff.

5. Correction of work

Mistakes made by the employees are usually corrected by them during working hours. If the work performed by a self-employed person is unsatisfactory, the client will expect him to make the corrections and not pay for the time taken to remedy the mistake.

6. Holidays

An employee gets holiday pay and sick pay from his company. The company pays a self-employed only for days when he works and not for holidays.

7. Number of people employed

Usually, employees work for one employer. Self-employed people normally work for a number of employers.

8. Mode of payment

Employees are paid weekly / monthly / yearly whereas the self-employed are paid per contract.

9. Position

Self-employed individuals are not an integral part of the business.

10. Obligation

The self-employed are not obliged to accept every work allotted to them.

Diagram 1: Determining factors of employment or self-employment

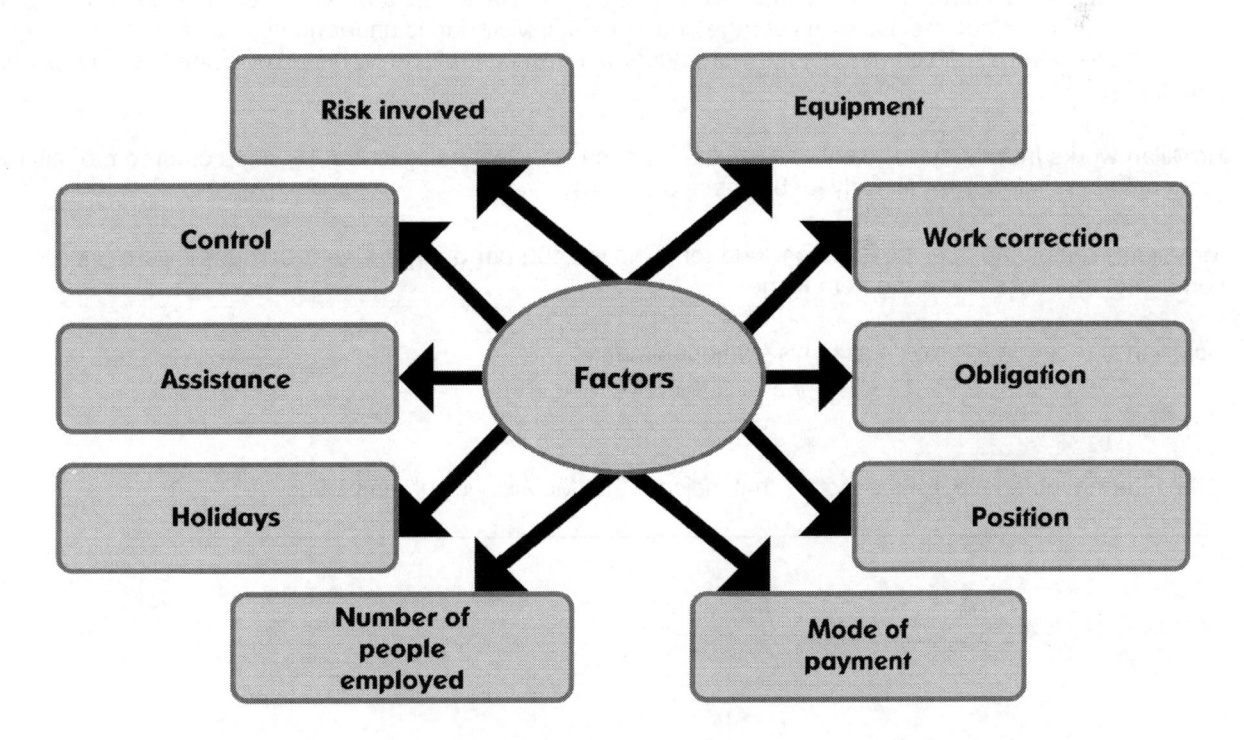

SUMMARY

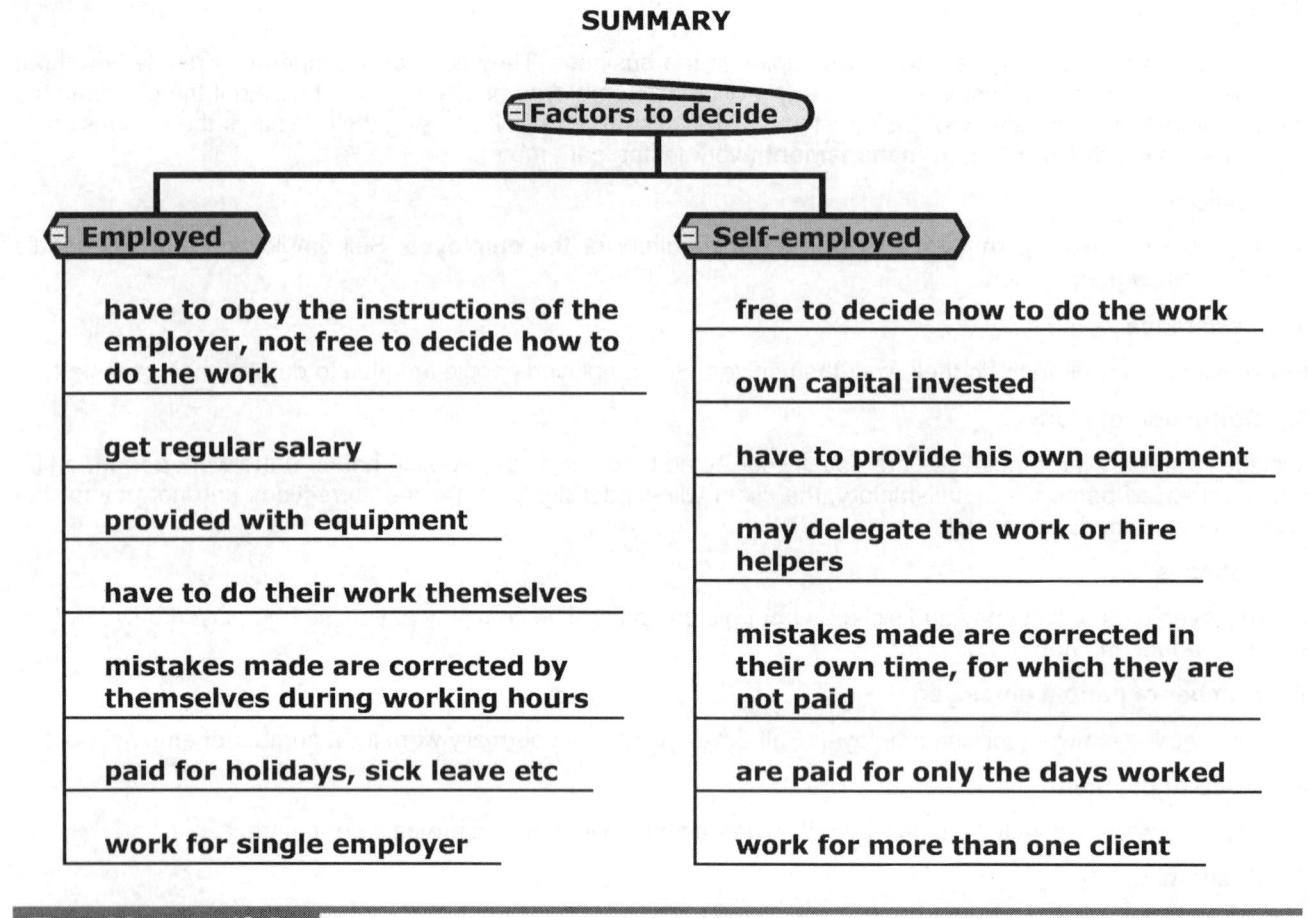

Factors to decide

Employed
- have to obey the instructions of the employer, not free to decide how to do the work
- get regular salary
- provided with equipment
- have to do their work themselves
- mistakes made are corrected by themselves during working hours
- paid for holidays, sick leave etc
- work for single employer

Self-employed
- free to decide how to do the work
- own capital invested
- have to provide his own equipment
- may delegate the work or hire helpers
- mistakes made are corrected in their own time, for which they are not paid
- are paid for only the days worked
- work for more than one client

Test Yourself 1

McMillan Byte is a computer programmer who started working for Web-Designs Ltd on 6 April 2009.

The following information is available in respect of the year ended 5 April 2010:

1. McMillan received income of £60,000 from Web-Designs Ltd. He is paid a fixed fee for each contract that he works on, and each contract lasts an average of two weeks. McMillan is under no obligation to accept any of the contracts offered, and carries out the work under his own control. He is, however obliged to do the work personally.

2. McMillan works from home, and never visits the premises of Web-Designs Ltd. He uses one room of his five room private residence exclusively for business purposes.

3. McMillan's telephone bills are £500 per quarter. This is £400 per quarter higher than they were prior to the commencement of his working from home.

4. McMillan is required to provide all of his own equipment.

Required:

From the information above, list the factors that indicate that McMilan is self-employed.

2. Recognise the basis of assessment for employment income.[2]
[Learning outcome b]

2.1 What is employment income?

Income that a person receives as the holder of an office or employment is charged to income tax as "employment income". The salary, wages or remuneration arising under a **contract of service** received by the employee in respect of employment is considered income from employment. The earnings received in any one tax year include the employee's earnings plus the "cash equivalent" of any taxable non-monetary benefits.

Earnings include

1. Bonus
2. Commission
3. Fees
4. Round sum expenses allowances
5. Payments on the termination of employment
6. Pensions arising from the employment and
7. Benefits

It is important to note that **all income generated from employment** is considered employment income i.e. income which is not received directly from the employer, but received as a result of employment, is considered employment income.

Example A restaurant waiter receives £2 as a tip from a customer for good service. The employer does not **directly** pay this income. However, he has received this income as a **result** of his employment. This income is, therefore, taxable as employment income for the waiter.

The income of directors is also treated as employment income.

2.2 When is employment income taxable?

An individual's employment income for a tax year is the income actually received in that year i.e. income from employment is taxable on a **receipt basis.**

Example An employee is entitled to a bonus for the year ended 31 March 2009. The amount of the bonus depends on the company's results for that year. The company's accounts for the year ended 31 March 2009 are finalised on 31 October 2009, and the employee's bonus of £5,000 is paid on 30 November 2009.

The bonus relates to 2008-09, however, as it is received in 2009-10 the bonus is taxable in full in 2009-10.

2.3 When is employment income received?

Income from employment is treated as received on the **earlier** of:

1. **For individual employees**

a) The date when payment is made. For example, the date when the salary cheque is received.

b) The date when an employee becomes entitled to payment.

Example If salary is paid monthly, the last day of the month would be treated as the date received, even if it was not actually paid until a later date.

2. For directors

Bonuses, Salaries and Director fees are treated as received on the earlier of:

a) The date that the earning (bonus) has been paid.

b) The date that entitlement to the earning (bonus) arises.

c) The date on which the income is **credited** to the director in the accounting records of the company.

> **Example**
> BBC Ltd accounted for a director's remuneration in its accounting records on 25 March 2009; however, it did not actually pay him the remuneration until 15 June 2009. The remuneration will be considered to be received by the director during the tax year 2008-09 when it was credited in the records of the company.

d) The end of the period of accounts, if the director's income for that period is determined **by then**.

> **Example**
> A company prepares its accounts for the year up to 31 December. On 1 May 2009, Chi was appointed as a director with a remuneration of £48,000 per calendar year. The company had actually paid £20,000 up to 31 December 2009. On 31 December 2009, in the accounts, Chi will be treated as though he has received £32,000 (eight months 8/12 x £48,000) even though he has actually only received £20,000 for the tax year 2009-10. Chi's taxable income is £32,000.

e) The date on which the amount is determined, **after the end** of the company's **period of accounts.**

> **Example**
> Assume that in the above example no remuneration was agreed upon for Chi at the time of his appointment as director. On 1 May 2010, the company decided to pay him £35,000 as his remuneration for his services to date. In this situation, the remuneration of £35,000 will be treated as received on 1 May 2010. It will be chargeable to tax in the tax year 2010-11.

> **Tip**
> The receipt basis does not apply to pension income. Pensions are taxed on an **accrual basis.**

2.4 Some other relevant points

1. An individual is taxed on his net taxable earnings of a tax year. Net taxable earnings are equal to **total taxable earnings less total allowable deductions.**

> **Tip**
> Net taxable earnings = Total taxable earnings – Total allowable deductions

2. Deductions are allowed to the **maximum** extent of the amount of **taxable earnings** i.e. deductions cannot create a loss; they can only reduce the net taxable earnings to nil.

> **Example**
> Jenny is employed with a company on a part time basis and her employment income for 2009-10 is £4,000. She is also entitled to statutory mileage allowance (explained in detail later in this Study Guide) of £4,050 as she drives 10,200 miles for business purposes.
>
> As Jenny's taxable employment income is £4,000, the maximum total deduction to which she is entitled is £4,000. However, the statutory mileage allowance to which she is entitled is more than £4,000 and the unused deduction is £50 (£4,050 - £4,000). But in such a case, she cannot claim that she has incurred a loss of £50.

3. If there is more than one employment in the year, separate calculations are required for each employment.

Example

Nancy worked for three companies during the tax year 2009-10. In this situation, separate calculations of earnings and deductions are required. Her net earnings from all these companies are to be calculated as follows:

Particulars	Company A £	Company B £	Company C £
Period of work	10 April 09 to 15 June 09	7 July 09 to 5 December 09	25 December 09 to 15 March 10
Total earnings	1,250	1,620	1,480
Less: Deductions			
Donations to charity made under the payroll deduction scheme operated by an employer	(310)	(180)	-
Mileage allowance	(120)	(340)	(120)
Contribution to approved pension scheme	(45)	-	(65)
Net earnings	**775**	**1,100**	**1,295**

SUMMARY

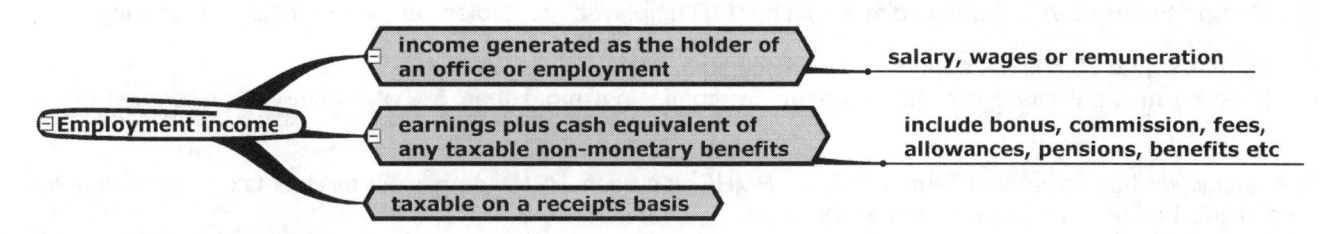

Employment income
- income generated as the holder of an office or employment → salary, wages or remuneration
- earnings plus cash equivalent of any taxable non-monetary benefits → include bonus, commission, fees, allowances, pensions, benefits etc
- taxable on a receipts basis

Test Yourself 2

Jo received a basic salary of £35,700 in 2009-10. She also receives an annual bonus (received in January) based on her performance in the previous calendar year.

Bonuses for the last three calendar years are as follows:

	£
Year ended 31 December 2007 (received in January 2008)	5,300
Year ended 31 December 2008 (received in January 2009)	6,550
Year ended 31 December 2009 (received in January 2010)	7,100

Required:

Compute her total income in 2009-10.

Test Yourself 3

State the rules that determine when a bonus paid to a director is treated as being received for tax purposes.

(December 2005)

Test Yourself 4

SP International Ltd is an advertising company. It prepares its accounts up to 31 March every year. It appointed David as its director on 1 January 2009. His remuneration was agreed to be £60,000 per calendar year, payable monthly in equal instalments. On 31 March 2009, the company accounted for £15,000 in David's account showing it as payable. On 2 April, it was decided to increase David's remuneration to £84,000 per calendar year retrospectively. The company had actually paid £12,000 to David on 5 May 2009.

Required:

When is David's employment income treated as received and how much is it?

3. Identify P11D employees.[1]

[Learning outcome g]

Employment income includes the value of benefits, i.e. income received in the form of goods and services, rather than money. Employees are divided into two classes for the purpose of assessing benefits:

1. **P11D (higher paid) employees:** P11D employees are taxed on any benefit regardless of whether or not it is convertible into cash. They are assessed on the marginal cost incurred by the employer providing that benefit.

2. **P9D (lower-paid) employees:** Employees other than P11D employees are called "lower-paid employees". Lower paid employment is where earnings for the tax year are less than £8,500. Lower paid employees are taxed only on those **benefits which are convertible into cash.**

P11D employees

Directors and employees who are not lower paid are referred to as P11D employees because their benefits are reported to HMRC on form P11D. P11D employees **are those who:**

a) **earn at least £8,500 per annum:** for calculating this £8,500,

i. all earnings are totalled including benefits valued as if the employee were a P11D employee,
ii. no expenses are to be deducted from earnings except contributions to an occupational pension scheme or to a payroll-giving scheme.

b) **Company directors:** company directors are P11D employees regardless of their earnings unless they:

i. earn less than £8,500 per annum and work full-time **AND**
ii. have no material interest in the company i.e. control not more than 5% of ordinary share capital of the company.

The employer has to submit form P11D to HMRC for each P11D employee for the tax year, listing the employee's benefits and any reimbursed expenses.

SUMMARY

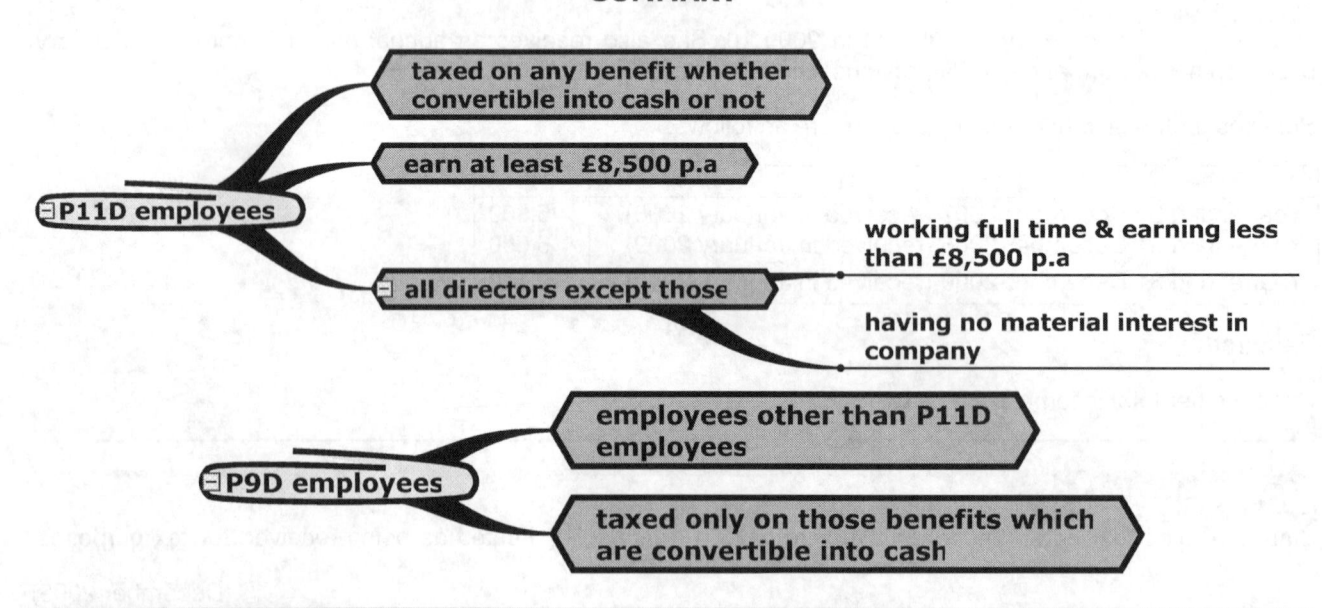

- **P11D employees**
  - taxed on any benefit whether convertible into cash or not
  - earn at least £8,500 p.a
  - all directors except those
    - working full time & earning less than £8,500 p.a
    - having no material interest in company
- **P9D employees**
  - employees other than P11D employees
  - taxed only on those benefits which are convertible into cash

Test Yourself 5

George retires from his job and joins Titan Ltd as a full time director in which he holds 25% of ordinary shares. His annual income from Titan Ltd is £7,000. Is he a P11D employee?

Test Yourself 6

Judi is an employee with a salary of £8,195 in 2009-10. She receives private health insurance in the year which costs her employer £400.

Is she a P11D employee?

4. Compute the amount of benefits assessable.[2]

[Learning outcome h]

The benefits are categorised as follows:
- exempt benefits
- benefits assessable on all employees
- benefits assessable on P11D employees

4.1 Exempt benefits

Exempt benefits include:

1. Meal vouchers up to 15p per day.

2. Free or subsidised meals in a staff canteen, if available to all employees.

3. The cost of staff parties, which are open to staff generally, up to £150 per person per year. The £150 limit may be split between several parties. However, if a function costs more than £150, **the whole amount is taxable,** not just the excess over £150.

4. The provision for a parking place at or near an employee's place of work.

5. Contributions by an employer towards additional household costs incurred by an employee who works at home (supporting evidence required if these costs exceed £2 per week).

6. The payment by an employer of an **employee's personal incidental expenses** when the employee is staying away from home overnight on business, of up to £5 per night within UK or £10 per night outside the UK. If the limit is exceeded the whole amount is taxable.

7. Reasonable removal expenses (up to a maximum of £8,000) paid for by an employer when an employee first takes up employment or transfers to a new location within the organisation.

8. An award of up to £5,000 made under a staff suggestion scheme.

9. Payments of up to £15,000 per academic year to an employee who is attending a full-time course at a recognised educational establishment. If the limit is exceeded the whole amount is taxable.

10. The provision of **one mobile phone** for an employee's use. If **more than one mobile phone** is provided then that is **taxable**.

Example

Excellent Plc provided Rower with two mobile phones throughout the tax year 2009-10 for her personal use. The mobile phones cost £180 each.

Benefits assessable for the tax year 2009-10 in respect of the second mobile = £180 x 20% = £36 (explained in point 4.3 under assets loaned for private use.) Rower will also be taxed on the running costs paid by Excellent plc in respect of the second mobile telephone.

---

11. The provision of workplace childcare or childcare vouchers up to £55 per week, sports or recreation facility.

12. The provision of welfare counselling service for employees generally.

13. The provision of pension information and advice if available to all the employees and costing less than £150 per employee per year.

14. Entertainment provided by a third party.

15. Gifts from third parties up to £250 per donor (if exceeded all taxable).

16. Long service awards.

17. Concessional interest on small loans not exceeding £5,000.

18. Job-related accommodation.

19. Contributions to employees' pension fund.

4.2 Benefits assessable on all the employees

This includes:

- Living accommodation
- Vouchers exchangeable for goods or services

1. Living accommodation

If an employee is provided with living accommodation such as a house or flat there are two possible benefits assessable on **ALL** employees.

Diagram 2: Taxable value for living accommodation

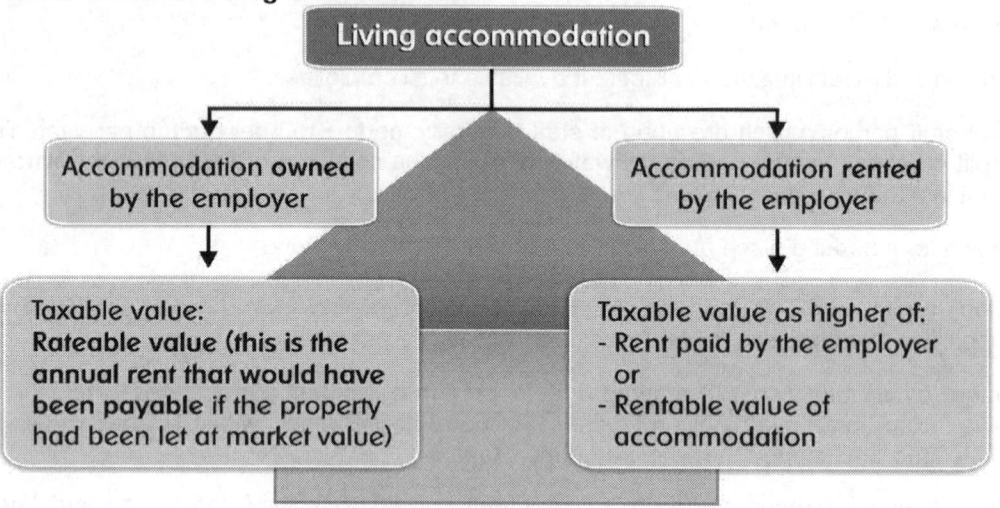

```
                    Living accommodation
                   /                    \
        Accommodation owned        Accommodation rented
          by the employer            by the employer
                 |                          |
        Taxable value:              Taxable value as higher of:
        Rateable value (this is the  - Rent paid by the employer
        annual rent that would have    or
        been payable if the property - Rentable value of
        had been let at market value)  accommodation
```

> **Tip:** Rateable value figure will be given in the exam.

a) Rented accommodation

Taxable benefit for living accommodation is calculated as:

	£
Higher of:	
Rent paid by employer	X
Annual value of property	
Less: Employee contribution	(X)
Taxable benefit	X

Example Honey is provided with living accommodation from 1 January 2009, which has a rateable value of £6,200. The employer pays rent of £7,400 for the property annually. Honey pays her employer £850 per annum towards the accommodation. Calculation of taxable benefits in 2009-10:

		£
Rent paid by employer = £7,400	higher	7,400
Annual value of property = £6,200		
Less: Employee contribution		(850)
Taxable benefit for living accommodation		**6,550**

b) Employer owned accommodation: expensive accommodation benefit

i. If the employer owns the accommodation and it **cost more than £75,000** then there is an additional charge on the employee. **This is in addition to the rateable value of accommodation.**

The amount of the expensive accommodation benefit is:

> (Cost of providing the accommodation - £75,000) x official rate of interest
> The official rate of interest for 2009 - 10 is 4.75%.

Tip Official rate of interest will be provided in the exam paper. However, limit for expensive accommodation of £75,000 will not be provided in the exam and you will have to memorise it.

Example Henry is provided with living accommodation from 1 January 2009 which has a rateable value of £6,200. The employer purchased the property in 2007 for £80,000 and spent £10,000 on improvements in August 2008. Henry pays his employer rent of £850 per annum. Calculate Henry's taxable benefits in 2009-10. The official rate of interest is 4.75% per annum.

	£
Rateable value	6,200
Expensive accommodation benefit	713
(£80,000 + £10,000 − £75,000) x 4.75%	
	6,913
Less : Employee contribution	(850)
Cost of benefits of accommodation	**6,063**

As the **property costs more than £75,000,** the **expensive accommodation** benefit must also be calculated.

(Cost of providing the accommodation - £75,000) x official rate of interest
= (£80,000 + £10,000 - £75,000) × 4.75%
= £15,000 × 4.75%
= £713

Total taxable benefit = £5,350 + £713 = £6,063

---

ii. Where the accommodation was purchased by the employer less than six years before being made available to an employee, the cost of providing the accommodation is:

> Cost of providing the property + improvement expenditure up to the start of the tax year

iii. Where the accommodation was acquired **more than six years before** being made available to an employee, the cost of providing the accommodation is:

> Market value of the property when first occupied by an employee
> + any subsequent improvements up to the start of the tax year

The taxable benefit for living accommodation is calculated as:

	£
Rateable Value	X
Add: Expensive accommodation benefit	
(£Cost - £75,000) x official rate of interest	X
Total	X
Less: Employee contribution	(X)
Taxable benefit	**X**

Example Jack was provided with a house by his employer in June 2009. He pays £125 per month for use of the house. The house had been purchased at £120,000 in 2000 and has an annual value of £1200. The house had a market value of £150,000 in June 2009. Calculate taxable benefits in 2009-10, assuming an official interest rate of 4.75% per annum.

Continued on next page

	£
Rateable value	1,200
Add: Expensive accommodation benefit (£150,000 – £75,000) @ 4.75% (note)	3,563
Total	**4,763**
For ten months (£4,763 x 10/12)	3,969
Less: employee contribution (£125 x 10 months)	(1,250)
Taxable benefit	**2,719**

Note: The house was acquired by Jack's employer more than six years before being provided to Jack. Hence, the market value of the house on the date when it was first occupied by Jack will be considered for calculating the expensive accommodation benefit.

c) Representative accommodation

No taxable benefit arises in respect of representative accommodation. Accommodation is treated as representative if it is

i. **Job related** i.e. it is **necessary** for the employee to reside in the accommodation for the **proper performance** of his duties.

Example It is necessary for a caretaker to live in his employer's premises for proper performance of his duties. Hence it will be treated as job related accommodation. (e.g. doctor's / nurses' residence or wardens of schools or prisons)

ii. The accommodation is provided for the **better performance** of the employee's duties and the employment is of the type where it is **customary** for accommodation to be provided (e.g. Prime Minister's / Arch Bishop's residence).

iii. The accommodation is provided as a part of a **security** arrangement because there is a special threat to the employee's security.

Test Yourself 7

An employee lives in accommodation which is owned by his employer. The house cost the employer £100,000 and has a rateable value of £1,200. The employee pays monthly rent of £120. The official rate of interest is 4.75%.

Required:

Calculate the taxable benefit.

Test Yourself 8

Nick lives in a company owned flat. The flat cost the company £120,000 in November 2005. The rateable value of the flat is £1,000 and Nick pays rent of £100 per month. Nick moved out of the flat on 1 January 2010 and bought his own house.

Required:

Calculate Nick's taxable benefit. The official rate of interest is 4.75%.

2. **Vouchers for goods or services:** Employees are taxed on the expense incurred by the person providing the vouchers. An employee may receive from his employer:

a) cash vouchers (vouchers exchangeable for cash such as gift vouchers),

b) credit token (such as a credit card) to obtain money, goods or services or

c) exchangeable vouchers (such as book tokens).

In such cases, the employer is taxed on the cost of providing the benefit, less any amount the employee contributes towards it.

All the employees, whether P9D (lower paid) or P11D, are assessed to tax on the cost to their employer for the vouchers exchangeable for goods or services.

Example Jimmy, an employed person, received a book token worth £120 from his company. In this case, £120 will be added to Jimmy's employment income. If Jimmy pays £20 to the employer for the book token then only £100 will be added to his employment income.

Exceptions

i. **First 15p per day** of meals vouchers are **not taxable**.

Example A company provided its employee's luncheon vouchers worth 80p for 260 days in 2009-10. The taxable value of luncheon vouchers = (80p – 15p) = 65p x 260 days = £169 which will be added to the employee's taxable income.

ii. Entertainment and hospitality vouchers provided by a person **other than the employer** or someone connected with the employer **are not taxable.**

Example A supplier of PMC Ltd provided all the purchasing department employees with musical show tickets, each costing £120. The value of the ticket is not taxable for the employees as these are not provided by the employer or someone directly connected with the employer.

4.3 Benefits assessable on P11D employees

This includes:
- cars provided for private use
- fuel provided for private use
- vans provided for private use
- beneficial loans
- assets loaned for private use
- ancillary services connected with living accommodation

Important rule about benefits

a) Benefits are time apportioned if only available for part of the year.
b) Benefits are reduced by any contribution made by employee (except fuel benefit).

1. Cars provided for private use

a) If a car is provided to an employee or members of his family for private use a taxable benefit arises.

The charge for the private use is based on the manufacturer's list price, and is calculated as follows:

	£
(Manufacturer's list price – Employee capital contribution) x Appropriate %	X
Less: Employee contribution for the provision of the car	(X)
Assessable benefit	**X**

Note: Employee's capital contribution cannot exceed £5,000.

Diagram 3: Manufacturer's list price

The manufacturer's list price is determined as follows:

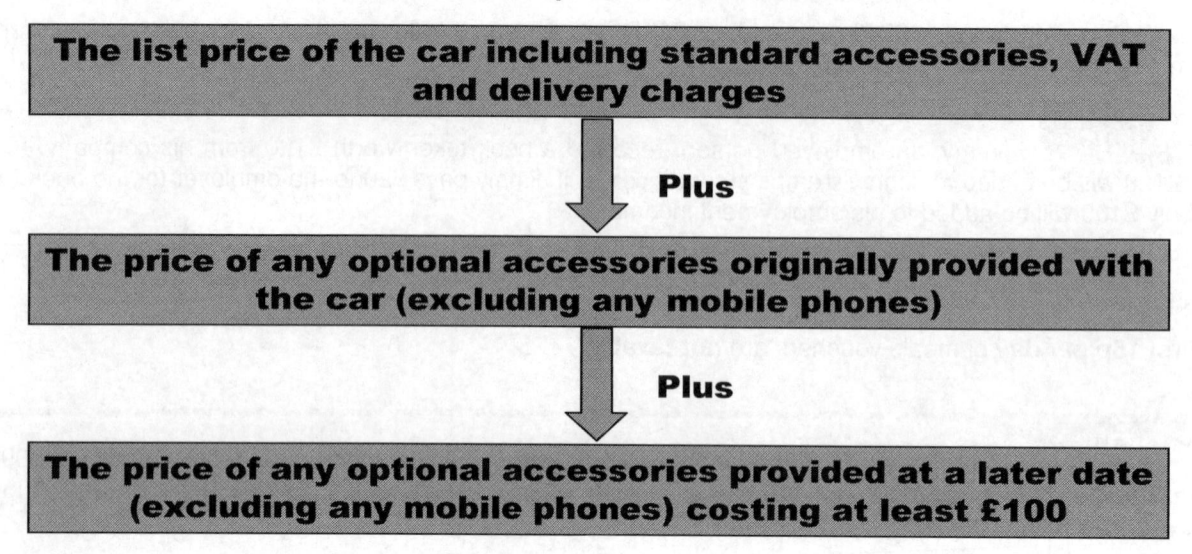

> The list price of the car including standard accessories, VAT and delivery charges

Plus

> The price of any optional accessories originally provided with the car (excluding any mobile phones)

Plus

> The price of any optional accessories provided at a later date (excluding any mobile phones) costing at least £100

The manufacturer's list price cannot exceed £80,000.

Example

George is employed as an accountant at a salary of £50,000 and is provided with a company car by his employer for his private use. His car is a Mercedes with a list price (when new) of £55,000, but his employer purchases the car second hand for £40,000. At the same time, accessories worth £2,000 were fitted in the car for George.

Calculate the list price of the car.

To calculate the taxable benefit, the list price of the car is:
£55,000 + £2,000 = £57,000

---

b) If the car is a "classic car" and its current market value is greater than the manufacturer's list price, then the market value is used.

What is a classic car?

A "classic car" is one which is more than 15 years old and whose market value at the end of the tax year is more than £15,000.

c) Where an employee contributes towards the capital cost of the car, (to enable a more expensive car to be purchased) the capital contribution is deducted from the manufacturer's list price, subject to a maximum of £5,000.

Example

If in the above example, George contributed £3,000 towards the cost of car, the list price will be £57,000 - £3,000 = £54,000.

---

d) **Appropriate percentage**

The appropriate percentage used to calculate the benefit depends on the carbon dioxide (CO_2) emissions rate of the car, and ranges from 15% to 35%. It is expressed in grams per kilometre (g/km), and if the CO_2 emissions do not exceed the lower threshold for the year the lower rate of 15% applies.

The 15% rate is increased by 1% for each 5g/km over the threshold up to a maximum of 35%.

The Finance Act 2008 has introduced a new lower rate of 10% for motor cars with a CO_2 emissions rate of exactly 120 grams per kilometre or less.

The threshold for 2009-10 for petrol cars is:

120 g/km or less	⟶	10%
121 g/km to 135 g/km	⟶	15%
Each additional 5 g/km	⟶	1% increase
Maximum (235 g/km or more)	⟶	35%

3% is added to the appropriate percentage if the car runs on diesel. The 3% supplement cannot take the appropriate percentage above 35%.

> **Tip**
> If the CO_2 emissions rate of the car is above 135 g/km and is not in multiples of five, it is **rounded down to the nearest 5 g/km level** for calculating the appropriate percentage.

Example Suppose, in George's case, (list price £54,000), the CO_2 emissions is 210g/km, the appropriate percentage is:

$$15\% + \frac{(210 - 135)}{5} = 30\%$$

The assessable benefit is = £54,000 x 30% = £16,200

Example Assume in the above example, the car runs on diesel.

The appropriate percentage is 30% + 3% = 33%

Example George was provided with a new diesel-powered company car with a list price of £15,200 and an official CO_2 emissions rate of 122 grams per kilometer.

The CO_2 emissions are below the base level of 135 grams per kilometer, so the appropriate percentage is 18% (15% + 3%)

The benefit would be £15,200 x 18% = £2,736

If George was provided with a petrol-powered car then the appropriate percentage would have been 15%. The benefit would have been £15,200 x 15% = £2,280

If George was provided with a new petrol-powered company car throughout the tax year 2009-10 with a list price of £15,200 and an official CO_2 emissions rate of 118 grams per kilometer, then as the CO_2 emissions are below 120 grams per kilometer, the lower rate of 10% applies. The vehicle was available throughout the tax year 2009-10, so the benefit is £15,200 x 10% = £1,520

e) Any contributions made by the employee to the employer for the private use of the car will be deducted from the taxable benefit.

Example If, in above example, George contributes £30 per month for the private use of the petrol driven car, the taxable benefit will be:

£1,520 – (£30 x 12) = £1,160

f) If a car is not available for the whole of the tax year or is unusable for a continuous period of at least 30 consecutive days, the benefit is pro-rated accordingly. Calculations are done to the nearest month.

Example Judi is employed with a salary of £45,000 and is provided a car with a list price of £20,000 and CO_2 emissions of 186 g/km. The car was made available from 6 November 2009. Calculate the benefits assessable in 2009-10.

Continued on next page

List price = £20,000
Relevant percentage

$$15\% + \frac{(185-135)}{5} = 25\%$$

Benefit assessable = £20,000 x 25% = £5,000 x 5 months/12 months
= £2,083

g) More than one car

If the employee is provided with more than one car, for e.g. a car is provided for his wife as well, then he is assessed on both cars.

h) Cars used for business only

If there is no private use of the car, there is no benefit.

i) Pool cars

No assessable benefit arises from the use of a pool car. A pool car is one which satisfies all the following criteria:

- It is available for use by more than one employee and is not ordinarily used by one employee exclusively.
- It is not normally kept at an employee's residence overnight.
- Any private use is incidental to its use for business purposes.

Test Yourself 9

Lily, a P11D employee, is provided with a car by her employer. The list price of the car is £15,300. Lily made a capital contribution of £1,200 and pays her employer £30 per month for the private use of the car. The car is available throughout 2009-10.

Required:

Calculate the benefits assessable in 2009-10 if the car is petrol driven and has an emissions rate of

1. 120 g/km
2. 164 g/km
3. 222 g/km
4. 280 g/km

The **car benefit** assessable on the employee **covers the provision of the car by his employer and any running costs** (i.e. insurance, road fund licence and maintenance). It does not cover the provision of private fuel.

Test Yourself 10

During the tax year 2009-10, Tip-Top Plc provided the following employees with company motor cars:

1. Neil was provided with a new diesel-powered company car throughout the year 2009-10. The motor car has a list price of £15,500, and an official CO_2 emissions rate of 192 grams per kilometer.

2. Bob was provided with a new petrol-powered company car from 5 September 2009. The motor car has a list price of £12,400, and an official CO_2 emissions rate of 129 grams per kilometer.

3. Simi was provided with a new petrol-powered company car throughout the tax year 2009-10. The motor car has a list price of £25,800, and an official CO_2 emissions rate of 282 grams per kilometer. Simi paid Tip-top plc £1,600 during the tax year 2009-10 for the use of the motor car.

Required:

Calculate the value of assessable benefits.

2. Fuel provided for private use

A separate benefit arises on the provision of **private fuel**, and is calculated as follows:

```
Fixed amount set by HMRC  x    Appropriate %
£16,900 for 2009 - 10          Same % as for car benefit
```

The benefit is calculated as above where there is any fuel provided for private use; the actual amount is irrelevant. The taxable benefit bears no resemblance to the amount of fuel actually paid for / reimbursed by the employer for the year. Therefore **any partial reimbursement by the employee will not affect the taxable benefit.**

No benefit will arise if:
a) the employee **fully reimburses** the employer **for any private fuel** provided, or
b) the **fuel is only provided for business use**

If the fuel is not provided for the whole tax year, the benefit is pro-rated.

If the employee does not fully reimburse the cost of the private fuel, the full fuel benefit is assessable.

If the employee makes a partial contribution towards the cost of private fuel, the benefit is not reduced by the contribution. This is an exception to the general rule.

Test Yourself 11

Mark is provided with a car on 1 July 2009 by his employer. The list price of the car is £24,000 and the CO_2 emissions is 167g/km. The car runs on unleaded petrol, and the employer pays for all fuel.
Mark contributes £100 per month for the private use of the car and a further £25 per month towards the cost of private fuel (which actually amounts to £45 per month on average).

Required:

Calculate the car benefit and fuel benefit assessable on Mark for 2009-10.

Test Yourself 12

Fernando is employed, earning £30,000 per annum. In January 2009 he was provided with a Renault car that runs on petrol (list price £12,000 and CO_2 emissions 148g/km).

On 1 July 2009, his employer exchanged the Renault for a Ford Focus (list price £14,000 and CO_2 emissions 134 g/km). The Ford Focus runs on diesel. The company reimburses Fernando for his business fuel costs.

Required:

Calculate Fernando's taxable benefit for 2009-10.

> **Tip** **NIC**
> Employers will pay Class 1A NIC at 12.8% on the taxable benefits.
> Employees have no NIC liability on the car and fuel benefits.

3. Vans provided for private use

a) A P11D employee is assessed on the private use of a van.
b) The benefit is a fixed amount of £3,000 and there is no reduction for older vans. The benefit is proportionately reduced if a van is unavailable for part of the tax year.
c) Unlike car benefit, while calculating benefit for private use of a van, the journey between home and work is not considered.
d) If a van is for private use by more than one employee, then the amount of benefit is divided equally among all the employees who use the van for private purposes irrespective of the amount of private use by each of the employee.
e) There will also be an additional benefit of £500 if fuel is provided for private mileage. The fuel benefit is proportionately reduced if a van is unavailable for part of the tax year, or if fuel is only provided for part of the tax year.

4. Beneficial loans

A beneficial loan is one made to an employee by the employer which is **either interest free or the interest paid is less than the official rate of interest.**

The **taxable benefit** is as follows:

	£
Interest on outstanding amount at the official rate of interest	X
Less: interest actually paid (if any)	(X)
Assessable benefit	**X**

Loans made in the ordinary course of the employer's **money-lending business are not taxable,** if made on the same terms and conditions as loans made to the general public.

No assessable benefit arises if the total amount outstanding does not exceed £5,000 at any time during the tax year.

A benefit arises on interest on the whole loan, if the loan exceeds £5,000 and not just on the excess of the loan over £5,000.

If any amount of the loan is written off a benefit equal to the amount written off arises.

Example

Alan has an annual salary of £30,000. He has taken a loan from his employer of £20,000 at 3% interest to purchase a yatch.

Calculation of assessable benefits assuming official rate of interest of 4.75%:
As the loan is more than £5,000, the amount of assessable benefit is calculated as £20,000 x (4.75% - 3%) = £350

There are two methods of calculating the assessable benefit:

a) the average method, and
b) the strict method.

The average method is always applied unless the taxpayer elects for the strict method to be used.

a) Average method

The official rate of interest is applied to the average of the balance at the beginning and at the end of the year. If the loan was repaid before the year end, then the balance at the time of repayment is taken.

Example

Mack is an employee of BBG Ltd with a salary of £40,000. On 1 January 2008 the company provided Mack with an interest free loan of £60,000 to purchase a boat. Mack repaid £45,000 of the loan on 5 May 2009.

The assessable benefit for 2009-10 is computed as follows:

The average amount of the loan outstanding during the tax year = (£60,000 + £15,000)/2 = £37,500

Thus, assessable value of beneficial loan = (£37,500 x 4.75%) = **£1,781**

Note: Official rate of interest is 4.75% for 2009-10.

---

b) Strict method

The official rate of interest is applied to the amount outstanding on a month by month basis.

Example

Right Plc provided Lai with an interest free loan of £30,000 on 1 January 2006. She repaid £20,000 of the loan on 30 June 2009, with the balance of £10,000 being repaid on 31 December 2009. Calculate the amount of benefit for the tax year 2009-10 using:

1. The average method
2. The strict method

Continued on next page

Average method

(£30,000 + £10,000)/2 = £20,000 x 4.75% x 9/12
= £713

Strict method

	£
£30,000 x 4.75% x 3/12	356
£10,000 x 4.75% x 6/12	238
Total	**594**

Hence, it is beneficial for the employee to have the taxable benefits calculated according to the strict method.

Test Yourself 13

An employee availed of a taxable cheap loan from his employer on 10 April 2009 of £38,000. On 31 December 2009, he repaid £22,000. The employee's earning is £16,000 per annum. The remaining balance of £16,000 was outstanding at 5 April 2010. Interest paid during the year was £380.

Required:

What was the taxable benefit for 2009-10, assuming that the official rate of interest was 4.75%?

5. Assets loaned to employee for private use

When an employer makes an asset available to an employee for his private use, the employee is **assessed annually on 20% of the market value of the asset** when first provided to the employee.

Example An employer provided a T.V. set costing £900 to his employee for private use. The assessable benefit is 20% of £900 i.e. £180.

If the asset is subsequently gifted or sold to the employee, the assessable benefit **is the greater of:**

a) The market value at the date of the gift / sale less employee contribution (if any).

b) The market value when first provided to the employee less annual 20% assessments less employee contribution (if any).

The loan of a bicycle and cycling safety equipment is exempt from tax if used wholly or mainly for the travel between office and home.

If an employee is gifted or sold a bicycle which is used privately by an employee, the benefit is the market value on the date of the gift / sale less employee contribution (if any) i.e. (b) above does not apply.

Example Excellent Plc provided Rower with a computer throughout the tax year 2009-10 for her personal use. The computer cost £1,500.

Benefits assessable for the tax year 2009-10 in respect of the computer = £1,500 x 20% = £300

Example On 6 April 2007 a P11D employee was provided by his employer, for his private use, a new camera costing £600. On 5 September 2009 he buys the camera from his employer for £70 when its value was £200. Calculate the assessable benefits for 2007-08 to 2009-10.

	£	£
2007-08		
20% of £600		120
2008-09		
20% of £600		120
2009-10		
20% of 600 x 5/12		50
Add: greater of (1) or (2) below		
1. £200 - £70	130	
2. £600 - £120 - £120 - £50 - £70	240	240
Total benefits assessed		**530**

Test Yourself 14

On 6 April 2008 an employee was provided by his employer, for his private use, with a new music system costing £800. On 6 April 2009 he bought the music system from his employer for £180 when its value was £350.

Required:

Calculate assessable benefits in 2008-09 and 2009-10.

---

6. Ancillary services connected with living accommodation

P11D employees are taxed on **related expenses paid by the employer**, in addition to the benefit of living accommodation. These related expenses are:

a) Heating, electricity, cleaning, decorating etc.
b) Repairs and maintenance, but not structural repairs: these are assessed according to the cost to the employer.
c) The use of furniture: this is calculated according to the rules in 5 above.

If the accommodation is job related, the assessable benefit of ancillary services and use of furniture **cannot exceed 10% of employee's net earnings** for the tax year. Net earnings mean total earnings for the year **without** considering ancillary services and use of furniture **less** allowable expenses.

Example

Jack, whose salary was £12,000 for 2009-10, is given living accommodation by his employer. His employer pays the electricity bill of £1,240, a gas bill of £300 and the gardener's salary of £600. Jack contributes £30 per month towards the cost of these services.

Computation of the assessable benefit of the ancillary services, assuming the accommodation is:
➢ not job-related
➢ job-related

1. Assuming the accommodation is not job-related

The ancillary benefits provided along with the living accommodation are taxable.

	£
Electricity bill	1,240
Gas bill	300
Gardener's salary	600
Total benefits	**2,140**
Less: Jack's contribution (£30 x 12)	(360)
Assessable benefit	**1,780**

2. Assuming the accommodation is job-related

If the accommodation is job related, the assessable benefit of ancillary services **cannot exceed 10% of the employee's net earnings** for the year.

Jack's net earnings for 2009-10 are £12,000.

	£
10% of Jack's net earnings (10% of 12,000)	1,200
Less: Jack's contribution	(360)
Assessable benefit	**840**

Example

Harry has a salary of £62,850 in 2009-10. He is provided with job-related accommodation, which has a rateable value of £2,720. In 2009-10 the company pays an electricity bill of £1,320, a gas bill of £420, gardener's salary of £680 and redecoration costs of £1,280. The company has also provided furniture costing £15,000 along with the accommodation. Harry makes a monthly contribution of £50 for his accommodation. Harry's taxable employment income for 2009-10 is calculated as follows.

	£	£
Salary		62,850
Accommodation benefits		
Rateable value: exempt (being job related)		
Ancillary services		
Electricity	1,320	
Gas	420	
Gardener salary	680	
Redecoration expenses	1,280	
Furniture (£15,000 x 20%)	3,000	
	6,700	
Restricted to 10% of £62,850 (note)	6,285	
Less: employee's contribution (£50 per month)	(600)	5,685
Taxable employment income		**68,535**

Note: The value of ancillary services is £6,700. However, if the accommodation is job related, the assessable benefit of ancillary services **cannot exceed 10% of employee's net earnings** for the year.

Test Yourself 15

Peter is provided with job-related accommodation. His annual salary for 2009-10 is £20,000 and his benefits are as follows.

	£
Private medical insurance	450
Electricity bill for the flat	2,500
Cleaning	1,400

Required:

Calculate Peter's taxable employment income for the year 2009-10.

Diagram 4: Summary of benefits assessable on P11D employees

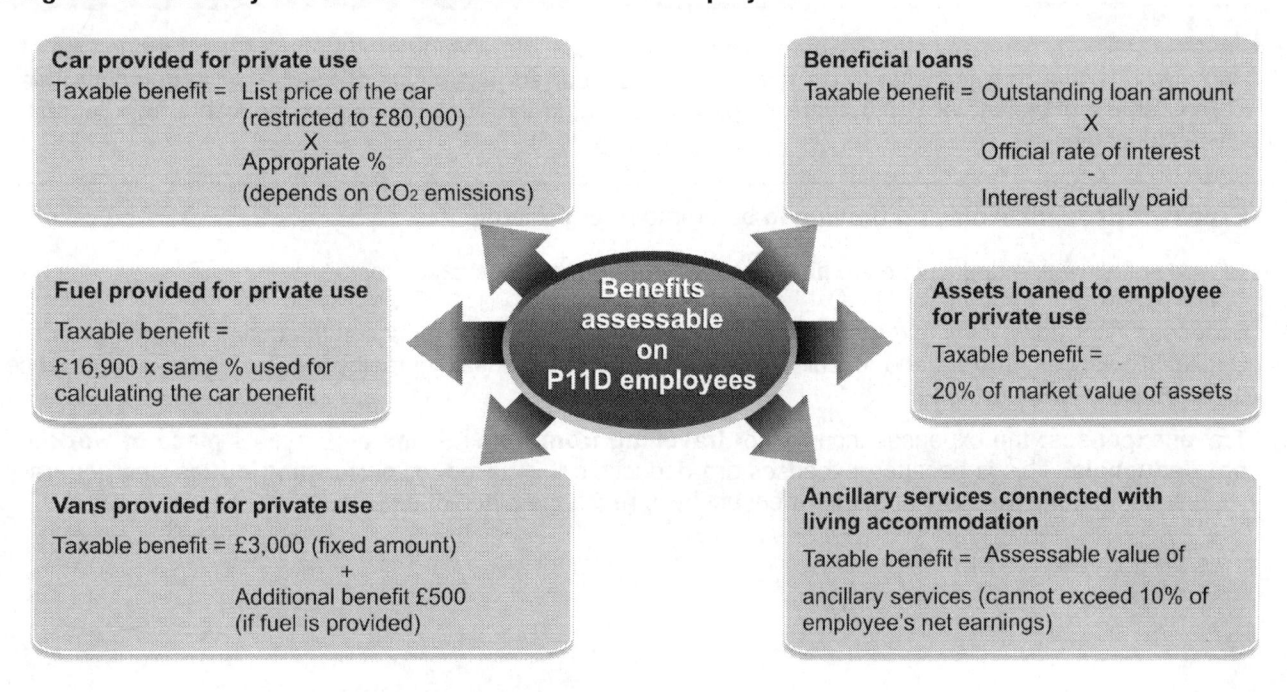

Car provided for private use
Taxable benefit = List price of the car
(restricted to £80,000)
X
Appropriate %
(depends on CO$_2$ emissions)

Beneficial loans
Taxable benefit = Outstanding loan amount
X
Official rate of interest
−
Interest actually paid

Fuel provided for private use
Taxable benefit =
£16,900 x same % used for calculating the car benefit

Assets loaned to employee for private use
Taxable benefit =
20% of market value of assets

Vans provided for private use
Taxable benefit = £3,000 (fixed amount)
+
Additional benefit £500
(if fuel is provided)

Ancillary services connected with living accommodation
Taxable benefit = Assessable value of ancillary services (cannot exceed 10% of employee's net earnings)

Benefits assessable on P11D employees

Test Yourself 16

Nancy is an employee of Anchor Ltd earning a salary of £30,000. Nancy was provided with living accommodation in the year 2001. The property was purchased in 1991 for £100,000 and was valued at £210,000 when first provided to Nancy. It has a rateable value of £6,000. The furniture provided with the property cost £10,000 and Anchor Ltd pays for the annual running costs of £4,000. The living accommodation is not job-related. Assume the official rate of interest is 4.75%.

Required:

What is Nancy's benefit for 2009-10?

---

5. Recognise the allowable deductions, including travelling expenses.[2]
[Learning outcome d]

Deductions allowable from taxable pay can be categorised as:
- expenses that are always deductible
- expenses that are deductible only on proving to be employment related

1. Always deductible

These include:

a) **Contributions to a registered occupational pension**.

b) **Subscriptions to professional bodies** approved by HMRC, if relevant to duties of employment.

Example
The annual subscription to the ACCA paid by a finance manager of a company is deductible from his employment earnings.

c) **Donations to charity made under the payroll deduction scheme operated by an employer.** Such donations are **deducted** from the employee's **gross earnings** to arrive at his net taxable earnings.

d) **Mileage allowance** relief (explained in Learning Outcome 6 in this Study Guide)

e) **Payment of employment related liabilities and for insurance against them.** If an employee or a director of a company incurs a liability related to his employment or pays for insurance against such liability, the cost incurred by him is allowable as deduction from his taxable pay. If such a liability is paid by the employer, on behalf of the employee then no taxable benefits arise to the employee.

Example
A company sued its manager for negligence. He was ordered to make good the losses of £5,000 caused by the manager due to his negligence. He incurred legal costs of £5,000 while defending his case. Thus, these expenses of £10,000 are employment related liabilities hence are deductible from taxable employment income.

2. Expenses deductible only on proving to be employment related

These types of allowable deductions are **limited to the following three** expenses.
- Travel expenses
- Expenses incurred **wholly, exclusively and necessarily** in the performance of the duties of employment
- Capital allowances on plant and machinery (excluding cars) necessarily provided for use in the performance of the duties of employment

a) **Travel expenses:** the expenses incurred for **travelling from home to the employee's place of work** are **not deductible.** This is because expenses are deductible if incurred for **performing duties** and generally you cannot perform any duty of employment until you reach the place of employment.

> **Example** Jessica is a finance manager of a company in London. She often travels for meetings at the company's head office in Southampton. As the journey is undertaken in performance of duties of employment, the full cost of these journeys is deductible.

Test Yourself 17

Annie resides in city A. She works with a construction company. Every day she has to report first to the company's office in city B and then has to go to a project site, which is in city C. From city C, she returns directly to her residence in city A.

Required:

What tax relief is available for Annie's travel costs?

However, the **costs of travel between home and work are allowable in the following situation:**

i. Travel costs incurred by an employee when undertaking business journeys which start from home. However relief will not be available if the journey is substantially the same as the employee's normal journey to work.

> **Example** Rita is a finance executive of a company. She resides in city A and has to go to city B where the office of the company is situated. However on every Monday and Friday, she has to go to city C to meet the company's bankers. On those days she goes directly to city C from city A. The distance between city A and city C is almost three times the distance between city A and city B.

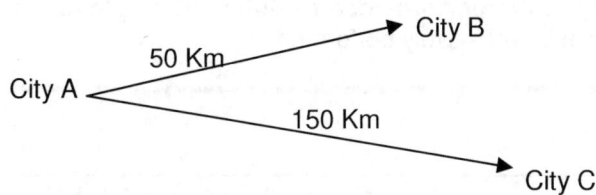

```
              City B
      50 Km ↗
City A
      150 Km ↘
              City C
```

In this case, the travelling costs from city A to city C are deductible.

However, instead of going to city C, if she has to attend a meeting in another part of city B, then as the journey is substantially the same, relief will not be available.

ii. Travelling costs **incurred by a "site-based" employee** travelling from home to the site are deductible. Site based employees are those who do not have a permanent workplace.

> **Example** Construction workers or management consultants who provide services at the customer's place.

However there is a **condition** that the employee does **not spend more than twenty-four months of continuous work** at any one site.

Test Yourself 18

Peter works for a company in London as a software developer. The company sets up a new branch in York and Peter is sent there to work full-time for 20 months, then he will return to work in London.

Required:

Is Peter entitled to deduct his commuting costs from London to York?

What will be your answer if Peter is appointed as the manager in charge of the new project at the York branch and the project lasts three years?

iii. Travel costs incurred by an employee who is seconded to a temporary workplace are deductible, provided it is expected that he will return to the normal workplace within **twenty-four months.**

If the secondment is initially expected to last up to twenty-four months, but it is extended, relief ceases to be due from the date the employee becomes aware of the change of period.

Example

Peter, a software engineer working in London, was sent to work full-time at a new branch of the company in Leeds for 20 months. At the end of the period he would return to the head office in London. He left for Leeds on 1 January 2010 and the project started on 15 January 2010. However, 3 months after the start of the project, it was clear that the project will continue for three years.

In this case, Peter ceases to get any deduction for travel costs to Leeds from the date he becomes aware that the project is extended to three years. That date is 3 months after the start of project i.e. 15 April 2010. Any traveling cost incurred up to 5 April 2010, can be deducted from his taxable earnings for 2009-10.

> **Tip: Quick revision of the rules relating to travelling expenses**
> a) Allow relief for the full cost of business travelling expenses.
> b) There is no relief for any costs relating to ordinary commuting (i.e. travel between home and a permanent workplace).
> c) There is no relief for any costs relating to private travel.
> d) Allow relief for travel in the performance of the employee's duties. It covers:
>   i. Travel costs incurred by an employee when undertaking business journeys which start from home.
>   ii. Travelling costs **incurred by a "site-based" employee** for travel from home to the site.
>   iii. If the employee is working at a particular workplace over a period of more than 24 months, that place is treated as his permanent workplace so travel between the work place and home is ordinary commuting for which there is no relief.

b) **Expenses incurred wholly, exclusively and necessarily in the performance of duties of employment**
i.e. expenses without which the duties of employment cannot be effectively performed.

Example
Cost of protective work clothes.

The word "wholly and exclusively" emphasises that any expenditure incurred for private purposes is not deductible. Whether expenditure is **"necessary"** for the performance of the duties of employment depends on if they could be **performed without this expenditure.**

Example
The expenses of joining a club that was virtually a requisite of an employment was not a deductible expense. This is so because it would have been possible to carry on the employment without the club membership, so the expense was not necessary.

Test Yourself 19

Which of the following expenses incurred by an employee would be deductible from his income for tax purposes?

1. The cost incurred by a production manager for a suit to wear for an office meeting.
2. The bank manager pays an annual subscription to the Association of Bankers.
3. A sales manager voluntarily pays an annual subscription to City Club. He visits the club only for the purpose of conducting meetings with clients.
4. An officer pays to attend study courses in the evenings so as to improve his prospects for promotion.

---

c) **Capital allowances:** Where plant or machinery is **necessarily provided** by an employee for use in the performance of his duties, capital allowances may be claimed for its business use.

Employees may not obtain capital allowances for cars, motorcycles or cycles.

Example
An employee uses his personal computer for performing his official duties. He can claim capital allowances on the computer, which will be deducted from his taxable employment income.

Income from Employment: B2.25

Diagram 5: Expenses deductible only on proving to be employment related

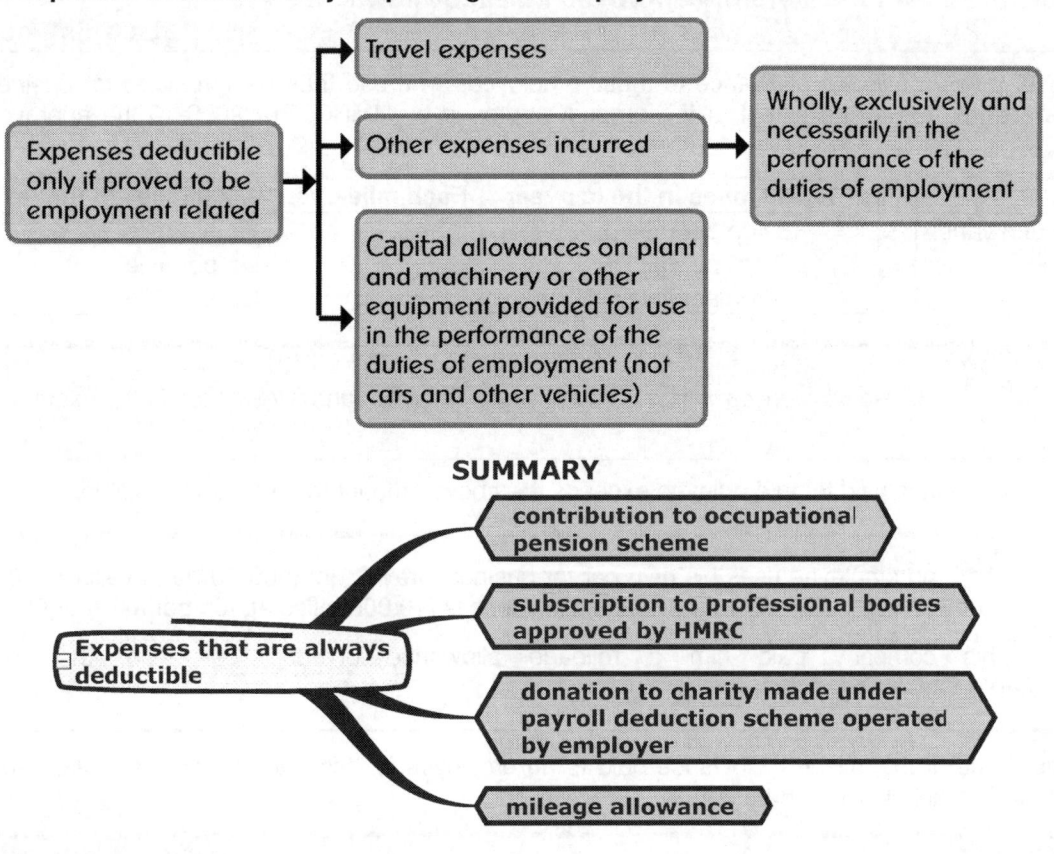

Expenses deductible only if proved to be employment related
- Travel expenses
- Other expenses incurred → Wholly, exclusively and necessarily in the performance of the duties of employment
- Capital allowances on plant and machinery or other equipment provided for use in the performance of the duties of employment (not cars and other vehicles)

SUMMARY

Expenses that are always deductible:
- contribution to occupational pension scheme
- subscription to professional bodies approved by HMRC
- donation to charity made under payroll deduction scheme operated by employer
- mileage allowance

Test Yourself 20

Joy Ltd spent £120 per employee on a Christmas party for all staff. What is the tax position for:

1. Joy Ltd
2. Each employee

Test Yourself 21

On 1 December 2009, Rocky commenced employment with Ajanta Plc. His salary is £25,000 per annum. During the period from 1 December 2009 to 5 April 2010 Rocky was provided with free meals in Ajanta Plc's staff canteen along with all other employees of the company. The total cost of these meals to the company was £1,800.

Required:

What is Rocky's taxable benefit in 2009-10?

Test Yourself 22

Susan is a chartered certified accountant working for TGT Ltd. Her annual salary is £15,000. She incurred the following expenses in the year ended 5 April 2010.
1. Her annual subscription fees for ACCA were £200.
2. She received an award of £150 under the staff suggestion scheme.
3. She received a bonus of £5,000 in the year in addition to her annual salary.
4. She threw a party on her birthday for all her colleagues in the office and incurred costs of £300.
5. She started contributing £300 per month to an occupational pension scheme from 1 August 2009.
6. She paid £200 as a deposit and £250 annual rent for her accommodation in the city.

Required:

What is Susan's taxable employment income for 2009-10?

6. Discuss the use of the statutory approved mileage allowances. [2]
[Learning outcome e]

The employer gives a mileage allowance to those employees who use their own vehicles for business. These allowances are tax-free to the extent of the amount approved by HMRC. For 2009-10 the approved mileage rates are:

	First 10,000 miles in the tax year	Each mile over 10,000 miles in the tax year
Motor cars and vans	40p per mile	25p per mile
Motor cycles	24p per mile	24p per mile
Bicycles	20p per mile	20p per mile

Tip

These allowances will be given to you in the rates and allowances in the exam.

If the mileage allowance paid to an employee exceeds the above amount the **excess** is taxable.

Example

An employee uses his own car for business travel. In 2009-10 he travelled 10,000 miles in the duties of his employment. The tax-free mileage allowance is (10,000 miles at 40p per mile) £4,000.

However, if his company paid him a mileage allowance of 60p per mile, the **excess** i.e. **£6,000 - £4,000 = £2,000 is taxable.**

On the other hand, if the mileage allowance paid to an employee is less than the sum calculated using these rates; the **deficit** is an allowable expense.

Example

Continuing with the above example, assume that he is paid 30p per mile. This is below the approved mileage allowance, and the deficit (£4,000 - £3,000 = £1,000) is deducted from his employment income.

If the employee **carries a passenger** on a **business trip**, the employer may pay the employee up to **5p per passenger per mile tax free**. However the employee cannot claim tax relief if the employer pays less than 5p per passenger per mile or pays nothing at all.

Test Yourself 23

Alan is employed with a salary of £25,000. He uses his own car when traveling, and in 2009-10 he drives 10,200 miles for business purposes.

Required:

Calculate his employment income if his employer pays him:
1. Nothing
2. 35p per mile
3. 45p per mile

Test Yourself 24

Lora is employed with Flex Plc. She used her private motor car for both business and private purposes during the period from 6 April 2009 to 31 December 2009. She received no reimbursement from Flex Plc for any of the expenditure incurred.

Lora's total mileage during this period was 17,480 miles, made up as follows:

	Miles
Normal daily travel between home and permanent workplace	6,650
Travel between home and permanent workplace in order to turn off a fire alarm	330
Private travel	5,950
Travel between home and a temporary workplace for a period of two months	3,800
Travel between permanent workplace and Flex plc's suppliers	750
	17,480

Required:

State which of the above travelling costs are deductible from employment income.

7. Compute the income assessable.[2]

[Learning outcome c]

The knowledge gained in the previous Learning Outcomes will now be tested.

Test Yourself 25

Jack works for LLH Ltd, and is in charge of controlling the sales activities in three cities (City B, C & D) in northern England and his annual salary is £36,000.

For the year 2009-10 he received a bonus of £1,500 and a performance incentive of £3,000 in December 2009. Jack contributes £500 to an occupational pension scheme every month.

Jack resides in city A and the company is based in city B. He works from city B and visits other cities in relation to his work. He has incurred the following travelling expenses during the year.

Travelling expenses incurred from:
City A to city B   -   £800
City B to city C   -   £700
City B to city D   -   £900
City D to city C   -   £1,000

LLH Ltd has provided him with a mobile phone. The company has incurred £2500 for mobile phone expenses excluding rental charges.

Required:

Calculate Jack's taxable employment income for 2009-10.

Test Yourself 26

Which of the following are exempt from income tax?

1. Meal vouchers of £1.30 per working day
2. Free meals in the company canteen
3. Removal expenses of £4,000
4. A cheque for £1,200 given to an employee on completing 25 years of service with his employer

Test Yourself 27

Which of the following expenses incurred by an employee would be deductible?

1. Travel cost between work and home
2. Travel cost between employment sites
3. The cost of a suit to wear at the office
4. Subscription to professional bodies

Test Yourself 28

Charles is an engineer working in a manufacturing company, Zeta Ltd, with an annual salary of £24,000. In 2009-10 he received the following:
1. a bonus of £1,800.
2. a gift voucher worth £1,500 at Christmas.
3. meal vouchers for 260 days worth 60p each.
4. staff Christmas party costing £200 per employee.

Required:

Calculate his employment income.

8. Explain the PAYE system.[1]

[Learning outcome f]

PAYE stands for **P**ay **A**s **Y**ou **E**arn. An employer deducts income tax from his employees' wages / salaries throughout the year and sends it to HMRC. This system of collecting income tax is known as PAYE.

PAYE is a way of spreading income tax over the tax year. The tax year starts on 6 April of one year and ends on 5 April in the next. Under PAYE, the employer deducts tax from weekly or monthly earnings and pays it over to the Inland Revenue. The employer is effectively acting as a collector of taxes on behalf of HMRC.

8.1 Features

The main features of the PAYE system:

1. Under the PAYE system, the employer has to deduct both **Income tax and National Insurance Contributions** (NIC) (refer Study Guide E1 and E2) from the employee's employment income, which includes wages / salaries, bonuses, commissions etc.

Example Simi is the employed director of BMC Software PLC. Her annual earnings are £40,000. How much income tax should BMC Software deduct for 2009-10 under PAYE?

Income tax liability of Simi

	£
Employment income	40,000
Less: personal allowance	(6,475)
Taxable income	**33,525**

Income tax	£
£33,525 @ 20%	6,705

Therefore, income tax to be deductible by BMC Software every month is £6,705 / 12 = £559

Tip For tax rates and computations refer to Study Guide B5.

2. Income tax and NIC must be paid to HMRC within **14 days** of the **end of the tax month**. In the case of electronic payment, payment must be made within 17 days. A tax month runs from the 6 of one month to the 5 of next month, so payment must be made on or before the **19 / 22** of every month (for electronic payment).

Example Zed Ltd pays its employees on the last day of every month. In January 2010, the total amount of tax deducted by the employer under PAYE was £36,000. The tax month ends on 5 February 2010, hence the amount must be paid within 14 days of the end of tax month i.e. on 19 February 2010.

3. The employers whose monthly PAYE payments do not exceed **£1,500 per month on average** are allowed to make **quarterly** payments instead of monthly payments. Tax quarters end on 5 July, 5 October, 5 January and 5 April. The employer can continue making payments quarterly during a tax year even if the monthly average payments reach or exceed £1,500.

However, a new estimate of average payments must be made at the start of each tax year.

> **Example**
> Fast transporters Ltd commenced trading in April 2009, with a staff of 4 employees and a proprietor. The tax deducted by the proprietor under PAYE in the first 6 months was £1,200 monthly. After 6 months, he employed another 4 employees and now deducts tax of £3,000 per month under PAYE.
>
> In this situation, as the proprietor's tax liability does not average £1,500 per month for the first 6 months, he can pay the amount due under PAYE on a quarterly basis. From the seventh month, his average monthly PAYE liability becomes £2,100, calculated as follows.
>
> $$\frac{(£1,200 \times 6) + (£3,000 \times 6)}{12}$$
>
> He can still continue to pay PAYE to HMRC quarterly. However, from April 10 the liability under PAYE has to be paid monthly, as his new average is £3,000 under PAYE.

4. If an employer fails to apply PAYE wherever it is applicable, **he must pay the tax that he should have deducted.** Such an employer is also liable to penalties. Interest will also be charged from **14 days after** the end of the tax month concerned on any underpaid PAYE.

> **Example**
> Roger, an employer fails to apply PAYE on the employment remuneration he paid to his employees. If the PAYE would have been applied, the tax that would have been deductible from the employees' employment income under PAYE is £4,500. In this case, he has to pay the tax of £4,500, which he should have deducted from the employees income immediately.

5. The officers of HMRC are given wide powers to inspect employer's records in order to satisfy themselves that the correct amounts of tax are being deducted and paid over to HMRC.

8.2 How does PAYE work?

To operate PAYE, an employer needs:

1. Tax codes
2. Tax tables
3. Deduction working sheets

1. Tax codes

a) The PAYE system is based upon the concept of "tax codes". The employer uses a tax code to calculate the amount of tax to deduct from wages / salaries. These codes are determined and amended by the Revenue.

b) A tax code is usually made up of one letter and several numbers,

> **Example**
> 117L or K497

The tax code represents the employee's tax free allowance. The figure is the employee's total allowances, **without the last digit.**

> **Example**
> If an employee's tax free allowances are £4,615, the code will be 461 followed by a letter. The tax code is issued by the HMRC to each employee for each tax year.

In order to decide the tax code, all the factors affecting the employee's income tax liability are to be considered. These factors include:

i. the personal allowance to which the employee is entitled

> **Example**
> Personal allowance for 2009-10 for an individual between 0 to 64 years of age is £6,475.

B2.30: Income Tax Liabilities

ii. allowable expenses (for example, professional subscriptions etc.)

iii. adjustments made for benefits

iv. adjustments for income against which tax was overpaid or underpaid in previous years (see Test Yourself 29 below)

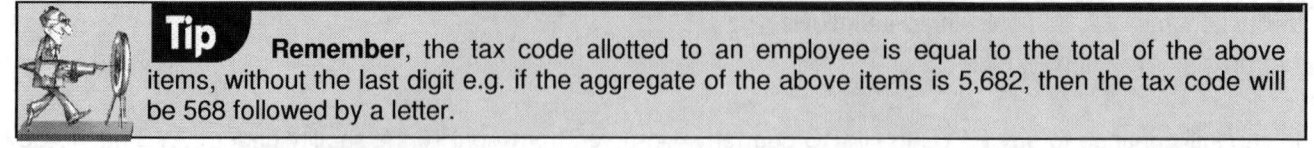

> **Tip** **Remember**, the tax code allotted to an employee is equal to the total of the above items, without the last digit e.g. if the aggregate of the above items is 5,682, then the tax code will be 568 followed by a letter.

How do you work out tax codes?

Diagram 6: Steps for working out tax codes

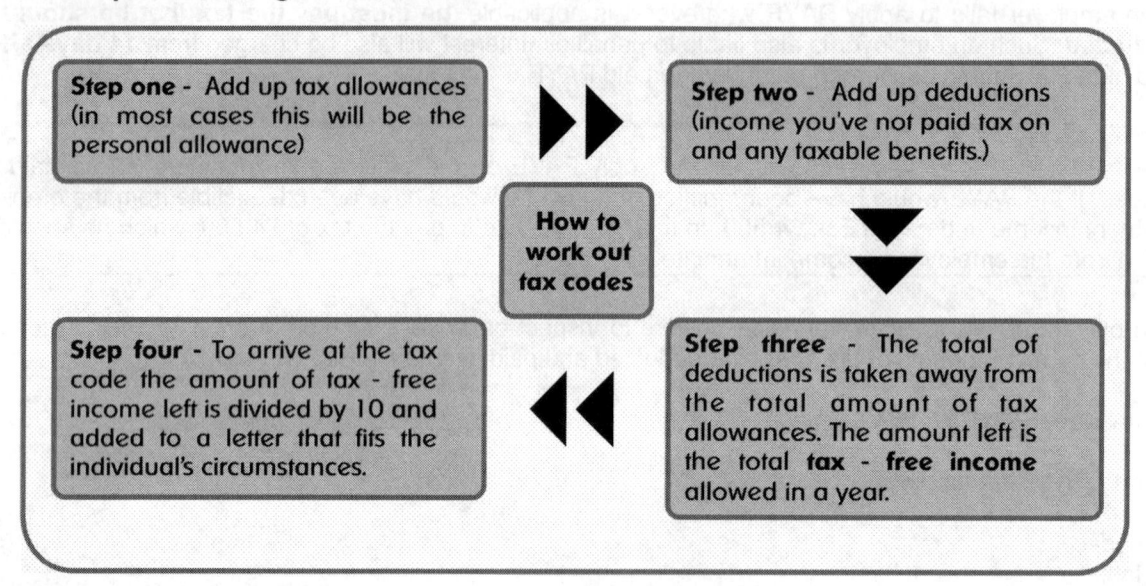

Step one - Add up tax allowances (in most cases this will be the personal allowance)

Step two - Add up deductions (income you've not paid tax on and any taxable benefits.)

Step four - To arrive at the tax code the amount of tax - free income left is divided by 10 and added to a letter that fits the individual's circumstances.

Step three - The total of deductions is taken away from the total amount of tax allowances. The amount left is the total **tax - free income** allowed in a year.

Test Yourself 29

Jimmy earns a salary of £18,000. He pays an allowable professional subscription of £138 and has benefits of £520 in 2009-10. His income for 2006-07 on which tax remains unpaid was £52.5. Jimmy is a basic rate taxpayer.

Calculate Jimmy's tax code for 2009-10.

---

1. Tax code suffixes

The tax code suffix indicates the type of allowance available to each employee.

The letter L is the most common tax code suffix issued to the employer and **indicates that the employee is entitled to the basic personal allowance only.**

The tax code suffix 'P' denotes that the employee is entitled to personal allowance for those aged 65-74.

K is a prefix. It denotes a negative code, which means the employee's benefits exceed his allowance.

2. Tax Tables

Tax tables are used with the code to deduct the correct amount of tax each month.

Mainly two types of tax tables are used:

a) **Table A:** It is also known as the **Pay Adjustment Table.** This table contains pages for each week or month of the year. The table shows, for each tax code, the amount of tax-free pay to which the employee is entitled for the year to date. This tax table spreads the employee's allowances evenly over the year, giving 1/12 of the allowances per month or 1/52 of the allowances per week.

b) **Table B:** It is also known as Taxable Pay Table. This table takes into account the employee's entitlement to tax-free pay and then the income tax liability is worked out.

8.3 PAYE Forms

Various forms are given to employees. Here is a summary of the most common.

Form	Contents	Date	To be given by the employer to
P9D	A year-end return showing the benefits and expenses of lower-paid employees.	6 July following the end of the tax year	HMRC
P11D	An end of year return showing the benefits and expenses of a director or employee earning at least £8,500.	6 July following the end of the tax year	HMRC and copy to employee
P14	An end of year return showing an **individual employee's** gross pay, tax paid and National Insurance paid for the year.	19 May	HMRC
P35	An end of year return showing and summarising **all employees'** gross pay, tax paid and National Insurance paid for the year.	19 May	HMRC
P45	This form has four parts and is used when an employee leaves employment. It shows the employee's tax code, gross pay to date and tax paid to date. Part 1 is sent to HMRC and Parts 2, 3 and 4 are given to the leaving employee. The employee gives Parts 2 and 3 to his or her new employer who retains Part 2 and sends Part 3 to HMRC. The employee retains Part 4	19 May	HMRC
P60	Certificate of gross pay and tax deducted.	31 May following the end of the tax year	employee

Test Yourself 30

Julian is the finance director of Solution Ltd. What are the forms that Solution Ltd must provide to him following the end of the tax year 2009-10 in respect of his earnings and benefits for that year? State the dates by which these forms have to be provided to him.

1. Records

The employer must keep records of each employee's pay and tax at each payday. The records containing details of National Insurance must also be maintained.

The employer can keep records in any of the following ways:
a) By using the official deductions working sheet (form P11).
b) By incorporating the figures in pay records prepared by the employer using a substitute document.
c) By retaining the figures on a computer.

Penalties on late submission of forms

a) A form P35 is due for submission to HMRC on **19 May** after the end of the tax year. However, in practice, a 7 day extension to the due date of 19 May is allowed. Thus practically the due date is **26 May.**

b) If an employer fails to submit form P35 on or before the due date, there is an automatic penalty of **£100 for every month or part-month per 50 employees.**

Example

A firm with 51 employees filed its P35 on 20 June 2010. The penalty amount would be calculated as if the submission was two months late. The fine would accordingly be £400.

This penalty applies for late submission in the 12 months after the due date.

B2.32: Income Tax Liabilities

c) If form P35 is not submitted within 12 months after the due date, a penalty of up to **100% of income tax plus National Insurance Contributions (NIC)** which remain unpaid at 19 April of following year may be charged.

> **Example**
>
> Sigma Ltd's PAYE liability for 2008-09 was £5,000. The company submitted form P35 on 20 July 2010. The delay is more than 12 months, so a penalty of 100% of the tax i.e. £5,000 may be charged.

d) For incorrect forms P35, there is a maximum penalty of 100% of any additional tax found to be due. This penalty can be mitigated.

Diagram 7: Summary of penalties

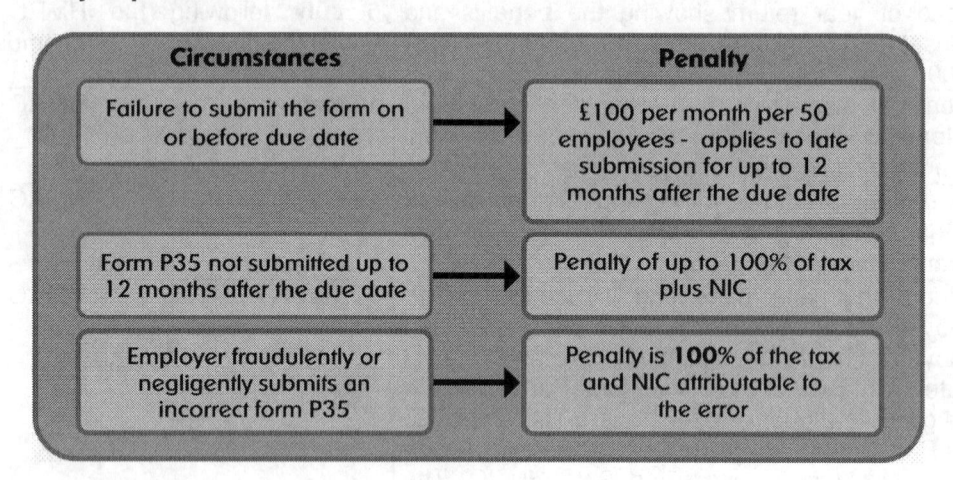

Circumstances	Penalty
Failure to submit the form on or before due date	£100 per month per 50 employees - applies to late submission for up to 12 months after the due date
Form P35 not submitted up to 12 months after the due date	Penalty of up to 100% of tax plus NIC
Employer fraudulently or negligently submits an incorrect form P35	Penalty is 100% of the tax and NIC attributable to the error

PAYE settlement agreements:

This is an arrangement for minor benefits under which employers can make a single payment to settle their employees' income tax liabilities.

The items covered by a PAYE settlement agreement do not have to be included on either Form P9D or P11D or on an employee's tax return.

The **due date** under the PAYE settlement agreement is **19 October following the end of the tax year.**

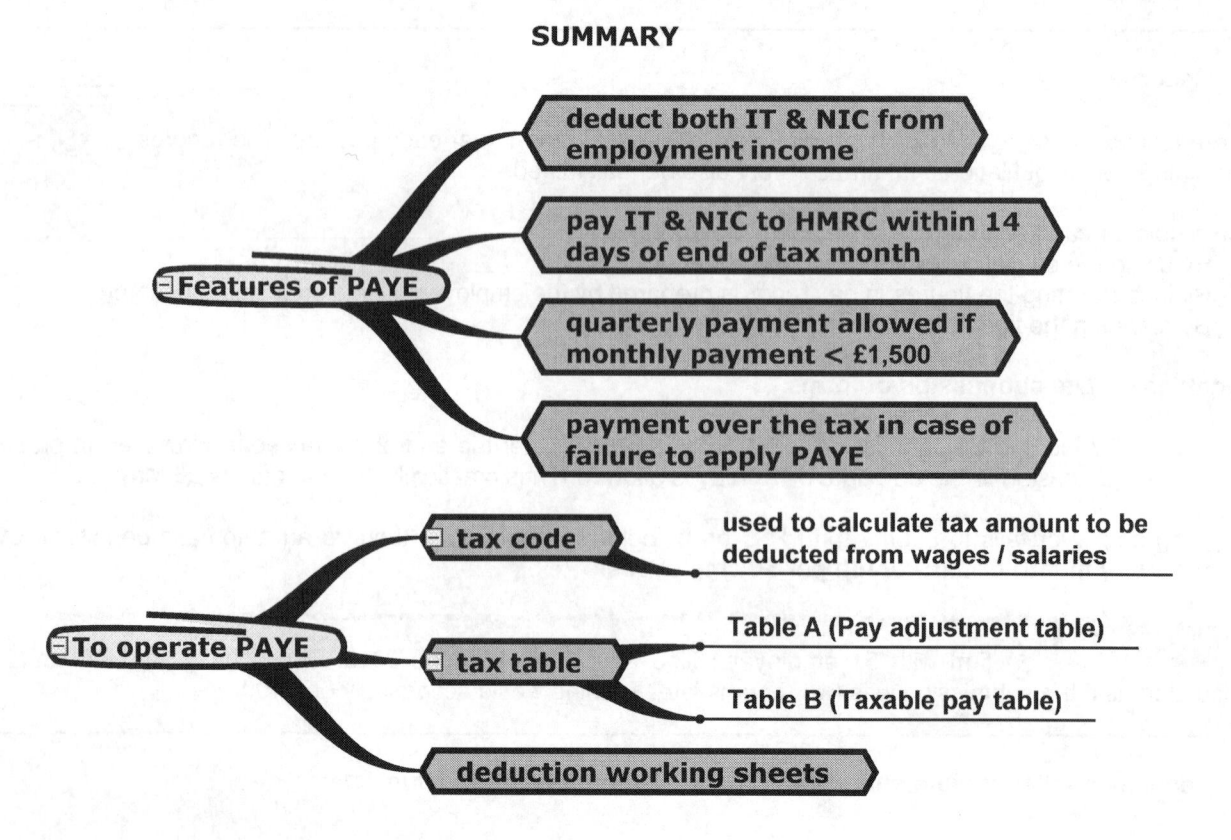

SUMMARY

Features of PAYE
- deduct both IT & NIC from employment income
- pay IT & NIC to HMRC within 14 days of end of tax month
- quarterly payment allowed if monthly payment < £1,500
- payment over the tax in case of failure to apply PAYE

To operate PAYE
- tax code — used to calculate tax amount to be deducted from wages / salaries
- tax table
  - Table A (Pay adjustment table)
  - Table B (Taxable pay table)
- deduction working sheets

9. Explain the purpose of dispensation from HM Revenue & Customs.[2]
[Learning outcome i]

Employers can save themselves the burden of completing forms P11D in respect of **deductible expense payments** made to directors or employees by applying to their Inspector of Taxes for a Dispensation.

While the dispensation remains in force, the employer need not return the expense payments on form P11D, and they do not need to be included on the employee's tax return.

The purpose of a dispensation is to reduce the administrative burden of completing and filing P11D returns on
- the person completing the returns on behalf of the employer,
- the person handling the returns in the tax office, and
- the employee who is required to complete a self-assessment tax return.

10. Explain how charitable giving can be made through a payroll deduction scheme.[1]
[Learning outcome j]

Employees can make donations to charities through a payroll deduction scheme, which allows them tax relief at their highest marginal rate. The charitable payment is deducted from employment income. Income tax is then calculated on earnings after deduction of the donation, through PAYE.

The charitable payment is paid gross, and deducted from employment earnings in the calculation of taxable income.

Answers to Test Yourself

Answer 1

1. McMilan carries out the work under his own control.
2. McMilan procures his own equipment when working on the contracts for Web-Designs Ltd.
3. McMilan is paid fee for each contract; payment is not made on hourly, weekly or monthly basis.
4. There is a financial risk for McMilan.
5. McMilan can earn profit from sound management.
6. The contracts are all for short periods.
7. McMilan is not an integral part of Web-Designs Ltd's business.
8. McMilan is not under any obligation to accept work that is offered to him.

The above factors indicate that McMilan is self-employed.

Answer 2

The assessment of employment income is made on a receipt basis. Therefore, Jo's assessable employment income for 2009-10 is £42,800 i.e. (£35,700 + £7,100). The bonus received in January 2010 is assessed in 2009-10, even though part of it was earned in 2008-09.

Answer 3

The bonus to director is treated to be received at the earliest of:
1. The date on which the bonus was received by the director.
2. The date on which the right to receive the bonus was established.
3. The date when the bonus is credited in the company's accounts
4. The end of the period of account if the bonus relates to that period, and has been determined before the end of the period.
5. The date that the bonus is determined if the period of account it relates to has already ended.

Answer 4

The income of a director is considered to be received **at earliest of** the following:

1. The date on which the income is actually **received** by the director i.e. **5 May 2009** when David received £12,000.

2. The date on which the **right to receive** the income is established i.e. on **31 March 2009** when right to receive £15,000 (3/12 x £60,000) is established as remuneration is payable monthly.

3. The date on which the income is **credited** to the director in the records of the company i.e. on **31 March 2009** when £15,000 is credited to his account in the company's records.

4. The end of the period of accounts, if the director's income for that period is determined **before the end of the period of accounts** of the company i.e. on **31 March 2009** as before that date, it was decided to pay him £5,000 per month. Hence £15,000 is income to be treated as received.

5. The date on which the director's income is determined, if director's income is determined **after the end** of the company's **period of accounts** i.e. on **2 April 2009** when David's remuneration was increased to £84,000 retrospectively. The increase of £24,000 is determined after the end of the company's period of account. **Hence on 2 April 2009, he is entitled to a salary of £21,000 (3/12 x £84,000).**
The **earliest date among all above dates is 31 March 2009.**
The amount to be treated as income is **£15,000.**

Answer 5

A director, **in order not be considered a P11D employee,** has to fulfill the following two conditions:

1. he has to be a director who earns **less than £8,500** per annum **and**
2. he should **not control more than 5% of ordinary share capital** of the company.

Both conditions have to be complied with simultaneously.

As George fulfills only the first condition, but not the second, **he is a P11D employee.**

Answer 6

The cost of the health insurance when added to her salary will take her earnings over £8,500; therefore she is a P11D employee.

Answer 7

	£
Rateable value	1,200
Add: Expensive accommodation benefit	
(£100,000 - £75,000) x 4.75%	1,188
Total	**2,388**
Less: Employee contribution (£120 x12)	(1,440)
Taxable benefit	**948**

Answer 8

	£
Annual value	1,000
Add: Expensive accommodation benefit	
(£120,000 - £75,000) x 4.75%	2,138
Total	**3,138**
For nine months (6/4/2009 to 1/1/2010) (£3,138 x 9/12)	2,354
Less: Employee contribution (£100 x 9)	(900)
Taxable benefit	**1,454**

Answer 9

1. **CO_2 emissions rate of 120 g/km**

   a) Lily's capital contribution is deducted from the list price
      £15,300 - £1,200 = £14,100
   b) As the CO_2 emissions rate is exactly 120 g/km, the appropriate percentage is 10%.
   c) The assessable benefit is:

	£
£14,100 x 10%	1,410
Less: contribution (30 x 12)	(360)
	1,050

2. CO_2 emissions rate of 164 g/km

The appropriate emissions rate is:

$$15\% + \frac{(160 - 135)}{5} = 20\%$$

The assessable benefit is = (£14,100 x 20%) - £360 = **£2,460**

3. CO_2 emissions rate of 222 g/km

$$15\% + \frac{(220 - 135)}{5} = 32\%$$

The assessable benefit is = (£14,100 x 32%) - £360 = **£4,152**

4. CO_2 emissions rate of 280 g/km

$$15\% + \frac{(280 - 135)}{5} = 44\%$$

However, the percentage is restricted to 35%
The assessable benefit is = (£14,100 x 35%) - £360 = **£4,575.**

Answer 10

Neil

The list price of the car is £15,500

The CO_2 emissions are above the base level figure of 135 grams per Kilometer. The CO_2 emissions figure of 192 is rounded down to 190 so that it is divisible by five.

Relevant percentage:

$$15\% + \frac{(190 - 135)}{5} = 26\%$$

So the relevant percentage is 29% (26% plus a 3% charge for a diesel car). The motor car was available throughout the tax year.
Therefore, the benefit assessable = £15,500 x 29% = **£4,495**

Bob

The list price of the car is £12,400

The CO_2 emissions are below the base level figure of 135 grams per kilometer. Therefore, the relevant percentage is 15%.

The motor car was available for seven months of the tax year 2009–10.

Therefore, the assessable benefit = £12,400 x 15% x 7/12
= **£1,085**

Simi

The list price of the car is £25,800

The CO_2 emissions are above the base level figure of 135 grams per kilometer. The CO_2 emissions figure of 282 is rounded down to 280 so that it is divisible by five.

Relevant percentage

$$15\% + \frac{(280 - 135)}{5} = 44\%$$

But the relevant percentage is restricted to 35%

The motor car was available throughout the tax year 2009-10.

Therefore, the assessable benefit = £25,800 x 35%
= 9,030 - 1,600 (note)
= £7,430

Note: The contributions made by Simi towards the use of the motor car reduce the benefit.

Answer 11

Assessable benefit for the car

The appropriate percentage is:

$$15\% + \frac{(165-135)}{5} = 21\%$$

	£
List price x appropriate %	
£24,000 x 21%	5,040
Less: contribution (£100 x 12)	(1,200)
	3,840
Available for 9 months	
Benefit £3,840 x 9/12	**2,880**

Assessable benefit for fuel

Assessable benefit for fuel = £16,900 x 21% = £3,549

As the car is provided only for 9 months, reduce the assessable benefits proportionately
£3,549 x 9/12 = £2,662
Total car and fuel benefits = £5,542 (£2,880 + £2,662)

Answer 12

	£
Renault car (3 months)	
List price of the car is £12,000	
Assessable benefit	
£12,000 x 17% [15% + (145 - 135) / 5 = 17%] x 3/12	510
Ford Focus car (9 months)	
List price of the car is £14,000	
Assessable benefit	
£14,000 x 18% [15% + 3%] x 9/12	1,890
(<135 g/km plus diesel supplement)	
Total benefit	**£2,400**

Note:
No fuel benefit is available as the employer pays for the business fuel and not for the private fuel.

Answer 13

Average method

	£
(£38,000 + £16,000)/2 x 4.75%	1,283
Less: interest paid	(380)
Benefit	**903**

Strict method

	£
38000 x 4.75% x 9/12	1354
16000 x 4.75% x 3/12	190
Total	**1544**
Less: interest paid	(380)
Benefit	**1164**

It is beneficial for the employee to have the taxable benefits calculated according to the average method.

Answer 14

The benefit in 2008-09 is £800 × 20% = £160

The benefit in 2009-10 is **£460**, being the greater of (1) or (2) below:

	£
1. Market value at date of purchase	350
Less: price paid	(180)
	170
2. Original market value	800
Less: assessed in 2008-09	(160)
	640
Less: price paid	(180)
	460

Answer 15

	£	£
Salary		20,000
Add: medical insurance (amount treated as earning)		450
		20,450
Add: Ancillary expenses		
Electricity bill	2,500	
Cleaning	1,400	
Total	**3,900**	
Restricted to 10% of £20,450 (Note 1)	2,045	2,045
Total employment income		**22,495**

Note:

Peter is living in a job related accommodation; hence the assessable value of ancillary services **cannot exceed 10% of employee's net earnings** for the year.

Answer 16

1. Rateable value = £6,000

2. Expensive accommodation benefit (£210,000 - £75,000) x 4.75% = £6,413

3. Furniture (10,000 at 20%) = £2,000

4. Running costs incurred by Anchor Ltd = £4,000

Total benefits = £18,413 i.e. (£6,000 + £6,413 + £2,000 + £4,000)

Note: The expensive accommodation benefit is based on the MV of £210,000 because the property cost is in excess of £75,000 and it was purchased more than six years before it was first provided to the employee.

Answer 17

Annie is entitled to a deduction in respect of costs incurred for travelling from city B to city C. However, she is not entitled to any tax relief for the cost incurred in travelling between city A to city B and from city C to city A since these are normal commuting costs.

Answer 18

Although Peter is spending all of his time at the new branch in York it will not be treated as his normal work place because his period of attendance will be less than 24 months. He can claim relief in full for the costs of travel to and from York.

However, if he spends more than 24 months at the site (three years in this case) it will be treated as his normal place of work. Hence the travel cost from home to York is not deductible from his employment income.

Answer 19

1. The cost of the suit is not deductible, even if worn for office meetings. A suit provides warmth and is appropriate for his work. It therefore has a dual purpose. The expenditure is not wholly and exclusively for business purposes.
2. The cost of the subscription will be allowed as relevant professional subscriptions of this nature are specifically allowed by statute.
3. The subscription is not deductible although it is used wholly and exclusively for business purposes. It was not necessary for performing his duties.
4. The cost of the course is disallowed, as it was not incurred in the performance of his duties.

Answer 20

1. **Joy Ltd:** the cost of the Christmas party is deductible.
2. **Each employee:** the party is not a taxable benefit as the cost is less than £150 per person.

Answer 21

No taxable benefit arises because the provision of meals in a staff canteen does not give rise to a taxable benefit if they are available to all employees.

Answer 22

	£	£	£
Annual employment income			15,000
Add: 1. Bonus		5,000	
2. Award under staff suggestion scheme (exempt)		-	
		5,000	
Less: Deductions			
1. Subscription to ACCA	(200)		
2. Contribution to retirement scheme (8 months x £300)	(2,400)		
	2,600	(2,600)	
		2,400	2,400
Taxable employment income			**17,400**

Notes:

1. The annual subscription fee to ACCA, being relevant to duties of employment, is fully deductible.
2. An award up to £5,000, received under a staff suggestion scheme is an exempt benefit.
3. Bonus received is taxable and hence added to employment income.
4. Expenses incurred on a birthday party, are not employment related expenses, and are not deductible.
5. Contribution to an occupational pension scheme is deductible from employment income. Susan started contributing to the scheme from 1 August 2009, therefore, contributions for eight months (from August 09 to April 10) are deductible from her employment income.
6. Annual rent and deposit paid for accommodation is her personal expense and hence not deductible from employment income.

Answer 23

1. As no amount is received by A, an allowable expense is calculated as follows:
   For first 10,000 miles @40p per mile = £4,000
   Next 200 mile @25p per mile = £50
   Total **allowable expense** = **£4,050**
   Total employment income = £25,000 - £4,050 = **£20,950**

2. Tax-free mileage allowance = £4,050(as calculated in (1) above)
   Mileage allowance received from employer = 10,200 miles x 35p per mile = £3,570
   The deficit of **£480** (£4,050 - £3,570) £480 can be set off against the total income from employment.
   Employment income £25,000 - £480 = **£24,520**

3. Tax-free mileage allowance = £4,050
   Mileage allowance received from employer = 10,200 miles x 45p per mile = £4,590. Excess received **£540** (£4,590 - £4,050) is taxable.
   Employment income £25,000 + £540 = **£25,540**

Answer 24

Ordinary commuting (travel between home and the permanent workplace, including the journey to turn off the fire alarm) is not deductible from employment income.

Cost of private travel is not deductible from employment income.

The travel to a temporary workplace is deductible from employment income as it is for a period lasting less than 24 months.

The amount of deduction is (3,800 miles @ 40p per mile) = £1,520

Cost of travel between permanent workplace and Flex plc's suppliers is deductible from employment income.

The amount of deduction is (750 miles @ 40p per mile) = £300

Answer 25

	£	£
Employment income		36,000
Add: Bonus (W1**)**		1,500
Performance incentive (W2)		3,000
Mobile phone expenses incurred by company (W3)		-
		40,500
Less: Deductions		
Contribution to occupational pension scheme (W4) (12 x £500 = £6,000)	(6,000)	
Business traveling expenses (W5) (£700 + £900 + £1,000)	(2,600)	(8,600)
Taxable employment income		31,900

Workings

W1 & W2 Bonus and performance incentives are part of employment income. They are assessed on receipt basis.

W3 The provision of a mobile is exempt.

W4 Contributions to an occupational pension scheme are deductible.

W5 Travel expenses for business purposes are deductible. Here travelling expenses from city A to city B (£700) are **not deductible** as travelling expenses from home to office are not deductible. However, other expenses are related to his work as a sales officer hence those are deductible.

Answer 26

1. 15p per day would be exempt. The remaining £1.15 i.e. (£1.30 - £0.15 = 1.15p) per day would be taxable.
2. Free meals in the company canteen are exempt if available to all employees
3. Removal expenses of up to £8,000 are exempt.
4. Long-service award made in cash is taxable.

Answer 27

1. Not allowable.
2. Allowable.
3. Not allowable even if worn only at office. A suit provides warmth and is appropriate attire. It is not wholly, exclusively and necessarily for the duties of employment.
4. Allowable if relevant to the employment.

Answer 28

	£
Employment income	24,000
Add:	
1. Bonus (W1)	1,800
2. Meal voucher (W2)	117
((60p - 15p) = 45p x 260 days)	
3. Gift Voucher (W3)	1,500
4. Christmas party (W4)	200
Taxable employment income	**27,617**

Workings

W1 Bonus is taxable on receipt basis.

W2 Meal vouchers of 15p per day exempt, any excess is taxable.

W3 A gift voucher is taxable.

W4 Staff parties costing up to £150 per head are exempt, if the cost exceeds £150 the whole cost is taxable.

Answer 29

Taking into account Jimmy's personal allowance, allowable expenses and adjustment for unpaid tax in the previous year, the tax code can be worked out as follows.

	£
Personal allowance	6,475
Add: Allowable expenses	138
Total	**6,613**
Less: income on which tax was unpaid in 2006-07 £52.5 x 100/22 (W1)	(239)
Less: Assessable benefits	(520)
Tax free income	**5,854**

Workings

W1

To collect unpaid tax, the amount must be grossed up by the individual's marginal rate of tax.
Tax code = 1/10 of £5,854 rounded down to a whole number. Therefore, tax code is **585 followed by a letter.**

Answer 30

Solution Ltd must provide the following forms to Julian.

1. Form P60 employee's certificate of pay, income tax and NIC must be given to Julian. Form P60 must be given by 31 May 2010.

2. A copy of form P11D detailing expense payments and benefits in kind. This must be given to Julian by 6 July 2010.

Quick Quiz

Answer in short.

1. What is the basis on which income from employment is taxable?

2. Are the expenses incurred for travelling from home to employee's place of work deductible?

3. What is the chargeable value of free meals provided to employees in a staff canteen?

4. If an employee travels 12,000 miles in a tax year by motor car, how much mileage allowance is he entitled to?

Answers to Quick Quiz

1. Income from employment is taxable on receipt basis.

2. No, as they are not considered to be incurred for performing duties of employment.

3. Benefits for free meals in a staff canteen are exempt from tax.

4.
10,000 miles x 40p per mile	=	£4,000
2,000 miles x 25p per mile	=	£500
Total mileage allowance	=	£4,500

Self Examination Questions

Question 1

When is the employment income received in case of:

1. an employee?

2. a director of a company?

Question 2

What are the tests which might be used to distinguish employment and self-employment?

Question 3

State the general rule which determines whether or not an employee's expenditure is deductible.

Question 4

Which of the following expenses incurred by an employee would be deductible when computing employment income?

1. The travelling cost from home to work place

2. The cost of business calls on a private telephone

3. The travelling cost between employment sites

4. Subscriptions to professional bodies

5. Donations to charity made under payroll deduction scheme operated by an employer

B2.42: Income Tax Liabilities © GTG

Question 5

Pillsbury is employed and earns a salary of £25,000. His employer reimbursed the following expenses incurred by Pillsbury in 2009-10.

	£
Entertaining expenses	444 (wholly for business)
Rail and taxi fares	326 (wholly for business)
Home telephone cost	182 (50% private use)

His employer provided the following benefits:

1. Private medical insurance costing £650 in 2009-10.

2. A car, with a list price of £13,650. The company paid all the costs of the car, including fuel. The car runs on petrol and the CO_2 emissions rate is 165 g/km.

Required:

Calculate Pillsbury's taxable employment income for 2009-10.

Question 6

On 5 July 2009 Harry resigned from Men-city plc, where he had been employed for some years.
The following information is available for 2009-10

1. Harry's gross salary was £36,000 per annum, PAYE of £2,680 was deducted in 2009-10.

2. Men-city Plc had provided Harry with a petrol driven car with a list price of £16,500. The CO_2 emissions rate was 278 g/km. Men-city Plc had also provided Harry with fuel for private journeys. Harry contributed £2,500 towards the cost of the motor car when it was first provided to him and paid £100 per month to Men-city Plc for the use of the car.

3. On 1 January 2008 Men-city Plc provided Harry an interest- free loan of £70,000 to purchase a boat. Harry repaid £45,000 of loan on 5 May 2009, and repaid the balance of the loan of £25,000 on 6 July 2009.

4. The company had provided Harry with free meals in the company staff canteen which is open to all employees. The total cost of these meals to the company was £280.

5. Harry has no other source of income in 2009-10.

Required:

Calculate Harry's income tax payable / repayable for 2009-10.

Answers to Self Examination Questions

Answer 1

1. Employee

The earlier of:
a) the date when payment is made
b) the date when an employee becomes entitled for payment

2. Director

The earliest of:
a) the two alternatives given in the rule for employees
b) the date on which the income is **credited** to the director in the accounting records of the company
c) the end of period of accounts, if the director's income for that period is determined by then
d) the date on which the amount is determined, if after the end of the company's period of accounts

Answer 2

1. Control
2. Financial risk involved
3. Equipment
4. Assistance
5. Work correction
6. Holidays
7. Number of persons contracted with
8. Mode of payment
9. Position
10. Obligation

Answer 3

Employee's expenses are **allowed only if they are incurred wholly, exclusively and necessarily in the performance of the duties of employment.**

Answer 4

1. Not deductible
2. Deductible
3. Deductible
4. Allowable if relevant to the duties of employment
5. **Specifically** deductible

Answer 5

Calculation of Pillsbury's taxable employment income

	Earned income	£	£	£
	Employment income			25,000
Add:	Reimbursed expenses			
	Entertaining		444	
	Rail and taxi fares		326	
	Home telephone		182	
			952	
Less:	Allowable expenses			
	Entertaining (W1)	(444)		
	Rail and taxi fares (W1)	(326)		
	Home telephone: 50% (W2)	(91)	(861)	91
Add:	Assessable value of benefits			
	Car (W3)		2,867	
	Fuel: £16,900 X 21%		3,549	
	Private medical insurance		650	7,066
Taxable employment income				**32,157**

Workings

W1 Entertaining expenses and rail and taxi fares incurred wholly for business purposes are deductible from employment income.

W2 Home telephone cost is allowed only up to 50% as any expenditure incurred for private purposes is not deductible.

W3 Assessable benefit of car

The list price of the car is £13,650
The appropriate percentage is:

$$15\% + \frac{(165 - 135)}{5} = 21\%$$

Therefore, assessable benefit =£13,650 x 21%= £2,867

Answer 6

Calculation of income tax payable / repayable by Harry for 2009-10

	£
Salary (£36,000 x 3/12)	9,000
Car benefit (W1)	925
Fuel benefit (W2)	1,479
Beneficial loan (W3)	475
Staff canteen (Note)	-
Total Income	11,879
Less: Personal allowance	(6,475)
Taxable Income	**5,404**
Income tax liability (£5,404 x 20%)	**1,081**
Less: PAYE deducted	(2,680)
Income tax repayable	**(1,599)**

Workings

W1 Assessable car benefit

The list price of the car is £16,500

Harry made a capital contribution of £2,500.

The appropriate percentage is 15% + ((275 -135)/5) = 43%
Restricted to 35%
The car was available for 3 months in 2009-10
Harry contributed £100 per month for the private use of the car.

The assessable car benefit is:

	£
(£16,500 – £2,500) x 35% x 3/12	1,225
Less: contribution (3 x 100)	(300)
	925

W2 Fuel benefit

£16,900 x 35% x 3/12 = £1,479

W3 Assessable value of beneficial loan

Average method

((£70,000 + £25,000)/2 x 4.75% x 3/12) = £564

Strict method

[(£70,000 x 4.75% x 1/12) + (£25,000 x 4.75% x 2/12)] = £475

Harry will elect to use the strict method, as this gives a lower assessment.

Note: The provision of meals in a staff canteen does not give rise to a taxable benefit.

SECTION B: INCOME TAX LIABILITIES

B3

STUDY GUIDE B3: INCOME FROM SELF-EMPLOYMENT (PART 1)

■ Get Through Intro

If an individual is trading via an unincorporated business, he is termed as a sole trader. He is the proprietor of his business.

We calculate the profits of the business as if it were separate from the proprietor. However, whereas the profits of a company are charged to corporation tax, the profits of an unincorporated business must be included in the calculation of the proprietor's taxable income.

This Study Guide discusses the calculation of taxable profits, the allowable deductions, the relief available for pre-trading expenses and the assessment of the profits of self-employed individuals, including the rules on commencement and cessation of a business.

As a tax consultant, you will need to ensure that your clients **compute their taxable profits correctly** and **make use of all available deductions and exemptions**. You will also need to ensure that your taxable income is correct.

A question on this topic appears in nearly every paper, and so you **must** have a thorough understanding of this Study Guide.

■ Learning Outcomes

a) Recognise the basis of assessment for self-employment income.
b) Describe and apply the badges of trade.
c) Recognise the expenditure that is allowable in calculating the tax-adjusted trading profit.
d) Recognise the relief that can be obtained for pre-trading expenditure.
e) Compute the assessable profits on commencement and on cessation.
f) Change of accounting date
   i. Recognise the factors that will influence the choice of accounting date.
   ii. State the conditions that must be met for a change of accounting date to be valid.
   iii. Compute the assessable profits on a change of accounting date.

Introduction

The rules on deductions of expenses are more generous than for employed individuals, and a much **wider range** of expenses are allowed against the income of self-employed individuals. The self-employed pay their tax later than employed individuals, **as they are required to make payments on account, and then a balancing payment after the end of the tax year.** An individual's employment status also affects his national insurance contributions. Self-employed individuals may pay **less NIC** than employees.

As a result, you must determine, when advising clients, whether they are employed or self–employed.

1. Recognise the basis of assessment for self-employment income.[2]
[Learning outcome a]

Income tax is charged for a **tax year**. A tax year is also called a "year of assessment". The tax year runs **from 6 April to the following 5 April**. However, traders may prepare their accounts to any date. They are not required to prepare them to 5 April.

> **Example**
> Lilly, a bookseller may prepare her accounts for the twelve months to 31 December every year.

Each individual trader may have a different period end. It would be very difficult for HMRC to determine the tax liability of different traders for different years. Hence it is necessary to establish a link between the accounting periods for which trading profits are calculated and the tax year in which those profits are charged to tax.

For tax purposes, the trading profits must be calculated in accordance with generally accepted accounting principles. An important point which must be noted here is that **the accrual basis** of accounting must be followed.

The accrual basis means profits and expenses are recognised when they are earned / incurred and accrued in the year, whether or not they are **actually received / paid** in that year.

Individuals are charged tax for the period 6 April to the following 5 April. If the accounts are not prepared to 5 April, special rules are needed to link the period of account to the tax year. Basis periods are used to link periods of account to tax years. The profits are taxed in the corresponding tax year.

The basic rule for taxing trading profits is the current year basis of assessment (CYB). The basis period (the period of profits taxed) for a tax year is the twelve month accounting period ending in the tax year.

> **Tip** What is a basis period?
> The basis period for a tax year is the twelve month accounting period ending in the tax year.

> **Example**
> A trader prepares accounts to 31 December each year. The twelve month period of account from 1 January 2009 to 31 December 2009 ends in the tax year 2009-10. The basis period for tax year 2009-10 will be the 12 month period ended on 31 December 2009.

Special rules apply on commencement of trade, on change of accounting date and on cessation. These rules are studied in Learning Outcome 5 and 6 of this Study Guide.

> **Example**
> Millie prepares her accounts to 31 October each year. Identify the basis period for tax year 2009-10.

The twelve month accounting period to 31 October 2009 ends during 2009 - 10. The basis period for 2009-10 is year ended 31 October 2009.

SUMMARY

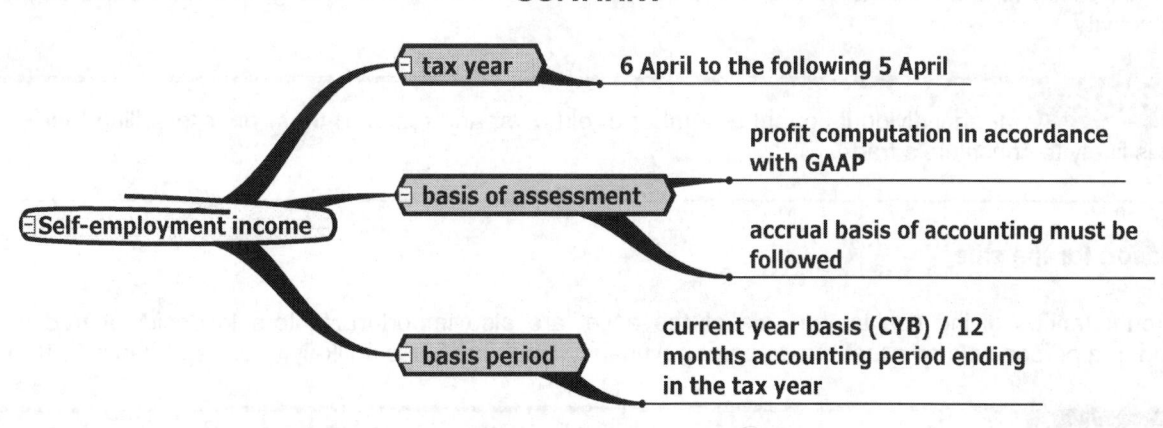

Self-employment income
- **tax year** — 6 April to the following 5 April
- **basis of assessment**
  - profit computation in accordance with GAAP
  - accrual basis of accounting must be followed
- **basis period** — current year basis (CYB) / 12 months accounting period ending in the tax year

2. Describe and apply the badges of trade.[2]

[Learning outcome b]

All the trading profits of a person who is a UK resident are chargeable to income tax.

When an individual disposes of assets, it is not always clear if those transactions constitute a trade or not. If an individual disposes of an asset, should that transaction be:
➤ treated as a **capital gain**, or
➤ treated as **trading income?**

The courts have interpreted what legislation means by 'trade' and how to determine if a trade exists in a given situation. Where there is doubt as to whether an activity constitutes a trade, a number of **key factors** have been identified through judicial decisions, known as the **badges of trade**. The badges of trade give guidance where it is not clear if certain activities constitute a trade.

2.1 Badges of trade

1. Subject matter of the transaction

There are three main reasons for purchasing an asset:
a) for personal use
b) as an investment, either to yield income, or for a long-term gain
c) to resell at a profit, which constitutes trading.

The **intentions** of the purchaser **at the time of purchase regarding the resale** of the article **are relevant.**

If the asset is **held as an investment or for personal use**, any profit on a later sale will be treated as a **capital profit.**

If an asset is **not held as an investment or for personal use**, any profit on its sale will be treated as a **trading profit.**

2. Length of period of ownership

Assets purchased for personal use or as an investment are normally held for a long period, whereas assets purchased as trading stock are usually held for a shorter term. The shorter the period of ownership, the more likely that the activity constitutes a trade.

3. Frequency of similar transactions

The number of similar transactions and the frequency of those transactions suggest that the activity constitutes trading.

> **Example**
> A taxpayer bought clothes at the local market each week, and sold them at a profit. The taxpayer is regularly performing the same transaction. This is likely to constitute as trading.

4. Supplementary work and marketing

Where a taxpayer performs some supplementary work on the asset, to make it more marketable, it is **more likely to be regarded as trading.**

If steps are taken to find purchasers e.g. if the sale occurred following advertising, this would also suggest a trading activity.

> **Example**
> If an individual bought a number of old cars, and restored them prior to selling them, the activity is likely to constitute a trade.

5. Reason for the sale

The circumstances giving rise to the sale of the asset are also important factors to decide if trading has occurred. If a person sold an asset due to personal financial problems, it is unlikely to be regarded as a trade.

> **Example**
> An individual sells one of his three motorcars to raise funds to pay for his mother's healthcare is unlikely to be regarded as trading.

6. Profit motive

The presence of a profit motive in the mind of the taxpayer **at the time of buying the asset** is a strong indication that a person is trading. An asset acquired other than by purchase, e.g. inheritance on the death of a relative, is unlikely to indicate a trading activity.

The badges of trade cannot be used as a checklist as no one factor is conclusive in deciding whether or not trading has occurred. All of the badges of trade are to be considered. It depends on the facts of the particular case to determine whether the transaction is a trade or not.

> **Tip** How do you remember these six elements?
> Make some meaningful sentence by using words from each of them.
> Like, **Frequency** and **length** of **profit** are **subject matter** not **supplementary reasons**.
>
> **Where:**
> **Frequency:** frequency of transactions
> **Length:** length of ownership
> **Profit:** profit motive.
> **Subject matter:** subject matter of transaction
> **Supplementary:** supplementary work and marketing
> **Reason:** reason for sale

Test Yourself 1

State the six main badges of trade.

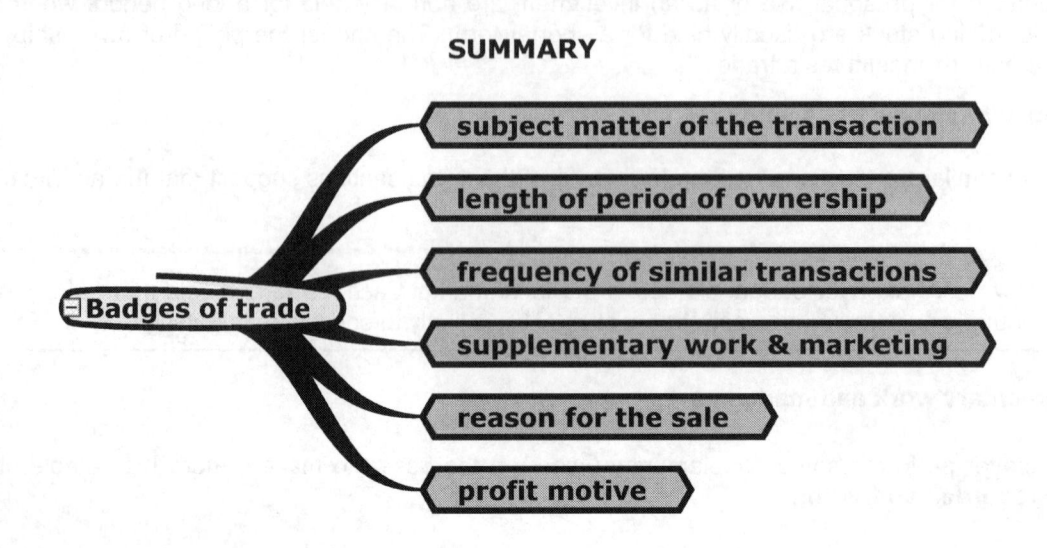

SUMMARY

Badges of trade
- subject matter of the transaction
- length of period of ownership
- frequency of similar transactions
- supplementary work & marketing
- reason for the sale
- profit motive

3. Recognise the expenditure that is allowable in calculating the tax-adjusted trading profit.[2]
[Learning outcome c]

In order to ascertain the taxable trading profits for an accounting period, the net profit shown in the accounts must be adjusted as the accounting conventions are different from the rules of taxation.

Adjustments to profits shown in the financial accounts would include:

1. **ADD:** Adding back depreciation, client entertaining, etc which **are not allowable for tax purposes.**

AND

2. **DEDUCT:** Deducting capital allowances, (which **are allowable for tax purposes).**

> **Tip**
> Capital allowances are a statutory form of depreciation giving relief on capital purchases.

After making these adjustments, we arrive at the trading profit for tax purposes.

Some examples of the types of adjustments required to the net profit per accounts are given in the overview below. The detailed rules are explained subsequently:

	Adjustment to profits calculation	£
	Net trading profits per accounts	X
Add:	**(I) Expenditure shown in the accounts but not deductible for tax purposes**	
	Customer entertaining	X
	Purchases of asset (capital expenditure)	X
	Increases in general provision	X
	(II) Trading income taxable but not included in the accounts	
	Goods taken for own consumption	X
Less:	**(I) Expenditure deductible for tax purposes but not shown in the accounts**	
	Business use of private telephone	(X)
	Short term lease premium paid by the trader	(X)
	(II) Income included in the accounts but not taxable as trading income	
	Dividends	(X)
	Property income	(X)
	Adjusted profit before capital allowances	X

> **Tip**
> Remember, you start with **net trading profits** per accounts, not gross profits.

The general rule is that only **expenditure which is wholly and exclusively for the purposes of trade is allowable.**

> **Example**
> Income tax paid by a trader is not allowed as it does not relate to the trade. It is a personal expense of the person carrying on the trade.

> **Tip**
> As a general rule, expenditure incurred wholly and exclusively for the purposes of trade is allowable, and expenditure, which does not relate to the trade, is not allowable.

3.1 Allowable and non-allowable deductions for calculating tax-adjusted trading profits.

Here we look at the main categories of business expenditure and their treatment, when calculating tax adjusted trading profits.

☑ This **denotes deductible**.

☒ This **denotes non deductible**.

1. Appropriation of profit ☒

Tax must be paid on all the profits of the business, so any amounts taken out of the business by the owner must be added back. This includes drawings, owner's salary (although a salary paid to the spouse is allowable), interest on capital, the owner's personal income tax and NICs.

2. Salaries to family members ☒

Salary to family members in excess of market rates is not deductible.

3. Expenses attributable to private use by owner ☒

Expenses attributable to private use by the owner e.g. telephone is **not allowable**.

4. Depreciation / amortisation ☒

Depreciation gives relief for the cost of a fixed asset over its useful life. As the accounting rules (depreciation) are different from the prescribed tax rules (capital allowances), depreciation is added back and capital allowances are deducted.

A detailed discussion on capital allowances is covered in the next section of this Study Guide.

5. Provisions ☒

A specific provision, that relates to revenue expenditure and is specifically quantifiable, is allowable.

General provisions are disallowable.

> **Example** A general provision for repairs would not be deductible as it is an estimated amount.

> **Tip** Remember, FRS 26 states that a general allowance cannot be made for debtors. Therefore, all allowances relating to debtors made in the accounts are deductible as they are specific allowances.

6. Capital expenditure ☒

Capital expenditure is specifically disallowed. Capital expenditure is not normally charged to the profit and loss account. However repairs and maintenance expenditure charged to the profit and loss account may contain items that are of a capital nature.

Expenditure on repairs (returning the asset to its original condition) and maintenance (redecoration) is allowable. If the expenditure relates to improvement or enhances the value of the asset, it is a capital expenditure and disallowed.

> **Example** The rebuilding of a wall that was damaged in an accident is repair expenditure and allowable.

The building of an entirely new wall is capital expenditure and disallowable.

Expenditure which relates to a capital asset is not allowable, **e.g.**

a) Legal and professional fees relating to the acquisition of a capital asset.
b) Losses on the disposal of fixed assets.
c) Purchase of a used asset: If an asset is purchased in a state of disrepair and is not useable, and the purchase price reflects the state of disrepair, any expenditure incurred in bringing the asset into a useable condition is treated as capital expenditure and disallowed.

7. Gifts ☑

a) Gifts to employees are allowable.
b) Gifts to customers are not allowable **unless:**
   i. They **cost not more than £50** per person per year.
   ii. They are **not food, drink, tobacco or vouchers** exchangeable for goods.
   iii. They **carry a conspicuous advertisement** for the business.

Example Expenditure on coffee mugs, that cost £20 each, with the business name printed on them would be allowable.

8. Entertaining ☑

- Entertaining employees is allowable.
- Entertaining **customers, suppliers** or anyone else is **not allowable.**

9. Donations ☒

A donation to a **national charity** is **not allowable.** Similarly, donations to a political party are not allowable.

Example A donation of £5,000 to UNICEF is not allowable, as it is not given to a local charity.

Gift aid donations are not allowable as a deduction from trading income. This is because the basic rate tax relief is given at the time the payments are made and by extension of the basic rate band for higher rate taxpayers.

Gifts of trading stock or used plant and machinery to charities and **UK educational establishments are allowable by statute.**

However, **small** gifts or donations to a **local charity** are **allowable** if it benefits the company's trade.

Example Anthony, a trader, made a cash donation of £200 to a local charity, and received free advertising in the local magazine. This is allowable because the amount is small; it is given to a local charity and the business benefits.

10. Subscriptions ☑

a) Subscriptions to professional and trade associations are **allowable if they relate to the trade.**

Example A trader's subscription to the Chamber of Commerce is allowable.

b) Political subscriptions and donations: not allowable

11. Legal and professional charges ☑

Allowable if they relate to revenue expenditure and incurred for the purposes of trade.

Allowable expenses include:

a) fees relating to an action for breach of contract.
b) fees paid to a lawyer in relation to trade debt collection.

c) Fees incurred in defending the title to a fixed asset.
d) Fees for audit and accountancy work, and agreeing tax liabilities with HMRC.

However, fees incurred in relation to tax appeals and investigations are not allowable.

Legal and professional fees relating to the following capital expenses are specifically allowable:

- legal costs incurred in **the renewal of a short (50 years or less) lease.**
- incidental costs relating to the **raising of long-term finance** (even if the loan is not obtained).
- costs incurred relating to the **registration of a patent or copyright**.

12. Interest ☑

Interest, including interest on business bank overdrafts, hire purchase and credit cards is allowable.

Note: Interest paid as a **result of the late payment of tax is disallowed.**

13. Bad debts ☑

a) Trade bad debts are allowable.
b) **Employee bad debts** or other non-trade loans written off are **not allowable.**

14. Penalties and fines ☒

Fines or penalties imposed due to infringements of the law are disallowed, e.g. penalties for late registration of VAT, speeding fines of the owner, fines for infringement of health and safety regulations.

An **exception is parking fines incurred by employees whilst on business, which** are allowable.

15. Staff- related expenses ☑

Staff-related expenses are deductible, and include the following:

a) Gross salaries and employer's National Insurance Contributions.
b) Employer's contributions into an occupational or personal pension scheme.
c) Redundancy payments and compensation for loss of office. If payment is made on the cessation of trade, payments up to three times the statutory amount, in addition the statutory redundancy payments are allowed (i.e. four times the statutory redundancy amount in total).
d) Counselling services for employees leaving employment.
e) Educational courses arranged for staff, if related to the trade.
f) Contributions to local enterprise agencies etc.

16. Removal expenses to new business premises ☑

Allowable, provided it is **not due to the expansion** of the business.

17. Illegal payments ☒

Payments, which constitute a criminal offence such as a bribe or illegal payments such as payments to blackmailers or extortionists, are not allowable.

18. Irrecoverable VAT ☑

Irrecoverable VAT is allowable if it relates to an item of allowable expenditure.

19. Staff defalcations ☑

Losses as a result of employee dishonesty are allowable. However, losses resulting from the owner's dishonesty are not allowable.

20. Travelling expenses ☑

The costs of business travel by the owner is allowable, but not travel from home to the office.

21. Car leasing and rental costs ☑

The cost of hiring, leasing or renting plant, machinery and equipment is allowable irrespective of the price of the car. However, there is a restriction on the allowable expenditure where the CO_2 emissions of the car exceed 160g/km. 15% of the leasing costs are disallowed and 85% are allowed while calculating taxable profits where the CO_2 emissions of the car exceed 160g/km.

Example

A trader pays hire charges of £3,800 per annum for a car with CO_2 emissions of 185g/km. Compute the allowable amount.

Answer

As the CO_2 emissions of the car exceed 160g/km, 15% of the hire charges will be disallowed and 85% will be allowed while calculating taxable profits.

Amount of hire charges disallowed = £3,800 x 15% = £570

Therefore, **the allowable amount is (£3,800 - £570) = £3,230.**

22. Short term lease premiums ☑

When a trader pays any short term lease premium, the deduction of lease premium paid is allowable from his trading profits. Such a premium is deductible each year for the period of the lease.

Rent premium deductible per year is calculated by using the following formula:

P – 2% of (P x (n-1)) / no. of years of lease

Where, P = Premium

n = period of lease

Diagram 1: Summary of allowable expenses

Type of expense	Deductible
Salaries to family members at market rates	✓
Expenses attributable to private use by owner	✗
Depreciation / amortisation	✗
Increase in general provision	✗
Capital expenditure	✗
Gifts to employees	✓
Gifts to customers (provided cost not more than £50, not food, drink etc)	✓
Staff entertainment	✓
Customer / supplier entertainment	✗
Trade subscriptions	✓
Political donations	✗
Trade-related legal and professional charges	✓
Interest (trading purposes)	✓
Penalties and fines	✗
Staff training	✓
Removal expenses, unless an expansionary move	✓
Redundancy pay in excess of statutory limit	✓
Contribution to pension schemes	✓
Appropriation of profit	✗
Lease premium	✗
Illegal payments	✗
Irrecoverable VAT, if relates to an item of allowable expeniture	✓
Staff defalcations	✓
Travelling expenses (business)	✓
Lease and rent payments for equipment	✓
Registration of patents and trademarks	✓

Test Yourself 2

Nick runs a restaurant, his profit and loss account for the year ended 31 March 2010 is as follows:

	£	£
Gross profit		27,430
Salaries	6,300	
Depreciation	2,500	
Bad debts written off	180	
Legal fees relating to the purchase of a new restaurant	350	
Increase in general provision	50	(9,380)
Net Profit		**18,050**

Required:

Compute the trading profit for tax purposes.

Trading income not shown in the accounts

The main example of trading income not shown in the accounts is goods taken by the trader for his personal use. The owner should be taxed on the profit as if the goods had been sold at market value. If he takes goods either without adjusting for them or adjusting for them at cost, the trading profit must be adjusted.

If the goods have been adjusted at cost, the profit must be added back.
If no adjustment has been made, the selling price must be added back.

Example

Thomas, a sports car dealer, gives one of the cars to his son. Its cost was £6,125 and normally sells for £8,000. Thomas does not account for the transaction in his books. £8,000, the selling price of the car, must be added to the accounting profit.

Test Yourself 3

Macho, a trader manufacturing cutting tools, incurred the following expenditure in the year to 31 December 2009. Explain the treatment of each of the following expenses to calculate tax-adjusted trading profits.

	£
Depreciation	3,160
Repairs to machinery	1,390
Construction of a new rest room for staff	9,600
Purchase of a car for the factory manager	2,000
General provision for repairs	1,890
Christmas lunch for staff	120
Christmas lunch for 50 customers	1,510
Wedding gift to staff	320
Wedding gift to a customer	680
Gifts to customers (20 pens, costing £45 each, with business name engraved)	900
Gift aid donation to a local charity	1,000
Legal fees for the collection of trade debts	1,000
Costs of renewing a 40 year lease	2,300
Costs of registering a business trademark	5,500

4. Recognise the relief that can be obtained for pre-trading expenditure.[2]
[Learning outcome d]

A trader may incur expenses before actually starting the trade, e.g., rent of business premises, interest on a loan for the purchase of machinery, legal charges etc. These expenses are known as pre-trading expenditure, and are treated as if incurred on the first day of trade. They are allowable provided they were incurred within seven years of the commencement of trade, and are related to the trade. These expenses must be of a type which, if incurred after trading had commenced, would be allowable i.e. capital expenditure incurred before the commencement of trade is not allowable.

Example

John started trading on 1 January 2009, incurring the following expenses before that date:

Expenses	Date	£
Legal fees for transferring the business premises to his name	12 August 2005	1,200
Rent for a workshop for the business	5 May 2005	300
Fees for a market survey	1 January 2004	1,450
Fees for making a project report and feasibility study	15 June 1997	620

Required:

Which expenses are allowable & which are not allowable?

Continued on next page

Answer

Expenses	Allowable / Not Allowable	Reason
Legal fees for transferring the business premises to his name	Not allowable	Relates to a capital asset
Rent for a workshop for the business	Allowable	Normal trading expenditure incurred within seven years of the commencement of trade
Fees for a market survey	Allowable	Normal trading expenditure incurred within seven years of the commencement of trade
Fees for making a project report and feasibility study	Not allowable	Incurred more than seven years before the commencement of trade

SUMMARY

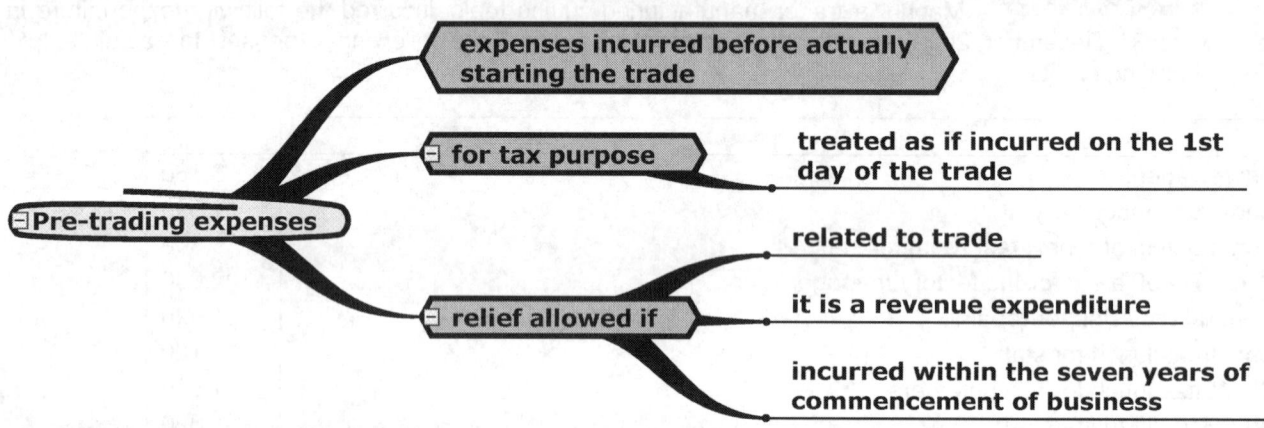

Pre-trading expenses
- expenses incurred before actually starting the trade
- for tax purpose — treated as if incurred on the 1st day of the trade
- relief allowed if:
  - related to trade
  - it is a revenue expenditure
  - incurred within the seven years of commencement of business

5. Compute the assessable profits on commencement and on cessation.[2]
[Learning outcome e]

5.1 Assessable profits

The owner of a business is charged to income tax on his trading profits. In order to determine the assessable amount, the following three steps are required:

1. Adjust the net profit figure per the accounts

The net profit per the accounts has been arrived at using accounting rules; this figure now needs to be adjusted according to the tax rules (refer to Learning Outcome 3).

2. Calculation of capital allowances

The trader has added back the depreciation charge in his accounts, and now calculates the relief for capital expenditure according to HMRC's prescribed rules (refer to Study Guide B3 Part 2).

3. Determine in which tax year the trading profits will be taxed

The adjusted profit is charged as trading income in the owner's income tax calculation. Special rules apply to determine the period assessed in each tax year (the basis period).

The trading income calculation

	£
Net profit per accounts	X
Add: Expenditure not allowable	X
Less: Income not taxable as trading income	(X)
Adjusted profits before capital allowances	X
Less: Capital allowances on plant and machinery	(X)
Capital allowances on industrial buildings	(X)
Adjusted profits after capital allowances	X

The individual pays income tax on the income in a tax year (the year 6 April to following 5 April). If a business prepares accounts to 5 April, then the profits for the year to 5 April 2010 will be taxed in 2009-10.

If an individual prepares the accounts to any other date, the accounts to the chosen date have to be linked to a tax year. The basic rule is to tax the twelve month period ending in the tax year. A trader preparing accounts for the year to 31 August 2009 will have those profits taxed in 2009-10. This is called the current year basis (CYB).

5.2 Commencement of trade

In the first years of trade, we cannot use the current year basis, as special rules are needed.

1. The first tax year: The period charged to tax (the basis period) in the first tax year of trade is determined according to the date the trade commences. It runs from **the date of the start of trade to the following 5 April.**

> **Example** Annie started trading on 1 January 2010, annually preparing accounts to 31 December. She started trading in 2009-10. The basis period is 1 January 2010 to 5 April 2010.

If the trade ceases to exist before 5 April, the basis period is from the date of start of trade to the date of cessation of trade.

> **Example** Jimmy started trading on 1 May 2009 and closed down the business on 31 January 2010. The basis period for 2009-10 is 1 May 2009 to 31 January 2010.

2. The second tax year: The basis period for the second tax year depends on the length of the accounting period that ends in the second tax year.

a) If the accounting period ending in the second tax year is **at least, or exactly twelve months** long, tax the **twelve months ending on that accounting date.**

> **Example** Rosy commenced her business on 1 January 2009 and prepares accounts to 31 December each year. Her first accounts are for the period to 31 December 2009.
> What is the basis period for 2008-09 and 2009-10?
>
> Rosy started trading in 2008-09. The basis period for the first tax year 2008-09 is 1 January 2009 to 5 April 2009.
>
> There is an accounting period of at least twelve months ending in the second tax year 2009-10, thus the basis period is twelve months, ending on that accounting date, i.e. 1 January 2009 to 31 December 2009.

b) If the accounting period ending in the second tax year is **less than twelve months** long, tax the **first twelve months of trading.**

> **Example** Lisa commenced trading on 1 November 2008 and prepares accounts to 30 June each year. Her first accounts are for the period to 30 June 2009.
> What are the basis periods for 2008-09 and 2009-10?
>
> The basis period for the first tax year 2008-09 is 1 November 2008 to 5 April 2009.
>
> There is an accounting period from 1 November 2008 to 30 June 2009 ending in the second tax year of 2009 - 10, but it is less than 12 months.
>
> Therefore, in this case the basis period is the first twelve months of trading, i.e. from 1 November 2008 to 31 October 2009.

c) If there is **no accounting period ending in the second tax year**, tax the **period 6 April to 5 April of the second tax year.**

B3.14: Income Tax Liabilities

> **Example**
> Garry commences trading on 1 February 2009 and prepares accounts to 30 June each year. His first accounts are for the period to 30 June 2010. What are the basis periods for 2008-09 and 2009-10?
>
> The basis period for the first tax year 2008 - 09 is 1 February 2009 to 5 April 2009.
>
> No accounting period ends in tax year 2009-10 as the accounting date 30 June 2009 falls in tax year 2010-11. Thus, the basis period for the second tax year 2009 - 10 is 6 April 2009 to 5 April 2010.

3. **The third tax year:** The basis period for the third tax year is:

a) If a twelve months accounting period **ends in the third tax year**, tax that period **(CYB)**.
b) If (a) is not possible, tax **twelve months to the accounting date in the third tax year.**

> **Example** — Continuing with the example of Garry
> The accounting period ending in the tax year 2010 - 11 on 30 June 2010 is of 17 months. As no twelve months accounting period ends in the third tax year, the basis period for the third tax year 2010 - 11 is twelve months to the accounting date in 2010 - 11 i.e. year ended 30 June 2010.

> **Example**
> A trader commenced trading on 1 May 2007 and prepares his first accounts to 30 September 2008 and then 30 September thereafter. Here, the basis periods for the first three years are as follows:
>
> | Tax year | Basis period |
> | --- | --- |
> | 2007 - 08 (note 1) | 1 May 2007 to 5 April 2008 |
> | 2008 - 09 (note 2) | 1 October 2007 to 30 September 2008 |
> | 2009 - 10 (note 3) | 1 October 2008 to 30 September 2009 |
>
> **Notes:**
>
> 1. For the first tax year the basis period runs from the commencement of trade to the following 5 April.
> 2. **There is an accounting period of at least 12 months ending in the second tax year**, so the basis period is 12 months to the accounting date in the second tax year.
> 3. Current year basis.

> **Tip** — **Exam tip:** Errors frequently arise, when deciding on the basis periods for the opening years. You must learn these rules. Expect to see these rules tested frequently in the exam.

4. **Subsequent tax years**

The basis period for the following tax years is the twelve month accounting period ending in the tax year – the current year basis.

> **Example**
> Merry has been trading for many years and prepares accounts to 31 October each year. What is the basis period for 2009 - 10?
>
> The year ended 31 October 2009 ends in 2009 - 10.
> The basis period for 2009 - 10 is the year to 31 October 2009.

> **Example**
> Alan has been trading for many years and prepares accounts to 30 June each year. What is the basis period for 2009 -10?
>
> The year ended 30 June 2009 ends in 2009 - 10.
> The basis period for 2009 - 10 is the year to 30 June 2009.

Diagram 2: Summary of basis periods for the opening years of assessment

Tax year		Basis period
First tax year		Date of commencement to 5/4
Second tax year	Does an accounting period end in tax year 2? **No**	6/4 to 5/4
	Yes → Is this accounting period at least 12 months long? **Yes**	Tax 12 months to accounting date
	No	Tax 12 months from commencement of trade
Third tax year	Normally CYB	12 months to accounting date ending in tax year 3

Test Yourself 4

A trader commences trading on 1 January 2009 and prepares accounts to 31 December each year.

Required:

Give the basis periods for the first three tax years.

Test Yourself 5

A trader commences trading on 1 January 2009 and prepares accounts to 30 April. His first accounts are for the period to 30 April 2010.

Required:

Give the basis periods for the first four tax years.

5. Overlap profits

If a trader prepares accounts to 5 April each year, all the profits will be taxed only once. If any other year end date is chosen, **some profits will be taxed more than once** in the opening tax years. We call these profits 'overlap' profits.

Example

Vicky started to trade on 1 January 2007 and prepares her first accounts to 30 June 2007 and annually thereafter. Her results are as follows:

	£
Six months to 30 June 2007	13,000
Year to 30 June 2008	27,000
Year to 30 June 2009	42,000

Calculate her taxable profits for the first four tax years, and show the overlap profits.

Continued on next page

Answer

Year	Basis Period	Working	Taxable (£)
2006 - 07	Actual (01/01/2007 - 05/04/2007)	£13,000 x 3/6	6,500
2007 - 08	First 12 months (01/01/2007 - 31/12/2007)	£13,000 + (£27,000 x 6/12)	26,500
2008 - 09	CYB (year to 30/06/08)(01/07/2007 – 30/6/2008)		27,000
2009 - 10	CYB (year to 30/06/2009)(01/07/2008 – 30/06/2009)		42,000

Overlap profits	£
01/01/2007 – 05/04/2007 (3 months) (W1) (£13,000 x 3 months/ 6 months)	6,500
01/07/2007 – 31/12/2007 (6 months) (W2) (£27,000 x 6months/12 months)	13,500
Total	**20,000**

Workings

W1
Profits during the period 01/01/07 to 05/04/07 are taxed twice, once in 2006 - 07 and again in 2007 - 08. The profits taxed more than once are overlap profit.

W2
Profits during the period 01/07/07 to 31/12/07 are taxed twice, once in 2007 - 08 and also in 2008 - 09.

Test Yourself 6

A trader commenced trading on 1 June 2008, and has the following results:

17 months to 31 October 2009	£25,500
Year to 31 October 2010	£18,500

Required:

Calculate the trading income assessments for the first three tax years. How much is the overlap profit?

Test Yourself 7

Ilyas started to trade on 1 January 2007 and makes up his first accounts to 30 June 2007, and then 30 June annually thereafter. His results are as follows:

	£
Six months to 30/06/2007	40,000
Year to 30/06/2008	60,000
Year to 30/06/2009	74,000

Required:

Calculate his trading income assessments for 2006 - 07 to 2009 - 10 and identify any overlap profits.

6. Cessation of trade

The final assessment of a sole trader is the tax year in which there is a cessation of trade. A cessation of trade may occur when the sole trader retires, sells the business or dies. The basis period for the tax year in which the cessation occurs is determined as follows:

a) If the trade commences and ceases in the same tax year, the basis period is the whole life of the business.

b) If the trade ceases in the second tax year, the basis period runs from 6 April at the start of the second year to the date of cessation. This rule overrides the usual commencement rules.

c) If the trade ceases in the third tax year or any subsequent year, the basis period runs from the end of the basis period for the previous tax year to the date of cessation of trade.

Tip The basis period for the last tax year could be less than 12 months, exactly 12 months or more than 12 months.

7. Overlap relief

a) Relief is available for the overlap profits arising on commencement, by deducting them from the final tax year assessment when a business ceases to trade. This ensures that the assessments over the life of the business equal the total tax-adjusted profits earned by the business. **If overlap profits are greater than the assessment for the final tax year, relief is available for the resulting loss.**

Example

Cinderella has been trading for many years, preparing accounts to 31 December each year. She ceases to trade on 31 May 2009, profits for the 5 months to that date are £12,300. The overlap profits from the opening years of her trade were £7,100.

Required:

Calculate her trading income assessment for 2009-10.

Answer

	£
Profit for five months: 01/01/2009 - 31/05/2009	12,300
Less: overlap relief	(7,100)
Taxable profit	**5,200**

b) Overlap profits may also arise or be deducted on a change of accounting date, depending on the situation. The rules regarding change of accounting date have been dealt with in detail in Learning Outcome 6 of this Study Guide.

> **Tip** Overlap profits will arise in all cases other than where the accounting date is 5 April. Don't forget to calculate overlap profits, and remember how they can be relieved.

SUMMARY

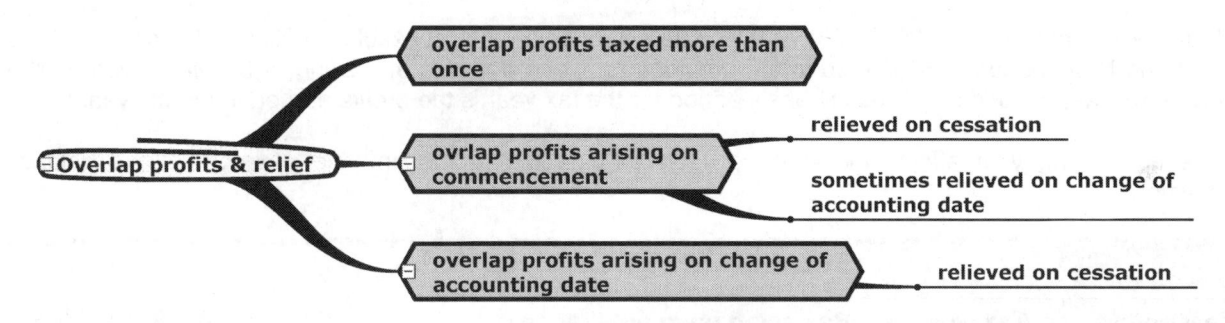

Overlap profits & relief
- overlap profits taxed more than once
- ovrlap profits arising on commencement
  - relieved on cessation
  - sometimes relieved on change of accounting date
- overlap profits arising on change of accounting date
  - relieved on cessation

Test Yourself 8

Brian has been trading for many years, preparing accounts to 30 November each year. He ceases to trade on 30 June 2009 and prepares his final accounts for the 7 months to that date.

Required:

What is the basis period for the tax year of cessation?

Test Yourself 9

Simi has been trading for many years, preparing accounts to 31 January each year. She ceases to trade on 31 July 2010 with recent profits as follows:

	£
Year to 31/01/2009	32,000
Six months to 31/07/2009	9,000

The overlap profits from commencement were £7,000.

Required:

Give the assessments for 2008 - 09 and 2009 - 10.

Test Yourself 10

What is the basis period for the tax year,
1. in which trade commences, and
2. in which trade ceases?

---

6. Change of accounting date
i. Recognise the factors that will influence the choice of accounting date.[2]
ii. State the conditions that must be met for a change of accounting date to be valid.[1]
iii. Compute the assessable profits on a change of accounting date.[2]

[Learning outcome f]

6.1 Factors influencing the choice of accounting date

The choice of accounting date is important for a sole trader as it affects the amount of overlap profits and the delay between earning the profits, and making the final tax payment (the balancing payment is due 31 January after the end of the tax year).

31 March accounting date end
- No overlap profits on commencement.
- Application of the basis period rules will be simplified.
- Time between earning the profits and the balancing payment is minimised (10 months).
- The maximum period of assessment in the final tax year will be 12 months.

30 April accounting date end
- Maximum period of overlap, with no relief until cessation (or possibly on future change of accounting date).
- Time between earning the profits and the balancing payment is maximised (21 months).
- The period of assessment in the final tax year could be up to 23 months long, less any relief for overlap profits.

1. If the profits are rising, a 30 April year end date will give lower assessable profits, as 11 months of profit from the basis period were earned in the previous tax year. If profits are falling, a 31 March year end will give lower assessable profits as the basis period for the tax year is the profits earned in the tax year.

2. The accounting year affects the time between earning the profits and the payment of the balancing payment.

Example

Year ended	Tax year	Balancing payment due on
31/03/2009	2008 - 09	31/01/2010
30/04/2009	2009 - 10	31/01/2011

> **Tip:** For details of due dates and balancing payments refer Study Guide G2.

Summary:

1. If profits fall, then 31/03 gives no overlap. Higher profits are not taxed twice.
2. If profits rise, then 30/04 gives overlap profits and earlier lower profits are taxed twice.
3. 30/04 year end gives an additional 11 months to prepare accounts and submit return.

6.2 Conditions that must be met for a change of accounting date to be valid

If a trader finds his current accounting date inconvenient, for any reason, he may change it.

The following conditions must be met:

- The change of accounting date **must be notified to HMRC by 31 January** following the tax year in which the change is made.
- The first accounts to the **new date must not exceed 18 months.**
- There must not have been a **change of accounting date in any of the 5 previous tax years**, or, if there has, the latest change is made for **genuine commercial reasons.**

6.3 Computation of assessable profit on change of accounting date

On a change of accounting date, **overlap will either be created or relieved**. No profits should escape tax on a change of accounting date.

On a change in accounting date there will be either an accounting period of less than 12 months, or an accounting period of more than 12 months. The basis periods are determined by applying the following rules:

1. When a change of accounting date results in an accounting period of less than 12 months ending in a tax year, the basis period for that tax year will be 12 months to the new accounting date. In this situation, overlap profits are created.

> **Example** Alan prepares his accounts to 31 December every year. He decides to change his accounting date to 30 June and prepares the accounts for the six months to June 2009. In this case, Alan's basis period for 2009 - 10 is the 12 month period ending on 30 June 2009. However, the basis period for 2008 - 09 was the year to 31 December 2008, which means that the six months to 31 December 2008, have been taxed twice. Overlap profits are for the period from 1 July 2008 to 31 December 2008.

2. When a change of accounting date results in an accounting period of more than twelve months ending in a tax year, the basis period for that tax year ends on the new accounting date. The basis period starts from the end of the basis period for the previous tax year and ends on the new accounting date. This means the basis period will exceed twelve months. In this situation, overlap profits brought forward can be relieved. The overlap can reduce the number of months of profit taxed down to twelve, but no further.

> **Example** A trader prepares his accounts to 31 May each year. He changes his accounting date to 31 August, and prepares the accounts for 15 months to 31 August 2009.
>
> The basis period for 2009 - 10 is the 15 month period from 1 June 2008 to 31 August 2009. Three months of overlap profits brought forward (if any) can be relieved in 2009 - 10.

> **Example** John prepares his accounts to 31 December each year. He has overlap profits of £6,000 from a 3 month period of overlap. John changed his accounting date to 28 February preparing accounts for the period from 1 January 2009 to 28 February 2010. The profit for this period was £15,000.

Required:

Calculate John's trading income assessment for 2009-10.

Answer

Determine which tax year the change of accounting date falls into.
28 February 2010 falls into 2009-10.
The basis period for 2009-10 is 14 months to 28 February 2010.

The trading income assessment is:

	£
Fourteen months: 01/01/2009 -28/02/2010	15,000
Less: Overlap relief (W1)	(4,000)
Trading income assessments for 2009-10	**11,000**

Workings

W1 Overlap relief used

Overlap profits brought forward relate to a 3 month period.

The basis period is 14 months long, which exceeds 12 months by 2 months.

Overlap relief is 2/3 x £6,000 = £4,000

John still has 1 month overlap profits to carry forward.

3. When a **change** of accounting date **results in no period of account ending in the tax year,** then the basis period is found by **deducting 12 months from the new accounting date, and taking 12 months to the resulting date.**

Example Akash prepares his accounts up to 31 March 2009. He changed his accounting date to 30 April and prepares the accounts for thirteen months to 30 April 2010.

Step 1: In which tax year does the change of accounting date fall?
2009 - 10

Step 2: Does an accounting period end in the tax year?
There is **no accounting period ending in 2009 - 10.**

Step 3: Deduct 12 months from the new accounting date i.e. 30 April 2010 less 12 months = 30 April 2009

Step 4: The basis period for 2009 - 10 is 12 months ending on 30 April 2009.

Overlap profits arise for the period 1 May 2008 to 31 March 2009 i.e. 11 months overlap profits, which can be carried forward for relief on cessation, or possibly on a future change of accounting date.

4. When a change in the accounting date results in two sets of accounts ending in a year, the basis period starts from the end of the previous basis period and ends on the new accounting date. Overlap relief can reduce the number of months of profit taxed down to 12.

Example Andrew prepares his accounts to 31 October. He changed his accounting date and prepares the accounts for 5 months to 31 March 2010.

There are two accounting periods ending in 2009 - 10, the 12 months to the old date i.e. 31 October 2009 and the five months to the new accounting date 31 March 2010.

The basis period for 2009 - 10 is the period from 1 November 2008 to 31 March 2010 i.e. 17 months.

Example Arnold commenced trading on 1 October 2007 and prepares his first accounts to 30 September 2008. His results show a profit of £24,000 (£2,000 per month). The profits assessable in 2007 - 08 and 2008 - 09 are as follows.

2007 - 08: 1 October 2007 to 5 April 2008 = £24,000 x 6/12 = £12,000

2008 - 09: 1 October 2007 to 30 September 2008 = £24,000

The period 1 October 2007 to 5 April 2008 (6 months).has been taxed twice, resulting in overlap profit of £12,000

Arnold decides to change his year end to 5 April and prepares accounts for the 18 months to 5 April 2010. The profits for the period are £20,000.

Continued on next page

The assessable trading profits for 2009 - 10 are as follows:

	£
18 months to 5 April 2010	20,000
Less: overlap relief b/f (note)	(12,000)
2009 - 10 assessable trading profit	**8,000**

Note: 18 months worth of profit is taxed in 2009 – 10, overlap relief b/f of 6 months may be used, to reduce the period taxed to 12 months.

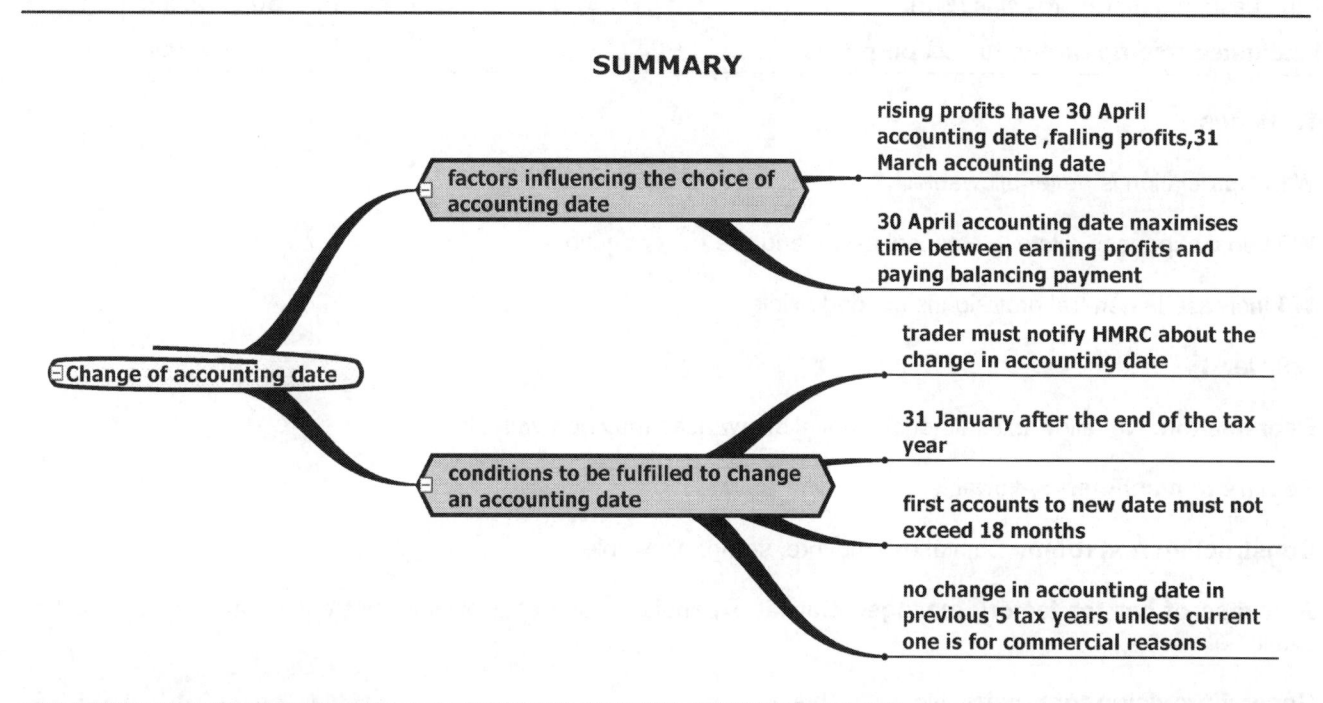

SUMMARY

Change of accounting date

- **factors influencing the choice of accounting date**
  - rising profits have 30 April accounting date, falling profits, 31 March accounting date
  - 30 April accounting date maximises time between earning profits and paying balancing payment
- **conditions to be fulfilled to change an accounting date**
  - trader must notify HMRC about the change in accounting date
  - 31 January after the end of the tax year
  - first accounts to new date must not exceed 18 months
  - no change in accounting date in previous 5 tax years unless current one is for commercial reasons

Test Yourself 11

1. Mary prepares accounts to 31 May each year. She changes her accounting date to 31 August and prepares the accounts for the period 1 June 2008 to 31 August 2009. The conditions necessary for a change of accounting date were all satisfied. Identify the basis period for 2009 - 10.

2. Bob began trading on 1 March 2006, preparing the accounts to 31 January 2007, and annually thereafter. He changed his accounting date to 30 April and prepares the accounts for the period 1 February 2009 to 30 April 2010. The conditions for change of basis period were all satisfied. Identify the basis periods for 2005 - 06 to 2011 -12 inclusive.

Answers to Test Yourself

Answer 1

Badges of trade are:

1. **Subject matter of transaction:** If the property is held for personal enjoyment or if the property yields income, this generally indicates an investment rather than a trading transaction.

2. **Frequency of transactions:** The repetition of a transaction generally indicates the existence of a trade.

3. **Length of ownership:** An intention to re-sell the asset in the short term might be a pointer towards a trading transaction, as opposed to an investment.

4. **Profit motive:** A transaction undertaken with the motive of realising a profit suggests trading.

5. **Supplementary work and marketing:** Work carried out on an asset prior to sale to make it marketable indicates trading.

6. **Reason for sale:** A forced sale to raise cash for an emergency indicates that the transaction is not trading.

Answer 2

	£	£
Net profits per accounts		18,050
Add: Expenditure shown in the accounts but not deductible for tax purpose		
Depreciation (W1)	2,500	
Legal expenses relating to the purchase of a capital asset (W2)	350	
Increase in general provision (W3)	50	2,900
Adjusted trading profits for tax purposes		**20,950**

Workings

W1 Depreciation is never allowable.

W2 Legal expenses relate to a capital asset, and are not deductible.

W3 Increase in general provision is not deductible.

Answer 3

Depreciation: Not allowable, although capital allowances may be available.

Repairs to machinery: Allowable.

Constructing rest room: Capital expenditure, so not allowable.

Purchase of car for factory manager: Capital expenditure, so not allowable, but capital allowances will be available.

General provision for repairs: Not allowable.

Christmas lunch for staff: Staff entertaining is allowable.

Christmas lunch for 50 customers: Customer entertaining is not allowable.

Wedding gift to staff: Allowable.

Wedding gift to customers: Not allowable.

Gift of 20 pens to customers, costing not more than £50 per person, not food, drink, tobacco or vouchers exchangeable for goods and has business logo engraved on it: Allowable.

Gift aid donation to local charity: Not deductible.

Legal fees incurred for collecting trade debts: Allowable as connected with the trade.

Costs of renewing 40 year lease: Allowable as cost of renewing a short lease (50 years or less).

Costs of registering business trademark: Allowable.

Answer 4

Tax year	Basis period
2008 - 09 (note 1)	1 January 2009 to 5 April 2009
2009 - 10 (note 2)	12 months to 31 December 2009
2010 - 11 (note 3)	12 months to 31 December 2010

Notes:

1. For the first tax year the basis period runs from the commencement of trade to the following 5 April.
2. There is an accounting period of at least 12 months ending in the second tax year, so the basis period is 12 months to the accounting date in the second tax year.
3. Current year basis.

Answer 5

Tax year	Basis period
2008 - 09 (note 1)	1 January 2009 to 5 April 2009
2009 - 10 (note 2)	6 April 2009 to 5 April 2010
2010 - 11 (note 3)	1 May 2009 to 30 April 2010
2011 - 12 (note 4)	12 months ended on 30 April 2011

Notes:

1. For the first tax year the basis period runs from the commencement of trade to the following 5 April.
2. No accounting period ends in the second tax year, so the basis period is 6 April to following 5 April.
3. Basis period is 12 months to the accounting date in the third tax year.
4. Current year basis.

Answer 6

Tax year	Basis period	Working	Trading Income (£)
2008 - 09 (note 1)	1 June 2008 to 5 April 2009	£25,500 x10/17	15,000
2009 - 10 (note 2)	1 November 2008 to 31 October 2009 (12 months to a/c date in year 2)	£25,500 x12/17	18,000
2010 - 11	Year to 31 October 2010	-	18,500

Notes:

1. The basis period for the first tax year runs from 1 June 2008 to 5 April 2009 i.e. 10 months.
2. There is an accounting period of at least 12 months ending in the second tax year, so the basis period is 12 months to the accounting date, i.e. 31 October 2009.
3. Profits during the period 1 November 2008 to 5 April 2009 (5 months) are taxed twice; therefore overlap profit is £7,500 (£25,500 x 5/17).

Answer 7

	£
2006 - 07 Actual (01/01/2007 – 05/04/2007) £40,000 x 3/6	20,000
2007- 08 First 12 months (01/01/2007 – 31/12/2007) £40,000 + £30,000 (£60,000 x 6/12)	70,000
2008 - 09 Current Year Basis (year to 30/06/2008)	60,000
2009 - 10 Current Year Basis (year to 30/06/2009)	74,000
Overlap profits 01/01/2007 – 05/04/2007 (£40,000 x 3/6) 01/07/2007 – 31/12/2007 (£60,000 x 6/12)	20,000 30,000
Total overlap profit	**50,000**

Answer 8

Step one: Determine the tax year of cessation.
2009 - 10

Step two: Determine the period of assessment for the previous tax year.
2008 - 09   year ended 30 November 2008

Step three: The remaining profits are taxed in the final tax year.
2009-10: 1 December 2008 to 30 June 2009 less any overlap profits b/f.

Answer 9

The date of cessation is 31 July 2009, which falls in 2009 - 10.
The assessment for 2008 - 09 is therefore on the CYB.

2008 - 09

Year to 31/01/2008   £32,000

2009 - 10

In the final tax year the basis period runs from the end of the basis period for the previous tax year to the date of cessation of trade.

	£
Six months: 01/02/09 – 31/07/09	9,000
Less: Overlap relief	(7,000)
Assessable trading profits	**2000**

Note: Overlap profits on commencement are relieved **when the trade ceases.**

Answer 10

1. The basis period for the first tax year runs from **the date of commencement to the following 5 April.**

2. The basis period for the tax year in which trade ceases:

a) If the trade ceases in the **first tax year,** the basis period is the **whole lifespan of the trade.**
b) If the trade ceases in the **second tax year,** the basis period runs from **6 April at the start of the second year to the date of cessation.** This rule overrides the normally applicable second year rule.
c) If the trade ceases in the **third year or any subsequent year,** the basis period runs from **end of basis period for the previous tax year to the date of cessation of trade.**

Answer 11

1. As the change of the accounting date results in an accounting period of more than 12 months, the new basis period is from the end of the previous basis period to the new accounting date. The new accounting date i.e. 31 August 2009 is more than 12 months after 31 May 2008, so the basis period for 2009 - 10 is 1 June 08 to 31 August 09. As this is a 15 month period, 3 months of overlap profits (if any) may be relieved in 2009 - 10, to reduce the number of months charged to tax to 12.

2. The accounting date is changed in the tax year 2009 -10. The basis period for 2008 - 09 is the year to 31 January 2009.

The new accounting date, 30 April 2010 falls in 2010 - 11, so the basis period for 2010 - 11 is 12 months to 30 April 2010.

The basis period for 2009 - 10 is determined by going back 12 months from 30 April 2010 i.e. 30 April 2009, and taking the 12 months to that date.

Basis periods for 2005 - 06 to 2011 - 12 are as follows:

2005 - 06	1 March 2006 to 5 April 2006
2006 - 07	1 March 2006 to 28 Feb 2007
2007 - 08	1 February 2007 to 31 January 2008 (year ended 31 January 08)
2008 - 09	1 February 2008 to 31 January 2009 (year ended 31January 09)
2009 - 10	1 May 2008 to 30 April 2009 (year ended 30 April 2009)
2010 - 11	1 May 2009 to 30 April 2010 (year ended 30 April 2010)
2011 - 12	1 May 2010 to 30 April 2011 (year ended 30 April 2011)

Overlap on commencement is 01/03/2006 – 05/04/2006 and 01/02/2007 – 28/02/2007 i.e. 2 months.
On change of accounting date, 9 additional months of overlap profits are created 01/05/2008 – 31/01/2009.

Quick Quiz

1. Explain the concept of badges of trade.

2. Bill started trading on 1 August 2009 and prepared his first set of accounts to 31 December 2009, and annually thereafter.

   What is the basis period for 2009 - 10?

3. State the general rule which determines if an expenditure is deductible when computing the trading income?

4. Brown starts trading on 1 July 2007 and prepares accounts to 30 June each year. Show the basis periods for the first three tax years, and identify the period of overlap profits.

5. What is the basis of assessment for the final tax year on cessation of trading?

6. Explain overlap profit and overlap relief.

Answers to Quick Quiz

1. Badges of trade are a set of various criteria, which may be used to distinguish between trading activities and non-trading activities.

2. **2009 - 10**
   01/08/09 – 05/04/10
   Profits assessed:
   5 Months to 31 December 2009 plus 3/12 of year to 31 December 2010.

3. The expenditure incurred must be wholly and exclusively for the purposes of trade.

4. **2007 - 08**
   1 July 2007 to 5 April 2008

   2008 - 09
   1 July 2007 to 30 June 2008

   2009 - 10
   1 July 2008 to 30 June 2009

   Period of overlap: 1 July 2007 to 5 April 2008.

5. Tax year in which cessation occurs: basis period is from the end of the basis period for the previous tax year to the date of cessation.

6. In the opening years, and sometimes on change of the accounting date, some profits are taxed twice. The basis periods for consecutive tax years contain a common period. The profits which are taxed twice are referred to as overlap profits.
   In the opening years of a business it is possible to have an overlap between tax year 1 and tax year 2.

   Relief for overlap profits:
   Overlap profits are relieved by deducting them from the assessable trading income of the year of cessation, or sometimes on a change of accounting date.

Self Examination Questions

Question 1
Jessica began trading on 1 January 2009 and prepares the accounts to 30 June. Her first accounts are prepared for the 18 months to 30 June 2010 and show an adjusted trading profit of £43,200. Compute Jessica's trading income for the first three tax years and calculate the amount of any overlap profits.

Question 2
Explain, with suitable examples, the rules for assessing profits in the first tax year of trade.

Question 3
Explain the rules for assessing profits in the second tax year of trade.

Question 4

Explain the rules for assessing profits in the third tax year of trade.

Question 5

Bill started trading on 1 January 2009, and prepared his first set of accounts to:
1. 30 June 2010
2. 31 December 2009
3. 30 June 2009
4. 31 March 2010

Give the basis periods for 2008 - 09 and 2009 - 10 for each of the above accounting dates.

Question 6

Bill Brown started trading on 1 January 2008, and prepares his accounts as follows:

1. to 30 June 2009 and annually to 30 June thereafter
2. to 31 December 2008 and annually to 31 December thereafter
3. to 30 June 2008 and annually to 30 June thereafter
4. to 31 March 2009 and annually to 31 March thereafter

Give the basis period for 2009 - 10 in each of the above cases.

Question 7

Juhi, a sole trader, started trading on 1 January 2009, preparing accounts up to 30 June 2009 and annually thereafter.

Her profit and loss account for the period ended 30 June 2009 was as follows:

	£	£
Gross Sales		75,380
Dividend received (net)		5,000
Interest on bank deposit		2,100
Goods taken for own use (at cost) (2)		8,000
Salary to self	1,360	
Salary to husband as Manager (1)	2,000	
Rent, business rates and insurance	3,120	
Repairs and maintenance (3)	6,220	
Motor expenses	1,650	
Depreciation on car	300	
Depreciation on equipment	250	
Loss on sale of equipment	960	
Car purchased for employee	12,000	
General repairs provision	1,800	
Legal fees for renewing a 40 year lease	2,490	
Interest on bank overdraft (4)	3,560	
Salaries and wages	9,400	
Hire purchase interest	1,230	(46,340)
Net profit		**44,140**

Notes:
1. The salary paid to her husband is at the market rate.
2. The goods taken for own use have a market value of £12,000.
3. Repairs to office building includes:
    - alterations to flooring in order to install a new machine £4,300
    - redecoration of offices £1,920
4. The overdraft was necessary to purchase stock.
5. Recovery from a debtor, previously written off not included in the profit and loss account £2,300.
6. She paid a trade subscription personally which is not included in the profit and loss account £1,000.

Required:

Compute Juhi's adjusted trading profits for tax purposes for the period ended 30 June 2009. Ignore capital allowances.

Question 8

John is a self-employed trader. His profit and loss account for the year ended 5 April 2010 is as follows:

	£	£
Gross profit		173,500
Expenses		
Depreciation	1,210	
Motor expenses (note 1)	6,250	
Professional fees (note 2)	3,090	
Repairs and renewals (note 3)	3,825	
Entertainment expenses (note 4)	4,860	
Wages and salaries (note 5)	68,530	
Other expenses (note 6)	67,370	(155,135)
Net profit		**18,365**

Notes:

1. **Motor expenses**
During the year John drove a total of 20,000 miles, of which 40% was private.

2. **Professional fees consist of:**
   £1,020 for accountancy,
   £1,620 for personal financial planning advice,
   £450 for debt collection

3. **Repairs and renewals:** this is made up of £525 for repairing the fence, and £3,300 for a new computer.

4. **Entertainment:** this is made up of £1,610 for entertaining suppliers and £3,250 for entertaining employees.

5. **Wages and salaries:** this includes a salary of £20,000 paid to John's wife. She works in the shop as a sales assistant. Other sales assistants doing the same job are paid a salary of £15,000 p.a.

6. **Other expenses:** this includes £125 for a wedding present to an employee, £125 for John's health club subscription, £125 as a donation to a political party, and £1,800 for a trade subscription.

7. **Business use of house:** John uses one of the six rooms in his house as an office. The total running costs of the house for the year were £8,720.

8. **Private telephone:** the total cost of John's private telephone for the year was £1,850, 45% of this related to business telephone calls. The cost of the private telephone is not included in the profit and loss account.

9. **Goods for own use:** during the year ended 5 April 2009 John took goods out of the shop for his personal use without paying for them, and no entry has been made in the accounts to record this. The goods cost £750, and have a selling price of £1,550.

Required:

Calculate John's tax adjusted trading profit for the year ended 5 April 2009. Ignore capital allowances.

Answers to Self Examination Questions

Answer 1

Tax year		Basis Period		£
2008 - 09	Actual	1 January 2009 to 5 April 2009	£43,200 x 3/18	7,200
2009 - 10	Tax year itself	6 April 2009 to 5 April 2010	£43,200 x 12/18	28,800
2010 - 11	12 months to accounting date	1 July 2009 to 30 June 2010	£43,200 x 12/18	28,800

Overlap period is of 9 months from 1 July 2009 to 5 April 2010. This period is taxed in 2009 - 10 and 2010 - 11.

Overlap Profits = £43,200 x 9/18 = **£21,600**

Answer 2

The taxable profit for the tax year in which a sole trader starts to trade is the amount **arising from the date of commencement of the trade to the end of that first tax year (i.e. 5 April).**

If a trader starts to trade on 1 July 2009, then the first tax year is 2009 - 10. In 2009 - 10 he will be assessed on the taxable profit for the period 1 July 2009 to 5 April 2010.

If a trader starts to trade on 1 August 2009, and prepares his first set of accounts to 31 December 2009, then he started trading in 2009 - 10, and the basis period is 1 August 2009 to 5 April 2010.

Answer 3

For the second tax year of trading, the amount of the taxable profit depends upon whether or not there is an accounting date ending in the second tax year.

The following three situations may arise:

1. **No accounting period ends in the second tax year.**
   The basis period is the tax year itself (i.e. 6 April to following 5 April).

2. **The accounting period ending in the second tax year is at least 12 months long.**
   The basis period is the 12 months to the accounting date in the second tax year.

3. **The accounting period ending in the second tax year is less than 12 months long.**
   The basis period is the first twelve months of trade.

Answer 4

In the third tax year of trade, the basis period is:

a) 12 month accounting period ending in the third tax year.
b) If there is no 12 month accounting period ending in the third tax year, take 12 months to the accounting date in the third tax year.

Answer 5

First tax year

Bill starts trading in 2008 - 09.

The basis period will be 1 January 2009 (i.e. the date the trade started) to 5 April 2009 (i.e. the end of that tax year in which the trade started) in all situations.

Second tax year 2009 - 10

1. **Accounts prepared to 30 June 2010**

There is no accounting period ending in 2009 - 10 as the first set of accounts is prepared to 30 June 2010.

Therefore the basis period for 2009- 10 is 6 April 2009 to 5 April 2010.

2. **Accounts prepared to 31 December 2009**
There is an accounting period ending in 2009 - 10 (31 December 2009) and it is exactly 12 months long.

Therefore the basis period for 2009 - 10 is 12 months to the accounting date i.e. 1 January 2009 to 31 December 2009.

3. **Accounts prepared to 30 June 2009**
There is an accounting period ending in 2009 - 10 (30 June 2009) and it is less than 12 months long.

Therefore the basis period for 2009 - 10 is the first twelve months of trading i.e. 1 January 2009 to 31 December 2009.

4. **Accounts prepared to 31 March 2010**.
There is an accounting period ending in 2009 - 10 (31 March 2010) and it is more than 12 months long.

Therefore the basis period for 2009 - 10 is the twelve months to 31 March 2010 i.e. 1 April 2009 to 31 March 2010.

Answer 6

2009 - 10 is the third tax year of trading:

1. 12 months to 30 June 2009 (as no accounting period ended in the second tax year).

In answers 2, 3 and 4 below an accounting period ends in the second tax year, so the basis period for the third tax year is the current year basis.

2. 1 January 2009 to 31 December 2009
3. 1 July 2008 to 30 June 2009
4. 1 April 2009 to 31 March 2010

Answer 7

	£	£
Net trading profits given per accounts		44,140
Add : (I) Expenses shown in accounts but not deductible for tax purposes		
Car purchase (capital expenditure)	12,000	
Salary to self	1,360	
General repairs provision	1,800	
Alteration to the flooring to install a new machine	4,300	
Depreciation (£300 + £250)	550	
Loss on sale of equipment	960	20,970
(II) Trading income taxable but not included in the accounts		
Goods taken for own use (at Market value) (£12,000 - £8,000)	4,000	
Recovery from a debtor, previously written off	2,300	6,300
Less: (I) Expenditure deductible for tax purposes but not shown in the accounts		
Trade subscriptions	(1,000)	(1,000)
(II) Income not taxable included in the accounts		
Dividend	5,000	
Income which is taxable under another heading such as interest, property income	2,100	(7,100)
Trading profits for tax purposes		**63,310**

Answer 8

Calculation of John's tax adjusted trading profits for the year ended 5 April 2010

	£	£
Net trading profits per accounts		18,365
Add : (I) Expenses shown in accounts but not deductible for tax purposes		
Depreciation	1,210	
Motor expenses (40% private use) (£6,250 x 40%)	2,500	
Fees for personal financial planning advice (private)	1,620	
Purchase of new computer (capital)	3,300	
Entertaining suppliers	1,610	
Salary to wife (the excess over market rate added back) (£20000 - £15000 = £5000)	5,000	
Health club subscription (private)	125	
Donation to a political party	125	15,490
(II) Trading income taxable but not included in the accounts		
Goods taken for own consumption (at MV)	1,550	1,550
Less: (I) Expenditure deductible for tax purposes but not shown in the accounts		
Use of home as office (W1)	1,453	
Telephone expenses (W2)	833	(2,286)
Trading profits for tax purposes		**33,119**

Workings

W1 Share in total running cost of house

Number of rooms is six; one is used for business purposes
Total running cost is divided proportionately
£8,720 x 1 room/6 rooms = 1,453

W2 Telephone expenses

Out of the total cost of private telephone, 45% is used for business purposes
Total telephone cost = £1,850
45% of £1,850 = £833

SECTION B: INCOME TAX LIABILITIES

B3

STUDY GUIDE B3: INCOME FROM SELF-EMPLOYMENT (PART 2)

Get Through Intro

Capital expenditure cannot be deducted when computing taxable income and no allowance is available for the depreciation in the value of assets. However, legislation allows **relief for capital expenditure** in the form of a **deduction, known as capital allowances, from taxable trade profits**.

The Finance Act 2008 and 2009 made substantial changes to the rules on capital allowances. These changes were applied from 6 April 2008 for individuals and 1 April 2008 for companies. For the purpose of your examination, only the new rules are examinable and therefore the examples in this Study Guide assume that the new rules have always applied.

It is necessary to understand the different provisions for the calculation of capital allowances in order to give proper guidance to your clients when calculating '**trading income**' in your capacity as a chartered certified accountant.

Capital allowances are a very important part of your syllabus as they will be examined, for a significant number of marks, in every exam.

Learning Outcomes

g) Capital allowances
   i. Define plant and machinery for capital allowances purposes.
   ii. Compute writing down allowances and the annual investment allowance.
   iii. Compute capital allowances for motor cars.
   iv. Compute balancing allowances and balancing charges.
   v. Recognise the treatment of short life assets.
   vi. Explain the treatment of assets included in the special rate pool.
   vii. Define an industrial building for industrial buildings allowance purposes.
   viii. Compute industrial buildings allowance for new buildings.

Introduction

Byron set up his business, and purchased a machine for £122,000. He anticipates that the machine will need replacing in about 6 years, and at that time he should be able to sell it for £5,000. The machine has cost him £117,000 over 6 years, and he is unsure how he will be given relief for this expenditure.

This Study Guide explains the relief available for different categories of capital expenditure, and the provisions for the disposal of assets.

1. Define plant and machinery for capital allowances purposes. [1]

[Learning outcome g (i)]

1.1 Definition of plant and machinery for capital allowances purposes

As discussed above, in this section, capital allowances are expenses that are deducted from profits in the financial accounts to arrive at trading profit for tax purposes. In other words, capital allowances are statuary form of depreciation giving relief on capital purchases. For example, the expenditures that are eligible to be deducted under capital allowance are plant and machinery and industrial buildings.

Legislation does not define the term plant and machinery. The definition of 'machinery' is not a problem; it includes all machines, vehicles, computers etc. However, the meaning of 'plant' is not so straightforward. Office furniture and equipment are plant and machinery, but expenditure on structures is not so easily dealt with.

In a leading case it was stated that plant includes whatever tool or apparatus is used by a businessman for carrying on his business, other than his stock in trade, but all goods and chattels, fixed or movable, live or dead, which he keeps permanently employed in the business.

Later case law has considered the 'functional test'.

a) If an asset is actively used in the business, then it is considered apparatus **with which** the business is carried on, and so is considered to be plant and machinery.

Example

➢ Storage platforms built in a warehouse are considered plant and machinery as the inventory cannot be stored without the platforms.
➢ Swimming pool of a health club is plant and machinery too, as clients probably would not come to the club if it didn't have a pool.

b) If an asset is **passively used in the business**, then it is considered to be the setting **in which** the business is carried on, and so it is not considered to be plant and machinery.

Example

The following are not considered to be plant and machinery:

➢ waste disposal or drainage systems of the building. However, they are considered part of the building.
➢ a false ceiling built to hide the electrical fittings, or floor of the restaurant making it attractive.

Hence, to identify plant for capital allowance purposes, a distinction is required to be made between **the setting in which the business is carried on** and **the apparatus with which the business is run**. However, some of the items seem to be part of the setting, but qualify as plant. For example, lifts and escalators qualify as a plant for capital allowance purposes. On the other hand, expenditure on flooring and ceiling in office premises will be considered part of the business setting and hence, will not qualify as a plant.

1.2 Expenditure which specifically qualifies as plant and machinery

Legislation lists the following expenditure as qualifying for relief:

1. Expenditure on the thermal insulation of any building used for a qualifying activity (e.g. a trade).

2. Expenditure incurred to comply with fire and safety regulations for premises used in trade.

3. Expenditure on building operations, incidental to the installation of plant and machinery.

4. Expenditure on sports ground which is necessary to comply with safety regulations.

5. Expenditure on a license to use computer software.

6. Expenditure on assets necessary to safeguard an individual's personal physical security.

> **Tip**
> Note that **'land' does not qualify** as plant and machinery.

Test Yourself 1

Can the following assets be considered plant and machinery?

1. An old ship used as a restaurant.
2. Central heating system in an office building.

SUMMARY

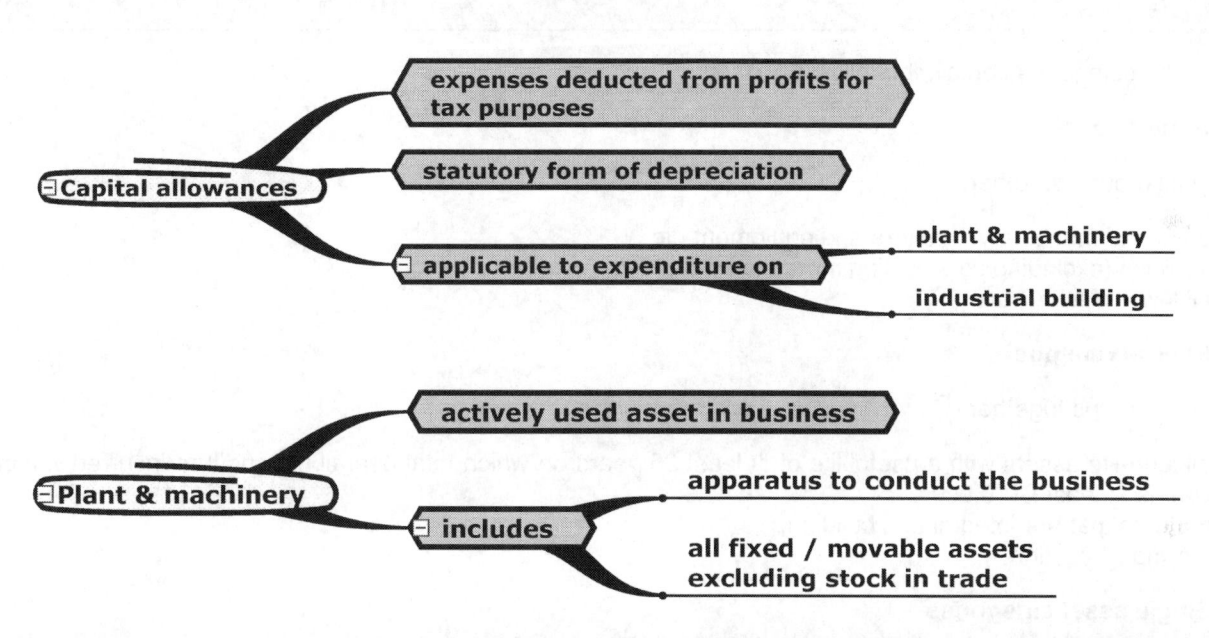

- **Capital allowances**
  - expenses deducted from profits for tax purposes
  - statutory form of depreciation
  - applicable to expenditure on
    - plant & machinery
    - industrial building

- **Plant & machinery**
  - actively used asset in business
  - includes
    - apparatus to conduct the business
    - all fixed / movable assets excluding stock in trade

2. Compute writing down allowances, first year allowance and the annual investment allowance. [2]
[Learning outcome g (ii)]

The allowances available on plant and machinery are:

➢ annual investment allowance (AIA)
➢ first year allowance (FYA)
➢ writing down allowances (WDA)

Capital allowances are not calculated separately for each item of plant and machinery purchased by a business. Instead, capital expenditure is categorised and capital allowances are given at different rates on different types of assets, in a way similar to accounting depreciation charges. When assets are grouped in the same category, it is known as 'pooling'.

The categories and the calculation of capital allowances are as follows:

	General pool £	Expensive car £	Private use asset £	Short life asset £	Special rate pool £	Capital Allowances £
TWDV b/f	X			X	X	
Additions	X	X	X		X	
Disposals	(X)				(X)	
	X				X	
Less: Allowances	(X)	(X)	(X)	(X)	(X)	X
TWDV c/f	X	X	X	X	X	
Allowances for the period						X

> **Tip** TWDV means tax written down value.

2.1 The categories contain the following assets:

1. General pool

The pool groups together:

- plant and machinery, furniture and equipment etc
- vehicles (excluding cars costing more than £12,000)
- all low emission cars

2. Special rate pool

The pool groups together:

- all long-life assets with a useful life of at least 25 years on which total overall expenditure incurred within a year is at least £100,000.
- features that are integral to a building.
- thermal insulation.

3. Single asset categories

- Expensive cars (cars costing more than £12,000 excluding low emission cars)
- Private use asset (an asset used for private purposes by the owner)
- Short life asset (an asset with a useful life of less than 5 years)

2.2 Annual investment allowance (AIA)

The annual investment allowance (AIA) was introduced in the Finance Act 2008 and is applicable for any expenditure on plant and machinery from 6 April 2008 (1 April 2008 for limited companies). This allowance is available to all kinds of businesses and allows a business to immediately write off the first £50,000 of expenditure on plant and machinery. This limit of £50,000 is applicable annually.

Expenditure which is over £50,000 will get first year allowance at the rate of 40%. The annual investment allowance is available to all expenditure on plant and machinery, **but not for cars**.

> **Example** Jake started trading on 6 April 2009 and prepares accounts to 5 April each year. On 10 April 2009, Jake purchased a plant for £70,000. Calculate the amount of annual investment allowance available to Jake for the year ended 5 April 2010.

Continued on next page

The AIA available for the year ended on 5 April 2010 is as follows:

	General pool (£)	Allowances (£)
Year ended 05/04/2010		
TWDV b/f		
Additions		
Not qualifying for AIA		
Qualifying for AIA	70,000	
Less: AIA (maximum)	(50,000)	50,000
TWDV c/f	**20,000**	
Allowances		**50,000**

Where the period of accounts is more or less than 12 months the limit of £50,000 is proportionately increased or decreased.

Example Mary commenced trading on 1 July 2009 and prepares accounts to 31 March each year. Her first accounts are for the period to 31 March 2010. Mary has a total expenditure of £64,000 on plant and machinery on 1 July 2009. Therefore the AIA would be £37,500 (50,000 x 9/12) for the nine month period of accounts.

	General pool £	Allowances £
9 months to 31/03/2010		
Additions qualifying AIA	64,000	
AIA	(37,500)	37,500
TWDV c/f	**26,500**	
Allowances		**37,500**

2.3 First year allowance (FYA)

According to the Finance Act 2009, the first year allowance of 40% will be available for expenditure on plant and machinery in the 12 month period from 6 April 2009 to 5 April 2010 (1 April 2009 to 31 March 2010 for companies). This allowance will be available on expenditure which exceeds the £50,000 AIA. FYA is not available for expenditure on cars, long life assets and expenditure that is included in the special rate pool.

However, expenditure incurred by any business on low emission motor cars is eligible for a 100% FYA. It has been discussed in detail in Learning Outcome 3 of this Study Guide.

Tip FYAs are available for expenditure on plant and machinery other than cars and long-life assets except low emission cars in which case FYA of 100% is available.

Unlike AIA, FYAs are not scaled up for an accounting period of more than 12 months, or down for an accounting period of less than 12 months. It is the date of expenditure that is relevant, not the length of the accounting period.

Example Jim started trading on 6 April 2009 and prepared accounts to 31 March each year. His first accounts covered the period from 6 April 2009 to 5 April 2010. During this period he made the following purchases:

		£
1 May 2009	Bought office furniture	39,500
1 May 2009	Bought plant	100,000

Continued on next page

Calculate the amount of AIA and FYA available for the year ended 5 April 2010.

Capital allowances for the year ended 5 April 2010 are as follows:

	FYA £	General pool £	Allowances £
Year ended on 05/04/2010			
TWDV b/f		-	
Additions			
Not qualifying for AIA: Car			
Qualifying for AIA:			
Office furniture	39,500		
Plant	100,000		
	139,500		
Less: AIA	(50,000)		50,000
	89,500		
Less: FYA 40%	(35,800)	53,700	35,800
TWDV c/f		61,900	
Allowances			85,800

2.4 Writing down allowance (WDA)

Writing down allowance (WDA) is given **at 20% per annum** on the **reducing balance basis**. The WDA is given for an accounting period.

This is calculated as follows:

➢ Any balance on the pool (i.e. the tax written down value TWDV) is brought forward.
➢ Expenditure on plant and machinery not qualifying for AIA and FYA is added (it includes cars except low emission cars).
➢ Disposal proceeds (limited to cost) are deducted.
➢ The WDA is deducted from the pool.
➢ The figure remaining (the TWDV) is carried forward to the next period.

> **Tip**
> If, in an accounting period, AIA and FYA are claimed for any asset, the asset does not additionally qualify for WDA. AIA and FYA on new assets are therefore dealt with after the WDA on other assets has been calculated.

Proforma for calculation of capital allowances

	FYA £	General pool £	Allowances £
TWDV b/f		X	
Additions not qualifying for AIA		X	
Disposals (limited to cost)		(X)	
		X	
WDA 20%		(X)	X
		X	
AIA and FYA additions (note)	X		
Less: AIA	(X)		X
	X		
Less: FYA 40%	(X)	X	X
TWDV c/f		X	
Allowances			X

Example

Jack prepares accounts to 31 March each year. Information for the year ending 31 March 2010 is as follows:

		£
1 April 2009	TWDV brought forward	65,000
10 April 2009	Bought plant	59,500
1 May 2009	Bought machinery	112,500

Capital allowances for the year ended to 31 March 2010 are as follows.

	FYA	General pool £	Allowances £
Year ended 31/03/2010			
TWDV b/f		65,000	
Additions not qualifying AIA & FYA		-	
Disposals		-	
		65,000	
WDA (£65,000 x 20%)		(13,000)	13,000
		52,000	
Additions qualifying AIA			
Plant	59,500		
Machinery	112,500		
	172,000		
Less: AIA	(50,000)		50,000
	122,000		
Less: FYA 40% (£122,000 x 40%)	(48,800)	73,200	48,800
Total		125,200	
Allowances			111,800

WDA when an accounting period is 12 months long

WDA is given for an accounting period. If the period is 12 months long the capital allowances will be 20% of the TWDV of the pool after making adjustments for additions and disposals. Whether the asset was bought on the first day of the accounting period or the last day of the accounting period the same allowances are available. It is the length of the accounting period that determines the allowance, not the date of purchase within the accounting period.

WDA when an accounting period is more or less than 12 months

Where a trader prepares accounts for a period longer or shorter than twelve months, the **WDA is increased or decreased accordingly.**

Example

Linda prepares accounts to 31 December each year. In March 2009, she decided to change her accounting date to 31 March, and prepares the accounts for 15 months to 31 March 2010. The balance of plant and machinery account as on 1 January 2009 was £10,000.
Her accounting period for the tax year 2009 – 10 is 15 months ending on 31 March 2010.
Capital allowances for the 15 month accounting period are calculated as follows:
£10,000 x 20% x 15/12 = £2,500

SUMMARY

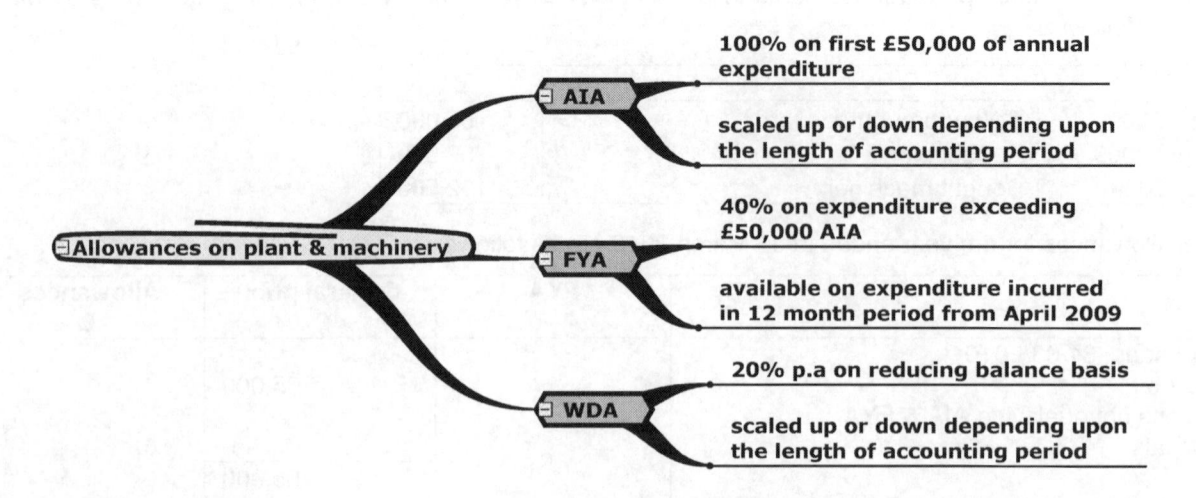

Allowances on plant & machinery

- **AIA**
  - 100% on first £50,000 of annual expenditure
  - scaled up or down depending upon the length of accounting period
- **FYA**
  - 40% on expenditure exceeding £50,000 AIA
  - available on expenditure incurred in 12 month period from April 2009
- **WDA**
  - 20% p.a on reducing balance basis
  - scaled up or down depending upon the length of accounting period

Test Yourself 2

Eric prepares accounts to 31 March each year. Information for the year ending 31 March 2010 is as follows:

	£
TWDV brought forward 1 April 2009	28,000
1 June 2009 purchased machinery	58,000
1 July 2009 sold plant (original cost £10,500)	12,000

Required:

1. Calculate the capital allowances for the year to 31 March 2010.
2. Calculate the capital allowances for the period to 31 March 2011, assuming there are no sales or purchases in the year.

Test Yourself 3

Malcolm started trading on 1 October 2008 and prepares accounts to 31 December each year. His first accounts are for the period to 31 December 2009. The only transaction in the period to 31 December 2009 was on 10 October 2009 when he bought machinery for £68,000.

Required:

Calculate the capital allowances for the period to 31 December 2009.

Test Yourself 4

Mack has been trading for many years with an annual accounting date of 30 April.

In the year to 30 April 2010 he bought and sold plant and machinery as follows:

		£
1 July 2009	Bought plant	22,500
30 July 2009	Sold plant (original cost £4,000 on 1/4/05)	3,000
29 March 2010	Bought plant	55,000

TWDV on the general pool at 1 May 2009 is £12,729.

Required:

Compute capital allowance for the year to 30 April 2010.

3. Compute capital allowances for motor cars. [2]

[Learning outcome g (iii)]

The Finance Act 2009 has introduced a new basis for calculation of capital allowances for motor cars. Before 6 April 2009 (1 April 2009 for limited companies), the calculation of capital allowances on motor cars was based upon the cost of the car. However, from the tax year 2009-10, the calculation of capital allowance will be based upon the CO_2 emissions rate of the car.

According to the Finance Act 2009, the capital allowance available for motor cars purchased on or after 6 April 2009 (1 April 2009 for limited companies) is determined with respect to the following categories:

- Cars with CO_2 emissions rate not exceeding 110g/km (low emission cars)
- Cars with CO_2 emissions rate between 110g/km and 160g/km
- Cars with CO_2 emissions rate exceeding 160g/km

Tip Note that these rules only apply to cars. Any other type of vehicle, such as a motorcycle, lorry or van, is treated as plant and machinery with AIA available for the first £50,000.

3.1 Low emission cars

1. **A low emission car is one** with a **CO_2 emission rate of 110g/km** or less, or an **electrically propelled** car.
2. **Low emission cars** are eligible for a **100% first year allowance** regardless of the cost of the car.
3. The FYA is given in full in the year the car is purchased, irrespective of the length of the accounting period.

Tip FYA at 100% is available on low emission cars.

Example Sally started trading on 1 June 2009 and prepared her first accounts to 31 March 2010. On 16 November 2009 she purchased a car with an emissions rate of 90g/km for £18,000. This was the only transaction in the accounting period.

Expenditure on cars does not qualify for FYAs unless it has an emissions rate of 110g/km or less, in which case 100% FYA is available.

Sally can claim an FYA of 100% i.e. £18,000

Note: A 10 month accounting period has no effect on FYAs.

3.2 Cars with CO_2 emissions rate between 110g/km and 160g/km

According to the Finance Act 2009, cars purchased on or after 6 April 2009 (1 April 2009 for limited companies) and with CO_2 emissions rate exceeding 110g/km but up to 160g/km, will go into the **general pool**. Writing down allowance (WDA) at the rate of 20% per annum will be available on these cars. However, these cars do not qualify for AIAs.

Example Jack has been trading for many years, preparing accounts to 5 April each year. On 1 February 2010 he bought a car with CO_2 emissions rate of 130g/km for £10,000. As the car was purchased after 6 April 2009 and CO_2 emissions rate of the car is between 110g/km and 160g/km, it will be included in the general pool and will not qualify for AIA.

Jack's capital allowances will be calculated as follows:

	General pool £	Allowances £
Year ended 05/04/2010		
TWDV b/f	-	
Additions	10,000	
WDA (£10,000 x 20%)	(2,000)	2,000
TWDV c/f	**8,000**	
Allowances		**2,000**

3.3 Cars with CO_2 emissions rate exceeding 160g/km

1. If these cars are purchased after 6 April 2009 (1 April 2009 for limited companies), they are **not pooled in the general pool** of plant and machinery.

2. **Each** of these cars is allocated to the **special rate pool and will have its own column.**

3. These cars **do not qualify for AIA.**

4. The WDA on these cars is calculated at the rate of 10% per annum on a reducing balance basis.

> **Important**
> The writing down allowance for the cars purchased before 6 April 2009 (1 April 2009 for limited companies) remains the same for the next five years and is calculated at the rate of 20% per annum. Cars costing less than £12,000 are included in the general pool and cars costing more than £12,000 are termed expensive cars. Each expensive car has its, own column. However, WDA on cars costing more than £12,000 is restricted **to a maximum of £3,000** per annum. If the accounting period is not **12 months long**, this limit of **£3,000** is scaled up or down **depending on the length of the accounting period.**

Example Dennis started trading on 1 April 2009, preparing accounts to 31 December 2009 and annually thereafter. He purchased a car for £16,210 with CO_2 emissions rate of 185g/km on 10 April 2009.

The calculation of the capital allowances for the first three accounting periods is as follows:

	Special rate car £	Allowances £
Year ended 31/12/2009		
Addition: Car	16,210	
WDA (W1)	(1,216)	1,216
TWDV c/f	**14,994**	
Allowances		**1,216**
Year ended 31/12/2010		
TWDV b/f	14,994	
WDA @ 10%	(1,499)	1,499
TWDV c/f	**13,495**	
Allowances		**1,499**
Year ended 31/12/2011		
TWDV b/f	13,495	
WDA 20%	(1,350)	1,350
TWDV c/f	**12,145**	
Allowances		**1,350**

Workings

W1

As the CO_2 emissions rate of the car purchased on 10 April 2009 is more than 160g/km, WDA at the rate of 10% will be applicable. WDA on the car at the rate of 10% is £1,621 (£16,210 x 10%).

As the AP is nine months long, (1 April 2009 to 31 December 2009) the WDA is scaled down proportionately.

WDA for the period ended 31 December 2009 is £1,216 (1,621 x 9/12).

Example

Jack started trading on 1 April 2009 and prepares accounts to 30 May each year. His first accounts covered the period from 1 April 2009 to 31 May 2010.

Jack's expenditure on plant and machinery qualifies for capital allowances.

In the period he made the following purchases:

		£
1 April 2009	Bought plant	59,500
1 May 2009	Bought motor car (CO_2 emissions rate of 120g/km)	12,500

Capital allowances for 14 months to 30 May 2010 are as follows:

	FYA £	General pool £	Allowances £
14 months to 31/5/2010			
TWDV b/f		-	
Additions not qualifying AIA (Car)		12,500	
Less: WDA (£12,500 x 20% x 14/12)		(2,917)	2,917
		9,583	
Additions qualifying AIA			
Plant	59,500		
Less: AIA (Scaled up for 14 month) (£50,000 x 14/12)	(58,333)		58,333
	1,167		
Less: FYA (£1,167 x 40%)	(467)	700	467
TWDV c/f		10,283	
Allowances			**61,717**

Notes

1. AIA applies to all expenditure on plant and machinery with the exception of cars.
2. As the CO_2 emissions rate of the car purchased was between 110g/km and 160g/km, it will be included in the general pool and the WDA rate of 20% per annum will be applicable.
3. As the AP is more than 12 months, AIA and WDA will be scaled up proportionately.

Diagram 1: Capital allowance for motor car

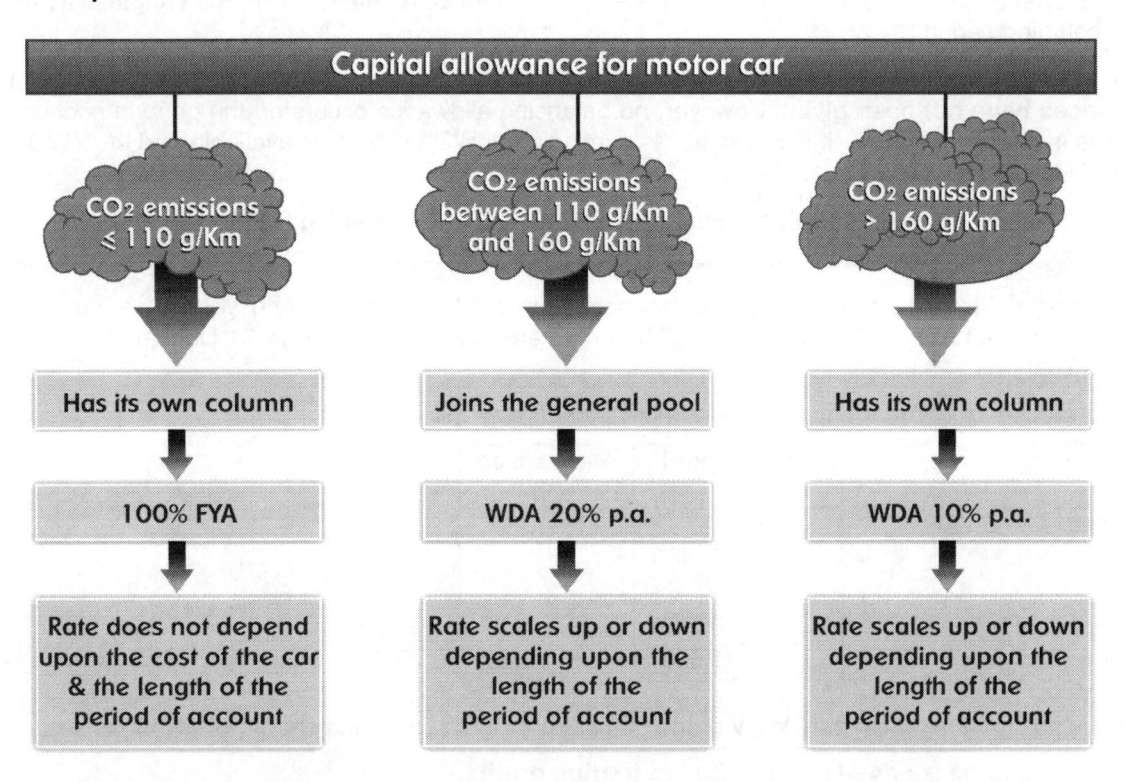

Capital allowance for motor car

- CO_2 emissions ≤ 110 g/Km → Has its own column → 100% FYA → Rate does not depend upon the cost of the car & the length of the period of account
- CO_2 emissions between 110 g/Km and 160 g/Km → Joins the general pool → WDA 20% p.a. → Rate scales up or down depending upon the length of the period of account
- CO_2 emissions > 160 g/Km → Has its own column → WDA 10% p.a. → Rate scales up or down depending upon the length of the period of account

Test Yourself 5

Robert has been trading for many years, preparing accounts to 31 December each year. The TWDV on his general pool on 1 January 2009 was £20,000. On 5 November 2009 he purchased a car for £15,000 with CO_2 emissions rate of 192g/km.

Required:

Calculate the capital allowances for the accounting period to 31 December 2009.

Test Yourself 6

Mack started trading on 1 June 2009 and prepared accounts to 31 March 2010 and annually thereafter. He bought cars as follows:

1 August 2009 (CO_2 emissions rate of 196g/km) = £14,000
2 September 2009 (CO_2 emissions rate of 105g/km) = £12,500
3 October 2009 = Purchased equipment for £61,400
The car bought in September is a low emission car.

Required:

Compute the capital allowances for the 10 months to 31 March 2010.

4. Compute balancing allowances and balancing charges. [2]

[Learning outcome g (iv)]

The aim of capital allowances is to compensate the business for the **net cost** of owning the asset. Capital allowances would have been given over the life of the asset. They may be greater or less than its net cost. On the disposal of an asset, adjustments can be made so that the total allowances equal the net cost of the asset (original cost less sale proceeds).

If insufficient allowances have been claimed, then additional allowances may be given by means of a balancing allowance. If the allowances claimed exceed the net cost of the asset, a balancing charge may arise, recovering some of the allowances already given.

The treatment of the disposal depends on whether the asset was in a pool, or in a column on its own.

4.1 Balancing adjustments on the general pool

1. If the **disposal value** of an asset **exceeds the TWDV** on the general pool, it means **too many allowances have been given in the past,** and a **balancing charge arises**. A balancing charge is simply a negative capital allowance, and is added to the tax adjusted trading profits. A balancing charge can arise at the end of any accounting period.

2. If the **disposal value** of the asset is **less than the TWDV** on the general pool, it means **sufficient allowances have not been given**. However, no balancing allowance occurs on the general pool unless the business is ceasing to trade. If the business is continuing, a WDA of 20% is available and the TWDV on the general pool is carried forward as normal.

3. These rules also apply to disposals from the special rate pool (refer Learning Outcome g (vi)).

Example

Ross, a trader, prepares his accounts to 31 December each year. The balance on the general pool on 1 January 2009 was £17,450. The only transaction in the year to 31 December 2009 was the sale of machinery for £19,000.

Capital allowances for the year ended 31 December 2009 are as follows:

	General pool (£)	Allowances (£)
Year ended 31/12/2009		
TWDV b/f	17,450	
Additions	-	
Disposal proceeds	(19,000)	
Balancing charge	**(1,550)**	**(1,550)**

Machinery is sold for more than the TWDV of the general pool, so a balancing charge of £1,550 arises.
The balancing charge is added to tax adjusted trading profits.

Example

Stephen, a trader, prepares accounts to 30 September each year. The balance on the general pool on 1 October 2009 was £24,250. He ceased trading on 31 December 2009, and sold all items in the general pool for £20,000.

Capital allowances for the period ending 31 December 2009 are as follows:

	General pool (£)	Allowances (£)
Period ended		
TWDV b/f	24,250	
Additions	-	
Disposal proceeds	(20,000)	
Balancing allowance	**4,250**	**4,250**

The machinery is sold for less than the TWDV of the general pool. As the business is ceasing to trade, a balancing allowance of £4,250 arises.

The balancing allowance is deducted from tax adjusted trading profits.

4.2 Balancing adjustments on single column assets e.g. expensive car

1. If the **disposal value** of the asset **exceeds the TWDV**, then excess allowances have been given, so a **balancing charge arises.**
2. If the **disposal value** of the asset is **less than the TWDV**, then insufficient allowances have been given, and a balancing allowance **arises.**

A balancing allowance on a single asset column can arise at any point in the life of a business, not just on cessation as for the general pool.

Example

Stuart, a trader, prepares accounts to 30 June each year. On 1 July 2009 the balance on an expensive car was £16,850. The car was sold in March 2010 for £12,000.

Capital allowances for the year to 30 June 2010 are as follows:

	Expensive car £	Allowances £
Period ended		
30/6/2009		
TWDV b/f	16,850	
Disposal proceeds	(12,000)	
Balancing allowance	**4,850**	**4,850**

As the disposal proceeds (i.e. £12,000) are less than the TWDV (i.e. £16,850) a balancing allowance of £4,850 arises.

Diagram 2: Balancing adjustments

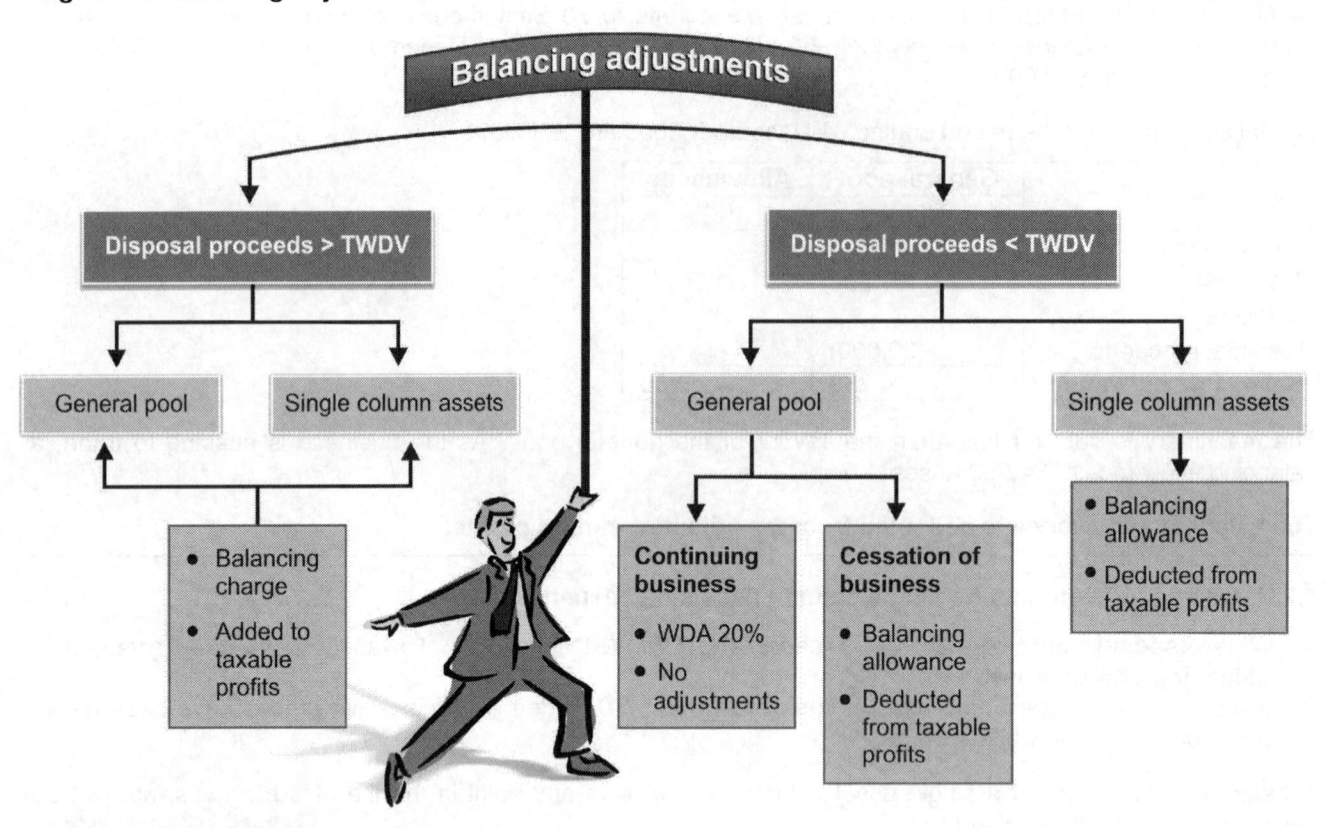

Balancing adjustments

- **Disposal proceeds > TWDV**
  - General pool
  - Single column assets
    - Balancing charge
    - Added to taxable profits

- **Disposal proceeds < TWDV**
  - General pool
    - Continuing business
      - WDA 20%
      - No adjustments
    - Cessation of business
      - Balancing allowance
      - Deducted from taxable profits
  - Single column assets
    - Balancing allowance
    - Deducted from taxable profits

Test Yourself 7

Glenda has been trading for many years, preparing accounts to 31 October each year. The TWDV of her general pool on 1 September 2009 is £28,000. On 1 October 2009, she purchased a car for £8,000 with CO_2 emissions rate of 146 g/km. Due to an illness, she decided to close the business on 31 January 2010, and sold all the general pool items (including her car) for £32,100.

Required:

Calculate the capital allowances for the period to 31 January 2010.

4.3 Private use of assets by the owner

Capital allowances are restricted where there is some private use **by the owner**. Capital allowances **can only be claimed on the business proportion.**

> **Tip** Remember, capital allowances are **not restricted** in this way if the private use of **an asset** is **by an employee (not the owner).**

An asset which is used **partially** for **business purposes** and partially for **private purposes** does not join the general pool but has its **own column**.

When the asset is disposed of balancing adjustments apply, but **only the business proportion is taken into account.**

Example

Michael, a trader, prepares accounts to 30 June every year.
He purchased a motor car with CO_2 emissions rate of 128g/km on 1 July 2009 for £5,000, with 60% private use agreed with HMRC. On 1 August 2009 he purchased a motor car for £15,000 with CO_2 emissions rate of 180g/km with 40% private use agreed with HMRC. No FYAs or AIA are available. On 1 February 2011 he sold the asset purchased in July 2009 for £4,800.

Compute the capital allowances for the two years to 30 June 2011.

Continued on next page

Answer

	General pool (£)	Business use 40% (£)	Special rate car (£)	Business use 60% (£)	Allowances (£)
Year ended 30/06/2010					
Addition not qualifying AIA (Car)	5,000		15,000		
WDA 20%/10%	(1,000)	400	(1,500)	900	1,300
TWDV c/f	**4,000**		**13,500**		
Allowances					**1,300**
Year ended 30/06/2011					
TWDV b/f	4,000		13,500		
Disposal	(4,800)				
Less: WDA 10%			(1,350)	810	810
Balancing charge (W1)	**800**	320			(320)
TWDV c/f			12,150		
Allowances					**490**

Working

W1

The private use asset is disposed of in the year ended 30 June 2011. **Disposal proceeds are greater than the TWDV, so a balancing charge of £800 arises.** We must then take into account the private use, so the balancing charge is 40%.
£800 x 40% = £320

Test Yourself 8

Lucy starts trading on 1 May 2009, preparing accounts to 30 April each year. On 10 May 2009 she purchased a car for £9,000 with CO_2 emissions rate of 152g/km. She agreed private use of 30% with HMRC.

Required:

Calculate the capital allowances for the two years to 30 April 2011.

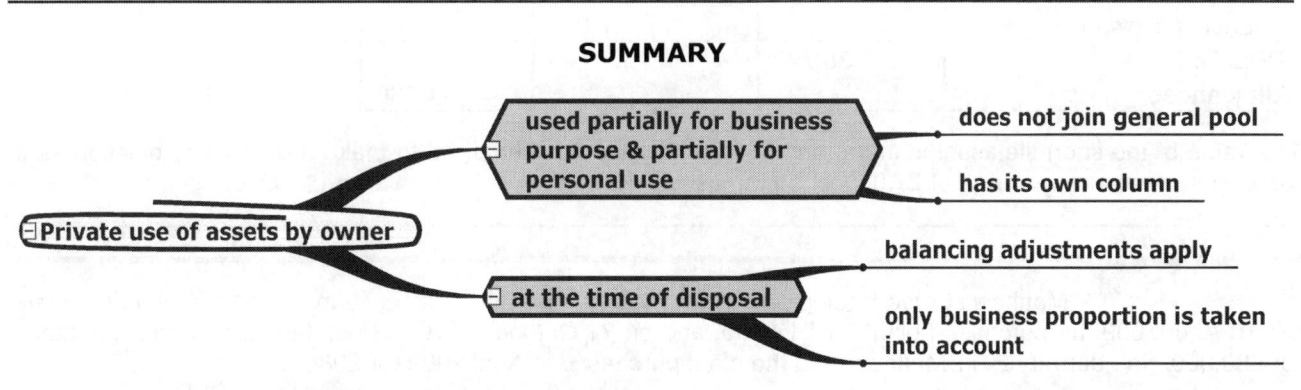

SUMMARY

- **Private use of assets by owner**
  - used partially for business purpose & partially for personal use
    - does not join general pool
    - has its own column
  - at the time of disposal
    - balancing adjustments apply
    - only business proportion is taken into account

---

5. Recognise the treatment of short life assets. [2]

[Learning outcome g (v)]

Short life asset is the asset which has an expected life of less than five years. An election can be made to **de-pool such item of asset (plant and machinery), which is normally accounted for in the general pool.**

1. The election is **not available** for **cars and private use assets.** (see above)

2. Each short life asset has **its own column for capital allowances.**

3. Expenditure on short life assets qualifies for the annual investment allowance of £50,000. However, if AIA covers the cost of a short life asset, making the de-pooling election will not be beneficial as it will result in a balancing charge when the asset is sold.

4. If the expenditure on a short life asset exceeds the £50,000 limit covered by AIA, then it is beneficial to make a de-pool election for that asset. Short-life assets purchased during the period from 6 April 2009 to 5 April 2010 (1 April 2009 to 31 March 2010 for limited companies) will qualify for FYA at the rate of 40%.

5. The availability of WDAs is the same as for the general pool. A balancing adjustment arises when the asset is disposed of.

6. If the asset is **not disposed** of by the end of the **fourth year** after the period of purchase, then the **TWDV of the asset is transferred to the general pool.**

7. The election **accelerates capital allowances** if the **asset is disposed of within five years** for a **price less than the TWDV.**

Example

Rob has been trading for many years, preparing accounts to 31 December each year. The TWDV on his general pool on 1 January 2009 was £48,000. On 5 November 2009 he purchased a plant for £70,000. Rob made a de-pooling election for the new plant purchased.

In March 2010, Rob sold the plant purchased in November 2009 for £5000.

The calculation of capital allowances is as follows:

	General pool £	Short life asset £	Allowances £
Year ended 31/12/2009			
TWDV b/f	48,000		
Less: WDA 20%	(9,600)		9,600
Additions qualifying AIA	-	70,000	-
Less: AIA	-	(50,000)	50,000
		20,000	
Less: FYA 40%		(8,000)	8,000
TWDV c/f	**38,400**	**12,000**	
Allowances			**67,600**
Year ended 31/12/2010			
TWDV b/f	38,400	12,000	
Less: WDA 20%	(7,680)		7,680
Less: Disposals		(5,000)	
Balancing allowance		7,000	7,000
TWDV c/f	**30,720**	**-**	
Allowances			**14,680**

The value of the short life asset is more than £50,000, hence it is beneficial to make a de-pooling election as it resulted in a balancing charge of £7,000 when the asset was sold.

Example

Matthew started trading on 7 April 2009 and prepares his accounts to 31 March each year. On 10 April 2009, he purchased plant for £12,400, and on 31 October 2010, he purchased an additional plant for £80,000. In February 2011 Matthew sold the plant purchased in April 2009 for £985.

Matthew made a de-pooling election for the plant purchased in April 2009. The **calculation of capital allowances is as follows:**

	General pool (£)	Short life asset (£)	Allowances (£)
Period ended 31/3/2010			
TWDV b/f	Nil		
Additions qualifying AIA	-	12,400	-
Less: AIA	-	(12,400)	12,400
TWDV c/f		-	
Allowances			**12,400**

The short life asset is not pooled in the general pool with the other assets; it has its own column.

Continued on next page

		Continued from last page
Year ended 31/3/2011		
TWDV b/f		-
Addition	80,000	
Less: AIA	(50,000)	50,000
	30,000	
Less: FYA 40%	(12,000)	12,000
Less: Disposals		(985)
TWDV c/f	**18,000**	
Balancing Charge		(985)
Allowances		**62,000**

Matthew opted for a de-pooling election but it was not beneficial as it has resulted in a balancing charge in the second year. Hence, the net capital allowances for the year ended 31/3/2011 are £61,015 (£62,000 – £985).

If Matthew doesn't make a de-pooling election, the calculation of capital allowances will be as follows:

	General pool (£)	Allowances (£)
Period ended 31/03/2010		
TWDV b/f		
Additions qualifying AIA	12,400	-
Less: AIA	(12,400)	12,400
TWDV c/f		
Allowances		**12,400**
Year ended 31/3/2011		
Additions qualifying AIA	80,000	
Less: AIA	(50,000)	50,000
	30,000	
FYA 40%	(12,000)	12,000
Disposals	(985)	
TWDV c/f	**17,015**	
Allowances		**62,000**

In this case, the net capital allowances for the year ended 31/3/2011 are £62,000. Hence, it will be more beneficial for Matthew to opt for not making a de-pooling election.

Example Jack has been trading for many years, making up accounts to 31 March each year. The TWDV of his plant and machinery on 1 April 2009 were:

	(£)
General pool	50,000
Expensive car (60% private use by Jack)	20,000
Short life asset (purchased 1 April 2007)	55,000

Jack bought plant and machinery as follows:

		(£)
1 May 2009	Bought car	10,800
10 May 2009	Bought machinery	10,000
30 May 2009	Bought equipment	62,000
1 June 2009	Bought van	15,000
1 July 2009	Bought car (CO_2 emissions of 187g/km) for employee (60% private use)	16,000

Jack makes a short life asset election for the equipment bought on 30 May 2009

> Remember, this car is used by the **employee** for private use, so capital allowance is **not restricted**.

Capital allowances are calculated as follows:

	General pool (£)	Expensive car (1) (£)	Business use 40% (£)	Special rate car (2) (£)	Short life asset (1) (£)	Short life asset (2) (£)	Allowances (£)
Year ended 31/03/2010							
TWDV b/f	50,000	20,000			55,000		
Non-AIA additions	10,800			16,000			
AIA additions	25,000					62,000	
(10,000 + 15,000)							
Less: AIA (100%)	(25,000)					(25,000)	50,000
	60,800					37,000	
Less: FYA 40%						(14,800)	14,800
Less: WDA 20%/10%	(12,160)	(3,000)	1,200	(1,600)	(11,000)		25,960
TWDV c/f	48,640	17,000		14,400	44,000	22,200	
Allowances							90,760

Notes:

1. Car purchased before 6 April 2009 and costing more than £12,000 is termed an expensive car and each expensive car has its own column.
2. The maximum WDA for an expensive car is £3,000 per annum.
3. The short life asset election made by Jack for the asset purchased on 31 May 2008 is beneficial as it exceeds the limit of £50,000 covered by AIA. Short life asset needs its own column, and qualifies for the annual investment allowance.
4. AIA is available to all businesses and provides FYA of 100% on the first £50,000 of expenditure on plant and machinery. The first £25,000 of the limit is utilised by the general pool, hence the balance of £25,000 is available for the short life asset. On the balance amount, FYA at the rate of 40% is available as it is purchased within 12 months from 6 April 2009.
5. The expensive car provisions do not apply to lorries or vans.

Test Yourself 9

Alice started her manufacturing business on 1 April 2009. She chose 31 March as her annual accounting date. On 10 April 2009, she purchased machinery for £54,800, and in May 2010 she purchased additional plant for £68,500. In August 2011, she sold the asset purchased on 10 April 2009 for £1,000.

Alice made a de-pooling election for the machinery purchased in April 2009.

Required:

Calculate the capital allowances for the three years to 31 March 2012.

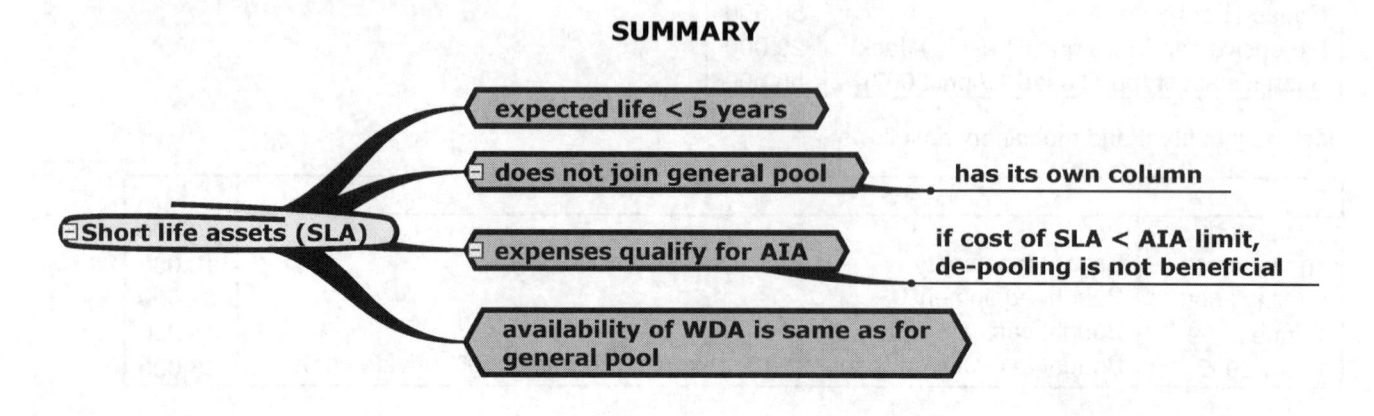

SUMMARY

Short life assets (SLA)
- expected life < 5 years
- does not join general pool — has its own column
- expenses qualify for AIA — if cost of SLA < AIA limit, de-pooling is not beneficial
- availability of WDA is same as for general pool

6. Explain the treatment of assets included in the special rate pool. [2]
[Learning outcome g (vi)]

A special rate pool has been introduced from 6 April 2008 (1 April 2008 for companies), with a WDA of 10%.

This special rate pool is for expenditure on:

- long-life assets
- features integral to a building
- thermal insulation

A number of items of plant and machinery are treated as being integral to a building, particularly:

- electrical and lighting systems
- cold water systems
- space or water heating systems
- powered systems of ventilation, cooling, or air purification
- lifts and escalators

Definition A long life asset is defined as:
- **an asset which, when new** has an **expected economic working life of at least 25 years,** and
- **TOTAL** expenditure on this type of asset **exceeds £100,000 in a 12 month period**

The following are not treated as long-life assets
a) Motor cars
b) Ships
c) Plant and machinery used in retail shops, showrooms, offices, hotels and dwelling houses

6.1 Treatment of expenditure on long life assets

1. If the expenditure on an asset with a life of at least 25 years is **less than £100,000** (pro-rata for short accounting periods), then they are not long life assets, and the assets go into the **general pool** as usual.
2. If the expenditure **exceeds £100,000**, then the assets go into the **special rate pool.**
3. **The WDA** on the special rate pool is 10% on the **reducing balance basis.**
4. Expenditure on assets in the special rate pool **qualifies for the annual investment allowance.** However, it does not qualify for FYA.
5. Balancing adjustments apply to the special rate pool in the same way as for the general pool.
6. It is beneficial to allocate AIA to the special rate pool initially as it will convert 10% WDA into 100% relief (which is more beneficial than converting 20% WDA into 100% relief).

Example Patrick has been trading for many years preparing accounts to 30 June every year. The TWDV on his special rate asset pool on 1 April 2009 was £74,200. In June 2010, he sold one of the long life assets for £82,000.

Capital allowances are as follows:

	Special rate pool (£)	Allowances (£)
Year ended 31/3/2010		
TWDV b/f	74,200	-
WDA 10%	(7,420)	7,420
WDV c/f	**66,780**	
Allowances		**7,420**
Year ended 31/3/2011		
TWDV b/f	66,780	
Disposal proceeds	(82,000)	-
Balancing charge	**(15,220)**	**(15,220)**

B3.50: Income Tax Liabilities   © GTG

Test Yourself 10

Jack is a trader preparing accounts to 30 April each year. The TWDV of the general pool on 1 May 2009 is £40,000. He purchased an asset on 15 April 2010 with an expected economic working life of 30 years.

Required:

Calculate the capital allowances for the year to 30 April 2010 assuming the purchase price of the asset is
(a) £90,000
(b) £190,000

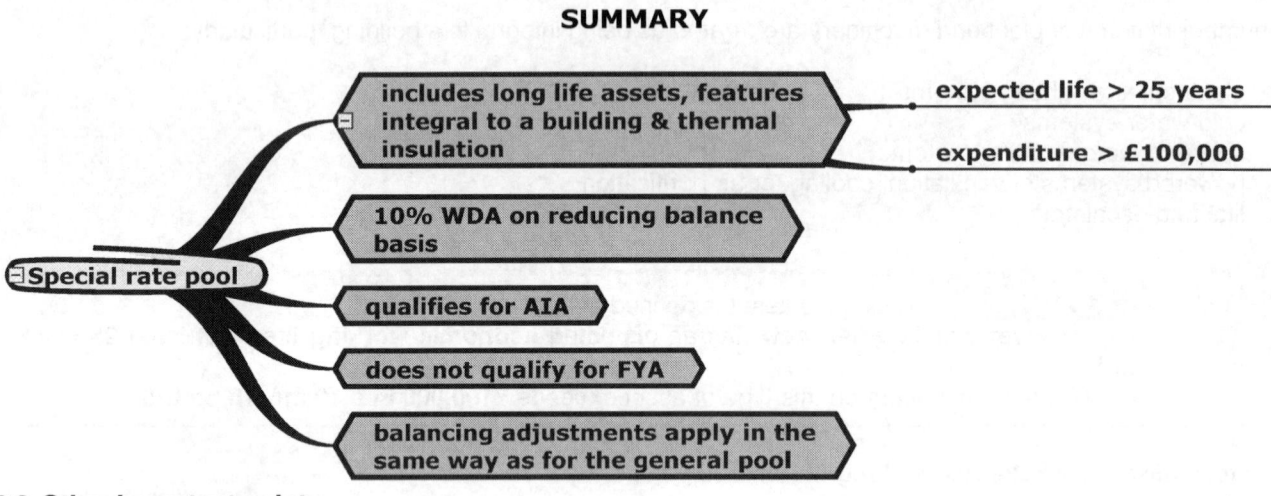

SUMMARY

Special rate pool
- includes long life assets, features integral to a building & thermal insulation
  - expected life > 25 years
  - expenditure > £100,000
- 10% WDA on reducing balance basis
- qualifies for AIA
- does not qualify for FYA
- balancing adjustments apply in the same way as for the general pool

6.2 Other important points

1. Second hand assets

The same allowances are available for a second hand asset as they are for a new one, including the annual investment allowance.

2. Part exchange transactions

A part exchange transaction is when a new asset is purchased, but instead of the asset being purchased for cash, the purchase is partly funded by trading a used asset. The remaining balance is paid in cash.

In other words, a new asset is purchased with a combination of an existing asset and cash.

For the capital allowances calculation, this is treated as two separate transactions. First, the disposal of one asset with the part exchange allowance being the disposal proceeds and second, the purchase of the new asset for the full amount.

Example

Jerry has been trading for many years, preparing accounts to 31 March each year. The balance on the general pool on 1 April 2009 is £24,000. He part exchanged a car used by an employee (original cost £7,750) for a new one with a CO_2 emissions of 140g/km. He was given a part exchange allowance of £4,150 on the old car, and paid an additional £6,700.

Capital allowances for the year to 31 March 2010 are as follows:

	General Pool (£)	Allowances (£)
Year ended 31/03/2010		
TWDV b/f	24,000	
Additions (£4,150 + £6,700)	10,850	
	34,850	
Less: Disposals	(4,150)	
	30,700	
WDA 20%	(6,140)	6,140
TWDV c/f	24,560	
Allowances		6,140

Note: FYA is not available on the purchase of a car. WDA at the rate of 20% will be available as the CO_2 emissions rate of the car is between 110g/km and 160g/km.

3. Hire purchase

a) Plant and machinery bought on hire purchase are treated in the same way as assets bought for cash.

b) Capital allowances are available for the **cash price (excluding interest)** on the date of the hire purchase agreement.

c) Interest included in the instalments is an allowable expense from the trading income.

Example John has been trading for many years and prepares his accounts to 31 July each year. The balance on the general pool on 1 August 2009 is £16,000.

John bought plant under a hire purchase agreement on 1 August 2009. He paid a deposit of £3,200 and 20 monthly instalments of £250. The price of the plant if purchased for cash is £7,000.

John's trading profits for the year to 31 July 2010, before deducting the capital allowances and interest from the hire purchase agreement are £80,000.

To calculate the adjusted trading profits, first calculate the capital allowances.

	General Pool (£)	Allowances (£)
Year ended 31/07/2010		
TWDV b/f	16,000	
AIA additions	7,000	
Less: AIA	(7,000)	7,000
	16,000	
WDA 20%	(3,200)	3,200
TWDV c/f	12,800	
Allowances		10,200

The interest element of the HP agreement is:
Total payments £3,200 + (20 x £250) = £8,200

Cash price £7,000
Interest element £1,200

The interest is an allowable expense, spread over the period of the contract.
Interest allowable in year ended 31 July 2010 is £1,200 x 12/20 = £720

Adjusted trading profits for year ended 31 July 2010

	(£)
Trading profit (given)	80,000
Less: Interest	(720)
Less: Capital allowances	(10,200)
Adjusted trading profits	**69,080**

4. Allowances in opening years

a) A trader will generally prepare accounts for a 12 month period, but it is not unusual for the first accounting period to be of a different length.

b) Capital allowances are calculated for an accounting period. If this period is not 12 months long, the allowances must be scaled up or down.

c) WDAs (10% / 20% and £3,000) must be pro-rated.

d) AIA is pro-rated, according to the length of the accounting period.

e) FYAs are NEVER pro-rated, regardless of the length of the accounting period.

Example

Michael started trading on 1 July 2009 and prepares accounts to 31 March every year. The following transactions took place over 3 years.

	(£)
1 August 2009, bought car (CO$_2$ emissions rate of 156g/km)	8,800
1 September 2009, bought plant	25,000
1 May 2010, sold car	6,200

The tax adjusted trading profits before capital allowances are as follows:

	(£)
Period ended 31/3/2010	250,000
Year ended 31/3/2011	100,000
Year ended 31/3/2012	200,000

We first compute the capital allowances for the accounting periods.

9 months to 31/03/2010

	AIA and FYA (£)	General pool (£)	Allowances (£)
Non-AIA additions		8,800	
WDA (£8,800 x 20% x 9/12)		(1,320)	1,320
		7,480	
AIA additions	25,000		
Less: AIA (note)	(25,000)	-	25,000
TWDV c/f		7,480	
Allowances			26,320

Note: AIA is scaled down to £37,500 (£50,000 x 9/12). Therefore full expenditure is allowed for AIA.

Year ended 31/03/2011

	General Pool (£)	Allowances (£)
TWDV b/f	7,480	
Disposal	(6,200)	
	1,280	
WDA 20%	(256)	256
TWDV c/f	1,024	
Allowances		256

Year ended 31/3/2012

	General Pool (£)	Allowances (£)
TWDV b/f	1,024	
WDA 20%	(205)	205
TWDV c/f	819	
Allowances		205

The adjusted **trading profits** for the three periods are as follows

	Period ended 31/03/2010 (£)	Year ended 31/03/2011 (£)	Year ended 31/03/2012 (£)
Trading profits given	250,000	100,000	200,000
Capital allowances	(26,320)	(256)	(205)
Adjusted trading profits after capital allowances	**223,680**	**99,744**	**199,795**

5. Pre-trading capital expenditure

a) Expenditure incurred on plant and machinery before trading commences is treated as if it was incurred on the first day of trading.

b) However, the rate of allowances goes by the **ACTUAL date of expenditure.**

6. Allowances on cessation

When trade ceases, all the plant and machinery is disposed of. Capital allowances in the final accounting period are calculated as follows:

a) Any purchases made in the final period are added to the TWDV b/f.

b) There are **no WDAs, FYAs or AIAs in the final period**.

c) Disposal proceeds (limited to cost) are deducted, giving rise to a balancing charge or balancing allowance. If the trader takes over an asset himself, then it is treated as sold at market value.

Example

Sunny has been trading for many years and prepares accounts to 31 March each year. The TWDV on the general pool on 1 April 2009 is £26,000.

On 1 May 2009 he bought plant for £10,600.

He ceased trading on 30 September 2009, and sold all general pool items for £29,800. The tax adjusted profits, before capital allowances, for the period to 30 September 2009 were £28,200.

Sunny has overlap profits brought forward of £2,600.

Calculate Sunny's trading income assessment for 2009-10.

First calculate capital allowances for the final period of trading.

	General Pool £
6 months to 30/09/09	
TWDV b/f	26,000
Additions	10,600
	36,600
Less: Disposal	(29,800)
Balancing allowance	**6,800**

Note: no AIA, FYA or WDA available in the final period of trading.

2009-10	£
Basis period 01/04/2009-30/09/2009	
Adjusted trading profits before capital allowances	28,200
Less: Balancing allowance	(6,800)
Less: Overlap relief	(2,600)
2009 -10 trading income assessment	**18,800**

7. Define an industrial building for Industrial buildings allowance purposes. [1]
Compute industrial buildings allowance for new buildings. [2]

[Learning outcome g (vii) and g (viii)]

Allowances are also available on qualifying industrial buildings, known as industrial building allowances (IBAs).

7.1 Definition

Industrial buildings include:

1. buildings **used for manufacturing goods (a factory)**
2. buildings used for the storage of goods or materials (a warehouse)
3. building used for the repair or maintenance of goods (a workshop)
4. buildings used for the welfare of employees in the manufacturing business (a canteen)
5. sports pavilion in any trade
6. drawing office (an engineer's office, technical drawing office) within or attached to an industrial building

The definition **specifically excludes**

i. Private houses
ii. Shops
iii. Showrooms
iv. Offices

However, if showrooms, offices and shops are an **integral part** of the industrial building, **and** this **expenditure does not exceed 25% of the total cost** of the building, then the **entire expenditure qualifies for an IBA**. **If the expenditure exceeds 25%,** then **none** of the **expenditure** on showrooms etc **qualifies.**

7.2 Qualifying expenditure

The industrial building allowance is based on the qualifying expenditure of the industrial building.

1. If the user constructs the building, then the qualifying expenditure is the cost of constructing the building.
2. If the building is bought from a builder, then the qualifying expenditure is the **amount paid to the builder.**
3. If the building is bought from someone other than a builder then the qualifying expenditure is the lower of:
    - price paid for the building
    - the original construction cost of the building

The qualifying cost does not include the cost of the land, and the legal fees relating to the purchase of the land. However, costs of preparing the land and professional fees relating to the building are qualifying expenditure.

Test Yourself 11

Henry purchases land and builds a factory for business purposes, incurring the following costs:

	£
Site preparation	16,000
Architect's fees	50,000
Factory building costs	1,000,000
Showroom cost	200,000
Land	450,000
Legal fees relating to purchase of land	24,000
	1,740,000

Required:

What is the qualifying expenditure for IBA purposes?

7.3 Industrial building allowances

1. Industrial building allowances are given on qualifying expenditure, and are available to the person who first uses the building.

2. Allowances are available to traders in two situations:
   - If the trader owns the industrial building
   - If the trader has a lease of more than 50 years on an industrial building and an election has been made to claim the allowances.

3. Allowances are given **for** accounting periods.

4. **The WDA is 2% per annum** on the **qualifying expenditure** on a **STRAIGHT LINE BASIS**.

5. Allowance is given if the building is in **industrial use (or temporary disuse)** at the **END** of the **accounting period.**

6. The allowance is given in full unless the **accounting period is not 12 months**. Then it is **pro-rated.**

7. The allowance is given in full even if the building is bought part-way through the accounting period.

8. The allowance is given in full even if the building was only in industrial use for part of the period, **provided it was in industrial use at the end of the period.**

9. The calculation for industrial buildings allowances is a separate calculation from plant and machinery capital allowances.

10. **The allowances are calculated for each industrial building on an individual basis, they are not pooled.**

Example

Robin prepares accounts to 31 March each year. On 10 April 2009 he bought a new factory for £120,000 (excluding land). He immediately put the building to industrial use.

Allowances for the year to 31 March 2010 are as follows:

	Qualifying cost £	Allowances £
Year ended 31/03/2010		
Cost excluding land	120,000	
WDA (2% x 120,000)	(2,400)	2,400
	117,600	

If the building is in non-industrial use, e.g. a factory used as a showroom, at the end of the period, no allowance is given. Instead a 'notional' allowance is deducted from the TWDV. Periods of temporary disuse are ignored.

SUMMARY

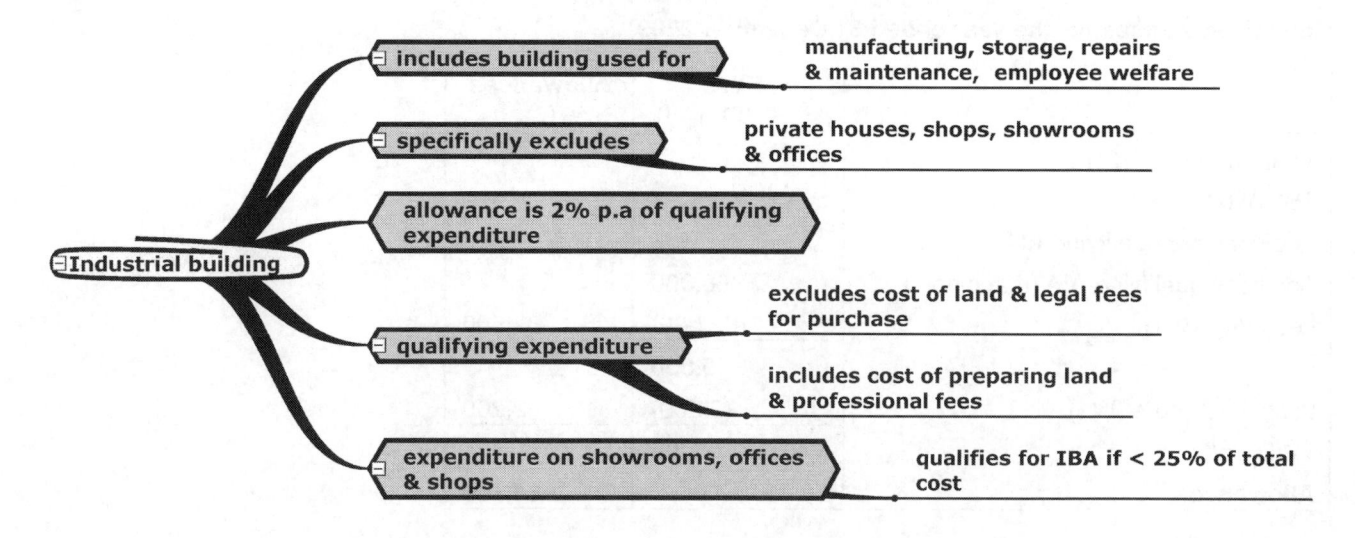

Industrial building
- includes building used for → manufacturing, storage, repairs & maintenance, employee welfare
- specifically excludes → private houses, shops, showrooms & offices
- allowance is 2% p.a of qualifying expenditure
- qualifying expenditure
  - excludes cost of land & legal fees for purchase
  - includes cost of preparing land & professional fees
- expenditure on showrooms, offices & shops → qualifies for IBA if < 25% of total cost

Answers to Test Yourself

Answer 1

1. The old ship is the setting for the business to be conducted. The structure used for carrying on the business is **not considered as plant and machinery.**
2. The central heating system will be considered plant and machinery as it is essential for proper functioning of the office.

Answer 2

1. Capital allowances for the year ended 31 March 2010

	FYA (£)	General pool (£)	Allowances (£)
Year ended 31/03/2010			
TWDV b/f		28,000	
Additions not qualifying AIA (machinery)		-	
Disposal (limited to cost)		(10,500)	
		17,500	
WDA 20%		(3,500)	3,500
		14,000	
Additions qualifying AIA			
Machinery	58,000		
Less: AIA	(50,000)		50,000
	8,000		
Less: FYA 40%	(3,200)	4,800	3,200
TWDV c/f		18,800	
Allowances			**56,700**

2. Capital allowances for the year ended 31 March 2011

	General pool (£)	Allowances (£)
Year ended 31/03/2011		
TWDV b/f	18,800	
WDA 20%	(3,760)	3,760
TWDV c/f	**15,040**	
Allowances		**3,760**

Answer 3

Capital allowances for the year ended 31 December 2009

	FYA (£)	Allowances (£)
Year ended 31/12/10		
TWDV b/f		
Additions not qualifying AIA		
Additions qualifying AIA (machinery)	68,000	
Less: AIA (W1)	(62,500)	62,500
	5,500	
Less: FYA 40% (W1)	(2,200)	2,200
TWDV c/f	**3,300**	
Allowances		**64,700**

Working

W1 AIA and WDA are scaled up or down according to the length of the accounting period.

Malcolm began trading on 1 October 2008. He prepares his first accounts to 31 December 2009. His first accounting period is fifteen months long, so the AIA is scaled up for 15 months.
Hence, AIA = £50,000 x 15/12 = £62,500

However, for calculation of FYA, the length of the accounting period is not relevant. FYA is available at the rate of 40% on the qualifying asset purchased in the 12 month period from April 2009.

WDA = £5,500 x 20% x 15/12 = £1,375

Answer 4

	FYA (£)	General pool (£)	Allowances (£)
Year ended on 30/04/2010			
TWDV b/f		12,729	
Non-AIA & non-FYA additions		-	
Disposals		(3,000)	
		9,729	
WDA (£9,729 x 20%)		(1,946)	1,946
		7,783	
Qualifying for AIA & FYA addition			
01/07/2009	22,500		
29/04/2007	55,000		
	77,500		
Less: AIA	(50,000)		50,000
	27,500		
Less: FYA 40%	(11,000)	16,500	11,000
TWDV c/f		24,283	
Allowances			62,946

Answer 5

	General pool £	Special rate car £	Allowances £
Year ended on 31/12/2009			
TWDV b/f	20,000		
Addition: car		15,000	
WDA 20%/10%	(4,000)	(1,500)	5,500
TWDV c/f	16,000	13,500	
Allowances			5,500

Note: The car with CO_2 emissions rate of more than 160g/km is not included in the general pool and WDA on the car is calculated at the rate of 10%.

Answer 6

	Special rate car £	FYA £	Allowances £
Period ended 31/3/2010			
TWDV b/f	-		
Additions not qualifying AIA			
Car	14,000	12,500	
Less: FYA 100%		(12,500)	12,500
		-	
Less: WDA at 10% (reduced proportionately for 10 months)	(1,167) W1		1,167
	12,833		
Additions qualifying for AIA			
Equipment		61,400	
Less: AIA (50,000 x 10/12)		(41,667)	41,667
		19,733	
Less: FYA 40%		(7,893)	7,893
TWDV c/f	12,833	11,840	
Allowances			**63,227**

Answer 7

	General pool £
Period ended 31/1/2010	
TWDV b/f	28,000
Addition: Car	8,000
	36,000
Disposal proceeds	(32,100)
Balancing allowance	**3,900**

Note: no WDA is given for the period in which the business ceases trading.

Answer 8

	General pool (£)	Business use 70% (£)	Allowances (£)
Year ended 30/04/2010			
Addition	9,000		
WDA 20% (W1)	(1,800)	1,260	1,260
TWDV c/f	7,200		
Allowances			**1,260**
Year ended 30/4/2011			
TWDV b/f	7,200		
WDA 20% (W1)	(1,440)	1,008	1,008
TWDV c/f	5,760		
Allowances			**1,008**

Working

W1

Motor cars are not eligible for AIA, the WDA is 20% per annum for cars with CO_2 emissions rate between 110g/km and 160g/km. Hence, allowances are £1,800 (£9,000 x 20%).

As Lucy has made private use of 30%, only the business proportion of the allowance (70%) can be claimed.

Capital allowances = £1,800 x 70% = **£1,260**

TWDV b/f £7,200 (i.e. £9,000 – £1,800)

Capital allowances for the second year = £ (7,200 x 20%) x 70% = **£1,008**

Answer 9

	General pool (£)	Short life asset (£)	Allowances (£)
Year ended 31/3/2010			
TWDV b/f		Nil	
Addition: Machinery		54,800	
Less: AIA		(50,000)	50,000
		4,800	
Less: FYA 40%		(1,920)	1,920
TWDV c/f		**2,880**	
Allowances			**51,920**
Year ended 31/03/2011			
TWDV b/f		2,880	
Additions: plant	68,500		
AIA	(50,000)		50,000
	18,500		
WDA 20%	(3,700)	(576)	4,276
TWDV c/f	**14,800**	**2,304**	
Allowances			**54,276**
Year ended 31/03/2012			
TWDV b/f	14,800	2,304	
Less: WDA 20%	(2,960)		2,960
Disposal proceeds		(1,000)	
TWDV c/f	**11,840**		
Balancing allowance		1,304	1,304
Allowances			**2,960**

Notes:

1. The short life asset election made by Alice for the asset purchased on 31 May 2008 is beneficial as it exceeds the limit of £50,000 covered by AIA. Short life asset needs its own column, and qualifies for the annual investment allowance. It qualifies for FYA at the rate of 40% also as it was purchased during the 12 month period from 6 April 2009 to 5 April 2010.

2. Plant purchased in May 2010 is eligible for AIA but is not eligible for FYA as it was not purchased during the 12 months period from 6 April 2009 to 5 April 2010.

Answer 10

1. Purchase price is £90,000

	FYA (£)	General Pool (£)	Allowances (£)
Year ended 30/04/2010			
TWDV b/f		40,000	
WDA 20%		(8,000)	8,000
AIA additions	90,000		
AIA	(50,000)		50,000
	40,000		
FYA 40%	(16,000)		16,000
TWDV c/f	**24,000**	**32,000**	
Allowances			**74,000**

2. Purchase price is £190,000

	Special rate pool £	General pool £	Allowances £
Year ended 30/04/2010			
TWDV b/f		40,000	
AIA additions	190,000		
Less: AIA	(50,000)		
	140,000		
WDA 10%/20%	(14,000)	(8,000)	22,000
TWDV c/f	126,000	32,000	
Allowances			22,000

Note: an asset with a life of 25 years or more is only treated as a long life asset if the expenditure exceeds £100,000 in the accounting period.

Answer 11

Qualifying expenditure for IBA purposes

	£
Site development expenses	16,000
Cost of construction	1,000,000
Architect's fees	50,000
Showroom	200,000
	1,266,000

The total expenditure excluding the cost of the land and legal fees relating to its purchase is £1,266,000. The cost of the showroom (£200,000) is less than 25% of the total cost (£1,266,000 x 25% = £316,500) so it becomes a qualifying expenditure for IBA purposes.

The **cost of the land and related professional fees are specifically excluded** from the qualifying expenditure.

Quick Quiz

1. How does a 9 month accounting period affect a WDA?
2. How does a 9 month accounting period affect an AIA?
3. What is a long life asset?
4. What expenditure qualifies for WDA when an industrial building includes a non-industrial part (offices, showrooms etc)?
5. When is a WDA available for an industrial building?

Answers to Quick Quiz

1. The WDA must be pro-rated in a 9 month accounting period.
2. The AIA is pro-rated in a 9 month accounting period.
3. A long life asset is one with an economic working life of more than 25 years, and where more than £100,000 has been spent on the asset in a year.
4. Where the non-industrial part is not more than 25% of the total cost of the building (excluding land) the whole building will qualify for WDAs. Where the non-industrial part exceeds 25% of the total cost, WDAs are available only on the industrial part.
5. A WDA is available for an industrial building if it is in industrial use at the end of the accounting period.

Self Examination Questions

Question 1

Della started business on 1 May 2009 and prepares accounts to 30 June 2010 and annually thereafter. Her adjusted trading profit before capital allowances for this period was £148,000.

She purchased the following assets:

		£
10 May 2009	Bought machinery	75,000
10 May 2009	Bought car (CO_2 emissions of 122g/km)	18,000
18 November 2009	Bought car (CO_2 emissions of 90g/km)	7,500

Compute the trading profits after capital allowances for the 14 months to 30 June 2010.

Question 2

Ivy prepares accounts to 5 April each year. The written down value of plant and machinery on 6 April 2009 was as follows:

	£
General pool	28,000
Expensive car	7,000

She made the following transactions during the year:

		£
30 May 2009	Sold car (acquisition cost £13,000)	2,500
20 August 2009	Bought plant	10,000

Required:

Calculate the capital allowances available to Ivy for the year to 5 April 2010.

Question 3

Sharon has been trading for many years, preparing accounts to 30 June 2009 each year.
She ceased trading on 10 March 2010.

Her TWDVs on 1 July 2009 were as follows:

	£
Main pool	18,200
Expensive car	12,800

Her transactions in the period to 10 March 2010 are:

		£
10 March 2010	Sold all general pool items	21,200
10 March 2010	Sold car	8,500

Required:

Calculate the capital allowances for Sharon's final accounting period.

Question 4

Raja prepares his accounts to 31 March each year. He purchased a motor car on 1 December 2009 for £81,000 with a CO_2 emissions rate of 140g/km. He agreed with HMRC to make 50% private use of the motor car. The motor car was sold on 1 September 2011 for £35,000.

Required:

Calculate the capital allowances available for the 3 years to 31 March 2012.

Question 5

Amanda started trading on 1 April 2009 and prepared her first accounts for the 13 months to 30 April 2010. She made the following purchases in the period:

		£
1 May 2009	Bought car (CO_2 emissions rate of 135g/km)	14,000
1 August 2010	Bought car (CO_2 emissions rate of 105g/km)	12,200

Required:

Calculate the capital allowances available to Amanda for the 13 months to 30 April 2010.

Answers to Self Examination Questions

Answer 1

Capital allowances computation

	FYA (£)	General pool (£)	Allowances (£)
14 months to 30/06/2010			
Additions not qualifying for AIA (Car)	7,500	18,000	
Less: FYA 100% (W1)	(7,500)		7,500
Less: WDA 20% (for 14 months) (W2)		(4,200)	4,200
	-	13,800	
Additions qualifying for AIA (machinery)	75,000		
Less: AIA (for 14 months) (W3)	(58,333)		58,333
	16,667		
Less: First year allowance (40%) (W3)	(6,667)	10,000	6,667
TWDV c/f	-	23,800	
Allowances			**76,700**

Calculation of adjusted trading profits

	£
Trading profits	148,000
Less: Capital allowances	(76,700)
Adjusted trading profits for 14 months ended 30/06/2009	**71,300**

Workings

W1

Cars with CO_2 emissions rate less than 110g/km are eligible for 100% FYA.

W2

Cars with CO_2 emissions rate between 110g/km and 160g/km are included in the general pool and are eligible for WDA at the rate of 20%. WDA is scaled up when the accounting period is more than twelve months.

The AP is 14 months, hence WDA for car is = £18,000 x 20% x 14/12 = £4,200

W3

Expenditure on plant and machinery (with the exception of cars) incurred by any business on or after 6 April 2008 is eligible for AIA at the rate of 100% for the first £50,000 expenditure on plant and machinery.

AIA is scaled up or down according to the length of the accounting period.

AIA for 14 months = £50,000 x 14/12 x = £58,333.

FYA is also available on the balance amount of expenditure (incurred during the period 6 April 2009 to 5 April 2010) at the rate of 40%. FYA is not scaled up or down according to the length of the accounting period.

Answer 2

Capital allowances computation

	FYA (£)	General Pool (£)	Expensive car (£)	Allowances (£)
Year ended 05/04/2010				
TWDV b/f		28,000	7,000	
Additions qualifying for AIA (Plant)	10,000			
Less: AIA	(10,000)	-		10,000
Less: Disposals			(2,500)	
Less: WDA @ 20%		(5,600)		5,600
TWDV c/f		22,400		
Allowances				15,600
Balancing Allowance			4,500	4,500

Total capital allowance available for the year to 5 April 2010 = £15,600 + £4,500 = £20,100

Notes:

1. The expenditure incurred by any business on plant and machinery on or after 6 April 2008 is eligible for AIA up to a limit of £50,000.

2. As the disposal proceeds of the car (£2,500) are less than the TWDV (£7,000), a balancing allowance of £4,500 is given.

Answer 3

Calculation of balancing adjustments

	General Pool (£)	Expensive car (£)	Allowances (£)
Period ended 10/03/2010			
TWDV b/f	18,200	12,800	
Disposal proceeds	(21,200)	(8,500)	
(Balancing charge)/allowance (W1)	(3,000)	4,300	1,300

Working

W1

No WDA and AIA are available in the final accounting period.

When the disposal proceeds are **more** than the TWDV, there is a **balancing charge** (i.e. negative capital allowance) which is added to the tax adjusted trading profits.

If the disposal proceeds are **less** than the TWDV, then a **balancing allowance** is given.

Answer 4

Calculation of capital allowances until the date of the sale

	Motor car (£)	Business use 50% (£)	Allowances (£)
Year ended 31/03/2010			
Additions not qualifying for AIA	81,000		
WDA @ 20% (W2)	(16,200)	8,100	8,100
TWDV c/f	64,800		
Allowances			8,100
Year ended 31/03/2011			
TWDV b/f	64,800		
WDA 20% (note 2)	(12,960)	6,480	6,480
TWDV c/f	51,840		
Allowances			6,480
Year ended 31/03/2012			
TWDV b/f	51,840		
Disposal proceeds	(35,000)		
Balancing allowance (note 3)	16,840	8,420	8,420

Notes:

1. A car that is used for both private as well as business purposes should not be included the general pool. It should be dealt with on an individual basis.

2. As the asset is used 50% for private use, the WDA allowance is also given at 50%.

3. If the disposal proceeds are less than the TWDV, then a balancing allowance is given.

Answer 5

Computation of capital allowance

	FYA (£)	General pool (£)	Allowances (£)
Period ended 30/04/2010 (13 months)			
Additions not qualifying for AIA (Car)	12,200	14,000	
Less: FYA 100%	(12,200)		12,200
Less: WDA 20% (W1)	-	(3,033)	3,033
TWDV c/f	-	10,967	
Allowances			15,233

Workings

W1

A car with CO_2 emissions between 110g/km and 160g/km is included in the general pool. The WDA on these cars is calculated at the rate of 20% per annum.

£14,000 x 20% = £2,800
The accounting period is 13 months, so scaled up accordingly.
£2,800 x 13/12 = £3,033.

W2

Cars with CO_2 emissions of less than 110g/km are eligible for 100% FYA.

SECTION B

INCOME TAX LIABILITIES

B3

STUDY GUIDE B3: INCOME FROM SELF-EMPLOYMENT (PART 3)

■ Get Through Intro

An important **job of an accountant** is to advise his client on how to make the best **use** of **all the statutory provisions** which are available to help the client **minimise his tax liability.**

A thorough knowledge of all the provisions for losses is essential, if relief for trading losses is to be used in the most beneficial way.

As a tax consultant, you should gain a good understanding of the loss relief provisions to ensure that they are used to the best advantage.

■ Learning Outcomes

h) Relief for trading losses
   i. Understand how trading losses can be carried forward.
   ii. Explain how trading losses can be carried forward following the incorporation of a business.
   iii. Understand how trading losses can be claimed against total income and chargeable gains.
   iv. Explain and compute the relief for trading losses in the early years of a trade.
   v. Explain and compute terminal loss relief.

Introduction

A trading loss occurs when a trader's adjusted profit after capital allowances gives a negative figure. A trading loss can also arise through capital allowances either creating a loss (turning a trading profit into a loss) or increasing a loss.

Points to note:

- The trading income assessment for the tax year of the loss will be nil. Never put a negative figure as trading income in the calculation of taxable income.
- Relief is available for the loss.

Different reliefs are available to a trader:

- in the previous tax year (thus generating a refund of tax)
- in the current tax year (reducing the current liability)
- in the future tax years (reducing a future liability, and thus delaying relief).

Special reliefs are available in the opening years of trade, in the final 12 months of trade and on incorporation.

Overview:

Main reliefs

Section 83 ITA 2007

The trading loss is carried forward and relieved against the first available future profits of the same trade.

Section 64 ITA 2007

The trading loss is relieved against total income (TI) of the current year and / or the preceding years.
A s64 claim can be extended and any unrelieved trading loss can be set against a trader's capital gains by a claim under s261B TCGA 1992.

A trading loss incurred in any of the first 4 tax years of trade can be relieved against TI of the previous 3 years, taking the earliest year first.

Section 89 of ITA 2007

A trading loss in the last 12 months of trading can be relieved against trading income of the previous 3 years taking the latest year first.

Section 86 ITA 2007

A trading loss incurred by an unincorporated business may be relieved against income received from a new company on incorporation.

> **Tip** Section numbers are from the Income Tax Act (ITA) 2007 and have been given for ease of identifying loss reliefs, but candidates will not be expected to quote section numbers as part of their answer in the exam.

A new **additional relief** has been introduced in the Finance Act 2009 for relief of trading losses of the tax year 2009-10 against trading income of the previous three tax years taking the latest year 2008-09 first.

All these provisions are discussed in more detail in this Study Guide.

1. Understand how trading losses can be carried forward.[2]

[Learning outcome h (i)]

1.1 Section 83 ITA 2007 – relief against future trading income

If no specific loss relief is claimed, the loss will be carried forward automatically, and relieved against the first available future trading profits.

The main provisions are:

1. The loss carried forward can only be set against **future trading profits**, not against any other income.
2. The set off must be against the **first available trading profits**.
3. It is not possible to restrict the set off of the loss, e.g., in order to avoid wasting personal allowances.
4. The relief is against future trading profits of the **same trade.**
5. There is **no time limit** on the carry forward – the loss can be carried forward indefinitely, until there are future trading profits.
6. It is not necessary to claim this relief - the loss will be carried forward automatically if **a trader does not choose to claim other reliefs, or if** a loss remains after other reliefs have been claimed.

Example

Larry has been trading for many years preparing accounts to 31 December each year. He made a trading loss of £32,600 in the year to 31 December 2008.

His anticipated taxable trading profits for the next three years are as follows.

	£
Year ended 31 December 2009	12,600
Year ended 31 December 2010	10,800
Year ended 31 December 2011	52,600

Larry also has property income of £2,000 every year.
If Larry makes no specific loss relief claim, his taxable income for 2008-09 to 2011-12 is as follows:
(Assume allowances continue unchanged in the future).

	2008-09 £	2009-10 £	2010-11 £	2011-12 £
Trading profits	-	12,600	10,800	52,600
Less: s83 relief	-	(12,600)	(10,800)	(9,200)
	-	-	-	43,400
Property income	2,000	2,000	2,000	2,000
Total Income	**2,000**	**2,000**	**2,000**	**45,400**
PA (restricted)	(2,000)	(2,000)	(2,000)	(6,475)
Taxable income	-	-	-	**38,925**

Notes:

1. The trading income assessment for the tax year 2008-09 is nil as the business incurred a loss.
2. The trading loss of year ended 31 December 2008 is carried forward and set against future trading profits until the entire loss is relieved.
3. Under s83, the loss is set off against future trading profits, and not against any other income (i.e. not against the property income). The maximum amount must be set off each year.
4. Personal allowances of £4,475 (£6,475 - £2,000) are wasted in 2009-10 and 2010-11.

Loss memorandum

	£
Loss for the year 2008-09	32,600
Set off:	
2009-10 (s83)	(12,600)
	20,000
2010-11 (s83)	(10,800)
	9,200
2011-12 (s83)	(9,200)

7. It is necessary to establish the amount of the loss with HMRC. This must be done within 5 years of 31 January following the tax year in which the loss arose (i.e. if a loss was incurred in year ended 31 December 2009, it falls in the tax year 2009-10, and the claim must be made by 31 January 2016).

8. Under s83 the relief is delayed, as it is given by means of a reduction in a future liability.

Test Yourself 1

Martin has been trading for many years, preparing accounts to 30 November each year. He made a trading loss of £37,550 in the year to 30 November 2008.

His anticipated taxable trading profits for the next three years are as follows:

Year ended	£
30 November 2009	9,600
30 November 2010	11,650
30 November 2011	39,750

Martin also had property income of £2,000 and building society interest of £1,800 (gross) each year.

Required:

Assuming Martin makes no specific loss relief claim, calculate his taxable income for 2008-09 to 2011-12. (Assume allowances continue unchanged in the future).

1.2 Drawbacks of relief under s83

1. Relief must be taken **to the maximum amount possible, and as soon as possible. It is not possible to restrict the relief, so** in some situations **personal allowances may be wasted.**
2. In future years if there is no sufficient trading income from the same business, then **relief is delayed** until sufficient profits are earned by the business.

Example

Henry has been trading for many years, preparing accounts to 31 December each year. He has the following results:

	£
Year ended 31/12/2008 trading loss	(2,500)
Year ended 31/12/2009 trading profit	7,000

In 2009-10 he pays interest charges of £900 on a loan for qualifying purposes. He has property income of £2,500 in both 2008-09 and 2009-10.

No specific loss relief claim is made.

His taxable income for 2008-09 and 2009-10 is as follows:

	2008-09 £	2009-10 £
Trading income	-	7,000
Less: s83 relief	-	(2,500)
	-	4,500
Property income	2,500	2,500
Total Income	2,500	7,000
Less: Interest paid	-	(900)
Net Income	2,500	6,100
PA (restricted)	(2,500)	(6,100)
Taxable income	-	-

Note: Personal allowance of £375 (£6,475 - £6,100) is wasted in 2009-10 as it is not possible to restrict the relief to claim the allowances.

SUMMARY

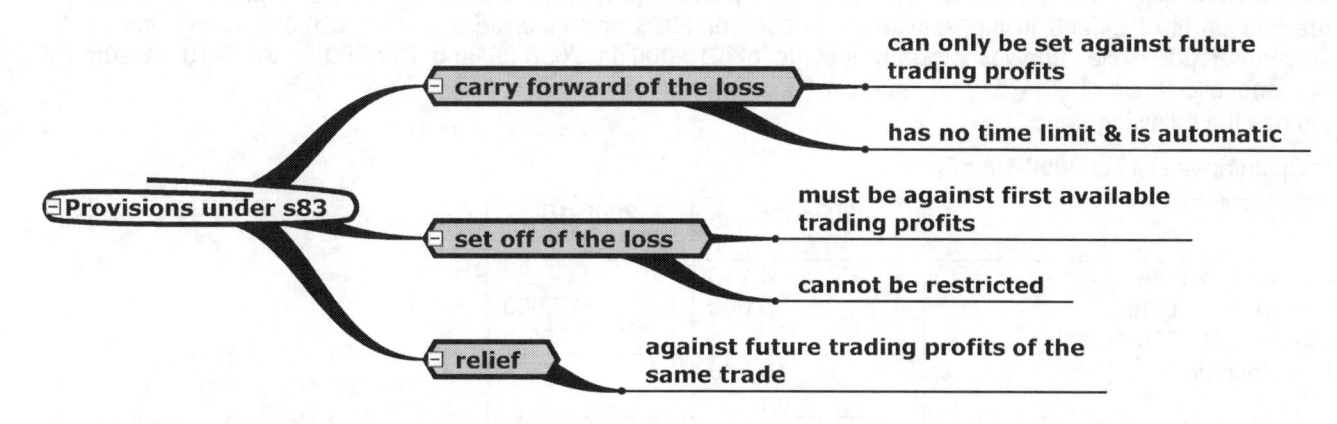

Provisions under s83
- **carry forward of the loss**
  - can only be set against future trading profits
  - has no time limit & is automatic
- **set off of the loss**
  - must be against first available trading profits
  - cannot be restricted
- **relief**
  - against future trading profits of the same trade

Test Yourself 2

Jack has been trading for many years, preparing accounts to 31 December each year. He has the following results:

	£
Year ended 31/12/2008 trading loss	(4,750)
Year ended 31/12/2009 trading profit	58,250

In 2009-10 he pays interest charges of £7,000 on a loan for a qualifying purpose. He has building society interest of £3,750 (gross) in both 2008-09 and 2009-10.

No specific loss relief claim is made.

Required:

Calculate his taxable income for 2008-09 and 2009-10.

---

2. Understand how trading losses can be claimed against total income and chargeable gains.[2]

[Learning outcome h (iii)]

2.1 Section 64 ITA 2007 – relief against TI of the current tax year and / or the previous tax year.

1. A trading loss arising in a tax year may be set against the trader's **total income (TI)** of the **current tax year and / or the previous tax year**.

Example

Jade has been trading for many years preparing accounts to 31 December. She incurs a loss in the year ended 31 December 2009.

This loss arises in the tax year in which the loss-making accounting period ends (2009-10) and so may be relieved against TI of the current year (2009-10) and/or previous year (2008-09).

2. These are **two separate claims** – a trader who incurs a loss in 2009-10 may claim against TI of:

a) 2009-10 only
b) 2009-10 and then 2008-09
c) 2008-09 only
d) 2008-09 and then 2009-10

> **Example**
>
> Jack has been trading for many years, preparing accounts to 31 December each year. He made a profit of £4,200 in the year to 31 December 2008 and incurred a loss of £20,000 in the year to 31 December 2009. He receives property income of £15,000 in 2008-09 and £17,000 in 2009-10. Assume a personal allowance of £6,475 each year.
>
> He has the following options:
>
> i. Claim against TI of 2009-10 only.
>
> | | 2008-09 £ | 2009-10 £ |
> | --- | --- | --- |
> | Trading income | 4,200 | - |
> | Property income | 15,000 | 17,000 |
> | **Less**: s64 2009-10 only | - | (17,000) |
> | Net Income | 19,200 | - |
> | PA | (6,475) | - |
> | **Taxable income** | **12,725** | **-** |
>
> The balance of the loss, (£3,000) will be carried forward and relieved against future trading profits under s83. The relief under s83 is delayed, and the future profitability is uncertain.
> The personal allowance is wasted in 2009-10.
>
> ii. Claim against TI of 2008-09 only.
>
> | | 2008-09 £ | 2009-10 £ |
> | --- | --- | --- |
> | Trading income | 4,200 | - |
> | Property income | 15,000 | 17,000 |
> | | 19,200 | 17,000 |
> | **Less**: s64 2008-09 only | (19,200) | - |
> | Net Income | - | 17,000 |
> | PA | - | (6,475) |
> | **Taxable income** | **-** | **10,525** |
>
> The balance of the loss, (£800) will be carried forward and relieved against future trading profits under s83. The relief under s83 is delayed, and the future profitability is uncertain.
> The personal allowance is wasted in 2008-09.
>
> iii. Claim against TI of 2009-10 and then 2008-09.
>
> | | 2008-09 £ | 2009-10 £ |
> | --- | --- | --- |
> | Trading income | 4,200 | - |
> | Property Income | 15,000 | 17,000 |
> | | 19,200 | 17,000 |
> | **Less**: s64 2009-10 then 2008-09 | (3,000) | (17,000) |
> | Net Income | 16,200 | - |
> | PA | (6,475) | - |
> | **Taxable income** | **9,725** | **-** |
>
> The personal allowance is wasted in 2009-10. All the loss is relieved.
>
> iv. Claim against 2008-09 and then 2009-10.
>
> | | 2008-09 £ | 2009-10 £ |
> | --- | --- | --- |
> | Trading income | 4,200 | - |
> | Property income | 15,000 | 17,000 |
> | | 19,200 | 17,000 |
> | **Less**: s64 | (19,200) | (800) |
> | Net Income | - | 16,200 |
> | PA | - | (6,475) |
> | **Taxable income** | **-** | **9,725** |
>
> The personal allowance is wasted in 2008-09. All the loss is relieved. There is a slight advantage of (iv) over (iii) as the taxpayer gets a refund of the tax paid for the year 2008-09 along with the interest.

3. If there are **losses in two consecutive years**, and a s64 claim is made for both the years, the first year's loss is dealt with first.

Example Ian has been trading for many years, preparing accounts to 31 March each year. In the years ending 31 March 2009 and 31 March 2010 he incurred a loss of £6,800 and £1,900 respectively. He receives a property income of £18,000 each year.

Ian claims relief under s64 for the loss for the year ended 31 March 2009 against TI of 2008 - 09. He also claims relief against TI of 2008 - 09 for the loss for the year ended 31 March 2010. Assume a personal allowance of £6,475 each year.

His taxable income for the 2008-09 and 2009-10 is as follows:

	2008-09 £	2009-10 £
Property income	18,000	18,000
Less: s64 loss of year ended 31/03/09	(6,800)	-
s64 loss of year ended 31/03/10	(1,900)	-
Net Income	9,300	18,000
PA (restricted)	(6,475)	(6,475)
Taxable income	2,825	11,525

In 2008-09 the loss for the year ended 31/03/09 is relieved in priority to the loss for the year ended 31/03/10. Alternatively, Ian may elect to carry forward this loss and set it off against his future trading income under s83.

4. It is **not possible to restrict the set off of the loss**, for example to avoid wasting personal allowances. However, the taxpayer has a choice to make a claim in one year, in both years, or not to make a claim at all.

5. If no s64 claim is made, or a loss remains unrelieved after a claim is made, the loss is **carried forward under s83** against future trading profits.

Example Mike has been trading for many years, preparing accounts to 31 August each year.

His recent taxable profits and (losses) have been as follows:

	£
Year ended 31 August 2006	3,000
Year ended 31 August 2007	(45,000)
Year ended 31 August 2008	18,000
Year ended 31 August 2009	20,000

He received property income of £10,000 each year.
Show Mike's taxable income for the years 2006-07 to 2009-10 assuming he claims relief for the loss as soon as possible.

Assume a personal allowance of £6,475 throughout.

Continued on next page

B3.72: Income Tax Liabilities

	2006-07 £	2007-08 £	2008-09 £	2009-10 £
Trading income	3,000	-	18,000	20,000
Less: s83	-	-	(18,000)	(4,000)
Property income	10,000	10,000	10,000	10,000
	13,000	10,000	10,000	26,000
Less: s64 2006-07 then 2007-08	(13,000)	(10,000)	-	-
Net Income	-	-	10,000	26,000
PA	-	-	(6,475)	(6,475)
Taxable income	-	-	3,525	19,525

Mike will make a s64 claim against TI of 2006-07 and 2007-08, relieving a total of £23,000 of the loss. There is still a loss of £22,000 (£45,000 - £23,000) unrelieved, which will automatically be carried forward and set against future trading profits under **s83**.

Loss memorandum

Year	£
Loss for the year ended 31/08/2009	45,000
Less: s64 2006-07	(13,000)
	32,000
Less: s64 2007-08	(10,000)
	22,000
Less: s64 2008-09	(18,000)
	4,000
Less: s83 2009-10	(4,000)
	-

If no s64 claims were made, the entire loss of £45,000 would have been carried forward and set off against future trading income.

6. Claim for relief under s64 must be made **within 12 months of 31 January following the tax year in which the loss arose.**

Example
If a loss arose in 2009-10, a s64 claim must be made by 31/01/2012.

7. A s64 claim will **reduce a current liability to tax**, or, if the loss is relieved in the **previous tax year** this will lead to a **repayment of tax. A s64 claim has a cash flow advantage over relief against future trading profits, as s83 leads to a reduction in the current liability.**

Important factors to consider
a) The rates of tax saved by the claim
b) Any loss of personal allowance
c) Cash flow as a result of the relief
d) Future anticipated profits

Test Yourself 3
Henry has been self-employed since 2002. He has the following taxable income and interest payments for the years 2006-07 to 2009-10.

	2006-07 £	2007-08 £	2008-09 £	2009-10 £
Trading profit/ (loss)	15,000	10,000	(12,500)	22,500
Building society interest (gross)	700	1,500	1,800	1,000
Interest paid	(2,000)	(2,500)	(2,500)	(2,600)

Required:

Calculate his taxable income for each of the tax years 2006-07 to 2009-10, assuming that Henry claims loss relief as early as possible. Assume a personal allowance of £6,475 throughout.

2.2 Additional loss relief to set off trading losses

Relief against trading income of the previous three tax years

1. The Finance Act 2009 has introduced an **additional loss relief** for set off of trading losses for the tax year 2009-10.

2. A trading loss arising in 2009-10 may be set against the trader's trading income of the previous three tax years taking the latest year first. Hence, if additional relief is claimed for the trading loss arising in the tax year 2009 - 10, it will be set first against the **trading profits** of the tax year 2008 - 09, then 2007- 08 and finally 2006 - 07.

3. If a claim is made against the trading profits of the tax years 2007 – 08 and 2006 - 07, it is restricted to £50,000 in total for the amount to be claimed as relief.

4. If a claim is made against the trading profits of the tax year 2008 – 09, there is no such restriction.

5. This relief is in addition to the trading loss relief under s64 against the trader's total income of the current year and / or previous year.

6. It is not possible to restrict the set off of the loss, e.g. to avoid wasting personal allowances. However, the taxpayer has a choice to make a claim in one year, in both years, or not to make a claim at all.

7. A trader who incurs a trading loss in 2009-10 will have to make a choice from the following three options for claiming loss:

	Option 1		Option 2		Option 3
	1st claim under s64 against		**1st claim under s64 against**		**1st claim under s64 against**
1	total income of tax year 2009 – 10	1	total income of tax year 2009 – 10	1	total income of tax year 2008 - 09
2	total income of tax year 2008 – 09				
	then claim under additional loss relief against		**then claim under additional loss relief against**		**then claim under additional loss relief against**
3	trading profits of tax year 2007 -08	2	trading profits of tax year 2008 -09	2	trading profits of tax year 2007 -08
4	trading profits of tax year 2006 -07	3	trading profits of tax year 2007 -08	3	trading profits of tax year 2006 -07
		4	trading profits of tax year 2006 -07		

8. The following factors should be considered while making a choice among the above mentioned three alternatives:
   - any loss of personal allowance
   - cash flow as a result of the relief
   - the rates of tax saved by the claim

9. If additional claim is made, or a loss remains unrelieved after a claim is made, the loss is carried forward under s83 against future trading profits.

Example

Lisa has been trading for many years, preparing accounts to 31 March every year.

Her taxable profits and (losses) for the years 2005 – 06 to 2009 – 10 are:

Year ended	£
31 March 2006	15,600
31 March 2007	35,800
31 March 2008	22,100
31 March 2009	18,500
31 March 2010	(81,400)

Continued on next page

B3.74: Income Tax Liabilities

Lisa also had property income of £3,500 and building society interest of £1,500 (gross) each year.

Show Lisa's taxable income for the years 2005 - 06 to 2009 – 10. Assume a personal allowance of £6,475 throughout.

	2005 - 06 £	2006 - 07 £	2007 - 08 £	2008 - 09 £	2009 - 10 £
Trading income	15,600	35,800	22,100	18,500	
Less: Additional loss relief (note 3)		(27,900)	(22,100)		
	15,600	7,900	0	18,500	0
Property income	3,500	3,500	3,500	3,500	3,500
Building society interest	1,500	1,500	1,500	1,500	1,500
	20,600	12,900	5,000	23,500	5,000
Less: s64 relief (note 2)				(23,500)	
	20,600	12,900	5,000	0	5,000
Less: Personal allowance	(6,475)	(6,475)	(5,000)		(5,000)
Taxable Income	**14,125**	**6,425**	**0**	**0**	**0**

Loss memorandum

Year	£
Loss of year ended 31/03/2010	81,400
Less: s64 2008 - 09	(23,500)
	57,900
Less: Additional loss relief 2007 - 08	(22,100)
	35,800
Less: Additional loss relief 2006 - 07	(27,900)
Balance loss to be carried forward (note 4)	7,900

Notes:

1. Additional loss relief has been introduced to claim the trading loss for the tax year 2009-10 against the trading profits of the previous three tax years taking the latest year first. This relief is in addition to the relief under section 64.
2. If Lisa claims trading loss against the total profits of the tax year 2009 – 10, it will result in wastage of personal allowance for that year. Hence, it is more beneficial for Lisa to first claim the trading loss under s64 against the total income of the tax year 2008 – 09. This will also lead to repayment of tax.
3. The remaining loss can be set against the trading profit of the tax years 2007 -08 and 2006 – 07 under additional loss relief. However, the relief amount is restricted to £50,000 if the relief is claimed in these two tax years.
   Hence, the relief available in the tax year 2007 – 08 is £22,100 (against trading profits).
   The relief available in the tax year 2006 – 07 is (£50,000 - £22,100) = £27,900.
4. The balance loss can be carried forward and set against the future trading profits under s83.
5. Personal allowance of £6,475 is wasted in 2008 – 09 and £1,475 (£6,475 - £5,000) is wasted in 2007 – 08 and 2009 – 10 as it is not possible to restrict the relief to claim the allowances.

Test Yourself 4

Garry has been self-employed since 2003. He has the following taxable income and interest payments for the tax years 2006 – 07 to 2009 – 10.

	2006 - 07 £	2007 - 08 £	2008 - 09 £	2009 - 10 £
Trading profit/ (loss)	35,000	30,000	12,500	(79,900)
Building society interest (gross)	9,700	10,500	11,800	10,200
Interest paid	(2,000)	(2,500)	(2,500)	(2,600)

Required:

Calculate his taxable income for each of the tax years 2006 – 07 to 2009 – 10 assuming that Garry claims the loss as early as possible. Assume a personal allowance of £6,475 throughout.

2.3 Section 261B Taxation of Chargeable Gains Act (TCGA) 1992 – relief against capital gains

1. After a s64 claim has been made against TI in a tax year, any remaining trading loss may be relieved by making a further claim under s261B TCGA 1992 to set it against the trader's capital gains for the same year. For the tax year 2009 – 10, the claim for any trading loss is first made against s64 relief and additional loss relief. The remaining loss, if any, is considered for relief under s261B.

2. The trading loss is effectively converted into a current year capital loss.

3. Relief is only available if a s64 claim has already been made against TI in the same tax year.

4. If the claim is made, the loss must be set off as far as possible, it cannot be restricted in order to preserve the annual exemption.

5. Claim for relief under s261B must be made within 12 months from 31 January following the tax year in which the loss arose.

6. **Important factors to consider**

a) The rates of tax saved by the claim
b) Any loss of annual exemption
c) Cash flow as a result of the relief
d) Future anticipated profits.

Example

Todd commenced trading on 1 April 2008 and prepares accounts to 31 March each year. In 2009-10 Todd incurred a loss of £12,000. He had no other income. His 2008-09 financial position is as follows:

	£
Trading income	6,400
Bank interest (gross)	1,200
Capital gains	12,650

The most beneficial way of calculating the losses to be relieved under s64 and s261B is as follows:

> **Tip — Steps to be followed**
> 1. Set off loss first against TI (For the tax year 2009 – 10, then set off against the trading profits of the previous three tax years)
> 2. Determine amount of loss remaining
> 3. Set off unrelieved loss against capital gains.

Calculation of income after relief under s64 and s261B

Step: 1 Set off of loss first against TI

In the tax year 2009-10, Todd has no other income. So, if he makes claim for loss relief under s64, he will have to set the loss against previous year's (i.e. 2008-09) total income.

Calculation of set off of loss against total income of the year 2008-09:

	2008-09 £
Trading income	6,400
Bank interest (gross)	1,200
	7,600
Less: Relief s64	(7,600)
Total Income	-

First set off of loss under s64 and then under s261B

Continued on next page

Step: 2 Determine amount of loss remaining

	£
Loss for 2009-10	12,000
Less: s64	(7,600)
Unrelieved loss	**4,400**

Claim to set off unrelieved losses under s261B:

Step: 3 Set off of unrelieved losses

	£
Capital gains 2008-09	12,650
Less: relief s261B	(4,400)
	8,250
Less: Annual exemption (restricted) (Refer to Learning Outcome 3, Study Guide C2)	(8,250)
Total chargeable capital gains	-

Relief under s261B is before annual exemption

> **Tip**
> A taxpayer may claim relief under s261B to relieve a trading loss against capital gains:
> 1. in the tax year in which the loss is incurred **OR**
> 2. the previous year **OR**
> 3. both the tax years.
>
> But remember that a s261B claim may only be made after the trading loss has first been set against TI in the year of the claim.
>
> Any remaining loss will be set against future trading income under s83.

The following summary gives details of relief under s64 against TI and s261B against capital gains:

SUMMARY

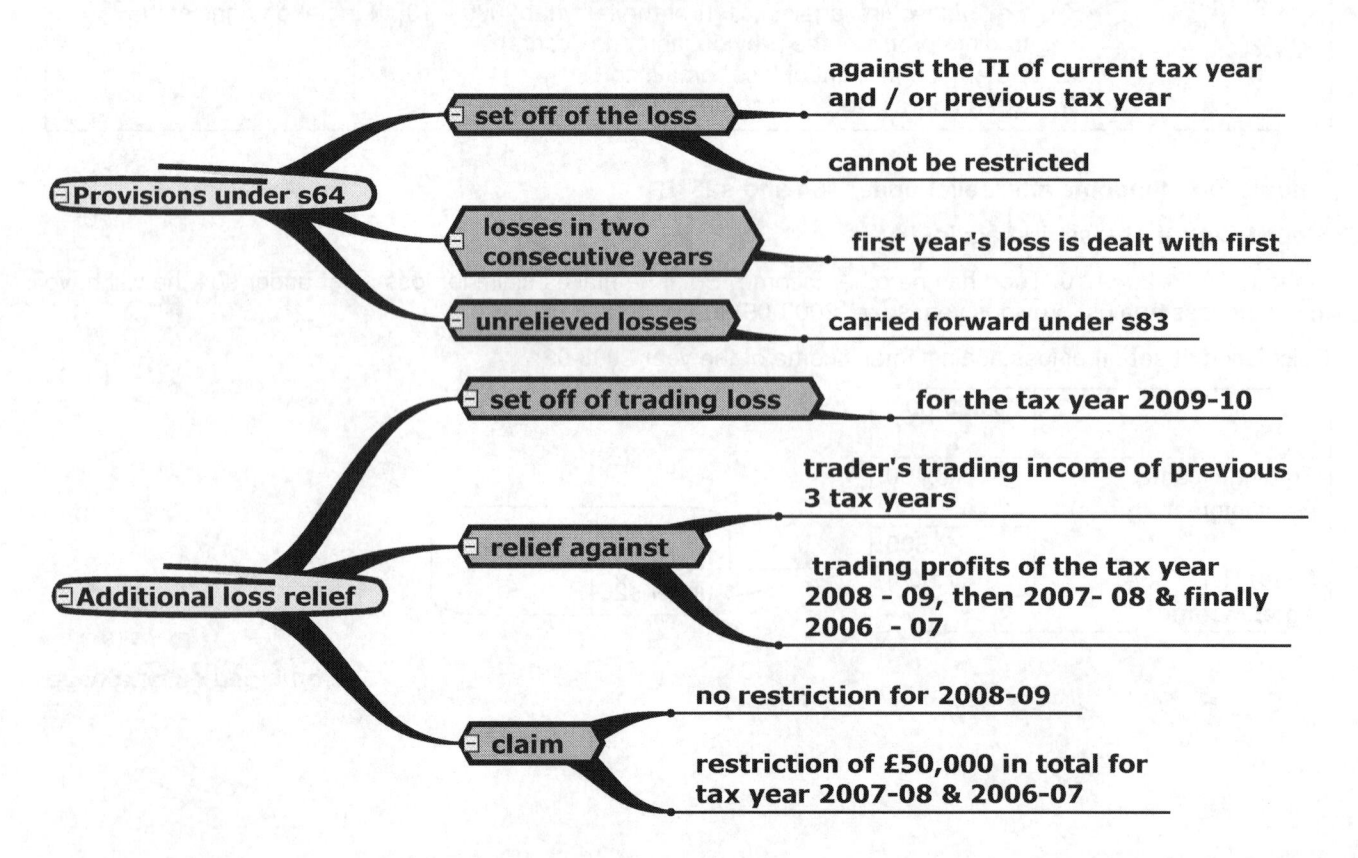

Provisions under s64
- set off of the loss
  - against the TI of current tax year and / or previous tax year
  - cannot be restricted
- losses in two consecutive years
  - first year's loss is dealt with first
- unrelieved losses
  - carried forward under s83

Additional loss relief
- set off of trading loss
  - for the tax year 2009-10
- relief against
  - trader's trading income of previous 3 tax years
  - trading profits of the tax year 2008 - 09, then 2007- 08 & finally 2006 - 07
- claim
  - no restriction for 2008-09
  - restriction of £50,000 in total for tax year 2007-08 & 2006-07

```
Provisions under s261B ─┬─ available only after s64 relief against TI
                        │
                        └─ set off of the loss ─┬─ against capital gains of the same tax year & previous tax year
                                                │
                                                └─ cannot be restricted
```

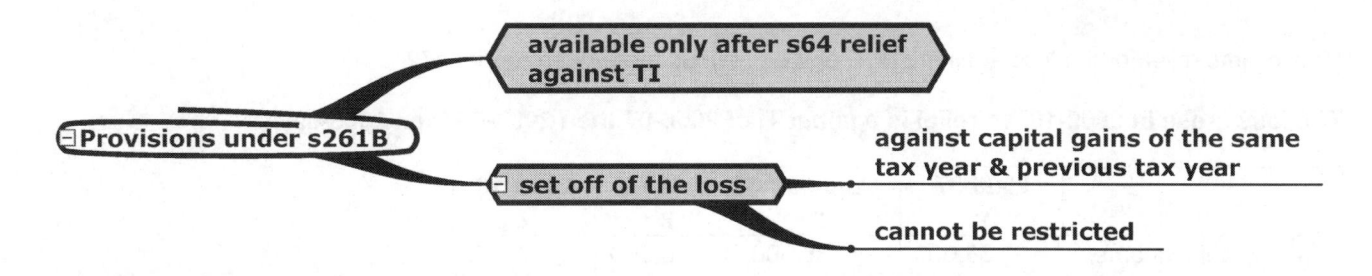

Test Yourself 5

Michael has been self-employed since 1999.

The following information is available for the years 2007-08, 2008-09 and 2009-10.

	2007-08 £	2008-09 £	2009-10 £
Trading profits / (loss)	9,000	(28,000)	23,500
Property income	1,000	1,600	3,000
Bank interest (gross)	500	600	400
Capital gains	17,000	8,000	11,000
Interest paid on loan for qualifying purposes	(2,500)	(2,200)	(3,000)

The capital gains are before the annual exemption.

Required:

Compute Michael's taxable income and chargeable gains for the three years on the assumption that he claims to relieve the trading loss against TI for 2007-08 under s64 and then against capital gains of the same year under s261B.

Assume rates and allowances for 2009-10 apply throughout.

---

3. Explain and compute the relief for trading losses in the early years of a trade.[1]
[Learning outcome h (iv)]

3.1 Section 72 ITA– relief against TI of the previous 3 years on a first in first out (FIFO) basis, available in the first four years of trade.

1. In the opening years of a business, a trading loss may be set against TI of the year of the loss and / or the previous year (s64) or it may be carried forward against future trading income under s83. In addition, there is a special loss relief available for trading losses arising in any of the first four tax years of a business.

2. A trading loss arising in any one of the first four tax years of trade may be set against the trader's total income (TI) of the previous 3 tax years, taking the earliest year first.

> **Example** Bill started a business on 6 April 2007 and prepares accounts annually to 5 April. He incurs a loss in the year to 5 April 2010.
>
> Bill started trading in 2007 - 08, as his loss arose in 2009 - 10, the third tax year of trade, he may relieve it against TI of the previous three years (2006 - 07 then 2007 - 08 then 2008 - 09).

3. If a s72 claim is made, relief must be taken against TI of all three years, it is not possible to make a partial claim.

> **Example** Mike has been employed for several years, earning £3,000 per month. He ceased employment on 31 December 2009 and started business as a sole trader on 1 January 2010, preparing accounts to 5 April each year. He incurs a loss of £100,000 in the period ended on 5 April 2010.
>
> He has unearned income of £5,000 (gross) each year.

Mike claims relief for the loss against the TI of the previous three years under s72.

The loss arose in 2009-10, so relief is against TI of 2006-07 then 2007-08 then 2008-09.

	2006-07 £	2007-08 £	2008-09 £	2009-10 £
Employment income	36,000	36,000	36,000	27,000
Unearned income	5,000	5,000	5,000	5,000
Total Income	**41,000**	**41,000**	**41,000**	**32,000**
Less: s72	(41,000)	(41,000)	(18,000)	-
Total income	-	-	23,000	32,000

	£	
Loss for 2009-10	100,000	(carry back to 2006 - 07, then 2007 - 08 and then 2008 - 09)
Set off s72 2006 - 07	(41,000)	
	59,000	
s72 2007 - 08	(41,000)	
	18,000	
s72 2008 - 09	(18,000)	
	-	

Tip Note that as the relief is against TI, the loss may be set against income earned before trade commenced.

4. The maximum relief possible must be taken for the loss; it is not possible to restrict the set off to preserve personal allowances.

5. If no claim is made in the opening years, or a loss remains after any claim is made, it is carried forward under s83 against future trading profits.

6. Claim for relief under s72 must be made within 12 months of 31 January following the tax year in which the loss arose.

Example If a loss arose in 2009 - 10, the claim must be made by 31/01/12.

7. Loss relief claimed under s72 will reduce the liability of earlier years and this will lead to a repayment of tax.

8. Important factors to consider:
   a) The rate of tax saved by the claim.
   b) Any loss of personal allowances.
   c) Cash flow as a result of the relief.
   d) Future anticipated profits.

9. Losses arising on the commencement of trade are allocated to tax years using the basis period rules for opening years of a business. When these rules are applied to a profitable business, some profit periods overlap and are taxed twice, with relief being given for those profits on cessation. Losses can only be relieved once. If a loss period overlaps, relief is given for the loss in the earlier period only.

Tip When there is overlap in the basis periods, then any loss arising during that period is treated as a loss of the earlier tax year.

Example

Anna ceased employment on 31 August 2007, and started her own business on 1 September 2007, preparing accounts to 31 August each year.

She incurred losses for the first two years as follows:

	£
Year ended 31/08/2008	34,140
Year ended 31/08/2009	18,900

Her employment income for the past four years was as follows:

	£
2004 - 05	12,900
2005 - 06	17,800
2006 - 07	27,500
Up to 31 August 2007	8,500

Anna claims relief for the losses against TI of the previous 3 years under s72.

The losses must be allocated to the tax years, using the opening year rules:

	Basis period	Workings	Trading loss £
2007 - 08	01/09/2007 to 05/04/2008	(£34,140) x 7/12	19,915
2008 - 09	Year ended 31/08/2008	(£34,140 – £19,915) (W1)	14,225
2009 - 10	Year ended 31/08/2009	(£18,900)	18,900

Workings

W1

The basis period for 2008-09 is the year ended 31/08/2008, which allocates the loss of £34,140 to tax year 2008-09. However, £19,915 of the loss has already been allocated to 2007-08, so only the loss remaining is treated as arising in 2008-09.

Relief under s72 is taken for the loss allocated to 2007-08 first, and then relief for the loss allocated to 2008-09.

	2004-05 £	2005-06 £	2006-07 £	2007-08 £
Employment income	12,900	17,800	27,500	8,500
Less: s72 relief for loss arising in 2007 - 08 first against 2004-05, then 2005-06	(12,900)	(7,015)	-	-
	-	10,785	27,500	8,500
Less: s72 relief for loss arising in 2008-09 first against 2005-06, then 2006-07		(10,785)	(3,440)	
	-	-	24,060	8,500
Less: s72 relief for loss arising in 2009-10 against 2006-07			(18,900)	
Total income	-	-	5,160	8,500

Note: Loss memorandum

	£	
Loss of 2007-08	19,915	(carry back to 2004-05 then 2005-06 then 2006-07)
Set off in 2004-05	(12,900)	
	(7,015)	
Set off in 2005-06	(7,015)	
	-	

Continued on next page

	£	
Loss of 2008-09 Set off in 2005-06	14,225 (10,785)	(carry back to 2005-06 then 2006-07 then 2007-08)
	3,440	
Set off in 2006-07	(3,440)	
	-	

	£	
Loss of 2009-10 Set off in 2006-07	18,900 (18,900)	(carry back to 2006-07 then 2007-08 then 2008-09)
	-	

Example

James started trading on 1 January 2007, preparing his first accounts for 18 months up to 30 June 2008 and annually thereafter. His results for the first two accounting periods are as follows:

	£
Period ended 30 June 2008 – Trading loss	(28,500)
Year ended 30 June 2009 – Trading profit	7,500

James' other gross income for the years 2003-04 to 2009-10 are as follows:

	Employment Income £	Bank interest £
2003-04	42,000	1,000
2004-05	40,000	1,200
2005-06	43,000	1,500
2006-07	36,000	1,800
2007-08	14,500	2,500
2008-09	-	2,600
2009-10	-	2,900

Losses can be relieved only once. Hence, the losses must be allocated to tax years, using the opening year rules:

	Basis period	Workings	Trading loss (£)	s72 relief
2006-07	01/01/2007 to 05/04/2007	£28,500 x 3/18	4,750	TI 2003-04, 2004-05 and then 2005-06
2007-08	06/04/2007 to 05/04/2008	£28,500 x 12/18	19,000	TI 2004-05, 2005-06 and then 2006-07
2008-09	Year ended 30/06/2008	(£28,500 - £19,000 - £4,750)	4,750	TI 2005-06, 2006-07 and then 2007-08

Note: If there is no accounting period ending in the second tax year, the basis period is 6 April to 5 April of the second tax year.)

James claims loss relief as early as possible against his TI, under s72.
His TI for the tax years 2003 - 04 to 2009 - 10 are as follows:

	2003-04 £	2004-05 £	2005-06 £	2006-07 £	2007-08 £	2008-09 £	2009-10 £
Employment income	42,000	40,000	43,000	36,000	14,500	-	-
Trading income	-	-	-	-	-	-	7,500
Bank interest	1,000	1,200	1,500	1,800	2,500	2,600	2,900
	43,000	41,200	44,500	37,800	17,000	2,600	10,400
Loss relief s72	(4,750)	(19,000)	(4,750)	-	-	-	-
Total income	**38,250**	**22,200**	**39,750**	**37,800**	**17,000**	**2,600**	**10,400**

SUMMARY

Provisions under s72
- **relief**: available for loss arising in the first 4 years of trade
- **set off**: against TI of previous 3 tax years, earliest year first; cannot be restricted
- **remaining loss**: carried forward under s83
- **loss in an overlap period**: can be relieved only once

Test Yourself 6

Jerry started trading on 1 November 2007, preparing accounts to 31 October each year. The results for first two years of trading are as follows:

	£
Year ended 31 October 2008 – Trading loss	(27,000)
Year ended 31 October 2009 – Trading profit	5,200

Jerry also had the following gross income for the tax years 2003 - 04 to 2009 - 10.

	Employment Income £	Property income £
2003 - 04	43,000	1,000
2004 - 05	40,200	1,200
2005 - 06	41,500	1,500
2006 - 07	36,500	1,800
2007 - 08	15,000	2,400
2008 - 09	-	2,500
2009 - 10	-	2,900

Required:

Compute his TI for each of the tax years 2003-04 to 2009-10, assuming that Jerry claims loss relief as early as possible against his TI under s72.

---

4. Explain and compute terminal loss relief.[1]

[Learning outcome h (v)]

4.1 Section 89 ITA 2007 – on cessation of trade, a loss arising in the last 12 months may be set against trading income of the final tax year and the previous 3 years, providing relief against the last year first.

In the case of a continuing business, a trader can relieve his loss by:

➢ carrying it forward and **setting it against future trading income** from the same trade (s83) **OR**

➢ relieving it against the TI of the current tax year **AND / OR** the previous year.

However, if there is a trading loss in the final 12 months of trade, it will not be possible to carry the loss forward against future trading income, and so there is a special loss relief allowing the loss of the last 12 months of trade to gain relief in the previous years.

1. The terminal loss is the loss of the final 12 months of trade and is calculated by adding:

a) trading loss after making adjustments for the profits, if any, for the period starting from the 6 April of the final tax year to the date of cessation of trade
b) trading loss for the period from the previous tax year which falls in the final 12 months of trade after making adjustments for the profits, if any, during that period, and
c) any overlap profits brought forward.

2. The terminal loss is set against:
a) the trading profits of the tax year in which the trader ceases trading and
b) the trading **profits** of the **previous three tax years,** latest first.
3. The claim for relief under s89 must be made within 5 years of 31 January following the tax year in which the cessation occurs. For example, if cessation occurs in 2009-10, a claim must be made by 31/01/2016.
4. A claim for terminal loss relief will reduce prior year liabilities; this will lead to repayment of tax.
5. On cessation, it is possible to claim relief against TI of the current tax year and /or the previous tax year (s64) instead of, or as well as terminal loss relief.

Example Brian has been trading for many years, preparing accounts to 31 December each year. He ceased trading on 31 December 2009. Any loss incurred in the twelve months from 1 January 2009 to 31 December 2009 can be relieved under terminal loss relief.
The loss of the last 12 months of trade may be set against the trading profits of the tax year 2009-10, then 2008-09, 2007-08 and 2006-07, in that order.

Example Monica has been trading for many years, preparing accounts to 31 July each year. She ceased trading on 31 July 2009. Her results for the last 5 years of trading were as follows:

	£
Year to 31 July 2005	17,200
Year to 31 July 2006	21,600
Year to 31 July 2007	18,000
Year to 31 July 2008	900
Year to 31 July 2009	(16,600)

She has overlap profits of £3,600 which have been brought forward.

Monica claims terminal loss relief.

Terminal loss is the loss of the final 12 months of trading, and is calculated as follows:

	£
Trading loss of the final 12 months of trading	
Final tax year 2009 -10	
(6 April 2009 to 31 July 2009) (4 months) (£16,600 x 4/12)	5,533
Previous tax year 2008 - 09	
(1 August 2008 to 5 April 2009) (8 months) (£16,600 x 8/12)	11,067
Unused overlap profits b/f	3,600
Terminal loss	**20,200**

Terminal loss relief is against the trading income for the year of the loss and the three preceding years, with the latest first.

	2005-06 £	2006-07 £	2007-08 £	2008-09 £	2009-10 £
Trading income	17,200	21,600	18,000	900	-
Loss relief s89		(1,300)	(18,000)	(900)	-
TI	17,200	20,300	-	-	-

Note: Loss memorandum

	£
Terminal loss	20,200
Set off in 2008-09	(900)
	19,300
Set off in 2007-08	(18,000)
	1,300
Set off in 2006-07	(1,300)
	Nil

4.2 Some general points

1. Availability of loss reliefs

a) In the opening years of a business, the following loss reliefs are available.

i. **Section 72** i.e. loss arising in any of the **first 4 tax years of trade,** may be **set against TI of the previous 3 years (FIFO).**

ii. **Section 64** i.e. **set off** of trading loss against **total income** of the current tax year **AND / OR** previous tax year.

iii. **Section 83** i.e. carried forward and **set off** against **trading income** of the same trade.

> **Tip**
> In the opening years it is possible to make both a s72 and a s64 claim, if the loss is large enough.

b) **In the continuing years of a business, the following loss reliefs are available**

i. s64 against the TI of the current and / or previous tax years.
ii. s83 against the future trading income.

c) **In the closing year of the business, the following loss reliefs are available**

i. s64 against the TI of the current and / or previous tax year.
ii. s89 i.e. loss of the last 12 months is set against trading income for the year of the loss and the preceding three tax years, latest first.

d) For trading losses incurred in the tax year 2009 – 10, an additional loss relief is available against the trading profits of the previous three tax years, starting with the latest year first. This relief is in addition to the relief under s64 and s83.

2. Disclaiming capital allowances

A trading loss automatically includes capital allowances. It is possible to reduce the capital allowances claimed. The reduced amount claimed is deducted from the pool, leaving a higher tax written down value to carry forward to the next period.

This would be useful if, for example, personal allowances would otherwise be wasted.

SUMMARY

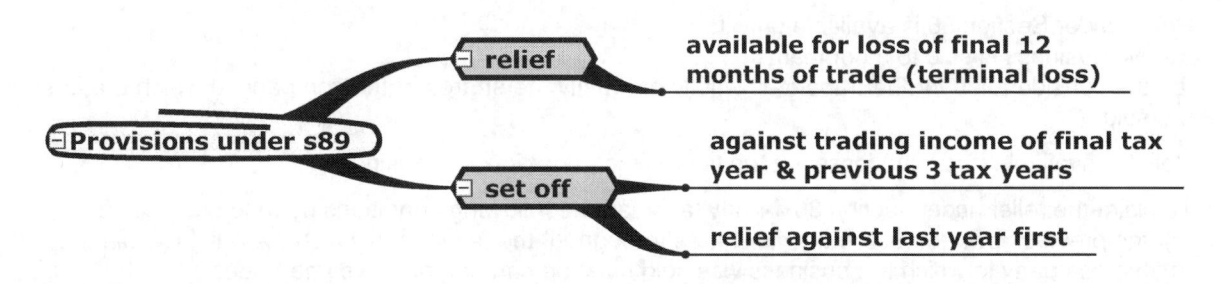

Provisions under s89
- **relief**: available for loss of final 12 months of trade (terminal loss)
- **set off**: against trading income of final tax year & previous 3 tax years
- relief against last year first

Test Yourself 7

Edwina has been trading for many years, preparing accounts to 31 March each year. She ceased trading on 31 March 2010.
Her trading results for the last five years were as follows:

Year ended	Trading profit / (loss) (£)
31 March 2006	14,000
31 March 2007	15,000
31 March 2008	11,200
31 March 2009	1,000
31 March 2010	(9,800)

Continued on next page

Edwina has unused overlap profits brought forward of £4,500.

Required:

Calculate total income for each of the tax years 2005-06 to 2009-10, assuming that Edwina claims terminal loss relief under s89.

Test Yourself 8

Jane has been trading for many years, preparing accounts to 31 December each year. She ceased trading on 31 August 2009. Her results for the last 5 years of trading were as follows:

	£
Year to 31 December 2005	27,400
Year to 31 December 2006	22,500
Year to 31 December 2007	20,000
Year to 31 December 2008	1,200
Eight months to 31 August 2009	(25,200)

Overlap profits of £2,200 arose when Jane started her business.

Required:

Assuming that Jane wants to claim terminal loss relief under s89, calculate her income for the tax years 2005-06 to 2009-10.

5. Explain how trading losses can be carried forward following the incorporation of a business.[2]

[Learning outcome h (ii)]

Section 86 ITA 2007 – relief of trading losses against future income received from a new company

1. When a trader incorporates his business, relief for the losses of an unincorporated business is available under
a) Section 64: against TI of the current year and / or the previous year
b) Section 89: against trading income of final and previous 3 tax years.

2. In addition, losses can be relieved under s86 against future income received by the taxpayer from the company to which the business is sold.

3. Relief under Section 86 is available only if:
   a) the business is sold to a company.
   b) the consideration for the transfer is wholly or mainly the shares of the company to which the business is sold.

4. Relief is available for all the losses at the time of incorporation of a business.

5. To claim the relief under section 86 for any tax year, the following conditions need to be fulfilled:
   c) the previous owner must retain his shares throughout the tax year in which the relief is claimed.
   d) the company to which the business was sold must be carrying on the same trade.

6. The set off must be against the first available income from the company which may be salaries, director's fees, interest or dividends.

Example

Robin has been trading for many years, preparing accounts to 31 March each year. He incorporated his business on 31 March 2009.
He incurred a loss in the final twelve months of trade of £32,000.
In the tax year 2009 - 10 he received a salary of £25,000 and interest of £10,000 (gross) from the company.

Robin does not relieve the loss against his TI under s64 or against trading income, under s89.

The trading loss of £32,000 is therefore carried forward and relieved against income from the company in 2009 - 10, £25,000 of the loss against his salary and remaining £7,000 against interest income.

SUMMARY

Provisions under s86

- **relief available**
  - if business is sold to a company
  - if whole consideration consists of shares
  - for all losses at the time of incorporation
- **conditions for claiming tax relief**
  - previous owner retains all shares throughout tax year
  - buying company still carries on same trade
- **set off**
  - must be against first available income from the company

Answers to Test Yourself

Answer 1

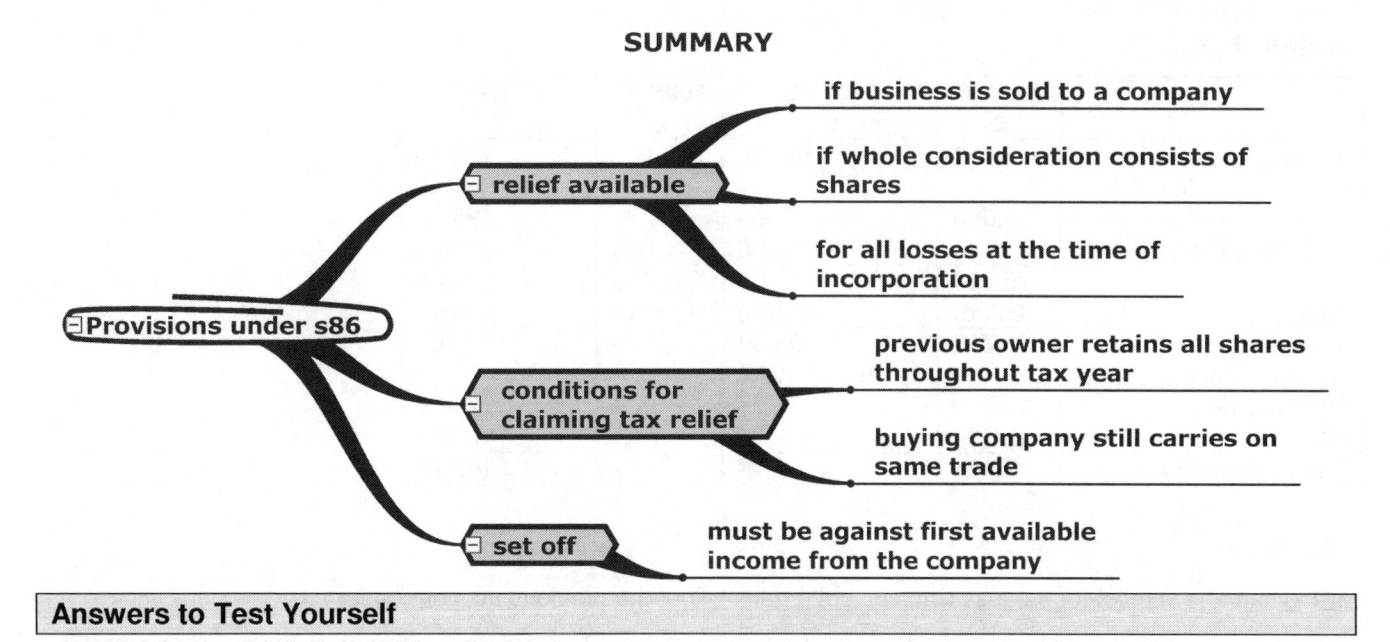

Calculation of taxable income:

	2008-09 £	2009-10 £	2010-11 £	2011-12 £
Trading profits	-	9,600	11,650	39,750
Less: s83 relief	-	(9,600)	(11,650)	(16,300)
	-	-	-	23,450
Building society interest	1,800	1,800	1,800	1,800
Property income	2,000	2,000	2,000	2,000
Total Income	**3,800**	**3,800**	**3,800**	**27,250**
PA (restricted)	(3,800)	(3,800)	(3,800)	(6,475)
Taxable income	**-**	**-**	**-**	**20,775**

Notes:

1. The trading loss arising in 2008-09 is carried forward to and set against future trading income until the whole loss is relieved.
2. Under s83, the loss is set off against trading profits only, not against any other income.

Loss memorandum

	£
Loss for the year 2008-09	37,550
Set off: 2009-10 (s.83)	(9,600)
	27,950
2010-11 (s83)	(11,650)
	16,300
2011-12 (s83)	(16,300)
	-

Answer 2

Taxable income is as follows:

	2008-09 £	2009-10 £
Trading income	-	58,250
Less: s83 relief		(4,750)
		53,500
Building society income	3,750	3,750
Total Income	**3,750**	**57,250**
Less: Interest Paid	-	(7,000)
Net Income	**3,750**	**50,250**
PA	3,750	(6,475)
Taxable income	**Nil**	**43,775**

Answer 3

	2006-07 £	2007-08 £	2008-09 £	2009-10 £
Trading income	15,000	10,000	-	22,500
Less: Loss relief s83	-	-	-	(3,500) (W2)
	15,000	10,000	-	19,000
Building society interest	700	1,500	1,800	1,000
	15,700	11,500	1,800	20,000
Interest paid	(2,000)	(2,500)	(1,800)	(2,600)
Total Income	13,700	9,000	-	17,400
Loss relief s64	-	(9,000) (W1)	-	-
Net Income	13,700	-	-	17,400
PA	(6,475)	-	-	(6,475)
Taxable Income	7,225	-	-	10,925

Workings

W1 The earliest relief for the loss is to set it off against TI of the previous tax year under s64.

W2 The remaining loss of £3,500 (£12,500 - £9,000) is carried forward and set against future trading profits under s83.

W3 Interest payments of £1,800 are relieved in 2008-09. The balance is unrelieved.

Answer 4

	2006 - 07 £	2007 - 08 £	2008 - 09 £	2009 - 10 £
Trading income	35,000	30,000	12,500	-
Less: Additional loss relief	(20,000)	(30,000)	-	-
	15,000	-	12,500	-
Building society interest	9,700	10,500	11,800	10,200
	24,700	10,500	24,300	10,200
Less: Interest paid	(2,000)	(2,500)	(2,500)	(2,600)
Total income	22,700	8,000	21,800	7,600
Less: s64 relief	-	-	(21,800)	(7,600)
Net income	22,700	8,000	-	-
Less: Personal allowance	(6,475)	(6,475)	-	-
Taxable income	16,225	1,525	-	-

Loss memorandum

Year	£
Loss of year ended 31/03/2010	79,900
Less: s64 2009 - 10	(7,600)
	72,300
Less: s64 2008 - 09	(21,800)
	50,500
Less: Additional loss relief 2007 - 08	(30,000)
	20,500
Less: Additional loss relief 2006 - 07	(20,000)
Balance loss to be carried forward	500

Notes:

1. To claim the loss relief as early as possible, Garry will first set the trading loss under section 64 against the total income of the current tax year 2009 – 10 and then against total income of the previous tax year 2008 – 09.

2. The remaining loss is set against the trading income of the previous tax years 2007 – 08 and 2006 – 07 under additional loss relief. This relief is limited to a maximum of £50,000.
3. Personal allowance is wasted for the tax year 2009 – 10 and 2008 – 09 as it is not possible to restrict the relief to claim the allowances.

Answer 5

	2007-08 £	2008-09 £	2009-10 £
Trading income	9,000	-	23,500
Less: s83 relief (W1)	-	-	(3,000)
	9,000	-	20,500
Property income	1,000	1,600	3,000
Bank interest	500	600	400
Total income	10,500	2,200	23,900
Less: Interest charges	(2,500)	(2,200)	(3,000)
	8,000	-	20,900
Less: s64 relief (W1)	(8,000)	-	-
Net income	-	-	20,900
PA	-	-	(6,035)
Taxable income	-	-	14,865
Relief under s261B			
Capital Gains	17,000	8,000	11,000
Less: s261B relief (W1)	(17,000)	-	-
	-	8,000	11,000
Less: Annual Exemption (Refer to Learning Outcome 3, Study Guide C2)	-	(8,000)	(10,100)
Chargeable Gains	-	-	900

Workings

W1

In 2007-08 £8,000 of the loss is relieved against TI under s64, £17,000 of the loss is relieved against capital gains, and the remaining loss of £3,000 (£28,000 - £8,000 - £17,000), is relieved against future trading profits under s83.

Loss Memorandum

	£
Loss of 2008-09	28,000
2007-08 s64	(8,000)
	20,000
2007-08 s261B	(17,000)
	3,000
2009-10 s83	(3,000)
	-

Answer 6

	2003-04 £	2004-05 £	2005-06 £	2006-07 £	2007-08 £	2008-09 £	2009-10 £
Employment income	43,000	40,200	41,500	36,500	15,000	-	-
Trading income	-	-	-	-	-	-	5,200
Property income	1,000	1,200	1,500	1,800	2,400	2,500	2,900
	44,000	41,400	43,000	38,300	17,400	2,500	8,100
Loss relief s72		(11,250)	(15,750)	-	-	-	-
Total income	44,000	30,150	27,250	38,300	17,400	2,500	8,100

B3.88: Income Tax Liabilities

Workings

W1

The losses must be allocated to tax years, using the opening year rules

	Basis period	Workings	Trading loss (£)	S72 relief
2007-08	1 November 2007 to 5 April 2008	£27,000 x 5/12	11,250	TI 2004-05, 2005-06 and then 2006-07
2008-09	Year ended 31 October 2008	£27,000 – £11,250	15,750	TI 2005-06, 2006-07 and then 2007-08

Note: Relief is given under s72 for losses allocated to the tax year 2007 – 08 against TI of 2004-05, 2005-06 and 2006-07 (i.e. previous three tax years, FIFO).

Answer 7

	2005-06 £	2006-07 £	2007-08 £	2008-09 £	2009-10 £
Trading income	14,000	15,000	11,200	1,000	-
Less: Loss relief s89		(2,100)	(11,200)	(1,000)	
Total income	**14,000**	**12,900**	**-**	**-**	**-**

Workings

W1 Calculation of terminal loss

	£
Trading loss of the final 12 months of trading	9,800
Overlap profits b/f	4,500
Terminal loss	**14,300**

W2 Loss memorandum

	£
Terminal loss	14,300
Set off in 2008-09	(1,000)
	13,300
Set off in 2007-08	(11,200)
	2,100
Set off in 2006-07	2,100
	-

Answer 8

Calculation of terminal loss:

	£	£
Trading loss of the final 12 months of trading		
Final tax year 2009 - 10		
6 April 2009 to 31 August 2009 (5 months) (£25,200 x 5/8)		15,750
Previous tax year 2008 - 09		
1 September 2008 to 5 April 2009 (7 months)		
Loss for the period from 1 January 2009 to 5 April 2009 (£25,200 x 3/8)	9,450	
Less: Profit for the period from 1 September 2008 to 31 December 2008 (£1,200 x 4/12)	(400)	9,050
Add: Unused overlap profits b/f		2,200
Terminal loss		**27,000**

Relief of terminal loss:

	2005-06 £	2006-07 £	2007-08 £	2008-09 £	2009-10 £
Trading income	27,400	22,500	20,000	1,200	-
Less: Loss relief s89	-	(5,800)	(20,000)	(1,200)	-
Total income	27,400	16,700	-	-	-

Note: Loss memorandum

	£
Terminal loss	27,000
Set off in 2008-09	(1,200)
	25,800
Set off in 2007-08	(20,000)
	5,800
Set off in 2006-07	(5,800)
	-

Quick Quiz

1. What happens to a trading loss if no specific claim is made to relieve it?
2. Give two loss reliefs available in the continuing years of a business.
3. Describe the loss relief available in the opening years of trade.
4. A trader has been trading for many years and incurs a loss. He wishes to claim relief against TI under s64. What options are available to him?
5. A trader has been trading for many years and incurs a loss. He wishes to relieve the loss against his capital gains of the previous tax year. How may he achieve this?
6. What relief is available for a trading loss on the cessation of a business?

Answers to Quick Quiz

1. The loss is automatically carried forward and set against future trading profits of the same trade.
2. i. Set off against TI of the current year and / or previous year.
   ii. Set off against future trading profits of the same trade.
3. A loss occurring in any of the first 4 tax years of a business may be set against TI of the previous three years, relieving the earliest year first.
4. He may claim against:
   - TI of the current year only
   - TI of the previous year only
   - TI of the current year and then the previous year
   - TI of the previous year and then the current year
5. He may claim against his capital gains of the current year and / or the previous year, but only after a claim has been made against TI of the year of the claim.
   In order to claim against the capital gains of the previous year, he must first claim against TI of the previous year under s64.
6. The loss of the last 12 months of trade (terminal loss) may be set against trading income for the tax year of cessation and the previous 3 tax years, latest first.

Self Examination Questions

Question 1

For the year ended 31 March 2010, Jack, a cold-drinks seller, incurred a loss of £22,000. Every year, apart from this trading income, he receives interest on gilt-edged securities of £12,000 (gross). Last year he had no trading income.

Jack is not sure of his future income. Thus he wants to claim relief as early as possible.

Required:

Calculate his taxable income for 2008-09 and 2009-10 assuming he claims relief under s64.

B3.90: Income Tax Liabilities

Question 2

Lisa was running a 'fish and chips' takeaway shop. In the year 2008-09 due to overall trade recession, she incurred a loss of £18,200. She is confident that she will earn profit in future.

Required:

1. Advise her, under which section she should make claim for relief of loss.
2. Show the calculation of total taxable income of 2009-10 assuming that she earned a profit of £11,000.
3. What will be the position of unrelieved loss?

Question 3

Sabrina started trading on 1 November 2007 preparing accounts to 31 December each year.

Her results are as follows:

	£
14 months to 31 December 2008	(28,000)
Year to 31 December 2009	21,000

Sabrina received property income as follows:

	£
2004-05	15,000
2005-06	14,000
2006-07	21,000
2007-08	20,000
2008-09	19,000
2009-10	18,000

She had no other sources of income.

Assuming Sabrina claims loss relief as early as possible against TI (under s72) calculate her TI for the tax years 2004-05 to 2009-10.

Question 4

Thornton has a wholesale chocolates business for the past many years, preparing accounts to 31 December every year. In the year 2009-10, he incurred a loss of £77,900. His taxable trading profits for the past three years are as follows:

	£
2006 - 07	22,400
2007 - 08	31,600
2008 - 09	20,700

Thornton also had property income of £2,500 and interest income of £800 (gross) each year.

Required:

Show the calculations of the loss to be relieved, assuming Thornton claims the loss as early as possible. Assume a personal allowance of £6,475 throughout.

Question 5

Michael has been trading for many years. He has the following income and allowable interest payments for the years 2007-08, 2008-09 and 2009-10.

	2007-08 £	2008-09 £	2009-10 £
Trading profits/(loss)	10,000	(22,000)	23,500
Property income/(loss)		1,600	3,000
Building society interest (gross)	500	600	400
Interest paid (gross)	(2,500)	(3,500)	(3,000)

Required:

Calculate Michael's taxable income for all three years, assuming that he makes no specific claim to relieve the loss, and that tax allowances for 2009-10 apply throughout.

Answers to Self Examination Questions

Answer 1

Calculation of Jack's taxable income after relief under s64

Under s64, Jack can claim relief against the TI of 2009 - 10 or total income of 2008 - 09 or both. As the claim under s64 is not automatic, Jack must elect for relief.

	2008-09 £	2009-10 £
Trading income	-	-
Interest on gilt-edged securities	12,000	12,000
Total income	**12,000**	**12,000**
Less: Relief under s64 (W1)	(12,000)	(10,000)
Net income	**-**	**2,000**
Less: Personal allowance		(2,000)
Taxable income	-	-

Workings

W1 Loss memorandum

	£
Loss for the year 2009-10	22,000
Less: Relief under section 64 against 2008-09 income	(12,000)
	10,000
Less: Relief under section 64 against 2009-10 income	(10,000)
Balance	-

Note: Jack should first set the loss against the income of the year 2008 - 09, as he will get a repayment of tax paid for the previous year along with the interest on it.

Answer 2

1. From the given facts, we can conclude that Lisa had no other income and she is confident about earning profits in future. She has to carry forward the loss to be set against future income (s83).

2. Computation of total income

	2009-10 £
Trading income	11,000
Less: Loss for the year 2008-09	(11,000)
Balance trading income	-

3. Loss memorandum

Year	£
Loss for the year 2008-09	18,200
Less: Set off against income of 2009-10	(11,000)
Balance unrelieved loss	**7,200**

Unrelieved loss of £7,200 can be carried forward to future years to be set against future profits from the same trade.

Answer 3

Step 1 - In the opening years of a trade we need to allocate the profit/ (loss) to tax years

	Basis period	Workings	Trading £	s72 relief
2007-08	01/11/2007 to 05/04/2008	(£28000) x 5/14	(10,000)	TI 2004-05, 2005-06
2008-09	01/01/2008 to 31/12/2008	(£28,000) x12/14 Less loss used in 2007-08	(24,000) 6,000 (18,000)	TI 2005-06, 2006-07
2009-10	Year ended 31/12/2009		21,000	

Step 2 - Calculate TI for years 2004-05 to 2009-10

	2004-05 £	2005-06 £	2006-07 £	2007-08 £	2008-09 £	2009-10 £
Trading income	-	-	-	-	-	21,000
Property income	15,000	14,000	21,000	20,000	19,000	18,000
	15,000	14,000	21,000	20,000	19,000	39,000
Loss relief s72	-	-	-	-	-	-
Loss of 2007-08	(10,000)	-	-	-	-	-
Loss of 2008-09	-	(14,000)	(4,000)	-	-	-
Total income	**5,000**	**-**	**17,000**	**20,000**	**19,000**	**39,000**

Workings

W1 Loss Memorandum

	2007-08 £	2008-09 £
Trading loss	10,000	18,000
Less: Set against TI of		
2004-05	(10,000)	-
2005-06	-	(14,000)
2006-07 (balance)	-	(4,000)
	-	-

Answer 4

Thornton can claim relief for the trading loss of 2009 -10 under s64 against the total income of the current tax year and the previous tax year 2008 – 09. He can also claim relief under additional loss relief against the trading profits of the previous three tax years taking the latest year first.

Calculation of Thornton's taxable income for the fours years is as follows:

	2006 - 07 £	2007 - 08 £	2008 - 09 £	2009 - 10 £
Trading income	22,400	31,600	20,700	
Less: Additional loss relief (note 2)	(18,400)	(31,600)		
	4,000	0	20,700	0
Property income	2,500	2,500	2,500	2,500
Building society interest	800	800	800	800
	7,300	3,300	24,000	3,300
Less: s64 relief			(24,000)	(3,300)
	7,300	3,300	0	0
Less: personal allowance	(6,475)	(3,300)		
Taxable income	**825**	**0**	**0**	**0**

Loss memorandum

Year	£
Loss of 2009 - 10	77,900
Less: s64 2009 - 10	(3,300)
	74,600
Less: s64 2008 - 09	(24,000)
	50,600
Less: Additional loss relief 2007 - 08	(31,600)
	19,000
Less: Additional loss relief 2006 - 07	(18,400)
Balance loss to be carried forward under s83	**600**

Notes:

1. Additional loss relief has been introduced to claim the trading loss for the tax year 2009-10 against the trading profits of the previous three tax years taking the latest year first. This relief is in addition to the relief under section 64.

2. The remaining loss after claiming relief under s64 can be set against the trading profit of the tax years 2007 - 08 and 2006 – 07 under additional loss relief. However, the relief amount is restricted to £50,000 if the relief is claimed in these two tax years.
   The relief available in the tax year 2007 – 08 is £31,600 (against trading profits).
   Hence, the relief available in the tax year 2006 – 07 is (£50,000 - £31,600) = £18,400.

3. Personal allowance of £6,475 is wasted in 2008 – 09 and 2009 – 10 and allowance of £3,175 (£6,475 - £3,300) is wasted in 2007 – 08 as it is not possible to restrict the relief to claim the allowances.

Answer 5

	2007-08 £	2008-09 £	2009-10 £
Trading income	10,000	-	23,500
Less: s83 relief (W1)			(22,000)
	10,000	-	1,500
Property income	-	1,600	3,000
Building society interest	500	600	400
	10,500	2,200	4,900
Less: Interest paid	(2,500)	(2,200)	(3,000)
Total income	**8,000**	**-**	**1,900**
PA (restricted)	(6,475)	-	(1,900)
Taxable income	**1,525**	**-**	**-**

Working

W1

As Michael has not made a specific claim to relieve the loss, it is carried forward and set against the first available trading profits under s83.

SECTION B: INCOME TAX LIABILITIES

B3

STUDY GUIDE B3: INCOME FROM SELF-EMPLOYMENT (PART 4)

Get Through Intro

This Study Guide deals with the income tax rules relating to partnerships. A partnership is a collection of individuals carrying on a business together. Accounts are prepared for the partnership, and the profits are allocated between the partners. Each partner's share of the profits is taxed in their individual income tax computation.

The partnership itself is not taxed. The profits are allocated to the individual partners, and they are each taxed as if they were a sole trader running their own business.

Professionals, like doctors or lawyers often work in a partnership. Once you pass your ACCA exam, you too can work in a partnership. However, you will need to know how your share of profits from the partnership will be assessed to tax. If you have clients operating their businesses as a partnership, you will need to be able to advise them.

Learning Outcomes

i) Partnerships and limited liability partnerships
   i. Explain how a partnership is assessed to tax.
   ii. Compute the assessable profits for each partner following a change in the profit sharing ratio.
   iii. Compute the assessable profits for each partner following a change in the membership of the partnership.
   iv. Describe the alternative loss relief claims that are available to partners.
   v. Explain the loss relief restriction that applies to the partners of a limited liability partnership.

Introduction

Apple, Mango and Banana have been trading for many years preparing accounts to 5 April each year. Their profit sharing ratio is 1:2:3.

The profit for the year to 5 April 2010 is £1,800,000.

The profits are allocated to the partners as follows:

	£
Apple	300,000
Mango	600,000
Banana	900,000

Mango retires from the partnership on 5 April 2010, and Apple and Banana share profits in the ratio of 2:3. In the year to 5 April 2011 the profit is £1,500,000.

The profits are allocated to the partners as follows:

	£
Apple	600,000
Banana	900,000

The principles which apply to sole traders also apply to partnerships, once the profits have been allocated to the individual partners. This Study Guide will help you appreciate how this operates.

> 1. **Explain how a partnership is assessed to tax.**[2]
> **Compute the assessable profits for each partner following a change in the profit sharing ratio.**[2]
> **Compute the assessable profits for each partner following a change in the membership of the partnership.**[2]
> [Learning outcomes i (i, ii and iii)]

1.1 How a partnership is assessed to tax

A partnership is a single trading entity, preparing accounts and computing tax adjusted trading income. However, the partnership is not a separate entity for tax purposes, and the partnership is not subject to tax.

The profits of the partnership are calculated, they are adjusted for tax purposes, and then they are allocated to the partners who are each taxed as sole traders in their income tax computations.

1. The tax adjusted trading income of the partnership is calculated in the same way as for a sole trader.

2. The tax adjusted trading income is then allocated to each partner in their profit sharing ratios (PSR).

3. Each partner is then taxed as a sole trader in the tax year determined on the basis of assessment rules.

> **Example**
> Alan and Bob have been trading for many years, preparing accounts to 31 December each year. They share profits in the ratio 2:3.
>
> Adjusted profits for the year to 31 December 2009 were £100,000.
>
> This figure is then allocated to the partners, in their profit sharing ratio. Alan's share is £40,000 and Bob's share is £60,000. Each partner is treated as a sole trader, so Alan has profits of £40,000 for the year ended 31 December 2009, which will be assessed as trading income in his income tax computation for 2009 - 10, and Bob will be assessed on £60,000 in his income tax computation.

4. A profit sharing agreement may specify that the partners are to be paid an annual salary, or given a fixed percentage of interest on their capital, and share the balance of the profits between them in their profit sharing ratios.

The salary is not employment income, and the interest is not taxed as savings income. They are both simply part of the arrangement for sharing profits. These are not deductible expenses. They are seen as drawings and are therefore added back to calculate the profits.

Example

Edwin, Fergus and George have been trading for many years, preparing accounts to 30 September each year. Adjusted profits for the year to 30 September 2009 were £160,000.

Profits were shared as follows:
Edwin was paid an annual salary of £10,000,
Interest was paid at 10% on their capital accounts.
Capital account balances:

	£
Edwin	50,000
Fergus	60,000
George	30,000

The remaining profits were shared:

Edwin	Fergus	George
20%	30%	50%

The profit for the year ended 30 September 2009 is shared as follows:

	Total £	Edwin £	Fergus £	George £
Year ended 30 September 2009				
Salary	10,000	10,000		
Interest (10% on capital)	14,000	5,000	6,000	3,000
Remaining profit in PSR (20:30:50)	136,000	27,200	40,800	68,000
	160,000	42,200	46,800	71,000

5. As previously explained, the tax adjusted trading income of the partnership is calculated in the same way as for a sole trader. Similarly, calculation of **capital allowances** for partnerships is also done in the same way as for a sole trader. The adjustment / deduction for capital allowances of partnerships are made before allocating profits to each partner.

Moreover when a **partner personally**, **owns an asset** e.g. his car, **capital allowances may be claimed** for that, with **adjustments for any private use**. However, the allowances are not set against the partner's share of the partnership profits; instead they are deducted from the partnership profits.

1.2 Change in profit sharing ratio

Profits are allocated to the partners according to their profit sharing arrangements during the accounting period. If the arrangements change during the accounting period, the profits must be allocated accordingly.

The change in the profit sharing ratio can take place due to the following reasons:
1. existing partners decide to change the profit sharing arrangement
2. a new partner joins the partnership
3. an existing partner leaves the partnership

While calculating the profit of each partner in case of a change in the profit sharing ratio, the accounting period is divided and the profits are allocated accordingly for each period.

Example

Harry, Ian and James have been trading for many years, preparing accounts to 30 June each year. Their recent tax adjusted profits have been as follows:

	£
Year ended 30 June 2009	147,000
Year ended 30 June 2010	171,000
Year ended 30 June 2011	180,000

They shared profits equally, until 31 October 2009 when they decided on the following arrangement:

	Harry	Ian	James
Salary	£19,500	£39,000	£49,500
Profit sharing %	50%	30%	20%

The partners' trading income assessments for 2009 - 10, 2010 - 11 and 2011 - 12 are as follows:

	Total £	Harry £	Ian £	James £
2009 - 10 (Year ended 30 June 2009)				
PSR 1:1:1	147,000	49,000	49,000	49,000
2010 - 11 (Year ended 30 June 2010)				
1 July 2009 to 31 October 2009 (4 months)				
PSR (1:1:1)	57,000	19,000	19,000	19,000
1 November 2009 to 30 June 2010 (8 months)				
Salary (8/12)	72,000	13,000	26,000	33,000
Remaining profit PSR (50:30:20)	42,000	21,000	12,600	8,400
	171,000	53,000	57,600	60,400
2011 - 12 (Year ended 30 June 2011)				
Salary	108,000	19,500	39,000	49,500
Remaining profit PSR (50:30:20)	72,000	36,000	21,600	14,400
	180,000	55,500	60,600	63,900

1.3 Changes in the membership of the partnership

A situation may arise where the business of the partnership continues, but the partners change. Can you think of any such situations?

1. A partner leaves the partnership.

2. A new partner joins the partnership.

In the above cases what is the basis period for individual partners?

a) The commencement rules are applicable only to new members of the partnership.

> **Tip**: The basis period for the first tax year runs from the date the trade started to the following 5 April.

b) The last year rules are applicable only to partners who have left partnership.

Example

Alan and Bob were in a partnership. The accounting period of the partnership is twelve months to 31 October each year.

Cathy joins the partnership on 1 January 2009. It is considered that she started her business on 1 January 2009. Hence her period of account will be from 1 January 2009 to 31 October 2009. The basis period for the first tax year runs from the date the trade started to the following 5 April. Thus her basis period for the tax year 2008 - 09 will be 1 January 2009 to 5 April 2009. Her basis period for the second tax year, 2009 – 10, will be twelve months from the commencement of trade i.e. from 1 January 2009 to 31 December 2009.

Similarly if Alan leaves the partnership on 31 May 2009, then it will be treated as if he has finished his business on that date. Alan's period of account will start from the beginning of the period of account, i.e. 1 November 2008, and will end on the day he leaves the partnership, i.e. 31 May 2009.

c) Partners who carry on business in partnership continuously (ignoring the other partners who join or leave) carry on using the period of account ending in each tax year as the basis period for the tax year.

d) When a partnership transfers its trade to a completely new owner or set of owners, the last year rules for basis period apply to old partners, while commencement rules apply to new owners.

1.4 Basis of assessment for partnership profits

1. Continuing partners

Partners who were partners both before and after the change in membership continue to be taxed on the current year basis as if a change had not occurred.

2. Partners joining

A new partner joining will be assessed under the commencement rules. If a partner joins part way through an accounting period, he will have a period which begins on the day he joined. The other partners continue to be assessed on the current year basis.

3. Partners leaving

A partner leaving the partnership will be assessed under the cessation rules. If a partner leaves part way through an accounting period, he will have a period which ends on the day he left. The other partners continue to be assessed on the current year basis.

Example Chris and Evan began a partnership on 6 April 2005, preparing accounts to 5 April. Chris resigned as a partner on 31 December 2009, and Greg joined as a partner on 1 January 2010. The partnership's trading profit for the year ended 5 April 2010 is £80,000.

Profits were shared as follows:

1. Evan was paid an annual salary of £5,000.
2. Interest was paid at the rate of 10% on the partners' capital accounts, the balances on which were:

	£
Chris	30,000
Evan	60,000
Greg (from 1 January 2010)	10,000

Chris's capital account was repaid to him on 31 December 2009.

3. The balance of profits were shared as follows:

	Chris %	Evan %	Greg %
6 April 2009 to 31 December 2009	60	40	
1 January 2010 to 5 April 2010		70	30

Required:

Calculate the trading income assessments of Chris, Evan and Greg for the tax year 2009 - 10.

Answer

Assessments 2009 - 10

	Total £	Chris £	Evan £	Greg £
Nine months to 31 December 2009 (£80,0000 x 9/12)				
Salary (£5,000 x 9/12)	3,750		3,750	
Interest (W1)	6,750	2,250	4,500	
Balance (60%/40%)	49,500	29,700	19,800	
	60,000	31,950	28,050	
Three months to 5 April 2010 (£80,0000 x 3/12)				
Salary (£5,000 x 3/12)	1,250		1,250	
Interest (W1)	1,750		1,500	250
Balance (70%/30%)	17,000		11,900	5,100
	20,000		14,650	5,350
Total assessment	80,000	31,950	42,700	5,350

Continued on next page

Workings

W1 Interest on capital

Chris: (£30,000 x 10% x 9/12) = £2,250
Evan: (£60,000 x 10% x 9/12) = £4,500

Evan: (£60,000 x 10% x 3/12) = £1,500
Greg: (£10,000 x 10% x 3/12) = £250

SUMMARY

Partnership
- trading income & capital allowance — calculated in the same way as for the sole trader
- tax adjusted trading income — allocated to each partner in their profit sharing ratio
- each partner is taxed — as a sole trader
- basis of assessment for profits:
  - continuing partner: current year basis, if change had not occurred
  - partners joining: commencement rules
  - partners leaving: cessation rules

Test Yourself 1

Cindy, Barbie and Cinderella began trading as a partnership on 1 January 2008, sharing profits in the ratio 1:2:3.

From 1 January 2009, the partners decided that:
1. Cinderella should receive a salary of £50,000 per annum.
2. All the partners should be entitled to interest on capital at 4% per annum.
3. The remaining profits should be shared in the ratio of 2:3:5.

The adjusted trading profits of the partnership are:
Year ended 31 December 2008   £240,000
Year ended 31 December 2009   £280,000

The fixed capital of the partners is as follows:
Cindy £120,000, Barbie £160,000 and Cinderella £210,000

Required:

Calculate the trading income assessments and the overlap profits for each of the partners for the years 2008 - 09 and 2009 - 10.

Test Yourself 2

Kelly and Millie started a business in partnership on 1 June 2006. The partnership makes up accounts for seventeen months up to 31 October 2007 in the first year, and to 31 October each year thereafter. On 1 December 2007, Celli joins the partnership. On 31 July 2009, Kelly left the partnership and started her own business.

Required:

State the basis periods and the overlap periods for the partners.

2. Describe the alternative loss relief claims that are available to partners. [1]

[Learning outcomes i (iv)]

2.1 Loss relief claims available to partners

The two steps for a partnership are

Step 1: share the profits between the partners in the profit sharing ratio of the accounting period.
Step 2: treat each partner as a sole trader.

These rules continue to be applied when the partnership incurs a loss.

The partnership loss is allocated to the individual partners in their profit / (loss) sharing ratio of the accounting period. Each partner may then claim their share of loss, as a sole trader. He may claim whatever loss relief is most beneficial to him.

Continuing partners may claim
- **Section 64:** against TI of the current and/or previous tax year
- **Section 83:** against future trading income
- **Additional loss relief:** against trading income of the previous three years, latest first (it is available for any trading loss arising from the tax year 2009-10)

Partners joining may claim
- **Section 72:** a loss in any of the first four tax years may be set against TI of the previous three years, earliest first.
- **Section 64:** against TI of the current and/or previous tax year
- **Section 83:** against future trading income

Partners leaving may claim
- **Section 89:** a loss of the last twelve months may be set against trading income of the last and previous three tax years, latest first.
- **Section 64:** against TI of the current and/or previous tax year.
- **Additional loss relief:** against trading income of the previous three years, latest first (it is available for any trading loss arising from the tax year 2009-10).

Test Yourself 3

Hira and Mira have been trading for many years, preparing accounts to 31 December each year. They share profits equally. Tara joined the partnership on 1 January 2008 and it was agreed to share profits equally among all the three partners. The partnership made a profit of £60,000 for the year ended 31 December 2008 Hira resigned as a partner on 31 December 2009. Mira and Tara continued and decided to share profits equally. The partnership made a loss of £90,000 in the year ended 31 December 2009.

Required:

Give the possible ways in which Hira, Mira and Tara can relieve their share of the trading loss. Assume Hira's overlap profit relief brought forward was £9,000.

3. Explain the loss relief restriction that applies to the partners of a limited liability partnership. [1]

[Learning outcome i (v)]

3.1 Limited Liability Partnerships (LLP)

1. This type of partnership has a distinct legal existence, separate from its partners. It can own property and sue or can be sued in the name of the corporation. It enjoys perpetual succession even if anything happens to the partners i.e. additions or departure of partners, death or insolvency of partners. It will have no effect on its continuation.

    Normally there is no limit to the amount that each partner is required to contribute towards partnership losses, debts and liabilities.

2. It is possible to form a limited liability partnership where the contribution to losses, debts and liabilities by each partner is limited by agreement.

3. The limited liability partnership is taxed in the same way as other partnerships.
4. Normal loss reliefs are available.

However, the amount of loss (relief under s.64 and s.72), which a partner of a limited liability partnership can set off against his non-partnership income, is restricted to the capital contributed by him in the partnership.

Example

Robert has been a member of an LLP for many years, introducing capital of £100,000 when he joined. The partnership prepares accounts to 5 April each year. The partnership incurred a loss in the year ended 5 April 2009 and 2010.

Robert's share is as follows:

| Year ended 5 April 2009 | £60,000 |
| Year ended 5 April 2010 | £72,000 |

What is the maximum relief that Robert may claim against his TI under s64?

Answer

Robert is entitled to s64 relief against his other income or gains as follows:

| 2008 - 09 | £60,000 | (£60,000 of contributed capital has been used up, £40,000 remaining) |
| 2009 - 10 | £40,000 | (s64 relief limited to capital contribution of £100,000. Loss of £40,000 relieved) |

Note: The balance of the loss, £32,000 (£72,000 - £40,000), can be carried forward and set against Robert's share of the LLP's profits from the same trade for later years. Alternatively, if Robert makes a further capital contribution in a later year, the balance of the loss can be set against his other income or gains, not arising from the partnership.

Test Yourself 4

Arnold joins an LLP on 6 April 2009. The capital contributed by him in the partnership is as follows:

| 6 April 2009 | £90,000 |
| 6 April 2010 | £25,000 |

Arnold's share of the partnership's trading profits and losses are:
Year ended 5 April 2010: Loss (£140,000)
Year ended 5 April 2011: Profit £60,000

Required:

Explain how loss relief can be claimed.

Test Yourself 5

Tom and Dick began trading as a partnership on 1 October 2006, sharing profits equally. They prepared accounts to 30 September each year.

On 1 January 2008 they agreed to admit Harry as a partner, and decided on the following profit sharing ratio:

Tom	Dick	Harry
50%	30%	20%

The adjusted trading profits of the partnership are as follows:

	£
Year ended 30/9/07	220,000
Year ended 30/9/08	250,000
Year ended 30/9/09	300,000

Required:

Calculate the trading income assessment for each partner for the years 2006 - 07 to 2009 - 10 and the overlap profits for each of the partners.

SUMMARY

LLP
- distinct legal existence — separate from its partners
- taxed — in the same way as other partnerships
- partner's contribution to losses, debts & liabilities — limited by agreement
- claim relief for losses — against non-partnership income but restricted upto capital contributed

Answers to Test Yourself

Answer 1

The allocation of trading profit for each accounting period is as follows:

	Total £	Cindy £	Barbie £	Cinderella £
Year ended 31/12/08				
PSR (1:2:3)	240,000	40,000	80,000	120,000
Year ended 31/12/09				
Salary	50,000			50,000
Interest on capital	19,600	4,800	6,400	8,400
Remaining profits (2:3:5)	210,400	42,080	63,120	105,200
	280,000	46,880	69,520	163,600

Each partner is treated as a sole trader who started trading on 1 January 2008, preparing accounts to 31 December each year.

The trading income assessments for each partner are as follows:

Cindy

	Basis period	Workings	Assessment £
2007 - 08	01/01/2008 to 05/04/2008	£40,000 x 3/12	10,000
2008 - 09	Year ended 31/12/2008		40,000
2009 - 10	Year ended 31/12/2009		46,880

Barbie

	Basis period	Workings	Assessment £
2007 - 08	01/01/2008 to 05/04/2008	£80,000 x 3/12	20,000
2008 - 09	Year ended 31/12/2008		80,000
2009 - 10	Year ended 31/12/2009		69,520

Cinderella

	Basis period	Workings	Assessment £
2007 - 08	01/01/2008 to 05/04/2008	£120,000 x 3/12	30,000
2008 - 09	Year ended 31/12/2008		120,000
2009 - 10	Year ended 31/12/2009		163,600

Overlap profits:

The overlap period is from 1 January 2008 to 5 April 2008.
The overlap profits are: Cindy £10,000, Barbie £20,000 and Cinderella £30,000.

Answer 2

Basis periods for Kelly

Tax Year	Basis period Working	
2006 - 07	01/06/2006 - 05/04/2007	
2007 - 08	01/11/2006 - 31/10/2007	W1
2008 - 09	01/11/2007 - 31/10/2008	
2009 - 10	01/11/2008 - 31/07/2009	W2

Workings

W1

In the second year, as the accounting period that ends in that tax year is more than twelve months after the start of trading (seventeen months), the basis period is twelve months to the accounting date.

W2 Cessation of trade

The basis period for the tax year in which the trade ceases, runs from the end of the basis period for the previous tax year, to the date of cessation of trade.

Step 1: Find out the date of cessation

The date of cessation is 31 July 2009.

Step 2: Determine the tax year of cessation

The tax year of cessation is 2009 - 10.

Step 3: Determine the tax year prior to the tax year of cessation

The tax year prior to the tax year of cessation is therefore 2008 - 09.

Step 4: Determine the basis period for the period decided in step 3

The basis period for 2008 - 09 is the period from 1 November 2007 to 31 October 2008.
The end of the basis period for this tax year is therefore 31 October 2008.

Therefore, for the tax year of cessation 2009 - 10, the basis period is 1 November 2008 to 31 July 2009.

Overlap periods for Kelly

1. Kelly will have an overlap period of five months from 1 November 2006 to 5 April 2007. This period is common to 2006 - 07 and 2008 - 09. The overlap profits are eligible for deduction when she ceases to trade. Hence, profits earned during this period will be deducted from the profits earned during 1 November 2008 to 31 July 2009.

Basis periods and overlap periods for Millie

Tax Year	Basis period Working
2006 - 07	01/06/2006 – 05/04/2007
2007 - 08	01/11/2006 – 31/10/2007
2008 - 09	01/11/2007 – 31/10/2008
2009 - 10	01/11/2008 – 31/10/2009

2. Millie's basis periods for 2006 - 07 to 2008 - 09 and the overlap period are the same as Kelly's.

Basis periods for Celli

Tax Year	Basis period Working	
2007 - 08	1/12/07 – 5/04/08	
2008 - 09	1/12/07 – 30/11/08	W4
2009 - 10	1/11/08 – 31/10/09	

W4

In the second year, as the accounting period that ends in the tax year is less than twelve months after the start of trading (eleven months), the basis period is the first twelve months of trading.

Overlap periods for Celli

Celli will have an overlap period of four months from 1 December 2007 to 5 April 2008 (period common to 2007 - 08 and 2008 - 09) and one month from 1 November 2008 to 30 November 2008 (period common to 2008 - 09 and 2009 - 10). The overlap profits are eligible for deduction when she ceases to trade.

Answer 3

The profits / (losses) will be divided as follows:

	Total	Hira	Mira	Tara
	£	£	£	£
Year ended 31 December 2008 PSR (1:1:1)	60,000	20,000	20,000	20,000
Year ended 31 December 2009 PSR (1:1:1)	(90,000)	(30,000)	(30,000)	(30,000)

Mira is a continuing partner, Tara is a joining partner and Hira is a leaving partner.

Tara joined the business on 1 January 2008. Her basis period assessments will be as follows:

2007 - 08	01/01/2008 - 05/04/2008	3/12 x £20,000	£ 5,000
2008 - 09	01/01/2008 - 31/12/2008	Year ended 31 December 2008	£20,000
2009 - 10	01/01/2009 - 31/12/2009	Year ended 31 December 2009	£(30,000)

Tara will have an overlap period of 3 months from 1 January 2008 to 5 April 2008. Her overlap profit for this period is 3/12 x £20,000 = £5,000

Mira will have losses of £30,000 for the year ended 31 December 2009.

Hira ceases to trade and her final assessment is a loss of £30,000 plus an overlap profit relief of £9,000. This will increase her loss to £39,000.

Hence, the relief available to each partner is as follows:

Mira (continuing partner)
1. Section 64 and additional loss relief: There are three possible ways to claim relief under s64 and additional loss relief:
   a) Mira can claim the loss of £30,000 against TI of 2009 - 10 and then 2008 – 09 under s64. She can claim any remaining loss against the trading income of the previous three tax years, 2008-09, 2007-06 and 2006-07.
   b) Mira can claim the loss of £30,000 against TI of 2009-10 and then against trading income of the previous three tax years, latest first.
   c) Mira can claim the loss of £30,000 against TI of 2008 -09 and then against the trading income of 2007-08 and 2006-07.

2. Section 83: Mira can carry forward the loss of £30,000, to set off against future trading profits.

Tara (joining partner)
1. Section 72: Tara can claim the loss of £30,000 against TI of 2006 - 07 to 2008 - 09.
2. Section 64: Tara can claim the loss of £30,000 against TI of 2009 - 10 and / or 2008 - 09.
3. Section 83: Tara can carry forward the loss of £30,000 to set off against the future trading profits.

Hira (resigning partner)
1. Section 89: Hira can claim the loss of £39,000 against trading profits of 2008 - 09, then 2007 - 08 then 2006 - 07.
2. Section 64 and additional loss relief: This relief is available in the same way as Mira's.

Answer 4

Arnold's capital contributions for the purposes of loss relief restrictions are:

At 5 April 2010	£90,000
At 5 April 2011	£115,000 (£90,000 + £25,000)

Loss relief that may be claimed against other income is restricted to the amount of Arnold's capital contribution on 5 April 2010 (£90,000). Thus, Arnold is entitled to claim relief either under section 64 or section 72 against his other income or gains as follows:

Relief under	Against other income	Year
Section 72	£90,000	2006 – 07
Section 64	£90,000	2008 – 09 & 2009 - 10

Note: The remaining loss of £50,000 out of a total loss of £140,000 suffered in 2009 - 10, for which relief cannot be given against Arnold's other income or gains, can be carried forward under s83, and set against his share of the partnership's trading profits for 2010 - 11 and later years.

Answer 5

The allocation of trading profit for each accounting period is as follows:

	Total £	Tom £	Dick £	Harry £
Year ended 30/09/2007 (1:1)	220,000	110,000	110,000	
Year ended 30/09/2008 01/10/2007 to 31/12/2007 (3 months) £250,000 x 3/12 PSR (1:1)	62,500	31,250	31,250	
1/1/08 to 30/09/2008 (9 months) £250,000 x 9/12 PSR (5:3:2)	187,500	93,750	56,250	37,500
	250,000	125,000	87,500	37,500
Year ended 30/09/2009 PSR (5:3:2)	300,000	150,000	90,000	60,000

Each partner is treated as a sole trader.
Each partner's assessment is as follows:

Tom

	Basis period	Workings	Assessment £
2006 – 07	01/10/2006 to 05/04/2007	£110,000 x 6/12	55,000
2007 – 08	Year ended 30/09/2007		110,000
2008 – 09	Year ended 30/09/2008		125,000
2009 - 10	Year ended 30/09/2009		150,000

Dick

	Basis period	Workings	Assessment £
2006 – 07	01/10/2006 to 05/04/2007	£110,000 x 6/12	55,000
2007 – 08	Year ended 30/09/2007		110,000
2008 – 09	Year ended 30/09/2008		87,500
2009 - 10	Year ended 30/09/2009		90,000

Harry

	Basis period	Workings	Assessment
			£
2007 – 08	01/01/2008 to 05/04/2008	£37,500 x 3/9	12,500
2008 – 09	01/01/2008 to 31/12/2008	£37,500 + (£60,000 x 3/12)	52,500
2009 - 10	Year ended 30/09/2009		60,000

Overlap profits

For Tom and Dick, the overlap period is 1 October 2006 to 5 April 2007; the overlap profit for both of them is £55,000.

For Harry, the overlap period is 1 January 2008 to 5 April 2008 and 1 October 2008 to 31 December 2008.

Overlap profits are £12,500 + (£60,000 x 3/12) = £27,500.

Quick Quiz

1. What are the two steps to follow when dealing with a partnership?

2. Explain the basis by which partners are assessed to tax when they join a partnership.

3. Arnold and Bob have been in partnership for many years, preparing accounts to 31 December each year. They always shared profits equally until 1 October 2009 when they decided that Arnold should have a salary of £12,000 per annum and the balance of the profits should be shared 2:3.

   The partnership profits for the year to 31 December 2009 were £100,000.

   Required:

   Show the partners' trading income assessments for 2009 - 10.

4. Candice and Diane have been in partnership for many years, preparing accounts to 30 June each year. Ethel joins them on 1 January 2010.

   Required:

   What will be the basis period for each partner for 2009 - 10?

5. Fiona, Gertrude and Henrietta have been in partnership for many years preparing accounts to 31 August each year. Fiona leaves the partnership on 31 December 2009.

   Required:

   What will be the basis period for each partner for 2009 - 10?

6. Iris and Jade have been trading for many years, preparing accounts to 31 December each year. Kerry joined the partnership on 1 June 2009, and Jade resigned from the partnership on 31 October 2009. The partnership incurred a loss in the year to 31 December 2009.

   Required:

   What loss reliefs are available to each partner?

Answers to Quick Quiz

1. Step 1: allocate the profits between the partners in the profit sharing ratio of the accounting period.
   Step 2: treat each partner as a sole trader.

2. Each partner is treated as a sole trader running a business. The commencement rules apply when a partner joins the partnership, with the first year of assessment being on an actual basis.

3. Partner's trading income assessments

	Total £	Arnold £	Bob £
Year ended 31 December 2009			
01/01/2009 to 30/09/2009 (9 months)			
(£100,000 x 9/12 = £75,000)			
PSR (1:1)	75,000	37,500	37,500
01/10/2009 to 31/12/2009 (3 months)			
(£100,000 x 3/12 = £25,000)			
Salary x 3/12	3,000	3,000	
Balance PSR (2:3)	22,000	8,800	13,200
	100,000	49,300	50,700

4. Candice and Diane: year ended 30 June 2009 (CYB)

   Ethel: 1 January 2010 – 5 April 2010 (opening year rules)

5. Fiona: 1 September 2008 – 31 December 2009 (closing year rules)

   Gertrude and Henrietta: year ended 31 August 2009 (CYB)

6. **Iris:**
   - Section 64 against TI of 2009 - 10 and / or 2008 - 09.
   - Additional loss relief against trading income of 2008-09, then 2007-08 and then 2006-07.
   - Section 83 against future trading income.

   Jade:
   - Section 64 against TI of 2009 - 10 and / or 2008 - 09.
   - Additional loss relief against trading income of 2008-09, then 2007-08 and then 2006-07.
   - Section 89 against trading profits of 2009 - 10 then 2008 - 09, 2007 - 08 and 2006 - 07.

   Kerry:
   - Section 72 against TI of 2006 - 07, 2007 - 08 and 2008 - 09.
   - Section 64 against TI of 2009 - 10 and / or 2008 - 09.

Self Examination Questions

Question 1

Edwin and Frank began trading as a partnership on 1 August 2006, sharing profits in the ratio 60:40. They prepared accounts to 31 December 2006 and annually thereafter. George joined the partnership on 1 May 2008 and they shared profits equally from that date. On 31 December 2009, Edwin resigned; Frank and George continued to share the profits equally.

The trading profits earned by the partnership are as follows:

	£
1/08/2006 to 31/12/2006	18,900
Year ended 31/12/2007	48,000
Year ended 31/12/2008	120,000
Year ended 31/12/2009	99,000

Required:

Show the allocation of profits to the partners for each accounting period.

Question 2

Continuing with Edwin, Frank and George calculate the trading income assessments for 2006 - 07 to 2009 - 10 and identify any overlap profits.

Answers to Self Examination Questions

Answer 1

Allocation of profits to the partners

	Total £	Edwin £	Frank £	George £
01/08/2006 to 31/12/2006				
PSR (60:40)	18,900	11,340	7,560	
Year ended 31/12/2007				
PSR (60:40)	48,000	28,800	19,200	
Year ended 31/12/2008				
01/01/08 – 30/4/2008 (4 months)				
(£120,000 x 4/12)				
PSR (60:40)	40,000	24,000	16,000	
01/05/2008 – 31/12/2008 (8 months)				
(£120,000 x 8/12)				
PSR (1:1:1)	80,000	26,667	26,667	26,666
	120,000	50,667	42,667	26,666
Year ended 31/12/09				
PSR (1:1:1)	99,000	33,000	33,0000	33,000

Answer 2

	Basis period	Working	Edwin £	Frank £	George £
2006 – 07	01/08/2006 - 05/04/2007	01/08/2006 – 31/12/2006	11,340	7,560	
		01/01/2007 – 05/04/2007			
		3/12 x Year ended 31/12/2007	7,200	4,800	
		Trading income assessment	18,540	12,360	
2007 – 08	01/01/2007 – 31/12/2007	Trading income assessment	28,800	19,200	
2008 - 09	01/01/2008 – 31/12/2008		50,667	42,667	
	01/05/2008 – 05/04/2009	01/05/2008 – 31/12/2008			26,666
		1/01/09 – 5/04/09			
		3/12 x Year ended 31/12/2009			8,250
		Trading income assessment	50,667	42,667	34,916
2009 - 10	01/01/2009 – 31/12/2009		33,000	33,000	33,000
		Less: Overlap (01/10/2007 to 05/04/2007)	(7,200)		
		Trading income assessment	25,800	33,000	33,000
		Overlap carried forward		4,800	8,250

Note:

The basis period for the first tax year runs from the date of the start of trade, to the following 5 April. Hence, the basis period for Edwin and Frank is 1 August 2006 to 5 April 2007 for their first tax year 2006 - 07. For George it is 1 May 2008 to 5 April 2009 for his first tax year 2008-09.

Closing year rules will be applicable to a partner leaving the partnership. Hence, the basis period for the tax year of cessation 2009 - 10 for Edwin is from 1 January 2009 to 31 December 2009. He is also eligible to deduct overlap profits from the profits earned during this period.

The overlap period for Edwin and Frank is 1 January 2007 – 5 April 2007, the overlap period for George is 1 January 2009 – 5 April 2009.

Edwin resigned on 31 December 2009, so he may relieve his overlap in 2009 – 10.

SECTION B: INCOME TAX LIABILITIES — B4

STUDY GUIDE B4: PROPERTY AND INVESTMENT INCOME

Get Through Intro

Property income, received from letting out properties, is taxed according to specific rules. **Income from investments** consists of **dividends received** from company shares and **interest received** on savings.

This Study Guide discusses the provisions for the computation of property business income, income from investments and tax exempt investments.

As a tax consultant, you need to be aware of all these provisions in order to compute the correct tax liability of your clients on their property business income and investment income. A **thorough knowledge of all these provisions** will **ensure that the best use is made of all the benefits and reliefs available**

This knowledge will help you to solve the questions in your examination with confidence.

Learning Outcomes

a) Compute property business profits.
b) Explain the treatment of furnished holiday lettings.
c) Describe rent-a-room relief.
d) Compute the amount assessable when a premium is received for the grant of a short lease.
e) Understand how relief for a property business loss is given.
f) Compute the tax payable on savings income.
g) Compute the tax payable on dividend income.
h) Explain the treatment of individual savings accounts (ISAs) and other tax exempt investments.

Introduction

On the death of her father, Jane inherits a house. Instead of disposing of the house and creating a potential capital gain, she decides to rent it out for additional income. The process of renting out a property for which one receives income is known as a "property business".

This income is known as unearned income. Most income received from land and property in the UK is taxed under the property income rules. In the following Study Guide we shall see how to compute income from lettings, what expenses are allowable against the income and the specific deductions available for the taxpayer.

> 1. **Compute property business profits.**[2]
>   **Compute the amount assessable when a premium is received for the grant of a short lease.**[2]
>
>   [Learning outcomes a and d]

For individuals, property income now falls within the scope of income tax.

1.1 What is property income?

Income from land and buildings

> **Example**
> Wilson rents out his flat to William at an annual rent of £12,000. In this case, rent received by Wilson (i.e. £12,000 per annum) is his property business income.

The main classes of property income are as follows:

1. **Rents of property**

> **Example**
> Sally lets out her flat to Mike for a monthly rent of £880. The rent received is her property business income.

2. **Lease premiums on short leases** (A short lease is a lease for a period less than 50 years.)

> **Example**
> Jo lets out a commercial property on a 20-year lease for an annual rent of £1,000 and a premium of £5,000. The rent (£1,000) as well as the lease premium will be her property business income.

The treatment of lease premiums is discussed in detail later in this Study Guide.

The following points are extremely important

1. **Accruals Basis:** the income should be computed on an accruals basis.

> **Example**
> Arnold, a trader, buys a new property on 1 July 2009. He let out the property for an annual rent of £12,000 payable in advance.
>
> Rent due for 2009–10 is £12,000 (being annual rent payable in advance).
>
> Rent accrued on 5 April 2010 is £12,000 x 9/12 = £9,000.

2. **Aggregation of expenses / income if more than one property:** when rent is generated from letting more than one property, all the rents and expenses for all the properties let out are pooled together, and a single amount is calculated.

Example John lets out one office for an annual rent of £5,000 and one shop for an annual rent of £6,000. He paid insurance of £300 for the office and £200 for the shop.

Here, property business income will be calculated as:

	£
Rent from office	5,000
Rent from shop	6,000
Total	**11,000**
Less: Insurance expenses (£300 + £200)	500
Property business income	**10,500**

3. **Deductible expenses from rental income:** as we have seen for a trading business, **expenses incurred wholly and exclusively for the property business** are deductible from rental income, to arrive at the taxable property income. Some examples of allowable expenses are:

a) expenses towards repairs and maintenance
b) insurance
c) agents fees
d) interest on loans to purchase / improve the property
e) the cost of providing services to the tenants
f) administrative and management costs
g) bad debts (if rents are not paid)

4. **Letting out furnished property:** when property is let out with furniture, the following two choices are given to the taxpayer. He will need to **opt for one of them**.

a) **Renewals basis:** in this option, no deductions are allowed for the cost of the original furniture. However, if the furniture is subsequently replaced, the **full cost of the replacement** of the furniture is treated as revenue expenditure, and hence is **fully deductible.** It is very important to note here that if the replacement cost includes any component attributable to improvement, as opposed to simple replacement, then the improvement portion is not deductible.

b) **10% wear and tear basis:** in this option, the actual cost of furniture is ignored and a straight **10% of rent** is allowed as a deduction. If any liabilities of the tenant are paid by the landlord, e.g. council tax and water rates, then such amounts are first deducted from the rent received. Then 10% of the remaining balance is allowed as a wear and tear allowance.

1.2 Premiums received for the grant of a short lease

A premium refers to lump sum payments made by a tenant to the landlord on the **grant of a lease** to the tenant. The tax treatment of these premiums depends upon the nature of the lease i.e. whether it is a short lease or a long lease.

Short Lease: if the lease is granted for a period of **50 years or less** then it is termed a short lease. Premiums received on a short lease are **assessable to property business income.** The amount to be assessed to property business income is equal to the amount of **premiums reduced by 2% for each year of the lease, except for the first year.**

Premium assessable to property business income
= P – P (2% x (n- 1))

Where, P = Premium
n = no. of years of lease

Diagram 1: Short lease

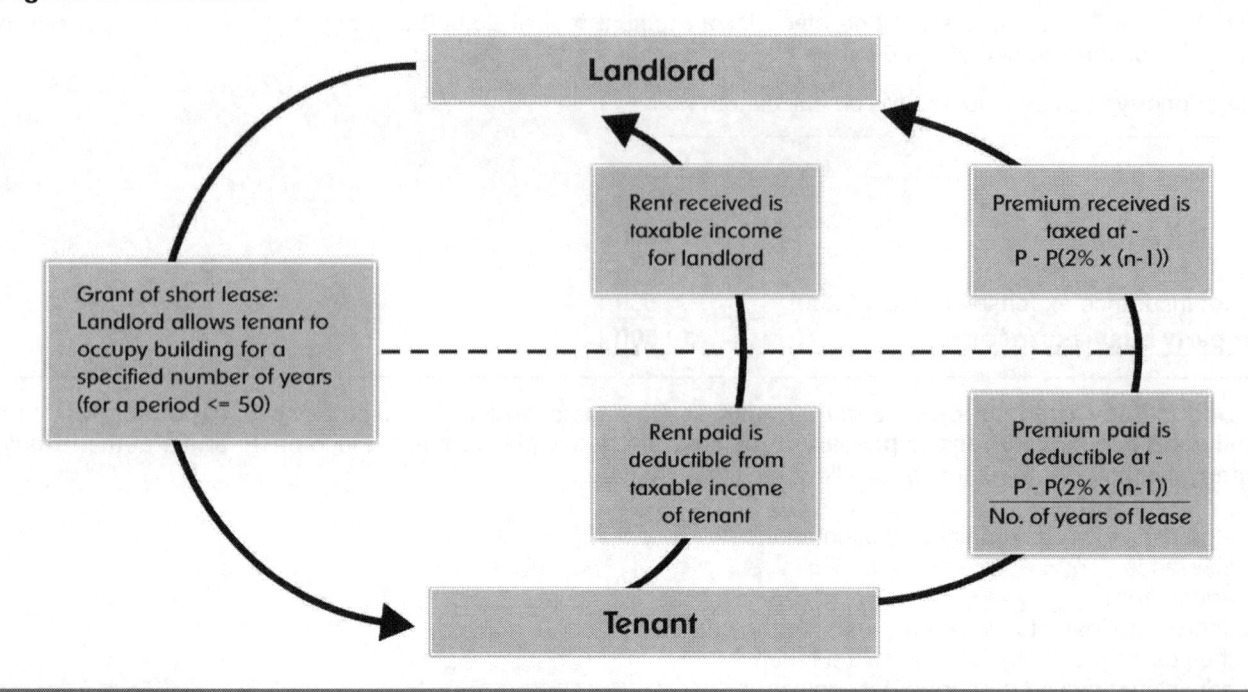

- **Grant of short lease:** Landlord allows tenant to occupy building for a specified number of years (for a period <= 50)
- **Rent received is taxable income for landlord**
- **Premium received is taxed at -** P - P(2% x (n-1))
- **Rent paid is deductible from taxable income of tenant**
- **Premium paid is deductible at -** P - P(2% x (n-1)) / No. of years of lease

Example

Frank, a trader, receives a premium of £20,000 from his tenant for the grant of a 20 year lease, in 2009 - 10. What is Frank's property income in respect of this premium?

The premium is reduced by 2% for property business income computation purposes. Therefore, by reducing 2% each year except for the first year, 38% (19 years x 2%) of the premium is deductible. Thus, the remaining 62% is taxable in the year of receipt.

Property business income for premium = P – P (2% x (n- 1))
= £20,000 – £20,000 (2% x (20 – 1))
= £12,400

The property business income for 2009 -10 for premium is £12,400.

SUMMARY

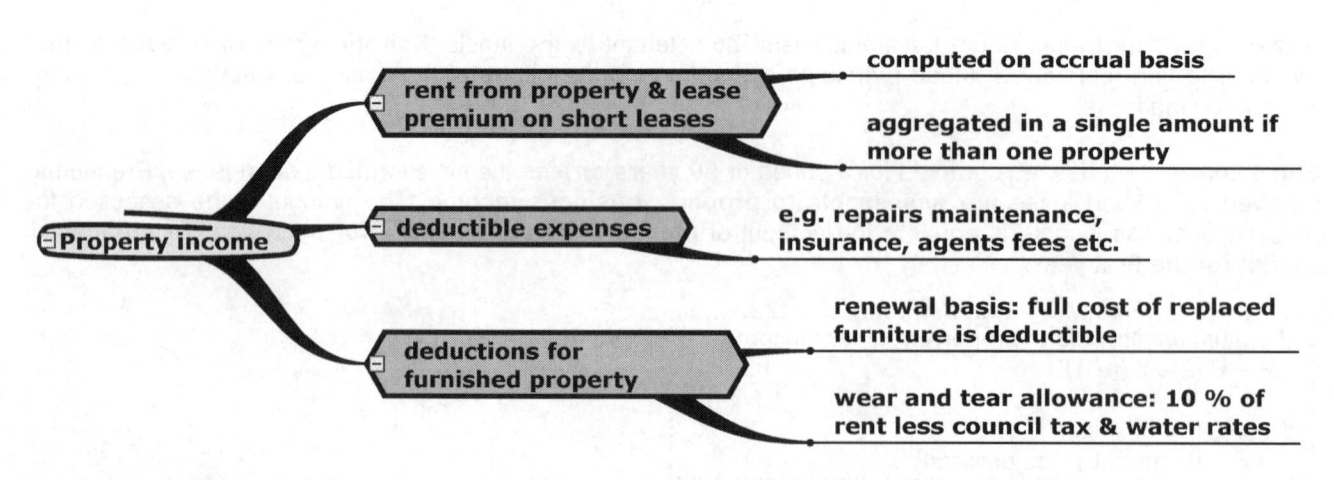

Property income
- **rent from property & lease premium on short leases**
  - computed on accrual basis
  - aggregated in a single amount if more than one property
- **deductible expenses**
  - e.g. repairs maintenance, insurance, agents fees etc.
- **deductions for furnished property**
  - renewal basis: full cost of replaced furniture is deductible
  - wear and tear allowance: 10 % of rent less council tax & water rates

---

Test Yourself 1

Fenny, a trader receives a premium of £12,000 from her tenant for the grant of a 12 year lease, in 2009-10. What is Fenny's property income in respect of this premium?

Test Yourself 2

Robert prepares his accounts up to 31 March every year. He owns three shops, a furnished flat and an office building, which he has rented out. Rent on the property is due monthly in advance on the 1st of every month.

The details of the property rented out during the year ended 31 March 2010 are:

1. Shop 1 was let out at £5,500 p.a. throughout the year.
2. Shop 2 was let out at £6,600 p.a. from 1 December 2009.
3. Shop 3 was let out at £7,500 p.a. to 30th June. On 31 May 2009, £1,000 was received. The tenant became bankrupt and the balance of the rent was not received.
4. The furnished flat was let out throughout the year as furnished accommodation at £2,500 p.a.
5. The office building was let out unfurnished on 1 October 2009 on a 10 year lease at a premium of £20,000 and annual rent of £6,000. The rent for one year was received in advance.

Robert incurs the following expenses

a) Repairs of shop 1 in June 2009, £2,000.
b) Insurance per shop £500 p.a., for flat £200, for office £2,100.
c) Interest on the loan taken to purchase shop 2, £1,500.
d) Advertisement expenses for obtaining tenants for shop 2, £1,200 and for the office £1,000.

Required:

Compute Robert's property income chargeable to tax.

---

2. Explain the treatment of furnished holiday lettings.[1]

[Learning outcome b]

Furnished holiday letting is also known as qualifying holiday accommodation.

If the letting of furnished property satisfies certain conditions, it qualifies as income from the "commercial letting of furnished holiday accommodation". **Such income is treated as income from trade and not as income from property business. It gives extra tax relief.**

Conditions to be satisfied to qualify as a holiday let are:

➢ available for commercial letting to the public for at least 140 days in a tax year, and

➢ actually let as holiday accommodation in this period for at least 70 days (excluding periods of long term occupation – explained below)

➢ periods of longer term occupation must not exceed 155 days.

A period of longer term occupation occurs when the property is in the same occupation for more than 31 days.

> **Tip**
> If a taxpayer owns two or more properties **which satisfy the 140 day** condition, **but do not satisfy the 70 day condition, then** the properties will be regarded as satisfying the 70 day rule, **if the average number of days let is at least 70 days.**

The benefits of treating income from furnished holiday lettings as a trading income

➢ Income is regarded as earned income and qualifies as "net relevant earnings" when determining the extent to which tax relief is available on contributions to pension scheme. (Net relevant earnings and pension contributions are discussed in detail in Study Guide B6).

➢ Losses arising are treated as trading losses, (not property business losses), and therefore relief is available accordingly.

➢ Capital gains tax and rollover relief may be available.

➢ Capital allowances are permitted in respect of furniture (wear and tear allowances and the renewals basis of allowances do not apply).

SUMMARY

Furnished holiday letting
- treated as income from trade
- **conditions**
  - available for commercial letting for at least 140 days
  - actually let as holiday accommodation for at least 70 days
  - periods of longer term < 155 days
- **benefits**
  - qualifies as " net relevant earnings"
  - losses are treated as trading losses
  - capital gains & rollover relief are available
  - capital allowance is permitted

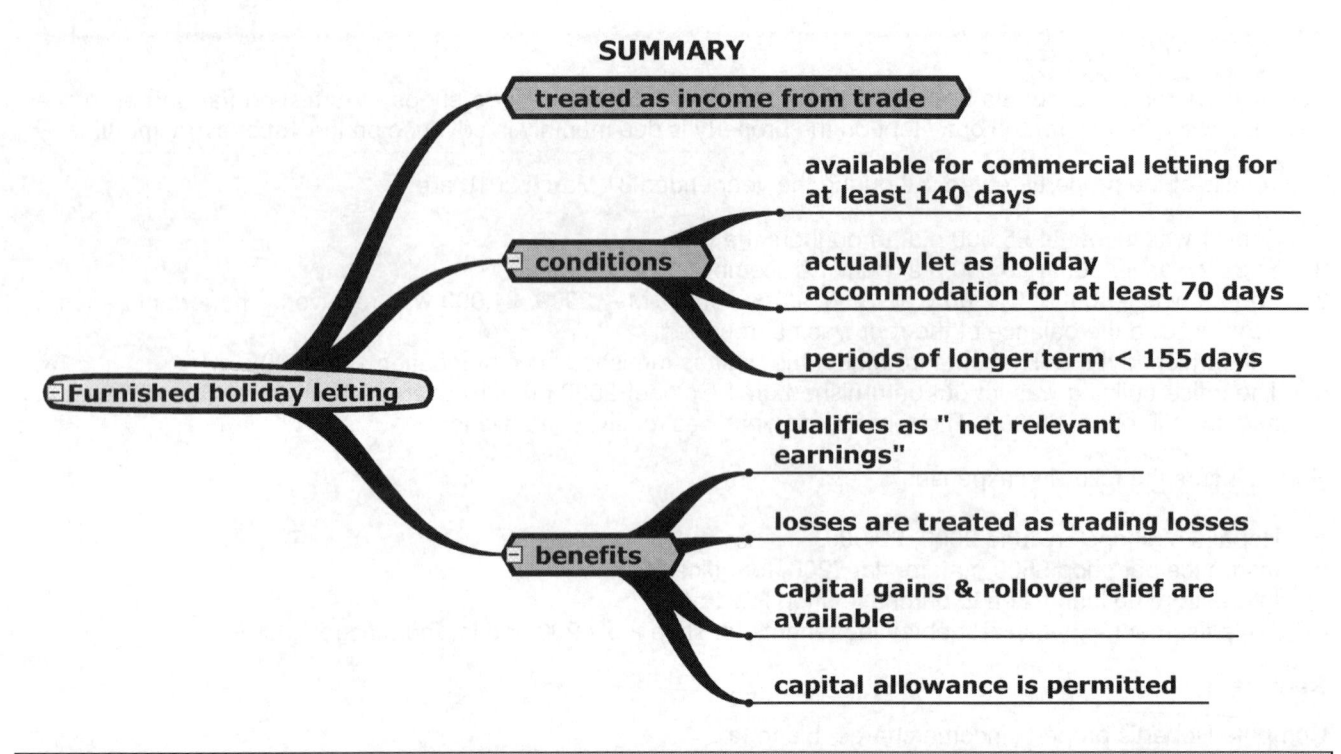

3. Describe rent-a-room relief.[1]

[Learning outcome c]

Gross rents (i.e. rents with no deduction for expenses) up to a specified limit (£4,250 for 2009 - 10) are exempt from income tax if they relate to the letting of furnished accommodation, **which is part of an individual's main residence.**

Example
Ming owns a house, which has 8 rooms. She rents out one of the rooms for £4,000 per annum. In this case, income up to £4,250 (total income of £4,000 in this case) is exempt from tax.

If the gross rent exceeds £4,250, the taxpayer may elect to either:

a) be assessed on the excess of gross rents over £4,250 with no expense deductions, or

b) apply normal property business income rules with no deduction for rent-a-room relief.

Example
Terri owns a house, which has 8 rooms. She rents out one of the rooms for £6,000 per annum. Terri has the following two options:

1. Either to apply normal property business income rules i.e. not to take up the rent-a-room exemption. The income assessable in this case will be £6,000 less any allowable expenses incurred, for example, repairs, wear and tear allowance, council tax etc.

2. To take up the exemption. However, in this case, any expenses incurred will not be deductible. In other words, the income assessable will be £6,000 - £4,250 = £1,750. Any expenses, for e.g. repairs incurred, will not be deductible.

This option is to be exercised by the taxpayer **by 31 January in the second tax year following the tax year to which the option relates.**

Example
For the tax year 2009 - 10 the taxpayer has until 31 January 2012 to elect whether he wants to use the rent-a-room exemption or whether he wants to apply normal property business income rules.

> **Tip:** Full exemption (i.e. £4,250) is available even if the property is not let out throughout the whole tax year. The exemption is not apportioned.

Test Yourself 3

Burley owns a house. He prepares his accounts up to 31 March every year. He rented out a room to a tenant on 1 June 2009 for £7,000 p.a. He incurred the following expenses for the let out portion of the property.

	£
Agent commission for obtaining tenant	350
Repairs to the staircase	420
Insurance	600

Required:

Calculate his property income by applying rent-a-room relief and applying normal business income rules for the year-ended 31 March 2010. Decide which is more beneficial.

---

4. Understand how relief for a property business loss is given.[2]

[Learning outcome e]

1. All property receipts and all property expenses are pooled to give an overall profit or loss figure for the year. The losses from the running of one property business are automatically **offset against other property income.**

2. The losses from running a property business are carried forward to the next tax year.

3. To carry forward a loss, it is necessary that the **property business must continue** i.e. if a property business ceases to exist, and then the carry forward of the property business loss is not allowed.

4. The carried forward loss can be set off against the first available property income, arising in the subsequent tax years.

Test Yourself 4

Ronny prepares his accounts up to 31 March every year. He owns two shops, and a flat, which he has rented out. Rent on the property is due quarterly, in advance, on 1 January, 1 April etc. The details of the property rented out during the year ended 31 March 2010 are:

➢ Shop 1 was let out at £1,800 p.a. throughout the year.

➢ Shop 2 was let out at £3,400 p.a. from 1 May 2009.

➢ The flat was let throughout the year at £1,300 p.a., and was unfurnished.

Ronny incurs the following expenses:

➢ Repairs to shop 1 in January 2010, £5,300.
➢ Insurance per shop £900 p.a., for flat £350.
➢ Interest on loan taken to purchase shop 2, £2,100.
➢ Advertisement expenses for obtaining tenants for shop 2, £200.

Required:

Compute property business income/loss. In the case of a loss, explain the loss relief provisions.

SUMMARY

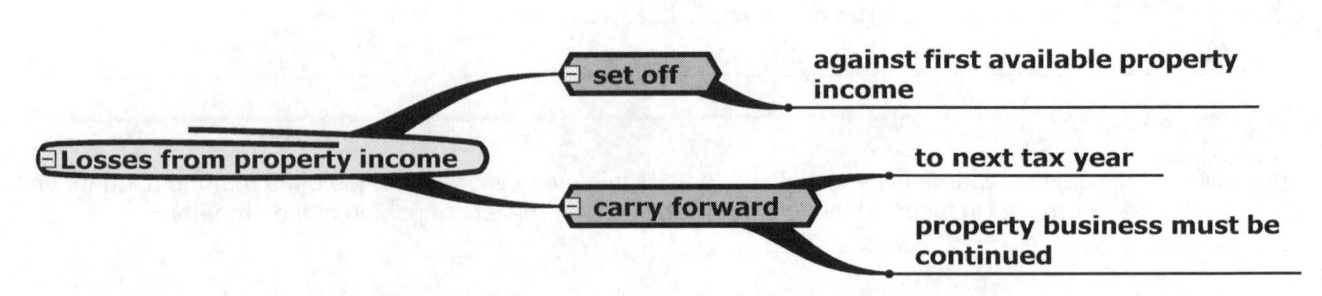

Losses from property income
- set off → against first available property income
- carry forward → to next tax year; property business must be continued

5. Compute the tax payable on savings income.[2]

[Learning outcome f]

Many people try to save a proportion of their salary for the future. HMRC states that savings income consists of:

- Interest on debentures and loan stock paid by UK companies to individuals
- Bank interest
- Building Society interest

> **Tip** — **Building society**: A building society is very similar to a bank. It is an organisation which offers customers the opportunity to invest their money in a variety of accounts for a given rate of interest. Building societies typically offer services such as mortgage lending and investment planning.

Savings income is usually received **net of tax at 20%, which** means at the time of receiving the income; the basic rate tax is already deducted at source. The amount received has to be grossed up, by multiplying it by **100/80** to include it as gross income in the income tax computation. The tax deducted at source is deducted while computing tax payable.

> **Tip** — In the exam, make sure you read the question carefully, whether the amount of saving income is given gross or net.

If the net amount received or credited is given, you should gross up the figure at the rate of 20%, for the tax computation.

Example

The interest received from a building society is £160. This amount is net of a 20% tax deduction.

The equivalent gross income is £160 × 100/80 = £200 on which tax of £40 (20% of £200) has been suffered.

Although the interest paid by banks and building societies to individuals is generally paid net of 20% tax, if a recipient is not liable to tax, he can either recover the tax suffered, or he can certify in advance that he is a non-taxpayer and can receive the gross interest.

Tax on savings income

Savings income is taxed after non-savings income.

Income tax is charged first on non-savings income, which is income from employment, self-employment and property, then on savings income and finally on dividend income. Tax rates and income tax calculations are covered in detail in Study Guide B5.

When is interest taxable?

Interest is taxable in the **tax year that it is paid to the taxpayer,** or credited to his account, **even if part of it has been earned in the previous tax year.** So, the taxpayer does not have to include the gross interest earned in the current year if it has not been paid yet.

Test Yourself 5

John Smith has the following income and payments for the tax year 2009 - 10.

- Salary £32,500 (gross; PAYE deducted of £2,500)
- Bank interest £2,400 (net)
- Building society interest £800 (net)
- Interest paid on loan for qualifying purposes £2,000 (net)

Required:

Compute his total income for 2009 - 10.

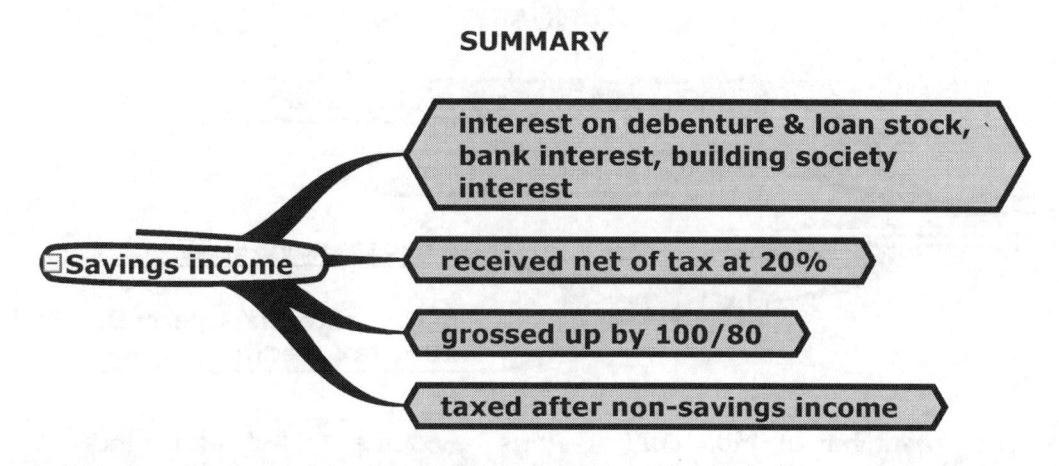

SUMMARY

Savings income
- interest on debenture & loan stock, bank interest, building society interest
- received net of tax at 20%
- grossed up by 100/80
- taxed after non-savings income

---

6. Compute the tax payable on dividend income.[2]

[Learning outcome g]

6.1 Dividend income

Dividends from UK shares are deemed to be received **net of a 10% tax credit. Therefore any dividend received needs to be grossed up by 100/90 for inclusion in income tax computation.**

Example

You receive £180 as a dividend from a UK company. Dividends are received net of a 10% tax credit. To find the gross amount of the dividend, multiply the net amount by 100/90.

In this case, the gross dividend is 180 x 100/90 = £200, which is the amount entered into the income tax computation, with a tax credit of £20 (£200 - £180).

The amount of dividend received from UK company shares is grossed up by multiplying it by **100/90**. The gross amount is included in the income tax computation. The tax credit can be **deducted** in computing tax payable, **but any excess tax credit cannot be repaid under any circumstances.** Therefore, tax credits on dividends should always be deducted first to reduce an individual's tax liability and to ensure that the credit is not lost.

The government provides a 'tax credit' to shareholders amounting to 10% of the dividend income, to take account of the fact that dividends are paid out of profits that have been already taxed (the company which is paying the dividend must have already paid tax, and a dividend is paid from profits remaining after paying corporation tax). Therefore, when dividends are issued, you will receive a statement showing both how much was paid and the amount of the tax credit.

6.2 Tax on Dividend Income

There are two levels of tax on dividends. Basic rate taxpayers are taxed at 10%, which is covered by the tax credit issued, so there is no further tax to pay. Higher rate taxpayers pay 32.5% less 10% tax credit (i.e. effective rate of tax of 22.5%).

The rate at which tax is payable depends on whether the overall taxable income (after allowances) falls within or above the basic rate income tax limit. Tax rates on dividends have been discussed in detail in Study Guide B5.

Test Yourself 6

Jack has taxable Income as follows:

- £52,500 Employment income (Gross, PAYE deducted £4,500)
- £4,000 Interest income (net)
- £4,200 Dividend income (net)

Required:

Compute Jack's total income.

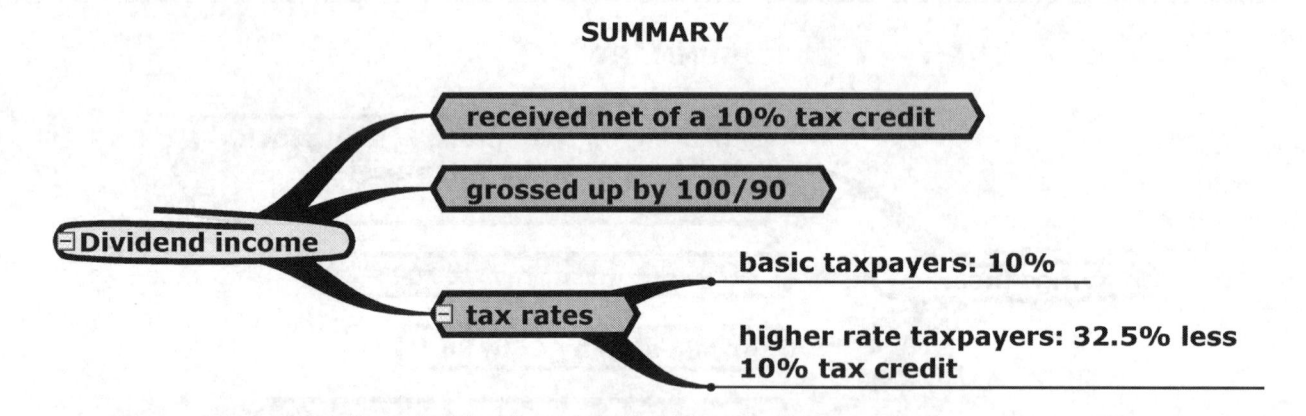

SUMMARY

Dividend income
- received net of a 10% tax credit
- grossed up by 100/90
- tax rates
  - basic taxpayers: 10%
  - higher rate taxpayers: 32.5% less 10% tax credit

---

7. Explain the treatment of individual savings accounts (ISAs) and other tax exempt investments.[1]

[Learning outcome h]

7.1 Individual Savings Account (ISA)

What is an Individual Savings Account (ISA)?

An ISA is a financial product available in the UK. It is a **tax efficient** way of **saving or investing**. An ISA investment will be free from UK personal income tax and capital gains tax.

An ISA can contain **two components**

1. A **cash** component: cash ISAs' allow savers to invest their money to accrue interest just like it would in an ordinary bank or building society account, but with the advantage of receiving interest tax-free. Cash ISAs can be a useful place to put money in order to receive tax-free interest and have easy access at relatively short notice.

2. A **stocks and shares** component: share ISAs' will invest in the stock market. As a consequence, the risk profile of the ISA may be anything from low to high. Share ISAs' should, like all stock market investments, be considered a long term investment.

Subscription limits for ISA

There are restrictions on how much an individual can invest in an ISA in each tax year (6 April to the following 5 April).

The amounts which may be deposited in an ISA in a tax year are fixed by law. The overall limit for investment in ISA in 2009 - 2010 is £7,200.

The individual limits for cash ISAs' and stocks and shares ISAs' are:

a) Cash ISA: up to a maximum of £3,600
b) Stocks and shares ISA: up to a maximum of £7,200
c) The overall limit for investment in both ISA's is £7,200.

Example: Nikon Ltd offers an ISA that contains a cash component and a stocks and shares component. Their investors can subscribe up to £3,600 to the cash component ISA, and can subscribe the remaining £3,600 to the stocks and shares component. Alternatively, investors could subscribe an overall amount of £7,200 to the stocks and shares component.

Example: Jones subscribes £2,000 to cash ISA in the year 2009-10. In that same year he can subscribe up to £5,200 in a stocks and shares ISA. Alternatively, he can also subscribe a further £1,600 to his cash ISA, and up to £3,600 in a stocks and shares ISA.

The Finance Act 2009 has introduced a separate limit for investment in ISAs' for **individuals aged 50 and above**. The overall limit for investment in ISAs' for these individuals for the tax year 2009-10 is £10,200. Individual limits for cash ISAs' and stocks and shares ISAs' are:

a) Cash ISA: up to a maximum of £5,100
b) Stock and shares ISA: up to a maximum of £10,200.
c) The overall limit for investment in both ISA's is £10,200.

Example: Lisa, who is 52 years old, subscribes £3,000 to the cash component of an ISA in 2009-10. She can subscribe a further £2,100 to the cash component of the ISA, with the balance up to the overall annual limit of £10,200 in the stocks and shares component. She can alternatively choose to put all the remaining balance of £7,200 into the stocks and shares component.

Important points to note

i. Any UK resident individual of at least eighteen years of age can invest in **one ISA,** with both components provided by a single financial institution.

ii. Alternatively, a person can invest in **two ISAs,** one for each component i.e. cash component and a stocks and shares component. The two ISAs' may be with two different providers if the investor wishes.

iii. UK resident individuals aged between 16 and 18 can also open cash ISAs', but can only allocate their investment to the cash component.

Example: Edward opens an ISA on 10 April 2008. He will be 18 years old on the 5 May 2008. He can subscribe up to £3,600 to the cash component of his ISA before he becomes 18, but chooses to subscribe only £1,000. After his 18th birthday he can subscribe up to £2,600 to the cash component and any balance remaining up to the overall annual limit of £7,200 to the stocks and shares component, before 6th April 2009.

Tax treatment of income arising from ISA

➤ **All income (dividends, interest and bonuses) received from ISA investments are tax-free.**
➤ **All capital gains arising on ISA investments are exempt from capital gains tax.**

> **Tip — ISA Rules**
>
> For individuals below the age of 50: max £3,600 per year in cash ISA & £7,200 per year in stocks and shares ISA, with an overall annual investment limit of £7,200.
>
> For individuals aged 50 and above: max £5,100 per year in cash ISA & £10,200 per year in stocks and shares ISA with overall annual investment limit of £10,200.

7.2 Other tax-exempt investments

National Saving Certificates

It is a tax efficient way of saving money. National saving products are a popular mode of investment mainly because of their risk-free nature.

National savings offer various investment products, some of which are tax-free e.g. national savings certificates, children's bonus bonds etc. The income from these investments is exempt from income tax as well as capital gains tax.

National savings also offers some taxable investment products e.g. investment accounts, easy access savings accounts etc. The income on these investments is usually paid in gross and taxed as savings income.

SUMMARY

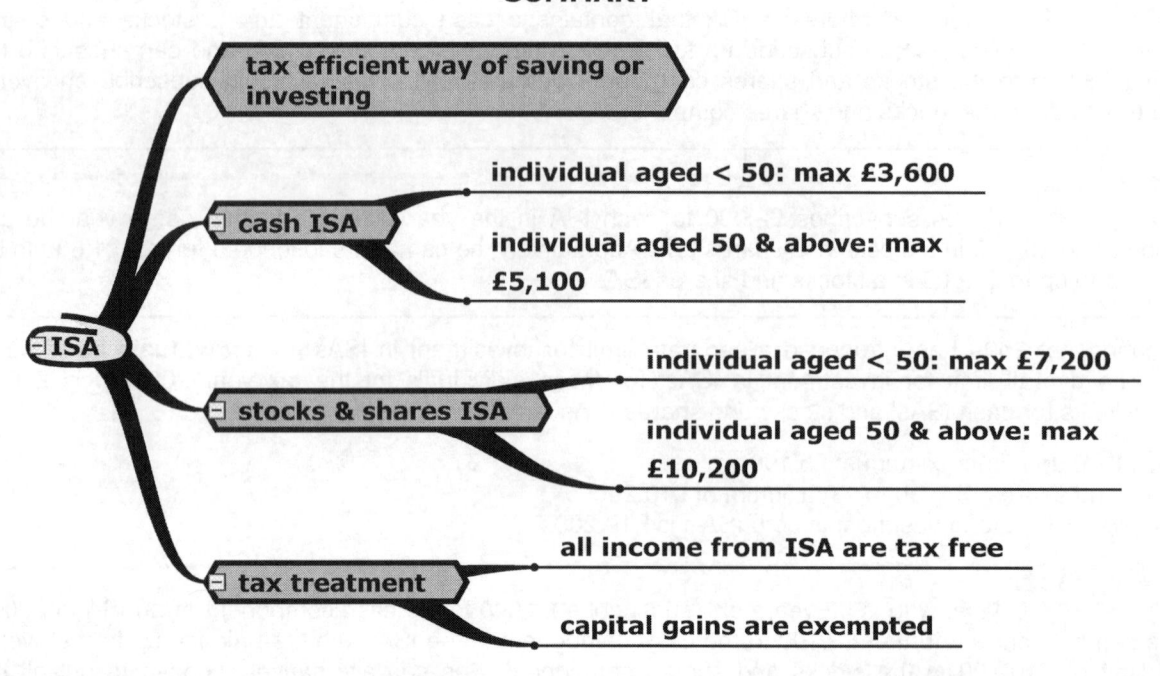

- **ISA**
  - tax efficient way of saving or investing
  - **cash ISA**
    - individual aged < 50: max £3,600
    - individual aged 50 & above: max £5,100
  - **stocks & shares ISA**
    - individual aged < 50: max £7,200
    - individual aged 50 & above: max £10,200
  - **tax treatment**
    - all income from ISA are tax free
    - capital gains are exempted

Answers to Test Yourself

Answer 1

	£
Gross premium	12,000
Less: £12,000 (2% x (12 -1))	(2,640)
Property business income for premium	9,360

Answer 2

	Shop 1 £	Shop 2 £	Shop 3 £	Flat £	Office £	Total £
Rent accrued						
Shop 1	5,500					5,500
Shop 2 (1/12/09 to 31/03/10) (£6,600/12 x 4)		2,200				2,200
Shop 3 (1/04/09 to 30/06/09) (£7,500/12 x 3)			1,875			1,875
Furnished flat				2,500		2,500
Office building						
Rent £6,000/12 x 6					3,000	3,000
Lease premium						
Gross premium 20,000						
Less: £20,000 x (2% x (10 - 1)) (3,600)						
Net lease premium = 16,400					16,400	16,400
Total rent accrued (a)	5,500	2,200	1,875	2,500	19,400	31,475
Less : Expenses						
Repairs	2,000					2,000
Bad debts			875			875
Insurance	500	500	500	200	2,100	3,800
Interest on loan		1,500				1,500
Advertising expenses for obtaining tenants		1,200			1,000	2,200
10% wear & tear on furnished flat (£2,500 x 10%) (note 3)				250		250
Total expenses incurred (b)	2,500	3,200	1,375	450	3,100	10,625
Property business profit (a - b)	3,000	(1,000)	500	2,050	16,300	20,850

Net property business profit is **£20,850**.

Only £1,000 could be recovered out of £1,875, so £875 is a bad debt.

Notes:

1. All property receipts and all property expenses are pooled to give an overall profit or loss figure for the year. The losses from the running of one property business are automatically **set-off against the income from other property businesses**

2. The property business loss of shop 2 is automatically set off against other property business income. (Refer to Learning Outcome 5).

3. 10% wear and tear allowance is allowed as a deduction for the furnished property. It is calculated at the rate of 10% of rent less any liabilities of the tenant paid by the landlord.

Answer 3

1. **By applying rent-a-room relief**

	£
Rent	5,833
Less: rent-a-room relief	(4,250)
Property business income assessable to tax	**1,583**

House rented on 1/06/09 to 31/03/10 i.e. 10 months. So, rent = £7,000 x 10/12 = £5,833

2. **By applying normal property business income rules**

	£	£
Rent		5,833
Less: expenses		
1) Agent commission for obtaining tenant	(350)	
2) Repairs of the staircase	(420)	
3) Insurance	(600)	(1,370)
Property business income assessable to tax		**4,463**

Thus, as income assessable to tax is lower in option 1, it is advisable to obtain rent-a-room relief and show £1,583 as income chargeable to tax.

Answer 4

	Shop 1 £	Shop 2 £	Flat £	Total £
Rent accrued				
Shop 1	1,800			1,800
Shop 2 (1/05/08 to 31/03/09) (£3,400/12 x 11)		3,117		3,117
Flat			1,300	1,300
Total rent accrued (a)	**1,800**	**3,117**	**1,300**	**6,217**
Less : Expenses				
Repairs	5,300			5,300
Interest on loan to purchase property		2,100		2,100
Insurance	900	900	350	2,150
Advertising expenses for obtaining tenants		200		200
Total expenses incurred (b)	**6,200**	**3,200**	**350**	**9750**
Property business profit (a - b)	**(4,400)**	**(83)**	**950**	**(3,533)**

Net loss is £3,533. This loss of the property business can be carried forward to the next tax year i.e. tax year 2010-11.

The carried forward loss must be set off against the first available property income arising in the subsequent tax years. For example in 2010-11, if Ronny's property business income is £6,500, then the carried forward loss of £3,533 will be first set off against this, so the taxable income for 2010-11 will be (£6,500 - £3,533 = £2,967).

For the carry forward of property business losses, it is necessary that the **property business should be continued.** Therefore, if Ronny ceases the property letting business, then the carry forward of property business losses is not allowed.

Answer 5

While calculating John's total income, ensure all his income has been grossed up.

John Smith's total income calculation for 2009 - 10 is as follows:

	Non savings £	Savings income £	Total income £
Income from employment	32,500		32,500
Building society interest (£800 x 100/80)	-	1,000	1,000
Bank interest (£2,400 x 100/80)	-	3,000	3,000
	32,500	4,000	36,500
Less: Interest paid	(2,000)		(2,000)
Total Income	**30,500**	**4,000**	**34,500**

Note: The building society and bank interest received were £800 and £2,400 respectively. They have each been grossed up by multiplying by 100/80 to take account of the 20% tax withheld at source.

Answer 6

Jack's total income is computed as follows:

	Non savings income £	Savings income £	Dividend income £	Total income £
Income from employment (W1)	52,500			52,500
Interest income (W1)		5,000		5,000
Dividend income (W1)		-	4,667	4,667
Total Income	**52,500**	**5,000**	**4,667**	**62,167**

Workings

W1

Jack's interest income and dividend income needs to be grossed up to take account of income tax deducted at source:
Savings income = £4,000 x 100/80 = £5,000
Dividend income = £4,200 x 100/90 = £4,667

Quick Quiz

State true or false

1. Rent a room relief is available in full even if the property was not let out throughout the year.

2. A short lease is a lease granted for a period of 30 years or less.

3. Non-savings income is taxed after savings income.

Answers to Quick Quiz

1. True, rent a room relief is never apportioned on a time basis.

2. False, a short lease is a lease granted for a period of 50 years or less.

3. False, savings income is taxed after non-savings income.

Self Examination Questions

Question 1

What are the advantages of property income being treated as income from furnished holiday accommodation?

Question 2

What is the treatment of a premium received on short lease?

Question 3

When is interest taxable?

Question 4

In 2009 - 10 Thelma received income from property. Details of the income and corresponding expenses were:

1. Rent from letting out a room in her house for £2,600. The repairs expenditure incurred on this room was £3,200.

2. Rent from a furnished flat. The flat had been let on a lease which expired on 30 June 2009 at an annual rent of £5,500. The property was re-let from 1st July 2009 on a nine-year lease, at an annual rent of £6,000. In addition, the incoming tenant was required to pay a premium of £4,000. Thelma elects to claim wear and tear allowance on this property.

    Expenditure in the year ended 5 April 2010 was:

    a) insurance of £350 was paid.

    b) water rates and council tax £1,400.

    c) sundry repairs £650.

    The rent on both leases was paid in advance on the usual quarter days, 25 March, 24 June, 29 September and 25 December.

3. The rent received from a furnished cottage was £5,200 and the following expenditure was incurred:

	£
Insurance	600
Water rates and council tax	900
Sundry repairs and decorating	350
Cleaning	240
Bad debts	200
Advertising	300
Capital allowances on furniture and fittings, adjusted for private use	500
	3,090

Thelma stayed in the cottage for the whole of August, but it was let out for the remainder of the year.

Required:

Calculate Thelma's property income for the year 2009 - 10.

Answers to Self Examination Questions

Answer 1

The tax advantages of property income being treated as income from furnished holiday accommodation are:

1. relief for losses sustained may be offset against other income as if they were trading losses,

2. the income qualifies as 'net relevant income' for the purpose of pension contributions,

3. certain capital gains tax reliefs, e.g. rollover relief, retirement relief and relief for gifts of business assets are available and

4. capital allowances may be claimed on furniture and fittings.

Answer 2

If the lease is granted for a period of **50 years or less** then it is termed a short lease. Premiums received on a short lease are **assessable to property** business income. The amount to be assessed to property income is equal to the amount of the **premium reduced by 2% for each year of the lease, except for the first year.**

> Premium assessable to property business income
> = P – P (2% x (n- 1))
>
> Where, P = Premium
> n = no. of years of lease

Answer 3

Interest is taxable in the **tax year that it is paid to the taxpayer,** or credited to his account, **even if part of it has been earned in the previous tax year.** So a taxpayer does not have to include the gross interest earned in the current year when working out his taxable income if it has not been paid yet.

Answer 4

	Room £	Furnished flat £	Cottage £	Total £
Rent accrued				
Room in house (note)	2,600			2,600
Furnished flat:				
Rent (£5,500/12 x 3)		1,375		1,375
Rent (£6,000/12 x 9)		4,500		4,500
Lease premium				
Gross premium 4,000				
Less: £4,000 x (2% x (9 - 1)) 640		3,360		3,360
Cottage			5,200	5,200
Total rent accrued (a)	**2,600**	**9,235**	**5,200**	**17,035**
Less: **Expenses**				
Repairs	3,200	650	321	4,171
Water rates and council rates		1,400	825	2,225
Insurance		350	550	900
Cleaning			220	220
Advertising			300	300
Bad debts			200	200
10% wear & tear (W1)		448	438	886
Total expenses incurred (b)	**(3,200)**	**(2,848)**	**2,854**	**8,902**
Property business profit (a - b)	**(600)**	**6,387**	**2,346**	**8,133**

Net property business profit is **£8,133.**

Note: If rent a room relief is claimed, the amount up to £4,250 is exempt. As the rent received is less than £4,250, if rent a room relief is claimed, the taxable income will be nil.
However, it is beneficial not to claim rent a room relief as a loss arising after deduction of allowable expenses, i.e. (£2,600 - £3,200 = £600) can be claimed to offset against other income.

Workings

W1

It is stated that the cottage was occupied by Thelma for the month of August. Hence the following expenses will be proportionately reduced for private use.

	Total expenses £	Deduction for private use £	Expenses allowed £
1) Repairs	350	29 (350/12 x 1)	321
2) Water rates and council rates	900	75 (900/12 x 1)	825
3) Insurance	600	50 (600/12 x 1)	550
4) Cleaning	240	20 (240/12 x 1)	220

Total expenses for 1 year are £350. Therefore for 1 month they are 350/12 = £29

W2 Wear and tear allowance.

The wear and tear allowance is available on letting out a the furnished property, hence it will be available on both furnished flat and furnished cottage.
The 'wear and tear' allowance is 10% of the rent (excluding lease premium) less the items which would normally be the tenant's responsibility, i.e. water rates and council tax.

	Furnished flat £	Cottage £
Rent:		
Furnished flat (£1,375 + £4,500)	5,875	
Cottage		5,200
Less: Water rates and council tax	1,400	(825)
	4,475	4,375
Wear and tear allowance 10%	448	438

SECTION B: INCOME TAX LIABILITIES

B5

STUDY GUIDE B5: THE COMPREHENSIVE COMPUTATION OF TAXABLE INCOME AND INCOME TAX LIABILITY

Get Through Intro

In this Study Guide we look at how the different types of an individual's income are classified, and the types of payment that are given tax relief. The sum of the different types of income, less allowable deductions gives the taxable income figure. We will then see how to calculate the income tax on this figure, noting that different types of income are taxed at different rates of income tax.

In your work as an accountant, you will need to calculate the income tax liability of clients, and also give advice on how to minimise their tax liability.

This Study Guide is very important from an exam point of view. The first question in your exam will be on income tax. In addition, aspects of this Study Guide are likely to be examined in other questions.

You need to make sure that you have a thorough understanding of this Study Guide.

Learning Outcomes

a) Prepare a basic income tax computation involving different types of income.
b) Calculate the amount of personal allowance available to people aged 65 and above.
c) Compute the amount of income tax payable.
d) Explain the treatment of interest paid for a qualifying purpose.
e) Explain the treatment of gift aid donations.
f) Explain the treatment of property owned jointly by a married couple, or by a couple in a civil partnership.

Introduction

McMilan is a sole trader, earning trading income. In addition he receives bank interest and dividends. These three different types of income are all charged to income tax at different rates.

You are given the rates in your tax rates and allowances in the exam, but it is essential that you know how to apply the rates.

This Study Guide explains the steps to follow in order to get the calculation correct.

1. Prepare a basic income tax computation involving different types of income.[2]
[Learning outcome a]

Income tax is a tax on the earnings or income of individuals, which they receive in different ways, and from different sources. Not all the income is taxable. Individuals are taxed only on 'taxable income' above a certain level. Income tax assessments of a taxpayer are computed for a tax year, taking into consideration his aggregate income for that year from all sources, and ignoring any income which is exempt from tax. Some basic concepts are as follows:

1. All adults and children are charged to income tax if they receive sufficient income to pay tax.
2. They are liable to income tax on their taxable income in a tax year.
3. A tax year runs from 6 April to the following 5 April. The exam will cover the period 6 April 2009 to 5 April 2010, written as 2009 - 10.
4. Taxable income is made up of:

- income from all sources
- payments that are tax deductible
- personal allowances

The basic calculation of income tax payable is as follows:

Calculation of income tax payable	£
Earned income	X
Investment income	X
Total Income	**X**
Less: Payments that are tax deductible	(X)
Net income	**X**
Less: Personal allowances	(X)
Taxable income	**X**
Income tax liability	X
Less: Tax suffered	(X)
Income tax payable	**X**

1.1 Taxable persons

Each individual is liable for tax on his own income. In general, a UK resident is liable to pay income tax for all his income earned during the tax year (whether it arises in the UK or abroad). Individuals who are not UK residents are generally only liable to pay tax on their UK income. Income tax is payable by:

1. **Adults:** on their income and on their share of income of a partnership.
2. **Children:** if they have taxable income.

1.2 Income tax computation

The total income of an individual comprises:

1. earned income
2. investment income

Earned income consists of:

- income from employment
- income from self-employment (as a sole trader or partner)

Investment income consists of:

- savings income (e.g. bank interest, building society interest)
- dividend income
- other income from investments (property income)

In order to calculate taxable income, we need to look at the various types of income.

Income is either:

- exempt from income tax, or
- taxable

Taxable income is either:

- taxed before it is received by the taxpayer (taxed at source), or
- tax is paid by the taxpayer through self assessment (income received gross).

In order to calculate taxable income, earned and investment income is aggregated. Exempt income is excluded.

Income taxed at source

All taxable income is included in the calculation of an individual's taxable income, whether it is received gross (and taxed by self assessment) or received net (tax already deducted before being paid to the individual).

The statement of taxable income consists of the gross amount of income from all sources as the amount of tax already deducted may be too small or too large. The gross amount is charged to tax, and then the tax already deducted is taken into account.

Income taxed at source may have different rates of tax deducted:

	Received net of
Building society interest	20% tax
Bank interest (except National Savings Bank interest)	20% tax
Debenture interest	20% tax
Patent royalties	20% tax
UK dividends	10% tax
Employment income	Various rates (paid net under PAYE – Pay As You Earn scheme)

Important point to note

- Most interest is received net of 20% tax.
- Building society interest is treated in the same way as bank interest.
- Care must be taken in the exam to determine if the income given to you is gross, or net (after the tax has been deducted).
- If bank interest, for example is given net, then multiply this figure by 100/80 to find the gross figure for the calculation of taxable income.
- If you are given the net figure for bank interest, to find the tax deducted, multiply the net figure by 20/80.

Income taxed by self assessment

Some income is received gross. The individual is liable to pay tax to HMRC via self-assessment at a later date.

The main types of income received gross are:

- trading income (income from self-employment or partnership income)
- property income (income from letting out land and buildings)
- interest received gross

Interest received gross

Most of the interest income is received net of 20% tax.

The main types of interest received gross are:

- National Savings Bank interest (NSB)
- Interest from Government securities

Taxable income is the total figure charged to tax, however, different categories of income are charged at different rates, so the taxable income needs to be categorised.

The categories are as follows:

- non-savings income
- savings income
- dividend income

Non-savings income	Savings income	Dividends
Employment income	Interest received gross	UK dividends
Pension income	Interest received net	
Trading income		
Property income		
Patent royalties		

The total income, less any tax deductible payments is known as **net income**.

Every individual is entitled to a personal allowance, and this is deducted from the **net income** to give the **taxable income.**

1.3 Income exempt from tax

Certain types of income are completely exempt from income tax. Some of the important sources of non-taxable income are:

1. Scholarship income
2. Interest on National Saving Certificates.
3. Winnings from betting, national lottery and premium bond prizes.
4. Income of up to £4,250 per annum received under the "rent–a-room" scheme (see Study Guide B4 for more details).
5. Statutory redundancy pay and the first £30,000 of compensation received for loss of employment.
6. Interest received from HMRC (repayment supplement).
7. Certain social security benefits like child benefit and housing benefit.

> **2. Calculate the amount of personal allowance available to people aged 65 and above.[2]**
> **[Learning outcome b]**

Personal Allowance (PA)

Every individual living in the UK is entitled to a personal allowance. This is available from the year of birth to the year of death.

The personal allowance for 2009 - 10 is £6,475. This figure is given to you in the rates and allowances in the exam. The personal allowance is deducted from net income. If there is insufficient income to absorb the allowance, it is lost.

> **Tip**: The personal allowance is never time apportioned. It is always allowed in full. It cannot be carried forward to the next year or be used to create a tax loss.

Income is categorised into non-savings, savings and dividend income. The personal allowance must be set off against non-savings income, then, if it is not fully utilised, against savings income and finally dividend income.

Personal Age Allowance (PAA)

As older people living off a pension are likely to have a smaller income than people working, they are given a higher age allowance, instead of the personal allowance.

The amount of the allowance is dependant on their age and their net income.

A personal age allowance is available to a taxpayer who is **65 or over** at any time in the tax year. These figures are given to you in the exam in rates and allowances, so you don't need to memorise them. The amounts of allowances available are as follows:

	2009 - 10 £
Personal allowance for people aged 65 - 74	9,490
Personal allowance for people aged 75 and over	9,640
Income limit for age-related allowances	22,900

> **Tip**
> A taxpayer is considered to be:
> ➢ 65 if his 65th birthday falls anywhere in the tax year.
> ➢ 75 if his 75th birthday falls anywhere in the tax year.
>
> A taxpayer born before 6 April 1945 is entitled to a personal age allowance.

Test Yourself 1

Calculate the personal allowances available to each of the following taxpayers in 2009 - 10.

1. Peter born on 31 July 1933
2. Mark born on 1 May 1929
3. Brian born on 12 November 1940
4. Alex born on 1 January 1983

The personal age allowances are reduced if the taxpayer's net income exceeds a set limit. The set limit for 2009 - 10 is £22,900. If a taxpayer's net income **exceeds £22,900**, the **personal age allowance** is **reduced by one half of the excess**.

> **Example**
> John, a taxpayer aged 67 has a net income of £23,100 for 2009 - 10. The maximum net income limit for 2009 - 10 is £22,900. Therefore, John's net income exceeds the limit by £200. The personal age allowance of £9,490 will be reduced by one half of the excess. John's allowance is (£9,490 - ½ x £200) = £9,390.

> **Tip**
> It is important to note that the reduction may reduce the personal age allowance to £6,475 but no further. The allowance of £6,475 is the minimum allowance available to everyone.

SUMMARY

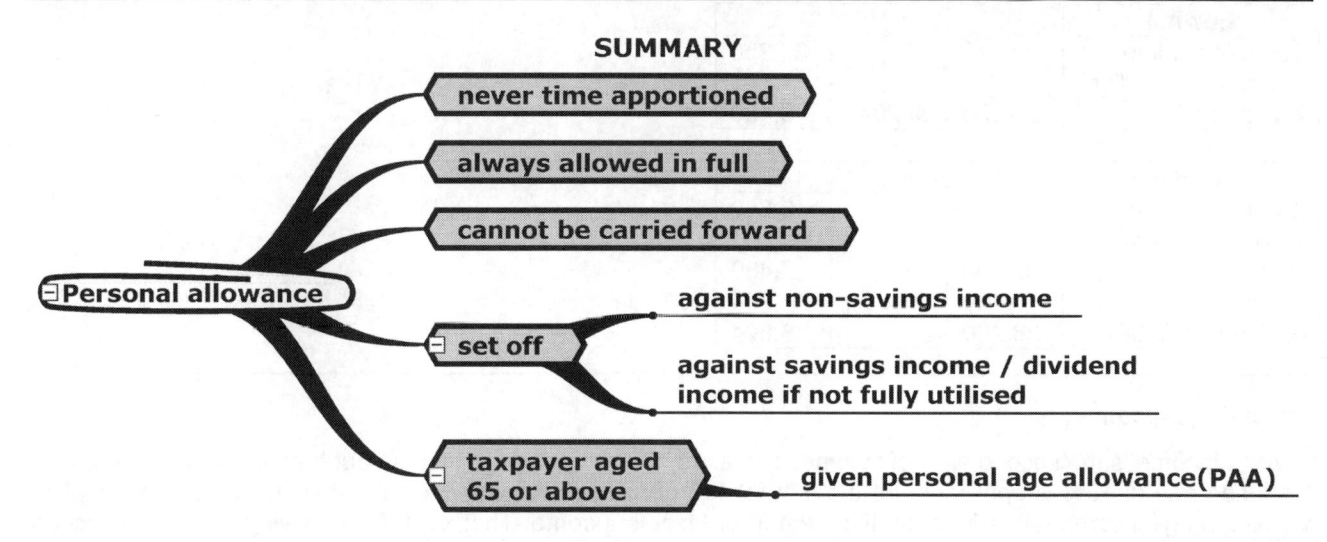

Personal allowance
- never time apportioned
- always allowed in full
- cannot be carried forward
- set off
  - against non-savings income
  - against savings income / dividend income if not fully utilised
- taxpayer aged 65 or above — given personal age allowance (PAA)

B5.6: Income Tax Liabilities © GTG

Test Yourself 2

Calculate the personal allowances available in 2009 - 10 for the following taxpayers:

1. Adam, born on 1 November 1931 with net income of £34,200 in 2009–10.
2. Barry, born on 12 January 1946 with net income of £32,000 in 2009-10.
3. Charles, born on 23 August 1944 with net income of £14,300 in 2009-10.
4. David, born on 10 July 1934 with net income of £9,800 in 2009–10.
5. Edwin, born on 5 October 1943 with net income of £24,100 in 2009-10.

3. Compute the amount of income tax payable.[2]

[Learning outcome c]

Once the income has been categorised and the personal allowance deducted (from non-savings income, then savings income and dividends) the income tax liability can be calculated.

It is necessary to arrange the taxable income in 'slices', with non-savings income at the bottom, followed by savings income then dividend income.

3.1 Non-savings income

In 2009 - 10 non-savings income, which is the bottom slice of taxable income, is taxed at the following rates:

Income tax band	Income tax rate
£1 - £37,400	Basic rate of 20%
Over £37,400	Higher rate of 40%

Example   In 2009 - 10 Arthur, Edwina and Cordelia receive the following non-savings taxable income, (after deducting personal allowances):

	£
Arthur	1,200
Edwina	27,250
Cordelia	40,860

They receive no other taxable income in 2009 - 10. Their tax liability for 2009 - 10 is as follows:

Arthur	£		£
Taxable income			1,200
Income tax liability			
Basic rate	1,200	at 20%	240

Edwina	£		£
Taxable income			27,250
Income tax liability			
Basic rate	27,250	at 20%	5,450

Cordelia	£		£
Taxable income			40,860
Income tax liability			
Basic rate	37,400	at 20%	7,480
Higher rate	3,460	at 40%	1,384
Income tax liability	38,260		8,864

3.2 Savings income

Savings income is the second slice of income; it is taxed after non-savings income but before dividend income. A starting rate of 10% is applicable for the first £2,440 of savings income. However this 10% rate only applies where savings income falls within the first £2,440 of taxable income. Therefore if non-savings income exceeds £2,440 the starting rate of 10% for savings will not apply. In this case the savings income will be taxed at the basic rate of 20% if it falls below the higher rate threshold of £37,400, and at the higher rate of 40% if it exceeds the threshold.

Example

Sophie aged 67 has an income from her pension that amounts to £11,200, and bank interest of £3,900 (net). Her income tax liability is as follows:

	Total £	Non-savings income £	Savings income £
Pensions	11,200	11,200	
Bank Interest (£3,900 x 100/80)	4,875		4,875
Total / Net income	**16,075**	**11,200**	**4,875**
Less: Personal allowance	9,490	9,490	-
Taxable income	**6,585**	**1,710**	**4,875**
Income tax:			
Non-savings income £1,710 at 20%	342		
Savings income (which falls within first £2,440 of taxable income) (£2,440 - £1,710) = £730 at 10%	73		
£4,145 at 20%	829		
Income Tax liability	**1,244**		

Note: non savings income does not exceed the starting rate threshold of £2,440, so £730 (£2,440 -£1,710) of the savings income is taxed at the starting rate of 10%, and the balance of the savings income, £4,145 (£4,875 - £730), is taxed at the basic rate of 20%.

Tip

The personal allowance is always set off against non-savings income first.

Example

Norman receives the following income in 2009 - 10:

	£
Salary	27,200
Bank deposit interest (amount received)	800

Norman's income tax payable for 2009 - 10 is as follows:

	Total £	Non-savings £	Savings £
Employment income	27,200	27,200	
Bank deposit interest (£800 x 100/80)	1,000		1,000
Total income / Net Income)	**28,200**	**27,200**	**1,000**
Less: PA	(6,475)	(6,475)	
Taxable income	**21,725**	**20,725**	**1,000**
Tax on taxable income:			
Non-savings: basic rate band (£21,725 at 20%)	4,345		
Savings: basic rate band (£1,000 at 20%)	200		
Income tax liability	**4,545**		
Less: tax deducted at source (£1,000 x 20%)	(200)		
Tax payable	**4,345**		

Notes:
1. Bank deposit interest is received net of 20% tax, so this is grossed up by 100/80.
2. The personal allowance is deducted from the non-savings income first.
3. The non-savings income is taxed first, fully utilising the starting rate band of 10% for the first £2,440 of savings income.
4. The savings income does not fall within the starting rate band of 10%, but falls in the basic rate band, so is taxed at 20%.
5. The income tax calculated is the 'tax liability'; this is the total liability to tax. Tax has already been deducted at source from the bank interest. This is deducted in order to arrive at the tax payable i.e. the amount of tax that is outstanding.
6. The salary will have been taxed under PAYE, which will further reduce the tax payable.

3.3 Dividend income

Dividend is declared by companies after they have paid corporation tax. Therefore when the dividend is received by an individual there is a 10% tax credit. This is why it is grossed up by 100/90. As long as the dividend income is below the base band of £37,400 it is taxed at 10%. Thus, the individual does not have to pay any further tax on the dividend with the 10% tax credit off setting the tax payable. If the dividend income falls outside the base band of £37,400 it will be taxed at 32.5% so that the individual will have to pay an additional tax of 22.5% (32.5% - 10%).

Dividend income is the top slice of income; it is taxed after non-savings and savings income. To the extent that dividend income falls in the basic rate band it is taxed at 10%, if it falls in the higher rate band, it is taxed at 32.5% (not 40% as for savings and non-savings income).

Remember, the personal allowance is always set off against non-savings income first. If non-savings income does not exceed the personal allowance, then the personal allowance is set off against savings income and finally dividend income.

Summary of tax rates

Income Tax Band	Non-savings income	Savings income	Dividend income
Starting rate band: £1 to £2,440		10%	
Basic rate band: £1 to £37,400	20%	20%	10%
Higher rate band: £37,400 and above	40%	40%	32.5%

For the tax year 2009 - 10, the first £2,440 of savings income is taxed at 10%. However, if non-savings income exceeds £2,440 the starting rate of 10% for savings will not apply. In this case savings income will be taxed at the basic rate of 20% if it falls below the higher-rate threshold of £37,400, and at the higher rate of 40% if it exceeds the threshold.

If non-savings income is below £2,440, then the starting rate of 10% will be applicable to savings income falling within the first £2,440 of taxable income. If non-savings income exceeds £2,440, then the starting rate of 10% will not apply to any savings income.

Dividends are taxed at the lower rate of 10% if they fall below the higher rate threshold of £37,400 and at the higher rate of 32.5% where they exceed the threshold.

> **Tip**
> The bands and rates for non-savings income are given to you in the exam. You are not given the rates for savings income and dividend income.

Diagram 1: Summary tax rates

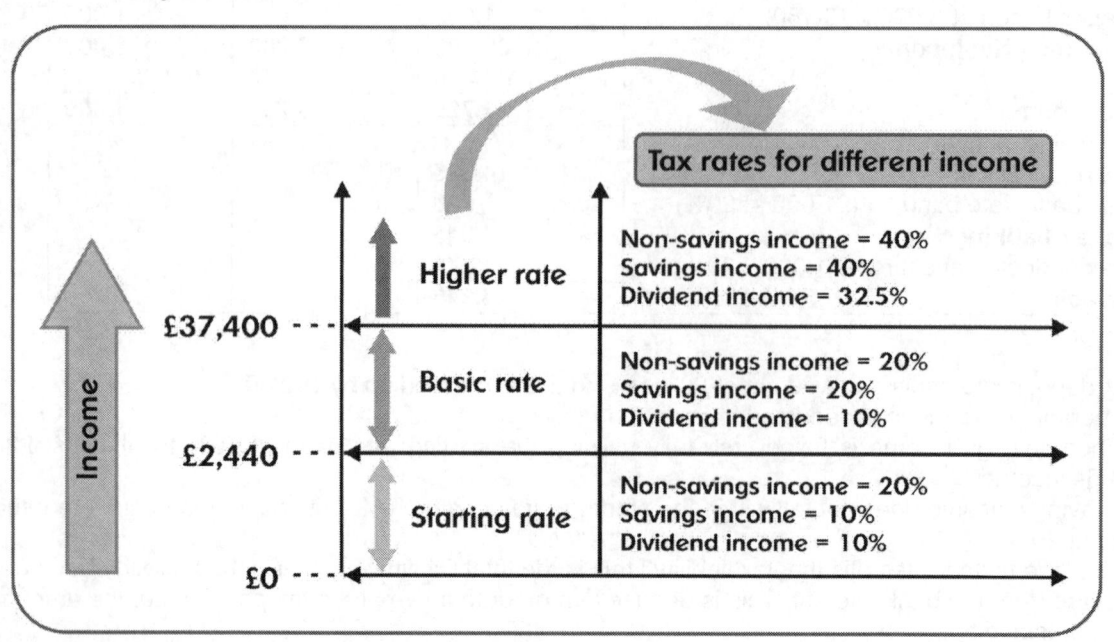

Income

£37,400 — Higher rate
- Non-savings income = 40%
- Savings income = 40%
- Dividend income = 32.5%

Basic rate
- Non-savings income = 20%
- Savings income = 20%
- Dividend income = 10%

£2,440 — Starting rate
- Non-savings income = 20%
- Savings income = 10%
- Dividend income = 10%

£0

Tax rates for different income

Total income tax liability is calculated by applying the tax rates as discussed above. **Income tax payable / repayable** is calculated by deducting the tax already suffered on the income, for example, PAYE deducted from salary income.

Example

James aged 35 has received the following income in 2009 - 10:

	£
Salary	22,500
Building society interest (cash amount received)	3,800
Dividends (cash amount received)	18,900

James's income tax liability for 2009 - 10 is computed as follows:

	Total £	Non-savings £	Savings £	Dividends £
Employment income	22,500	22,500		
Building society interest (£3,800 x 100/80)	4,750		4,750	
Dividend income (£18,900 x 100/90)	21,000			21,000
Total / Net Income	48,250	22,500	4,750	21,000
Less: PA	(6,475)	(6,475)		
Taxable income	41,775	16,025	4,750	21,000
Income tax				
Non-savings: basic rate band (£16,025 x 20%)	3,205			
Savings: basic rate band (£ 4,750 x 20%)	950			
Dividends: basic rate band (£16,625 x 10%)	1,663			
£ 37,400				
Dividends: higher rate band (£4,375 x 32.5%)	1,422			
Income tax liability	7,240			

Steps for calculation of income tax liability

Step 1
Ensure that all James's income has been grossed up if any income tax has been deducted before James received it:

Salary: £22,500 (this is the gross amount).
Building society interest: £3,800 x 100/80 = £4,750 (tax of 20% has been deducted).
Dividend income: £18,900 x 100/90 = £21,000 (cash amount of dividends must be grossed up by 100/90).

Step 2
Deduct personal allowance. This is always deducted from non-savings income first, leaving £16,025 (£22,500 - £6,475) of taxable non-savings income.

Step 3
Compute the income tax liability for each category of income, starting with non-savings income, then savings and finally dividend income.

Non-savings income

The first £37,400 of non-savings income is taxed at the basic rate of 20%.
£16,025 x 20% = **£3,205**

Savings income

The savings income of £4,750 is taxed at 20%.
£4,750 x 20% = **£950**

(This is because the sum of non-savings income of £16,025 plus savings income of £4,750 i.e. £20,775 is still within the basic rate band of £37,400).

Dividend income

The dividend income falls partly in the basic rate band and partly in the higher rate band.

The amount falling in the basic rate band is £16,625 (£37,400 - £20,775) and is taxed at 10%.
£16,625 x 10% = **£1,663.**

The amount falling in the higher rate band is £4,375 (£21,000 - £16,625) and is taxed at 32.5%.
£4,375 x 32.5% = £1,422.

The figure of £7,240 is the income tax liability. If asked for the income tax payable, then PAYE and tax suffered is deducted from this figure.

B5.10: Income Tax Liabilities © GTG

Test Yourself 3

In 2009 - 10, Jo aged 35 has trading income of £17,450, and receives bank interest of £640 (amount received).

Required:

Calculate Jo's income tax payable for 2009 - 10.

Test Yourself 4

In 2009 - 10 George aged 55 Years, Harry aged 62 years and Duncan aged 40 years receive the following income:

	Employment Income £	Pension Income £	Savings Income (Net) £
George	18,750		1,200
Harry		8,000	3,200
Duncan	56,400		1,800

Required:

Calculate their income tax payable or repayable for the tax year 2009 - 10.

4. Explain the treatment of interest paid for a qualifying purpose. [2]
[Learning outcome d]

Certain payments of eligible interest made by a taxpayer are entitled to tax relief. These payments are deducted from taxable income.

Eligible interest

Eligible interest is paid gross, and deducted in the calculation of taxable income.

The loan must be used for a qualifying purpose, which includes:
1. The purchase of plant and machinery by an employee which is used in the performance of his duties.
2. The purchase of plant or machinery by a partner which is used in the business.
3. The purchase of an interest in a partnership or contribution to the partnership by way of capital or loan.

Treatment of interest paid for a qualifying purpose

The gross amount of the interest is deducted from income, to give net income. The interest is deducted first from non-savings income, then savings income and finally from dividend income, in the same way as personal allowances.

The taxpayer will obtain full tax relief as the interest is reducing the amount of income taxed.

Example

In 2009-10 Anthony and Bob both aged 35 years, have trading income of £45,000 and £26,200 respectively. Anthony paid interest on a loan for qualifying purposes of £200 (gross).

Their income tax liabilities are calculated as follows:

	Anthony £	Bob £
Trading income	45,000	26,200
Less: Interest paid	(200)	
Net Income	**44,800**	**26,200**
Less: Personal allowance	(6,475)	(6,475)
Taxable Income	**38,325**	**19,725**
Income tax		
£37,400 / £19,725 at 20%	7,480	3,945
£925 at 40%	370	-
	7,850	3,945

5. Explain the treatment of gift aid donations.[1]

[Learning outcome e]

The gift aid scheme allows tax relief for gifts of money by individuals to charities.

The relief applies to all charitable donations other than gifts through the payroll giving scheme.

A donation must be a payment of a sum of money.

The conditions for gift aid relief to apply are as follows:

1. The payment must not be repayable to the individual.
2. The donor must give the charity a gift aid declaration.

Payments of any amount may qualify for gift aid relief; there is no minimum or maximum amount.

Tax relief for gift aid payments

Tax relief is given at the individual's highest marginal rate of tax. This is achieved as follows:

Basic rate relief

The payments are treated as if they have been paid net of the basic rate tax (20%) which the charity then recovers from HMRC.

If the taxpayer made a gift of £800 (the amount of cash paid) to a charity, the charity would receive a total (gross gift) of £1,000. This is made up of the cash of £800 from the taxpayer, and the tax of £200 (£800 x 20/80) which the charity would recover from HMRC.

If the individual is a basic rate taxpayer, relief is given at the time of payment (he paid it net of 20% tax) and no further relief is available. The gift aid payment does not feature in the calculation of taxable income or the income tax liability.

If the individual is a higher rate taxpayer, he has received relief of 20% as the payment was made net of basic rate tax. He receives the additional 20% (40% - 20%) relief by extending the basic rate band by the gross amount of the payment.

Example

Charles, David and Edgar each have trading income of £47,225 in 2009 - 10. Charles makes a gift aid payment of £320 (amount paid) and David pays an interest of £400 on a loan for qualifying purposes. Edgar makes no payments.

Their income tax liabilities are calculated as follows:

	Charles £	David £	Edgar £
Trading income	47,225	47,225	47,225
Less: interest paid	-	(400)	-
Net Income	47,225	46,825	47,225
Less: Personal allowance	(6,475)	(6,475)	(6,475)
Taxable Income	40,750	40,350	40,750

Income tax					Charles	David	Edgar
Charles	David	Edgar					
37,800 (W1)	37,400	37,400	at 20%		7,560	7,480	7,480
2,950	2,950	3,350	at 40%		1,180	1,180	1,340
40,750	40,350	40,750					
Income tax liability					**8,740**	**8,660**	**8,820**

Working
W1

Charles's basic rate band is extended by the gross amount of the payment - £400 (£320 x 100/80) to £37,800 (£37,400 + £400).

Charles and David have both made tax deductible payments of £400 (gross) which should reduce their tax bill by £160 (£400 x 40%).

The difference between Edgar's and David's income tax liability is £160 (£9,516 - £9,356).

Charles and David have both made the same payments:

	Charles £	David £
Gift aid payment / interest payment	320	400
Income tax liability	8,740	8,660
Total	**9,060**	**9,060**

B5.12: Income Tax Liabilities © GTG

SUMMARY

Tax relief for gift aid payments
- **basic rate taxpayer**
  - relief of 20% given at time of payment
  - not taken into account in calculation of taxable income
- **higher rate taxpayer**
  - relief of 20% given at time of payment
  - additional relief of 20% given by extending basic rate band by gross amount of payment

Test Yourself 5

Mike aged 54 years, earns a salary of £48,250 per annum. He makes a gift aid payment of £2,080 (amount paid) in 2009 - 10.

Required:

Calculate his income tax liability for 2009 - 10.

Proforma for tax calculation

	Total	Non-savings	Savings	Dividends
Trading income	X	X	---	---
Employment income	X	X	---	---
Property income	X	X	---	---
Bank interest (gross)	X		X	---
Dividends (gross)	X		---	X
Total Income	X	X	X	X
Less: Interest paid for a qualifying purpose	(X)	(X)	---	---
Net income	X	X	X	X
Less: Personal allowance	(X)	(X)	---	---
Taxable income	X	X	X	X
Income tax liability	X			
Less: Tax credits	(X)			
Less: Tax deducted at source	(X)			
Income tax payable	X			

Test Yourself 6

Abraham aged 45 years has the following income in 2009 - 10:

	£
Salary (PAYE deducted £5,454)	31,000
Building society interest (amount received)	410
Bank deposit interest (amount received)	500
Dividend income (amount received)	12,600

Calculate his tax payable or repayable for 2009 - 10.

Test Yourself 7

Merry started trading on 1 January 2010 and had the following results for the period to 5 April 2010:

	Notes	£	£
Gross profit			36,075
Less :			
Depreciation		910	
Motor expenses	1	4,580	
Professional fees	2	3,090	
Sundry expenses	3	2,695	
Entertaining	4	4,060	
Business rates		3,930	(19,265)
Net profit			**16,810**

Continued on next page

Additional information

1. **Motor expenses:** it has been agreed with HMRC that 60% of motor expenses relate to business use.

2. **Professional fees** consist of:

	£
Legal costs in defending a claim for allegedly faulty work	1,320
Personal financial planning advice	1,240
Debt collection	530
	3,090

3. **Sundry expenses consist of:**

	£
Merry's health club subscription	125
Donation to local charity (Merry received free advertising in the charity's magazine)	45
Printing and stationery	645
Gifts of 35 umbrellas bearing Merry's logo.	680
Subscription to a trade association	1,200
	2,695

4. **Entertaining;** £2,312 for entertaining customers, £1,748 for entertaining employees.

5. The cost of Merry's private telephone for the period 1 January 2010 to 5 April 2010 was £2,650. It has been agreed with HMRC that 35% of this related to business calls. Telephone costs are not included in the profit and loss account.

6. Merry took goods from stock that cost £1,250, and had a selling price of £1,550. No entry was made in the accounts.

7. No capital allowances were claimed.

Merry was employed up to 31 December 2009 earning a monthly salary of £4,200.

Her employer provided Merry with a petrol-powered car which had a list price of £18,500. Merry contributed £2,300 towards the capital cost of the car. The official CO_2 emission rate for the car was 278 grams per kilometre. The employer paid for all the fuel for private journeys. Merry paid £110 per month to her employer for the private use of the car.

On 1 January 2008 Merry was given an interest free loan of £65,000 to purchase a residential flat. On 5 May 2009 she repaid £35,000, and the balance of £30,000 was repaid on 31 December 2009. The official rate of interest was 4.75%.

PAYE paid during employment was £6,980.

Merry received interest from her bank account of £380 on 31 December 2009.
She also received dividend income of £1,233 (amount received) during 2009 - 10.

Required:

Calculate the income tax payable by Merry for 2009 - 10.

---

6. Explain the treatment of property owned jointly by a married couple, or by a couple in a civil partnership. [1]

[Learning outcome f]

A married couple or civil partners who live together may hold property in their joint names. If the jointly held asset is a building society account or bank account, any income needs to be allocated between the couple.

The couple is treated as if they own the property in equal proportions, and the income is divided equally between them. This happens regardless of the actual ownership.

If couples own the property in unequal proportions, they may make a declaration to HMRC of their actual ownership, and are then taxed on the proportion of income to which they are actually entitled.

> **Example**
>
> Linda and her husband Jerry deposited £100,000 into a joint building society account.
>
> Linda contributed £40,000 and Jerry £60,000. They received interest of £4,800 in 2009 - 10.
>
> Linda and Jerry will each be taxed on £3,000 (£4,800 x 100/80 x1/2) and will be treated as owning the asset in equal shares.
>
> However, if they make a declaration to HMRC as to the actual ownership, Linda will be taxed on £2,400 (£4,800 x 100/80 x 4/10) and Jerry will be taxed on £3,600 (£4,800 x 100/80 x 6/10).

Answers to Test Yourself

Answer 1

1. Peter is 76 during 2009 - 10 so his personal allowance is £9,640.
2. Mark is above 75 in 2009 - 10 so his personal allowance is £9,640.
3. Brian is above 65 but below 75 in 2009 - 10 so his personal allowance is £9,490.
4. Alex is aged below 65 in 2009 - 10 so his personal allowance is £6,475.

Answer 2

1. Adam

He is 79 years old at the end of the tax year.

	£
Personal age allowance	9,640
Less: reduction	
1/2 (£34,200 – £22,900) (restricted)(W1)	(3,165)
Personal age allowance	**6,475**

Workings

Adam has net income which exceeds the limit by (£34,200 - £22,900) = £11,300. His personal age allowance is reduced by one-half of the excess:

PAA = (£9,640 – 1/2 x £11,300) = £3,990
The PAA cannot be reduced to below the PA of £6,475, so Adam is entitled to an allowance of £6,475

2. Barry

He is 64 years old at the end of the tax year.

	£
Personal allowance	6,475

Barry is less than 65 at the end of the tax year, so he is entitled to a PA of £6,475.

3. Charles

He is 66 years old at the end of the tax year.

	£
Personal age allowance	9,490
Less: reduction	Nil
Personal age allowance	**9,490**

Charles reaches the age of 66 during 2009 - 10 and his net income is below £22,900 so he is entitled to a PAA of £9,490.

4. David

He is 76 years old at the end of the tax year.

	£
Personal age allowance	9,640
Less: reduction	Nil
Personal age allowance	**9,640**

David reaches the age of 76 during 2009 - 10 and his net income is below £22,900 so he is entitled to a PAA of £9,640.

5. Edwin

He is 67 years old at the end of the tax year.

	£
Personal age allowance	9,490
Less: reduction 1/2 (£24,100 – £22,900)	(600)
Personal age allowance	**8,890**

Edwin is 67 at the end of 2009 - 10 and his net income exceeds the limit by (£24,100 - £22,900) = £1,200. The PAA to which he is entitled is reduced by one-half of the excess. PAA = (£9,490 – 1/2 x £1,200) = £8,890.

Answer 3

Income tax payable 2009 - 10

	Total £	Non-savings £	Savings £
Trading income	17,450	17,450	
Bank interest £640 x 100/80	800		800
Net Income	**18,250**	**17,450**	**800**
Less: PA	(6,475)	(6,475)	
Taxable Income	**11,775**	**10,975**	**800**

Income Tax

	Income £	Rate	Tax £
Non-savings : basic rate band	10,975	x 20%	2,195
Savings : basic rate band	800	x 20%	160
	11,775		
Income tax liability			**2,355**
Less: Tax credits (£800 x 20%)			(160)
Income tax payable			**2,195**

Non-savings income occupies the whole of the starting rate band of savings income. Hence, savings income falls entirely in the basic rate band and is taxed at 20%.

Answer 4

(a) George's tax calculation for 2009 - 10

	Total £	Non-Savings income £	Savings income £
Income from Employment	18,750	18,750	
Income from Bank interest (W2)	1,500	0	1,500
Net income	**20,250**	**18,750**	**1,500**
Less: Personal allowance	(6,475)	(6,475)	0
Taxable income	**13,775**	**12,275**	**1500**
Income tax liability (W1)	2,755		
Less: Tax credit on interest (W2)	(300)		
Tax Payable	**2,455**		

Note:
The starting rate of 10% for savings income is not applicable as taxable non-savings income, i.e. £12,275 exceeds the starting rate threshold of £2,440.

Workings

W1 Calculation of George's tax liability

	Income (£)	Rates	Tax Liability (£)
Non-Savings Income - Basic rate band	12,275	20%	2,455
Savings income : Basic rate band (Note 1)	1,500	20%	300
Income tax liability	**13,775**		**2,755**

W2 Calculation of gross interest and tax credit on interest

Interest is net of 20% tax, it has to be grossed-up by multiplying by 80%.

Therefore, interest = £1,200 x 100/80 = £1,500

Tax credit on interest = £1,500 - £1,200 = £300

(b) Harry's tax calculation for 2009 - 10

	Total £	Non-Savings income £	Savings income £
Pension Income	8,000	8,000	
Building society interest (W2)	4,000		4,000
Net income	**12,000**	**8,000**	**4,000**
Less : Personal allowance	(6,475)	(6,475)	
Taxable income	**5,525**	**1,525**	**4,000**
Income tax liability (W1)	1,014		
Less: Tax credit on saving income (W2)	(800)		
Tax payable	**214**		

Workings

W1 Calculation of Harry's total tax liability

	Income (£)	Rates	Tax Liability (£)
Non- saving income : basic rate	1,525	20%	305
Savings income : starting rate (£2440 - £1,525) (note)	915	10%	92
	2,440		
On savings income - basic rate	3,085	20%	617
	5,525		**1,014**

W2 Calculation of gross interest and tax credit on interest

Interest is net of 20% tax, it has to be grossed-up by multiplying by 80%.
Therefore, interest = £3,200 x 100/80 = £4,000

Tax credit on saving income = £4,000 x 20% = £800

Note:

In Harry's case, the starting rate of 10% is applicable for saving income, as his non-saving income does not exceed £2,440. It is applicable on his saving income falling in the first £2,440 of taxable income after deducting non-saving income amount. Balance of saving income not falling in the first £2,440 of taxable income is taxed at the basic rate of 20%.

(c) Duncan's tax calculation for 2009 - 10

	Total £	Non-Saving income £	Saving income £
Income from employment	56,400	56,400	
Building society interest (W2)	2,250		2,250
Net income	**58,650**	**56,400**	**2,250**
Less: Personal allowance	(6,475)	(6,475)	
Taxable income	**52,175**	**49,925**	**2,250**
Income tax liability (W1)	13,390		
Less: Tax credit on saving income(W2)	450		
Tax payable	**12,940**		

Workings

W1 Calculation of Duncan's total tax liability

	Income (£)	Rates	Tax Liability(£)
Non- saving income : Basic rate band	37,400	20%	7,480
Higher rate band	12,525	40%	5,010
Savings income : Higher rate band	2,250	40%	900
	52,175		13,390

W2 Calculation of gross interest and tax credit on interest

Interest is net of 20% tax, it has to be grossed-up by multiplying by 80%.
Therefore, interest = £1800 x 100/80 = £2,250

Tax credit on saving income = £2,250 x 20% = £ 450

Note:

The starting rate of 10% for saving income is not applicable as taxable non-savings income exceeds £ 2,440. Saving income also exceeds the higher rate threshold of £ 37,400, and so is taxed at 40%.

Answer 5

Mike's income tax liability is as follows:

	£
Employment income	48,250
Less: PA	(6,475)
Taxable income	**41,775**
Income tax	
Basic rate band (W1) £40,000 at 20%	8,000
Higher rate band £1,775 at 40%	710
Income tax liability	**8,710**

Working

W1

Mike's basic rate tax band is extended to £40,000 (£37,400 + £ 2,600) by the gross amount of the payment i.e. £2,600 (£2,080/80 x 100)

Answer 6

Calculation of Abraham's income tax payable / repayable for 2009 - 10

		Total £	Non-savings £	Savings £	Dividend £
Employment income		31,000	31,000		
Building society income (£410 x 100/80) (Note1)		512		512	
Bank interest (£500 x 100/80) (Note 2)		625		625	
Dividend income (£12,600 x 100/90) (note 3)		10,000			14,000
Net income		46,137	31,000	1,137	14,000
Less: PA		(6,475)	(6,475)		
Taxable income		39,662	24,525	1,137	14,000
Income tax					
Non-savings income: basic rate band	24,525 x 20%	4,905			
Savings income : basic rate band (Note 5)	1,137 x 20%	227			
Dividends (Note 6): basic rate band	11,738 x 10%	1174			
	37,400				
Dividends higher rate band	2,262 x 32.5%	735			
	39,662				
Income tax liability		7,041			
Less: tax credits / deducted at source					
Dividends (£14,000 x 10%)		(1,400)			
Interest (£1,137 x 20%)		(227)			
PAYE		(5,454)			
Income tax repayable		**(40)**			

Notes:

1. Building society interest is received net of 20% tax. All income must be included gross: the calculation is £410 x 100/80.

2. Bank interest is received net of 20% tax. All income must be included gross: the calculation is £500 x 100/80.

3. Dividend income has a tax credit of 10%. All income must be included gross: the calculation is £9,000 x 100/90.

4. Non-savings income is taxed first.

5. Savings income is taxed next as it falls in the basic rate band it is taxed at 20%.

6. Dividend income falls partly in the basic rate band, partly in the higher rate band. Non-savings and savings income totals £25,662 (£24,525 + £1,137). This leaves £11,738 (£37,400 - £25,662) of the basic rate band. Dividends in the basic rate band are taxed at 10%. The remaining £2,262 (£14,000 - £11,738) falls in the higher rate band and is taxed at 32.5%.

Answer 7

Calculation of Merry's income tax payable / repayable for 2009 - 10

		Total income £	Non-savings income £	Savings income £	Dividend income £
Trading income (W1)		23,851	23,851		
Employment income (W2)		46,706	46,706		
Bank interest (W6)		475		475	
Dividend income (W7)		1,370			1,370
Net income		72,402	70,557	475	1,370
Less : Personal allowance		(6,475)	(6,475)		
Taxable Income		65,927	64,082	475	1,370
Income tax					
Non-savings income: basic rate	£37,400 x 20%	7,480			
higher rate	£26,682 x 40%	10,673			
	£64,082				
Savings income	£475 x 40%	190			
Dividend income	£1,370 x 32.5%	445			
	£ 65,927	18,788			
Less: tax credits/deducted at source					
Dividends at 10% (Note)		(137)			
Interest at 20%		(95)			
PAYE		(6,980)			
Tax payable		**11,576**			

Note:

Tax credit of dividends is deducted while computing tax payable. However any excess tax credit cannot be repaid under any circumstances, so it is deducted in priority over other tax credits and PAYE.

Workings

W1 Calculation of Merry's tax adjusted trading profits for the year ended 5 April 2010

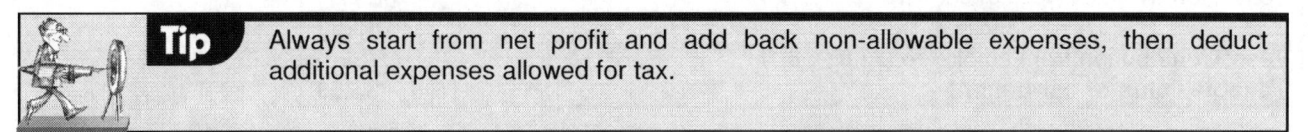

> **Tip** Always start from net profit and add back non-allowable expenses, then deduct additional expenses allowed for tax.

	Notes	£	£
Net profit per accounts			16,810
Add: Disallowable expenditure:			
Depreciation		910	
Private element of motor expenses	1	1,832	
Private element of professional fees	2	1,240	
Health club subscription	3	125	
Entertaining	4	2,312	
		6,419	
Add: Goods taken out of business by owner	5	1,550	7,969
Less: Business expenditure borne personally by the owner			
Telephone	6		(928)
Adjusted profits for tax purposes			**23,851**

Notes:

1. Private element of motor expenses: 40% x £4,580 = £1,832

B5.20: Income Tax Liabilities

2. Professional fees:
   - Legal cost in defending a claim for allegedly faulty work is business expenditure, hence allowed.
   - Private financial planning is Merry's personal expenditure: add back £1,240.
   - A professional fee for debt collection is also business expenditure, hence allowed.
3. Sundry expenses:
   - Merry's health club subscription is personal expenditure: add back £125.
   - Donation to local charity is allowable as it benefits the trade through advertising in the charity's magazine.
   - Printing and stationery and subscription to a trade association are allowable expenses.
   - Gifts of 35 umbrellas bearing Merry's logo are allowable as they carry a conspicuous advertisement for the business, and do not cost more than £50 per person (£645 / 35 = £18 per umbrella) and are not food, drink or tobacco vouchers exchangeable for goods.

4. Customer entertaining not allowed: add back £2,312

5. Market value of goods taken are added back: £1,550

6. Business call allowable: 35% x £2,650 = £928.

W2 Employment income

	£
Salary (April to December 2009 = £4,200 x 9)	37,800
Car benefit (W3)	3,263
Fuel benefit (W4)	4,436
Beneficial loan (W5)	1,207
Employment income	**46,706**

W3 Car benefit

	£
List price of the car when new	18,500
Less: Capital contribution from Merry	(2,300)
	16,200
% based on CO_2 emissions 15% + ((275 -135)/5)) = 43% restricted to 35%	35%
	5,670
Less: Non availability £5,670 x 3/12	(1,417)
	4,253
Less: Contribution from employee (£110 x 9)	(990)
Taxable value of car benefit	**3,263**

W4 Fuel benefit

Fuel benefit = £16,900 x % based on CO_2 x number of months available
 = £16,900 x 35% x 9/12
 = £4,436

W5 Beneficial loan

Average method

	£
$\left(\dfrac{\text{Loan balance at Start of year} + \text{Loan balance at end of year}}{2} \right)$ x official rate of interest x number of months	
= $\dfrac{£65,000 + £30,000}{2}$ x 4.75% x 9/12	1,692

Alternative method: strict method

	£
April 2009 £65,000 x 4.75% x 1/12	257
May – December 2009 £30,000 x 4.75% x 8/12	950
	1,207

Merry would elect for the strict method.

W6

Bank interest is received after deduction of 20% tax. The gross figure is shown in the taxable income computation, so the amount received is multiplied by 100/80.

Gross bank interest is £380 x 100/80 = £475
The tax deducted is   £475 x 20%   = £95.

W7

Dividend income has a credit of 10%. The gross figure is shown in the taxable income computation, so the amount received is multiplied by 100/90.

Gross dividend is £1,233 x 100/90 = £1,370
The tax credit is £1,370 x 10%   = £137

Quick Quiz

1. What is total income?

2. What is taxable income?

3. How are personal allowances and charges deducted in the income tax calculation?

4. At what rates are the following types of income taxed?
   a) Non-savings income
   b) Savings income
   c) Dividend income

Answers to Quick Quiz

1. **Total income** is the aggregate of all income i.e. savings, non-savings and dividend income less interest paid for qualifying purpose. Note **this is before personal allowances**.

2. It is Net income less personal allowances.

3. First from non-savings income, then from savings income, then from dividend income.

4.
a) Non-savings income 20% and 40%.
b) Savings income 10%, 20% and 40%.
c) Dividend income 10% and 32.5%.

Self Examination Questions

Question 1

Nancy is employed by Pillsbury plc as a manager. The information relevant to her income is as follows:

a) She is paid a gross annual salary of £36,000.

b) Throughout 2009-10 Nancy was provided with an 1800 cc petrol powered car, which has a list price of £14,000. Nancy made a capital contribution of £2,000 towards the cost of the car when it was first provided. The official CO_2 emission rate for the car is 225 grams per kilometre. Pillsbury plc paid for all the running costs of the car during 2009 - 10 including petrol used for private journeys.

c) Pillsbury has provided Nancy with living accommodation since 2009. The property was purchased in 2005 for £110,000. It has an annual value of £4,250. Nancy pays the company £2,800 towards living accommodation.

d) Nancy pays a gross interest of £705 on a loan for qualifying purposes.

e) During 2009-10 Nancy received building society interest of £1,800 (net).

f) During 2009-10, Nancy received dividends of £2,250 (net).

Required:

Calculate Nancy's income tax payable for 2009 - 10.

B5.22: Income Tax Liabilities

Question 2

Farah was born in 1939. The following information is relevant:

a) Farah owns a cottage, which was originally purchased as a holiday home for her. This cottage, which is furnished, has been let to the public from the summer of 2004 for holiday use. Farah ceased using it privately as from this day. The cottage was let on a commercial basis for 25 weeks in 2009 - 10 with each individual letting not expected to exceed 2 weeks in duration. The letting generated total rental income of £7,850. She incurred advertising costs of £1,000, maintenance costs of £5,600 and loan interest costs of £1,900 in the tax year. The maintenance costs relate to roof repairs following gale damage. The tax written down value of furniture in the cottage at 5 April 2009 was £3,500.

b) She received bank interest of £3,800 in 2009 - 10.

c) She received net dividends of £2,340 in 2009 - 10 from a UK Company.

d) She received net building society interest amounting to £5,400.

e) She also received a taxable state retirement pension amounting to £5,750.

f) She pays interest of £1,000 gross on a loan taken for qualifying purposes.

Required:

Calculate Farah's income tax payable or repayable for 2009 - 10.

Answers to Self Examination Questions

Answer 1

Income Tax Computation for Nancy 2009 – 10

	Total £	Non-saving income £	Saving income £	Dividend income £
Income from Employment (W1)	48,650	48,650		
Income from UK Dividends. (W5)	2,500			2,500
Income from Building society Interest (W6)	2,250		2,250	
Total Income	53,400	48,650	2,250	2,500
Less: Interest paid	(705)	(705)		
Net Income	52,695	47,945	2,250	2,500
Less: Personal Allowance	(6,475)	(6,475)		
Taxable Income	46,220	41,470	2,250	2,500
Income tax liability (W7)	10,821			
Less: Tax credit on Dividends(W5)	(250)			
Less: Tax deducted at source on building society interest (W6)	(450)			
Income Tax payable	10,121			

Workings

W1 Taxable employment income

Employment income		£
Salary		36,000
Car benefit	(W2)	3,960
Fuel benefit	(W3)	5,577
Living accommodation	(W4)	3,113
Taxable employment income		**48,650**

W2 Car benefit

	£
List price of the car when new	14,000
Less: Capital contribution from Nancy	(2,000)
	12,000
% based on CO_2 emissions 15% + ((225 -135)/5))	33%
Taxable value of car benefit	**3,960**

W3 Fuel benefit

Fuel benefit = Base figure x % based on CO_2 x number of months given by HMRC emissions
= £16,900 x 33%
= **£5,577**

W4 Living accommodation

	£
Annual value	4,250
Add: Additional annual rent if cost £75,000 (£110,000 - £75,000) x 4.75%	1,663
Total	**5,913**
Less: Employee contribution	(2,800)
Taxable benefit	**3,113**

W5

Dividend is net of 10% tax hence it has to be grossed up by multiplying it by 90%.

Therefore, gross dividend = £2250 x 100/90 = £2,500

Tax deducted at source = £2,500 – £2,250 = £250

W6

Building society interest is net of 20% tax, it has to be grossed-up by multiplying it by 80%.

Therefore, gross building society interest = £1,800 x 100/80 = £2,250

Tax deducted at source = £2,250 – £1,800 = £450.

W7 Income Tax liability

	£		£
Non-savings : basic rate band	37,400	20%	7,480
higher rate band	4,070	40%	1,628
Savings : higher rate band	2,250	40%	900
Dividends : higher rate band	2,500	32.5%	813
	46,220		
Tax Liability			**10,821**

Answer 2

Income Tax Computation for Farah 2009 - 10

	Total Income £	Non-savings Income £	Savings Income £	Dividend Income £
Pension	5,750	5,750		
Income from UK Dividends. (W1)	2,600			2,600
Income from Bank Interest. (W2)	4,750		4,750	
Income from building society interest (W3)	6,750		6,750	
Total Income	19,850	5,750	11,500	2,600
Less: Interest paid	(1,000)	(1,000)		
Less: Loss from furnished holiday lettings (W4)	(1,350)	(1,350)		
Net Income	17,500	3,400	11,500	2,600
Less: Personal Allowance (W5)	(9,490)	(3,400)	(6,090)	
Taxable Income	8,010	-	5,410	2,600
Total tax liability (W6)	1,098			
Less: Tax credit on dividends (W1)	(260)			
Less: Tax credit on bank interest (W2)	(950)			
Less: Tax credit on building society interest (W3)	(1,350)			
Tax repayable	(1,462)			

Workings

W1

Dividend is received net of 10%. The gross amount is calculated as the amount received multiplied by 100/90.

Therefore, gross dividend = £2,340 x 100/90 = £2,600

Tax credit = £2,600 – £2,340 = £260

W2

Bank interest is received net of 20% tax. The gross amount is calculated as the amount received multiplied by 100/80.

Therefore, gross bank interest = £3,800 x 100/80 = £4,750

Tax deducted at source = £4,750 – £3,800 = £950

W3

Building society interest is received net of 20% tax. The gross amount is calculated as the amount received multiplied by 100/80.

Therefore, gross building society interest = £5,400 x 100/80 = £6,750

Tax deducted at source = £6,750 – £5,400 = £1,350

W4

If the letting of furnished property satisfies certain conditions, it qualifies as income from the "commercial letting of furnished holiday accommodation." **Such income is treated as income from trade, and not as income from a property business.**

To qualify as a furnished holiday letting, the property must satisfy the following conditions:

➢ available for commercial letting to the public for at least 140 days in a tax year,
➢ is actually so let in this period for at least 70 days, and
➢ is not normally in the same occupation for more than 31 days at a time, any longer term occupation must not exceed 155 days.

The cottage passes all three conditions. Therefore, it will be regarded as furnished holiday accommodation.

The net assessable letting income for 2009 - 10 is calculated as follows:

	£	£
Rental income		7,850
Less: Expenses		
Advertising	(1,000)	
Maintenance (repairs to roof allowable)	(5,600)	
Loan interest	(1,900)	
Capital allowances £3,500 @ 20%	(700)	(9,200)
Loss		**(1,350)**

W5

The taxpayer is over 65 and her net income is below the income limit of £22,900. Therefore, she is entitled to the full PAA of £9,490.

If the personal allowance exceeds the total for non-savings income, deduct the surplus from the savings income and then dividend income.

W6 Total income tax liability

	£		£
Non-savings income	-	-	-
Savings income: starting rate band	2,440	10%	244
basic rate band	2,970	20%	594
	5,410		
Dividends income: basic rate band	2,600	10%	260
	8,010		
Tax liability			**1,098**

SECTION B: INCOME TAX LIABILITIES

B6

STUDY GUIDE B6: THE USE OF EXEMPTIONS AND RELIEFS IN DEFERRING AND MINIMISING INCOME TAX LIABILITES

Get Through Intro

Pension is the most efficient way of availing tax relief along with savings for old age.

In this Study Guide we will discuss various pension schemes available to self-employed people, as well as non-earners and the employed.

We will also see how a self-employed person may join either a 'personal pension scheme' or a 'retirement annuity contract.'

As a tax consultant, you should have thorough knowledge of all these provisions so that you can guide your clients through the associated tax planning.

Learning Outcomes

a) Explain and compute the relief given for contributions to personal pension schemes, using the rules applicable from 6 April 2006.
b) Describe the relief given for contributions to occupational pension schemes, using the rules applicable from 6 April 2006.
c) Explain how a married couple or couple in a civil partnership can minimise their tax liabilities.

Introduction

A pension is a means by which you will financially support yourself when you retire from employment. Currently there are **four sources** from which an individual may draw a pension in the UK. These are:

- **The state pension scheme**: a scheme based upon National Insurance contributions.
- **An occupational pension scheme**: one which is based upon an individual's employment and length of service with a particular employer.
- **A personal pension scheme**: a scheme with which an individual may choose to save a part of their earnings for use in their later years.
- **A stakeholder pension**: this is a portable pension in which an individual saves and can take with them when they change employment.

The UK government encourages investment in a pension scheme in order to reduce the reliance upon the state pension scheme. Accordingly most investments attract tax relief and contributions are made under very favorable tax incentives.

1. Explain and compute the relief given for contributions to personal pension schemes, using the rules applicable from 6 April 2006.[2]
[Learning outcome a]

A state pension is available when an individual retires, but the government encourages individuals to provide additional funds for their retirement. An individual can save additional funds for their retirement by contributing to pension schemes. Tax relief is given on contributions to a pension fund. However, the tax relief is available only if the pension scheme is registered with HMRC.

There are two types of pension schemes
- Personal pension scheme
- Employer's occupational pension scheme *(Discussed in Learning Outcome 2 of this Study Guide)*

1. Personal pension scheme

a) An individual can contribute any amount, **regardless of their earnings,** into a personal pension fund even if they already belong to an occupational pension fund.

b) There is no restriction on the number of pension schemes in which an individual can contribute. However, tax relief available on the contribution is subject to certain restrictions.

c) **Tax relief is available** for pension contributions up to the amount of an individual's net relevant earnings ("net relevant earnings" is employment income and trading income). If the individual does not have any earnings, relief is available on gross contributions of up to **£3,600** (this figure is given in the rates and allowances in the exam).

Hence, the maximum amount of gross pension contribution in a tax year on which an individual can get tax relief is the higher of:

i) an individual's earnings for the tax year

ii) £3,600

d) There is an **annual allowance** which restricts the amount of contributions that can qualify for tax relief even though it is calculated as discussed above.

i) For 2009 - 10 this amount is **£245,000** (given in tax rates and allowances in the exam).

ii) Any **contributions** in **excess** of this limit and on which tax relief has been given are **taxed at the rate of 40%.** The annual allowance charge cancels out the tax relief that has been given on the excess contribution.

iii) There is **no 40% charge where contributions have not qualified for tax relief.**

iv) Tax is paid under the self assessment system.

e) If the individual is an employee, their employer may make contributions into their personal pension fund. These contributions:

   i) are exempt benefits.
   ii) have no limit for the employer.
   iii) count towards the annual allowance.

2. Method of giving relief

a) Personal pension contributions are made net of basic rate tax of 20% by both employed and self-employed contributors.

b) Tax relief has therefore been given to all except higher-rate taxpayers at the time of contribution itself, and hence contributions are ignored in the income tax calculation.

c) Higher rate tax payers have already obtained 20% relief, the additional 20% (40% - 20%) relief is obtained by extending the basic rate band by the gross contribution when calculating income tax.

d) If the contribution is made in excess of the annual allowance by the contributor and tax relief is given on that contribution, then that excess amount will be taxed at the rate of 40%.

Example

For the tax year 2009 - 10, Ted, Rob, Mary, Mark, Terry and Mike had trading profits and made gross personal pension contributions as follows:

	Trading Profits £	Gross pension contributions £
Ted	--	6,000
Rob	25,000	17,000
Mary	25,000	30,000
Mark	65,000	30,000
Terry	65,000	85,000
Mike	355,000	255,000

Ted

The maximum amount of gross pension contribution on which tax relief is available is the higher of:
- Ted's earnings - NIL
- £3,600

He has no earnings for the tax year 2009 - 10. Tax relief is available only for gross contributions of £3,600. Therefore, tax relief = £720 (£3,600 at 20%).

Amount to be paid to the personal pension company by Ted is £5,280 (£6000 - £720).

Rob

The maximum amount of gross pension contribution on which tax relief is available is the higher of:
- Rob's earnings - £25,000
- £3,600

The gross contribution made by Rob of £17,000 is less than the maximum amount of contribution on which tax relief is available i.e. £25,000. Therefore, his entire contributions of £17,000 qualify for tax relief.

Tax relief = £3,400 (£17,000 at 20%).

Amount to be paid to the personal pension company by Rob is £13,600 (£17,000 - £3,400).

Since Rob is not a higher-rate taxpayer, the contributions are ignored as regards his income tax computation.

Mary

The maximum amount of gross pension contribution which Mary can make is the same as Rob i.e. £25,000. Therefore, only £25,000 of her contributions out of £30,000 qualifies for tax relief.

Tax relief = £5,000 (£25,000 at 20%).

Amount to be paid to the personal pension company by Mary is £25,000 (£30,000 - £5,000).

Since Mary is not a higher-rate taxpayer, the contributions are ignored as regards her income tax computation.

Mark

The maximum amount of gross pension contribution on which tax relief is available is the higher of:
- Mark's earnings
- £3,600

Mark has earnings of £65,000 for the tax year 2009-10. All of his contributions of £30,000 qualify for tax relief.

Therefore, tax relief = £6,000 (£30,000 at 20%)

Amount to be paid to the personal pension company by Mark is £24,000 (£30,000 - £6,000).

Since Mark is a higher-rate taxpayer, he is eligible for higher-rate tax relief. Thus, his basic rate tax band is extended by £67,400 (£37,400 + £30,000).
His income tax liability for the tax year 2009-10 is as follows:

	£
Trading profit	65,000
Less: personal allowance	(6,475)
Taxable income	**58,525**
Income tax:	
£58,525 at 20%	11,705
Tax liability	**11,705**

Terry

The maximum amount Terry can contribute is the same as Mark i.e. £65,000. Therefore, only £65,000 out of his total contributions of £85,000 qualifies for tax relief.

The amount of tax relief = £13,000 (£65,000 at 20%).

Amount to be paid to the personal pension company by Terry is £72,000 (£85,000 - £13,000).

Since Mark is a higher-rate taxpayer, he is eligible for higher-rate tax relief. Thus, his basic rate tax band is extended by £102,400 (£37,400 + £65,000).

His income tax liability for the tax year 2009 - 10 is therefore the same as Mark's (£11,705).

Mike

Mike has earnings of £355,000 for the tax year 2009 - 10. Therefore, all of his contributions of £255,000 qualifies for the tax relief.

Therefore, tax relief = £51,000 (£255,000 at 20%).

Amount to be paid to the personal pension company by Mike is £204,000 (£255,000 - £51,000).

Since Mike is a higher-rate taxpayer, he is eligible for higher-rate tax relief. Thus, his basic rate tax band is extended by £292,400 (£37,400+ £255,000).

In addition, there will be a tax charge at the rate of 40% on the excess of contributions above the annual allowance of £245,000.

Continued on next page

His income tax liability for the tax year 2009 - 10 is as follows:

	£
Trading profit	355,000
Less: Personal allowance	(6,475)
Taxable income	348,525
Income tax:	
£292,400 at 20%	58,480
£56,125 at 40%	22,450
	80,930
Excess contribution charge	
£10,000 (£255,000 - £245,000) at 40%	4,000
Tax liability	**84,930**

Lifetime allowance

The tax treatment of any income arising from the amount contributed and accumulated in the pension schemes is as follows:

➢ All income (interest and bonuses) received from pension schemes are tax-free.
➢ All capital gains arising on capital disposal of investments made are exempt from capital gains tax.

The funds contributed to the pension schemes and the income arising from it is tax free up to a certain maximum amount. This maximum amount is known as lifetime allowance and is £1,750,000 for the tax year 2009 - 10.

If the value of the pension fund exceeds this amount, there is an **additional tax charge** when funds are **withdrawn** as a pension. The additional charge is as follows:
➢ If the funds are withdrawn at once, the excess fund amount is taxed at the rate of 55%.
➢ If the funds are used to provide a pension, the excess fund amount is taxed at the rate of 25%.

> **Tip**
> The examiner has stated that this rule will not be examined in any detail.

SUMMARY

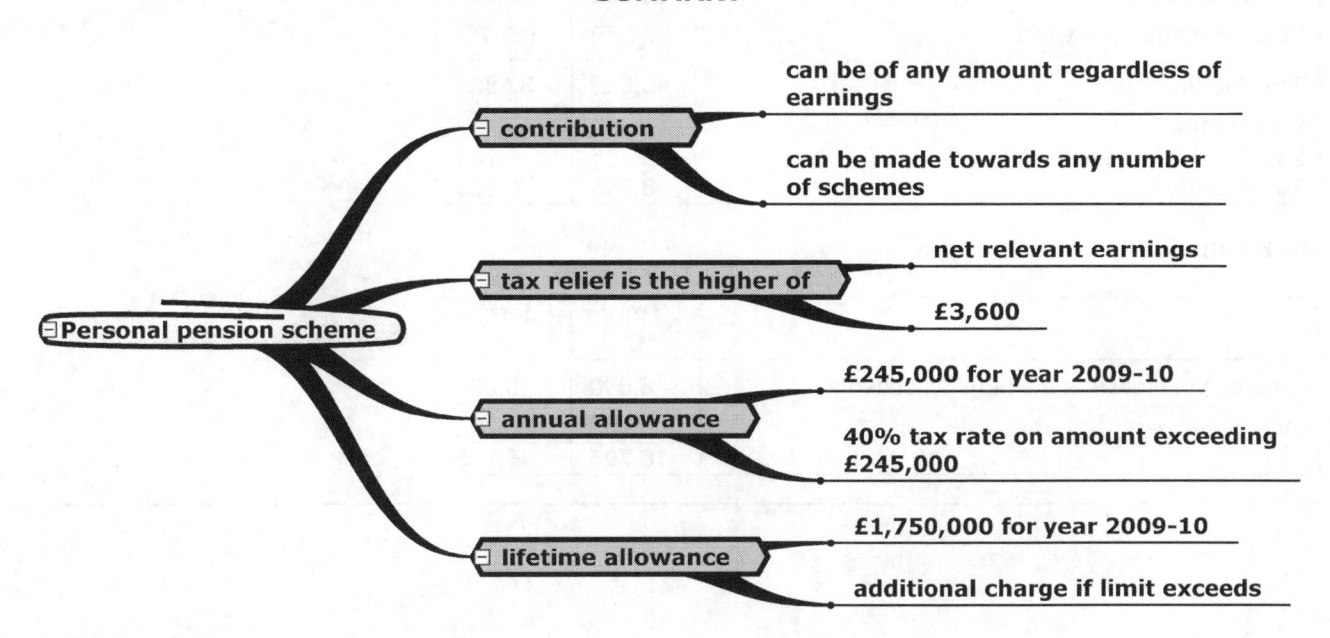

Personal pension scheme
- **contribution**
  - can be of any amount regardless of earnings
  - can be made towards any number of schemes
- **tax relief is the higher of**
  - net relevant earnings
  - £3,600
- **annual allowance**
  - £245,000 for year 2009-10
  - 40% tax rate on amount exceeding £245,000
- **lifetime allowance**
  - £1,750,000 for year 2009-10
  - additional charge if limit exceeds

2. Describe the relief given for contributions to occupational pension schemes, using the rules applicable from 6 April 2006.[1]

[Learning outcome b]

An occupational pension scheme is one set up by an employer for his employees. The employer generally contributes to the scheme. Some schemes require the employee to contribute, whereas some are non-contributory.

The same rules apply to occupational pension schemes as to personal pension schemes.

Method of giving relief

1. An occupational scheme will usually **operate net pay arrangements**.
2. The employer deducts the gross pension contributions from the individual's earnings before applying PAYE.

Tax relief is therefore given automatically at the appropriate rate.

Example

Tom and Jerry are employed with Cheese Ltd earning a salary of £50,000. Tom contributes £10,000 into a personal pension scheme and Jerry contributes £10,000 into an occupational pension scheme.

Tom has earnings of £50,000 for the tax year 2009 – 10 which are higher than his contribution to the pension scheme. Therefore, all of his contributions of £10,000 qualify for tax relief.

Tax relief = £2,000 (£10,000 at 20%).

Amount to be paid to the personal pension company by Tom is £8,000 (£10,000 - £2,000).

Since Tom is a higher-rate taxpayer, he is eligible for higher-rate tax relief. Thus, his basic rate tax band is extended by £47,400 (£37,400 + £10,000).

Jerry contributes to occupational pension scheme. This contribution is deductible from taxable employment income.

Their tax computations will appear as follows:

	Tom £	Jerry £
Income from employment	50,000	50,000
Less: Contribution to occupational pension scheme	-	(10,000)
Net income	50,000	40,000
Less: Personal allowance	(6,475)	(6,475)
Taxable income	43,525	33,525
Income tax		
£43,525/ £33,525 at 20%	8,705	6,705
Tax liability	**8,705**	**6,705**

Cash outflow

	Tom £	Jerry £
Amount paid towards the pension scheme	8,000	10,000
Income tax paid	8,705	6,705
	16,705	16,705

Summary

Personal pension scheme	Occupational pension scheme
Paid net of basic rate tax	Paid gross
Is not deducted while calculating taxable income	Is deducted while calculating taxable income
Basic rate band is extended by the gross contribution to give additional 20% relief.	No extension of basic rate band.

3. Explain how a married couple or couple in a civil partnership can minimise their tax liabilities.[2]

[Learning outcome c]

Since 1990, husbands and wives are taxed separately on their income and capital gains. Hence, both have their own allowances, lower and basic rate tax bands for income and capital gains tax purposes and are responsible for their own tax affairs. Since December 2005, the same tax treatment applies to same-sex couples who have entered into a civil partnership under the Civil Partnership Act.

Tax planning opportunities

1. Income tax allowances and tax bands

Everyone is entitled to a basic personal allowance which is £6,475 for tax year 2009 - 10.

This allowance **cannot,** however, **be transferred between spouses**.

The married couples should try to ensure that they both fully use their allowance since there is no facility to transfer it from one spouse to the other. This can make a huge difference to the overall income tax liability for the year because:

a) The total taxable income of the couple will be reduced by twice the amount of personal allowance.

Example If a couple's total income of £80,000 is split between the spouses, each spouse will get a personal allowance of £6,475 for the tax year 2009-10. Thus, the couple's overall taxable income will be £67,050 (£80,000 – (£6,475 + £6,475))

b) As the income is reduced, it will fall under the lower tax band. This can be better understood with the help of the following example.

Example Nick's total income is £79,895 and his wife, Amy, has NIL income. In this case, Nick's tax liability will be as follows:

	£
Total income	79,895
Less: Personal allowance	(6,475)
Taxable income	73,420
Tax borne	
£37,400 @20%	7,480
£36,020 @ 40%	14,408
Total	21,888

Instead, if Nick transfers some of his income, say £25,000 to his wife, their total tax liability will be as follows:

	Nick	Amy
	£	£
Total income	54,895	25,000
Less: Personal allowance	(6,475)	(6,475)
Taxable income	48,420	18,525
Tax borne		
(£37,400/£18,525) @20%	7,480	3,705
£11,020 @ 40%	4,408	-
Total	11,888	3,705

Continued on next page

Thus, the couple's total tax liability will be £15,593 (£11,888 +£3,705) i.e. reduced by £6,295 as compared to £21,888.

This reduction is because of the following reasons:

➤ The total income of £79,895 is reduced by £12,950 (£6,475 +£6,475).
➤ Instead of £36,020 being taxed at 40%, only £11,020 is taxed at 40%. Thus, as the tax band is reduced, the tax is also reduced.

c) In the case of those aged 65 and over

Taxpayers aged at least 65 should consider how to make full use of the available age allowances.

Income tax allowances	2009 - 10 £
Personal allowance for people aged 65-74	9,490
Personal allowance for people aged 75 and over	9,640

The higher allowances are gradually withdrawn once income exceeds £22,900 (for tax year 2009 - 10) (refer to Study Guide B5).

Test Yourself 1

Darren and Lynn have total annual taxable income of £100,000. What will be their tax liability if:

1. The total income is to be taxed on either of the spouses alone.

2. The income is split between the couple equally.

2. Married couple allowance (MCA)

If either of the spouses were born before 6 April 1935, a married couple's allowance is available. This is given to the spouse with higher income, although it is possible, by election, to transfer it to the other spouse.

A married couple allowance is available **only if the following conditions** are fulfilled.

➤ The couple is legally married and lives together for at least part of the tax year.
➤ At least one of the spouses was born before 6 April 1935.

In the case of couples married **before 5 December 2005**, the MCA is given to the **husband.** In the case of couples married **on or after 5 December 2005 (and civil partners)**, the MCA is normally given to the **spouse with the higher income.**

a) It is important to note here that:

i. The husband and wife **jointly may decide** that a minimum amount of MCA (£2,670 for 2009 - 10) should be set against the wife's tax.

ii. The **wife unilaterally may decide** that 50% of the MCA should be set against her tax.

iii. If one spouse is unable to fully utilise the MCA, the **unused MCA can be transferred** to the other spouse.

b) The amount of allowance

For 2009 - 10, the allowance is:

i. If either of the spouse was born before 6 April 1935 but is under 75 years of age (i.e. 65 to 74) - allowance is not available.

ii. If either of the spouse is 75 years of age or above – allowance is 10% of £6,965.

> **Tip**
> Remember, MCA is deducted from tax payable and not from TI.

Like age allowance, this allowance also starts to be withdrawn once income goes over the income threshold i.e. £22,900 for tax year 2009 - 10 (refer Study Guide B5).

Income tax allowances	2009 - 10
Married couple's allowance for people born before 6 April 1935 but aged under 75	N.A.
Married couple's allowance - aged 75 or more	10% of £6,965
Minimum amount of married couple's allowance	10% of £2,670

Test Yourself 2

Henry is 76 and is married to Alice who is 72. Henry receives his state pension of £3,470 and also a pension from his former employer of £8,000, from which the employer deducted £443 as tax. He also has £2,000 bank interest that has had tax taken off at 20% leaving him with £1,600.

Required:

Calculate Henry's tax liability and determine whether any tax is repayable to him in 2009 – 10.

The MCA can be used to minimise the tax liability of the couple overall. Where the person who is entitled to a married couple's allowance is unable to use his full MCA in any tax year he can ask for the balance to be transferred to his spouse.

Test Yourself 3

Peter and Susan are married. Peter is 78 and works part-time. Susan is 71 and also works. They have a joint bank account, which pays gross interest of £1,200, from which the bank has taken off 20% in tax leaving them with £960. Peter earns £9,500. He also has half of the gross bank interest, £600, and half of the tax £120 that the bank has already deducted.

Susan has income of £10,000 in wages from which her employer deducted £395 tax through PAYE, plus half of the gross interest on her joint account with Peter, £600.

Required:

Determine how the MCA can be used to reduce the tax liability of the couple.

---

3. Jointly owned assets

It is often the case that married couples own assets jointly. The normal rule is to split income from such assets equally between them for tax purposes. This applies even where the asset is owned in unequal shares unless an election is made to split the income in proportion to the ownership of the asset.

> **Example**
> A let property is owned by a married couple in the proportion 95:5. The rental income arising can be split between them for tax purposes either 50:50 or by election, 95:5. This can be a useful mechanism for achieving a more desirable split of income for tax purposes without needing the underlying capital ownership to follow.

The one exception to this rule is dividends from jointly owned shares in 'close' companies (broadly those owned by the directors or five or fewer people) which are taxed according to the actual ownership of the shares.

This option can prove to be a very efficient measure to reduce the tax liability of each spouse.

Example

A let out property was owned by a married couple (John and Jenny) in the proportion 90:10. The rent received from this property is £20,000. John's employment income is £30,000 and Jenny has no income.

If the property income is **not split between them 50:50**, the tax liability would be as follows:

	John £	Jenny £
Employment income	30,000	-
Property income (90:20)	18,000	2,000
Net Income	**48,000**	**2,000**
Less: Personal allowance	(6,475)	(2,000)
Taxable income	**41,525**	-
Tax borne		
£37,400 at 20%	7,480	-
£4,125 at 40%	1,650	-
Total tax liability	**9,130**	-

If the property income is **split between them 50:50**, the tax liability would be as follows:

	John £	Jenny £
Employment income	30,000	-
Property income (50:50)	10,000	10,000
Net income	**40,000**	**10,000**
Less: Personal allowance	(6,475)	(6,475)
Taxable income	**33,525**	**3,525**
Tax borne		
(£33,525/ £3,525) at 20%	6,705	705
Total tax liability	**6,705**	**705**

Thus, total tax liability of the couple is £7,410 (£6,705 + £705). **The couple has actually saved tax of £1,720** (£9,130 - £7,410) by using the 50:50 split of jointly owned property income.

---

4. Capital gains

Transfers of assets between spouses or persons who are civil partners and who are living together will be on a no-gain no-loss basis, and thus not attract an immediate CGT charge.

Each spouse has their own annual capital gains tax (CGT) exemption, currently £10,100. Any gains above this level are taxed on each spouse separately by reference to their own disposals of assets. For 2009 - 10 capital gains are taxed at a single rate of 18% regardless of the amount of taxable gains or taxable income.

So the option of transferring the asset to the spouse and realising the capital gain in the hands of the lower income partner is another measure of a married couple's tax planning. A considerable CGT saving may be made by ensuring that maximum advantage is taken of annual exemptions and to utilise any capital losses the other spouse or partner may have.

> **Example**
>
> Smith bought a non-business asset for £5,000 in March 1985. He sold the asset to his wife for £50,000 in September 2008 when they were living together. The asset is deemed to have transferred for an amount, which gives neither a gain nor a loss on transfer. The actual amount paid by Mrs. Smith is ignored.
>
> The deemed disposal proceeds are calculated as follows:
>
> Smith has neither a gain nor a loss.
>
> The deemed cost to Mrs. Smith for any future disposal of the asset is £5,000 (cost to Mr. Smith when he originally purchased the asset).
>
> Mrs. Smith sells the asset for £80,000 in June 2009.
>
> The gain arising is:
>
> | | £ |
> |---|---|
> | Disposal proceeds | 80,000 |
> | **Less:** Cost | (5,000) |
> | **Net chargeable gain** | 75,000 |
> | **Annual exemption** | (10,100) |
> | **Taxable gain** | 64,900 |

Answers to Test Yourself

Answer 1

1. If the total income is to be taxed in either of the spouse alone

	£
Income	100,000
Less: Personal allowance	(6,475)
Taxable income	93,525
Tax borne	
£37,400 20%	7,480
£56,125 40%	22,450
Total tax liability	29,930

2. Instead, if the couple split this income equally, the tax liability of each of them would be as follows:

	Darren £	Lynn £
Income	50,000	50,000
Less: Personal allowance	(6,475)	(6,475)
Taxable income	43,525	43,525
Tax borne		
£37,400 20%	7,480	7,480
£6,125 40%	2,450	2,450
Total tax liability	9,930	9,930

Hence Darren's tax liability is £9,930 and Lynn's tax liability is also £9,930.
The couple's total liability is £19,860.

Thus almost £10,070 (i.e. £29,930 - £19,860) of tax can be saved every year.

Answer 2

Henry's income is calculated for tax as follows:

	Total income £	Non-savings income £	Savings income £
State pension	3,470	3,470	
Employer's pension	8,000	8,000	
Bank interest	2,000		2,000
Net income	13,470	11,470	2,000
Less: Personal allowance (Note 1)	(9,640)	(9,640)	-
Taxable income	3,830	1,830	2,000
Tax on taxable income			
Non saving income			
Basic rate £1,830 at 20%	366		
Saving income			
Starting rate (£2,440 - £1,830) £610 at 10% (Note 3)	61		
Basic rate £1,390 at 20%	278		
Tax payable	705		
Less: Married couple's allowance (£6,965 at 10%) (Note 1)	(697)		
Net tax payable	8		
Less: Tax already paid			
Bank interest	(400)		
Employer's pension	(443)		
Repayment due	(835)		

Notes:

1. Henry is entitled to the age related personal allowance of £9,640 as he is aged over 75. He is also entitled to married couple's allowance of 10% of £6,965 as he is aged over 75.

2. As his income is less than £22,900, none of the age-related elements of his allowances needs to be reduced.

3. Non savings income £1,830 does not exceed the starting rate threshold of £2,440, so £610 (£2,440 - £1,830) of the savings income is taxed at the starting rate of 10% and the balance of the savings income, £1,390 (£2,000 - £610), is taxed at the basic rate of 20%.

Answer 3

Peter's income is taxed as follows:

	Total income £	Non-savings income £	Savings income £
Gross bank interest (i.e. before tax is taken off)	600		600
Add: Wages	9,500	9,500	
Net income	10,100	9,500	600
Less: Personal allowance	(9,640)	(9,500)	(140)
Taxable income	460	-	460
Tax on taxable income			
Saving income (£460 at 10%) (Note 2)	46		
Tax Payable	46		
Less: MCA (£6,965 at 10%)	(697)		
Amount of married couple's allowance unused (£697-£46)	651		
Net Tax payable	-		
Less: Tax already paid (Bank Interest) (£600 x 20%)	(120)		
Repayment due	(120)		

Peter's unused MCA can be transferred to Susan, which she can set against her income as follows:

	Total income £	Non-savings income £	Savings income £
Gross bank interest (i.e. before tax is taken off)	600		600
Add: Wages	10,000	10,000	
Net income	**10,600**	**10,000**	**600**
Less: Personal allowance	(9,490)	(9,490)	
Taxable income	**1,110**	**510**	**600**
Tax on taxable income			
Non saving income £510 x20%	102		
Saving income (£600 at 10%) (Note 2)	60		
Total tax due	**162**		
Less: unused MCA from Peter £651	(162)		
Tax payable	-		
Less: Tax already paid			
Tax deducted from bank interest	(120)		
Tax deducted by employer under PAYE	(395)		
Repayment due	**(515)**		

Notes:

1. Peter is entitled to the age-related personal allowance of £9,640 and married couple's allowance because he is aged above 75.

2. For tax year 2009 - 10, there is a 10% starting rate for the first £2,440 saving income subject to non-saving income not exceeding £2440.

3. Unused MCA will be £651 – £162 = £489 which would now be wasted.

Quick Quiz

Fill in the blanks

1. Employee's contribution to a _____ pension scheme is deducted in calculation of taxable income.

2. Personal pension contribution is paid _____ of basic rate tax.

3. If the individual does not have any earnings, relief is available on gross contributions of up to _____.

4. Annual allowance for 2009 - 10 is _____.

Answers to Quick Quiz

1. occupational

2. net

3. £3,600

4. £245,000

Self Examination Questions

Question 1

What is the amount of relief available to an individual if he does not have any earnings?

Question 2

What is lifetime allowance?

Question 3

Which two conditions are to be satisfied for the availability of married couple allowance?

Answers to Self Examination Questions

Answer 1

The amount of relief is available on gross contributions of up to £3,600 to an individual if he does not have any earnings.

Answer 2

The maximum value for a pension fund is called the lifetime allowance and it is £1,750,000.

Answer 3

Married couple allowance is available only if the following two conditions are satisfied:

a) The couple should be legally married and live together for at least part of tax year.
b) At least one of the spouses should be born before 6 April 1935.

SECTION C: CHARGEABLE GAINS

C1

STUDY GUIDE C1: THE SCOPE OF THE TAXATION OF CAPITAL GAINS

Get Through Intro

Capital gains tax is a charge on the increase in the value of an asset over the period of ownership, with an allowance for inflation.

'Capital Gains tax' is an important topic of your syllabus. Also, as a tax consultant to companies as well to individuals, you need to possess a **complete and in-depth knowledge of the scope, applicability and requirements of capital gains tax.**

In the course of the next six Study Guides, we will take you through all the related provisions of capital gains tax.

In this Study Guide we shall discuss the **scope of capital gains tax** and how the **classification of individuals** as **resident and ordinarily residents affects** the **applicability** of capital gains tax.

Learning Outcomes

a) Describe the scope of capital gains tax.
b) Explain how the residence and ordinary residence of an individual is determined.
c) List those assets which are exempt.

C1.2: Chargeable Gains

Introduction

Case Study

During the past ten years, Maria was a resident of the UK. She was permanently residing in Manchester. In July 2007, she left Manchester to take a job in Canada. After going to Canada, she had to send some money to her parents in the UK. Therefore she sold a painting for £30,000 and sent all the money to the UK. This transaction resulted in her making a capital (profit) gain of £10,000.

Maria thought that this gain was neither taxable in the UK nor in Canada and she didn't pay any tax. However, when the UK tax authorities made a demand for capital gains tax, she was surprised.

Maria is liable to capital gains tax on the disposal of the painting as she was, until recently, a resident of the UK.

In this Study Guide we will see how residential status affects the capital gains tax liability of a person, the scope of capital gains tax and the assets which attract capital gains tax.

1. Describe the scope of capital gains tax.[2]
List those assets which are exempt.[1]

[Learning outcomes a and c]

Capital gains tax is a charge on the increase in value of an asset over the period of ownership. This is the capital profit made or realised. In the case of an individual this profit is computed by deducting only the cost. However in the case of companies after deducting the cost a further deduction is made as an allowance for inflation known as indexation allowance.

The capital gains of a limited company and an individual have similarities but many differences too.

1. A limited company's capital gains are part of profits chargeable to corporation tax (PCTCT), and are charged to corporation tax.

2. An individual's capital gains are charged to capital gains tax which is totally separate from income tax. Capital gains tax is treated as though it is another element of savings income for the year of assessment.

3. An indexation allowance (to allow for inflation) is given for a company in the calculation of its gains.

4. **Reliefs** available to **individuals**
   - Rollover relief
   - Entrepreneur's relief on disposal of a business or a part of a business
   - Holdover relief for the gift of business assets
   - Rollover relief when a business is incorporated

5. **Reliefs** available to a **company**
   - Rollover relief

1.1 Scope of capital gains tax

A liability to tax arises if there is a **chargeable disposal** of a **chargeable asset** by a **chargeable person**.

1. **Chargeable disposal**

   1. The sale of an asset.
   2. The sale of part of an asset (e.g. selling a 40% share of a house).
   3. The gift of an asset (e.g. giving an expensive necklace to your daughter as a present).
   4. The loss or destruction of an asset (e.g. an insurance receipt in respect of a property damaged by fire).

The chargeable disposal occurs on the date of the contract. Transfers of assets on death are exempt disposals.

2. Chargeable asset

All capital assets are chargeable, unless specifically exempt by law or other regulations. This applies to all assets wherever they are in the world.

A list of exempt assets is given below:

a) **An individual's home** (principal private residence (refer to Study Guide C5). If he owns more than one home then it will be the one he elects.

b) **Motorcars** including veteran and vintage cars.

c) **Cash (sterling currency** and **foreign currency** for an individual's own use or maintenance of assets abroad).

d) **Wasting chattels** (tangible, moveable property with a predicted life of not more than 50 years (refer to Study Guide C4)).

e) **Chattels** which are not wasting **if sold for £6,000 or less** (refer to Study Guide C5).

f) **Compensation or damages** received for personal or professional wrongs or injury.

g) **Prizes** and **betting** winnings.

h) **Life insurance policies** but only when disposed of in the hands of the original owner or beneficiaries.

i) **Gifts** to charities or certain sports clubs.

j) **SAYE** (save as you earn) deposits, **savings certificates and premium bonds**.

k) **Government securities** and qualifying companies **loan stock**.

l) All **debts** except debts on security.

m) **Pensions** and **annuity rights**.

> **Tip**
> Gains on the sale of the above exempt assets are not liable to capital gains tax. In the same way, a loss arising from the disposal of the above assets is not eligible for set off.

3. Chargeable person

a) A liability arises to capital gains tax if an individual **resident or ordinary resident in the UK** makes a chargeable disposal.

b) Companies pay tax on their chargeable disposals, but pay corporation tax, rather than capital gains tax.

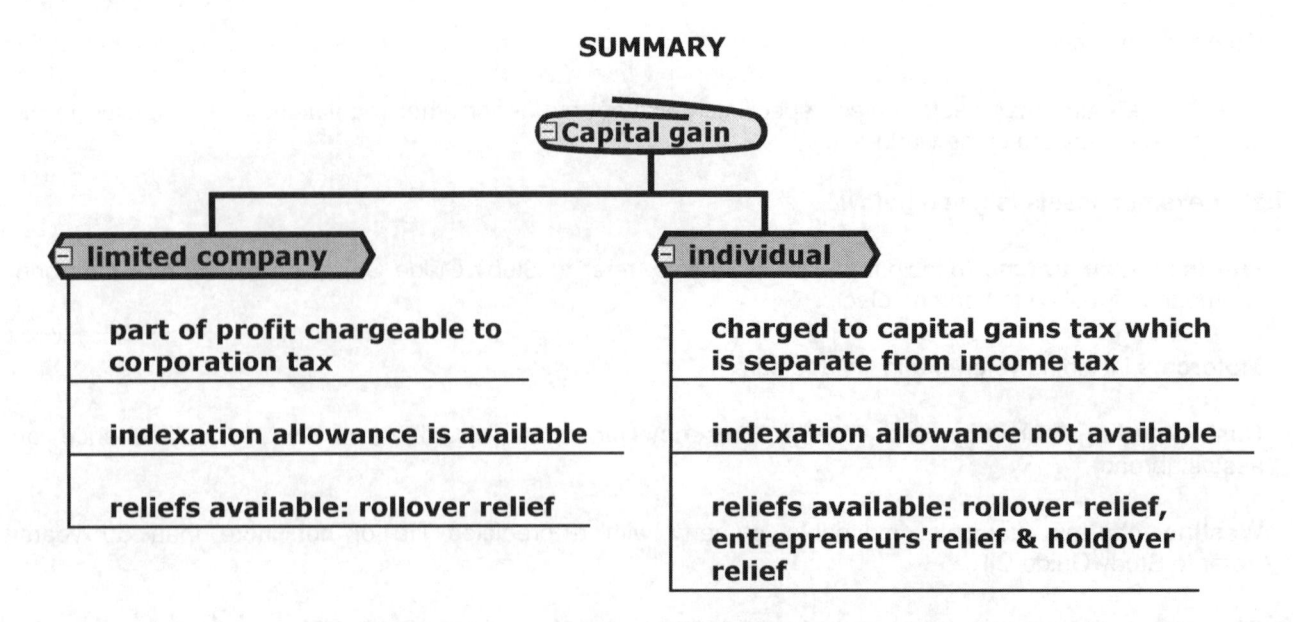

SUMMARY

Capital gain

limited company
- part of profit chargeable to corporation tax
- indexation allowance is available
- reliefs available: rollover relief

individual
- charged to capital gains tax which is separate from income tax
- indexation allowance not available
- reliefs available: rollover relief, entrepreneurs' relief & holdover relief

2. Explain how the residence and ordinary residence of an individual is determined.[2]
[Learning outcome b]

2.1 Residence of an individual

1. An individual **physically present in the UK for at least 183 days** is a UK **resident** for the **whole tax year**.

2. An individual returning to the UK for visits will be a UK resident for the whole tax year if he makes regular and substantial (average at least 91 days per tax year) visits to the UK. This is in respect of each of four or more consecutive years.

   An individual is either a resident or a non resident for the entire year of assessment. They **cannot be partly resident**.

3. A non-UK resident starting to make regular and substantial visits to the UK will be a UK resident from the earlier of:

a) the start of the fifth tax year, or
b) the start of a tax year where an intention to continue long-term visits is apparent.

2.2 Ordinary residence

The ordinary residence of an individual is the country where he normally resides year after year.

An individual who is ordinarily resident in the UK but who is temporarily abroad during a particular tax year (i.e. not present in the UK for the minimum 183 days but not absent for the entire tax year) is deemed to be a UK **resident** for the whole of that tax year.

> **Tip**: It is possible to be a UK resident but not ordinarily resident, and vice-versa. For more details, refer to Study Guide B1.

2.3 Chargeability to capital gain tax – individuals

An individual resident or ordinary resident in the UK is liable for:
- assets owned and sold in the UK
- assets owned and sold outside the UK (overseas assets)

An individual non resident or ordinarily resident is not liable to capital gains tax on any assets whether sold in the UK or outside the UK. The only exception is where a non resident carrying on a permanent trade disposes of an asset in the UK.

Example

Tina is a resident of Brazil. She runs a modelling class in London. She sold her classroom building for £70,000 and made a capital gain of £21,000.

Tina is a non-resident individual of the UK but as she carries on a permanent trade in the UK and sells the business asset in the UK, she is liable to capital gains tax on gain from such disposal in the UK.

Test Yourself 1

Joydeep has been a UK resident since his birth. On 10 May 2009, he leaves the UK to take up a permanent job in the US. However, he didn't like it there, so on 4 March 2010, he returned to the UK.

During the period when he was in the US, he sold his diamond gold Omega wrist watch which he had purchased there, for £21,000 and made a capital gain of £2,000. As a tax consultant, is this capital gain taxable in the UK?

Answer to Test Yourself

Answer 1

Joydeep is a resident of the UK as well as UK domiciled. However, during the tax year 2009 - 10, he was present in the UK for only 67 days.

6/4/09 to 30/4/09	25 days
1/5/09 to 9/5/09	9 days
5/3/10 to 31/3/10	27 days
1/4/10 to 5/4/10	5 days
Total	**66 days**

Although, Joydeep was not present in the UK for the minimum 183 days, he was not absent for the whole year. Hence, Joydeep is considered a resident. As a resident and UK domiciled, Joydeep is liable to capital gains tax on all world gains.

As a result, Joydeep is liable to capital gains tax on a gain arising on the disposal of a foreign asset (i.e. diamonds).

Quick Quiz

State whether the following disposals are chargeable.

1. James had two plots of land. Out of these he gave one plot of open land to his married daughter as a gift.

2. Garry sold his private motor car for £8,000 and made a gain of £500.

3. Mark sold government securities for £21,000, which originally cost £20,500.

Answers to Quick Quiz

1. The definition of chargeable disposal includes the gift of a chargeable asset. Therefore, the gift to his daughter is a chargeable disposal.

2. Capital gains arise on sale or disposal of a chargeable asset. However, a private motor car is an exempt asset. Hence the gain on disposal of a private motor car is not chargeable to capital gains tax.

3. Government securities are exempt assets, hence the disposal is not a chargeable disposal.

Self Examination Questions

Question 1

John, who is ordinarily resident in the UK, likes to travel. During 2009 - 10, he spent only one month in the UK. For the remainder of the year he was in Tasmania, Australia. During the year 2009 - 10 he sold his farmhouse in Tasmania and made a capital gain of £50,100.

Advise John as to whether he is liable for capital gains tax in the UK on this capital gain of £50,000.

Question 2

Annett from Germany arrived in the UK on 15/08/2009 and stayed there until 31/10/2009. After this date she left to live in Germany permanently. During her stay in the UK, she purchased 100 shares of Sleep-Well Ltd. Over the next 10 days, the share prices of Sleep-Well increased by £7. She sold all the shares she had purchased and made a capital gain of £35,500.

Advise her as to whether or not she is liable for capital gains tax.

Answers to Self Examination Questions

Answer 1

An individual who is ordinarily resident in the UK but who is not present in the UK for the minimum 183 days is deemed to be resident in the UK for the year provided he was not absent for the entire tax year.

Here, John is ordinarily resident in the UK but was not present in the UK for the minimum 183 days during 2009 - 10. However, he was not absent for the entire tax year. Hence, he is deemed to be resident in the UK for 2009 - 10.

A person who is ordinarily a resident in the UK is liable for capital gains tax on UK assets as well as on foreign assets.

Hence, John must pay capital gains tax on capital gains arising from the sale of foreign assets.

Answer 2

An individual who is physically present in the UK for at least 183 days during a tax year (excluding days of arrival and departure) is deemed to be resident in the UK for the whole tax year.

Annett was present in the UK for (15/8/2009 to 31/10/2009) i.e. 77 days. Therefore, she is a non-resident.

A person who is a non-resident of the UK is not liable to capital gains tax on any asset whether sold in the UK or outside the UK. Hence, Annett is not liable to pay capital gains tax on the gain of £35,500 arising from the disposal of shares in the UK.

SECTION C: CHARGEABLE GAINS

STUDY GUIDE C2: THE BASIC PRINCIPLES OF COMPUTING GAINS AND LOSSES

Get Through Intro

This Study Guide discusses the **computation of capital gains, calculation of capital gains tax for individuals, treatment of capital losses,** and introduces you to the **concept of the indexation allowance.**

It is essential that you pay considerable attention to this Study Guide as proper computation of capital gains and **paying the proper amount** of tax calculated according to the principles of the Act is **important** for both the government and the taxpayer.

Knowledge of these principles is essential in your professional life.

Learning Outcomes

a) Compute capital gains for both individuals and companies.
b) Calculate the indexation allowance available to companies.
c) Compute the amount of capital gains tax payable.
d) Explain the treatment of capital losses for both individuals and companies.

Introduction

Capital gains tax (CGT) was introduced with effect from 6 April 1965 to tax the gains of individuals, personal representatives and trustees. Most CGT rules apply to companies as well, except for some important differences. However, a company's gains are charged to corporation tax and not CGT.

In general, CGT applies when a **chargeable person** makes a **chargeable disposal** of a **chargeable asset**. A gain arises where the proceeds received are greater than the cost of acquisition plus any enhancement costs.

A simple example is as follows:

John bought a rental property as an investment for £42,000. He incurred acquisition costs of £3,200 and installed a new bathroom which cost £5,000. He later sold the cottage for £80,000. In simple terms the gain subject to CGT would be £29,800.

In this Study Guide, we will look at the basics of capital gain calculations, including allowable deductions and the concept of indexation allowance.

1. Compute the capital gains for both individuals and companies.[2]
[Learning outcome a]

In the previous Study Guide, we discussed the assets chargeable to CGT and the persons liable to capital gains tax. In this Study Guide, we will explain how to calculate capital gains (and losses) for individuals and companies.

1.1 Basis of assessment

A person's CGT liability is calculated on the basis of the assets disposed of during the tax year. In the case of **individuals, the** tax year is the period between **6 April and 5 April** of the following year, whereas in the case of **companies**, the tax year is the period between **1 April and 31 March** of the following year.

> **Example**
> On 6 April 2009, Peter sold 1,000 shares of Success Ltd and made a capital gain of £5,000. This gain is chargeable to tax during the tax year 2009 -10 (as the tax year for individuals is the period between 6 April and 5 April).
>
> Suppose the asset is sold by Delta Ltd on 6 April 2009. The gain on the disposal of the asset, if any, is chargeable on the basis of the accounting period in which the disposal takes place during the financial year 2009 – 10.

1.2 Basic computation of gain / loss

Proforma for Individuals

	£
Disposal consideration	X
Less: Incidental costs of disposal	(X)
Net disposal consideration	X
Less: Allowable deductions	
Acquisition costs (including incidental costs)	(X)
Enhancement expenditure	(X)
Net gain / (loss)	X/(X)

Proforma for Companies

	£
Disposal consideration	X
Less: Incidental costs of disposal	(X)
Net disposal consideration	X
Less: Allowable deductions	
Acquisition costs (including incidental costs)	(X)
Enhancement expenditure	(X)
Unindexed gain	X
Less: Indexation allowance	**(X)**
Net indexed gain / (loss)	X/(X)

> **Tip:** The indexation allowance is applicable only to companies and was withdrawn for individuals from 6 April 2008.

Let us look at each term in detail.

1. Disposal consideration

This is the cash or cash equivalent value received on disposal of the asset. A gain or loss may be realised on the sale or gift of an asset. However, transfers on death are exempt from CGT.

Method of disposal	Disposal proceeds
Sale	Sale proceeds
Sale to a connected person	Market value
Gift	Market value
Transfer to spouse / civil partner	Special rules (refer to Study Guide C3)

> **Tip:** Market value is the value the asset can expect to realise if sold on the open market.

Connected person

On a disposal to a connected person, the market value is used as disposal proceeds.

a) **A person is connected with:**

i. His spouse / civil partner.
ii. His relatives (brothers, sisters, ancestors (parents, grandparents etc) and lineal descendants (children, grandchildren etc).
iii. His spouse / civil partner's relatives and their spouse / civil partners.

b) **A company is connected with**

i. The persons controlling it.
ii. Companies under the same control are connected with each other.

Example: Doll Plc and Dot Plc are sister companies (i.e. both companies are managed by the same group of people). During 2009 - 10, Doll Plc sold its industrial building to Dot Plc for £100,000, when the actual market value of the same building was £150,000.

As the transaction is between two connected persons, the market value on the date of sale (i.e. £150,000) is deemed to be sale proceeds and not the actual amount paid (i.e. £100,000), for the calculation of capital gains.

2. Incidental costs of disposal

Incidental costs of disposal, which are allowable deductions include:

a) legal fees e.g. legal fees paid to lawyers for legal advice when devising agreements
b) estate agent's fees
c) advertising costs e.g. advertisements given in a newspaper
d) auctioneer's fees

> **Tip:** Auction is the sale of an asset by giving public notice; the asset is sold to the person who is ready to give the highest price for the asset.

3. Allowable deductions

a) If purchased, acquisition cost.

b) If acquired as a gift, market value at the date of acquisition.

c) If acquired from a connected person, market value at the date of acquisition.

d) If inherited (acquired as a result of an individual's death), probate value (market value on the date of death).

Example George's grandfather gave him a golden ring on his eighteenth birthday. On that day, the market value of the ring was £2,000. On 2 May 2009, Jorge sold the ring for £2,100.

In this situation, when calculating chargeable gains, the cost of acquisition of the ring by Jorge is considered to be £2,000 i.e. the market value of the ring on the day it was given.

e) Incidental costs of acquisition (valuation fees, legal fees).

f) Enhancement expenditure (capital costs of additions and improvements).

Example Tracy bought a piece of land in Manchester for £40,000. In May 2009, she constructed a new industrial building on this land. The cost of constructing this industrial building was £20,000.

She disposed of the industrial building in June 2009 for £120,000. The total cost will be the cost of land (£40,000) and the expenditure incurred on the industrial building (£20,000) which is reflected in the asset on the date of its disposal. Tracy can deduct this expenditure from sales proceeds.

Example Linda bought a shop in May 2001 for £50,000. She paid £2,000 towards her lawyer's fees and stamp duty to register the title of the shop in her name. Due to an earthquake in June 2009, the walls of the shop cracked. She spent £1,000 on repairing the walls. At the same time, she spent £6,500 on redecorating the shop.

In December 2009, Linda sold the shop for £80,000.

Here, capital gain is calculated as follows:

	£
Disposal consideration	80,000
Less: Incidental costs of disposal	-
Net disposal consideration	**80,000**
Less: Allowable deductions	
Acquisition costs (£50,000 + £2,000)	(52,000)
Enhancement expenditure	-
Net gain	**28,000**

Notes:

1. Repairs and maintenance expenses are not considered to be enhancement expenditure as they are not of a capital nature.

2. Redecoration is not enhancement.

SUMMARY

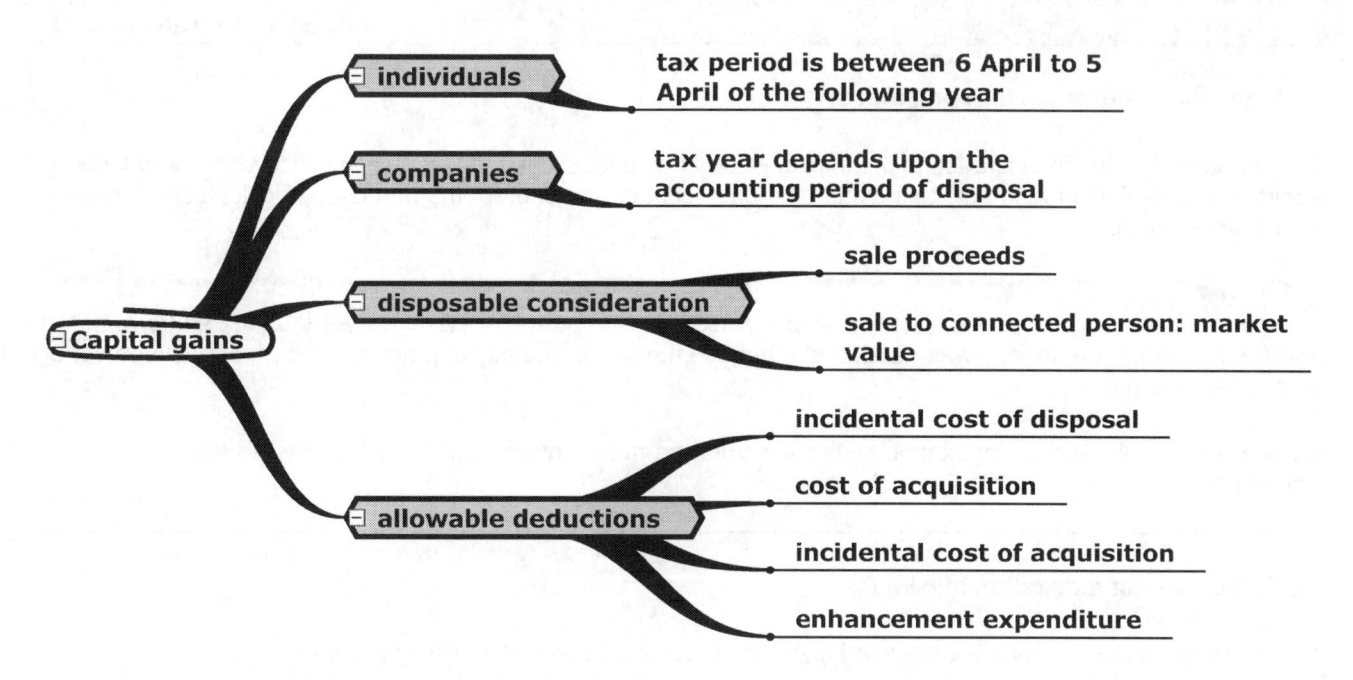

Capital gains
- **individuals**: tax period is between 6 April to 5 April of the following year
- **companies**: tax year depends upon the accounting period of disposal
- **disposable consideration**:
  - sale proceeds
  - sale to connected person: market value
- **allowable deductions**:
  - incidental cost of disposal
  - cost of acquisition
  - incidental cost of acquisition
  - enhancement expenditure

Test Yourself 1

Malcolm purchased a business asset in April 2002 for £40,000. In order to purchase machinery he took out a bank loan. To obtain this bank loan he had to pay £500 to a legal advisor as well as registration charges.

In June 2006, he spent £10,000 on machinery to improve the utility of the asset. In September 2009, he sold the asset for £30,000. To help him sell the asset, he appointed an agent, whom he paid £500.

Required:

Calculate chargeable gains / losses.

Test Yourself 2

On 20 April 2009, Margaret gave her diamond jewellery to her daughter Iris as a wedding present. On the day of the gift, the market value of the gift was £20,000. Margaret had originally purchased this diamond jewellery for £15,000.

Required:

Advise Margaret as to whether she is liable for CGT.

Test Yourself 3

In May 2004, William purchased a business asset for £50,000. He used this asset for five years and sold the same in December 2009 for £60,000.

To sell this asset, he placed an advertisement in the daily newspaper. The total expenditure on this advertisement was £500.

Required:

Show the calculation of chargeable gain / loss.

2. Calculate the indexation allowance available to companies.[2]

[Learning outcome b]

2.1 Indexation allowance for companies

The intention is to tax the increase in the capital value of an asset. The indexation allowance was introduced as a relief against inflation, and acts to increase the base cost of an asset for the purposes of calculating a capital gain on a disposal.

Example In 2008, it was possible to purchase 1 litre of petrol for £2. However in 2009, a litre of petrol cost £3. In short, more money was needed to purchase the same quantity of petrol i.e. the purchasing power of money had decreased.

Companies are allowed an indexation allowance from the month of acquisition of an asset to the month of its disposal.

2.2 Calculation of indexation allowance

1. The indexation allowance is calculated using the movement in the RPI (Retail Price Index).

2. Each item of allowable expenditure is multiplied by the indexation factor.

The formula for the indexation factor is:

$$\frac{\text{RPI for the month of disposal - RPI for the month of acquisition}}{\text{RPI for the month of acquisition}}$$

Tip You will be given the RPIs in the exam if you need them.

3. The indexation allowance must be **rounded to three decimal places**.
4. The **indexation allowance cannot** be used to **create or increase a loss**.
5. The indexation allowance is calculated separately for each item of expenditure (such as cost of disposal, enhancement expenditure etc).

Example Good Ltd purchased an asset in May 1997 (RPI 156.9) for £28,500. The company sold it in June 2009 for £54,100 (RPI 213.4). In this situation, the capital gains after indexation allowances are calculated as follows:

	£
Disposal consideration	54,100
Less: Incidental costs of disposal	-
Net disposal consideration	54,100
Less: Allowable deductions	
Acquisition costs	(28,500)
Unindexed gain	25,600
Less: Indexation allowance	
£213.4 - £156.9 = (0.360) x £28,500	
£156.9	
	(10,260)
Indexed gain	**15,340**

Rounded to three decimal places

> **Example**
>
> Multi Ltd acquired a chargeable asset in April 2001. The cost of acquisition was £21,000. The company sold the asset in August 2009. The calculations of chargeable gain assuming actual sales proceeds were as follows:
> 1. £26,500
> 2. £22,800
> 3. £17,920
>
> (RPI of April 2001 – 173.1, RPI of August 2009 – 214.4)

	1 £	2 £	3 £
Disposal consideration	26,500	22,800	17,920
Less: Allowable deductions			
Acquisition costs	(21,000)	(21,000)	(21,000)
Unindexed gain / (loss)	5,500	1,800	(3,080)
Less: Indexation allowance	(5,019)	(5,019)	-
	(W1)	(note 1)	(note 2)
Indexed gain / (loss)	481	-	(3,080)

Working

W1 Indexation allowance = $\dfrac{(£214.4 - £173.1)}{£173.1} \times £21,000$

= 0.239 × £21,000

= £5,019

Note:

1. Indexation allowance is restricted to £1,800, as indexation allowance cannot be used to create a loss.
2. The company cannot claim indexation allowance, as indexation allowance cannot be used to increase loss.
3. The amount of capital gain will be charged to corporation tax.
4. The loss will be set off against other capital gains.

> **Example**
>
> Rosary Inc purchased a business asset on 20 August 2000 (RPI 170.5) for £27,800. The company incurred enhancement expenditure of £5,000 in December 2003 (RPI 183.5).
>
> Rosary Inc sold the asset in August 2009 (RPI 214.4) for £41,500. Chargeable gains on the disposal of the business asset are calculated as follows:

Calculation of chargeable gains of Rosary Inc

	£
Disposal consideration	41,500
Less: Allowable deductions	
Acquisition costs	(27,800)
Enhancement expenditure	(5,000)
Unindexed gain	8,700
Less: Indexation allowance (W1)	(7,985)
Indexed gain / (loss)	715

Note:

The amount of gain will be charged to corporation tax.

Working

W1 Indexation allowance

	£
1. On cost of acquisition $\dfrac{214.4 - 170.5}{170.5} = (0.257) \times £27,800$	7,145
2. On enhancement expenditure $\dfrac{214.4 - 183.5}{183.5} = (0.168) \times £5,000$	840
Total	**7,985**

C2.8: Chargeable Gains

> **Tip**
> Although you may be required to calculate the indexation allowance, the examiner has said that it is not examinable in detail. In many cases the actual indexation allowance figure will be provided as part of the question, or the figure given for the cost of an asset will already take account of indexation.

SUMMARY

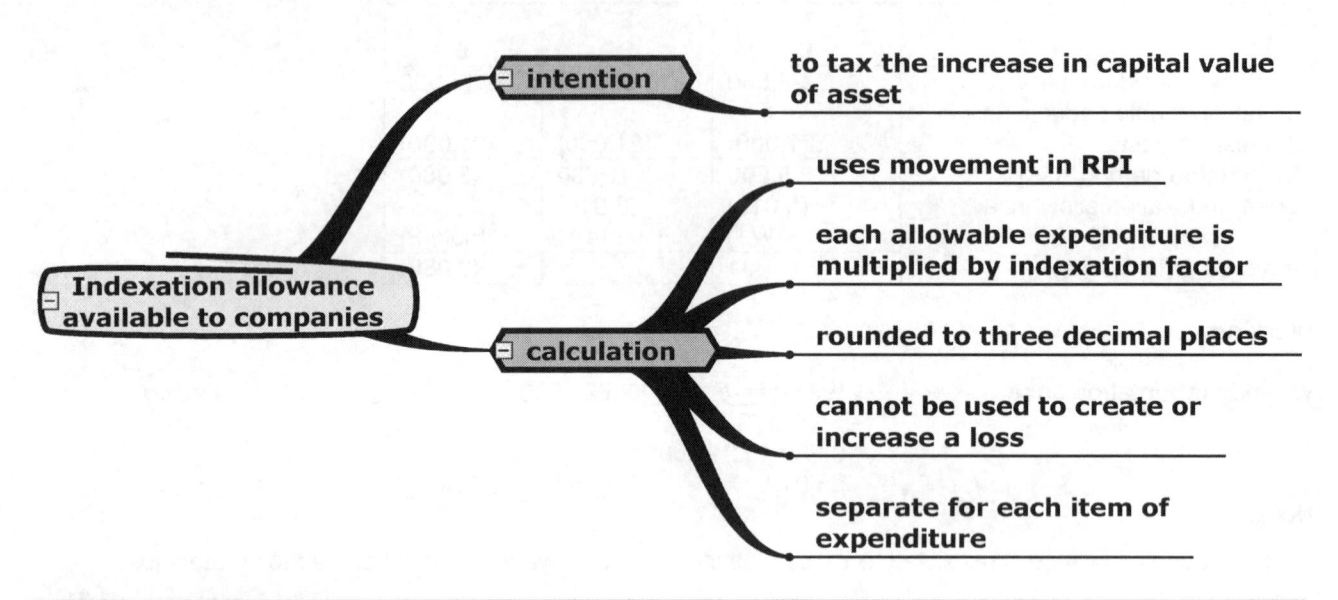

Indexation allowance available to companies
- **intention**: to tax the increase in capital value of asset
- **calculation**:
  - uses movement in RPI
  - each allowable expenditure is multiplied by indexation factor
  - rounded to three decimal places
  - cannot be used to create or increase a loss
  - separate for each item of expenditure

Test Yourself 4

In July 2000 (RPI 170.5) Arc Ltd purchased an asset for £35,300, and disposed of the asset in April 2009 (RPI 211.5) for £38,000.

Required:

a) Show the calculation for capital gains.

b) Suppose Lisa, a professional, owns this asset, what is the chargeable gain on disposal of the asset?

Test Yourself 5

Mars Ltd purchased a factory on 14 October 1996 (RPI 153.8) for £175,000. During March 1998 (RPI 160.8), the company incurred a cost of £40,000 for the extension of the factory.

During May 1999 (RPI 165.6), a fire occurred and the roof of the factory was damaged. So, the roof was repaired and the cost incurred for this purpose was £3,000.

On 25 May 2009 (RPI 212.8), Mars Ltd sold the factory for £400,000.

Mars Ltd incurred the following legal fees both at the time of purchasing the factory and at the time of sale.

Legal fees	£
At the time of purchase	4,000
At the time of sale	7,500

Required:

Calculate the chargeable gains of Mars Ltd.

3. Compute the amount of capital gains tax payable.[2]

[Learning outcome c]

3.1 Capital gains tax

An individual pays capital gains tax on his taxable gains.

Taxable gains are calculated as follows:

a) **Deduct** current capital losses and brought forward capital losses from net capital gains, to give chargeable gains.

b) Chargeable gains are **reduced by the annual exemption** to give taxable gains.

   Annual exemption:
   Every individual is entitled to an annual exemption which is deducted from capital gains income. The annual exemption limit for the tax year 2009 - 10 is £10,100.

c) Capital gains are calculated on this amount at the rate of 18%.

d) Capital gains tax is collected as **part of the self-assessment process**. It is **due on 31 January following the tax year.** Payments on account are not needed. So, capital gains tax liability for the tax year 2009 - 10 will be payable on 31 January 2011.

Proforma for calculation of taxable gains

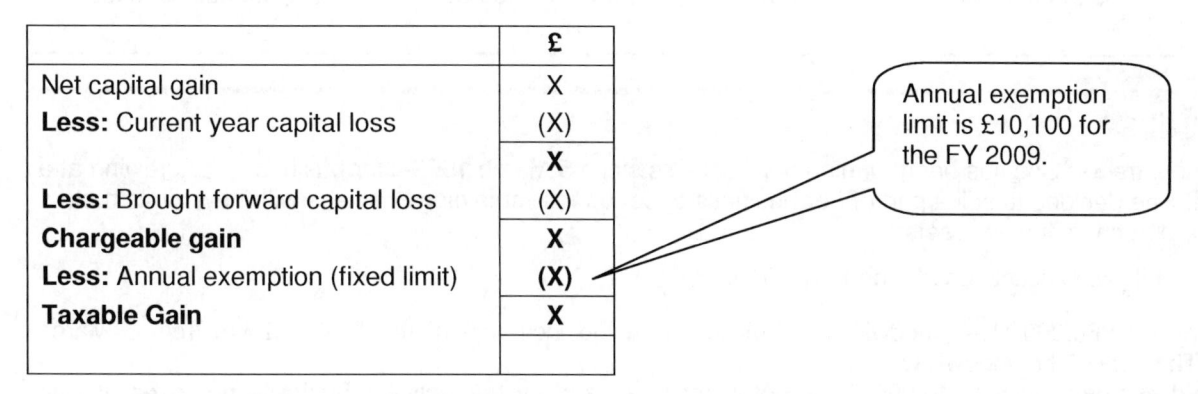

	£
Net capital gain	X
Less: Current year capital loss	(X)
	X
Less: Brought forward capital loss	(X)
Chargeable gain	X
Less: Annual exemption (fixed limit)	(X)
Taxable Gain	X

> Annual exemption limit is £10,100 for the FY 2009.

e) If the sum of the chargeable gains for a year is less than the annual exemption, the assessment is **nil** and any **unused annual exemption is lost.**

Example

During 2009 - 10, Sweety made a capital gain of £20,000. Sweety cannot claim her personal allowance (£6,475) against capital gain but she can claim it only against her net income while computing income tax. However, for capital gains annual exemption is available. Her capital gains tax liability is calculated as follows:

	£
Net chargeable gain	20,000
Less: Annual exemption	(10,100)
Taxable gain	9,900
Total capital gain tax liability @ 18%	1,782

Example

Naomi has chargeable capital gains of £16,600 during the tax year 2009 - 10. Her trading profits for 2009 – 10 are £38,000. Calculate Naomi's total tax liability.

Calculation of income tax payable

	£
Trading profits	38,000
Less: Personal allowance	(6,475)
Taxable income	**31,525**
Tax liability	
Income tax (£31,525 x 20%)	6,305

Calculation of capital gains tax liability

	£
Chargeable capital gains	16,600
Less: Annual exemption	(10,100)
Taxable capital gains	**6,500**
Tax liability	
Capital gain tax (£6,500 x 18%)	1,170

Naomi's total tax liability is £7,563 (£6,305 + £1,170)

Since £31,525 falls in the basic rate tax band of £37,400, it will be taxed at 20%. The capital gain is taxed at a single rate of 18%.

Example

Suzy is a sole trader. She has been running her business since 5 March 1999. Her business was growing at a rapid pace. She decided to sell a part of her business to set up the remaining business with new infrastructure through the purchase of new assets.

She sold the following assets on 25 February 2010:

1. Goodwill for £60,000. The goodwill was built up from the inception of the business i.e. from 5 March 1999. The cost of the goodwill was nil.
2. She sold a motor car for £40,000. The motor car was used by her only for business purposes. It was purchased on 2 November 2007 for £30,000.
3. A freehold office building was sold for £150,000. The office building was used by Suzy only for business purposes. The office building was purchased by her on 2 July 2008 for £120,000.
4. A freehold warehouse was sold for £160,000. This warehouse was never used by her for business purposes. It was purchased on 5 March 1999 for £96,000.

Suzy's property income for 2009 - 10 was £31,000.

Compute Suzy's total tax liability for 2009 - 10.

To compute the capital gains for the year, we have to compute the gain derived from each individual transaction as follows:

Goodwill

	£
Sale proceeds	60,000
Less: Acquisition cost	-
Net gain	**60,000**

Freehold office building

	£
Sale proceeds	150,000
Less: Acquisition cost	(120,000)
Net gain	**30,000**

Continued on next page

Freehold Warehouse

	£
Sale proceeds	160,000
Less: Acquisition cost	(96,000)
Net gain	**64,000**

Notes:

1. Capital gain is calculated separately for each asset disposed.
2. Motor car is exempt from capital gains tax.

Computation of total taxable gains

	£
Goodwill	60,000
Freehold office building	30,000
Freehold warehouse	64,000
Chargeable gains	**154,000**
Less: Annual exemption	(10,100)
Taxable gains	**143,900**
Capital gains tax at 18%	**25,902**

Suzy's tax liability is calculated as follows:

	£
Property income	31,000
Less: Personal allowance	(6,475)
Taxable income	**24,525**
Income tax	
On £24,525 @20%	4,905

Test Yourself 6

For the year 2009-10, Colin's salary income is £7,135. This income is before deduction of personal allowance. During the tax year, he made a capital gain of £62,000 on disposal of his business asset.

Required:

Calculate the tax payable by Colin during 2009-10.

4. Explain the treatment of capital losses for both individuals and companies.[1]
[Learning outcome d]

4.1 Treatment of capital losses for companies

1. A capital loss is **first set against any CAPITAL gains in the same accounting period**.

2. **If any capital loss remains**, it is **carried forward and set against the first available capital gains in future** accounting periods.

3. When a company incurs a capital loss, the capital gain in the PCTCT calculation is nil, **(never a negative figure). Capital losses are never set against other income.**

Example

Margaret Ltd has been engaged in a trading business for many years.

The results of its trading and other incomes for two years are as follows:

	Year ended 31 March 2009 £	Year ended 31 March 2010 £
Adjusted trading profit / (loss)	60,000	(20,500)
Property business income	5,000	12,000
Capital gain / (loss)	(10,000)	90,000

The taxable income of Margaret Ltd for the two years is calculated as follows:

	Year ended 31 March 2009 £	Year ended 31 March 2010 £
Adjusted trading profit	60,000	-
Property business income	5,000	12,000
Capital gain (W1)	-	80,000
Total income	**65,000**	**92,000**
Less: Loss relief	-	(20,500)
PCTCT	**65,000**	**71,500**

Working

W1 Capital gains

Capital Gains for year ended 31 March 2010 = £90,000 - £10,000 (loss b/f of year ended 31 March 2009) = £80,000.

4.2 Treatment of capital losses for individuals

1. **Current year losses**

a) Must be **set off against current year capital gains**, and **cannot be restricted** to preserve annual exemption.

b) Are set off **before brought forward capital losses and annual exemption.**

Example

Information relating to three friends is shown below.

	Tom £	Dick £	Harry £
Capital gains for 2009 - 10	12,000	15,000	13,000
Capital losses for 2009 - 10	13,400	800	10,500

Continued on next page

Calculation of taxable gains is as follows:

	Tom £	Dick £	Harry £
Capital gain for 2009 - 10	12,000	15,000	13,000
Less: Current year capital loss (note)	(12,000)	(800)	(10,500)
Brought forward capital loss	-	-	-
Chargeable gain	-	14,200	2,500
Less: Annual exemption	-	(10,100)	(2,500)
Taxable gain / (loss)	-	4,600	-

Note:

The current year's losses must be **set off against the current year's gains**, and **cannot be restricted** to preserve annual exemption.

Therefore for Tom, it is not possible to restrict the current year's losses to £1,900 (£12,000 - £10,100) to preserve the annual exemption of £10,100. Tom's remaining loss of £1,400 (£12,000 - £13,400) can be carried forward and set against the first available capital gains in future tax years.

Also, for Harry it is not possible to restrict the current year's losses. He has to set off the current year's losses in full, even though his annual exemption to the extent of £7,600 (i.e. £10,100 - £2,500) is wasted.

2. Capital losses b/f

a) Must be set off against the first available net gains in the future.
b) Losses brought forward are only set off to reduce current year capital gains (after current year losses) to the annual exempt amount. Note, this means that the b/f losses are deducted up to the amount which makes up the total net gains equal to the exempt amount.

Example

The following is the available information for the three friends.

	Tom £	Dick £	Harry £
Capital gains for 2009 - 10	8,000	15,000	21,000
Capital losses for 2009 - 10	13,400	800	10,500
Carried forward capital losses for 2008 - 09	600	1,000	5,000

Calculation of taxable gains is as follows:

	Tom £	Dick £	Harry £
Capital gain for 2009 - 10	8,000	15,000	21,000
Less: Current year capital loss	(8,000)	(800)	(10,500)
Current year net capital gain	-	14,200	10,500
Brought forward capital loss	-	(1,000)	(400) (note)
Chargeable gain	-	13,200	10,100
Less: Annual exemption	-	(10,100)	(10,100)
Taxable gains / (loss)	-	3,100	-

Working

W1 Loss memorandum

	Tom £	Dick £	Harry £
b/f capital losses for 2008 - 09	600	1,000	5,000
Less: Set off against gains for 2009 - 10	-	(1,000)	(400)
Add: Current year unrelieved capital loss 2009 - 10 (£13,400 - £8,000)	5,400		
Loss c/f to 2010-11	6,000	-	4,600

Note: After set off of current year capital losses, the balance of the gain remaining is £10,500. Brought forward losses are set off to reduce current year capital gains up to the annual exemption amount, hence loss relief for brought forward losses is restricted to £400, so as to leave net gains exactly equal to the annual exemption amount of £10,100 (£10,500 – £400).

Example

In August 2009, Robin sold a business asset and made a capital gain of £25,000. He also sold gold coins realising a capital loss of £1,500. He has a brought forward capital loss of £3,000. His business income for the tax year 2009 - 10 is £30,000. His tax liability is calculated as follows:

Step 1 Computation of capital gains tax liability

	£
Capital gain	25,000
Less: Current year capital loss	(1,500)
Current year net capital gain	23,500
Brought forward capital loss	(3,000)
Net chargeable gains	20,500
Less: Annual exemption	(10,100)
Taxable gains	10,400
Capital gains tax at 18%	1,872

Step 2 Computation of income tax liability

	£
Trading profits	30,000
Less: Personal allowance	(6,475)
Taxable income	23,525
Income Tax	
£23,525 @20%	4,705

3. Losses on disposal to a connected person

a) Losses on disposals to a connected person **cannot be set off** against all chargeable gains.
b) They can **only be set against gains made on disposals to the same connected person** in the same or future years.

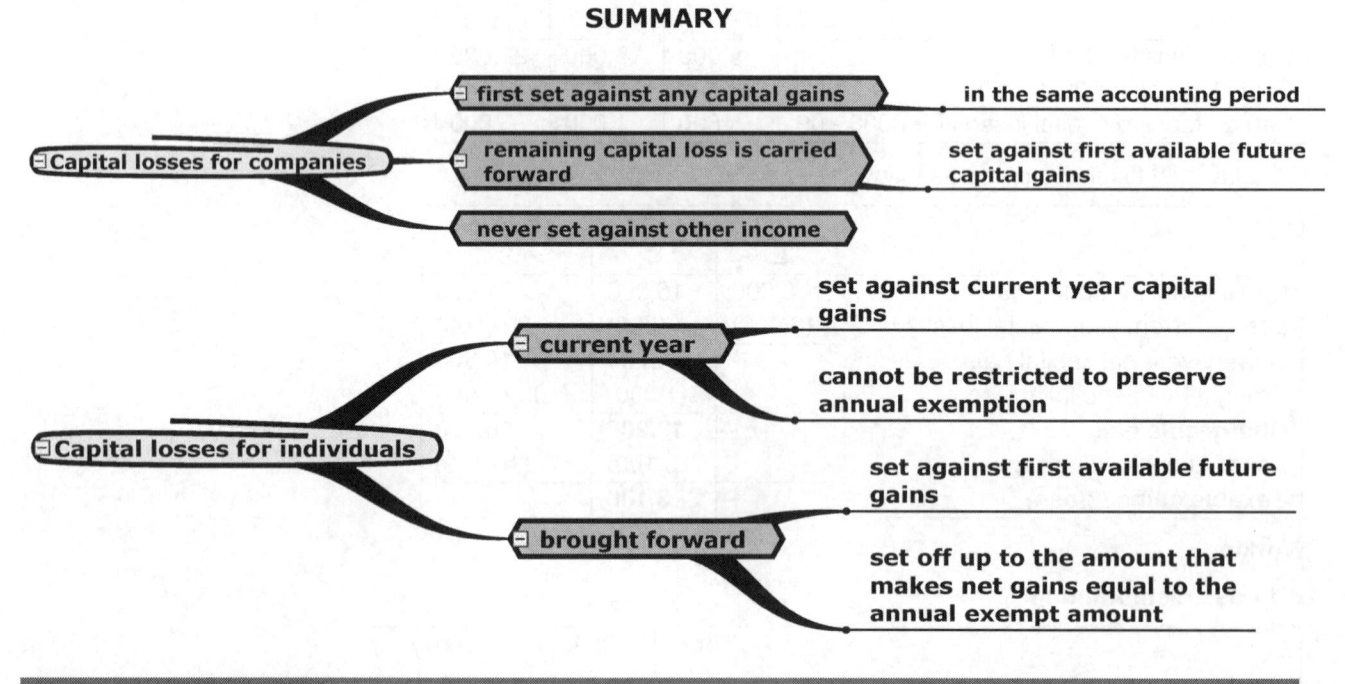

SUMMARY

Capital losses for companies
- first set against any capital gains — in the same accounting period
- remaining capital loss is carried forward — set against first available future capital gains
- never set against other income

Capital losses for individuals
- current year
  - set against current year capital gains
  - cannot be restricted to preserve annual exemption
- brought forward
  - set against first available future gains
  - set off up to the amount that makes net gains equal to the annual exempt amount

Test Yourself 7

Alan has a loss of £37,100 carried forward from the previous year (2008 - 09). His current year's (2009 - 10) capital gain is £32,500, and his capital loss is £2,700.

Required:

Show the calculation of chargeable gains for the tax year 2009 - 10.

Answers to Test Yourself

Answer 1

Calculation of chargeable gains

	£
Disposal consideration	30,000
Less: Incidental costs of disposal	(500)
Net disposal consideration	**29,500**
Less: Allowable deductions	
Acquisition costs (including incidental costs) (£40,000 + £500)	(40,500)
Enhancement expenditure	(10,000)
Gain / (loss)	**(21,000)**

Note: £10,000 spent on machinery will be treated as enhancement expenditure, as it improves the utility of the asset.

Answer 2

Margaret had given her diamond jewellery to her daughter as a present. As the gift of an asset is also considered to be a chargeable disposal, chargeable gain is calculated as follows:

	£
Disposal consideration (note)	20,000
Less: Incidental costs of disposal	-
Net disposal consideration	**20,000**
Less: Allowable deductions	
Acquisition costs	(15,000)
Gain / (loss)	**5,000**

Note: When an asset is disposed of by way of a gift, the disposal consideration is the market value of an asset on the day of the gift.

Answer 3

Calculation of chargeable gains / losses

	£
Disposal consideration	60,000
Less: Incidental costs of disposal	(500)
Net disposal consideration	**59,500**
Less: Allowable deductions	
Acquisition costs	(50,000)
Chargeable gain / (loss)	**9,500**

Answer 4

a) Calculation of indexed capital gains of Arc Ltd

	£
Disposal consideration	38,000
Less: Allowable deductions	
Acquisition costs	(35,300)
Unindexed gain	**2,700**
Less: Indexation allowance (W1)	(2,700)
Indexed gain / (loss)	**-**

Working

W1 Indexation allowance = $\frac{£211.5 - £170.5}{£170.5}$ = (0.240) x £35,300

= £8,472

However, the allowable indexation allowance is £2,700, as indexation allowance cannot convert gain into loss.

b) Computation of indexed capital gains of Lisa

	£
Disposal consideration	38,000
Less: Allowable deductions	
Acquisition costs	(35,300)
Gain	**2,700**

Note: Indexation allowance is withdrawn for individuals from 6 April 2008.

Answer 5

Computation of indexed capital gains / losses

	£
Disposal consideration	400,000
Less: Incidental costs of disposal	(7,500)
Net disposal consideration	**392,500**
Less: Allowable deductions	
Acquisition costs (£175,000 + £4,000)	(179,000)
Enhancement expenditure	(40,000)
Unindexed gain	**173,500**
Less: Indexation allowance (W1)	(81,656)
Indexed gain / (loss)	**91,844**

Working

W1 Indexation allowance

	£
1. On cost of acquisition $\frac{£212.8 - £153.8}{£153.8}$ = (0.384) x £179,000	68,736
2. On enhancement expenditure $\frac{£212.8 - £160.8}{£160.8}$ = (0.323) x £40,000	12,920
Total	**81,656**

Note:

1. Repairs and maintenance expenses are not considered to be enhancement expenditure as they are not of a capital nature.

2. The amount of indexed gain will be charged to corporation tax.

Answer 6

Calculation of Colin's income tax liability for 2009-10

	£
Salary income	7,135
Less: Personal allowance	(6,475)
Total taxable income	660
Tax liability	
Income tax (£660 @ 20%)	132

Calculation of Colin's capital gains tax liability for 2009-10

	£
Total capital gain	62,000
Less: Annual exemption	(10,100)
Taxable gain	51,900
Capital gains tax liability (£51,900 @18%)	9,342

Answer 7

Calculation of taxable gains

	£
Capital gain for 2009 - 10	32,500
Less: Current year capital loss	(2,700)
Current year net capital gain	**29,800**
Brought forward capital loss (note)	(19,700)
Chargeable gains	**(10,100)**
Less: Annual exemption	(10,100)
Taxable gains / (loss)	-

Note: Relief for brought forward capital losses is restricted to £19,700 so that Alan can take full advantage of annual exemption. The remaining loss of £17,400 (£37,100 – 19,700) can be carried forward to set off against future capital gains.

Working

W1 Loss memorandum

	£
Capital losses b/f from 2008 - 09	37,100
Less: Set off against gains for 2009 -10	(19,700)
Loss c/f to 2010 - 11	**17,400**

Quick Quiz

1. What is market value?

2. What is the purpose of providing indexation to assets?

3. Is indexation allowance given to individuals?

Answers to Quick Quiz

1. The market value is the value the asset can achieve if sold in the open market.

2. The indexation allowance was introduced as a relief against inflation and is available only to companies.

3. For individuals, indexation allowance is not available from 6 April 2008.

Self Examination Questions

Question 1

Stuart purchased an asset in July 1990 for £28,000. In May 2007, he incurred additional expenditure of £2,500 to improve the working life of the asset.

In November 2009, he sold this asset for £40,000. The incidental expenditure of the sale was £800.

Required:

Show the calculation of the capital gains tax for 2009 - 10, assuming that he carried forward the previous year's capital loss of £8,100.

Question 2

Fire Plc purchased a chargeable asset on 9 March 1983, for £15,000 (RPI 83.1). The company incurred enhancement expenditure of £4,600 on 20 April 2001 (RPI 173.1).
The asset was sold in May 2009 (RPI 212.8) for £51,000.

Required:

Compute the chargeable gains.

Question 3

Canara Ltd purchased a non-business asset in March 1983 for £15,400 (RPI 83.1). In August 2000 (RPI 170.5), the company incurred additional enhancement expenditure of £2,100 on the asset to improve its utility. In June 2009 (RPI 213.4), the company sold this asset for £37,000.

Required:

Calculate the amount of chargeable gains.

Answers to Self Examination Questions

Answer 1

Calculation of capital gain

	£
Disposal consideration	40,000
Less: Incidental cost of disposal	(800)
Net disposal consideration	39,200
Less: Cost of acquisition	(28,000)
Net capital gain	11,200
Less: Current year capital loss	-
Current year net capital gain	11,200
Less: Brought forward capital loss	1,100
Chargeable gain	10,100
Less : Annual Exemption	(10,100)
Net capital gain	-
CGT @ 18%	-

Notes:

1. Additional expenditure is allowable expenditure for the calculation of chargeable gains, provided it enhances the utility of the asset.

    Stuart incurred additional expenditure to improve the working life of an asset. It did not enhance the utility of the asset. Hence it is not an allowable expenditure.

2. Relief for brought forward capital losses is restricted to £1,100 i.e. (£11,200 − £10,100) so that full advantage of annual exemption can be taken.

Answer 2

Calculation of chargeable gains

	£	£
Disposal consideration		51,000
Less: Allowable deductions		
Cost of acquisition	15,000	
Enhancement expenditure	4,600	(19,600)
Unindexed gain		31,400
Less : Indexation allowance		
Cost of acquisition		
$\frac{(£212.8 - £83.1)}{£83.1} = (1.561) \times £15,000$	23,415	
Enhancement expenditure		
$\frac{(£212.8 - £173.1)}{£173.1} = (0.229) \times £4,600$	1,053	(24,468)
Chargeable gain		**6,932**

Answer 3

Computation of chargeable gains of Canara Ltd

	£
Disposal consideration	37,000
Less: Allowable deductions	
Cost of acquisition	(15,400)
Enhancement expenditure	(2,100)
Unindexed gain	**19,500**
Less: Indexation allowance	
Cost of acquisition	(19,500)
$\frac{(£213.4 - £83.1)}{£83.1}$ = (1.568) x £15,400	(note)
Enhancement expenditure	
$\frac{(£213.4 - £170.5)}{£170.5}$ = (0.252) x £2,100	-
Indexed gain	**-**

Note:

Indexation allowance for the actual cost of acquisition is £24,147 (calculated above).
However, as indexation allowance cannot be used to create or increase a loss, it is restricted to £19,500.

For the same reason, no indexation allowance is given for enhancement expenditure.

SECTION C: CHARGEABLE GAINS

C3

STUDY GUIDE C3: FURTHER PRINCIPLES OF COMPUTING GAINS AND LOSSES

■ Get Through Intro

This Study Guide explains the treatment of transfers between a husband and wife, the treatment to be given to an asset which is lost, damaged or destroyed and the computation of allowable expenditure for part disposal of a chargeable asset.

A thorough understanding of these principles is a must so that in future you can easily tackle these complex issues.

Knowledge of these principles is essential both from the examination point of view and also for your future professional life.

■ Learning Outcomes

a) Explain the treatment of transfers between a husband and wife or between a couple in a civil partnership.
b) Compute the amount of allowable expenditure for a part disposal.
c) Explain the treatment where an asset is damaged, lost or destroyed, and the implications of receiving insurance proceeds and reinvesting such proceeds.

C3.2: Chargeable Gains

Introduction

Case Study

Suzanne had a good collection of antique furniture. The total furniture was worth around £200,000. On 4 May 2008, due to fire, most of the furniture was destroyed. Fortunately she had taken out insurance coverage for the furniture.

In the month of January 2009, the insurance company paid her compensation of £150,000. As it was antique furniture, she could not replace the furniture and she retained the whole amount.

When she received a notice from HMRC to pay tax, she was surprised. From her point of view, she had lost her furniture and had duly received compensation from the insurance company. Why should she then have to pay tax on that?

We will try to understand the provisions relating to compensation for a destroyed or damaged asset in detail, but first let us look at transfers between husband and wife.

1. Explain the treatment of transfers between a husband and wife or between a couple in a civil partnership.[2]

[Learning outcome a]

1. Disposal between husband and wife / civil partners is **not exempt**.
2. If transfer is after 6 April 2008, original cost of the asset to the spouse disposing the asset is considered the disposal value for the spouse acquiring the asset so that neither a chargeable gain nor an allowable loss arises. (No gain / no loss transfer).

Tip — Situations before 6 April 2008 are not examinable.

3. Market value is used if transfer is between connected persons, but the market value is not used as a disposal proceeds in this case.
4. On a subsequent disposal, the acquisition cost for the spouse making the disposal is the value taken into account to reach a no gain / no loss position on the original transfer.

Example

In January 2001 Roger purchased 2000 shares for £20,000. In May 2008, Roger transferred these shares to his wife, Camilla. The market value of the shares on that date was £35,000.

As the disposal is between husband and wife, neither a chargeable gain nor an allowable loss arises. Hence, it is considered that the shares are transferred to the spouse (wife) at the original cost of £20,000.

In October 2009, Camilla sold these shares for £47,000. Calculation of chargeable gain on this disposal of shares is as follows:

	£
Disposal consideration	47,000
Less: Allowable deductions	
Acquisition costs (note1)	(20,000)
Net chargeable gain	**27,000**

Note:

In the case of the disposal of an asset between husband and wife, the acquiring spouse is treated as having acquired the asset at its original cost to the other spouse to make a no gain / no loss transfer. In the case of Camilla, it is assumed that she had acquired these shares for £20,000.

Test Yourself 1

Michael sold a piece of land on 10 May 2009 for £250,000. This land was purchased by Margaret, Michael's wife for £190,000 on 25 July 2006. She transferred the land to Michael on 20 November 2008 for £225,000. On this date, the market value of the land was £210,000.

Required:

Calculate Michael's chargeable gains.

> **2. Compute the amount of allowable expenditure for a part disposal.**[2]
> [Learning outcome b]

We have already seen in Study Guide C1, that a chargeable disposal **includes the disposal of part of an asset**. As only a part of the asset is sold (e.g. John sold only the first floor of his house and kept the ground floor for himself), only part of the original cost of the entire asset can be used as the acquisition cost.

Important points to note

1. The **original cost** is **allocated** between the **part disposed of** and the **part retained**.
2. The **cost is allocated according to the market values** at the time of disposal of the part disposed of and the part retained.
3. The cost is **not allocated based on size** (e.g. if part of a plot of land is sold).
4. When the part retained is eventually sold, the balance of the original cost is used.

The cost of the part disposed of is calculated as:

Cost of the part disposed = Total Cost x A/(A+B)

Where:

A is the market value of the part being disposed of, and
B is the market value of the part being retained.

Example

Jack purchased 5 acres of land on 15 July 2007 for £250,000. He sold 3 acres of land for £290,000 on 20 February 2010. The land was never used for business purposes. The market value of the unsold acres of land as on 20 February 2010 was £110,000.

Here, we will have to calculate the cost of the piece of land that was sold first.
Out of 5 acres of land, 3 acres were sold.

Therefore, the cost relating to the three acres of land = Total Cost x A/(A+B)

= £250,000 x £290,000/ (£290,000+£110,000)
= £250,000 x £290,000/£400,000
= £181,250

This is how you should present the answer in the examination:

	£
Disposal consideration	290,000
Less: Allowable deductions	
Acquisition costs (including incidental costs)	(181,250)
Chargeable gains	**108,750**

Example

In December 1996 (RPI 154.4), Alistair Ltd bought a chargeable asset for £32,000. In July 2009 (RPI 213.4), it sold 40% of the interest in the asset for £14,000. The cost of disposing the asset was £480. The market value of the remaining 60% of interest in the asset is £38,000.

The calculation of chargeable gain on part disposal is as follows:

	£
Disposal consideration	14,000
Less: Incidental costs of disposal	(480)
Net disposal consideration	13,520
Less: Allowable deductions	
Part acquisition costs £14,000/(£14,000 + £38,000) x £32,000	(8,615)
Gain	**4,905**
Less: Indexation allowance (note) $\frac{213.4 - 154.4}{154.4}$ = (0.382) x £8,615	(3,291)
Chargeable gain	**1,614**

Note: companies are eligible for indexation allowance from the date of acquisition until the date of disposal.

Test Yourself 2

In December 1997 (RPI 160.0), Soft Ltd purchased a chargeable asset for £50,000. In May 2009 (RPI 212.8), it sold 35% of the interest in the asset for £22,000. The cost of disposing the asset was £1,400.

The market value of the remaining 65% of interest in the asset was £56,000. In August 2009 (RPI 214.4), Soft Ltd disposed of the remaining part of the asset for £56,000.

Required:

Calculate the chargeable gains of Soft Ltd.

---

3. **Explain the treatment where an asset is damaged, lost or destroyed, and the implications of receiving insurance proceeds and reinvesting such proceeds.**[2]

[Learning outcome c]

3.1 Asset lost / destroyed entirely

> **Tip** Asset lost and asset destroyed receive the same treatment.

This covers the following situations

1. No compensation received
2. Compensation received, but no replacement
3. Compensation received, asset replaced

1. No compensation received

If an asset is entirely lost or destroyed, then there is a **disposal** for capital gains tax purposes, giving rise to an **allowable loss**.

Example

Merry bought a painting for £50,000 in May 2004. It was destroyed by fire in August 2009, and no compensation was received.

Here, she realises an allowable loss of £50,000 (as the proceeds are nil).

2. Compensation received, but no replacement

If an asset is totally destroyed, and compensation or insurance proceeds are received, this is treated as a **CGT disposal**, with the **money received being the proceeds**.

Example Continuing with the example of Merry

She received insurance proceeds of £65,000 in October 2009 as a compensation for the painting.

	£
Sale proceeds (Insurance proceeds)	65,000
Less: cost of acquisition	(50,000)
Gain	15,000

Here, the transaction is treated as disposal of the painting. The disposal proceeds are £65,000 and cost of acquisition is £50,000. Accordingly capital gains of £15,000 (£65,000 - £50,000) will be charged to CGT.

3. Compensation received, asset replaced

a) If all the proceeds are used to buy a replacement asset within 12 months, the gain arising on destruction of the asset can be deferred by deducting the gain from the base cost of the replacement asset.

Example Continuing with the example of Merry,

In March 2010, Merry purchased a replacement asset costing £67,000.

	£
Sale proceeds (Insurance proceeds)	65,000
Less: cost of acquisition	(50,000)
Deferred gain	15,000

Here, as all the insurance proceeds of £65,000 are used to buy a replacement asset within 12 months, the gain of £15,000 can be deferred by deducting the gain from the base cost of the replacement asset.
Therefore, the deemed or base cost of the replaced asset will be

	£
Cost of Replaced Asset	67,000
Less : deferred gain	(15,000)
Deemed cost of replaced Asset	52,000

b) If the full proceeds are not used on the replacement asset, the gain (up to the amount of proceeds not reinvested) is chargeable now, and the balance of the gain is deducted from the base cost of the replacement asset.

Example Glory bought a painting for £50,000 in May 2004. It was destroyed by fire in August 2009. Glory received insurance proceeds of £65,000.

In March 2010, Glory purchased a replacement asset costing £63,000.

	£
Sale Proceeds (Insurance proceeds)	65,000
Less: cost of acquisition	(50,000)
Total gain	15,000
Less: Amount not re-invested (£65,000 - £63,000) chargeable to capital gains	(2,000)
Deferred gain	13,000

Continued on next page

Here, out of total insurance proceeds of £65,000, only £63,000 is used on the replacement asset. Therefore, out of a total gain of £15,000, £2,000 (£65,000 - £63,000) is chargeable to capital gain tax immediately. The balance gain of £13,000 can be deferred by deducting the gain from the base cost of the replacement asset. Therefore, the base cost or deemed cost of the replaced asset will be

	£
Cost of Replaced Asset	63,000
Less : deferred gain	(13,000)
Deemed cost of replaced Asset	50,000

Diagram 1: Asset entirely lost or destroyed

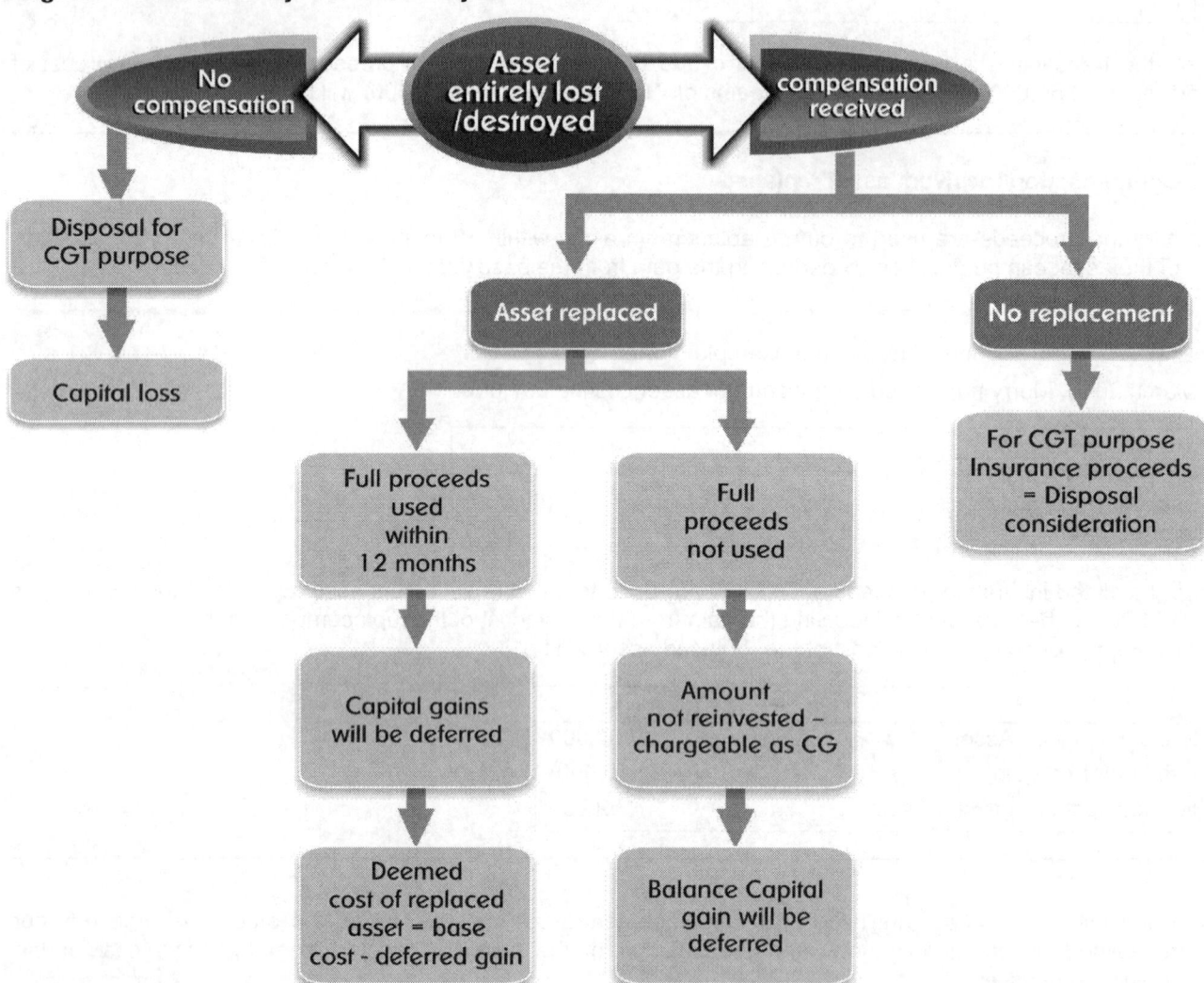

```
                    Asset entirely lost/destroyed
            ←                                        →
      No compensation                        compensation received
            ↓                                        ↓
    Disposal for                      ┌──────────────┴──────────────┐
    CGT purpose                  Asset replaced              No replacement
            ↓                         ↓                            ↓
      Capital loss         ┌──────────┴──────────┐         For CGT purpose
                      Full proceeds         Full              Insurance proceeds
                      used within          proceeds           = Disposal
                      12 months            not used           consideration
                           ↓                    ↓
                     Capital gains        Amount
                     will be deferred     not reinvested –
                           ↓              chargeable as CG
                     Deemed                    ↓
                     cost of replaced     Balance Capital
                     asset = base         gain will be
                     cost - deferred gain deferred
```

3.2 Asset damaged, compensation received

When an asset has been damaged, and compensation or insurance proceeds are received, this is **treated as a part disposal** (for part disposal, refer to Learning Outcome 2 above). The market value of the asset in its damaged condition is considered the market value of the part retained.

If compensation is used to restore the asset, the taxpayer may claim that instead of being treated as a part disposal, the sum received can be deducted from the allowable expenditure when the gain is computed on the subsequent disposal of the asset.

To claim this, one of the following conditions must be met

a) All of the sum received must be spent on restoring the asset **OR**
b) The amount not spent on restoring the asset is 'small' **OR**
c) The amount received is '**small**'

Definition of 'small'

For this purpose, the sum is regarded as small, if the sum received / not used for restoration is **less than 5% of the proceeds received,** restricted to **maximum of £3,000**.

Example — If all of the compensation amount is used to restore the asset

Alan bought an asset for £10,000. The asset was damaged and the value of the asset in its damaged condition was £2,000. Alan received compensation of £4,000. He spent all the compensation on restoring the asset.

Here, as all the proceeds were used in restoration, a claim may be made to deduct the proceeds from the cost of the asset i.e. not to treat this as part-disposal.

The allowable expenditure on **subsequent disposal** is £10,000 calculated as follows

	£
Cost of asset	10,000
Less: Compensation receipt	(4,000)
	6,000
Add: Expenditure on restoration	4,000
Adjusted cost	**10,000**

Example — If compensation not used in restoring the asset is small

Alan bought an asset for £10,000. The asset was damaged and the value of the asset in its damaged condition was £2,000, Alan received compensation of £4,000. He spent £3,900 of the compensation on restoring the asset.

Therefore, £100 of the compensation was not used to restore the asset. This does not exceed 5% of the capital sum received and is also less than £3,000, so a claim may be made to deduct the proceeds from the cost of the asset i.e. to not treat this as part-disposal.

The allowable expenditure on **subsequent disposal** is £9,900 calculated as follows:

	£
Cost of asset	10,000
Less: Compensation received	(4,000)
	6,000
Add: Expenditure on restoration	3,900
Adjusted cost	**9,900**

> **Tip:** If the compensation remaining is not small, then all proceeds would be treated as part disposal.

Example — If compensation not used in restoring the asset is not small

In April 2003, Winston purchased an antique statue for £100,000. On 5 May 2009, the statue was damaged by fire. In December 2009, the insurance company paid him compensation of £28,000.

Winston did not use the sum received from the insurance company for restoring the statue. The market value of the damaged statue was £150,000.

Continued on next page

C3.8: Chargeable Gains

Here, the capital gains are calculated as follows

	£
Disposal consideration	28,000
Less: Allowable deductions	
Part acquisition costs £28,000/(£28,000 + £150,000) x £100,000	(15,730)
Net gain	**12,270**

Note:

1. Winston can carry forward the balance of allowable expenditure, £84,270 (£100,000 - £15,730) and can use the same in the calculation of the gain arising on subsequent disposal.

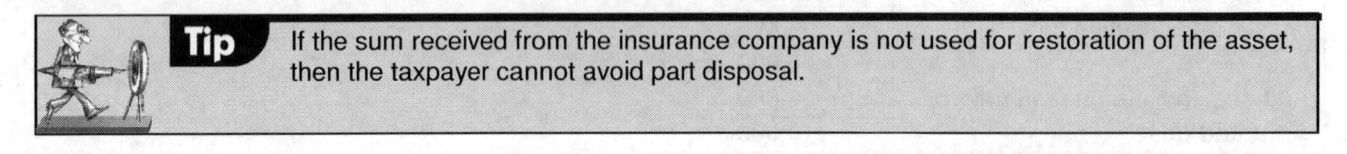

> **Tip:** If the sum received from the insurance company is not used for restoration of the asset, then the taxpayer cannot avoid part disposal.

It is possible to claim to have part of the capital sum which was applied in restoring the asset deducted from the acquisition cost of the asset. The proceeds not applied in restoring the asset are treated as a part-disposal.

Diagram 2: Asset damaged

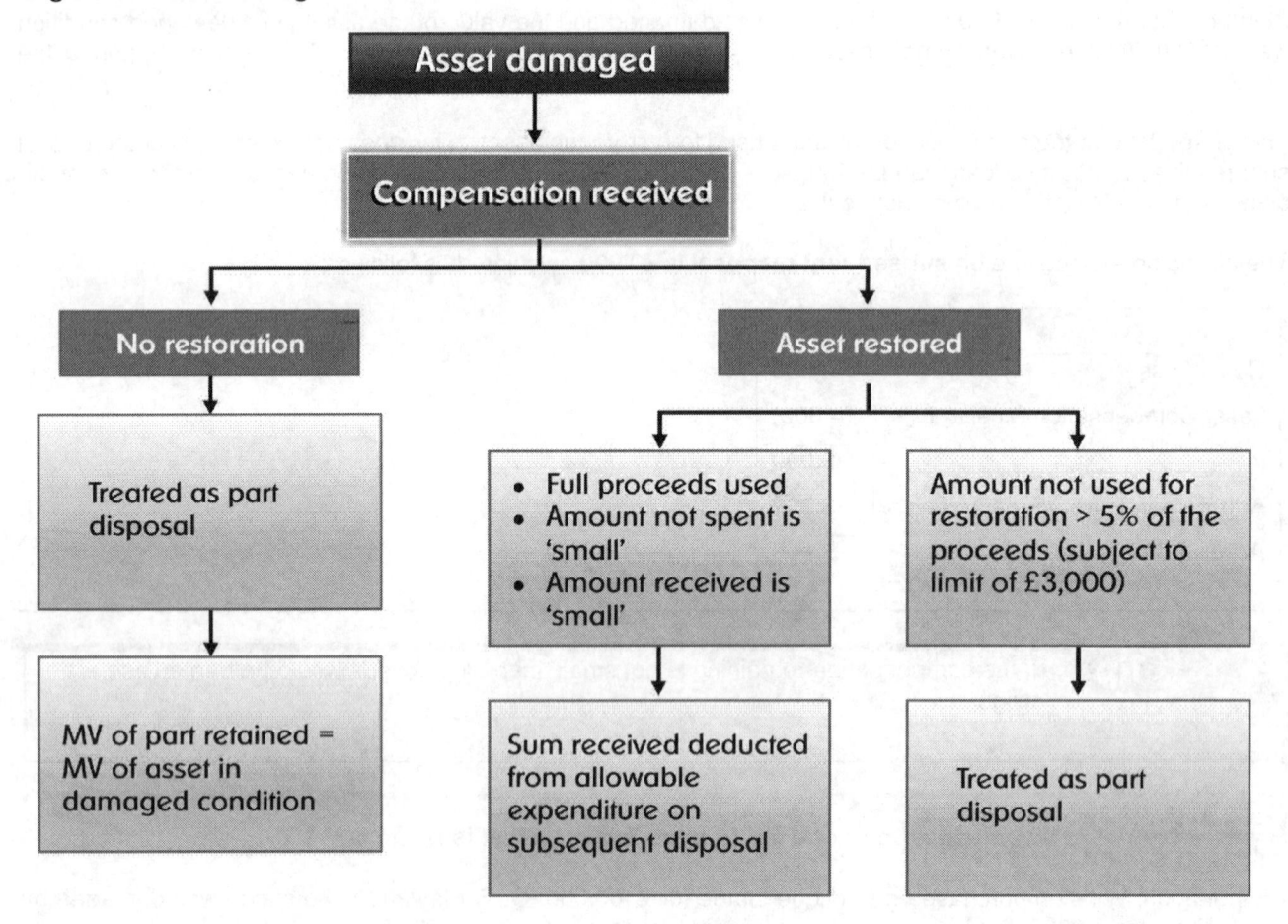

```
                    Asset damaged
                          │
                          ▼
                 Compensation received
                    │            │
         ┌──────────┘            └──────────┐
         ▼                                  ▼
   No restoration                     Asset restored
         │                          │              │
         ▼                          ▼              ▼
   Treated as part          • Full proceeds    Amount not used for
   disposal                   used             restoration > 5% of the
         │                  • Amount not       proceeds (subject to
         ▼                    spent is         limit of £3,000)
   MV of part retained =      'small'                │
   MV of asset in           • Amount received         ▼
   damaged condition          is 'small'        Treated as part
                                  │             disposal
                                  ▼
                           Sum received deducted
                           from allowable
                           expenditure on
                           subsequent disposal
```

Test Yourself 3

Jill purchased a painting for £41,000 in January 2006. On 3 May 2009, the painting was destroyed due to a fire. In August 2009, she received a sum of £48,000 from the insurance company. She spent £49,000 to replace the painting.

Required:

Show the computation of chargeable gains.

Answers to Test Yourself

Answer 1

	£
Disposal consideration	250,000
Less: Allowable deductions	
Acquisition costs (note)	(190,000)
Chargeable gains	**60,000**

Note: in the case of the disposal of an asset between husband and wife, the acquiring spouse is treated as having acquired the asset at its original cost to the other spouse. In the case of Michael, it is assumed that he had acquired the land for £190,000. The value at which Michael purchased the asset from his wife and the market value of the land are not relevant where the transfer is between a husband and wife or between civil partners.

Answer 2

Calculation of chargeable gains on disposal of 35% interest in the asset

	£
Disposal consideration	22,000
Less: Incidental costs of disposal	(1,400)
Net disposal consideration	**20,600**
Less: Allowable deductions	
Part acquisition costs	(14,103)
£22,000/(£22,000 + £56,000) x £50,000	
Gain	**6,497**
Less: Indexation allowance	
$\frac{212.8 - 160.0}{160.0}$ = (0.330) x £14,103	(4,654)
Indexed gain	**1,843**

Note: companies are eligible for indexation allowance from the date of acquisition until the date of disposal. The cost when a part of an asset is sold is allocated according to the market value at the time of the part disposal of the part disposed of and the part that is retained.

Calculation of chargeable gains on disposal of remaining 65% interest in the asset

	£
Disposal consideration	56,000
Less: Allowable deductions	
Part acquisition costs (note)	(35,897)
(£50,000 - £14,103)	
Gain	**20,103**
Less: Indexation allowance	
$\frac{214.4 - 160.0}{160.0}$ = (0.340) x £35,897	(12,205)
Indexed gain	**7,898**

Note: The acquisition cost of 65% interest in the asset is calculated as follows:

Part acquisition cost (65% interest) = Total cost – cost allocated on sale of 35% interest
= £50,000 - £14,103 = £35,897

Answer 3

Computation of chargeable gains

	£
Disposal consideration	48,000
Less: Cost of acquisition	(41,000)
Chargeable gains	**7,000**

£7,000 may be deducted from the cost of the painting purchased to replace the original painting. So, the cost of the new painting will be £42,000 (£49,000 - £7,000).

Due to this, Jill's capital gain tax liability is postponed until she sells the painting that she had purchased to replace the original.

Quick Quiz

1. Fill in the blanks.

   (a) In the case of part disposal of an asset, the original cost is allocated between the part _____ and the _____.

   (b) If an asset is totally destroyed, and compensation is received, then this transaction is treated as a ____ for capital gain tax purposes.

2. What is the effect of transfer of assets between spouses or civil partners?

Answers to Quick Quiz

1.
(a) Disposed of, part retained

(b) Disposal

2. When an asset is transferred between spouses or civil partners, it is not a chargeable disposal, as the asset is deemed to be transferred at no gain / no loss. However, the **subsequent transfer** of the asset is treated as a chargeable disposal.

Self Examination Questions

Question 1

Henry sold a plot of land on 5 March 2010 for £500,000.

This land was purchased by Jerry, Henry's wife for £200,000 on 20 July 2008. She transferred the land to Henry on 5 November 2009 for £250,000. On this date, the plot of land was valued at £300,000.

Required:

Calculate Henry's chargeable gains.

Question 2

Mack purchased 5 acres of land on 20 July 2008 for £500,000. He sold 3 acres of land for £550,000 on 25 February 2010. The market value of the unsold acres of land on 25 February 2010 was £220,000.

Required:

Calculate Mack's chargeable gains.

Question 3

Lisa purchases a set of diamond necklace and earrings for £120,000 in June 1996.

She sells the diamond earrings for £40,000 in April 2009. The incidental cost of sale is £450. On the date the earrings were sold, the market value of the necklace was £160,000.

Required:

Show the calculation of chargeable gains.

Answers to Self Examination Questions

Answer 1

	£
Disposal consideration	500,000
Less: Allowable deductions	
Acquisition costs (W1)	(200,000)
Chargeable gains	**300,000**

Working

W1

In the case of the disposal of an asset between husband and wife, the acquiring spouse is treated as having acquired the asset at its original cost, along with any incidental costs and enhancement expenditure to the other spouse. Therefore, the acquisition cost of the land for Henry is £200,000. The price at which Henry purchased the asset (£250,000) from his wife and the market value of the plot of land at the date of acquisition (£300,000) are not considered for calculation of CGT.

Answer 2

	£
Disposal consideration	550,000
Less: Allowable deductions	
Acquisition costs (including incidental costs) (W1)	(357,143)
Chargeable gains	**192,857**

Working

W1

Cost is allocated according to the market values of the part disposed of and the part retained at the time of part disposal.
Here, we will have to calculate the cost of the land that was sold. Out of 5 acres of land, 3 acres of land was sold.

The cost relating to three acres of land sold = £500,000 x £550,000/(£550,000 + £220,000)
= £500,000 x £550,000/£770,000
= £357,143

Answer 3

Computation of chargeable gains

	£
Disposal consideration	40,000
Less: Incidental cost of disposal	(450)
Net disposal consideration	39,550
Less: Cost of acquisition $\dfrac{£40,000}{(£40,000 + £160,000)} \times £120,000$	(24,000)
Chargeable Gain	15,550

Note: Cost of acquisition is allocated according to the market values of the part disposed of (diamond earrings) and the part retained (diamond necklace) at the time of part disposal.

SECTION C: CHARGEABLE GAINS

C4

STUDY GUIDE C4: GAINS AND LOSSES ON THE DISPOSAL OF MOVABLE AND IMMOVABLE PROPERTY

Get Through Intro

Capital gains tax has a wide scope and can be split into various sections for the purpose of easy understanding. One **new section** which has been introduced in the new syllabus deals with **capital gains tax on the disposal of movable and immovable property.**

Movable and immovable property forms a **major section** of capital assets of both individuals and companies and its disposal normally is a **major component of capital gains tax**.

This Study Guide discusses the principles of identification of chattels and wasting assets and introduces you to the important **concept of a principal private residence**. It also deals with the treatment of capital gains tax on their disposal.

Learning Outcomes

a) Identify when chattels and wasting assets are exempt.
b) Compute the chargeable gain when a chattel is disposed of.
c) Calculate the chargeable gain when a wasting asset is disposed of.
d) Compute the exemption when a principal private residence is disposed of.
e) Calculate the chargeable gain when a principal private residence has been used for business purposes.
f) Identify the amount of letting relief available when a principal private residence has been let out.

Introduction

Case Study

Sam owns various assets such as an antique table, shares in Sun Ltd, a television set and a watercolour painting. He has owned these assets for many years.

On 5 May 2009, he sold the antique table, the shares in Sun Ltd and the watercolour painting for £500,000, £200,000 and £450,000 respectively.

Are all these assets chargeable to capital gains tax under the same provisions?

The answer to this question is - 'No'. There are different provisions that apply to different classes of assets.

These provisions are explained in depth in this Study Guide.

1. Identify when chattels and wasting assets are exempt.[1]
[Learning outcome a]

1.1 Chattel

A chattel is tangible, movable property: something touchable and not fixed, for example, painting, jewellery etc. Examples of properties which are not chattels are:

- Shares (intangible)
- House (immovable)

1.2 Wasting asset

A wasting asset is an asset which has a predictable life of less than 50 years at the time of acquisition, e.g. plant and machinery. Such assets may also include copyrights or registered designs.

1.3 Types of chattels

- **Wasting chattel:** a wasting chattel is a chattel with an expected life of less than 50 years. Wasting chattels are exempt e.g. greyhounds, racing horse etc.

- **Non-wasting chattel:** a non-wasting chattel is a chattel with an expected life of more than 50 years, e.g. antiques, paintings etc.

1.4 Exempt chattels

The disposal of following chattels is exempt:

1. **Wasting chattels** (unless used in a business and eligible for capital allowances).
2. **Non-wasting** chattels when **sold for £6,000 or less, realising a gain.**

Test Yourself 1

1. Katherine had a painting. Is the gain on disposal of this painting chargeable to CGT?

2. Tina acquired an item of plant for £8,000. The plant has a working life of 20 years. She used the plant for business purposes for 5 years. After 5 years, Tina wanted to sell the plant for £10,000. Advise her as to whether the gain on this disposal will be liable to capital gains tax.

SUMMARY

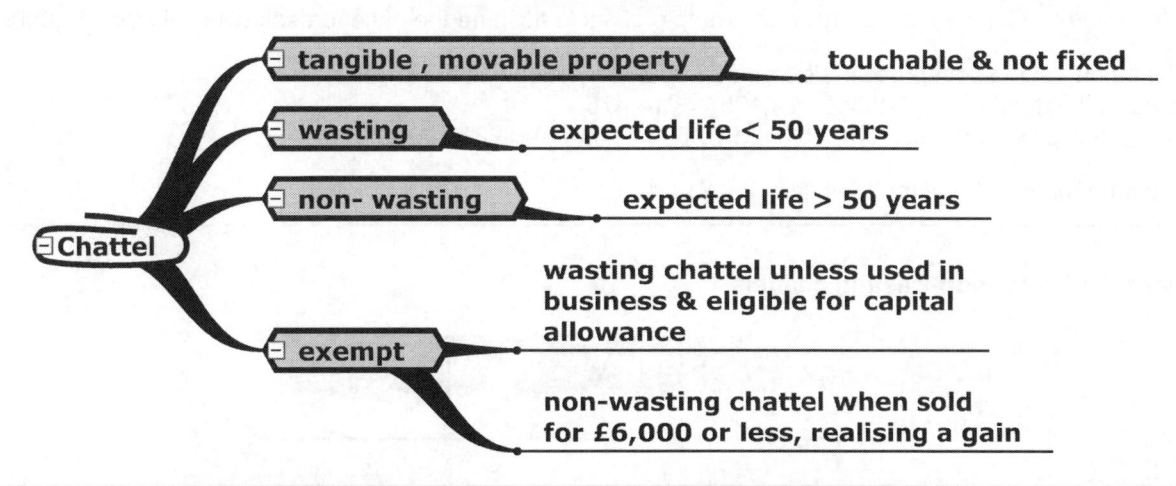

- **Chattel**
  - **tangible, movable property** — touchable & not fixed
  - **wasting** — expected life < 50 years
  - **non-wasting** — expected life > 50 years
  - **exempt**
    - wasting chattel unless used in business & eligible for capital allowance
    - non-wasting chattel when sold for £6,000 or less, realising a gain

2. Compute the chargeable gain when a chattel is disposed of.[2]

[Learning outcome b]

2.1 Rules for computing CGT on disposal of non-wasting chattels

1. If gross sale proceeds are **£6,000 or less**, any **gain is exempt.**

Example
Alan bought a painting for £4,250 in January 2007 and sold it in November 2008 for £5,800. As the sale proceeds are less than £6,000, the gain is fully exempt.

2. If gross sale proceeds are **less than £6,000**, any **loss is allowable**, but gross **sale proceeds** are **deemed** to be **£6,000**.

Example
Rex bought an antique vase for £7,650 in October, 2007 and sold it for £5,250 in February, 2010. As the gross sale proceeds are less than £6,000, when calculating the chargeable gains, the actual sale proceeds are deemed to be £6,000.

Therefore, the allowable loss will be £1,650 (£7,650 - £6,000).

3. If gross sale proceeds **exceed £6,000**, the gain is the **lower of**:
a) The normal net gain
b) 5/3 x (gross proceeds - £6,000)

Example
Jack bought an antique desk for £4,125 in December 2007 and sold it for £7,200 in January 2010. As the sale proceeds exceed £6,000, the net gain is the **lower of**:
1. the normal net gain
2. 5/3 x (gross proceeds - £6,000)

	£
Disposal consideration	7,200
Less: Allowable deductions	
Acquisition costs (including incidental costs)	(4,125)
Net gain	**3,075**

Therefore the net gain is the **lower of**:
1. £3,075
2. 5/3 of (£7,200 - £6,000) = £2,000

Hence, the net gain is £2,000.

Example

Continuing the previous example of Jack, assume the antique desk was sold for £18,600.

In this situation, as the sale proceeds exceed £6,000, the net gain is the lower of:
1. the normal net gain, i.e. (£18,600 - £4,125) = £14,475
2. 5/3 x (gross proceeds - £6,000) = 5/3 x (£18,600 - £6,000) = £21,000

Hence, the net gain is the normal net gain, i.e. £14,475.

Diagram 1: Rules for non-wasting chattels

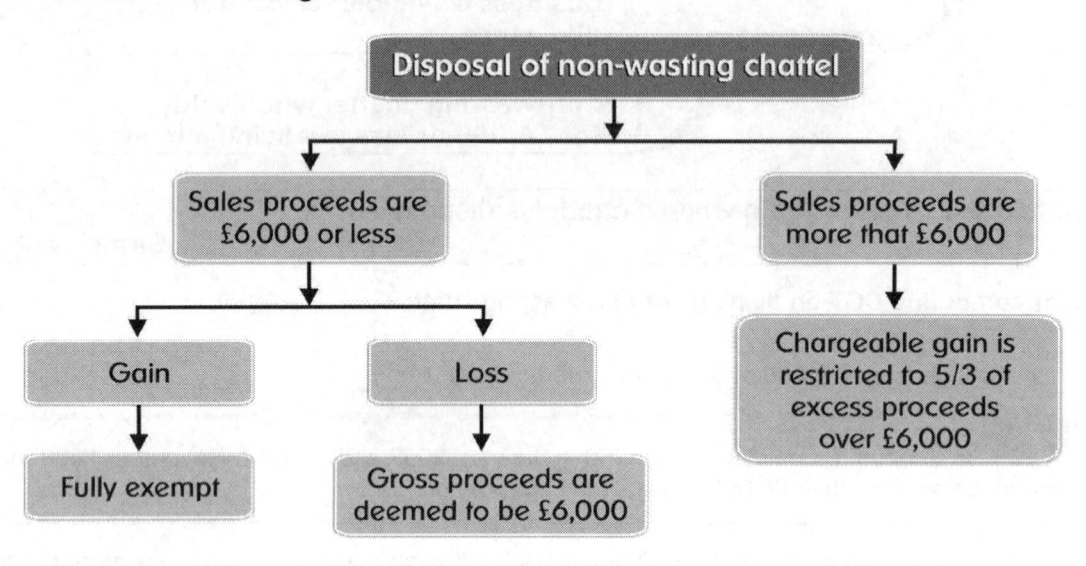

```
                    Disposal of non-wasting chattel
                    /                              \
        Sales proceeds are                  Sales proceeds are
        £6,000 or less                      more than £6,000
          /        \                                |
        Gain      Loss                    Chargeable gain is
         |         |                      restricted to 5/3 of
     Fully      Gross proceeds are        excess proceeds
     exempt    deemed to be £6,000        over £6,000
```

2.2 Rules for computing CGT on disposal of wasting chattel

1. A gain on the disposal of a wasting chattel is **exempt,** unless it is used in a business and eligible for capital allowances (in such a case, it is treated as a non-wasting chattel).

Example

In December 2009, Cathy disposed of a greyhound for £7,250, bought for £3,150 in February 2009. As this is a wasting asset not used in business and not eligible for capital allowances, the gains arising on its disposal are exempt.

2. The rules for computation of CGT on disposal of the wasting chattels used in business and **eligible for capital allowances** (plant and machinery) are as follows:

➢ If they are sold at a loss, then CGT computation is not considered, as the loss has already been given as capital allowance. While computing CGT, the net amount of capital allowances given (after deducting balancing charges on disposal) are deducted from allowable expenditure so that neither a chargeable gain nor an allowable loss arises.

➢ If they are sold at a gain, then capital gain is calculated normally by treating it as a disposal of the non-wasting chattels. Hence, the rules for computing CGT on disposal of non-wasting chattels will be applicable.

Example

Peter disposed of machinery which was used in his business, for £7,440 in November 2009. This machinery was originally bought for £15,250 in September 08.

As the machinery was sold at a loss, the net amount of capital allowances given will be deducted from the allowable expenditure while computing CGT so that neither a chargeable gain nor an allowable loss arises.

Continued on next page

The capital allowances on machinery will be computed as follows:

	FYA £	Allowances £
Year ended 31/03/08		
Additions qualifying for AIA	15,250	
Less: AIA	(15,250)	15,250
TWDV c/f	-	
Allowances		**15,250**
Year ended 31/03/09		
TWDV b/f	-	
Less: Disposal	(7,440)	
Balancing charge	**(7,440)**	**(7,440)**

The capital loss on sale of machinery will be computed as follows:

		£
Disposal consideration		7,440
Less: Allowable deductions		
Acquisition costs	15,250	
Less: Net capital allowances given (£15,250 - £7,440)	(7,810)	(7,440)
Net gain / loss		**-**

Example — Continuing the previous example of Peter

Assume the machinery was bought for £4,250 in September 08. In this situation, although the machinery is a wasting chattel (expected life being not more than 50 years), it is treated as a non-wasting chattel as it is used in the business, is eligible for capital allowances and is sold at a gain. Therefore, the capital gain will be calculated normally and the rules for non-wasting asset (as discussed above) will be applicable.

Capital allowance computation is as follows:

	FYA £	Allowances £
Year ended 31/03/08		
Additions qualifying for AIA	4,250	
Less: AIA	(4,250)	4,250
TWDV c/f	-	
Allowances		**4,250**
Year ended 31/03/09		
TWDV b/f	-	
Less: Disposal (restricted to cost)	(4,250)	
Balancing charge	**(4,250)**	**(4,250)**

The capital gain on sale of machinery will be computed as follows:

		£
Disposal consideration		7,440
Less: Allowable deductions		
Acquisition costs	4,250	
Less: net capital allowances given (£4,250 - £4,250)	-	(4,250)
Net gain		**3,190**

As the sale proceeds exceed £6,000, chargeable gain is the lower of:
1. the normal net gain which is £3,190
2. 5/3 of excess proceeds over £6,000 which is 5/3 (£7,440 - £6,000) = £2,400

Hence, the net gain is £2,400.

3. **No losses** are allowable.

> **Example** Merry disposed of a greyhound for £7,250, in December 2009, originally bought for £8,150 in February 2009. Here, as this is a wasting asset, losses arising on its disposal are not allowable.

Test Yourself 2

Jack purchased antique furniture a few years ago for £2,900. He decided to replace this furniture and sold it for £8,200.

Required:

Show the calculation of chargeable gains on the disposal of furniture.

Test Yourself 3

Jay is a trader. On 9 February 2005, he purchased a machine for £41,000. This machine was eligible for capital allowances. He used this machine for four years for business purposes and then on 20 April 2009 Jay sold the machine.

Required:

Show the calculation of chargeable gains on disposal of machinery assuming the disposal value is:
1. £25,000
2. £49,000
3. £5,000

3. Calculate the chargeable gain when a wasting asset is disposed of.[2]
[Learning outcome c]

A wasting asset is one which is not a chattel and which has a predictable life of less than 50 years when acquired. Such assets may include copyrights or registered designs. The allowable cost to be used in calculating the chargeable gain must be apportioned so that only the part relating to the remaining life of the asset is taken into account.

The asset is depreciated on a straight line basis over its useful life.

> **Example** Katie sold a registered design of her latest dress creation. This was a business asset with a 35 year life when acquired. It had a remaining useful life of 15 years on disposal. The registered design was sold for £20,000 in January 2010. The design had originally cost £10,000 in January 1990.
>
> The calculation of chargeable gain is as follows:
>
> | | £ |
> | --- | --- |
> | Disposal consideration | 20,000 |
> | **Less:** Cost of acquisition (allowable cost 15/35 x £10,000) | (4,286) |
> | **Chargeable gain** | 15,714 |

Note: The allowable cost represents the 15 years of life remaining out of the 35 years predictable total life of the asset.

4. Compute the exemption when a principal private residence is disposed of.[2]

[Learning outcome d]

4.1 Principal private residence

1. The disposal of an **individual's only or main residence** (principal private residence) **is fully exempt** if the **property** is **occupied** by the owner **throughout the period of ownership**.

   This is known as principal private residence relief **(PPR relief)**.

2. If the property has been **unoccupied for a part of the period of ownership**, then **part of the gain** may be **chargeable**.

   The exempt part of the gain (PPR relief) is:

   $$\frac{\text{Periods of occupation}}{\text{Total period of ownership}} \times \text{net gain}$$

   > **Tip**
   > The period of residence and the period of ownership are calculated to the nearest month.

3. Periods of occupation include periods of actual occupation and periods of deemed occupation.

4. Some periods of absence are deemed to be periods of occupation which are as follows:

   a) the **last 36 months – always exempt** i.e. the taxpayer will get full PPR relief whether or not, during the last 36 months, the taxpayer was using the property as his residence and whether or not the taxpayer owns another PPR.
   b) any length of period whilst the individual is **employed overseas.**
   c) a total of up to **4 years where the individual is working** (employed or self-employed) **elsewhere in the UK.**
   d) a total of **3 years for any reason.** This period **need not be a consecutive period** of thirty six months.
   The periods of occupation mentioned in (b) to (d) above are treated as periods of occupation only if:
   i. the taxpayer **claims no other property as his principal private residence,** and
   ii. at **some time both before and after the period of absence** there is a **period of actual residence.**

5. It is the **net gain** that is **exempt**.

> **Example**
> Brian owned a house in London. He had purchased this house on 1 June 1995 for £35,000. He used this apartment as his main residence until 31 May 2003. On 1 June 2003, he moved to a rented house. The apartment was then unoccupied until it was sold on 31 May 2009 for £75,000.

In this situation the chargeable gain (after PPR exemption) is calculated as follows:
Step -1 Calculate total chargeable gain before PPR
Step -2 Calculate PPR exemption
Step -3 Calculate chargeable gain after PPR

Step 1 Calculate total chargeable gain before PPR

	£
Disposal consideration	75,000
Less: Cost of acquisition	(35,000)
Net gain	**40,000**

Step 2 Calculate PPR exemption

Calculation of periods of occupation by Brian:

	Total (Months)	Exempt (months)	Chargeable (months)
1 June 1995 to 31 May 2003 (actual occupation)	96	96	
1 June 2003 to 31 May 2009 (absence- any reason) (Note)	72	36	36
	168	132	36

Last 36 months are always exempt

Continued on next page

Note: Brian's period of absence for any reason will not be considered deemed occupation for principal private residence relief as there should be an actual period of residence both before and after the period of absence. As Brian has not returned after he left his residence on 31 May 2003, PPR relief will not be available for this period. However, the last 36 months of ownership are always exempt.

PPR relief = Period of actual and deemed residence x net gain
                       Period of ownership
= 132 x £40,000
    168
= **£31,429**

Step 3 Calculate chargeable gain after PPR

	£
Net gain	40,000
Less: PPR relief	(31,429)
Chargeable gain	**8,571**

Test Yourself 4

On 1 February 2010, Melanie sold a residential property for £80,000. She had purchased this property on 1 April 1986 for £15,000 and occupied it as her principal residence from the date of purchase until 31 May 2000. The property was then unoccupied until it was sold on 1 February 2010.

Required:

Calculate chargeable gain (after PPR exemption).

Example

Henry purchased a house in Birmingham on 1 April 1989 for £150,000. He occupied this house as his main residence from the date of purchase until 30 June 1993. On 1 July 1993, he shifted to a rented flat in Norwich due to change in his job. He again occupied the house from 1 January 1996 to 31 July 2003 as his main residence. After that, he shifted to Canada due to his job and remained there until he sold his house on 31 December 2009 for £300,000.

Henry's chargeable gains (after PPR exemption) shall be calculated as follows:

Step 1 Calculate total chargeable gain before PPR
Step 2 Calculate PPR exemption
Step 3 Calculate chargeable gain after PPR

Step 1 Calculate total chargeable gain before PPR

	£
Disposal consideration	300,000
Less: Cost of acquisition	(150,000)
Net gains	**150,000**

Step 2 Calculate PPR relief

Calculation of periods of occupation by Henry:

	Total (months)	Exempt (months)	Chargeable (months)
1 April 1989 to 30 June 1993 (Actual occupation)	51	51	
1 July 1993 to 31 December 1995 (employed elsewhere in the UK) (Note 1)	30	30	
1 January 1996 to 31 July 2003 (Actual occupation)	91	91	
1 August 2003 to 31 December 2009 (unoccupied) (Note 2)	77	36	41
	249	**208**	**41**

Continued on next page

Notes:

1. A total of up to four years where an individual is employed elsewhere in the UK is deemed to be period of occupation for calculation of PPR relief, only if the property was occupied both before and after the period of absence.
2. Any period where an individual is employed to work abroad is considered deemed occupation for principal private residence relief but there should be an actual period of residence both before and after the period of absence. As Henry has not returned after he left his residence to work abroad on 1 August 2003, PPR relief will not be available for this period. However, the last thirty-six months of ownership are always exempt.

$$\text{PPR relief} = \frac{\text{Period of actual and deemed residence}}{\text{Period of ownership}} \times \text{Net gain}$$

= 208/241 x £150,000
= **£129,461**

Step 3 Calculate chargeable gain after PPR

	£
Net gains	150,000
Less: PPR relief	(129,461)
Chargeable gain	**20,539**

Test Yourself 5

On 1 May 1993, Pinky purchased a residential property in Wick for £28,000. She occupied this house until 30 June 1998. On 1 July 1998 she moved to the USA, to start a new job there. She was in the USA for 3 years and 4 months. On 1 November 2001 Pinky returned to the property, but on 31 December 2001 she moved to Leeds to be closer to her family. The property has been unoccupied ever since.

On 1 April 2010, she sold her house in Wick for £58,000.

Required:

Calculate Pinky's chargeable gain (after PPR exemption).

4.2 Important points to remember

While computing gain from disposal of principal private residence we must remember the following points:

1. For tax purposes, the taxpayer has only one principal private residence. If he owns more than one principal private residence then he has to **elect** which property is to be considered his principal private residence.

    This election must be made **within 2 years** of commencing occupation of the second residence.

Example Clara owns an apartment in Skegness and another in Lincoln. Normally she stays in Skegness. However once a month she goes to Lincoln for her business work. Even though most of the time Clara uses the property in Skegness as the main residence, she may elect which property is to be treated as her PPR.

2. A married couple or civil partners living together may have **only one main principal private residence between them**. If they own more than one main house, then they have to elect which property is to be treated as their PPR.

Example Merry and Cherry are husband and wife. Both of them are working with a software company. Before marriage, Merry owned a house at Leicester and Cherry owned a house in Nottingham. Now, after marriage, they are staying together in Leicester.

After marriage, they must elect which property is to be treated as their PPR.

SUMMARY

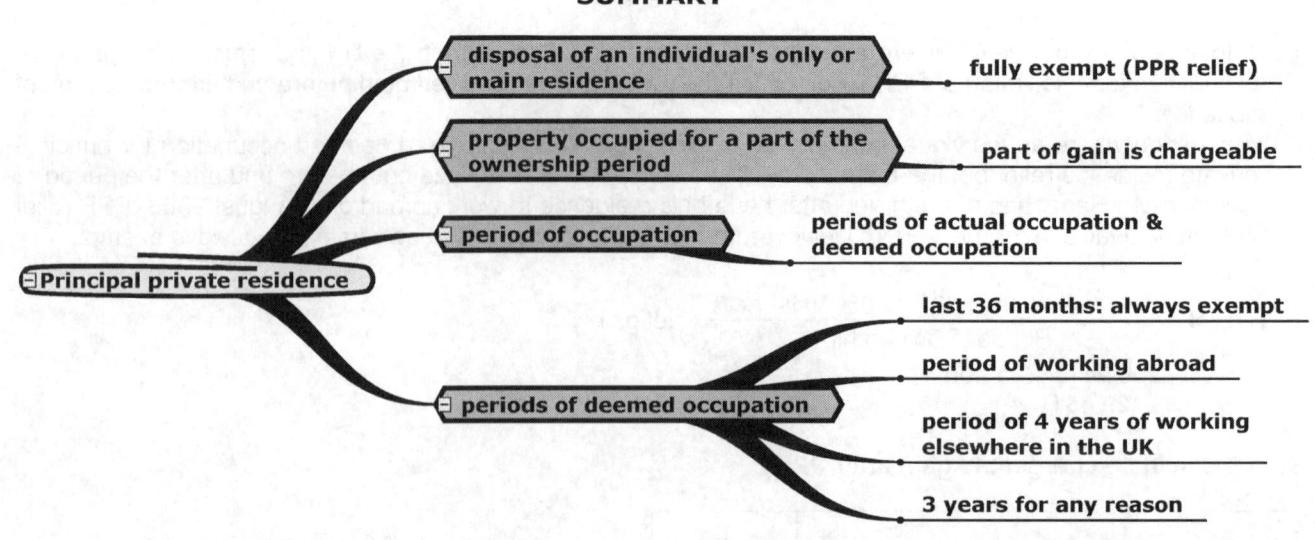

- **Principal private residence**
  - disposal of an individual's only or main residence → **fully exempt (PPR relief)**
  - property occupied for a part of the ownership period → **part of gain is chargeable**
  - period of occupation → periods of actual occupation & deemed occupation
  - periods of deemed occupation
    - last 36 months: always exempt
    - period of working abroad
    - period of 4 years of working elsewhere in the UK
    - 3 years for any reason

5. Calculate the chargeable gain when a principal private residence has been used for business purposes.[2]

[Learning outcome e]

If an individual has used part of his principal private residence for business purposes, that **proportion of the gain will be chargeable** for the period the residence was used for business purposes.

The PPR exemption for the **last 36 months** of ownership is **not applicable** to the **part of the property** which is used exclusively for **business purposes throughout the period of the ownership**.

However, if that part of the main residence was used for business purposes for only part of the period of ownership, then the last 36 months of exemption will be **applicable** to the **whole of the property** despite the fact that there has been some business use.

Example

Rick purchased a house on 1 June 1995 for £13,000 and was using half of the house for his business purposes throughout the period of ownership. On 1 April 2010, he sold this house for £65,000.

Here, chargeable gain is calculated as follows:

Step 1 Calculation of total chargeable gain

	£
Disposal consideration	65,000
Less: Cost of acquisition	(13,000)
Net capital gain	**52,000**
Less: PPR relief (Note)	
£52,000 x 50%	(26,000)
Chargeable gains	**26,000**

Note:

The house was occupied by Rick throughout the period of ownership; hence the entire capital gain is eligible for PPR relief.

However, the PPR exemption for the last 36 months of ownership will not be applicable for half of the house used for business purposes as it was used exclusively for business purposes throughout the period of ownership.

SUMMARY

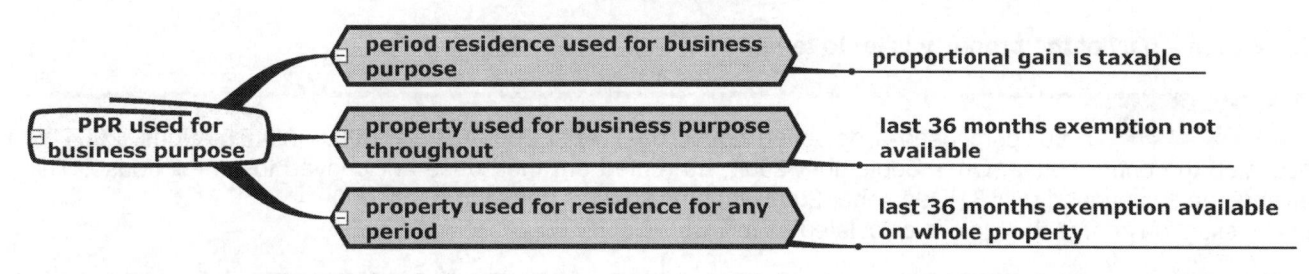

PPR used for business purpose:
- period residence used for business purpose → proportional gain is taxable
- property used for business purpose throughout → last 36 months exemption not available
- property used for residence for any period → last 36 months exemption available on whole property

Test Yourself 6

Mohammed was working with Excellence Plc as a marketing manager. During his period of service, he purchased a house for £16,400. The date of purchase of the house was 1 April 1993.

On 1 May 2005, he left the job and started a new business. From that date until the date of sale of the house i.e. 1 May 2009, he was using the house for business as well as domestic purposes. He sold the house for £59,200. 35% of the property was used for business purposes.

Required:

Show the calculation of chargeable gain on the disposal of the house.

---

6. **Identify the amount of letting relief available when a principal private residence has been let out.**[2]

[Learning outcome f]

- Where a principal private residence has been let out to tenants, **letting relief may be available.**
- Principal private residence relief (**PPR relief**) is deducted from the net gain first, then letting relief is deducted.
- Letting relief is the **lowest of:**
  ✓ PPR relief
  ✓ £40,000
  ✓ the gain that arose in the letting period
- Letting relief can reduce a gain to nil, but **cannot create a loss.**

Proforma

	£	£
Disposal consideration		X
Less: Cost of acquisition		(X)
		X
Less: PPR relief		
Gain x Period of actual and deemed residence / Period of ownership		(X)
Gain after PPR relief		X
Less: Letting relief		
Lowest of:		
PPR relief	X	
£40,000	X	
The gain that arose in the letting period	X	(X)
Net gain		**X**

There are two situations where letting relief applies:

1. **Where a part of the property is let to tenants**

Example

Peter purchased a detached house on 1 April 2003 for £88,000. Until 31 August 2004 he occupied the entire house. On 1 September 2004, he rented out the house and moved to a new house. This arrangement continued until 31 December 2009 when he sold his house for £182,000.
In this situation chargeable gain is calculated as follows:

	£	£
Disposal consideration		182,000
Less: Cost of acquisition		(88,000)
		94,000
Less: PPR relief (W1)		(61,506)
Gain after PPR relief		**32,494**
Less: Letting relief		
Lowest of:		
PPR relief	61,506	
£40,000	40,000	
The gain that arose in the letting period (£94,000 x 28/81)	32,494	(32,494)
Chargeable gain		**-**

Workings

W1 Calculation of PPR exemption

Calculation of periods of occupation by Peter:

	Total (months)	Exempt (months)	Chargeable (months)
1 April 2003 to 31 August 2004 (Actual occupation)	17	17	
1 September 2004 to 31 December 2009 (64 months) (Note 4)	64	36	28
	81	53	28

Notes:

1. **Total ownership period is 81 months.**
2. Out of this total ownership period, the house was used for **domestic purposes** only for **17 months.**
3. PPR relief is available for the last 36 months of ownership.

Workings

W1 PPR relief

PPR relief is available for the gain related to the part of the property that is used for domestic purposes (actual plus deemed).

$$\text{PPR relief} = \frac{\text{Period of actual and deemed residence} \times \text{Gain}}{\text{Period of ownership}}$$

$= (53/81) \times £94,000$
$= £61,506$

2. Where the entire property is let out during periods of absence

Example

Jeremy owned a house in London, which he bought on 1 April 2000 for £31,740. On 30 June 2005, he purchased a new apartment in Brighton. He moved into the new house immediately. On 1 December 2005, he let out the property in London. The property was let out until it was sold on 1 April 2010.

The London property was sold for £75,000. The calculation of chargeable gain on the disposal of the London property is as follows:

	£	£
Sale proceeds		75,000
Less: : Cost of acquisition		(31,740)
		43,260
Less: PPR relief (W1)		(35,689)
Gain after PPR relief		**7,571**
Less: Letting relief		
Lowest of:		
PPR relief	35,689	
£40,000	40,000	
The gain that arose in the letting period (£43,260 x 16/120)	5,768	(5,768)
Chargeable gain		**1,803**

Workings

W1

The total period of ownership of 120 months (1 April 2000 to 1 April 2010) needs to be broken down into the following periods:

	Total (months)	Exempt (months)	Chargeable (months)
1 April 2000 to 30 June 2005 (actual occupation)	63	63	
1 July 2005 to 30 November 2005 (unoccupied and not let out)	5		5
1 December 2005 to 31 March 2010 (52 months)(let out)	52	36	16
Total	**120**	**99**	**21**

PPR exemption

Out of the total ownership period of 120 months, the house was actually occupied for domestic purposes for 63 months. The last 36 months are always exempt. No relief is available for the 5 month period when the house was not occupied as Jeremy did not re-occupy the property after the period of absence.

PPR relief = 99/120 x gain = 99/120 x £43,260 = £35,689

SUMMARY

PPR let out
- letting relief available
  - deducted after PPR relief
  - cannot create loss
- letting relief lowest of
  - PPR relief
  - £40,000
  - gain that arose in the letting period

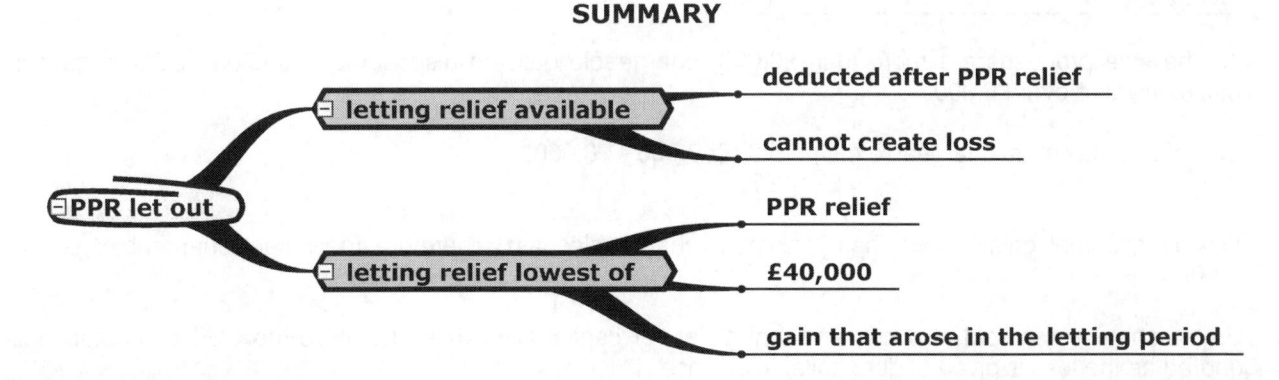

Test Yourself 7

Wendy has an apartment in London which she bought on 1 April 1999. On 1 June 2002, she changed her job and found the earlier accommodation to be too far from her workplace.

She rented out her apartment and bought a new studio apartment close to her new workplace. On 31 October 2009, she sold her apartment in London and made a gain of £12,000.

Required:

Calculate her chargeable gain.

Answers to Test Yourself

Answer 1

1. A painting is a tangible movable property, therefore can be classified as a chattel. A painting's expected life is more than 50 years hence it is a non-wasting chattel. Therefore, gains arising on disposal of a painting are liable to CGT.
However, if the disposal value of the chattel is £6,000 or less, then gain on disposal is not liable to CGT.

2. The plant is a business asset eligible for capital allowance. Any gain on disposal of plant and machinery used for business purposes gives rise to capital gains tax. Therefore, Tina is liable to capital gains tax on disposal of plant.

Answer 2

Calculation of chargeable capital gain on the disposal of a non-wasting chattel

	£
Disposal consideration	8,200
Less: Allowable deductions	
Acquisition costs (including incidental costs)	(2,900)
Chargeable gain	**(5,300)**

As the gross sale proceeds are more than £6000, the chargeable gain is the **lower of:**
1. The normal net gain = £5,300
2. 5/3 x (gross proceeds - £6,000) = 5/3 of £2,200 (i.e. £8,200 - £6,000) = £3,667

Therefore, the chargeable gain is restricted to £3,667.

Answer 3

1. As the machinery (wasting chattel eligible for capital allowances) was sold at a loss, the capital gain computation is ignored as the loss had already been given as capital allowance. The net amount of capital allowances given is deducted from allowable expenditure so that neither a chargeable gain nor an allowable loss arises.
Hence, the net capital gain / loss in this situation is nil.

2. As the machinery was sold at a gain, capital gain will be calculated normally. For CGT purpose, it will be treated as a **non-wasting chattel and** therefore, rules for non-wasting chattels will be applicable.

	£
Disposal consideration	49,000
Less: Acquisition cost	(41,000)
Net gain	**8,000**

As the sale proceeds are more than £6,000, chargeable gain on disposal is restricted to 5/3 of excess disposal value over £6,000.

Therefore, maximum chargeable gain = 5/3 (£49,000 - £6,000)
= £71,667.

However, actual gain is less than maximum chargeable gain. Therefore the actual chargeable gain is £8,000.

3. The machinery was sold at a loss and it qualifies for capital allowance, therefore the CGT computation is ignored as the loss is given under capital allowance.
Hence, the net capital gain / loss in this situation is nil.

Answer 4

Step 1 Calculate total chargeable gain before PPR
Step 2 Calculate PPR exemption
Step 3 Calculate chargeable gain after PPR

Step 1 Calculate total chargeable gain before PPR

	£
Disposal consideration	80,000
Less: Cost of acquisition	(15,000)
Net gain	**65,000**

Step 2 Calculate PPR relief

Calculation of periods of occupation by Melanie:

	Total (Months)	Exempt (months)	Chargeable (months)
1 April 1986 to 31 May 2000 (Actual occupation)	170	170	
1 June 2000 to 31 January 2010 (absence- any reason) (Note)	116	36	80
	286	206	80

Total period of ownership = 206 + 80 = 286 months

Notes:

Melanie has not returned after she left her residence on 31 May 2000. Hence, PPR relief will not be available for this period. However, the last 36 months of ownership are always exempt.

$$\text{PPR relief} = \frac{\text{Period of actual and deemed residence}}{\text{Period of ownership}} \times \text{Net gain}$$

$$= \frac{206 \times £65,000}{286}$$

$$= £46,818$$

Step 3 Calculate chargeable gains after PPR

	£
Net gain	65,000
Less: PPR relief	(46,818)
Chargeable gain	**18,182**

Answer 5

In this situation chargeable gain on disposal of property in Wick is calculated as follows:

	£
Disposal consideration	58,000
Less: Cost of acquisition	(28,000)
Net gain	**30,000**
Less: PPR relief (W1)	(20,690)
Chargeable gain	**9,310**

Workings

W1 Calculation of PPR

Pinky's ownership period of the house in Wick is split into exempt and chargeable periods as follows:

	Total (months)	Exempt (months)	Chargeable (months)
1 May 1993 to 30 June 1998 (Actual occupation)	62	62	-
1 July 1998 to 31 October 2001 (unoccupied -working abroad) (Note 1)	40	40	-
1 November 2001 to 31 December 2001 (Actual occupation)	2	2	
1 January 2002 to 31 March 2010 (unoccupied – any reason) (Note 2)	99	36	63
Total	**203**	**140**	**63**

Notes:

1. The actual period of residence is always exempt when calculating chargeable gain on the disposal of a residence.

Pinky was working abroad for three years and four months. Any period of absence during which the taxpayer is working abroad is exempt provided the property was occupied both before and after the period of absence.

2. The last thirty six months of ownership are always exempt.

Therefore, out of 203 months of ownership, 140 months are exempt. Hence, PPR exemption is calculated as follows:

$$\text{PPR relief} = \frac{\text{Period of actual and deemed residence}}{\text{Period of ownership}} \times \text{Net gain}$$

$$= \frac{140 \times £30,000}{203}$$

$$= £20,690$$

Answer 6

	£
Disposal consideration	59,200
Less: Cost of acquisition	(16,400)
Net capital gain	**42,800**
Less: PPR relief (W1)	
Actual occupation (181/193 x £42,800)	(40,139)
	2,661
Less: PPR relief (W1)	
Domestic as well as business use (12/193 x £42,800) x 65%	(1,730)
Chargeable gain	**931**

Workings

W1

Out of the total usage of the house, 35% usage is for business purposes and 65% (100% – 35%) is for domestic purposes.

	Total (months)	Exempt (months)	Chargeable (months)
1 April 1993 to 30 April 2005 (only domestic use)	145	145	
1 May 2005 to 30 April 2009 (domestic as well as business use) (Note)	48	36	12
	193	**181**	**12**

The exemption for the final 36 months will be applicable to the whole of the property as 35% of the property was not used for the business throughout the period of ownership. It was used wholly for residential purpose for some part of the period of the ownership.

The period for which the property was used for both domestic as well as business purposes is 48 months. But 35% usage for business purposes for 48 months will be considered only for 12 months after deducting last 36 months' exemption. i.e. (48 months – 36 months).

Answer 7

Calculation of chargeable gains

	£	£
Gain		12,000
Less: PPR relief (W1)		(6,992)
Gain after PPR relief		**5,008**
Less: Letting relief		
Lowest of:		
PPR relief	6,992	
£40,000	40,000	
The gain that arose in the letting period	5,008	(5,008)
Chargeable gain		**-**

Workings

W1 Total ownership period is broken down as follows:

		Total (months)	Exempt (months)	Chargeable (months)
1 April 1999 to 31 May 2002	Self-occupied	38	38	
1 June 2002 to 31 October 2009 (89 months)	Let out	89	36	53
Total ownership period		**127**	**74**	**53**

Out of a total ownership period of 127 months, Wendy let out the property for 89 months. Out of these 89 months, she will get PPR exemption for the last 36 months.

PPR relief

Out of a total ownership period of 127 months, gain apportioned to 74 months (38 + 36) will get PPR relief.

Therefore, total PPR relief is calculated as follows:

= 74/127 x £12,000 = £6,992

W2 Calculation of gain that arose during letting period

The only chargeable period is the 53 months during which property was let out. The gain apportioned to these 53 months is calculated as follows:

= 53/127 x £12,000 = £5,008

Quick Quiz

Classify the following assets into chattels and wasting assets.

1. Gold jewellery
2. Lease building (lease period – 31 yrs)
3. An antique
4. Car
5. Trademark (with life of 20 years)

Answers to Quick Quiz

1. Chattels
2. Wasting assets
3. Chattels
4. Wasting assets
5. Wasting assets

C4.18: Chargeable Gains

Self Examination Questions

Question 1

In May 2009, Eric sold his diamond cutting machinery for £8,500 which he had purchased for £4,000. He had used this machinery for three years for business purposes. He wants your help to calculate the chargeable gain on disposal of the diamond cutting machinery.

Question 2

On 1 January 2010, Damon sold an antique wall clock. He had purchased this wall clock in March 2000 for £12,000.

Required:

Show the calculation of allowable loss assuming the disposal value of the wall clock is:
1. £8,600
2. £5,600

Question 3

Raj, who is a wholesaler of woollen cloth, purchased a new apartment in Dundee on 1 February 1997 for £38,000. He lived in this apartment until 31 May 2002.

On 1 June 2002, he started a new job in Bristol. Until 31 December 2008, he lived in a rented house in Bristol. On 1 January 2009, he purchased a new apartment in Bristol and elected that apartment as his PPR.

On 1 January 2010, Raj sold his apartment in Dundee for £99,000.

Required:

Show the calculation of capital gain on disposal of the apartment in Dundee.

Question 4

In April 1999, Matthew purchased an antique picture for £1,000. In July 2009, he sold this picture for £8,200 having incurred incidental expenditure of £320.

Required:

Calculate chargeable gain.

Question 5

Linda is a practising chartered accountant. She bought a house for £28,000 on 1 January 2002. From that date she started using one room out of the four rooms of the house for business purposes.

On 31 May 2009, she purchased another house and sold her first house for £98,000.

Required:

What will be the chargeable gain?

Question 6

On 2 April 1999, Jaydeep purchased a house for £73,000. However, from 1 January 2000, he rented out 40% of the house. The tenant vacated the house on 31 March 2009. On 1 April 2010, Jaydeep sold the house for £148,300 in order to work in the USA.

Required:

Show the calculation of chargeable gain.

Question 7

David works in the IT industry. Due to his job he travels all over Europe. On 1 June 2002, he purchased a new house for £98,000. He lived in the house until 31 August 2003. He then went to India due to his employment for four years. On 1 December 2009 he sold his house for £258,000.

Required:

Calculate the chargeable gain arising from the transaction.

Answers to Self Examination Questions

Answer 1

Calculation of chargeable capital gain on the disposal of chattel

	£
Disposal consideration	8,500
Less: Cost of acquisition	(4,000)
Gain on disposal	**4,500**
Restricted to	**4,167**

Workings

W1

As the disposal value is more than £6,000, chargeable gain on disposal is restricted to maximum chargeable gain (5/3 of excess disposal value over £6,000).

The maximum chargeable gain = 5/3 (£8,500 − £6,000)
= £4,167

The actual chargeable gain is £4,167.

Answer 2

1. **Disposal value of wall clock is more than £6,000.** (calculation of capital loss in the usual way)

Calculation of allowable loss

	£
Disposal consideration	8,600
Less: Cost of acquisition	(12,000)
Allowable loss	**3,400**

2. **Disposal value is less than £6,000.**
(Disposal value is less than £6,000. Hence, while calculating allowable loss, replace disposal value with £6,000).

Calculation of allowable loss

	£
Disposal value	6,000
Less: Acquisition cost	(12,000)
Allowable loss	**6,000**

Note: Actual loss is £6,400 (£12,000 - £5,600) but allowable loss is £6,000 as calculated above.

Answer 3

	£
Disposal consideration	99,000
Less: Cost of acquisition	(38,000)
Net gain	**61,000**
Less: PPR relief (W1)	(39,355)
Chargeable gain	**21,645**

Workings

W1 Calculation of PPR

Raj's ownership period of house in Dundee is split into exempt and chargeable periods as follows:

	Total Period	Exempt period	Chargeable period
1 February 1997 to 31 May 2002 (note 1)	64	64 months	-
1 June 2002 to 31 December 2008 (note 2)	79	36 months	43 months
1 January 2009 to 31 December 2009 (note 3)	12		12 months
Total	**155**	**100 months**	**55 months**

Notes:

1. Actual period of residence is always exempt when calculating chargeable gain on the disposal of a residence.

2. A total of up to four years of absence where an individual is employed elsewhere in the UK is deemed to be period of occupation for calculation of PPR relief provided that there is an actual period of occupation both before and after the period of absence. As Raj has not come back after he left the property in June 2002, that period will not be treated as an exempt period. However, the last 36 months of ownership (in this case, before electing the other apartment in Bristol as his PPR) are always exempt.

3. Raj had declared the apartment in Bristol as his PPR. Hence, this period cannot be counted as deemed residence.

Therefore, total exemption is available for 143 months (100 + 43). The gain apportioned to the 12 month period is chargeable to tax.

$$\text{PPR relief} = \frac{\text{Period of actual and deemed residence}}{\text{Period of ownership}} \times \text{Indexed gain}$$

$$= \frac{100}{155} \times £61,000$$

$$= £39,355$$

Answer 4

Calculation of chargeable gain

	£
Disposal consideration	8,200
Less: Incidental cost of disposal	(320)
Net Disposal consideration	**7,880**
Less: Allowable deductions	
Acquisition cost	(1,000)
Net gain	**6,880**

Note:

If the gross sales proceeds of chattel exceed £6,000 then chargeable gain should not exceed 5/3 of (sale proceeds - £6,000.) Hence, the gain is restricted to:

$$= (£8,200 - £6,000) \times 5/3$$
$$= £3,667$$

Answer 5

Calculation of chargeable gain

	£
Disposal consideration	98,000
Less: Allowable deductions	
Acquisition cost	(28,000)
Net gain	**70,000**
Less: PPR exemption (W1)	
(1/4 x £70,000)	(17,500)
Chargeable gain	**52,500**

Workings

W1

Linda used one out of the four rooms of her house for business purposes throughout the period of ownership. To that extent she lost the PPR exemption.

Answer 6

Calculation of chargeable gain

	£	£
Disposal consideration		148,300
Less: Allowable deductions		
Acquisition cost		(73,000)
Net gain		**75,300**
Less: PPR exemption (W1)		(55,448)
		19,852
Less: Letting relief		
Lowest of:		
PPR relief	55,448	
£40,000	40,000	
The gain that arose in the letting period		
£75,300 x 87 x 40%	19,852	(19,852)
132		
Chargeable gains		**-**

Workings

W1 Calculation of total ownership period

Period between dates	Exempt (months)	Chargeable (months)
2 April 1999 to 31 December 1999 (only domestic purpose)	9	
1 January 2000 to 31 March 2009 (40% let out) (111 months)	24	87
1 April 2009 to 31 March 2010) (only domestic purpose)	12	
	45	87

PPR exemption

i. **Total ownership period is 132 months** (i.e. 45 months + 87 months).
ii. Out of this total ownership period, for the first 9 months and the last 12 months, the house was used only for domestic purposes
iii. Total period of ownership during which property was used for domestic purposes as well as let out is 111 months.
iv. PPR relief is available for the last 36 months of ownership. Out of this last 36 months, 24 months are covered during the period when the property was let out.

PPR exemption is available for the gain related to the part of the property that is used for domestic purposes (actual plus deemed). 40% of the property was let out for some period hence, PPR exemption will be available only for 60% of the property used for domestic purposes during that period.

$$\text{PPR relief} = \frac{\text{Period of actual and deemed residence} \times \text{Gain}}{\text{Period of ownership}}$$

	£
(45/132) x £75,300	25,670
(87/132) x £75,300 x 60%	29,778
	55,448

Answer 7

Calculation of chargeable gain

	£
Disposal consideration	258,000
Less: Allowable deductions	
Acquisition cost	(98,000)
Net gain	**160,000**
Less: PPR exemption	
$\frac{51 \times £160,000}{90}$	(90,667)
Chargeable gain	**69,333**

Workings

W1

Calculation of total ownership period and exempt and chargeable period

	Exempt (months)	Chargeable (months)
1 June 2002 to 31 August 2003 (actual occupation)	15	
1 September 2003 to 30 November 2009 (Note 1)	36	39
	51	39

Total ownership period = 90 months (51 + 39)

Notes:

1. Any period of absence during which the taxpayer is working abroad is exempt provided that the property was occupied both before and after the period of absence. The period between 1 September 2003 and 30 November 2009 cannot be covered under PPR exemption, as the property was not actually occupied after the period of absence.

2. The last thirty six months of ownership are always exempt.

SECTION C: CHARGEABLE GAINS

C5

STUDY GUIDE C5: GAINS AND LOSSES ON THE DISPOSAL OF SHARES AND SECURITIES

■ Get Through Intro

This Study Guide deals with the **calculation of capital gains** that arise because of the **disposal of shares and securities.**

Identification of the share matching rules is the **core ingredient** in the recipe required to prepare the dish called 'capital gains due to disposal of shares and securities'. An **improper identification** will lead to an **incorrect calculation** of capital gains and therefore this principle needs to be understood thoroughly.

This Study Guide discusses how **share matching rules** and **certain exemptions are different** for **companies** and for **individuals.** It also explains the pooling provision and states the treatment applied to bonus issues, rights issues, takeovers and reorganisations.

It is important that you try to grasp the principles underlying the calculations as they will help you tackle the questions in the examination with confidence, and guide you to give the correct advice in your professional life as a tax consultant.

■ Learning Outcomes

a) Calculate the value of quoted shares where they are disposed of by way of a gift.
b) Explain and apply the identification rules as they apply to individuals and to companies, including the same day, nine day, and thirty day matching rules.
c) Explain the pooling provisions.
d) Explain the treatment of bonus issues, rights issues, takeovers and reorganisations.
e) Explain the exemption available for gilt-edged securities and qualifying corporate bonds.

Introduction

Case Study

On 5 May 2003, Lily purchased 500 shares of Mega Ltd for £2 each. In May 2008, Mega Ltd made a bonus issue of 1 for 2, at the time of the bonus issue the market price of the shares was £5.

As she received 250 shares free of cost, she gave them to her daughter, Millie. One morning she received a notice from HMRC asking her to pay capital gains tax on the transfer of the shares, by way of a gift.

Lily was confused, she had received the bonus shares free of cost and rather than selling them, she had given them to her daughter as a gift. Why then should she pay capital gains tax?

In this Study Guide let us absorb the various provisions related to capital gains tax on the disposal of shares & securities.

1. Calculate the value of quoted shares where they are disposed of by way of a gift.[2]
[Learning outcome a]

Quoted Shares are the shares **listed on a recognised stock exchange**. These shares are also called listed shares.

We have already seen in Study Guide C1, that disposal of an asset by way of a gift is considered to be chargeable disposal. In the case of disposal by way of a gift, the **market value** of the asset on the day of disposal is considered to be the **sale proceeds**.

> **Tip**
> Market value is used when assets are disposed of by way of a gift.

Shares and securities which are listed on the Stock Exchange are valued at the lower of:

1. Lower quoted price +1/4 x (higher quoted price − lower quoted price) ('quarter up' rule)

2. The average of the highest and lowest recorded bargains.

Example

Kim, a seventy year old lady, gifted 200 shares of IBM plc to her son, Jim on 5 June 2009. On that day the shares were quoted at £200 - £208 with bargains marketed at £200, £202, £205, £206. In this situation, the market value of these quoted shares on the day of transfer is calculated as follows:

The valuation of quoted shares as on the day of transfer is the lower of the following:

1. Lower quoted price +1/4 (higher quoted price - lower quoted price)
   = £200 + 1/4(£208 - £200) = £202

2. The average of the highest and lowest recorded bargains
   = (£200 + £206)/2 = £203

Therefore, the value per share for CGT purposes is £202 and the value of 200 shares will be charged accordingly.

> **Tip**
> On the date of disposal by way of gift, if information relating to transactions or bids or bargains is not given, then the average of the range (the highest and lowest quoted price) is considered for calculating the average of the highest and lowest recorded bargains.

Example

Jack owns 20,000 ordinary shares of Jupiter Ltd. He had purchased these shares on 15 April 1995 for £25,000. On 23 June 2009, he gave all the shares to his son. On that day the shares were quoted on the Stock Exchange at £5.05- £5.13.

The disposal consideration for the purposes of capital gains should be calculated as follows:

As the bargains on the day of disposal by way of gift are not given, highest and lowest quoted price will be used for calculating average of the highest and lowest recorded bargains.

The valuation of quoted shares as on the day of transfer is the lower of the following:

Lower quoted price +1/4(higher quoted price - lower quoted price)
= £5.05+1/4(£5.13-£5.05) = £5.07

The average of the highest and lowest recorded bargains
= (£5.05 + £5.13)/2 = £5.09

Therefore, the value per share for CGT purposes will be £5.07 and the value of 20,000 shares will be charged accordingly.

The disposal consideration will be 20,000 ordinary shares x £5.07 = £101,400

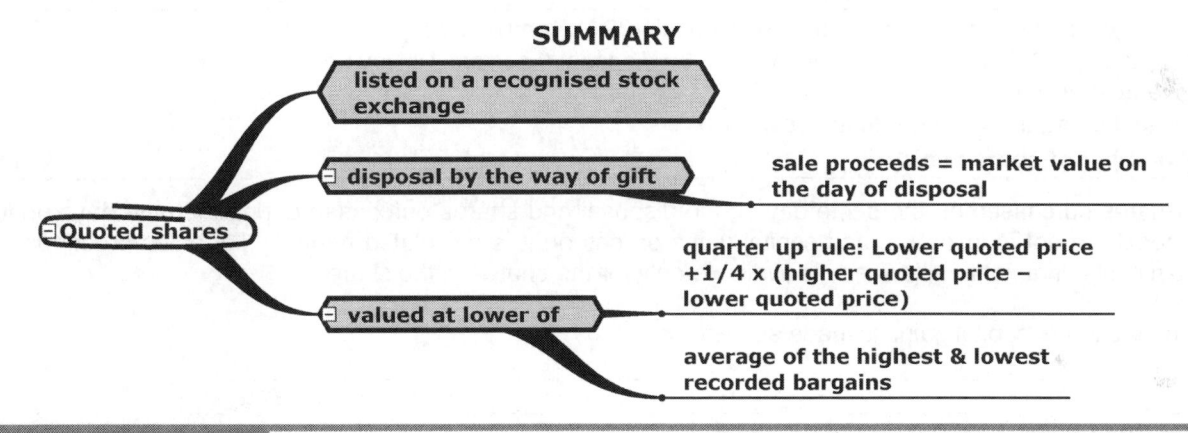

SUMMARY

Quoted shares
- listed on a recognised stock exchange
- disposal by the way of gift → sale proceeds = market value on the day of disposal
- valued at lower of:
  - quarter up rule: Lower quoted price +1/4 x (higher quoted price – lower quoted price)
  - average of the highest & lowest recorded bargains

Test Yourself 1

On 1 September 2007 River Plc made a gift of 2,000 shares of Rain Ltd to Sea Plc. On the day of transfer, shares in Rain Plc were quoted at £120 - £130p. The highest and lowest marked bargains were £122 and £129.

Required:

What would be the market value for CGT purposes?

> 2. **Explain and apply the identification rules as they apply to individuals and to companies, including the same day, nine day, and thirty day matching rules.**[2]
> **Explain the pooling provisions.**[2]
>
> [Learning outcomes b & c]

2.1 Share identification rules applicable for companies

When a company makes various acquisitions of shares in the same company over a period of time, and then disposes of some of them, special matching rules are required to determine which shares are being disposed.

1. **The disposal of shares is matched with purchases** in the following **order**:
a) Shares purchased on the **same day** as the disposal.
b) Shares purchased **during the nine days prior to the disposal.**
c) Shares **in the 1985 pool.**

All purchases are aggregated in the 1985 pool, except for those purchased on the **same day or the previous nine days**. They are **treated as a single asset**.

2. Operation of the 1985 pool

a) The pool **records** the number of shares, their cost and their indexed cost.
b) The pool must be **indexed up before each 'operative event.'** These events are acquisitions, disposals and rights issues.
c) The movement in the RPI is **not rounded to 3 decimal places**.
d) Disposals are taken out at **average cost and average indexed cost.**

> **Tip**
> Indexation allowance is not available for shares purchased on the same day as the disposal, and during the nine days prior to the disposal. Unlike other disposals, the movement in RPI is not rounded to three decimal places when shares are disposed.

Example Sun Ltd purchased 20,000 shares in Moon Ltd on 16 November 2009 for £100,000 and an additional 5,000 shares on 23 November 2009 for £30,000. Sun Ltd sells 12,000 shares in Moon Ltd on 23 November 2009 for £84,000.

First, we will match the disposal of shares with the purchases in the following order:

	No. of shares
Shares purchased on the same day as the disposal (23 November 2009)	5,000
Shares purchased during the nine days prior to the disposal (i.e. from 14 November 2009 to 22 November 2009)	7,000
Shares in the share pool (other than above two)	-
Total number of shares sold	**12,000**

Note: Shares purchased on the same day as the disposal and shares purchased during the nine days prior to the disposal are not indexed up, and capital gains or loss on it is calculated normally i.e. sales proceeds less allowable costs. Indexation allowance is available only for the shares in the share pool.

The computation of capital gains is made as follows:

	£	£
Shares purchased on same day of disposal		
Disposal consideration (£84,000 X 5,000/12,000)	35,000	
Less: Acquisition cost of shares	30,000	5,000
Shares purchased nine days prior to the disposal		
Disposal consideration (£84,000 X 7,000/12,000)	49,000	
Less: Acquisition cost of shares (£100,000 x 7,000/20,000)	35,000	14,000
Chargeable gains		**19,000**

Example Saturn Ltd purchased 50,000 shares in Neptune Ltd on 10 June 1998 (RPI 163.4) for £200,000. It purchased an additional 40,000 shares on 22 August 2002 (RPI 176.4) for £190,000. Saturn Ltd sold 60,000 ordinary shares in Neptune on 20 April 2009 (RPI 211.5) for £350,000.

First, we will match the disposals of shares with the purchases in the following order:

	No. of shares
Shares purchased on the same day as the disposal (20 April 2009)	-
Shares purchased during the nine days prior to the disposal (i.e., from 11 April 2009 to 19 April 2009)	-
Shares in the share pool (other than above two)	60,000
Total number of shares sold	**60,000**

Continued on next page

The computation of capital gains is as follows:

	£
Disposal consideration	350,000
Less: Acquisition cost of shares (W1) (Note 2)	(260,000)
Un-indexed gain	90,000
Less: Indexation allowance (£324,453 - £260,000) (W1)	(64,453)
Chargeable gain	25,547

Workings

W1 Indexed cost

	Number of shares	Cost (£)	Indexed cost (£)
Purchased in June 1998	50,000	200,000	200,000
Indexation to August 2002			
(176.4 -163.4/163.4) x £200,000			15,912
			215,912
Purchased in August 2002	40,000	190,000	190,000
	90,000	390,000	405,912
Indexation to April 2009			
(211.5 - 176.4/176.4) x £405,912			80,768
	90,000	390,000	486,680
Less: Disposal April 2009			
(Cost x 60,000/90,000)	(60,000)	(260,000)	(324,453)
Balance c/f	30,000	130,000	162,227

£486,680 x 60,000/ 90,000

Notes:

1. As all the shares are related to the share pool, indexation allowance will be available while calculating capital gain or loss on it. The share pool will record the number of shares, their cost and indexed cost and will be indexed up before each operative event. In this case, there is one operative event on 22 August 2002 on the purchase of 40,000 shares, and another on 20 April 2009 on the disposal of 60,000 shares. Hence, indexation is done before each of these events.

2. Disposals are taken out at average cost and average indexed cost.

3. The unindexed cost of sale for 60,000 shares amounting to £260,000 is matched first and then the indexation of £84,453 (£324,453 – £260,000) is deducted from the gain. This is to ensure that the indexation does not give rise to loss nor increase a loss.

2.2 Share identification rules applicable for individuals

The disposal of shares from 6 April 2008 onwards by individuals, is matched with purchases, in the following order:

1. Shares purchased on the **same day** as the disposal.
2. Shares purchased within the **following 30 days.**
3. Shares in the share pool.

The above rule 2 of matching against the future purchase is very uncommon. This is to prevent a person establishing a gain or a loss by selling shares at the close of business and buying them back at the start of business on the following day. The purpose is to trigger a chargeable gain equivalent to the annual exemption of £10,100 which cannot be carried forward.

This was known as **bed and breakfasting**, and allowed a gain or a loss to be established without a genuine disposal being made.

The share pool aggregates all purchases except for those made on the same day as the disposal, or within the following 30 days. Disposals are taken out at average cost for the shares in the share pool. Indexation allowance is not available to individuals.

C5.6: Chargeable Gains

Example The following are the details of acquisitions and disposals of shares by Barber over several years. Show the sequence in which the disposals will be matched against the acquisitions from the following data:

Date of transaction	Transaction acquisition	Number of shares
20 April 1992	Acquisition	200
9 September 1998	Acquisition	200
1 October 2002	Acquisition	1,200
20 March 2008	Acquisition	100
12 April 2008	Acquisition	100
12 April 2008	Disposal	(300)
30 April 2008	Acquisition	125
5 January 2009	Acquisition	150
15 April 2009	Disposal	(350)

1. Disposal of 300 shares on 12 April 2008 are matched in the following order:

	No. of shares
Shares purchased on the same day as the disposal (12 April 2008)	100
Shares purchased within next 30 days of the disposal (i.e. up to 12 May 2008)	125
Shares from the share pool acquired before date of disposal	75
Total number of shares sold	**300**

2. The 350 shares disposed on 15 April 2009 are matched in the following order:

	No. of shares
Shares purchased on the same day as the disposal (15 April 2009)	-
Shares purchased within next 30 days of the disposal (i.e. up to 15 May 2009)	-
Shares in the share pool acquired before date of disposal	350
Total number of shares sold	**350**

Example On 10 May 2009, Mack purchased 2,000 shares in Mars Ltd for £20,500. Mack found that the value of the shares fell drastically, so on 1 December 2009 he sold them for £4,000. He repurchased the shares on 12 December 2009 for £3,500.

In this case, the capital gain will be calculated as follows:

The transaction satisfies the condition of the 30 day matching rule. So, the sale of shares for £4,000 on 1 December 2009 will match the purchase made on 12 December 2009. Therefore, the capital gain for 2009 – 10 is £4,000 - £3,500 = £500.

Example Juliet purchased 50,000 ordinary shares in Jumbo Ltd on 20 June 2007 for £150,000. On 8 April 2009, Juliet purchased an additional 2,000 shares in Jumbo Ltd for £8,000, and sold 6,000 ordinary shares in Jumbo Ltd for £30,000 on the same day. She purchased 2,500 more shares in Jumbo Ltd for £12,000 on 30 April 2009.

Disposal of 6,000 shares on 8 April 2009 is matched in the following order:

	No. of shares
Shares purchased on the same day as the disposal (8 April 2009)	2,000
Shares purchased within next 30 days of the disposal (i.e. up to 8 May 2009)	2,500
Shares from the share pool acquired before date of disposal (against acquired on 20 June 2007)	1,500
Total number of shares sold	**6,000**

Continued on next page

The capital gain for 2009 - 10 is computed as follows:

	£	£
Shares (2,000) purchased on same day of disposal		
Disposal consideration (£30,000 X 2,000/6,000)	10,000	
Less: Acquisition cost of shares	8,000	2,000
Shares (2,500) purchased within next 30 days of disposal		
Disposal consideration (£30,000 X 2,500/6,000)	12,500	
Less: Acquisition cost of shares	12,000	500
Shares (1,500) in the share pool acquired before disposal		
Disposal consideration (£30,000 X 1,500/6,000)	7,500	
Less: Acquisition cost of shares (£150,000 x 1,500/50,000)	4,500	3,000
Chargeable gains		**5,500**

SUMMARY

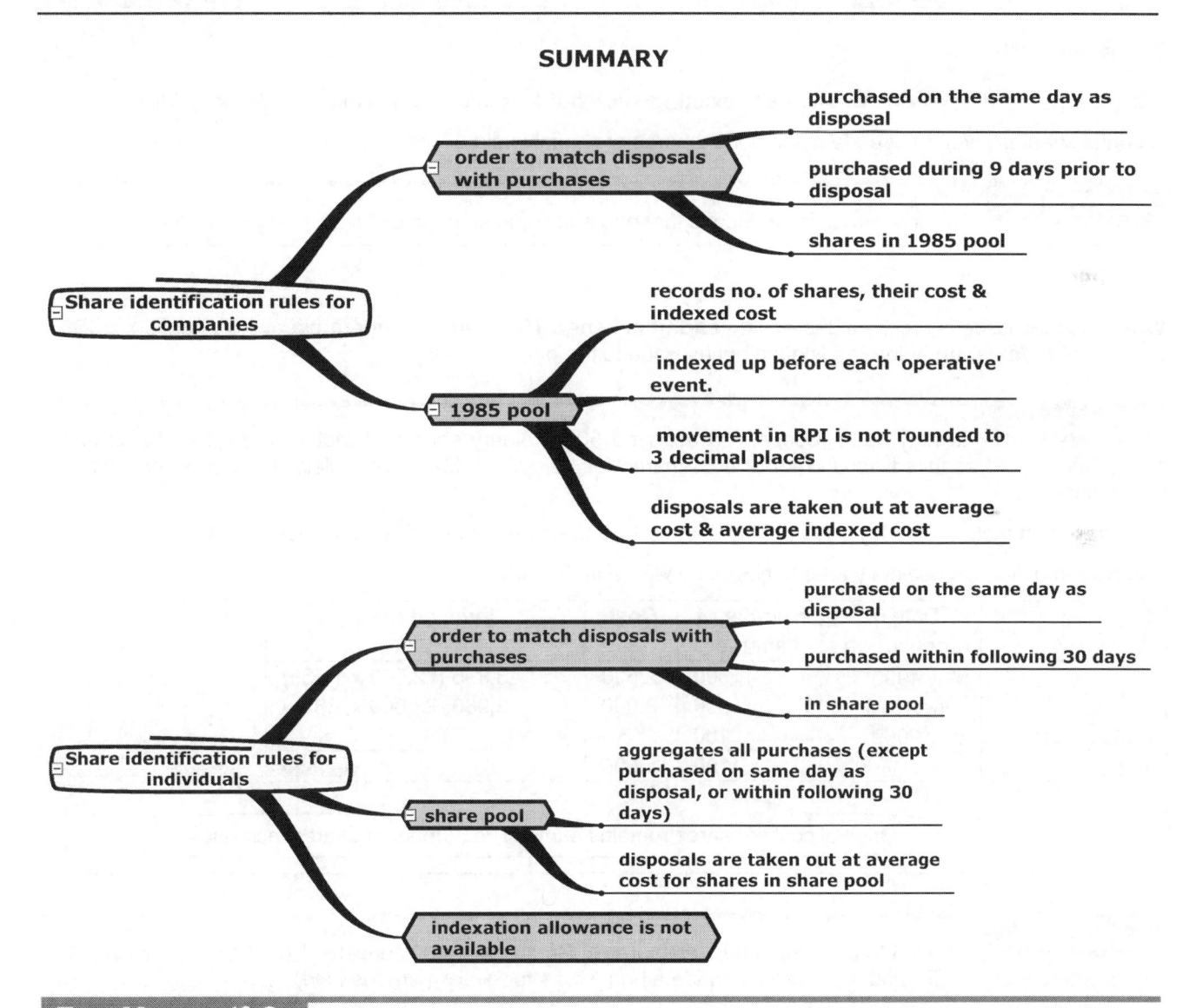

Share identification rules for companies
- order to match disposals with purchases
  - purchased on the same day as disposal
  - purchased during 9 days prior to disposal
  - shares in 1985 pool
- 1985 pool
  - records no. of shares, their cost & indexed cost
  - indexed up before each 'operative' event.
  - movement in RPI is not rounded to 3 decimal places
  - disposals are taken out at average cost & average indexed cost

Share identification rules for individuals
- order to match disposals with purchases
  - purchased on the same day as disposal
  - purchased within following 30 days
  - in share pool
- share pool
  - aggregates all purchases (except purchased on same day as disposal, or within following 30 days)
  - disposals are taken out at average cost for shares in share pool
- indexation allowance is not available

Test Yourself 2

Henry purchased 19,000 shares in Huge Plc on 10 December 2008 for 65,000. As the position of the company was very sound, he purchased another 15,000 shares on 25 August 2009 for £30,000. Henry sold 20,000 shares to Jerry on 20 February 2010. On that date the shares were quoted at £6.40 - £6.60.

Required:

Compute Henry's capital gain for 2009 - 10.

C5.8: Chargeable Gains

Test Yourself 3

Jerry had the following transactions relating to the sale and purchase of shares of Jupiter Ltd.

5 June 1997	Purchased 4,000 shares for £8,500
25 April 2007	Purchased 2,000 shares for £7,500
20 May 2007	Purchased 1,000 shares for £5,000
20 February 2010	Sold 5,000 shares for £30,000

Required:

Calculate the capital gains.

---

3. Explain the treatment of bonus issues, rights issues, takeovers and reorganisations.[2]

[Learning outcome d]

3.1 Bonus issue

A bonus issue is a **free issue of shares** to **existing shareholders** in proportion to their existing holding.

A bonus share is given for a certain number of shares previously held.

Example '1 for 4' bonus issue means that one additional share is given for every 4 shares held.

1. Companies

When a bonus issue is received, there is **no additional cost**. This is **not an 'operative event'**, hence the 1985 pool is **not indexed up** before adding the bonus issue to the pool.

Example In May 1993, Cooper Ltd acquired 500 ordinary shares of Metal Plc for £2,500. In June 1998, Cooper Ltd acquired another lot of 500 shares for £3,000. In May 2009, Metal Plc issued one for ten bonus shares.

The indexation factor from May 1993 to May 2009 is 1.558 and from June 1998 to May 2009 is 1.320.

The share holding, immediately after bonus issue will be as follows:

	Date of acquisition	Number of shares	Cost £	Indexed cost £
	May 1993	500	2,500	3,895 (£2,500 x 1.558)
	June, 1998	500	3,000	3,960 (£3,000 x 1.320)
Bonus issue	May 2009	100	-	-
Total		**1100**	**5,500**	**7,855**

Original cost of shares remains same. The number of shares increases.

Example Strong Ltd purchased 50,000 shares in Smart Ltd on 20 June 1991 (RPI 134.1) for £40,000. On 15 October 2006 (RPI 200.4), Smart Ltd made a bonus of 1 for every 4 shares held.

Strong Ltd sold 30,000 shares in Smart Ltd for £125,000 on 25 April 2009 (RPI 211.5).

The capital gains for 2009 - 10 are calculated as follows:

	£
Disposal consideration	125,000
Less: Acquisition cost of shares (W1)	(19,200)
Un-indexed gain	105,800
Less: Indexation allowance	
£30,282 - £19,200	(11,082)
Chargeable gain	**94,718**

Continued on next page

Workings

W1

	Number of shares	Cost (£)	Indexed cost (£)
Purchased in June 1991	50,000	40,000	40,000
Bonus issue October 2006 (50,000 x 1/4)	12,500		
	62,500	40,000	40,000
Indexation to April 2009			
(211.5 – 134.1/134.1) x £40,000			23,087
	62,500	40,000	63,087
Disposal April 2009 Cost x 30,000/62,500	(30,000)	(19,200)	(30,282)
Balance c/f	**32,500**	**20,800**	**32,805**

2. Individuals

The bonus shares are given based on the original holding. Therefore it is **treated as having been acquired on the same date as the original holding that qualified for the bonus.**

Example

Alan purchased the following shares:

- 1 June 2003 800 shares purchased
- 1 December 2006 1,200 shares purchased
- 1 June 2009 bonus issue 1 for 4

He will receive an additional 500 shares on 1 June 2009 ((800 + 1,200) x 1/4)

These bonus shares will be treated as acquired as follows:

- 200 (800 x 1/4) on 1 June 2003
- 300 (1,200 x 1/4) on 1 December 2006

Example

On 20 December 2008, Oliver acquired 1,000 shares of Archid Ltd for £5,000. On 18 March 2010, the company made a bonus issue of 3 for 10. Immediately after the bonus issue, Oliver sold all the shares for £10 each.

Calculation of capital gains on disposal of all these shares is as follows:

	£
Sale proceeds (W1) (£1,300 x 10)	13,000
Less: Acquisition cost	(5,000)
Chargeable gains	**8,000**

Workings

W1 Share holding

	Number of shares	Cost (£)
Shares acquired on 20 December 2008	1,000	5,000
Bonus shares (1,000/10) x 3	300	
	1,300	**5,000**

SUMMARY

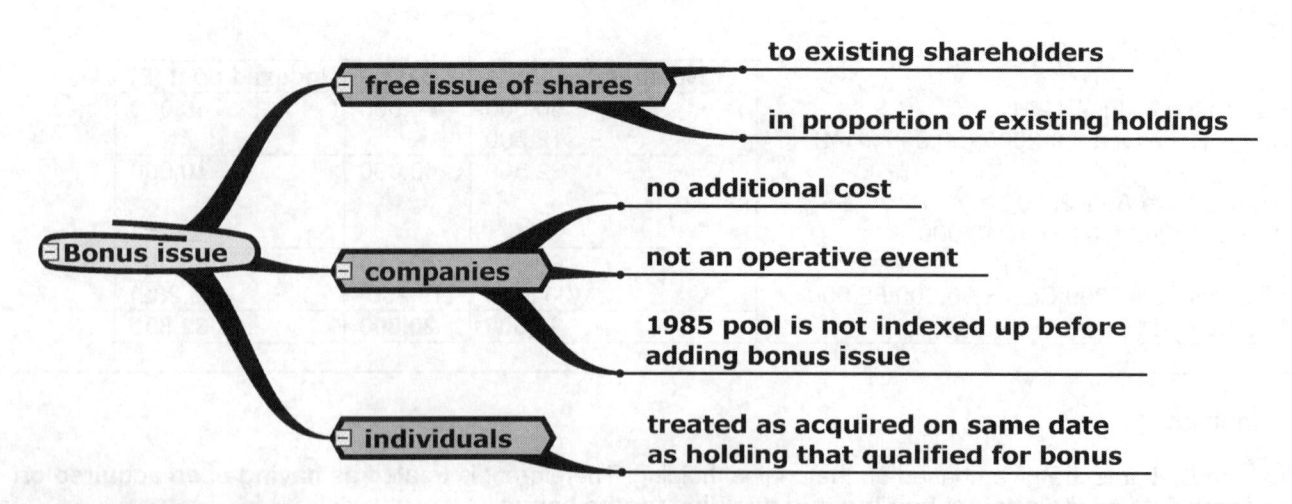

Bonus issue
- free issue of shares
  - to existing shareholders
  - in proportion of existing holdings
- companies
  - no additional cost
  - not an operative event
  - 1985 pool is not indexed up before adding bonus issue
- individuals
  - treated as acquired on same date as holding that qualified for bonus

Test Yourself 4

Circle Plc acquired the following preference shares in Square Ltd.

Date	No. of shares	Cost (£)
01/01/1991	2,000	8,000
20/04/1995	500	3,000
09/09/2001	400	2,000

On 1 December 2007, the company made a 2 for 5 bonus issue. On 1 June 2009, Circle Plc sold all the shares of Square Ltd for £28,420.

The Retail Price Indices are as follows:

Month	RPI
January 1991	130.2
April 1995	149.0
September 2001	174.6
December 2007	210.9
June 2009	213.4

Required:

Show the calculations of capital gains for Circle Plc.

Test Yourself 5

Ivon Ltd purchased 35,000 shares in Koyna Ltd on 15 February 2005 for £100,500. The indexed value of the 1985 pool on 5 January 2010 was £112,000. Koyna Ltd made a bonus issue on 5 January 2010 in the ratio of 1 for 2 shares.

Ivon Ltd sold 35,000 shares in Koyna Ltd on 25 January 2010 for £160,500.

Required:

Calculate the capital gains.

3.2 Rights issue

A rights issue is an offer to existing shareholders to buy additional shares in proportion to their existing holdings. These additional shares are purchased; they are not free.

1. Companies

The purchase of rights issue shares is an 'operative event'. The 1985 pool must be indexed up to the date of the rights issue, before the shares are added to the pool.

Example

Matthew Ltd purchased 35,000 shares in Michael Ltd on 10 February 2007 for £120,000. The indexed value of the 1985 pool on 4 January 2010 was £150,000.

Michael Ltd made a rights issue of 1 for 2 rights on 4 January 2010. Matthew Ltd paid for the rights issue at £2.20 for each new share issued.

On 26 January 2010, Matthew Ltd sold 35,000 shares in Michael Ltd for £75,000. As a rights issue is made by one company and exercised by another company, the calculation of capital gains will be made as follows:

First of all, we have to calculate the number and cost of the rights shares.
Number of rights shares = 35,000 x 1/2 = 17,500 shares.

Cost = No. of shares x rate of one share
     = 17,500 x £2.20
     = £38,500

Therefore, total cost of all shares = £120,000 + £38,500 = £158,500.

Cost of the number of shares sold = £158,500 x 35,000/(35,000 + 17,500)
                                  = £105,667

		£
Sale proceeds		75,000
Less: Acquisition cost of shares (W1)		(105,667)
Capital loss		**(30,667)**
Less: Indexation allowance (£125,667 - £105,667) (note 1)	20,000	-
Net capital loss		**(30,667)**

Workings

W1 Calculation of acquisition cost and indexed cost of shares sold

	No. of shares	Cost	Indexed cost
Purchased on 10 Feb 2007	35,000	1,20,000	1,20,000
Indexation to 4 Jan 2010			30,000
	35,000	120,000	150,000
Rights shares purchased on 4 Jan 2010	17,500	38,500	38,500
	52,500	158,500	188,500
Less : Disposal on 26 Jan 2010 (note 2) (Cost x 35,000/52,500)	(35,000)	(105,667)	(125,667)
	17,500	52,833	62,833

Notes:

1. Indexation allowance cannot be used to create or increase a loss.
2. The rights issues were purchased and sold in the same month, i.e. January 2010, in which case the RPI will be the same and hence pool will not be indexed up before the disposal of the shares (operative event).

C5.12: Chargeable Gains

Example Sun Ltd purchased 10,000 shares in Moon Ltd on 23 March 2010 for £30,000. On 26 March 2010, Moon Ltd made a rights issue of 1 for 1. Sun Ltd paid £3.50 for each new share issued. Sun Ltd sold 15,000 ordinary shares in Moon Ltd on 31 March 2010 for £60,500.

A rights issue is made by Moon Ltd and it has been exercised (purchased) by Sun Ltd the capital gains are calculated as follows:

First of all, we have to calculate the cost of the rights shares.
Cost = No. of shares x rate of one share
     = 10,000 x £3.50
     = £35,000

Therefore, total cost of all shares = £30,000 + £35,000 = £65,000

Cost of the number of shares sold = £65,000 x 15,000/(10,000 +10,000)
                                  = £48,750

	£
Sale proceeds	60,500
Less: Acquisition cost of shares	(48,750)
Chargeable gain	11,750

Note: Shares sold were purchased during the nine days prior to the disposal, hence cost will not be indexed up. Moreover, all the transactions were in the same month in which case the RPI will be the same and hence there will be no inflation (indexation allowance).

Example Mars Ltd purchased 40,000 shares in Venus Ltd on 15 February 2006 for £100,000. The indexed value of the 1985 pool on 5 January 2010 was £145,000. Venus Ltd made a rights issue of 1 for 2 rights on 5 January 2010. Mars Ltd paid for the rights issue @ £2.00 for each new share issued.

On 25 January 2010, Mars Ltd sold 40,000 shares in Venus Ltd for £160,000.

As the rights issue made by Venus Ltd has been exercised (purchased) by Mars Ltd, the calculation of capital gains will be made as follows:

First of all, we have to calculate the number and cost of the rights shares.
Number of rights issue = 40,000 x 1/2 = 20,000 shares.

Cost = No. of shares x rate of one share
     = 20,000 x £2.00
     = £40,000

	£
Disposal consideration	160,000
Less: Acquisition cost of shares (W1)	(93,333)
Un-indexed gain	66,667
Less: Indexation allowance (W1) (£123,333 – £93,333)	(30,000)
Chargeable gain	36,667

Working

W1 Calculation of acquisition cost and indexation allowance of shares sold

	No. of shares	Cost	Indexed cost
Indexed value on 5 Jan 2010	40,000	100,000	145,000
Rights shares purchased on 5 Jan 2010	20,000	40,000	40,000
	60,000	140,000	185,000
Less : Disposal on 25 Jan 2010 (Cost x 40,000/60,000)	(40,000)	(93,333)	(123,333)
	20,000	46,667	61,667

2. Individuals

The rights shares are **treated as** having been **acquired on the same date as the original holding** that qualified for the rights.

Example

Tania's investment folder shows the following transactions:

Date	Transaction	Number of shares (Cool Ltd)	Cost £
5 March 2004	Purchase	500	500
20 May 2006	Purchase	1,000	4,000

On 21 August 2009, the company made a 1 for 5 rights issue at £7 per share. Tania purchased her full quota of rights shares.

Tania's share holding immediately after the rights issue will be as follows:

	Number of shares	Cost £
Bought 5 March 2004	500	500
Bought 20 May 2006	1,000	4,000
	1,500	**4,500**
Rights issue on 21 August 2009 at £7 per share (1:5 ratio)	300	2,100
	1,800	**6,600**

These rights shares will be treated as acquired as follows:
- 100 shares (500 x 1/5) on 5 March 2004
- 200 shares (1000 x 1/5) on 20 May 2006

Example
Continuing the previous example of Tania's investment

In continuation of the above example, assume that Tania sold all the above shares for £16,200 on 28 March 2010.

Calculation of capital gains will be as follows:

	£
Sale proceeds	16,200
Less: Acquisition cost	(6,600)
Chargeable gain	**9,600**

Example

Henry purchased 40,000 shares in Venus Ltd on 15 February 2006 for £120,000.

Venus Ltd made a rights issue of 1 for 2 rights on 5 January 2010. He paid for the rights issue @ £2.00 for each new share issued.

On 25 January 2010, Henry sold 40,000 shares in Venus Ltd for £160,000.

Calculation of capital gains will be as follows:

First of all, we have to calculate the number and cost of the rights shares.
Number of rights issue = 40,000 x 1/2 = 20,000 shares.

Cost = No. of shares x rate of one share
= 20,000 x £2.00
= £40,000

Therefore, total cost of all shares = 120,000 + £40,000 = £160,000
Cost of number of shares sold = £160,000 x 40,000/(40,000 + 20,000)
= £106,667

	£
Sale proceeds	160,000
Less: Acquisition cost of shares	(106,667)
Chargeable gain	**53,333**

SUMMARY

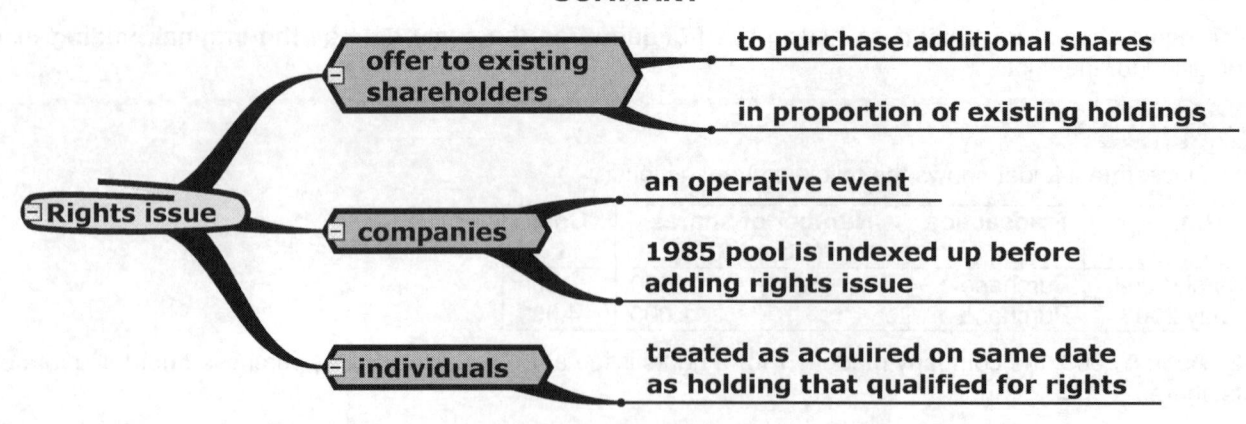

Rights issue

- **offer to existing shareholders**
  - to purchase additional shares
  - in proportion of existing holdings
- **companies**
  - an operative event
  - 1985 pool is indexed up before adding rights issue
- **individuals**
  - treated as acquired on same date as holding that qualified for rights

3.3 Takeovers and reorganisations

1. Companies

a) When **one company takes over another company**, the new company acquires shares in the old company in exchange for shares in the new company.

b) Known as '**paper for paper**' transaction.

c) This transaction does **not give rise to a chargeable gain.**

d) **New shares** take the place of the old shares, and are **treated as having been purchased at the same time and for the same cost.**

e) There is **no gain at the time of the takeover** if all the consideration is in the form of shares in the new company.

f) If the consideration is partly in shares and partly in cash and the consideration received in cash is not 'small', then the gain related to cash consideration will be chargeable immediately. The sum is regarded as 'small' if the cash consideration received is less than 5% of the total consideration received, restricted to **maximum of £3,000.**

While calculating chargeable gains, the part of the cost of the original shares attributable to the cash consideration received will be calculated as follows:

$$\text{Cost of original shares} \times \frac{\text{Cash received}}{\text{Total value of consideration from company}}$$

Where,
Total value of consideration from company = cash received + market value of new shares received

g) There is a **gain when the new shares are disposed of.**

h) If **more than one class of the new share** is acquired (e.g. ordinary shares and preference shares) the **cost of the original shares must be allocated** according to the market value of the new shares at the time of the takeover.

> **Example**
> **Example to show allocation of original cost**
>
> Tip top Plc bought 10,000 shares in Armco Plc in June 2007 for £25,000. In June 2009 Braun Plc took over Armco Plc.
>
> For every 2 shares in Armco Plc, Tip top Plc received 3 ordinary shares and 1 preference share in Braun Plc.
>
> At the time of the takeover Braun Plc's ordinary shares were quoted at £2.00, and their preference shares at £3.00.
>
> **Continued on next page**

Allocation of original cost:

Consideration of takeover for Tip top Plc	£
(10,000 x 3/2) 15,000 ordinary shares in Braun Plc at £2.00	30,000
(10,000 x 1/2) 5,000 preference shares in Braun Plc at £3.00	15,000
	45,000

Original cost allocated to	£
Ordinary shares: £25,000 x £30,000/£45,000	16,667
Preference shares: £25,000 x £15,000/£45,000	8,333
	25,000

Example

Saturn Ltd purchased 20,000 ordinary shares in Sun Ltd on 1 July 2009 for £100,000.

On 15 July 2009, Sun Ltd was taken over by Moon Ltd. Saturn Ltd received one £1 ordinary share and one £1 preference share in Moon Ltd for each £1 ordinary share held in Sun Ltd.

When Sun Ltd was taken over by Moon Ltd, the shares were quoted at different rates. Each £1 ordinary share in Moon Ltd was quoted at £5.10 and each £1 preference share was quoted at £1.75.

Saturn Ltd sold 12,000 £1 ordinary shares in Moon Ltd on 31 July 2009 for £40,000.

The RPI for July 2009 is 213.4.

The calculation of the capital gains of Saturn Ltd is as follows:

Due to takeover, Saturn Ltd receives a number of ordinary shares = 20,000
Number of preference shares = 20,000

Cost attributable to shares in Moon Ltd from the takeover is allocated on the basis of the market value of the new shares at the time of the takeover.
Market value of the shares in Moon Ltd:
➢ Ordinary shares = 20,000 x £5.10 = £102,000
➢ Preference shares = 20,000 x £1.75 = £35,000

Hence, cost attributable to 20,000 ordinary shares in Moon Ltd
= £100,000 x £102,000/(£102,000 + £35,000)
= £100,000 x £0.74
= £74,000

The cost attributable to 12,000 ordinary shares sold
= £74,000 x 12,000/20,000
= £44,400

	£
Sale proceeds	40,000
Less: Acquisition cost of shares	(44,400)
Capital loss	4,400

Note: As all the transactions were in the same month, there will be no indexation allowance. Moreover, indexation allowance cannot be used to create or increase a loss.

Example

Early Ltd purchased 15,000 shares in Weak Ltd on 2 May 2001 for £20,000. The indexed value of the 1985 pool on 5 March 2010 was £24,500.

On 5 March 2010, Weak Ltd was taken over by Strong Ltd. Early Ltd received two £1 ordinary shares and one £1 preference shares in Strong Ltd for each £1 ordinary share held in Weak Ltd.

Continued on next page

After the takeover each £1 ordinary share in Strong Ltd was quoted at £3.00, and each preference share was quoted at £2.00.

Early Ltd sold all the £1 ordinary shares in Strong Ltd on 29 March 2010 for £30,000.

The capital gain of Early Ltd is calculated as follows:

Due to the takeover, Early Ltd receives:
Number of ordinary shares = 15,000 x 2 = 30,000
Number of preference shares = 15,000 x 1 = 15,000

Market value of these shares at the time of the takeover:
Ordinary shares = 30,000 x £3.00 = £90,000
Preference shares = 15,000 x £2.00 = £30,000

Cost attributable to ordinary shares = £20,000 x £90,000/(£90,000+ £30,000)
= £20,000 x £90,000/£120,000
= £15,000

	£
Sale proceeds	30,000
Less: Acquisition cost of shares	(15,000)
Un-indexed gain	15,000
Less: Indexation allowance (W1)	(3,375)
Capital gains	11,625

Working

W1

Indexation allowance is calculated as follows:
Indexed value – original cost indexed for total value of ordinary shares.
= £24,500 – £20,000
= £4,500

Indexation allowance attributable to ordinary shares:
= £4,500 x £90,000/(£90,000 + £30,000)
= £3,375

2. Individuals

The **same principle** is applied where an individual is concerned except indexation allowance, as from 6th April 2008, it is no longer available to individuals.

Also from 5th April 2008, a shareholder who received a paper to paper transaction may elect to have the event treated as a disposal. This is to use their annual exemption or claim entrepreneur's relief.

Example

Roger purchased 20,000 shares in Splendid Ltd on **2 May 2002** for £24,000

Splendid Ltd was taken over by Blue Ltd on 5 March 2010.

Roger received two £1 ordinary shares and one £1 preference share in Blue Ltd for each £1 ordinary share held in Splendid Ltd.

After the takeover each £1 ordinary share in Blue Ltd was quoted at £2.00 and each preference share was quoted at £1.00.

Roger sold his entire holding of £1 ordinary shares in Blue Ltd on 29 March 2010 for £60,000.

The calculation of capital gain is made as follows:

Due to the takeover, Roger receives a number of ordinary shares = 20,000 x 2 = 40,000 shares

Number of preference shares = 20,000 x 1 = 20,000 shares

Value of the shares = Ordinary shares = 40,000 x £2.00 = £80,000

Preference shares = 20,000 x £1.00 = £20,000

Continued on next page

Cost attributable to ordinary shares =24,000 x £80,000/(£80,000 + £20,000)
=24,000 x £80,000/£100,000
= £19,200

	£
Sale proceeds	60,000
Less: Acquisition cost of shares	(19,200)
Net gain	40,800

Example

Rosy purchased 18,000 shares in Superb Ltd on 2 May 2002 for £20,000. Superb Ltd was taken over by White Ltd on 5 March 2010.

Rosy received two £1 ordinary shares and one £1 preference share in White Ltd and £1.25 in cash for each £1 ordinary share held in Superb Ltd. After the takeover, each £1 ordinary share in White Ltd was quoted at £2.75 and each preference share was quoted at £1.75.

Rosy sold her entire holding of £1 ordinary shares in White Ltd on 29 March 2010 for £60,000.

The computation of capital gains is made as follows:

Due to the takeover, Rosy received

Number of ordinary shares = 18,000 x 2 = 36,000 shares

Number of preference shares = 18,000 x 1 = 18,000 shares

Cash consideration = 18,000 x 1.25 = £22,500

Market value of these shares:

Ordinary shares = 36,000 x £2.75 = £99,000

Preference shares = 18,000 x £1.75 = £31,500

Hence, total value of consideration = £22,500 + £99,000 + £31,500 = £153,000

There is no gain at the time of takeover for the consideration received in shares. However, the gain related to cash consideration will be chargeable immediately as the cash consideration received of £22,500 is more than the 5% of the total consideration, i.e. £7,650 (£153,000 x 5%).

Cost attributable to cash consideration = Cost of original shares x cash received / Total value of consideration
= £20,000 x £22,500/(£22,500 + £99,000 + £31,500)
=£20,000 x £22,500/£153,000
= £2,941

The computation of capital gains at the time of takeover is as follows:

	£
Sale proceeds (cash)	22,500
Less: Acquisition cost of shares attributable to cash consideration	(2,941)
Capital gain	19,559

The calculation of capital gain on sale of entire holding of ordinary shares is as follows:

Cost attributable to ordinary shares = £20,000 x £99,000/(£22,500 + £99,000 + £31,500)
=£20,000 x £99,000/£153,000
= £12,941

	£
Sale proceeds	60,000
Less: Acquisition cost of shares attributable to ordinary shares	(12,941)
Capital gains	47,059

SUMMARY

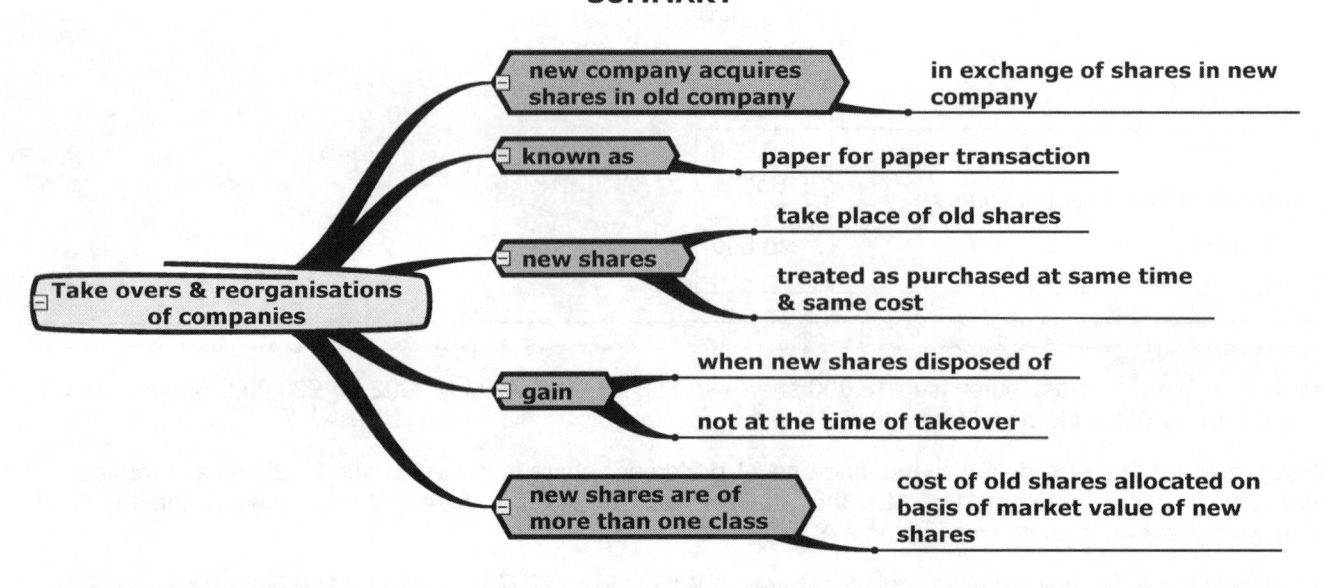

Take overs & reorganisations of companies
- new company acquires shares in old company — in exchange of shares in new company
- known as — paper for paper transaction
- new shares
  - take place of old shares
  - treated as purchased at same time & same cost
- gain
  - when new shares disposed of
  - not at the time of takeover
- new shares are of more than one class — cost of old shares allocated on basis of market value of new shares

Test Yourself 6

On 1 November 2000 (RPI 172.1), Galaxy Plc purchased 1,000 shares of Supernova Ltd for £5,000. In April 2009 Supernova Ltd made a takeover bid to the shareholders of Galaxy Plc to acquire their shares @ £12 per share. On 20 August 2009 (RPI 214.4), the offer was accepted by the shareholders of Galaxy Plc. Supernova Ltd made the payment to the shareholders of Galaxy Plc in cash.

Required:

Calculate the chargeable gain of Galaxy Plc

Test Yourself 7

Harry is a shareholder of Arco Ltd. He purchased 1,000 shares of Arco Ltd in April 1995 (RPI 149.0) for £3 per share. In June 2009, Lasso Ltd offered 1 share of Lasso Ltd for each share of Arco Ltd. On the day of the offer, each share of Lasso Ltd was worth £4.

Required:

Advise Harry whether any capital gain arises out of this transaction.

---

4. Explain the exemption available for gilt-edged securities and qualifying corporate bonds.[1]
[Learning outcome e]

Disposals of gilt-edged securities and qualifying corporate bonds are **exempt for individuals – not for companies.**

Example of gilt-edged securities

2½%	Treasury Stock 1975
12¾%	Treasury Loan 1992
12¼%	Exchequer Stock 1992
10½%	Treasury Convertible Stock 1992

Qualifying corporate bonds are debentures and other fixed interest securities of companies which represent a normal commercial loan.

Diagram 1: Gain on disposal of Gilt and Qualified corporate bond

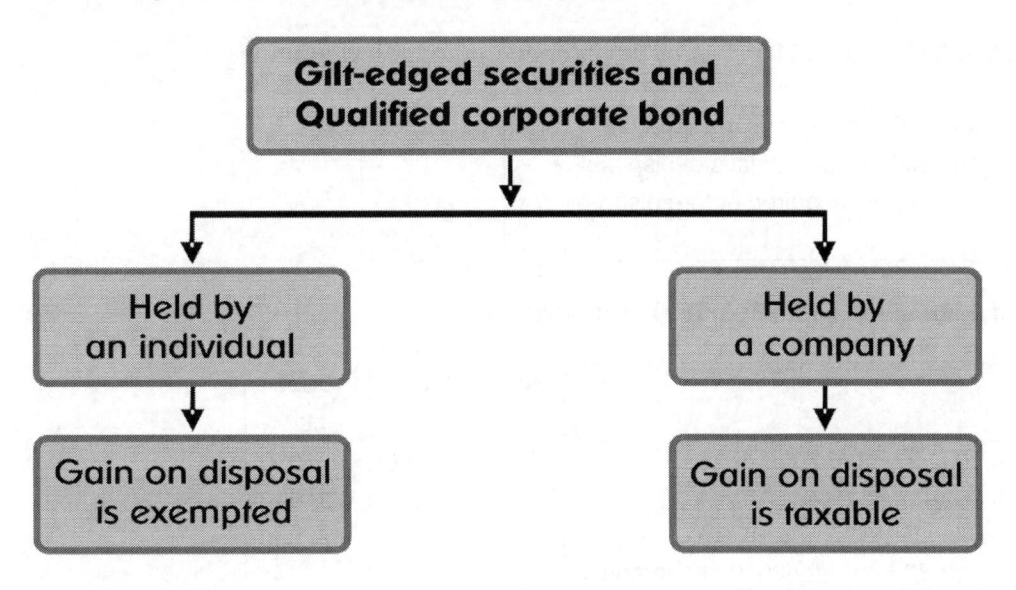

```
            Gilt-edged securities and
            Qualified corporate bond
           /                          \
       Held by                      Held by
    an individual                  a company
          |                            |
    Gain on disposal            Gain on disposal
      is exempted                  is taxable
```

Answers to Test Yourself

Answer 1

The value will be the **lower of:**

1. Lower quoted price +1/4(higher quoted price - lower quoted price)
   = £120 + 1/4 x (£130 – £120) = £122.5

2. The average of the highest and lowest recorded bargains
   = (£122 + £129)/2 = £125.5

Therefore, the value per share for CGT purpose will be £122.5. The value of 2,000 shares will be charged accordingly. The market value of the shares will be 2,000 x £122.5 = £245,000

Answer 2

	£
Disposal consideration (W1)	129,000
Less: Acquisition cost of shares (W2)	(55,882)
Chargeable gain	**73,118**

Workings

W1

The valuation of quoted shares as on the day of the transfer is calculated as follows:
The value will be the **lower of:**

1. Lower quoted price +1/4 (higher quoted price - lower quoted price)
   = £6.40 + 1/4 x (£6.60 – £6.40) = £6.45

2. The average of the highest and lowest recorded bargains
   = (£6.40 + £6.60)/2 = £6.50

Therefore, the value per share for CGT purposes will be £6.45. The value of 20,000 shares will be changed accordingly.

Hence, disposal consideration will be 20,000 ordinary shares x £6.45 = £129,000.

W2

Disposal of 20,000 shares on 20 Feb 2009 is matched in the following order:

Shares purchased on same day as the disposal	-
Shares purchased within next 30 days of disposal	-
Shares in the shares pool acquired before disposal	20,000
	20,000

Calculation of acquisition cost of shares in the share pool

	No. of shares	Cost
		£
Purchased on 10 December 2008	19,000	65,000
Purchased on 25 August 2009	15,000	30,000
	34,000	95,000
Less: Disposal on 20 February 2010 at average cost (£95,000 x 20,000/34,000)	(20,000)	(55,882)
	14,000	39,118

Answer 3

Disposal of 5,000 shares on 20 February 2010 is matched in the following order:

	No. of shares
Shares purchased on the same day as the disposal (20 February 2010)	-
Shares purchased within next 30 days of the disposal (i.e. up to 22 March 2010)	-
Shares from the share pool acquired before date of disposal	5,000
Total number of shares sold	**5,000**

	£
Shares in the share pool:	
Disposal consideration	30,000
Less: Acquisition cost of shares (W1)	(15,000)
Chargeable Gains	**15,000**

Workings

W1 Calculation of the cost of acquisition of shares in the share pool is as follows:

	No. of	Cost
Purchased on 5 June 1997	4,000	8,500
Purchased on 25 April 2007	2,000	7,500
Purchased on 20 May 2007	1000	5,000
	7,000	21,000
Less: Disposal on 20 February 2010 (at average cost) (£21,000 x 5,000/7,000)	5,000	15,000
	2,000	6,000

Answer 4

	£
Disposal consideration (4,060 shares)	28,420
Less: Acquisition cost of shares	(13,000)
Un-indexed gain	**15,420**
Less: Indexation allowance (£19,853 - £13,000) (W1)	6,853
Chargeable gain	**8,567**

Workings

W1 Share holding

	Number of shares	Cost (£)	Indexed cost (£)
Purchased on 01/01/1991	2,000	8,000	8,000
Indexation to April 1995			
(149.0 - 130.2/130.2) x £8,000			1,155
	2,000	8,000	9,155
Purchased on 20/04/1995	500	3,000	3,000
	2,500	11,000	12,155
Indexation to September 2001 (174.6 -149.0/149.0) x £12,155			2,088
	2,500	11,000	14,243
Purchased on 09/09/2001	400	2,000	2,000
	2,900	13,000	16,243
Bonus issue on 1 December 2007 (2,900 x 2/5)	1,160	-	-
	4,060	13,000	16,243
Indexation to June 2009			
(213.4 - 174.6/174.6) x £16,243			3,610
	4,060	13,000	19,853

Answer 5

	£
Disposal consideration	160,500
Less: Acquisition cost of shares (note 3)	(67,000)
Un-indexed gain	93,500
Less: Indexation allowance (note 4)	(7,667)
Chargeable gain	85,833

Notes:

1. Koyna Ltd made the bonus issue in the ratio of 1 for each 2 shares held.
   Therefore, bonus issue = 35,000 shares x 1/2 = 17,500 shares.

2. Cost of bonus shares is always 0.
   So, £100,500 is the cost of the total number of shares, including bonus shares i.e. 35,000 + 17,500 = 52,500 shares.

3. The cost of 35,000 shares sold = £100,500 x 35,000/(35,000 + 17,500) = £67,000

4. Indexation Allowance is calculated as follows:
   Indexed value – Purchase value
   = £112,000 - £100,500 = £11,500

   For 35,000 shares sold = £11,500 x 35,000/(35,000 + 17,500) = £7,667

Answer 6

Calculation of capital gains of Galaxy plc

	£
Disposal consideration (£12 x 1,000)	12,000
Less: Cost of acquisition	(5,000)
Un-indexed gain	7,000
Less: Indexation allowance	
(214.4 - 172.1/172.1) x £5,000	(1,229)
Chargeable gain	5,771

Answer 7

In the case of a paper for paper takeover, capital gains will not arise until the taxpayer sells the shares of the acquirer company. Merely a paper for paper exchange will not give rise to any capital gains.

When Harry sells the shares of Lasso Ltd, then a chargeable gain will arise.

Quick Quiz

1. How is a disposal of shares matched with purchases in the case of a company?

2. How is a disposal of shares matched with purchases in the case of an individual?

3. What is meant by a 'paper for paper' transaction?

Answers to Quick Quiz

1. **Disposal of shares is matched with purchases** in the following **order**:

a) Shares purchased on the **same day** as the disposal.

b) Shares purchased **during the nine days prior to the disposal.**

c) Shares **in the share pool.**

All purchases are aggregated in the share pool except for those purchased on the **same day or the previous nine days**. They are each **treated as a single asset**.

2. The disposal of **shares is matched** as follows:

a) Shares purchased on the **same day** as the disposal.

b) Shares purchased in the **following 30 days.**

c) Shares in **the share pool.**

All purchases are aggregated in the share pool except for those purchased on the same day or the following 30 days. They are each treated as single assets.

3. When **one company takes over another company**, the new company acquires shares in the old company in exchange for shares in the new company. This is known as a **'paper for paper'** transaction. It does not give rise to chargeable gain.

Self Examination Questions

Question 1

Lisa acquired shares in CD Plc on different dates. The details regarding the date of acquisition, number of shares and cost are as follows:

Date of acquisition	Number of shares	Cost (£)
01/09/1997	20,000	40,000
09/02/2005	7,200	10,800
10/10/2009	500	500
12/02/2010	1,000	1,500

Date of sale	Number of shares	Sales price (£)
09/02/2010	1,500	4,500

Required:

Show the calculations of capital gains arising on the disposal of shares.

Question 2

Nadia sold 300 qualifying corporate bonds at a loss of £200, which she had purchased in the previous month. Can she adjust this capital loss against the current year's capital gains?

Question 3

In July 2005, Prem purchased 300 shares of Lazy Ltd. In April 2009, Hate Ltd made an offer to the shareholders of Lazy Ltd to acquire their shares on the basis of 1 share of Hate Ltd for each share of Lazy Ltd.

Prem accepted the offer and exchanged his shares in return for 300 shares of Hate Ltd.

Required:

Calculate the amount of capital gains tax Prem is required to pay after this transaction.

Answers to Self Examination Questions

Answer 1

Disposal of 1,500 shares on 09/02/2010 are matched in the following order:

	No. of shares
Shares purchased on the same day as the disposal	-
Shares purchased within next 30 days of the disposal	1,000
Shares from the share pool acquired before date of disposal	500
Total number of shares sold	**1,500**

Calculation of acquisition cost of shares in the share pool

	No. of shares	Cost £
Purchased on 01/09/1997	20,000	40,000
Purchased on 09/02/2005	7,200	10,800
Purchased on 10/10/2009	500	500
	27,700	51,300
Less : Disposal on 09/02/2010 at average cost (£51,300 x 500/27,700)	(500)	(926)
	27,200	50,374

The capital gain for 2009 - 10 is computed as follows:

	£	£
Shares purchased on same day of disposal		
Disposal consideration	-	
Less: Acquisition cost of shares	-	-
Shares purchased within next 30 days of disposal		
Disposal consideration: 1000 shares (W1)	3,000	
Less: Acquisition cost of shares	(1,500)	1,500
Shares in the share pool acquired before disposal		
Disposal consideration: 500 shares (W2)	1,500	
Less: Acquisition cost of shares	(926)	574
Chargeable gains		**2,074**

Workings

W1

Total Disposal consideration for 1,500 shares is £4,500. Therefore, for 1,000 shares
= £4,500 x 1,000/1,500
= £3,000

W2

Total Disposal consideration for 1,500 shares is £4,500. Therefore, for 500 shares
= £4,500 x 500 /1,500
= £1,500

Answer 2

For capital gains purposes, the qualifying corporate bonds are not a chargeable asset. Therefore any gain arising from the disposal of qualifying corporate bonds is not a chargeable gain. In the same way, any loss on disposal of these bonds is not an allowable loss.

Therefore, Nadia cannot adjust the loss arising out of disposal of qualifying corporate bonds against the current year's capital gains.

Answer 3

In the case of a paper to paper transaction, the chargeable gain will arise only at the time when the shares of the acquired company are **sold** by the taxpayer.

Therefore, in the case of Prem, he is not liable to any capital gains tax on unrealised gains arising from the takeover transaction.

SECTION C: CHARGEABLE GAINS

C6

STUDY GUIDE C6: THE USE OF EXEMPTIONS AND RELIEFS IN DEFERRING AND MINIMISING TAX LIABILITIES ARISING ON THE DISPOSAL OF CAPITAL ASSETS

Get Through Intro

Proper tax planning requires an **in-depth knowledge** of all the rules, provisions and loopholes existing in the Tax Law.

This means that for the calculation of capital gains tax, the taxpayer or his consultant should be aware of all the reliefs – such as **entrepreneurs' relief, rollover relief, holdover relief, gift relief, and incorporation relief** - that the legislation has made available to him, along with all the other provisions relating to the calculation of capital gains.

This Study Guide explains the calculation of rollover relief (which is available to both individuals and companies) and the calculation of **entrepreneurs' relief, holdover relief** and **incorporation relief**, which is available only to individuals.

Learning Outcomes

a) Explain and apply entrepreneurs' relief as it applies to individuals.
b) Explain and apply rollover relief as it applies to individuals and companies.
c) Explain and apply holdover relief for the gift of business assets.
d) Explain and apply the incorporation relief that is available upon the transfer of a business to a company.

Introduction

Case Study

Kathy owned an industrial building in London. Until January 2005, she used this building for manufacturing toys. However, due to old age, she was unable to manage the business and her profits started to decline. As her daughter Laura was not interested in running the business, Kathy sold all her business assets except the industrial building.

Kathy wanted to give the industrial building to her daughter, Laura. However, she was avoiding this because she knew that the tax treatment of the transfer of the asset as a gift would trigger a chargeable disposal. This would require her to pay capital gains tax, which she did not want to do.

In this Study Guide we will see all the provisions relating to holdover relief and whether or not Kathy can give her daughter the business asset without having to pay any capital gains tax.

1. Explain and apply entrepreneurs' relief as it applies to individuals.[2]
[Learning outcome a]

1.1 Entrepreneurs' relief

1. Entrepreneurs' relief was introduced from 6 April 2008 as a replacement for taper relief previously available to individuals.

2. This relief is available when an individual disposes of a business or part of a business.

3. The relief is available on the **first £1 million of qualifying gains** that a person makes during his lifetime. Hence, this limit is known as the **lifetime limit**. The £1 million limit is reduced every time an individual makes a qualifying gain.

4. Relief reduces qualifying gains by a **factor of 4/9th** to give an effective capital gains tax rate of 10% (18% x 5/9th) for the gains covered by the relief.

5. Gains in excess of the £1 million limit are taxed at the normal capital gains tax rate of 18%.

6. Conditions to qualify for this relief:

a) there is no age requirement to qualify for this relief.

b) assets disposed of should have been owned for one year, prior to the date of their disposal.

c) the asset disposed of must be a qualifying asset (see below).

7. The following are the **qualifying disposals** to claim this relief:

a) disposal of the **whole or part of the business** operated individually or in a partnership. It will include only the capital gains arising from the disposal of the **trading assets** (in use for the purpose of the business) and will exclude capital gains arising from non-trading assets, such as investments.

b) disposal of **shares in a trading company** where:
   ➢ an individual has a shareholding of 5% in the company, and
   ➢ is also an employee of that trading company.

   In this case, there is no restriction on the amount of relief, even if the assets disposed of are non-trading assets such as investments, subject to the condition that the company is a trading company.

8. In case of disposal of the trading assets after the cessation of a business, the disposal needs to be within three years of the cessation of the business, and the asset must have been a qualifying asset for the 12 months up to the date of cessation, not to the date of disposal, in order to claim entrepreneur's relief.

9. This relief is available before the current year losses, brought forward losses and annual exemption.

Example

In the tax year 2009 - 10 John made the following disposals:

1. John sold a business on 30 June 2009, which he had started on 1 January 2003. He made the following capital gains:

Goodwill	£234,000
Freehold property	£333,000
Freehold warehouse	£153,000

The assets were owned prior to one year to the date of disposal. John did not use the warehouse for business purposes at all.

2. John sold a 30% shareholding in Jacket Lamb Ltd on 25 January 2010. Jacket Lamb Ltd is an unquoted trading company. There was a capital gain of £505,000. John had purchased the shares on 1 March 2004 and was an employee of Jacket Lamb Ltd from 1 March 2004 till the date the shares were disposed of.

Required:

Calculate John's capital gains tax liability for the tax year 2009 - 10.

Answer

John's capital gains tax liability for the tax year 2009 - 10 is as follows:

	£	£
Goodwill	234,000	
Freehold office building	333,000	
Shareholding in Jacket Lamb Ltd (note 2)	505,000	
	1,072,000	
Less: Entrepreneurs' relief (£1,000,000 x 4/9ths) (note 3)	(444,444)	627,556
Freehold warehouse (note 1)		153,000
Chargeable gains		**780,556**
Less: Annual exemption		(10,100)
Taxable gains		**770,456**
Capital gains at 18%		138,682

Notes:

1. Entrepreneur's relief is available on the disposal of whole or part of the business, and is available only on disposal of the trading assets used in the business. Hence, it is available on the disposal of goodwill and the freehold office building. However, as the warehouse was not used for business purposes at all, entrepreneurs' relief will not be available on its disposal.

2. Entrepreneurs' relief is available on the disposal of shares in Jacket Lamb Ltd, as John was an employee of the company, and had more than 5% of the company's shares.

3. Relief is available on the first £1 million of qualifying gains that a person makes during his lifetime.

C6.4: Chargeable Gains

Example

Rex purchased machinery (an asset) on 6 April 2003. The machinery was used for trading purposes until 15 April 2008. However, due to old age, he shut down his business. On 1 May 2009, he sold the machinery and made a gain of £45,000.

Required:

Calculate Rex's capital gains tax liability.

Answer

Total number of years of ownership (complete years) = 5 years

Rex's capital gains tax liability for 2009 - 10 is as follows:

	£
Machinery	45,000
Less: Entrepreneur's relief (£45,000 x 4/9)	(20,000)
Chargeable gain	25,000
Less: Annual exemption	(10,100)
Taxable Gain	14,900
Capital gains at 18%	2,682

Note:

Entrepreneur's relief is not available on the sale of an individual business asset in a continuing trade. However, if the asset is sold as a part of disposal of the whole or part of the business, it can be claimed. As Rex sold the machinery after cessation of business and within time limit of 3 years after cessation, entrepreneurs' relief is available on net gains arising on it. It was used for the purpose of the business and was held for more than a year before the cessation of the business.

Test Yourself 1

Ben, a toy manufacturer, sold part of his business due to a financial crisis. He was in the business for many years.

His gains from the disposal were:

	£
Moulds	250,000
Goodwill	150,000
Freehold land	200,000
Warehouse	300,000

All these assets were owned by him from the start of the business. Ben held the freehold land as an investment.

He was also employed by Clarks Ltd, an unquoted trading company, for the last 5 years, and held 15% of the company's shares. He sold 10% of his shares in Clarks Ltd at a gain of £200,000.

These were the only disposals made by him in 2009 - 10.

Required:

Calculate Ben's capital gains tax liability for 2009 - 10.

SUMMARY

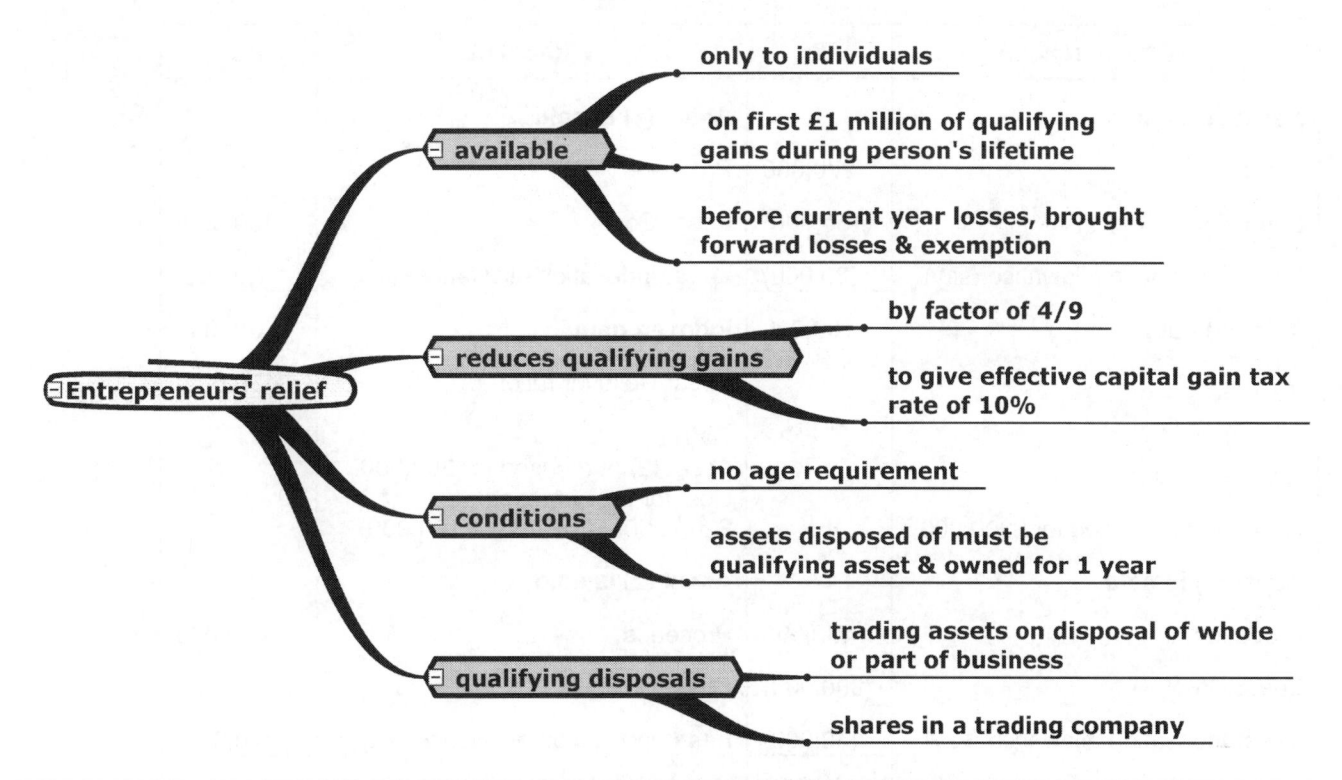

Entrepreneurs' relief

- **available**
  - only to individuals
  - on first £1 million of qualifying gains during person's lifetime
  - before current year losses, brought forward losses & exemption
- **reduces qualifying gains**
  - by factor of 4/9
  - to give effective capital gain tax rate of 10%
- **conditions**
  - no age requirement
  - assets disposed of must be qualifying asset & owned for 1 year
- **qualifying disposals**
  - trading assets on disposal of whole or part of business
  - shares in a trading company

2. Explain and apply rollover relief as it applies to individuals and companies. [2]
[Learning outcome b]

As the name suggests, when an old business asset is replaced by a new business asset, the gain arising on the disposal of the old asset is rolled over (carried forward) against the cost of the new asset.

Rollover relief is **available to companies and individuals.**

> **Tip:** The taxpayer has to claim rollover relief. It is not automatic.

2.1 Companies

1. **Rollover relief:** also known as replacement of business asset relief.

2. **Purpose:** to encourage businesses to re-invest in capital assets.

3. **Problem:** if a business asset is sold and realises a gain, money must be made available to pay tax on the gain, rather than re-investing in new assets.

4. **Solution:** calculate gain, but no tax charged now, gain is postponed ('rolled over') until disposal of the replacement asset.

5. **Capital gain is deferred** where the disposal proceeds of the first asset are re-invested in a new asset.

6. The deferral is achieved by deducting the capital gain from the base cost of the new asset.

How this relief operates in the case of companies

Without relief	£	With relief	£
Asset (1) is sold		**Asset (1) is sold**	
Proceeds	270,000	Proceeds	270,000
Less: Cost	(150,000)	**Less:** Cost	(150,000)
Less: Indexation allowance (say)	(20,000)	**Less:** Indexation allowance (say)	(20,000)
Indexed gain	100,000	**Indexed gain**	100,000
		Less: Rollover relief	(100,000)
		Gain	-
Asset (2) purchased for £300,000		Asset (2) purchased for 300,000. Cost for tax purposes £200,000 (£300,000 - £100,000)	
Asset (2) is sold		**Asset (2) is sold**	
Proceeds	480,000	Proceeds	480,000
Less: Cost	(300,000)	**Less:** Cost	(200,000)
Less: Indexation allowance (say)	(40,000)	**Less:** Indexation allowance (say)	(40,000)
Indexed gain	140,000	**Indexed gain**	240,000

The total gains are the same in both situations. **With relief, the indexed gain is deferred until the disposal of the replacement asset.**

2.2 Conditions

1. The old and the new asset **must be qualifying business assets (QBA)**:
   a) Land and buildings
   b) Fixed plant and fixed machinery

2. The asset sold and the replaced assets do **not need** to be in the **same category.**

3. **The purchase of the replacement asset must take place in the period one year before and three years after the disposal of the old asset.**

4. The asset sold and replaced assets **must both be qualifying business assets and used for business purposes.**

5. The replaced asset must be brought into **business use at the time it is acquired.**

Example

Victory Ltd purchased a warehouse in August 2001(RPI 174.0) for £200,000. The company sold the warehouse on 20 February 2009 (RPI 211.4) for £400,000.

The company decided to re-invest the sale proceeds by purchasing a building for £420,000. The company purchased the building on 15 May 2009.

In this example, it is clear that the whole proceeds are reinvested and the purchase is made within three years after the date of sale, so the entire indexed gain realised on sale of the warehouse can be rolled over.

Continued on next page

The calculation of **indexed gain** on sale of warehouse is as follows:

	£
Disposal consideration	400,000
Less: Cost of acquisition	(200,000)
Unindexed gain	200,000
Less: Indexation allowance $\frac{(211.4 - 174.0)}{174.0} = (0.215) \times 200,000$	(43,000)
Indexed gain	157,000
Gain Rolled Over	(157,000)
Chargeable now	**NIL**

As a result of rollover relief, the gain on the disposal of the warehouse is not immediately chargeable. However, the cost of the new building is reduced by the amount of gain on the disposal of the warehouse.

Hence, the cost of the new building purchased will be £263,000 (£420,000 - £157,000).

a) Partial re-investment

Rollover relief is available, as shown above, if all the proceeds of the disposal of the old asset are used to acquire the new asset.

If **only a part** of the proceeds are used, the amount of **rollover relief is restricted.** The amount not re-invested reduces the amount of the capital gain that can be rolled over.

A gain will arise equal to the sale proceeds not re-invested or the actual gain whichever is lower. The balance of the gain can be rolled over.

If the amount not re-invested is greater than the capital gains, no rollover relief is available.

Example

Win Ltd sold a warehouse on 20 February 2009 for £400,000.

This sale transaction resulted in the capital gain of £95,000. The company decided to re-invest the sale proceeds by purchasing a building for £320,000.

The company purchased the building on 15 May 2009.

In this example, it is clear that the total proceeds are not re-invested, so, the complete capital gain cannot be rolled over.

As the sale proceeds are not fully re-invested, the amount not reinvested of £80,000 (£400,000 - £320,000) cannot be rolled over, and is chargeable immediately.

The remaining capital gain of £15,000 (£95,000 - £80,000) will be rolled over and deducted from the base cost of the new building.

The base cost of the new building will be £320,000 – £15,000 = £305,000.

Example

Swing Ltd purchased a freehold factory in September 2001. The company sold the factory in January 2009 for £80,000. This sale transaction gave rise to an indexed gain of £20,500.

In June 2009, a replacement factory was purchased for £70,000.

The rollover gain is calculated as follows:

	£
Total indexed gain	20,500
Less: Amount not re-invested (£80,000 - £70,000)	(10,000)
Rollover gain	**10,500**

Continued on next page

The amount of the proceeds not reinvested i.e. £10,000 will be chargeable immediately. The balance of the gain can be rolled over.

The base cost of the replaced factory will be calculated after deducting rollover relief as follows:

	£
Cost of replaced factory	70,000
Less: Rollover gain	(10,500)
Base cost of new factory	**59,500**

b) Re-investment in a depreciating asset

Definition: A depreciating asset is one which has an **expected life of 60 years or less.** For example, a leasehold factory on a 35 years lease.

Fixed plant and fixed machinery are **always depreciating assets.**
Where the **replaced asset is a depreciating asset**, the gain on the old asset is not rolled over; instead it is **'held over'**.

A held over gain does not reduce the cost of the replaced asset; instead it is **'frozen'** until the **earliest of:**
i. **10 years after the purchase** of the replaced asset
ii. The **replaced asset stops being used** for purpose of the business
iii. The **replaced asset is sold**

Example: Victory Ltd sold a warehouse on 20 February 2009 for £400,000. The sale transaction resulted in a capital gain of £95,000.

The company decided to re-invest the sale proceeds to acquire a leasehold factory on a 50-year lease for a premium of £550,000. The company purchased the building on 15 May 2009.

In this example, it is clear that the whole proceeds are re-invested, so the complete capital gain can be held over.

As the re-investment is made into a depreciating asset, the base cost of the factory will not be adjusted as a held over gain does not reduce the cost of the replaced asset; instead it is **'frozen'** until the **earliest of:**

1. **10 years after the purchase** of the replaced asset.
2. The **replaced asset stops being used** for business purposes.
3. The **replaced asset is sold.**

So, the gain is held over until the earlier of May 2017 (i.e. first condition 10 years from the date of purchase) or the date the replaced asset is sold or stops being used for business purposes.

2.3 Individuals

Rollover relief entitles an individual to defer the net gain.

Qualifying assets for individuals

1. Land and buildings
2. Fixed plant and fixed machinery
3. Goodwill

Rollover relief for an individual **entitles the individual to defer the net gain,** where the disposal proceeds of the first asset are re-invested in a new asset.

The deferral is achieved by deducting the capital gains from the base cost of the new asset.

Example Jack sold a freehold factory for £200,000 on 25 November 2008. He had purchased the factory on 5 August 2005 for £140,000. The asset was a business asset.

The disposal of the factory resulted in a gain. The gain was rolled over against the purchase cost of a freehold warehouse for £200,000 on 20 February 2009.

The warehouse was sold by Jack on 28 March 2010 for £250,000.

Jack used both the assets for business purposes.

As the sale proceeds of £200,000 were fully re-invested, so, the whole gain of £60,000 (£200,000 - £140,000) realised on the sale of the freehold factory can be rolled over and deducted from the base cost of the warehouse purchased.

Hence, cost of the new warehouse will be = Base cost of the warehouse – Rolled over gain
= £200,000 - £60,000 = £140,000

Calculation of chargeable gain on the sale of the warehouse is as follows:

	£	£
Disposal consideration		250,000
Less: Cost	200,000	
Rolled over gain	(60,000)	(140,000)
Chargeable gain		110,000

Example Mack purchased an office building on 5 May 2009 for £150,000. He sold it on 15 March 2010 for £220,000.

Mack also sold a warehouse on 20 April 2009 for £152,000 which was purchased on 12 November 2003 for £98,000.

Mack used the office building and warehouse for business purposes. He wanted to claim the benefit of rollover relief and so, he made the claim to rollover the gain, resulting from the sale proceeds of the warehouse against the cost of the building.

To calculate the chargeable gain we have to first calculate the amount of capital gains that cannot be rolled over.

	£
Sale proceeds	152,000
Less: Acquisition cost	98,000
Total gain	54,000
Less : Amount not reinvested in office building (£152,000 - £150,000)	2,000
Rolled over gain	52,000

Amount not reinvested of £2,000 will be chargeable to CGT immediately. The remaining capital gains of £52,000 can be rolled over, and deducted from the cost of the new office building.

The base cost of the office building will be calculated after deducting roll over relief as follows:

	£
Cost of building	150,000
Less: Rolled over gain	52,000
Cost for tax purpose	98,000

Continued on next page

Computation of chargeable gain on disposal of the office building is as follows:

	£
Disposal consideration	220,000
Less: Cost	(98,000)
Chargeable gain	122,000

Example Michael sold the warehouse on 15 February 2009 for £200,000. This sale transaction resulted in a capital gain of £55,000.

The company had an idea to purchase a freehold office building for £200,000 however; it finally decided to re-invest the sale proceeds by acquiring a leasehold factory on a 20-year lease for a premium of £220,000.

The company purchased the factory on 5 May 2009.

Would these two alternatives have had any impact on Michael's chargeable gains?

When the warehouse was sold and it was decided to re-invest the sale proceeds in the leasehold factory, the gain of £55,000 was **held over**, as a leasehold factory is a depreciating asset and the entire sale proceeds have been re-invested.

As the re-investment is made into a depreciating asset, the base cost of the factory is not adjusted. The gain will be held over until the earliest of:

1. 10 years after the purchase of the new asset.
2. The new asset stops being used for business purposes.
3. The new asset is sold.

However, if the company had purchased a freehold office building, then, because the total sale proceeds are re-invested, the total gain would be eligible for rollover relief and would have been deferred by deducting it from the base cost of the new office building.

Diagram 1: Rollover relief on reinvestment of proceeds of old asset in new asset

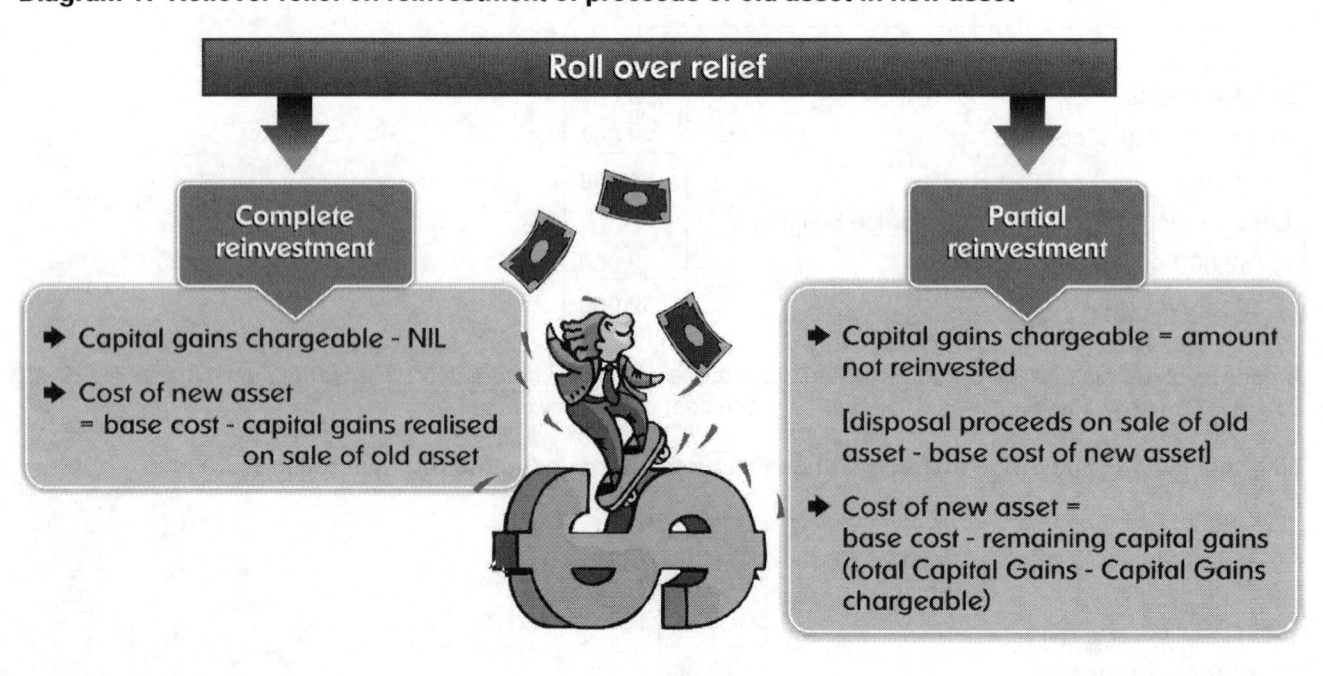

Roll over relief

Complete reinvestment
- Capital gains chargeable - NIL
- Cost of new asset
  = base cost - capital gains realised on sale of old asset

Partial reinvestment
- Capital gains chargeable = amount not reinvested
  [disposal proceeds on sale of old asset - base cost of new asset]
- Cost of new asset =
  base cost - remaining capital gains (total Capital Gains - Capital Gains chargeable)

2.4 Non-business use

Rollover relief is available when qualifying assets are used for business purposes.

Where an asset disposed of is **not entirely used for business purposes** then **only the gain relating to the business use qualifies for rollover relief.**

> **Example**
> Henry purchased a factory on 20 January 2001.
>
> He sold the factory on 15 November 2009 for £200,000. The sale of the factory resulted in a capital gain of £85,000.
>
> Henry used 60% of the factory for business purposes. The remaining 40% was kept for his personal use.
>
> Henry purchased another factory on 20 November 2009 for £250,000. This new factory was wholly used for business purposes.
>
> When we calculate Henry's chargeable gain, we will first calculate the amount of capital gains that are not allowed to be rolled over.
>
> Total capital gains = £85,000
> Utilisation of factory for non-business purposes is 40%
> Therefore, the amount of sale proceeds related to non-business purposes = £200,000 x 40% = £80,000
> Similarly, the proportion of capital gains for non-business purposes = £85,000 x 40%
> = £34,000.
>
> Thus, the amount of £34,000 does not qualify for roll-over relief. Hence to claim roll-over relief, re-investment is not required for the sale proceeds of £80,000 related to non-business purposes.
>
> As the 60% of the sale proceeds used for business purposes, i.e. £120,000 (£200,000 x 60%) was fully re-invested, the balance capital gain (£85,000 - £34,000 = **£51,000**) can be **rolled over.**
>
> As the sale proceeds are not re-invested into a depreciable asset, the cost of the new asset will be adjusted.
>
> The cost of the new factory = £250,000 - £51,000
> = £199,000.
>
> Calculation of chargeable gain is as follows:
>
> | | £ |
> |---|---|
> | Capital gain | 85,000 |
> | **Less:** Roll over relief | (51,000) |
> | **Chargeable gain** | **34,000** |

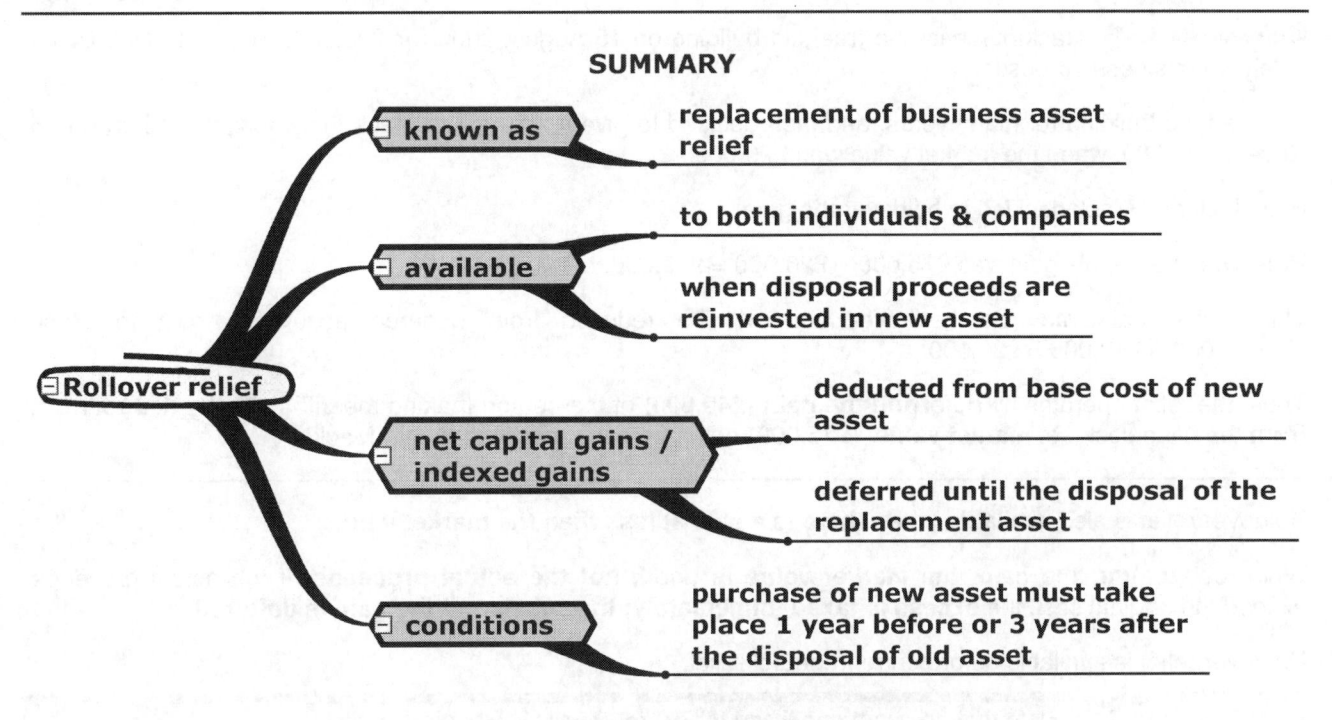

SUMMARY

Rollover relief
- **known as**: replacement of business asset relief
- **available**:
  - to both individuals & companies
  - when disposal proceeds are reinvested in new asset
- **net capital gains / indexed gains**:
  - deducted from base cost of new asset
  - deferred until the disposal of the replacement asset
- **conditions**: purchase of new asset must take place 1 year before or 3 years after the disposal of old asset

Test Yourself 2

In May 2003 (RPI 181.5) Cargo Ltd purchased an office building for £300,000. Due to its expansion the company decided to purchase a new office building. So in May 2009 (RPI 212.8) the company sold the old office building for £399,500. The company purchased a new office building for £560,000 in December 2009.

Required:

Calculate the chargeable gains on the disposal of the old office building assuming the company has elected for rollover relief.

---

3. Explain and apply holdover relief for the gift of business assets.[2]

[Learning outcome c]

Holdover relief for the gift of business assets (gift relief) is **only available to individuals.**

> **Tip**
> The taxpayer has to claim the holdover relief. It is not automatic.

When an individual gives a business asset as a gift, or sells it at less than market value, **disposal proceeds are taken to be at market value, even though no proceeds are received.** The person receiving the gift has a base cost in the asset equal to the market value as at the date of the gift, even though no expenditure was incurred.

Holdover relief allows a **capital gain on the gift of a qualifying asset to be deferred** (held over). The relief operates by **deferring the gain** of the person making the gift by **deducting it from the base cost** (i.e. **market value**) of the person receiving the gift. Both parties have to claim the relief.

3.1 Assets qualifying for gift relief include the following:

1. Assets used for business purposes by a sole trader.
2. Shares in unquoted trading companies (any size of holding).
3. Shares in a personal company.

A personal company is a one where an individual can exercise at least 5% of the voting rights. It must be a trading company.

> **Example**
> Jack purchased a freehold building on 15 August 2000 for £26,000. He used this building solely for business purposes.
>
> He used the building for many years, and then decided to give it as a gift to Mack, his younger brother, on 25 November 2009, when the market value was £75,000.
>
> Both Jack and Mack decided to holdover the gain.
>
> Here, the chargeable gain was £75,000 – £26,000 = £49,000.
>
> This whole gain may be held-over and will be reduced from deemed acquisition cost to Mack i.e. £75,000 – £49,000 = £26,000.
>
> Thus, the relief operates by **deferring the gain (£49,000)** of the person making the gift (Jack) by **deducting it from** the base cost (i.e. **market value**) (£75,000) of the person receiving the gift (Mack).

Holdover relief is also **available when there is a sale at less than the market value.**

When **calculating the gain, the market value is used, not the actual proceeds.** If the actual proceeds exceed the original cost, the **excess is taxed immediately; the balance of the gain is deferred.**

Holdover relief is available before entrepreneurs' relief.

> **Tip** Note that an asset qualifying for gift relief will be a business asset.

Example

Susan sold to her son Jack, 15,000 £1 ordinary shares in Sun Ltd, an unquoted trading company on 20 April 2009 for £120,000.

On that date, the market value of the shares was £150,000. Susan had purchased the shareholding on 15 July 2002 for £45,000.

They both decided to holdover the gain as a gift of a business asset.

As both Susan and her son are connected persons, for the purpose of calculating chargeable gains, the market value of the shares is used. Hence, **chargeable gain is calculated** as follows:

	£
Deemed proceeds (at market value)	150,000
Less: Cost of acquisition	(45,000)
	105,000
Less: Holdover relief **(W1)**	(30,000)
Chargeable gain	**75,000**

Workings

W1

The consideration paid of £120,000 for the shares is greater than the original cost by £75,000 i.e. (£120,000 - £45,000). Hence, £75,000 is chargeable to tax immediately.

Therefore holdover relief = £105,000 - £75,000 = £30,000 (i.e. the undervalue on the sale to her son)

Example

Continuing the above example of Susan and Jack. Let us suppose Jack at a later date sold 15,000 £1 ordinary shares in Sun Ltd for £175,000, the chargeable gain would be calculated as follows:

The cost of Jack's shares would be the market value of the shares less hold over relief.
Hence, the cost of the shares for Jack would be (£150,000 - £30,000) = £120,000 (i.e. the actual sales proceeds amount).

	£	£
Disposal consideration		175,000
Less: Cost of acquisition	150,000	
Holdover gain	30,000	(120,000)
Chargeable gain		**55,000**

3.2 Non Business use

Holdover relief is available when qualifying assets are used for business purposes. However, if an asset is used for both business and non-business purposes by the person giving the gift, then only the gain relating to the business use qualifies for holdover relief.

3.3 Restriction of holdover relief on the gift of the shares.

Holdover relief may be restricted if the shares (quoted or unquoted) are given as a gift and they are in the personal company of the person making the gift.

A personal company is one where an individual can exercise at least 5% of the voting rights. It must be a trading company.

The **gain to be deferred (holdover relief) is:**

$$\text{Net gain on the gift} \times \frac{\text{Market value of the company's chargeable business assets}}{\text{Market value of the company's total chargeable assets}}$$

> **Tip**
> You will be given the values of the chargeable assets and chargeable business assets in the exam.

C6.14: Chargeable Gains

Chargeable assets are all assets (business or non-business) which would be subject to capital gains if sold. Hence, stock, debtors and cash are not chargeable assets as no capital gains arise from their sale.

Chargeable business assets are chargeable assets used for business purposes excluding investments.

Example

Jack gave his shareholding of 60,000 shares (a 65% holding) in Jupiter Ltd (an unquoted trading company) to his brother Jimmy on 10 December 2009. On that date the market value of the shares was £300,000. Jack had bought the shares from the company on 10 January 2008 for £90,000.

The market values of Jupiter Ltd's assets on 10 December 2009 were as follows:

	£
Land	65,000
Office Building	105,000
Factory	50,000
Stock	35,000
Cash	10,000
Debtors	40,000
Investment in shares	80,000

Both Jack and Jimmy elected to holdover the gains.

Required:

Calculate Jack's chargeable gain.

Answer

The shareholding is 65%, i.e. Jimmy holds at least 5% of the shares. When a person owns at least 5% of the shares in a trading company (quoted or unquoted) holdover relief is available, but may be restricted, depending on the underlying assets of the company.

The gain to be deferred is:

Net gain on the gift x $\dfrac{\text{Market value of the company's chargeable business assets}}{\text{Market value of the company's total chargeable assets}}$

Chargeable assets of Jupiter Ltd on 10 December 2009 were £300,000 i.e. (£65,000 + £105,000 + £50,000 + £80,000)

Chargeable business assets on that day amounted to £220,000 i.e. (£65,000 + £105,000 + £50,000)

Thus, chargeable gain is calculated as follows:

	£
Deemed proceeds	300,000
Less: Cost of acquisition	(90,000)
	210,000
Less: Holdover relief (£210,000 x £220,000/£300,000)	(154,000)
Chargeable gain	56,000

Test Yourself 3

Ronny purchased a building for his business on 9 February 2003 for £45,000. He sold the building to his son, Kane on 20 April 2009 on the cessation of his business. On that date the market value of the building was £250,000. Kane paid his father £60,000 for the building.

Kane sold the building on 30 November 2009 for £260,000.

Required:

Calculate the chargeable gains for Ronny and Kane, assuming that they made an election for holdover relief. Assume that the current rules have always been used.

SUMMARY

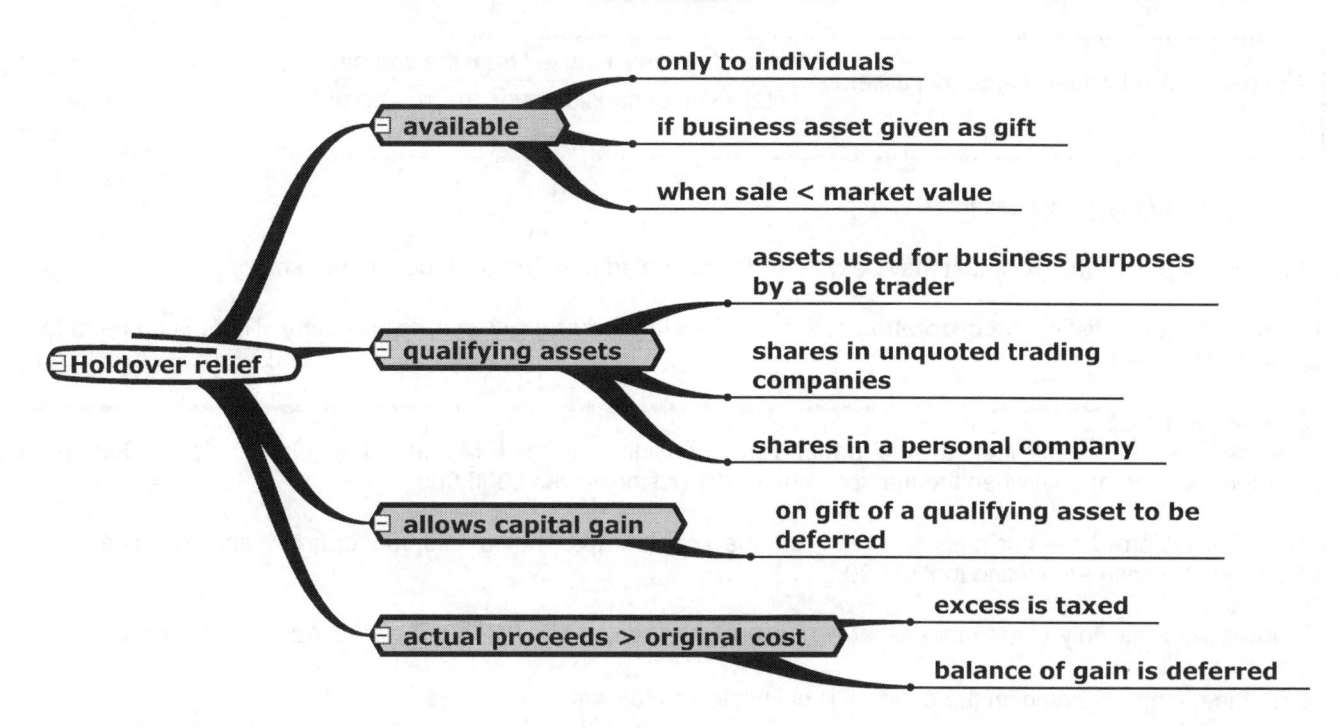

Holdover relief
- **available**
  - only to individuals
  - if business asset given as gift
  - when sale < market value
- **qualifying assets**
  - assets used for business purposes by a sole trader
  - shares in unquoted trading companies
  - shares in a personal company
- **allows capital gain**
  - on gift of a qualifying asset to be deferred
- **actual proceeds > original cost**
  - excess is taxed
  - balance of gain is deferred

---

4. Explain and apply the incorporation relief that is available upon the transfer of a business to a company.[2]

[Learning outcome d]

Incorporation relief is **only available to individuals**; either as sole traders or partnerships.

4.1 General introduction

- An individual is a sole trader who decides to incorporate his business.
- Sole trader ceases to trade, and a new company starts trading.
- Incorporation is achieved by transferring all the assets of the sole trader's business to the company (at market value) in exchange for shares in the company, or a mixture of shares and cash (known as 'consideration').
- The value of consideration will equal the total value of the sole trader's business.
- The assets of the sole trader have therefore been disposed of. Capital gains may arise on some of the assets (those chargeable to capital gains tax).

Consider some of the assets that may be transferred:

	Chargeable asset	Non-chargeable asset
Land and buildings	X	
Goodwill	X	
Motor car – exempt		X
Net current assets		X

Incorporation relief allows the capital gains arising on the disposal of the chargeable assets **to be deferred**.

This is achieved by **deducting the gains from the value of the shares received from the unincorporated company.**

This defers the gain until the individual disposes of the shares in the company.

4.2 Conditions

1. The transfer must be of a business as a **going concern.**
2. **All** of the assets **apart from cash** must be **transferred.**
3. The **consideration** for the transfer must be **wholly or partly in the form of shares.**

If all of the consideration received from the company is in the form of shares, all of the gains can be deferred.

If only part of the consideration is in the form of shares, only part of the gains can be deferred:

$$\text{Net gains on individual chargeable assets} \times \frac{\text{Value of shares received from the company}}{\text{Total value of consideration from company}}$$

The balance of the gain is taxable.

The gain (or part of the gain) that may be deferred is deducted from the base cost of the shares.

If conditions are satisfied, **incorporation relief can be claimed and given automatically.** There is no need to apply for this relief.

Example

Michael, a sole trader ran a business from 1 March 2006. On 10 April 2009 he incorporated a company, when the market value of the business was £300,000.

Michael transferred his business to Mars Ltd, the consideration being 225,000 ordinary shares valued at £225,000 and cash amounting to £75,000.

Goodwill was the only chargeable asset of the business, valued at £120,000 on 10 April 2009. The cost of goodwill is nil.

Here, the chargeable gain on the goodwill is calculated as follows:

	£
Disposal consideration	120,000
Less: Cost of acquisition	-
	120,000
Less: Incorporation relief (W1)	(90,000)
	30,000
Less: Entrepreneur's relief (£30,000 x 4/9) (note)	(13,333)
Chargeable gain	**16,667**

Note: Entrepreneur's relief is available on disposal of whole or part of the business. Hence, as the sole trader business is ceasing, relief will be available.

Workings

W1 Incorporation relief

The consideration is in the form of shares and cash. The proportion of the gain relating to the cash consideration is not eligible for incorporation relief.

So, the amount of capital gains that can be deferred as incorporation relief is:
= (Gain on chargeable asset) x (Value of shares / Total consideration)
= £120,000 x £225,000/£300,000
= £90,000

The deferred gain will be reduced from the market value of the shares to give the base cost of the shares.

	£
Market value of shares	225,000
Less: Deferred gain	(90,000)
Base cost of shares	**135,000**

Example

Continuing the above example of Michael and Mars Ltd,

Let us suppose Michael sold 75,000 £1 ordinary shares in a new limited company (an unquoted trading company) for £175,000 on 10 May 2009.

As Michael sold the shares to the company, we have to first calculate the base cost of the shares.

Base cost of the shares = Value of shares – Incorporation relief
= £225,000 - £90,000 = £135,000.

Out of a total 225,000 ordinary shares, 75,000 ordinary shares are sold.

Therefore the proportionate cost of 75000 shares = £135,000 x 75,000/225,000 = £45,000

	£
Disposal consideration	175,000
Less: Cost	(45,000)
Chargeable gains	**130,000**

Note: Entrepreneur's relief will not be available as the shares have not been owned for one year prior to the date of disposal.

Example

Simran was operating as a sole trader from 5 May 2006. She incorporated a company on 31 January 2010.

On 31 January 2010 the market value of the business assets was £800,000.

	Market value £	Cost £
Goodwill	200,000	-
Freehold warehouse	175,000	150,000
Freehold shop	250,000	185,000
Net current Assets	175,000	100,000
	800,000	435,000

The goodwill of the business had been built up from 5 May 2006.

Simran used both the freehold warehouse and the freehold shop solely for business purposes. Both these assets were purchased by her on 5 May 2006.

Simran transferred all the business assets to a new limited company, Sun Ltd, the consideration being made up of 500,000 £1 ordinary shares valued at £550,000 and cash of £250,000.

1. We assume that Simran does not take advantage of any of the reliefs available.

The chargeable gains are calculated as follows:

	£	£
Goodwill		
Market value	200,000	
Less: Cost	-	200,000
Freehold Warehouse		
Market value	175,000	
Less: Cost	(150,000)	25,000
Freehold Shop		
Market value	250,000	
Less: Cost	(185,000)	65,000
Net gains		**290,000**
Less: Entrepreneur's relief (£290,000 x 4/9)		(128,889)
Chargeable gains		**161,111**

Note: Entrepreneur's relief is available as the entire business is being sold and was owned for more than one year prior to the date of disposal.

Continued on next page

2. We assume that Simran takes advantage of incorporation relief.

Consideration comprises of shares and cash. So the proportion of gain relating only to shares is eligible for incorporation relief.

Therefore, £161,111 x £550,000/£800,000 = **£110,764 of the gain can be deferred as incorporation relief.**

Thus, **chargeable gains** = £161,111 - £110,764 = £50,347

3. We can further assume that Simran sells 400,000 £1 ordinary shares in her newly incorporated company on 31 March 2010 for £420,000.

Chargeable gain on the disposal of the shares in new company is calculated as follows:

	£
Disposal consideration	420,000
Less: Cost (W1)	(280,500)
Chargeable gains	**139,500**

Note: Entrepreneur's relief will not be available as shares were owned for less than one year prior to the date of disposal.

Workings

W1

Amount of gains rolled over:
= Total gains – Gain to be immediately charged
= £290,000 – £90,625
= £199,375

Base cost of 500,000 shares = £550,000 – £199,375
= £350,625

Therefore, cost of 400,000 shares sold = £350,625 x 400,000/500,000
= £280,500

Example In April 2009 Martha transferred her business of manufacturing ice creams to Cool-Chill Ltd. In exchange for that the company gave her shares worth £60,000 and paid cash of £20,000. From this transfer of the business, Martha had a capital gain of £15,500.

Martha did not make an election in respect of incorporation relief. In this situation calculation of capital gains is as follows:

$$\text{Incorporation relief} = \text{Net gains on individual chargeable assets} \times \frac{\text{Value of shares received from the comapny}}{\text{Total value of consideration from the company}}$$

$$= £15,500 \times \frac{£60,000}{£(60,000 + 20,000)}$$

$$= £11,625$$

Notes:

1. In effect, the chargeable gain is £3,875 (£15,500 - £11,625).
2. Incorporation relief is automatic. Even though Martha did not make an election for incorporation relief, she is eligible unless she elects for it to be disapplied.

Test Yourself 4

Merry ran a business for 10 years. On 20 April 2009, her business was taken over by Coca Ltd, in return for which Merry received consideration of shares of Coca Ltd worth £90,000. The capital gain from this transfer is £38,000.

Merry may wish to claim incorporation relief. Show the calculations for the amount that can be held over.

How will you answer if the business is exchanged for cash of £10,000 and shares worth £80,000?

SUMMARY

Incorporation relief
- **available**: when an individual incorporates his business
- **conditions**:
  - transfer must be of a business as a going concern
  - all of the assets apart from cash must be transferred
  - consideration for transfer must be in the form of shares
- **net capital gains**:
  - arising on the disposal of the chargeable assets is deferred
  - is deducted from the value of the shares received

Tax planning

➢ Transfer between husband and wife is a no gain / no loss transaction, so this mechanism could be used to ensure both annual exemptions are used.

➢ Delaying a disposal until 6 April to use next year's annual exemption, as there is often an increasing trend in the amount of the annual exemption limit. In addition, the capital gains tax liability of an individual will be delayed until the following year.

➢ The fact that gifts on death are not subject to capital gains tax.

Example

Suzy has been a sole trader from 5 April 1990. Though she is of 79 years old, she is a very hard working woman.

On 31 March 2010, she transferred her entire business to her son Sam. As a result of the transfer, the following assets were sold to Sam:

1. A freehold warehouse that has a market value of £300,000.

This warehouse was purchased on 2 April 1990 for £90,000 and was never used by her for business purposes.

Sam paid £150,000 for the warehouse.

2. A freehold shop that has a market value of £310,000.

This shop was purchased on 2 July 2005 for 120,000, and was always used for business purposes.

Sam paid £175,000 for the shop.

Continued on next page

C6.20: Chargeable Gains

Suzy and Sam have elected to holdover any gains arising.

Answer the following:

a) If Suzy had postponed the transfer of her business until 6 April 2010, explain how it would have been beneficial for capital gains tax purposes.

b) If Suzy had retained the business until her death, explain what the tax implications would be.

Answer

a) If Suzy had postponed the transfer of her business until 6 April 2010, the gains would not be assessed in the 2009 - 10 but in 2010 - 11.

The payment of the capital gains tax liability would not be due on 31 January 2011, but would instead be due on 31 January 2012 (refer Study Guide G2).

The warehouse is not a business asset, therefore it does not qualify for holdover relief.

b) If Suzy had retained the business until her death, when the transfer of assets would be made on the death of a person, then the transfer of assets is not subject to capital gains tax (although there may be a charge to inheritance tax on any assets not qualifying for relief from inheritance tax).

On such a transfer, Sam would have inherited the freehold warehouse and freehold shop.

Answers to Test Yourself

Answer 1

Ben's capital gains tax liability for the tax year 2009 - 10 is as follows:

	£	£
Moulds	250,000	
Goodwill	150,000	
Warehouse	300,000	
Shareholding in Clarks Ltd	200,000	
	900,000	
Less: Entrepreneurs' relief (£900,000 x 4/9ths)	(400,000)	500,000
Freehold Land		200,000
Chargeable gains		**700,000**
Less: Annual exemption		(10,100)
Taxable gains		**689,900**
Capital gains at 18%		124,182

Notes:

1. Entrepreneurs' relief will not be available for freehold land as it is not a business asset.

2. The relief is available on the first £1 million of qualifying gains that a person makes during his lifetime. The £1 million limit is reduced every time an individual makes a qualifying gain. Therefore, Ben will have a balance of £100,000 (£1,000,000 − £900,000) of qualifying gains available in the future.

Answer 2

	£
Disposal consideration	399,500
Less: Cost of acquisition	(300,000)
Unindexed gain	**99,500**
Less: Indexation allowance $\frac{(212.8 - 181.5)}{181.5} = (0.172) \times £300,000$	(51,600)
Chargeable gains	**47,900**
Gain Rolled Over	**(47,900)**
Chargeable now	**NIL**

Note:

As the entire sale proceeds are invested to purchase the new office building, and the purchase is made within three years after the date of sale, Cargo Ltd is entitled to rollover relief.

As a result of rollover relief, the gain on the disposal of the old office building is not immediately chargeable. However, the cost of the new office building is reduced by the amount of gain on the disposal of the old office building.

Hence, the cost of the new office building is £512,100 (£560,000 - £47,900).

Answer 3

1. **Computation of Ronny's chargeable gains:**

	£
Deemed sale proceeds (market value)	250,000
Less: Cost of acquisition	(45,000)
Gains	**205,000**
Less: Holdover relief (note)	(190,000)
Net gain	**15,000**
Less: Entrepreneurs' relief (15,000 x 4/9)	(6,667)
Chargeable gains	**8,333**

2. **Computation of Kane's chargeable gains:**

	£
Disposal consideration	260,000
Less: Cost (£250,000 - £190,000)	(60,000)
Chargeable gains	**200,000**

Note:

Holdover Gains = Market value – Actual proceeds
= £250,000 - £60,000 = £190,000

Answer 4

1. The whole amount of capital gains of £38,000 can be held over, as the whole consideration was received in shares.
2. Where consideration is received partly in cash and partly in shares.

$$\text{Incorporation relief} = \text{Net gains on individual chargeable assets} \times \frac{\text{Value of shares received from the company}}{\text{Total value of consideration from company}}$$

= 38,000 x (£80,000/£90,000)
= £33,778

As such, the gain of £33,778 can be heldover until a subsequent disposal takes place. However, the gain of £4,222 (£38,000 - £33,778) is immediately chargeable to tax.

Quick Quiz

1. State which of the following reliefs are automatic (i.e. no claim for relief is required).
   a) Rollover relief
   b) Holdover relief
   c) Incorporation relief

2. What are the required conditions to claim incorporation relief?

3. What are the various business assets for claiming entrepreneur's relief?

Answers to Quick Quiz

1. Incorporation relief is automatic.

2. To claim incorporation relief the following are the required conditions:

   a) All the business assets, except cash are transferred to the company.
   b) The business is transferred as a going concern.
   c) The consideration is in the form of shares (wholly / partly).

3. The most relevant types of business assets for claiming entrepreneur's relief are as follows:

   a) Assets **used for trade purposes** by a sole trader.
   b) **Shares in a personal trading company (quoted or unquoted)** where an individual either has a 5% shareholding or is an **employee** of the company.

Self Examination Questions

Question 1

In June 1997 (RPI 157.5) Mix Ltd acquired a building for business purposes for £48,000. In May 2009 the company sold the building for £89,500 (RPI 212.8). The following month the company purchased another building for use in its business.

Required:

Assuming the company made a claim for rollover relief; show the calculations for chargeable gain if the purchase price of the new building is:

1. £85,000
2. £95,000

Question 2

Peter sold his machinery to his daughter Shina on 12 November 2009, for £150,000 on cessation of his trade. On the date of sale the actual market price of the machine was £200,000. Peter had originally purchased this machinery in May 2005 for £100,000.

Required:

What is the chargeable gain in the hands of Peter assuming he makes a claim for holdover relief?
Calculate the chargeable gains arising.

Question 3

In January 2010 Mica transferred all his business assets to Takeover Ltd and received a total consideration of £75,000. It was decided that he will receive 2/3 of the consideration by way of shares in the company, and the remaining 1/3 in cash.

Assume the gain arising on the transfer was £25,000. Show the amount of capital gains immediately chargeable and the amount which is held over.

Answers to Self Examination Questions

Answer 1

Calculation of gain on disposal of original building:

	£
Disposal consideration	89,500
Less: Original cost of building	(48,000)
Un-indexed gain	41,500
Less: Indexation Allowance (W1)	(16,848)
Indexed gains	**24,652**

W1

Indexation Allowance = $\frac{(212.8 - 157.5)}{157.5}$ (0.351) x £48,000

= £16,848

1. Purchase price £85,000

Total sale proceeds	= £89,500
Purchase price of new building	= £85,000
So, company retained	= £4,500

£4,500 is immediately chargeable to tax.

Amount of gains rolled over
= Indexed Gains – Gain to be immediately charged
= £24,652 - £4,500
= £20,152 is the remaining amount of chargeable gain, which may be rolled over.

Therefore, the base cost of the new building = £85,000 - £20,152
= £64,848

2. Purchase price 95,000

Purchase price of the new building	= £95,000
Sale proceeds	= £89,500

It is clearly evident that the company has spent the entire sale proceeds for the purchase of the new building. Therefore the entire gains may be rolled over.

Thus, allowable cost of new building = £95,000 - £24,652
= £70,348

Answer 2

Peter's CGT position for 2009 – 10:

	£
Disposal consideration (market value)	200,000
Less: Acquisition cost	(100,000)
Gain	**100,000**
Less: Holdover relief (W1)	(50,000)
Net Gain	**50,000**
Less: Entrepreneurs' relief (W2)	(22,222)
Chargeable gains	**27,778**

Workings

W1

When the transaction is not at an arm's length price, we deem the market value to be the sales proceeds. The difference between the market value of the asset and the actual sale price (i.e. the discount element of the sale) is the maximum gain eligible for holdover relief (£200,000 - £150,000 = £50,000).

W2

Entrepreneurs' relief is also available to Peter for the gain on the disposal of his business. The asset disposed of was a business asset and was owned one year prior to the cessation of the business.

£50,000 x 4/9 = £22,222

Answer 3

Mica's total sales consideration:

£75,000 x 2/3 = £50,000	in the form of shares
£75,000 x 1/3 = £25,000	in cash

As Mica receives sales consideration partly in cash and partly in shares, the held over gain is calculated by applying the following formula:

$$\text{Net gains on individual chargeable assets} \times \frac{\text{Value of shares received from the company}}{\text{Total value of consideration from the company}}$$

= (£50,000/£75,000) x £25,000

= £16,667 (can be held over)

Calculation of the amount of gain immediately chargeable to tax:

	£
Total capital gain	25,000
Less: Holdover relief	(16,667)
	8,333
Less: Entrepreneur's relief (£8,333 x 4/9)	(3,704)
Chargeable gains	**4,629**

Note: Entrepreneur's relief is available as the whole of the business was transferred.

SECTION D: CORPORATION TAX LIABILITIES

STUDY GUIDE D1: THE SCOPE OF CORPORATION TAX

Get Through Intro

A tax is a compulsory charge paid by individuals, unincorporated businesses or incorporated businesses (companies) to the government. A company is a separate legal entity. This Study Guide deals with corporation tax i.e. tax paid by companies.

In this Study Guide, we will study the meaning of some basic terms and principles of corporation tax and also the tax rates applicable to companies.

Learning Outcomes

a) Define the terms 'period of account', 'accounting period', and 'financial year'.
b) Recognise when an accounting period starts and when an accounting period finishes.
c) Explain how the residence of a company is determined.

Introduction

Case Study

Bob is the owner and Managing Director of Acme Ltd. However, Bob & Acme Ltd are two different entities in the eyes of law. The chargeability of income of these two entities varies. Bob is liable to pay income tax on his salary, bonus and dividend income from Acme Ltd. At the same time, Acme Ltd is liable to corporation tax on the profits it has made during the accounting period.

> **Tip:** Corporation tax is tax paid by companies on their profits chargeable to corporation tax for each accounting period.

1. Define the terms 'period of account', 'accounting period' and 'financial year'.[1]

[Learning outcome a]

Before proceeding further, we need to understand some important concepts.

1. Company

Any incorporated body whether limited or unlimited is a company. Any corporate body or unincorporated organisation **chargeable to corporation tax is also a company.** The term also includes unincorporated associations which are not run as partnerships, such as members' clubs, societies and associations, sports club or a political association.

> **Tip:** Remember tax paid by individuals and partnerships is known as income tax and not corporation tax.

2. Period of Account and Accounting Period

We will frequently be using these two terms while calculating the corporation tax liability. So let us first try to understand what "Period of Account" and "Accounting Period" mean and how they differ from each other.

a) Period of Account: this is the period for which a company prepares its set of accounts. No specific period of account is specified by law, so companies can prepare their accounts for any period as they see fit. Therefore, the length of a period of account can be 6 months, 12 months, 18 months, 30 months, or any other length that the company decides. However, usually it is 12 months.

> **Example:** Alpha Ltd prepares its accounts for 12 months period from 01/01/09 to 31/12/09 (i.e. year ended 31 December 2009).
> Beta Ltd prepares its accounts for 9 months period from 01/01/09 to 30/09/09 (i.e. 9 months ended on 30 September 2009).
> Gamma Ltd prepares its accounts for 15 months from 01/01/09 to 31/03/10 (i.e. 15 months ended on 31 March 2009).

b) Accounting Period: the accounting period is the period for which the government charges corporation tax. The accounting period can never exceed 12 months. The accounting period may be less than 12 months.

> **Example:** Continuing the above example of Alpha, Beta and Gamma Ltd
>
> Alpha Ltd makes up its accounts to year ended 31 December 2009. The accounting period will be the 12 month period ended on 31 December 2009.
> Beta Ltd makes up its accounts for 9 months ended on 30 September 2009. The accounting period will be the 9 month period ended on 30 September 2009. This is less than 12 months.
> Gamma Ltd makes up accounts for 15 months ended on 31 March 2009. This period is longer than 12 months. Therefore the accounting period will be divided into two periods. The first period will be the first twelve months from 01/01/09 to 31/12/09 (i.e. 12 months ended on 31 December 2009). The next period will be the remaining period from 01/01/10 to 31/03/10 (i.e. 3 months period ended on 31 March 2010).

3. **Financial year:** the financial year is:

a) the period for which the rates of corporation tax are fixed by the government

b) the period that runs from 1 April to the succeeding 31 March

c) identified by the calendar year in which it begins

> **Example**
> The financial year (FY) 2008 covers the period from 1 April 2008 to 31 March 2009 and FY 2009 covers the period from 1 April 2009 to 31 March 2010.

For each FY the government decides the tax rates.

> **Example**
> The small company rate of corporation tax in FY 2009 is 21%.
>
> The full rate of corporation tax for FY 2009 is 28%.

The important point to consider here is which corporation tax rate should you consider to tax the profits if the accounting period does not match with the financial year?

> **Example**
> The accounting period of a company is the 12 months ended 31 August 2009.
>
> This accounting period falls in two financial years. The first 7 months fall in FY 2008 (FY starting from 1 April 2008 to 31 March 2009) and the next 5 months fall in FY 2009 (FY starting from 1 April 2009 to 31 March 2010).
>
> Here, the chargeable profits will be apportioned between the two FYs in the ratio of the months falling in each FY. The profits falling into FY 2008 will be taxed at the rates applicable to FY 2008 and the profits falling into FY 2009 will be taxed at the rates applicable to FY 2009.

2. Recognise when an accounting period starts and when an accounting period finishes.[1]
[Learning outcome b]

Diagram 1: Start and end of accounting period

The Accounting Period Starts on the earliest of these events
1. Company starts to trade
2. Company becomes liable to corporation tax
3. Immediately after end of previous accounting period

The Accounting Period Ends on the earliest of these events
1. At the end of company's period of account
2. After the 12 month period from the start of accounting period
3. On commencement of winding up proceedings
4. On company's ceasing to be liable to corporation tax
5. On a change in the residential status of company (i.e. on the company's ceasing to be resident in the UK)

As we have already seen, it is not necessary that a period of account must be 12 months. A company can prepare its set of accounts for any period consisting of any length. **What if, then, the set of accounts covers a period either less than 12 months or more than 12 months?**

Diagram 2: Accounting period

There are two possibilities

- A company's set of accounts consists of period **less than 12 months** e.g. 6 months ended 30/06/08
  - So the accounting period is also 6 months ended 30/06/08

- A company's set of accounts consists of period **more than 12 months** e.g. 18 months ended 30/06/08
  - Then the period covered by the set of accounts will be divided into 2 or more accounting periods
    - The first 12 months will be assessed as first accounting period e.g. 12 months ended 31/12/07
    - The remaining period will be assessed as next accounting period e.g. 6 months ended 30/06/08

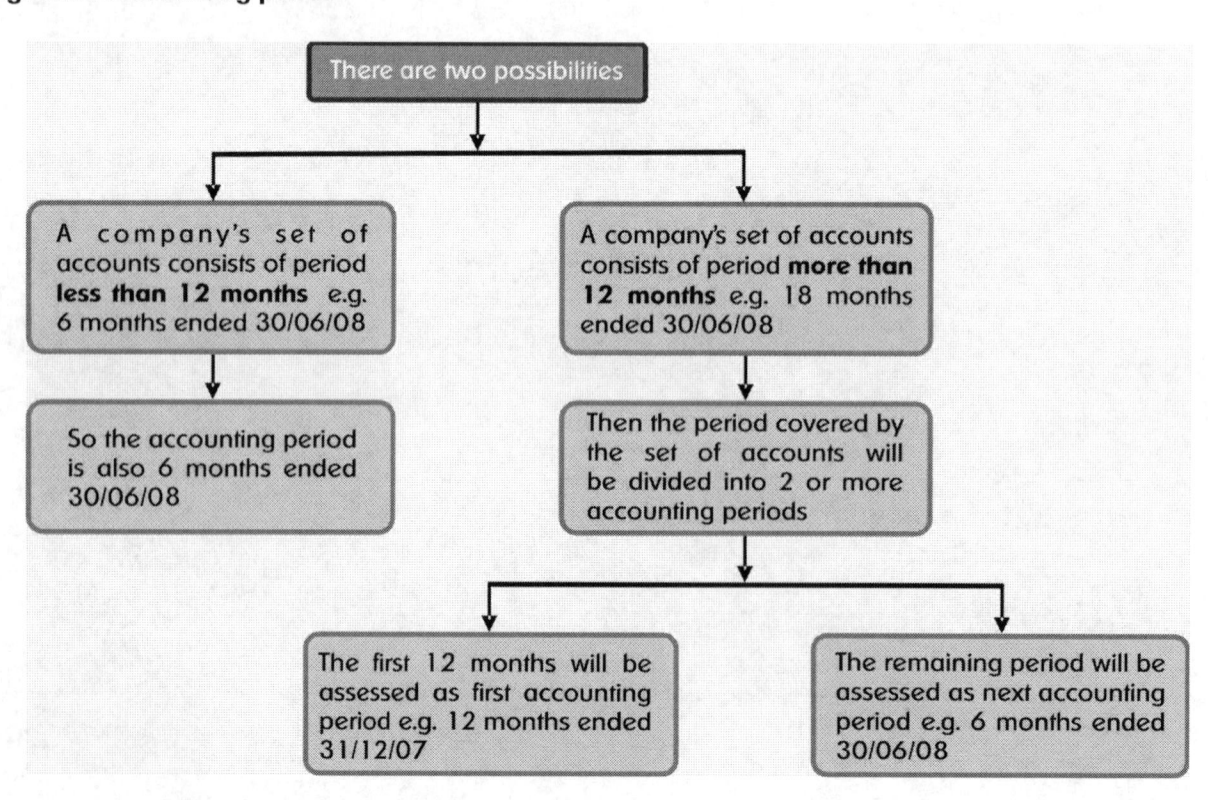

Test Yourself 1

From the given periods of accounts, identify the relevant accounting periods.

1. The set of accounts of Sun Ltd is prepared for year ended 31/12/09.

2. The set of accounts of Kelvin Ltd is prepared for six months ended 30/06/09.

3. The set of accounts of Woods Ltd is prepared for sixteen months ended 31/12/09.

4. The set of accounts of Shop Zone Ltd is prepared for twenty months ended 31/03/10.

---

3. Explain how the residence of a company is determined.[2]
[Learning outcome c]

Residence of a company depends upon where the company is incorporated.

1. If a **company is incorporated in the UK, then it is resident in the UK.**

2. A **non-UK incorporated company** is treated as **resident** in the UK **if its central management and control is exercised in the UK.**

Example
A company is incorporated in a country other than the UK, say France, but its Board of Directors conducts its affairs through meetings held in the UK. In this case, is the company resident in the UK or in France?

The answer is that the company is **resident in the UK** because its affairs are conducted (central management and control) through meetings of Board of Directors in the UK.

Summary

There can be three different situations depending upon the place of incorporation of a company:

Place where the company is incorporated	Whether resident in the UK
1. Company incorporated in the UK	**Resident** in the UK
2. Company incorporated in a place other than the UK	**Non-resident** in the UK
3. Company incorporated in a place other than the UK but control & management of the company situated in the UK	**Resident** in the UK

It is important to determine the residential status of a company as the companies which are **resident in the UK** are **liable to corporation tax on all the profits and chargeable gains arising worldwide**.

Test Yourself 2

Determine whether the following companies are UK residents for the purposes of corporation tax:

1. Adobe Ltd is incorporated in the UK and operates in Spain.

2. Bake Ltd is incorporated, managed and controlled from Ukraine.

3. China Chop Ltd is incorporated in Australia but is managed and controlled centrally from the UK.

D1.6: Corporation Tax Liabilities

Answers to Test Yourself

Answer 1

1. The period of 12 months ended on 31/12/09 is an accounting period in itself.

2. The period of 6 months ended on 30/06/09 is an accounting period in itself.

3. The accounting period can never exceed 12 months. Hence, the period of 16 months from 01/09/08 to 31/12/09 is divided into two accounting periods – one for the first 12 months from 01/09/08 to 31/08/09 and the other for the remaining 4 months from 01/09/09 to 31/12/09.

4. The period of 20 months from 01/08/08 to 31/03/10 is divided into two accounting periods - one for the first 12 months from 01/08/08 to 31/07/09 and the other for the remaining 8 months from 01/08/09 to 31/03/10.

Answer 2

1. Adobe Ltd – UK resident as it is incorporated in the UK

2. Bake Ltd – Non-resident in the UK as it is neither incorporated in the UK nor managed and controlled centrally from the UK.

3. China chop Ltd - UK resident as it is managed and controlled centrally from the UK.

Quick Quiz

1. Explain the term accounting period.

2. What period is the financial year 2009?

3. The period of accounts of LMN Ltd is of 13 months ended 31 May 2009. Identify its accounting periods.

Answers to Quick Quiz

1. The accounting period is the period for which the government charges corporation tax on the company's profits. The accounting period can never exceed 12 months.

2. 1 April 2009 to 31 March 2010.

3. The period of accounts of 13 months is divided into two accounting periods:

    a) One for the first 12 months from 01/05/08 to 30/04/09 and
    b) The other for the remaining 1 month i.e. May 09.

Self Examination Questions

Question 1

When does an accounting period start for corporation tax purposes?

Question 2

When does an accounting period end for corporation tax purposes?

Question 3

The following information is provided in respect of three companies:

1. Red Ltd: the chargeable profits for the year ended on 31 March 2010 are £120,000.
2. Yellow Ltd: the chargeable profits for the year ended on 31 December 2009 are £180,000.
3. Orange Ltd: the chargeable profits for the 15 months period ended on 31 March 2009 are 300,000.

Required:

The corporation tax rates of which financial years are applicable to these profits?

Answers to Self Examination Questions

Answer 1

An accounting period starts at the earliest of these events:

1. When a company starts to trade
2. When its profits become liable to corporation tax
3. Immediately after the end of the preceding accounting period

Answer 2

An accounting period ends at the earliest of these events:

1. At the end of a company's period of account.
2. 12 months after the beginning of the accounting period.
3. When a company commences winding up proceedings.
4. When its profits otherwise cease to be liable to corporation tax.
5. When a company ceases to be UK resident.

Answer 3

1. The accounting period of Red Ltd is the 12 month period ended on 31 March 2010. This entire period falls in the financial year 2009 (i.e. 1 April 2009 to 31 March 2010). Hence, the corporation tax rate of FY 2009 will be applicable to the profits of £120,000 of Red Ltd.

2. The accounting period of Yellow Ltd for the year ended on 31 December 2009 falls in two financial years, i.e. FY 2008 (1April 2008 to 31 March 2009) and FY 2009 (1 April 2009 to 31 March 2010). The period of 3 months up to 31 March 2009 falls in the FY 2008 and the remaining period of 9 months up to 31 December 2009 falls in the FY 2009.

Accounting period	Corporation Tax Rate applicable (FY 2008)	Corporation Tax Rate applicable (FY 2009)
12 months ended on 31 December 2009 (chargeable profits of £180,000 in the ratio of 3:9)	£180,000 x 3/12 = £45,000	£180,000 x 9/12 = £135,000

3. The accounting period can never exceed 12 months. As the accounting period of Orange Ltd is more than 12 months (15 months), first it will be divided into two accounting periods.- first accounting period of 12 months ended on 31 December 2009 and the second accounting period of 3 months ended on 31 March 2009.

    Chargeable profits for the first accounting period of twelve months ended on 31 December 2009 are (£300,000 x 12/15) = £240,000

    Chargeable profits for the second accounting period of three months ended on 31 March 2009 are (£300,000 x 3/15) = £60,000

    The first accounting period (year ended on 31 December 2009) falls into two financial years, hence chargeable profits for this period are required to be split according to the financial year for determining the rates of corporation tax applicable.

    The first 3 months (1 January 2009 to 31 March 2009) fall in FY 2008 and the next 9 months (1 April 2009 to 31 December 2009) fall in FY 2009.

    The second accounting period (3 months period ended on 31 March 2009) falls into FY 2009.

Accounting period	Corporation Tax Rate applicable (FY 2008)	Corporation Tax Rate applicable (FY 2009)
12 months ended on 31 December 2009 (chargeable profits of £240,000 in the ratio of 3:9)	£240,000 x 3/12 = £60,000	£240,000 x 9/12 = £180,000
3 months period ended on 31 December 2009	-	£60,000
	60,000	**240,000**

SECTION D: CORPORATION TAX LIABILITIES

D2

STUDY GUIDE D2: PROFITS CHARGEABLE TO CORPORATION TAX (PART 1)

Get Through Intro

Corporation tax is charged on the trading profits of companies, and on their other income and chargeable gains. A company's taxable income is charged with reference to income or gains arising in its accounting period. It is essential to correctly identify and calculate the profits chargeable to corporation tax to determine corporation tax liability. In this chapter, we will learn what the profits chargeable to corporation tax are and how to calculate chargeable profits from trade.

Learning Outcomes

a) Recognise the expenditure that is allowable in calculating the tax-adjusted trading profit.
b) Explain how relief can be obtained for pre-trading expenditure.
c) Compute capital allowances (as for income tax).
d) Compute property business profits.
e) Explain the treatment of interest paid and received under the loan relationship rules.
f) Explain the treatment of gift aid donations.

Introduction

Case Study

Superb Ltd is a fast growing company. It deals in the manufacture of personal computers. This is its third year of operation.

It has incurred different types of expenditures during the current year, including purchase of assets; expenses incurred entertaining customers, gifts to employees, trade subscriptions, political donations, staff training and travelling expenses.

Superb Ltd is not sure which expenses are deductible and which are not, while calculating chargeable profits.

The company approaches you for advice about the calculation of chargeable profits.

This Study Guide will teach you how to calculate the chargeable profits of Superb Ltd and other companies.

1. Recognise the expenditure that is allowable in calculating the tax-adjusted trading profit.[2]
[Learning outcome a]

If a company is liable to pay corporation tax, then it must work out its tax liability. In order to calculate the tax liability, you need to know how much taxable or **chargeable profits** you have made in the **accounting period**. Corporation tax is charged on income and gains that fall within certain headings, all of which are defined by legislation. A company's chargeable profits consist of income in the form of trading profits, income from non-trading loans, income from property and chargeable gains. In other words, a company's total income is the addition of the following different categories of income and gains:

1. Trading profits
2. Property income
3. Profits arising from loan relationship (commonly referred to as interest income)
4. Income from foreign securities and possessions
5. Chargeable gains

Tip

1. Dividends received by a company are **not included in the profits chargeable** to corporation tax.
2. Dividends paid by a company are not deductible from chargeable profits.

The pro-forma for computation of corporation tax is as follows:

	£	£
1. Trading profits	X	
Less: Brought forward trading losses	(X)	X
2. Property income		X
3. Profits from loan relationship (interest income)		X
4. Profits from foreign securities and possessions		X
5. Chargeable gains	X	
Less: Allowable capital losses brought forward	(X)	X
Total income		X
Less: Reliefs		
Property business losses	X	
Trading losses relieved under S393A	X	
Gift aid payments	X	(X)
Profits chargeable to corporation tax (PCTCT)		**X**

Now let us see the part **trading profits** in detail.

The profits arising from a company's trade are termed **trading profits.** The starting point is to take the net profits before tax from the financial statements and make various adjustments which will give the adjusted trading profits. The format you may follow to arrive at the adjusted profits is shown here:

	£
Net Profits given in the accounts	X
Add:	
(i) Expenditure shown in the accounts but not deductible for tax purposes	X
(ii) Income taxable but not included in the accounts	X
Less:	
(i) Expenditure deductible for tax purposes but not shown in the accounts	(X)
(ii) Income included in the accounts but not taxable as trading income	(X)
Adjusted trading profits	X

An important step in the calculation of trading profits for tax purposes **is recognising which expenses are deductible and which are non-deductible for tax purposes**. We have already seen the deductible and non-deductible expenses in Study Guide B3 (part 1). Let us quickly revise them here.

Type of expense	Deductible
Depreciation / amortisation	✗
Increase in general allowance	✗
Capital expenditure	✗
Gifts to employees	✓
Gifts to customers (provided cost not more than £50, not food, drink etc)	✓
Staff entertainment	✓
Customer / supplier entertainment	✗
Trade subscriptions	✓
Political donations	✗
Trade-related legal and professional charges	✓
Interest (trading purposes)	✓
Penalties and fines	✗
Staff training	✓
Removal expenses, unless an expansionary move	✓
Redundancy pay in excess of statutory limit	✓
Contribution to pension schemes	✓
Lease premium	✗
Illegal payments	✗
Irrecoverable VAT, if relates to an item of allowable expenditure	✓
Staff defalcations	✓
Travelling expenses (business)	✓
Lease and rent payments for equipment	✓
Registration of patents and trademarks	✓

D2.4: Corporation Tax Liabilities

There are differences in treatment of some of the items while calculating the trading profits for tax purposes for an individual and a company, which are as follows:

1. Private use adjustments
2. Capital Allowances (Learning Outcome 3)
3. Interest paid and received under loan relationship (Learning Outcome 5)
4. Gift aid payments (Learning Outcome 6)

Private use adjustments

Expenses attributable to private use by a sole trader are not allowable. Adjustments are made for the private use by an owner. But, **in the case of a company, directors are employees and therefore no such adjustments are made for private use**. Hence, any expenses attributable to the private use by a director or an employee of the company are fully allowable while calculating tax adjusted trading profits.

Test Yourself 1

Sunshine Ltd incurred the expenditure below:

	£
New Year's dinner for 18 employees	1,800
New Year's dinner for 10 customers	2,000

Required:

Explain whether the above expenditure is allowable or not allowable for calculating trading income.

Test Yourself 2

True Ltd incurred legal and professional charges relating to the following items:

	£
Purchase of a new machine	8,300
Collection from trade debtors	1,100
Obtaining bank loan	1,500
Costs of renewing a 30-year lease	4,000
Costs of registering the company's trademark	1,500

Required:

What is the treatment for each of these items of expenditure for calculating trading income?

Test Yourself 3

Dolphin Ltd incurred the following expenditure:

Christmas gifts for staff (£100 each)
Christmas gift vouchers for 10 customers of £65 each
15 watches, with company name engraved (costing £45 each) as Christmas gift for customers

Required:

Identify which expenses are allowable and which are not allowable for calculating trading income.

Test Yourself 4

GTG Ltd made the following donations:

	£
Cash donation to a political party	5,000
Cash donation to UNICEF	2,500
Cash donation to local charity, for which free advertising for the company was received in the local magazine	250
Gift aid donation to local charity	1,000

Required:

What is the tax treatment for each item?

Test Yourself 5

Given below is the profit and loss account of Varieties Ltd:

	£	£
Gross operating profit		21,930
Salaries	(6,000)	
Depreciation	(2,500)	
Bad debts written off	(220)	
Property income	1,300	
Legal expenses relating to issue of shares	(1,500)	
Increase in general allowance	(50)	
Loss on sale of fixed assets	(70)	(9,040)
Net Profit		**12,890**

Required:

Calculate trading income of Varieties Ltd.

---

2. Explain how relief can be obtained for pre-trading expenditure.[1]

[Learning outcome b]

A company may incur expenses before actually starting to trade, e.g. rent of business premises, interest on loan for the purchase of machinery, legal charges etc. These expenses are known as pre-trading expenditure, and are **treated as if incurred on the first day of the trade**. They are **allowable** provided they were incurred **within seven years of the commencement of trade** and are related to the trade. Such expenses must be of the type which, if incurred after commencement of trade, had been allowable i.e. **capital expenditure** incurred before commencement of trade is **not allowable**. However, **capital allowance is available on capital expenditure** incurred before commencement of trade and is treated as if incurred on the first day of the trade.

SUMMARY

Pre-trading expenditure:
- expenses incurred — before actually starting trade
- for tax purpose — treated as if incurred on 1st day of trade
- deductible if — incurred within 7 years of commencement of trade; related to trade
- capital allowance — available on capital expenditure incurred before commencement of trade

Test Yourself 6

M & C Ltd was incorporated on 1 Jan 2006. The first three years of operation were the research phase and so there was no revenue during this period. The phase of research included the development of products, market research and production setup. M & C Ltd started trading on 1 December 2009 and, by that date, had already incurred the following expenses.

	Date	£
Rent for the office and warehouse for business	15/10/06 – 15/10/07	15,000
Purchase of own office place and permanent warehouse	01/10/07	200,000
Legal charges for purchase of office place and warehouse	10/12/06	5,000
Marketing and advertising expenses	01/06/09 – 01/11/09	46,000
Land purchased in 1998 for business use	24/05/99	70,000

Required:

Explain with reasons whether the expenses are deductible under relief of pre-trading expenses.

3. Compute capital allowances (as for income tax).[2]

[Learning outcome c]

We have already seen various provisions relating to capital allowances in Study Guide B3 (part 2). All the provisions of capital allowances relating to self-employed individuals are equally applicable to corporate entities except the differences mentioned below:

1. Unlike self employed individuals, there is **no private use restriction** by a director or an employee, where a company is involved.

2. The AP of a company can't exceed 12 months, so there is **no need to scale up WDAs or the AIAs**. However, if the accounting period of a company is less than 12 months, then WDA or AIA will be scaled down proportionately.

But, the rule for the FYA is the same as it is given in full in the year the asset is purchased, irrespective of the length of the accounting period.

Your knowledge of capital allowance provisions will be tested below.

Refer to Learning Outcome 1 from Study Guide B3 (part2) - Define plant and machinery for capital allowances purposes

Test Yourself 7

State whether the following assets are eligible for capital allowance:

1. Computer hardware
2. Rented software
3. Plant purchased on hire purchase basis
4. Old railway wagon used as primary school classroom
5. Cold storage room in ice factory

Refer to Learning Outcome 2 from Study Guide B3 (part2) – Compute writing down allowances (WDA), first year allowance (FYA) and annual investment allowance (AIA)

Test Yourself 8

Trans Ltd was incorporated on 1 April 2009. The company purchased the following plant and machinery during the year. The dates of purchase are as follows:

		£
10 May 2009	Purchased plant	80,000
1 September 2009	Purchased machinery	22,000
1 October 2009	Purchased car (with CO_2 emissions rate of 125g/km)	9,000

Required:

Show the calculations of capital allowance for the years ended 31 March 2010 and 31 March 2011.

Test Yourself 9

Speed Ltd manufactures sports bikes. The company started operations on 1 January 2009 and decided to prepare its accounts to 31 August each year. It's first accounts are for the period to 31 August 2010. During the first accounting period, the company bought the following plant and machinery:

		£
12 April 2009	Plant	55,000
1 November 2009	Equipment	7,500
10 January 2010	Machinery	48,000

Required:

Show the calculations of capital allowance for the accounting period ended on 31 August 2010.

Refer to Learning Outcome 3 from Study Guide B3 (part2) – Compute capital allowances for motor car

Test Yourself 10

On 1 January 2009 Bat Ltd started its new business. The company is a dealer of various types of balls. The company chose 30 June as its annual accounting date. However its first accounting period was until 30 June 2010 (i.e. 18 months).

On 1 January 2009 the company purchased a car with CO_2 emissions of 80g/km for £18,000. On 1 June 2009 the company purchased another car with CO_2 emissions of 185g/km for £21,000.

On 10 January 2010, the company purchased another car costing £10,000 with CO_2 emissions of 140g/km for the directors of the company.

Required:

Show the calculation of capital allowance for the accounting period ended 30 June 2010. Assume that the new capital allowance rules for cars have always been applied.

Refer to Learning Outcome 4 from Study Guide B3 (part2) – Compute balancing allowances and balancing charges

Test Yourself 11

In July 2004 Fat Ltd started its business. The company follows 30 June as its annual accounting date. On 30 June 2009, WDV of plant and machinery was as follows

	£
General Pool	15,200
Expensive car	7,400

The following is the summary of sale and purchase transactions for the period ended 30 June 2010.

			£
1 December 2009	Sell	Expensive car	5,000
10 December 2009	Purchase	Plant	65,000

Required:

Show calculations of capital allowance and balancing adjustments for the company for the year ended 30 June 2010.

Refer to Learning Outcome 5 from Study Guide B3 (part2) – Rocognise the treatment of short life asset

Test Yourself 12

On 5 April 2009, Hot Ltd purchased a plant for £72,000. The useful life of the plant was three years. However, in the second year, the company sold the plant for £7,500. The date of sale is 5 June 2010.

Required:

Show the calculations of the balancing adjustment assuming the company prepares its annual accounts to 30 June every year.

Refer to Learning Outcome 6 from Study Guide B3 (Part2) – Explain the treatment of assets included in the special rate pool

Test Yourself 13

Lucky Plc is a soap manufacturing company. On 15 July 2009 the company purchased new machinery for £150,000. The machinery has a useful life of thirty years.

Required:

Show the calculation of capital allowance for the company assuming that the company prepares its accounts to 31 October every year.

Refer to Learning Outcome 7 from Study Guide B3 (part 2) – Define an industrial building for industrial buildings allowance purposes

Test Yourself 14

Swan Ltd purchased a building site for £120,000. The company incurred the following expenses for developing the site and constructing an industrial building:

	£
Construction cost	800,000
Land development cost	80,000
Professional fees paid to architect	20,000

Required:

(a) What is the company's qualifying expenditure for the IBA?
(b) What would the qualifying expenditure for IBA have been if the company had purchased this building from a builder for £1,100,000 and this amount included £200,000 as cost of land?

---

4. Compute property business profits.[2]

[Learning outcome d]

4.1 We have already seen in Study Guide B4, how property business profits are calculated.

Let us quickly revise some of the following points related to property business profits which are extremely important:

1. The property must be situated in the UK
2. The income should be computed on an accruals basis.
3. Aggregation of expenses / income if more than one property
4. Deductible expenses from rental income: expenses incurred wholly and exclusively for the property business are deductible from rental income to arrive at the taxable property income. Some examples of allowable expenses are:
   a) Expenses towards repairs and maintenance
   b) Insurance
   c) Agent's fees
   d) Bad debts (if rent not paid for some part of the accounting period).

However, the treatment for the companies differs from the individuals in respect of the following points:

1. In the case of a company, the property business profits are calculated on the basis of the accounting periods and not tax years.

2. **Treatment of interest paid on loan taken to buy a property, which is let out:** For individuals, interest on loans to buy or improve properties is treated as an expense (on an accruals basis).

However, for companies, such interest is dealt with under the loan relationships rules, which is discussed later in this Study Guide. **Such interest is not deductible in calculating property business income of companies.**

3. In the case of an individual, all property receipts and all property expenses are pooled to give an overall profit or loss figure for the year and any balance loss is carried forward to set off against the first available property income.

However, in the case of a company, first all property receipts and all property expenses are pooled to give an overall profit or loss figure for the period and if there is any balance loss, it can be set off against total profit chargeable to corporation tax (PCTCT) of the current accounting period before gift aid payments. Then, it can be carried forward to set off against total profit chargeable to corporation tax of the future accounting period.

Example

Excellent Ltd receives a premium of £25,000 on 1 January 2009 from its tenant Goggle Ltd for granting 20 years lease, in the accounting period ending on 31 December 2009.

The property income of Excellent Ltd is calculated as follows:

If the lease is granted for a period of 50 years or less than 50 years then it is termed a short lease. Premiums received on a short lease are assessable to property business income. The amount to be assessed to property income is equal to the amount of premiums reduced by 2% for each year of the lease except for the first year.

Therefore, property income = P – P x (2% (n -1))
= £25,000 – £25,000 x (2% x (20 – 1))
= £15,500

4.2 Lease premiums paid by the company

When a company pays any short lease premium, then the deduction of lease premiums paid is allowable from the company's trading profits. The amount of deduction is the **lease premium assessable on the landlord divided by the number of years.** Such a premium is deductible each year for the period of lease.

Example Continuing the example of Excellent Ltd,

The lease premiums deductible for Goggle Ltd are calculated as follows:
Excellent Ltd declared £15,500 as its property lease premium chargeable to tax.
Goggle Ltd can deduct **£15,500/20 years = £775** per year for 20 years of the lease period.

4.3 Assigning a sublease

> **Tip**
> Assigning just means selling

When a tenant sublets a property, it is termed a **lease assignment.**

The following are important issues in relation to the sublease:

1. Any premiums received on a sublease are treated as rent received in full.
2. If the tenant originally paid a premium to his landlord for the grant of a lease, the premium received on his sublease is reduced in the following ratio:

Portion of head lease premium treated as rent x sublease duration / head lease duration

D2.10: Corporation Tax Liabilities

Test Yourself 15

Head Ltd granted a lease to Face Ltd on 1 January 2005 for a period of 25 years for a premium of £20,000. On 1 January 2009, Face Ltd granted a sublease to Neck Ltd for 15 years. The sublease premium payable by Neck Ltd was £40,000.

Required:

Calculate the amount assessable as property income for Face Ltd.

Test Yourself 16

Creamy Ltd owns two offices for several years, which it has rented out. The details of property rented out during the year ended 31/03/10 are as follows:

➢ Office 1 was let out on lease on 01/08/09 for 20 years to Icy Ltd. The initial lease premium was £25,000 and annual rent of £5,100 p.a. is payable by Icy Ltd.

➢ Office 2, a furnished office, was let out at £1,200 p.a. from 01/05/09. The tenant leaves on 31/08/09 and a new tenant moves in on 01/02/10, paying £1,800 p.a.

Creamy Ltd incurred the following expenses

➢ Repairs of Office 2 in January 10, £600
➢ Insurance per office, £600 p.a.
➢ Interest on loan taken to purchase office, 1, £2,300
➢ Advertisement expenses for finding tenants for office, 2, £150

Required:

Calculate Creamy Ltd's property income for the year ended 31/03/10.

---

5. Explain the treatment of interest paid and received under the loan relationships rules.[1]
[Learning outcome e]

5.1 What is a loan relationship?

A company is said to have a loan relationship if the company borrows or lends money.

Diagram 1: Loan Relationship

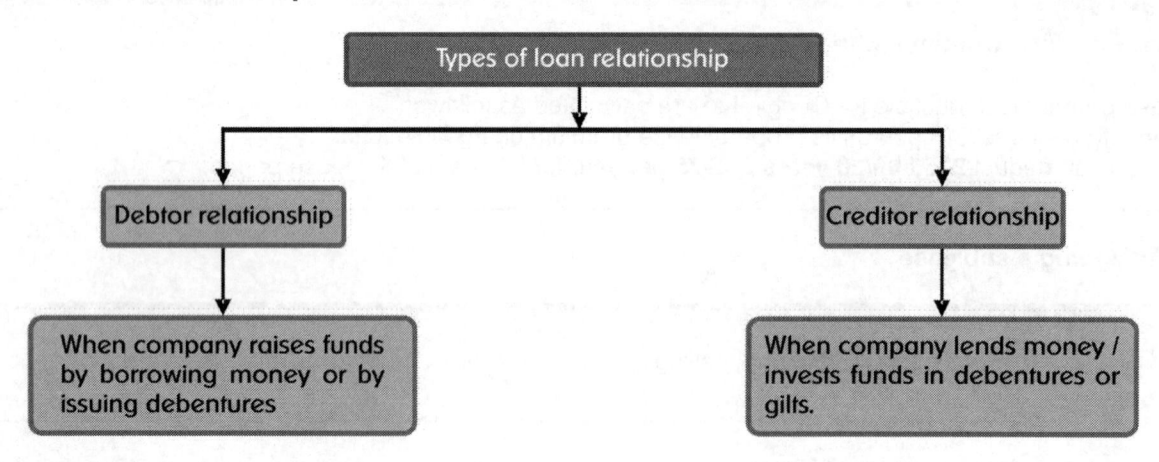

```
              Types of loan relationship
                        |
          ┌─────────────┴─────────────┐
   Debtor relationship          Creditor relationship
          |                             |
  When company raises funds     When company lends money /
  by borrowing money or by      invests funds in debentures or
  issuing debentures            gilts.
```

Tax Treatment of loan relationships

The tax treatment of loan relationships depends upon whether the loan relationship entered into is a **trading loan relationship or a non-trading loan relationship.**

1. **Trading loan relationships**: are when a loan is taken or issued for trading purposes.

a) The interest paid or payable on a loan taken for trading purposes is treated as a **trading expense** and hence is **fully deductible.**

b) The interest received or receivable can be of a trading nature only if the company is engaged in the business of lending money. In this case, the interest is treated as **trading income.**

Test Yourself 17

Low Ltd took a bank loan of £20,000 to purchase raw material for business. The interest paid during the year ended 31 March 2010 towards this loan was £1,260. How will the interest be treated while calculating the company's taxable profits?

> **Tip**
> In the case of a trading loan relationship, the income arising is trading income.

2. **Non-trading loan relationships:** if a loan is given for purposes other than trading, then any income arising out of such a relationship is **assessable as income from loan relationships. Similarly, if a loan is taken for purposes other than trading then any expenditure (e.g. interest payable) arising** out of such a relationship is **treated as expense from loan relationships.**

> **Example**
> Loan to purchase a property intended for letting out is a non-trading loan relationship.

5.2 How is income from loan relationship calculated?

If the **income from non-trading loan relationships** is **more than the expenses relating to non-trading loan relationships** then the **excess income is chargeable as income from loan relationship.**

Some examples of interest income which is assessable as income from loan relationships are:

1. Interest received on bank accounts.
2. Interest received on overpaid corporation tax
3. Interest received on government securities

> **Tip**
> Companies receive gross interest, hence grossing it up is not required for calculation of corporation tax purposes.

5.3 Accounting methods of loan relationships

While accounting for loan relationships, the company can opt for either of the following two methods:

1. **Accruals basis**: This refers to the practice of recognising income and expenses as soon as they become due. The actual receipt of income or payment of expenses is not relevant. If the income has become receivable, although not actually received by the end of the accounting period, the income is still considered for taxation purposes.

Test Yourself 18

Tree Ltd received gross bank interest of £8,200 for the year ended 31 March 2010. Bank interest owed to the company at the end of the year is £1,900. The corresponding amount at the start of the year was zero.

Required:

Calculate Tree Ltd's taxable interest.

2. **Mark to market basis**: In this method, at the end of each accounting period, the fair value of the loan relationship is determined.

SUMMARY

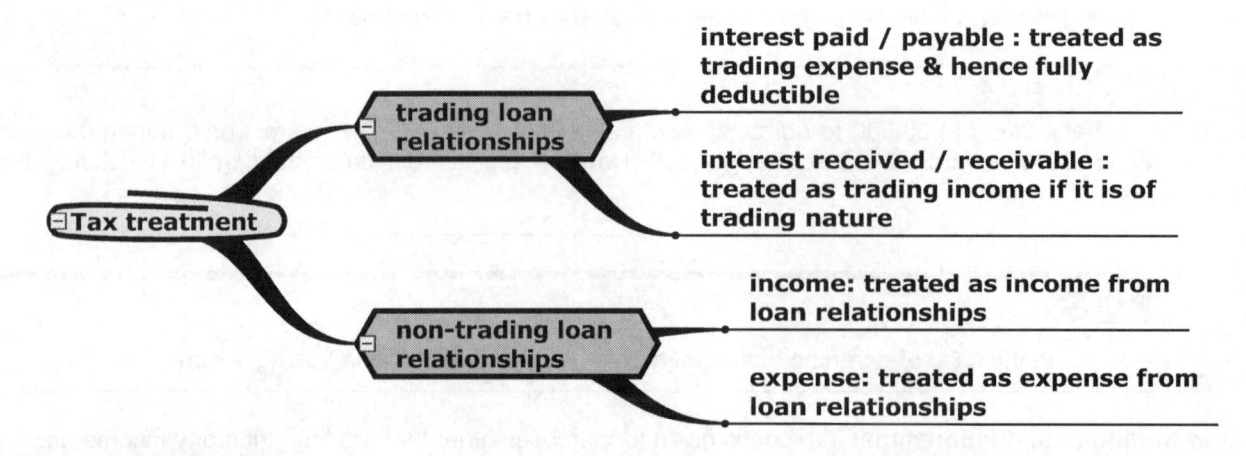

Tax treatment

- **trading loan relationships**
  - interest paid / payable : treated as trading expense & hence fully deductible
  - interest received / receivable : treated as trading income if it is of trading nature
- **non-trading loan relationships**
  - income: treated as income from loan relationships
  - expense: treated as expense from loan relationships

Test Yourself 19

Zebra Ltd's results for the year ended 31 March 2010 are as follows:

	£
Trading income	25,300
Income from property	11,000
Bank interest received (gross)	5,600
Government securities interest received (gross)	12,000
Chargeable gains	40,000

The following information is relevant:

1. Gross bank interest of £5,600 was received during the year and a further £890 was owed to the company at the end of the year. Bank interest of £300 was owed to the company at the start of the year.

2. Zebra Ltd acquired government securities on 30 June 2009. Interest of £12,000 (gross) is payable to the company on 1 January and 1 July every year.

Calculate Zebra Ltd's profits chargeable to corporation tax for the year to 31 March 2010.

---

6. Explain the treatment of gift aid donations.[2]

[Learning outcome f]

Gift aid donations made by a company are **relieved from chargeable profits** as a **deduction from total income**.

Example

Suppose Zebra Ltd (refer to Test yourself 20) paid a gift aid donation of £12,000. What will be its profits chargeable to corporation tax for the year ended 31 March 2010?

	£
Trading income	25,300
Property income	11,000
Income from loan relationship (W1)	24,190
Chargeable gains	40,000
	100,490
Less: Gift aid donation	(12,000)
Profits chargeable to corporation tax (PCTCT)	**88,490**

Test Yourself 20

Sun silk Ltd's profit and loss account for the year ended 31 March 2010 shows a trading profit of £215,000. The operating expenses include:

	£
Directors' fees	12,000
Depreciation	2,300
Gift aid donation paid	3,400
Customer entertaining expenses	2,600

All the remaining operating expenses are allowable as trading expenses. Sun silk Ltd also has property income of £25,000, and chargeable gains of £13,550.

Required:

Calculate Sun silk Ltd's profits chargeable to corporation tax for the year ended 31 March 2010.

Answers to Test Yourself

Answer 1

New Year's dinner for 18 employees - £1,800 is allowable.

Gifts to customers are deductible as expenses **only if:**
1. they cost less than £50 per recipient per year.
2. they **are not** food, drink, tobacco or vouchers exchangeable for goods or services.
3. they carry a conspicuous advertisement for the company making the gifts.

New Year's dinner for 10 customers is in the **form of food**, hence not allowable.

Answer 2

Purchase of new machinery	Not allowed (note)
Collection from trade debtors	Allowed being business-related
Obtaining bank loan	Allowed being business-related
Costs of renewing a 30-year lease	Allowed as renewal relates to short term lease (less than 50 years)
Costs of registering the company's trademark	Allowed being business-related

Note: A charge for the purchase of new machinery is in relation to an item of capital expenditure. These will be added to the cost of the new machinery and capital allowance will be allowed on the entire cost of machinery.

Answer 3

Item	Treatment
Christmas gift for staff	Allowable (Note 1)
Christmas gift vouchers for 10 customers of £65 each	Not allowable as **cost more than £50** per person (Note2)
15 watches, with company name engraved (costing £45 each) as Christmas gift for customers	Allowable (Note 2)

Notes:

1. Gifts and entertainment expenditure for the employees are fully allowable.
2. Gifts to customers are allowable provided they cost less than £50 per person per year and are not food, alcohol, tobacco or vouchers exchangeable for goods, and they carry a conspicuous advertisement for the business.

Answer 4

Item	Tax Treatment
Cash donation to a political party	Not deductible
Cash donation to UNICEF	Not deductible as not given to local charity
Cash donation to local charity	Deductible as it is small in amount, given to a local charity and benefits the company
Gift aid donation to local charity	Not deductible but tax relief is given as a deduction from total income

Answer 5

	£	£
Net Profits given according to accounts		12,890
Add: Expenditure shown in the accounts but not deductible for tax purposes		
Depreciation (Note 1)	2,500	
Legal expenses relating to issue of shares (Note 2)	1,500	
Increase in general allowance (Note 3)	50	
Loss on sale of fixed asset (Note 4)	70	4,120
Less: Income not taxable but included in the accounts		
Property income		(1,300)
Adjusted trading profits		**15,710**

Notes:

1. Depreciation is never deductible and hence is added back.
2. As the legal expenses relate to the issue of shares, these are considered to be capital expenses and hence are not deductible.
3. General allowances are never deductible.
4. Loss on sale of fixed asset is not deductible from trading profits as it is a capital loss. It is added back.

Answer 6

Expenses	Deductible / non-deductible	Reason
Rent for the office and warehouse used for business	Deductible	Being incurred not more than 7 years before the date of actual trading and revenue in nature
Purchase of own office place and permanent warehouse	Not deductible	Being capital expenditure. However, capital allowance will be available as it is treated as incurred on 1 December 2009 (first day of trade)
Legal charges for purchase of office place and warehouse	Not deductible	Relates to a capital asset. It will be added to the cost of office and warehouse.
Marketing and advertising expenses	Deductible	Being normal trading expenses
Land purchased in 1998 for business use	Not deductible	Being capital expenses and incurred more than 7 years before commencement of trade.

Answer 7

1. Expenditure on computer hardware is always eligible for capital allowance.

2. When software forms part of the computer (such as operating systems, utility programs) it is considered plant and machinery for the purposes of capital allowance. However if software is acquired on a rental basis, rent is charged against the profit for the tax year. Hence, it is not eligible for capital allowance purposes.

3. Plant purchased on a hire purchase basis is eligible for capital allowance purposes. The cash price of the plant is considered to be expenditure on plant and machinery and is eligible for capital allowance purposes as soon as the plant comes into use. However, hire purchase charges (e.g. interest) are not eligible for capital allowance purposes as they are charged against the profit.

4. An old railway wagon is used for conducting primary school classes. In effect, it is used merely as a structure. It does not perform an active role in the functioning of the school. Hence, it is not considered to be plant for capital allowance purposes.

5. In an ice factory, a cold storage building is essential for storing ice once it is manufactured. Therefore the cold storage building performs an active role in the functioning of the factory. It is therefore considered to be plant for capital allowance purposes.

Answer 8

	FYA £	General Pool £	Capital allowance £
Year ended 31 March 2010			
Additions not qualifying for AIA			
Car		9,000	
Less: WDA at 20% (Note 3)		(1,800)	1,800
		7,200	
Additions qualifying for AIA			
Plant	80,000		
Machinery	22,000		
	102,000		
Less: AIA (note 1)	(50,000)		50,000
	52,000		
Less: FYA at 40% (£52,000 x 40%) (note 2)	(20,800)	31,200	20,800
TWDV c/f		**38,400**	
Allowances			**72,600**
Year ended 31 March 2011			
TWDV b/f		38,400	
Additions		-	
Less: WDA @20%		(7,680)	7,680
TWDV c/f		**30,720**	
Allowances			**7,680**

Notes:

1. The expenditure incurred during the year by any business on plant and machinery except cars is eligible for annual investment allowance up to a limit of £50,000.
2. FYA is available at the rate of 40% on the qualifying asset purchased in the 12 month period from April 2009.
3. As the CO_2 emissions of the car purchased is between 110g/km and 160g/km, it is eligible for WDA at the rate of 20% per annum.

Answer 9

Speed Ltd's first accounting period is of twenty months (period between January 2009 and August 2010). This period of twenty months must be split into two accounting periods for corporation tax purposes.

The first chargeable period will be of twelve months (ending on 31 December 2009) and the second period will be of eight months (ending on 31 August 2010).

Calculation of the capital allowance is as follows:

	FYA £	General Pool £	Allowance £
Year ended 31 December 2009			
Additions qualifying for AIA			
Plant	55,000		
Equipment	7,500		
	62,500		
Less: AIA	(50,000)		50,000
	12,500		
Less: FYA 40%	(5,000)	7,500	5,000
TWDV c/f		**7,500**	
Total capital allowance			**55,000**
8 months to 31 August 2010			
TWDV c/f		7,500	
Less: WDA 20% (£7,500 x 20% x 8/12)		(1,000)	
		6,500	
Additions qualifying for AIA			
Machinery	48,000		
Less: AIA (£50,000 x 8/12) (note 2)	(33,333)		33,333
	14,667		
Less: FYA 40%	(5,867)	8,800	5,867
TWDV c/f		**15,300**	
Total capital allowance			**39,200**

Notes:

1. The expenditure incurred by any business on plant and machinery except cars is eligible for annual investment allowance at 100% up to an annual limit of £50,000.
2. AIA is scaled up or down according to the length of the accounting period,
3. FYA is available at the rate of 40% on the qualifying asset purchased in the 12 month period from 1 April 2009 to 31 March 2010

Answer 10

Bat Ltd's first period of account is of eighteen months (period between January 2009 and June 2010). This eighteen month period must be split into two accounting periods for corporation tax purposes.

The first chargeable period will be of twelve months (ended on 31 December 2009) and the second period will be of six months (ended on 30 June 2010).

Calculation of the capital allowance is as follows:

	FYA £	General Pool £	Special rate pool £	Allowance £
Year ended 31 December 2009				
Additions not qualifying for AIA			-	
Low emission car (note 1)	18,000			
Less: FYA 100% (Note 1)	(18,000)			18,000
Car (note 2)			21,000	
Less: WDA @ 10%			(2,100)	2,100
TWDV c/f	nil		18,900	
Total Capital Allowance				**20,100**
6 months to 30 June 2010				
TWDV b/f			18,900	
Additions not qualifying for AIA				
Car (note 3)		10,000		
Less: WDA @ 20%/ 10% for 6 months (note 4)		(1,000)	(945)	1,945
TWDA c/f		9,000	17,955	
Total capital allowance				**1,945**

Notes:

1. Cars with CO_2 emissions of less than 110g/km are known as low emission cars and are eligible for a 100% first year allowance regardless of the cost of the car and length of the accounting period.
2. Cars with CO_2 emissions exceeding 160g/km are included in the special rate pool and WDA is available at the rate of 10%
3. Cars with CO_2 emissions between 110g/km and 160g/km are included in the general pool and WDA is available at the rate of 20%.
4. WDA is scaled up or down according to the length of the accounting period.

Answer 11

	FYA £	General Pool £	Expensive Motor car £	Allowance £
Year ended 30 June 2010				
TWDV b/f		15,200	7,400	
Less: Disposal (limited to cost)			(5,000)	
Less: WDA 20%		(3,040)		3,040
		12,160		
Additions qualifying for AIA				
Plant	65,000			
Less: AIA	(50,000)			50,000
	15,000			
Less: FYA 40%	(6,000)	9,000		6,000
TWDV c/f		21,160		59,040
Balancing allowance			2,400	2,400
Total capital allowance				**61,440**

Notes:

1. Expensive motor cars do not join the pool. Capital allowance on expensive cars is calculated on an individual basis.
2. On the disposal of an asset, if the disposal proceeds are less than the TWDV, then a balancing allowance is given.
3. The expenditure incurred by any business on plant and machinery except cars in an accounting period is eligible for annual investment allowance at 100% up to an annual limit of £50,000.
4. FYA is available at the rate of 40% on the qualifying asset purchased in the 12 month period from 1 April 2009 to 31 March 2010.

Answer 12

	Short life asset £	Allowance £
Year ended 30 June 2009		
Additions qualifying for AIA		
Plant	72,000	
Less: AIA	(50,000)	50,000
	22,000	
Less: FYA 40%	(8,800)	8,800
TWDV c/f	**13,200**	
Allowances		**58,800**
Year ended 30 June 2010		
TWDV b/f	13,200	
Less: Disposal value	(7,500)	
Balancing allowance	**5,700**	

Notes:

1. Short life assets are not pooled. For capital allowance purposes, these assets are considered separately.
2. AIA is available to all businesses for expenditure on plant and machinery at 100% up to a limit of £50,000, and above this limit, it is chargeable for FYA @ 40% if the asset is purchased in the 12 month period from April 2009 to March 2010.
3. If the disposal value of the asset is less than TWDV, a balancing allowance arises which is deducted from tax-adjusted trading profits.

Answer 13

Calculation of capital allowance in relation to long life asset

	Special rate pool £	Allowance £
Year ended 31 October 2009		
TWDV b/f	-	
Additions qualifying for AIA		
Machinery	150,000	
Less: AIA	(50,000)	50,000
	100,000	
WDA @ 10%	(10,000)	10,000
TWDV c/f	**90,000**	
Total capital allowance		**60,000**
Year ended 31 October 2010		
TWDV b/f	90,000	
Less: WDA @10%	(9,000)	9,000
TWDV c/f	**81,000**	
Total capital allowance		**9,000**

Notes:

1. An asset with a life of 25 years or more is only treated as a long life asset if the expenditure on such asset exceeds £100,000 in the accounting period. For capital allowance purposes, these assets are considered separately in a special rate pool.
2. AIA is available on long life asset (special rate pool asset) at 100% up to a limit of £50,000, and above this limit, it is chargeable for WDA @ 10%. However, FYA is not available on long life assets.

Answer 14

1. **The qualifying amount for construction includes:**

a) Construction cost if the building is constructed by the user himself
b) Professional fees paid to the architect
c) Land preparation / development charges

So, in the case of Swan Inc, qualifying expenditure for IBA is calculated as follows:

	£
Construction cost	800,000
Land development cost	80,000
Professional fees paid to architect	20,000
Total qualifying expenditure	**900,000**

Note: Land cost is not eligible for industrial building allowance.

2. If Swan Inc had purchased this industrial building from the builder for £1,100,000 then all the costs excluding land cost should be considered for calculation of IBA. (i.e. 1,100,000 - 200,000).

Therefore the company's qualifying expenditure for IBA is £900,000.

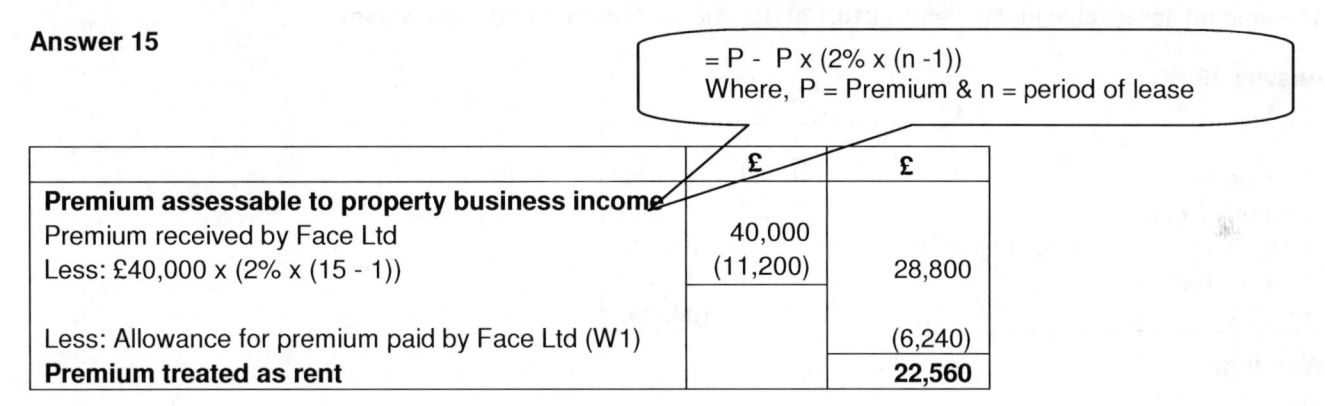

Answer 15

$= P - P \times (2\% \times (n - 1))$
Where, P = Premium & n = period of lease

	£	£
Premium assessable to property business income		
Premium received by Face Ltd	40,000	
Less: £40,000 x (2% x (15 - 1))	(11,200)	28,800
Less: Allowance for premium paid by Face Ltd (W1)		(6,240)
Premium treated as rent		**22,560**

Workings

W1 Allowance for premium paid

	£
Premium paid by Face Ltd	20,000
Less: £20,000 x (2% x (25 - 1))	9,600
	10,400

This amount paid will be reduced in the following ratio
= Portion of head lease premium treated as rent x sublease duration / head lease duration
= £10,400 x 15 / 25
= £6,240

Answer 16

	£
Lease premium received (office 1)	25,000
Less: £25,000 x (2% x (20 - 1))	(9,500)
Premium treated as rent	**15,500**
Rent (office 1) £5,100 x 8/12 (W1)	3,400
Rent (office 2) (W2)	700
	19,600
Less: Expenses	
Repairs	(600)
Insurance (£600 x 2 as 2 offices)	(1,200)
Advertisement expenses	(150)
Property income	**17,650**

Workings

W1 Office 1 was let out for 8 months (from 01/08/09 to 31/03/10) during the year.

W2 Office 2

£1,200 x 4/12 (from 01/05/09 to 31/08/09) = £400
£1,800 x 2/12 (from 01/02/10 to 31/03/10) = £300

                                              £700

Note: The interest on the loan is dealt with under the loan relationship rules. It is not a property business expense.

Answer 17

As the loan was taken for trading purposes, the interest paid on the loan is a trading expense. Hence, £1,260 will be fully deducted from the company's trading profits.

Answer 18

The bank interest is income from a non-trading loan relationship and is assessed on the accrual basis.

The amount assessable for the year is **£10,100** (£8,200 received + £1,900 receivable)

Answer 19

	£
Trading income	25,300
Property income	11,000
Income from loan relationship (W1)	24,190
Chargeable gains	40,000
PCTCT	**100,490**

Workings

W1

Bank interest and interest on government securities is income from a non-trading loan relationship and is assessed on the accrual basis.

	£
Bank interest received	5,600
Add: Receivable at the end of the year	890
Less: Receivable at the start of the year	(300)
	6,190
Government securities interest received	12,000
Add: Accrued (from 1 January to 31 March 10)	6,000
	18,000

Total income from loan relationship (£6,190 + £18,000) = **£24,190**

Answer 20

	£
Trading profits (W1)	223,300
Property income	25,000
Chargeable gains	13,550
	261,850
Less: Gift aid donation	(3,400)
PCTCT	**258,450**

Workings

W1 Trading profits

	£
Profits according to the accounts	215,000
Add: Expenditure shown in the accounts but not deductible for tax purposes.	
Depreciation	2,300
Gift aid donation	3,400
Customer entertaining expenses	2,600
Trading income	**223,300**

Quick Quiz

1. Are dividends paid deductible in arriving at profits chargeable to corporation tax?

2. Better Enterprises Ltd incurred the expenditure below:

	£
Depreciation on building	30,000
Depreciation on machinery	14,000
New office constructed near existing building	21,000
Repairs to machinery	9,000

Which expenditure is deductible for computation of trading profits?

Answers to Quick Quiz

1. No, dividends paid are not included in ANY calculation.

2. Only repairs to machinery (£9,000) are allowable. The new office constructed is a capital expenditure hence not deductible. Depreciation is never deductible.

Self Examination Questions

Question 1

SOCI (income statement) of OK Ltd is given below. Calculate trading profits.

	£	£
Gross operating profit		81,050
Office salaries & expenses	16,000	
Advertising & selling expenses	5,000	
Donation to a political party	7,000	
Depreciation on building & furniture	6,500	
Expenses of lunch given to customers on company annual day	6,600	
Professional fees paid for collection from trade debtors	2,350	43,450
Net profit		**37,600**

Question 2

Given below is the SOCI (income statement) of Wonderful Ltd. You are required to calculate the trading profits of Wonderful Ltd.

	£	£
Gross operating profit		211,930
Salaries	(36,800)	
Depreciation	(23,070)	
Bad debts written off	(2,120)	
Property income	18,200	
Legal expenses relating to issue of shares	(3,500)	
Entertainment of customers	(5,320)	
Loss on sale of fixed assets	(710)	(53,320)
Net Profit		**158,610**

Question 3

Delicious Ltd prepares its accounts up to 31 March every year. The company owns two warehouses, and an office, which it rents out. Rent of the property is due quarterly in advance on 1 January, 1 April and so on. The details of property rented out during the year ended on 31/03/10 are as follows:

1. Warehouse 1 was let out at £8,900 p.a. throughout the year.
2. Warehouse 2 was let out at £5,400 p.a. from 1 May 09. The company received a premium of £50,000 for the grant of 15 years' lease.
3. Office was let out until 31 December 2009 at an annual rent of £3,600 p.a. On that date, the tenant left without paying three months rent which the company is not able to recover.

Delicious Ltd incurs the following expenses:

a) Repairs of warehouse 1 in January 09, £3,900
b) Insurance per warehouse £1,300 p.a., for office £2,350
c) Interest on loan taken to purchase warehouse 2, £3,200
d) Advertisement expenses for obtaining tenants for warehouse 2, £2,600

Calculate property business income of Delicious Ltd.

Answers to Self Examination Questions

Answer 1

	£	£
Net Profits given in Accounts		37,600
Add:		
(i) Expenditure shown in the accounts but not deductible for tax purposes		
Donation to a political party	7,000	
Depreciation on building & furniture	6,500	
Expenses of lunch given to customers on company annual day	6,600	20,100
Adjusted trading profits		**57,700**

Answer 2

	£
Net Profits given in Accounts	158,610
Add:	
(i) Expenditure shown in the accounts but not deductible for tax purpose	
Depreciation (W1)	23,070
Legal expenses relating to issue of shares (W 2)	3,500
Entertainment of customers (W3)	5,320
Loss on sale of fixed asset (W4)	710
(ii) Income taxable but not included in the accounts	
	191,210
Less:	
(ii) Income not taxable but included in the accounts	
Property income	(18,200)
Adjusted trading profits	**173,010**

Notes:

1. Depreciation is never deductible hence added back.
2. As the legal expenses relate to the issue of shares, these are considered to be capital expenses and hence not deductible.
3. Entertaining employees is allowable but entertaining **customers, suppliers** or anyone else is **not allowable.**
4. Loss on sale of a fixed asset is not deductible in the calculation of trading profits.

Answer 3

	Warehouse 1 £	Warehouse 2 £	Office £	Total £
Rent accrued				
1. Warehouse 1	8,900			8,900
2. Warehouse 2 (01/05/09 to 31/03/10) (£5,400/12 x 11)		4,950		4,950
Lease premium received £50,000				
Less: £50,000 x (2% x (15-1)) (£14,000)		36,000		36,000
Office (£3,600 x 9/12)			2,700	2,700
Total rent accrued (a)	8,900	40,950	2,700	52,550
Expenses				
1. Repairs	3,900			3,900
2. Insurance	1,300	1,300	2,350	4,950
3. Advertising expenses for obtaining tenants		2,600		2,600
4. Bad debts (£3,600 x 3/12)			900	900
Total expenses incurred (b)	5,200	3,900	3,250	12,350
Property business profit (a – b)	3,700	37,050	(550)	40,200

The net property business profit is £40,200.
Note: Interest on loan taken to purchase warehouse is dealt with under loan relationship.

SECTION D: CORPORATION TAX LIABILITIES

STUDY GUIDE D2: PROFITS CHARGEABLE TO CORPORATION TAX (PART 2)

Get Through Intro

The **main job of a tax consultant** is to advise his client on how to make **optimal use** of **all the provisions of the Income Tax Act,** which will help the client **minimise his tax liability.**

A thorough knowledge of all the provisions related to this topic becomes imperative, if 'relief for trading losses' is to be used **as the effective tax planning tool that it is.**

You should devote a considerable amount of time to the study of this topic, so that you become fully aware of all the ins and outs of this effective tax planning provision. Needless to say, it is also frequently examined!

Learning Outcomes

g) Understand how trading losses can be carried forward.
h) Understand how trading losses can be claimed against income of the current or previous accounting periods.
i) Recognise the factors that will influence the choice of loss relief claim.
j) Explain how relief for a property business loss is given.
k) Compute profits chargeable to corporation tax.

Introduction

A trading loss occurs when a trader's adjusted profit after capital allowances (CAs) gives a negative figure. It can also arise by CAs either creating a loss (turning a trading profit into a loss) or increasing a loss.

Points to note:

➢ The trading income assessment for the current accounting period will be nil – never put a negative figure as trading income.

➢ Relief is available for the loss.

Different reliefs are available in the current accounting period (reducing the current liability) in the previous 12 months (therefore generating a refund of tax) and in future accounting periods (reducing a future liability, and therefore delaying relief).

A special relief is available in the final 12 months of trade.

Overview:

Main reliefs

Section 393(1) ICTA 1988

Trading loss carried forward and relieved against future trading profits of the same trade.

Section 393A (1) ICTA 1988

Trading loss relieved against total profits before gift aid donations of the current accounting period and then against total profits of the previous 12 months.

On cessation of trade, the carry back period is extended to 36 months.

> **Tip**
> Section numbers have been given for ease of identifying loss reliefs, but candidates will not be expected to quote section numbers as part of their answer in the exam

In this Study Guide we will see various provisions such as carry forward of trading losses, reliefs available for trading losses against incomes of previous or current accounting periods etc.

1. Understand how trading losses can be carried forward.[2]

[Learning outcome a]

1.1 Section 393(1) ICTA 1988: Relief against future trading income

1. Loss carried forward can **only be set off against future trading profits, not against any other income.**

2. The **set off must** be **against the first available trading profit.**

3. It is **not possible to restrict the set off** of the loss.

4. The relief is against future trading profits of the same trade. If there is any change in the nature of the business or if the company starts a new business then it cannot claim the relief for trading loss against the income from the changed or new business.

> **Example**
>
> Extraction Plc is in the business of extracting oil from various seeds such as coconut, groundnut etc. In the years ended on 31 March 2009 and 31 March 2010 the company incurred losses of £38,000 and £64,000 respectively.
>
> In October 2009, the company started manufacturing cosmetics. In the first year, the company earned a profit of £51,500 from the cosmetics business.
>
> However, as the activities conducted by both the businesses are different, **Extraction Plc cannot claim relief for loss from the oil business against the cosmetics business.**

5. There is **no time limit on the carry forward**: it may be carried forward until there are future trading profits.

6. It is **not necessary to claim** this relief: it **is automatically** done if a loss remains after other reliefs, if any, have been claimed.

7. Loss relief is delayed as it means a reduction in future liability.

> **Example**
>
> For the year ended on 31 March 2008, Citizen Ltd incurred a trading loss of £280,000. The company wants to set off losses under section 393(1). The company's trading results for the next two years are as follows:
>
> | | Year ended 31 March 2009 £ | Year ended 31 March 2010 £ |
> |---|---|---|
> | Trading profits | 132,400 | 144,590 |
> | Property income | 8,000 | 8,000 |
> | Chargeable gains | - | 27,500 |
>
> The calculation of company's profits chargeable to corporation tax for the year ended on 31 March 2009 and 31 March 2010 after the set off of the trading losses is as follows-
>
> | | Year ended 31 March 2009 £ | Year ended 31 March 2010 £ |
> |---|---|---|
> | Trading profits | 132,400 | 144,590 |
> | Less: relief s393(1) | (132,400) | (144,590) |
> | | -- | -- |
> | Property income | 8,000 | 8,000 |
> | Chargeable gains | -- | 27,500 |
> | PCTCT | 8,000 | 35,500 |
>
> **Notes:**
>
> 1. The trading loss of the year ended on 31 March 2008 is carried forward and set off against future trading profits.
>
> 2. Under section 393(1), the loss is set off against the future trading profits only and not against any other income (i.e. in this case against property income or chargeable gains).

Continued on next page

3. Loss memorandum

Year		£
Year ended 31 March 2008	Loss for the year	280,000
Year ended 31 March 2009	Loss set off	(132,400)
	Loss c/f	**147,600**
Year ended 31 March 2010	Loss set off	(144,590)
	Loss carried forward	**3,010**

The trading loss of £3,010 is carried forward to the future year to be set off against the first available trading profits of the same trade in the future.

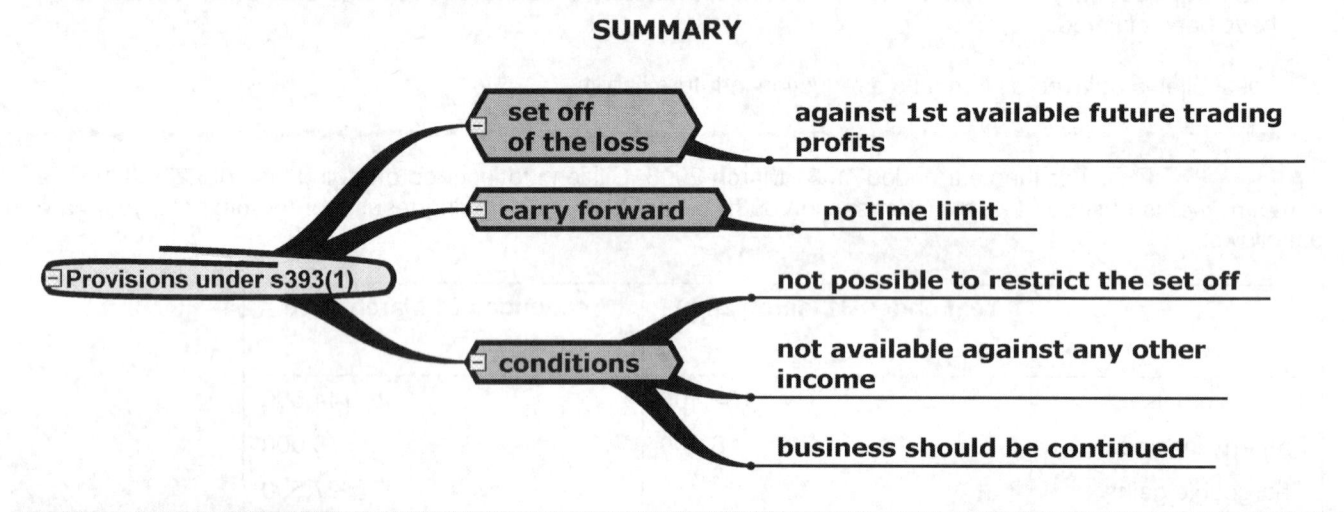

SUMMARY

Provisions under s393(1)
- set off of the loss → against 1st available future trading profits
- carry forward → no time limit
- conditions:
  - not possible to restrict the set off
  - not available against any other income
  - business should be continued

Test Yourself 1

The following are the trading results of Comfort Ltd:

	Year ended 31 December 2007 £	Year ended 31 December 2008 £	Year ended 31 December 2009 £
Trading profits	(347,400)	157,200	248,700
Property income	100,000	100,000	100,000
Chargeable gains	120,000	-	-

Assume that Comfort Ltd wants to carry forward its trading loss under section 393(1). Calculate the profits chargeable to corporation tax of the company for the three years.

2. Understand how trading losses can be claimed against income of the current and previous accounting periods.[2]

[Learning outcome b]

2.1 Section 393(A) ICTA 1988 – relief against total profits of the current accounting period and then against total profits of the previous 12 months

A trading loss arising in an accounting period may be set off against **total profits before deducting gift aid payments of the loss-making accounting period. Gift aid donations** may remain **unrelieved**. In short, the loss should be set off first.

Example

The following are the results of Tamco Ltd for the year ended 31 December 2009

	£
Trading loss before deducting gift aid donations	(40,000)
Property business profits	10,000
Building society interest receivable	10,000
Chargeable gains	48,000

During the year ended on 31 December 2009, the company paid £32,000 towards gift aid donations

In this situation '**total profits**' for section 393 (A) are:

	£
Trading profits	-
Property business income	10,000
Income from loan relationship	10,000
Chargeable gains	48,000
Total profits before gift aid payments	**68,000**

PCTCT calculations will be as follows

	£
Total profits	**68,000**
Less: Relief s393 (A)	(40,000)
	28,000
Less: Gift aid donation	(28,000)
PCTCT	-

Note:

Gift aid donations of £4,000 (£32,000 - £28,000) are unrelieved.

Test Yourself 2

Zenta Ltd gives its trading results for the year ended to 31 March 2010 as follows

	£
Trading loss	(32,000)
Building society interest	3,500
Chargeable gains	21,000
Property business profits	20,000
Gift aid donation	2,000

1. Once a claim has been made **against total profits of the loss-making accounting period**, a further claim may be made **to relieve any remaining loss** against the **total profits of the previous 12 months.**

PROFORMA

	£
Trading profit	X
Less: Trading loss brought forward	(X)
	X
Property business profit	X
Chargeable gains	X
	X
Less: Current year loss relief	(X)
Less: Carry back loss relief	(X)
	X
Less: Gift aid donation	(X)
PCTCT	**X**

The Finance Act 2009 has extended the carry back period of relief for the losses arising during the accounting periods (AP) ending between **24 November 2008 and 23 November 2010**. The relief for losses of these accounting periods can be claimed against the total profits of the previous **36 months** i.e. carry back period is extended from 12 months to 36 months (i.e. further 24 months), taking the latest accounting period first.

The **maximum amount of relief** that can be claimed against the total profits of the extended period of 24 months is **£50,000**. However, there is no limit for claiming relief against the total profits of the previous 12 months.

If the loss making accounting period for which the claimed carry back relief of 36 months is less than 12 months, then the maximum limit of £50,000 will be scaled down according to the length of the accounting period.

> **Tip**
>
> The maximum limit of relief of £50,000 for the extended period and the accounting periods for which this extended relief is applicable, (i.e. the accounting periods ending between 24 November 2008 and 23 November 2010) will be provided to you in the exam.

2. The **carry back claim** is **only possible once a claim against the total profits of the current year has been made.** It is not compulsory to claim carry back relief. The company can claim current year relief and then can opt to carry the balance forward to set off against future trading profits of the same trade.

3. It is **not possible to restrict the set off**, e.g. to relieve gift aid payments.

4. If **no s 393(A) claim is made**, or **trading loss remains** after a claim, the **remaining loss** is **carried forward** under section **393(1)** against **future trading profits.**

5. **Claim** for relief under s **393(A)** must be made **within 2 years from the end of the accounting period in which the loss arose.**

Example

If the loss arose in the year ended 31/12/08, the claim must be made by 31/12/10.

Example

Tetra pack Ltd has the following financial results for the last four periods:

	Year ended 31 March 2007 £	Year ended 31 March 2008 £	Year ended 31 March 2009 £	Year ended 31 March 2010 £
Trading profits / loss	58,800	16,400	20,150	(114,000)
Rental income	12,000	12,000	12,000	-
Chargeable gains	2,000	-	8,000	-
Gift aid donation	10,000	10,000	10,000	-

Assuming that the company has made a claim under section 393A for the last 36 months, the company's PCTCT for these four years is as follows

	Year ended 31 March 2007 £	Year ended 31 March 2008 £	Year ended 31 March 2009 £
Trading profit	58,800	16,400	20,150
Property business profit	12,000	12,000	12,000
Chargeable gains	2,000	-	8,000
	72,800	28,400	40,150
Less: Carry back loss relief (note 3)	(21,600)	(28,400)	(40,150)
	51,200	-	-
Less: Gift aid donation	(10,000)	-	-
PCTCT	**41,200**	**-**	**-**

Workings

W1 Loss memorandum

		£
Year ended 31 March 2010	Loss incurred	114,000
Year ended 31 March 2009	Less: Relief s393 (A)	(40,150)
	Balance	**73,850**
Year ended 31 March 2008	Less: Relief s393 (A)	(28,400)
	Balance	**45,450**
Year ended 31 March 2007	Less: Relief s393 (A)	(21,600)
	Balance	**23,850**

Notes:
1. The loss arising during the accounting period ending on 31 March 2010 can be relieved against the total profits of the previous 36 months (extended loss relief) as this period ends between 24 November 2008 and 23 November 2010.
2. There is no limit for claiming loss relief against the total profits of the previous 12 month period.
3. There is a maximum limit of £50,000 to claim relief against the total profits of the remaining 24 months (extended period). Hence, after claiming relief of £28,400, the amount which can be claimed as relief against the total profits for the year ended 31 March 2007 is £21,600 (£50,000 – £28,400).
4. The remaining loss of £23,850 can be carried forward to set off against the future trading profits.

Test Yourself 3

Magic pot Ltd prepares its accounts to 31 March every year. It has decided to change its accounting date to 31 December and prepares the accounts for the nine months to December 2009.
The results for the last four accounting periods are as follows:

	Year ended 31 March 2007 £	Year ended 31 March 2008 £	Year ended 31 March 2009 £	Period ended 31 December 2009 £
Trading profits	44,100	23,800	14,500	(96,300)
Property business income	10,000	10,000	10,000	10,000
Gift aid donation	2,000	2,000	2,000	2,000

Required:

Assume the company has made a claim for relief under section 393A. Show the calculation of PCTCT after set off of loss for the year ended 31 March 2009.

---

6. The **carry back period is not 12 months** – it may be necessary to **apportion the total profits figure if the carry back periods** before the loss-making period are not 12 months.

Example

Moon Plc's results are as follows:

	15 months period ended on 31 July 2007 £	Year ended on 31 July 2008 £	Year ended on 31 July 2009 £	Year ended on 31 July 2010 £
Trading profits	30,000	24,600	15,200	(84,600)
Bank interest	-	-	-	5,000

Assuming that the company claims relief for trading losses under section 393A, unrelieved loss is calculated as follows:

	Year ended on 30 April 2007 £	3 months to 31 July 2007 £	Year ended 31 July 2008 £	Year ended 31 July 2009 £	Year ended 31 July 2010 £
Trading profit	24,000	6,000	24,600	15,200	-
Income from loan relationship	-	-	-	-	5,000
	24,000	**6,000**	**24,600**	**15,200**	**5,000**
Less: Current year loss relief s393 (A)	-	-	-	-	(5,000)
Less: Carry back loss relief s393 (A)	(18,000)	(6,000)	(24,600)	(15,200)	-
PCTCT	**6,000**	-	-	-	-

Continued on next page

Workings

W1 Loss memorandum

		£
Year ended 31 July 2010	Loss incurred	84,600
Year ended 31 July 2010	Less: current year relief s393 (A)	(5,000)
	Balance	**79,600**
Year ended 31 July 2009	Less: carry back relief s393 (A)	(15,200)
	Balance	**64,400**
Year ended 31 July 2008	Less: carry back relief s393 (A)	(24,600)
	Balance	**39,800**
3 months period ended 31 July 2007	Less: carry back relief s393 (A)	(6,000)
	Balance	**33,800**
Year ended 30 April 2007	Less: carry back relief s393 (A)	(18,000)
	Balance carried forward to set off against future trading profits under s393(1)	**15,800**

Notes:

1. The carry back period is extended to 36 months for the loss arising in the accounting period ending between 24 November 2008 and 24 November 2010. Out of these 36 months, loss will be set off first against the 12 month accounting periods ending on 31 July 2008 and 31 July 2009. The remaining 12 months fall in the accounting period ended on 31 July 2007.

2. The accounting period in which the last 12 month period falls is of fifteen months. So, it will be divided into two accounting periods, first accounting period of 12 months ended on 30/04/07 and second accounting period of 3 months ended on 31/07/07.
Hence, the loss should first be set off against profits for the accounting period of 3 months ended on 31/07/07 i.e. £30,000/15 x 3 = £6,000
Then, the remaining loss can be set off against profit for the 9 months' period which falls in the year ended on 30/04/07 i.e. (£24,000 x 9/12) = £18,000.

3. There is a limit of £50,000 for the relief which can be claimed against the profits of the extended period of 24 months. However, this limit remained unutilised for the amount of £1,400 i.e. (£50,000 - £24,600 - £6,000 - £18,000) as the profits against which the relief was claimed for the last 12 months were less than £50,000.

Test Yourself 4

Sonja Ltd has the following financial results for the last five periods:

	Year ended 31 March 2006	Year ended 31 March 2007	Year ended 31 March 2008 £	Period ended 31 December 2008 £	Year ended 31 December 2009 £
Trading profits / (loss)	34,800	22,100	18,000	8,000	(68,200)
Bank interest	2,000	2,000	2,000	2,000	2,000

Required:

Show how it will set off its trading losses.

2.2 Terminal Loss Relief

1. If a **loss arises in the last 12 months of trading**, the **carry back period** is **extended to 36 months**.

    The loss is set off against the **total profits** before deducting gift aid payments **of the same accounting period,** and **then** against the **total profits** before deducting gift aid payments of **the previous 36 months**, relieving against **later years first**.

D2.34: Corporation Tax Liabilities

Example

Superior Ltd has been trading for many years, preparing accounts to 31 March every year. It ceased trading on 31 March 2010. Her results for the last 5 years of trading were as follows:

	Year ended 31/03/06 £	Year ended 31/03/07 £	Year ended 31/03/08 £	Year ended 31/03/09 £	Year ended 31/03/10 £
Trading profit / (loss)	197,000	234,000	176,000	58,000	(647,000)
Property business profits	6,800	12,000	8,000	4,200	4,000
Gift aid donation	(10,500)	(10,500)	(10,500)	(10,500)	(10,500)

We assume that the company claims the maximum possible relief for its trading losses.

Calculation of the **chargeable profits** is made as follows:

	Year ended 31/03/06 £	Year ended 31/03/07 £	Year ended 31/03/08 £	Year ended 31/03/09 £	Year ended 31/03/10 £
Trading profit	197,000	234,000	176,000	58,000	-
Property business profits	6,800	12,000	8,000	4,200	4,000
	203,800	246,000	184,000	62,200	4,000
Less: Current Year Loss relief u/s.393 (A)	-	-	-	-	(4,000)
Less: Terminal loss relief for year ended 31 March 2010	-	(246,000)	(184,000)	(62,200)	
	203,800	-	-	-	-
Gift aid donation	(10,500)	-	-	-	-
PCTCT	193,300				

Note:

Terminal loss in the last 12 months of trading can be set off against total profits of the current accounting period and then against the total profits available of previous 36 months without any restriction, relieving the loss against the later years first. There is no limit of £50,000 in case of loss arising in last 12 months of trading (terminal loss).

Workings

W1 Loss memorandum

		£
Year ended 31 March 2010	Loss incurred	647,000
Year ended 31 March 2010	Less: current year relief s393 (A)	(4,000)
	Balance	643,000
Year ended 31 March 2009	Less: carry back relief s393 (A)	(62,200)
	Balance	580,800
Year ended 31 March 2008	Less: carry back relief s393 (A)	(184,000)
	Balance	396,800
Year ended 31 March 2007	Less: carry back relief s393 (A)	(246,000)
	Unrelieved losses	**150,800**

2. If there are **losses in different periods**, they are **dealt with chronologically** i.e. claims are made for the **earlier loss before the later loss**.

3. If the **carry back periods before the loss-making period are not 12 months** – it may be necessary to **apportion the total profits figure**.

Example

Yamazaki Ltd prepares its accounts to 31 March every year. In April 2008, it has decided to change its accounting date to 31 July and prepares the accounts for the four months to 31 July 2008 and thereafter to 31 July every year. It ceased trading on 31 July 2009. The trading results for the last five accounting periods are as follows:

	Year ended 31/03/06 £	Year ended 31/03/07 £	Year ended 31/03/08 £	Period ended 31/07/08 £	Year ended 31/07/09 £
Trading profit / (loss)	246,000	69,500	26,500	(50,200)	(350,200)
Property business profits	7,500	14,000	7,000	5,000	-
Capital gains	-	-	6,000	-	25,500
Gift aid donation	(1,500)	(1,200)	-	-	(1,000)

To calculate the company's chargeable profits for the years ended 31 March 2006, 2007 and 2008, the four month period ended 31 July 2008, and the year ended 31 July 2009, we have to first calculate the profits available in the different years.

We assume that the company claims the maximum possible relief for its trading losses.

Calculation of the **chargeable profits** is made as follows:

	Year ended 31/03/06 £	Year ended 31/03/07 £	Year ended 31/03/08 £	Period ended 31/07/08 £	Year ended 31/07/09 £
Trading profit / (loss)	246,000	69,500	26,500	-	-
Property business profits	7,500	14,000	7,000	5,000	-
Capital gains	-	-	6,000	-	25,500
	253,500	83,500	39,500	5,000	25,500
Less: Current Year Loss relief u/s.393 (A)	-	-	-	(5,000)	(25,500)
Less: Carry back loss relief 393(A)			(39,500)		
Less: Terminal loss relief for year ended 31 July 2009	(169,000)	(83,500)			
	84,500	-	-	-	-
Gift aid donation	(1,500)	-	-	-	-
PCTCT	**83,000**				

Loss Memorandum

	Period ended 31 July 2008 £	Year ended 31 July 2009 £
Loss for the period	50,200	350,200
Less: Loss relief		
Current year loss relief 393(A)	(5,000)	(25,500)
Carry back loss relief (previous 12 months) (Year ended 31/03/08)	(39,500)	
Terminal loss relief (previous 36 months)		
1 April 08 to 31 July 08 4 months		-
Year ended 31 March 08 12 months		-
Year ended 31 March 07 12 months		(83,500)
1 August 05 to 31 March 06 8 months		(169,000)
36 months		
Unrelieved losses	**5,700**	**72,200**

Notes:

1. For the year ended 31/03/06, loss relief is restricted to £253,500 x 8/12 = £169,000.
2. Loss for the period ended 31 July 2008 may be set off only against total profits of the current AP and then against total profits of the previous 12 months (year ended 31 March 08). Extended relief of 24 months will not be available in this case as it is available only for the losses arising during the accounting period ending in between 24 November 2008 and 23 November 2010.

Continued on next page

3. Terminal loss in the last 12 months of trading can be set off against total profits of the current AP and then against total profits available of previous 36 months (without any restriction) relieving the losses against the later years first.
4. Gift aid donation of £1,200 and £1,000 for the years ended 31/03/07 and 31/07/09 respectively are unrelieved.

SUMMARY

Provisions under s393(A)

- **set off of loss**: against current accounting period's total profits
- **remaining loss**: carry back to set off against previous 12 month's total profits
- **extended relief**:
  - for losses of APs ending between 24 Nov 2008 & 23 Nov 2010
  - carry back period extended to 36 months
  - maximum relief: £50,000 for extended period of 24 months
- **terminal loss relief**:
  - for loss arising in the last 12 months of trading
  - carry back period extended to 36 months

3. Recognise the factors that will influence the choice of loss relief claim.[2]
[Learning outcome c]

3.1 A company may claim relief for a trading loss under:

1. S393(1) i.e. trading losses are carried forward to be set off against **future trading profits** or

2. S393A(1) (a) i.e. trading losses incurred during the accounting year are set off against **total profits of the same accounting period** and

3. S393A(1) (b) i.e. trading losses incurred during the accounting year are set off against **total profits of the 12 month period prior to the loss-making period.**

3.2 Some of the **factors that will influence the choice of loss relief claim** are as follows:

a) **Corporation tax rate** in the year the loss was incurred and the future tax rates when the losses are set off (if there is a decreasing trend, companies normally tend to set off trading losses at the lower rates in order to reduce current tax bills).

b) **Expectations about the future trading profits** of the company.

c) **A company's cash flows** (i.e. where a company suffers from cash shortage, generally it is sensible to set off losses at the earliest and avoid cash outflows).

4. Explain how relief for a property business loss is given.[1]

[Learning outcome d]

1. All property income, receipts and expenses are pooled to give an overall profit or loss figure for the year. The losses from running one property business are automatically **set off against income from other property business.**

2. The net loss from running a property business is **first set off against non-property income and gains of the same accounting period.**

3. Any excess loss, which could not be set off as above, is carried forward to the next accounting period.

4. For the carry forward of property business losses, it is necessary that the property business **should continue** i.e. if a property-letting business is ceased, then the carry forward of the property business loss is not allowed.

5. The carried forward loss can be set off against the total profits of subsequent tax years.

Test Yourself 5

Precious Ltd prepares its accounts to 31 March every year. Its trading profits for the year ended 31 March 2010 are £4,500 and it had received bank interest of £5,000. The company owns two shops, and an office which it had rented out. Rent on the property is due quarterly in advance on 1 January, 1 April and so on.

The details of property rented out during the year ended 31/03/10 are as follows.

a) Shop 1 was let out at £3,800 p.a. throughout the year

b) Shop 2 was let out at £5,400 p.a. from 1 May 09

c) Office was let out at £3,300 p.a. throughout the year

Precious Ltd incurs the following expenses.

a) Repairs of shop 1 in January 10, £7,300

b) Insurance per shop £2,900 p.a., for office £2,350 p.a.

c) Interest on loan taken to purchase shop 2, £4,100

d) Advertisement expenses for obtaining tenants for shop 2, £2,200

Required:

Calculate the property business's income / loss. Explain the loss relief provisions, in the case of loss.

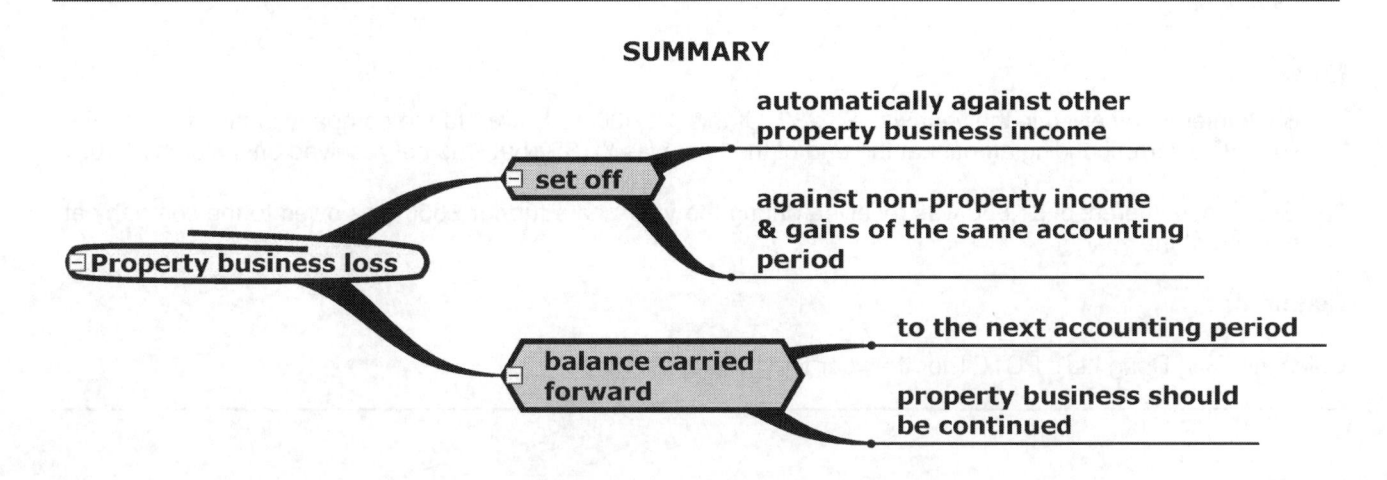

SUMMARY

Property business loss
- set off
  - automatically against other property business income
  - against non-property income & gains of the same accounting period
- balance carried forward
  - to the next accounting period
  - property business should be continued

5. Compute profits chargeable to corporation tax.[2]

[Learning outcome e]

After aggregating all trading income, property income, income from loan relationships, chargeable gains net of any capital losses and deducting gift aid payments, the total income is the profit chargeable to corporation tax (PCTCT).

We can present it as:

	£	£
1. Trading profits	X	
Less: Brought forward trading losses	(X)	X
2. Property income		X
3. Profits from loan relationship		X
4. Profits from foreign securities and possessions		X
5. Chargeable gains	X	
Less: Allowable capital losses brought forward	(X)	X
Total income		X
Less: Reliefs		
1. Property business losses	X	
2. Trading losses relieved under s393A	X	
3. Gift aid donations	X	(X)
Profits chargeable to corporation tax (PCTCT)		X

Test Yourself 6

Ding Dong Ltd, a manufacturing company has the following results for the year to 31 March 2010.

	£
Property income	15,500
Trading income	745,200
Bank interest (Note 1)	4,589
Loan interest receivable (Note 2)	2,400
Dividends from UK company	13,500
Chargeable gains	11,200
Gift aid donation	21,000

Notes:

1. Bank interest received in the year was £3,232. Of this, £1,000 was owed to the company at the start of the year. The corresponding amount at the end of the year was £2,357 but was not received until March 2010.

2. Gross loan interest of £1,850 was received during the year and a further £550 was owed to the company at the end of the year.

Required:

Calculate Ding Dong Ltd's PCTCT for the year to 31 March 2010.

Test Yourself 7

Green plant Ltd's profit and loss account for the year to 31 March 2010 is as follows.

	£	£
Gross trading profits		240,000
Income from property (Note 4)		6,000
Bad debts recovered (previously written off)		1,420
Building society interest (gross)		2,100
		249,520
Less:		
General expenses (Note 1)	(60,112)	
Directors' fees	(30,000)	
Repairs and renewals (Note 2)	(12,000)	
Bad debts written off	(1,100)	
Depreciation	(23,100)	
Registering patent	(6,600)	
Legal and accountancy charges (Note 3)	(10,000)	(142,912)
Net profit for the year		**106,608**

Note:

1. General expenses include £450 towards customers' entertainment and £1,000 towards donation to a political party.

2. Repairs and renewals include £200 towards refurbishing the premises and £300 towards constructing a new staff room.

3. Legal and accountancy charges are made up as follows.

	£
Collections from debtors	2,200
Purchasing land	2,300
Cost of renewing 45 year lease	4,500
Audit and accountancy	1,000
	10,000

4. The property was let out on 1 December 2009 at a rent of £2,000 per month payable in advance on 1 December, 1 March, 1 June and 1 September. There were no allowable expenses in the year to 31 March 2010.

Required:

Calculate Green plant Ltd's profits chargeable to corporation tax for the year ended 31 March 2010.

Test Yourself 8

Jasmine Ltd is a manufacturing company. The company's summarised Profit & Loss account for the year ended 31 March 2010 is as follows.

	£	£
Gross trading profits		1,919,920
Less: Operating expenses		
Bad debts written off	(14,230)	
Professional fees	(20,150)	
Depreciation	(95,500)	
Rent and rates	(121,480)	
Gift aid donations paid	(12,000)	
Other expenses	(197,630)	
Gifts and donations	(5,930)	(466,920)
		1,453,000
Income from investment		
Bank interest		14,400
		1,467,400
Interest on debenture paid		(100,000)
Net profit before taxation		1,367,400

Note:

1. Bad debts are as follows

	£
Trade debts recovered from earlier years	(4,020)
Employee bad debts	4,250
Non-trade loans written off	14,000
	14,230

2. Professional fees are as follows

	£
Cost of registering trademark	1,900
Legal fees in connection with share capital	15,000
Audit fees	3,250
	20,150

3. Rent and rates include a premium of £45,000 paid on 1 April 2009 for the grant of a 15 years lease on an office building.

4. Gifts and donations include

	£
Gift of pens (£20 each) displaying name Jasmine	2,600
Donations to a political party	3,330
	5,930

5. Other expenses include Christmas party expenses of £7,500 for entertaining employees and £4,500 for entertaining customers. The remaining expenses are all allowable.

6. Bank interest was received on bank deposit held for non-trading purposes.

7. Debenture interest was the actual amount paid during the year. The 10% Debentures for 1,000,000 was issued on 1st January 2009 to raise capital to build a new factory for manufacturing. The interest is payable half yearly on 30th September and 31st March each year.

Required:

Calculate Jasmine Ltd's profits chargeable to corporation tax for the year.

Test Yourself 9

Tasty Ltd's trading profits for the year ended 31/12/09 were £523,500, calculated as follows.

	£		£
Depreciation	25,000	Gross profit	550,000
Gift aid donation paid	11,000		
Bad debt written off	9,500		
Penalties and fine	10,000		
General allowance for repairs	12,000		
Net profit	482,500		
	550,000		**550,000**

Tasty Ltd's other income is as follows:

1. Tasty Ltd owned two warehouses. The first warehouse was let out from 1 April 2009 for an annual rent of £24,000. The company received a premium of £40,000 for grant of a 12 year lease. Rent is payable in advance on the first of every month.

   The second warehouse was let until 30 September 2009 at an annual rent of £12,000. On that date, the tenant left without paying three months' rent which the company is not able to recover. The roof of the warehouse was repaired at a cost of £2,500 during October 2009. The company had taken a loan to purchase the warehouse. The interest paid on the loan was £2,000.

2. Debenture interest received on 31 December 2009 was £35,000. Debenture interest owed to the company at the end of the year is £5,000.

3. The details of the income from bank interest are as follows.

	£
Bank interest receivable on 1 January 2009	2,000
Received	6,000
Receivable on 31 December 2009	3,000

Required:

Calculate chargeable profits for the year ended 31 December 2009.

Answers to Test Yourself

Answer 1

Step 1 Calculation of trading profits after relief under s393(1)

	Year ended 31 December 2007 £	Year ended 31 December 2008 £	Year ended 31 December 2009 £
Trading profits	-	157,200	248,700
Less: Relief under s393(1)	-	(157,200)	(190,200)
Trading profits	**-**	**-**	**58,500**
Property income	100,000	100,000	100,000
Chargeable gains	120,000	-	-
PCTCT	**220,000**	**100,000**	**158,500**

Working

W1 Loss memorandum

Accounting periods		£
Year ended 31 December 2007	Loss for the year	347,400
Year ended 31 December 2008	Loss set off	(157,200)
	Balance	**190,200**
Year ended 31 December 2009	Loss set off	(190,200)
	Balance	**-**

Notes:

1. The trading loss for the year ended on 31 December 2007 is carried forward to set off against future trading profits.
2. Under section 393(1), the loss is set off against the trading profits of the same trade only and not against any other income. (such as, in this case, property income, chargeable gains)

Answer 2

Calculation of chargeable profits after set off of trading loss under s.393(A)

	£
Income from loan relationship	3,500
Property business profits	20,000
Chargeable gains	21,000
Total profits	**44,500**
Less: Relief under s.393(A)	(32,000)
Balance	12,500
Less: Gift aid donation	(2,000)
Chargeable profits	**10,500**

Answer 3

Calculation of PCTCT after relief under s 393(A) and 393(A)

	Year ended 31 March 2007 £	Year ended 31 March 2008 £	Year ended 31 March 2009 £	Period ended 31 December 2009 £
Trading profit	44,100	23,800	14,500	
Property business profit	10,000	10,000	10,000	10,000
	54,100	33,800	24,500	
Less: Current year loss relief 393(A)	-	-	-	(10,000)
Less: Carry back loss relief 393(A)	(3,700)	(33,800)	(24,500)	-
	50,400	-	-	-
Gift aid donation	(2,000)	-	-	
PCTCT	**48,400**	**-**	**-**	

Working

W1 Loss memorandum

		£
Period ended 31 December 2009	Loss incurred	96,300
Period ended 31 December 2009	Less: current year relief s393(A)	(10,000)
	Balance	86,300
Year ended 31 March 2009	Less: carry back relief s393(A)	(24,500)
	Balance	61,800
Year ended 31 March 2008	Less: carry back relief s393(A)	(33,800)
	Balance	28,000
Year ended 31 March 2007	Less: carry back relief s393(A)	(3,700)
	Balance carried forward to be set off under sec 393(1)	24,300

Notes:

1. Relief under Sec 393(A) is available first against total profits of the current accounting period and then against total profits of previous 12 months. However, for the accounting period ending between 24 November 2008 and 24 November 2010, the carry back period has been extended to 36 months from 12 months. As the loss making accounting period ends during this period, relief is available up to the accounting period ending on 31 March 2007.
2. There is no restriction on the relief amount that can be claimed against the total profits of the previous 12 months. However, the relief is restricted up to the maximum amount of £50,000 for the extended period of 24 months.
3. The maximum limit of £50,000 is scaled down if the loss making accounting period is less than 12 months. As the loss making accounting period is of 9 months, the relief is restricted up to the amount of £37,500 (£50,000 x 9/12). Hence, the amount of loss that can be set off against the total profits of the year ended 31 March 2007 is restricted to £3,700 (£37,500 - £33,800).

Answer 4

	Year ended 31/3/06	Year ended 31/3/07	Year ended 31/3/08 £	Period ended 31/12/08 £	Year ended 31/12/09 £
Trading profit	34,800	22,100	18,000	8,000	-
Income from loan relationship	2,000	2,000	2,000	2,000	2,000
	36,800	24,100	20,000	10,000	2,000
Less: Current year loss relief s393(A)				-	(2,000)
Less: carry back loss relief s393(A) (previous 12 months) (note 2)			(5,000)	(10,000)	
Less: Carry back loss relief s393(A) (extended 24 months)	(9,200)	(24,100)	(15,000)		
PCTCT	27,600	-	-	-	-

Notes:

1. Sonja Ltd can first claim relief against the total profits of the current year, then against the total profits of the previous 12 months prior to loss making. This carry back relief has been extended for a further period of 24 months if the loss making accounting period ends between 24 November 2008 and 23 November 2010.

2. There is no restriction on the amount to be claimed against the previous 12 months profit but there is a restriction of £50,000 on the amount which can be claimed against the total profits of the extended period of 24 months.

Hence, carry back relief will be first claimed against the profits of the previous 12 months (i.e. period between 1 January 2008 and 31 December 2008). Out of these twelve months:
➢ nine months fall in the chargeable period ended 31 December 2008 and
➢ the remaining three months fall in the year ended 31 March 2008

Hence, the relief that can be claimed against the profits of the period ended 31 December 2008 is £10,000
And the relief against the three months falling in the year ended 31 March 2008 is (£20,000 x 3/12) = £5,000.

There is a restriction of £50,000 on the amount that can be claimed as a relief against the profits of the extended period of 24 months. Hence, the amount that can be claimed against the total profits of the year ended 31/03/06 is £10,900 (£50,000 - £15,000 - £24,100). However, the amount of profits against which the relief can be claimed is £9,200(£36,800 x 3/12).
Hence, the relief available against the accounting period ending on 31 March 2006 is £9,200.

Loss memorandum

		£
Year ended 31/12/09	Trading loss incurred	68,200
Year ended 31/12/09	Less: current year relief s393(A)	(2,000)
	Balance	**66,200**
Period ended 31/12/08	Less: carry back relief s393(A)	(10,000)
	Balance	**56,200**
Year ended 31/3/08	Less: carry back relief s393(A)	(20,000)
	Balance	**36,200**
Year ended 31/3/07	Less: carry back relief s393(A)	(24,100)
	Balance	**12,100**
Year ended 31/3/06	Less: carry back relief s393(A)	(9,200)
	Balance carried forward s393(1)	**2,900**

Answer 5

	Shop 1 £	Shop 2 £	Office £	Total £
Rent accrued				
Shop 1	3,800	-	-	3,800
Shop 2 (1/05/09 to 31/03/10) (£5,400 x 11/12)	-	4,950	-	4,950
Office	-	-	3,300	3,300
Total rent accrued	**3,800**	**4,950**	**3,300**	**12,050**
Less: Expenses				
1. Repairs	7,300			7,300
2. Insurance	2,900	2,900	2,350	8,150
3. Advertising expenses for obtaining tenants		2,200		2,200
Total expenses incurred	10,200	5,100	2,350	17,650
Property business loss	(6,400)	(150)	950	(5,600)

Net property business loss is £5,600

This £5,600 of property business loss can be first set off against current year non-property business income.

Precious Ltd's chargeable profits

	£
Trading profits	4,500
Income from loan relationship (W1)	900
	5,400
Property income (restricted)	(5,400)
PCTCT	**-**

Excess loss of £200 (£5,600 - £5,400) which cannot be set off can be carried forward to the next accounting period.

Such carried forward loss can be set off against the total income arising in subsequent accounting periods. Hence in the next accounting period, if Precious Ltd's total income is £6,500, then the carried forward loss of £200 will be first set off against it and the taxable income will be (£6,500 - £200 = £6,300).

For such carry forward of property business loss, it is necessary that the property business is continued. Therefore, if Precious Ltd ceases its property business then the carry forward of property business loss is not allowed.

Note: The interest on the loan is dealt with under the loan relationship rules. It is not a property business expense.

W1 Income from loan relationship

	£
Bank interest received	5,000
Less: Interest on loan taken to purchase shop 2	4,100
	900

Answer 6

	£
1. Trading profits	745,200
2. Property income	15,500
3. Income from loan relationship (£4,589 +£2,400) (W1& W2)	6,989
4. Chargeable gains	11,200
	778,889
Less: Gift aid donation	(21,000)
Profits chargeable to corporation tax (PCTCT)	**757,889**

Workings

W1

Bank interest of (£3,232 - £1,000 + £2,357) = **£4,589** is taxable for the year to 31 March 2010 under loan relationship. Because we follow the accrual basis, £1,000 must be accounted for in the previous year although it is actually received this year. Also, £1,357, although actually not received until March 2010, is accrued for the year and hence to be taken into consideration when calculating the chargeable profits for the year ended 31 March 2010.

W2

Loan interest: it is assumed that the loan was not made for trade purposes. Hence **£2,400** (£1,850 + £550) is part of income from loan relationships.

W3

The dividends from a UK company are franked investment income (discussed in detail in Learning Outcome 2 Study Guide D3) and do not form part of the company's profits chargeable to corporation tax.

Answer 7

Computation of profits chargeable to corporation tax of Green plant Ltd

	£
1. Trading profits (W1)	125,658
2. Property income (W2)	8,000
3. Income from loan relationship	2,100
Profits chargeable to corporation tax (PCTCT)	**135,758**

Workings

W1

	£
Net Profits according to accounts	**106,608**
Add: 1. Expenditure shown in the accounts but not deductible for tax purposes:	
Depreciation (note 1)	23,100
Customer entertainment (Note2)	450
Donation to political party (note 3)	1,000
Construction of a new staff room (note 4)	300
Legal charges for purchasing a property (note 5)	2,300
	133,758
Less: Income not taxable as trading income included in the accounts	
Income from property	(6,000)
Building society interest	(2,100)
Trading profit	**125,658**

Note:

1. Depreciation is never deductible, hence added back.
2. Entertaining customers is not allowable.
3. Donations to a political party are not allowable.
4. Construction of a new staff room is a capital expenditure, hence not allowable.
5. Legal charges for purchasing land are capital expenditure and will be added to the cost of the land.

W 2 Property income

Rent: 1 December 2009 to 31 March 2010

(£2,000 x 4) = £8,000

Answer 8

Calculation of profits chargeable to corporation tax for Jasmine Ltd

	£
Trading profits (W1)	1,544,420
Income from loan relationship (W2)	14,400
	1,558,820
Gift aid donation	(12,000)
Profits chargeable to corporation tax (PCTCT)	**1,546,820**

Workings

W1 Calculation of adjusted trading profits

	£	£
Net profit according to accounts		1,367,400
Add: Expenditure shown in the accounts but not deductible for tax purposes		
Employee bad debts and non-trade loans written off	18,250	
Professional fees in connection with issue of share capital (capital expenditure)	15,000	
Depreciation (not allowed)	95,500	
Premium for 25 year lease (W2)	45,000	
Gift aid donations	12,000	
Donation to political party (not allowed)	3,330	
Entertaining customers (not allowed)	4,500	193,580
Less: Income not taxable as trading income included in the accounts		
Short lease premium (W2)	(2,160)	
Bank Interest	(14,400)	(16,560)
Trading profits		**1,544,420**

Note: Gifts (i.e. pens) displaying the company's name are allowed as they cost less than £50 per person per year and are not food, alcohol, tobacco or vouchers exchangeable for goods and carry a conspicuous advertisement for the business.

W2

The amount of premium assessed under property business income for the landlord is

= P – P x (2% x (n-1))
= £45,000 - £45,000 x (2% x (15 -1)) = £32,400

Jasmine Ltd can deduct £2,160 (£32,400/15) per annum when calculating its trading profits. Hence, the total amount of premium of £45,000 which was deducted as operating expenses from gross trading profits will be added back and the amount of £2160 will be deducted for calculation of tax adjusted trading profits.

Answer 9

Calculation of profits chargeable to corporation tax

	£
Trading profits (W1)	540,500
Property income (W2)	52,700
Income from loan relationships (W3)	45,000
	638,200
Less: Gift aid donation	(11,000)
Profits chargeable to corporation tax (PCTCT)	**627,200**

Workings

W1

	£	£
Net profit according to accounts		482,500
Add: 1. Expenditure shown in the accounts but not deductible for tax purposes:		
Depreciation	25,000	
Gift aid donations	11,000	
Penalties and fines	10,000	
Provision for repairs	12,000	58,000
Trading profits		**540,500**

Notes:

1. As fines and penalties are not incurred exclusively for purpose of the trade, they are not deductible from trading profits.
2. General allowance for repairs is not allowable.

W2

	£	£
Property income		
Warehouse 1		
Premium	40,000	
Less: £40,000 x (2% x (12 -1))	(8,800)	
Premium treated as rent	31,200	
Rent (1 April 2009 to 31 December 2009) (£24,000 x 9/12)	18,000	49,200
Warehouse 2		
Rent (1 January 2009 to 30 September 2009) (£12,000 x 9/12)	9,000	
Less: Bad debts (three months' rent) (£12,000 x 3/12)	(3,000)	
Repair of roof	(2,500)	3,500
Property income		**52,700**

Note:

Interest on loan to purchase the warehouse is taken care of under loan relationship.

W3

	£	£
Income from loan relationship		
Debenture interest	35,000	
Add: Receivable	5,000	40,000
Bank interest received	6,000	
Less: Receivable on 1 January 2009	(2,000)	
Add: Receivable on 31 December 2009	3,000	7,000
		47,000
Less: Interest paid on loan taken to purchase warehouse 2		(2,000)
Income from loan relationship		**45,000**

Quick Quiz

Fill in the blanks.

1. Under section 393(1) ICTA 1988, trading loss can be carried forward and relieved against _____ of the same trade.

2. On cessation of trade, the carry back period is extended to _____ months.

3. Claim for relief under section 393(A) must be made within _____ of the accounting period in which the loss arose.

Answers to Quick Quiz

1. Future trading profit

2. 36

3. 2 years

Self Examination Questions

Question 1

Twins Ltd provides its financial results for the last three years:

	Year ended 31 March 2008 £	Year ended 31 March 2009 £	Year ended 31 March 2010 £
Trading profits	(30,000)	25,000	47,500
Property income	5,000	10,000	10,000
Income from loan relationship	2,000	2,000	2,000

The company knew that loss was a temporary situation. As a result, the company wanted to claim relief for trading loss under s 393(1).

Calculate its profits chargeable to corporation tax after relief under s 393(1).

Question 2

Power Ltd gives the following information for the year ended 31 March 2010.

	£
Trading income	(90,100)
Rental income	14,000
Non-trade interest	2,000
Chargeable gains	78,400

Assume that the company has made a claim for relief under s 393(A). The company has made gift aid donations totalling £5,000 during the year.

Show the calculation of PCTCT.

Question 3

Sparks Ltd is a UK resident company that commenced trading on 1 July 2008 as a producer of electrical accessories. The company's results for the nine-month period ended 31 March 2009 were as follows

	£
Trading profit	192,500
Income from loan relationship	6,500
Gift aid donations	(1,000)

The company's results for the year ended 31 March 2010 are as follows.

	£
Trading loss	175,000
Income from loan relationship	8,500
Chargeable gains	16,000

Calculate the chargeable profits of the company for both the accounting periods.

Question 4

Thunder Ltd is a manufacturer of ready-to-use electronic goods. The following information is available in respect of the year ended 30 September 2010.

Trading Loss

The trading loss is £85,000. (This amount is after taking account of capital allowances).

Property Income

Property income is £82,500. (This amount is after giving effect to rent receivable and bad debts).

Loan Interest Received

Loan interest of £10,000 was received on 30 June 2010, and £4,500 was accrued on 30 September 2010. The loan was made for non-trading purposes.

Calculate the company's chargeable profits assuming that the company claims relief for its trading loss against total profits under section 393(A) ICTA 1988.

Question 5

Toss Ltd has the following results for the accounting period ended 30 June 2009.

	£
Trading loss	(41,200)
Bank interest	15,000
Chargeable gains	30,000
Gift aid donation	2,000

Assuming Toss Ltd made a claim for loss relief under section 393(A), calculate the company's PCTCT for the year.

Question 6

During the accounting period ended on 31 March 2010 Music Ltd incurred a trading loss of £10,000. If the company wants to make a claim for relief under section 393(A), by which date should the company make this claim?

Answers to Self Examination Questions

Answer 1

Calculation of PCTCT after relief under s393(1)

	Year ended 31 March 2008 £	Year ended 31 March 2009 £	Year ended 31 March 2010 £
Trading profits	-	25,000	47,500
Less: Relief under s393(1)	-	(25,000)	(5,000)
	-	-	42,500
Property income	5,000	10,000	10,000
Income from loan relationship	2,000	2,000	2,000
PCTCT	**7,000**	**12,000**	**54,500**

Working

W1 Loss memorandum

Accounting periods		£
Year ended 31 March 2008	Loss for the year	30,000
Year ended 31 March 2009	Loss set off	(25,000)
	Balance	5,000
Year ended 31 March 2010	Loss set off	(5,000)
	Balance	-

Answer 2

	Year ended 31 March 2010 £
Trading profit	-
Less: Trading loss brought forward	-
	-
Property income	14,000
Income from loan relationship	2,000
Chargeable gains	78,400
	94,400
Less: Current year loss relief 393(A)	(90,100)
Less: Carry back loss relief 393(A)	-
	4,300
Gift aid donation	(4,300)
PCTCT	**-**

Note:

The company was able to relieve the gift aid donations of £4,300. The remaining amount of £700 (£5,000 – £4,300) cannot be relieved.

Answer 3

	Period ended 31 March 2009 £	Year ended 31 March 2010 £
Trading profit	192,500	
Income from loan relationship	6,500	8,500
Capital gain	-	16,000
	199,000	24,500
Less: Loss relief u/s 393(A)	(150,500)	(24,500)
	48,500	-
Less: Gift aid donations	(1,000)	
PCTCT	**47,500**	

Working

W1 Loss memorandum

		£
Year ended 31 March 2010	Loss incurred	175,000
Year ended 31 March 2010	Less: Current year relief s393(A)	(24,500)
	Balance	**150,500**
Period ended 31 March 2009	Less: Carry back relief s393(A)	(150,500)
	Balance carried forward to be set off under sec 393(1)	**-**

Answer 4

Thunder Ltd

Calculation of chargeable profits for the year ended 30 September 2010.

	£
Property income	82,500
Income from loan relationship (£10,000 + £4,500)	14,500
	97,000
Less: current year loss relief u/s 393A	(85,000)
PCTCT	**12,000**

Answer 5

	£
Income from loan relationship	15,000
Chargeable gains	30,000
Total profits (note)	**45,000**
Less: Relief under s393(A)	(41,200)
Balance	**3,800**
Less: Gift aid donations	(2,000)
PCTCT	**1,800**

Note: For set off of trading loss under section 393(A), total profit should be considered before deducting charges.

Answer 6

Music Ltd had incurred a trading loss during the accounting period ended on 31 March 2010. As the company wants to set off its loss under s393(A), the company should make an election for loss relief within two years from the end of the accounting period (i.e. 31 March 2010) during which the company incurred the loss. Hence, the company should make this claim up to 31 March 2012.

SECTION D: CORPORATION TAX LIABILITIES

D3

STUDY GUIDE D3: THE COMPREHENSIVE COMPUTATION OF CORPORATION TAX LIABILITY

Get Through Intro

As we discussed earlier, a company's trading and other income are charged to corporation tax under different headings. After ascertaining a company's chargeable profits for an accounting period, the next step is to calculate the actual corporation tax liability for that period.

In this Study Guide, we will see how to carry out a complete corporation tax calculation. We will look at how to consolidate the different elements and consider the deductions to be made in calculating a company's corporation tax liability.

Learning Outcomes

a) Compute the corporation tax liability and apply marginal relief.
b) Explain the implications of receiving franked investment income.
c) Explain how exemptions and reliefs can defer or minimise corporation tax liabilities.

D3.2: Corporation Tax Liabilities

Introduction

Case Study

Superb Ltd manufactures personal computers.

In the year ended on 31 March 2010 it has earned trading profits of £290,000, property income of £25,000, dividend income of £12,000 and chargeable gains of £15,000.

The company is of the view that all the above-mentioned income will be chargeable to tax at different rates.

The company approaches you to calculate its tax liability for the year ended 31 March 2010.

The calculation of the tax liability of Superb Ltd shall be done taking into consideration the corporation tax rate applicable to the income streams and also the marginal relief which is available.

This Study Guide will guide you through the calculation of corporation tax liability.

---

1. Compute the corporation tax liability and apply marginal relief.[2]
Explain the implications of receiving franked investment income.[2]
[Learning outcomes a and b]

1.1 Tax rates applicable to Corporation Tax

The rate of corporation tax for the companies is determined on the basis of the financial year i.e. from 1 April to 31 March of the following year and not on the basis of tax years (6 April to the following 5 April) as for individuals. The rate of corporation tax to be applied also depends upon the profits of the company. Profits of the company here mean PCTCT and franked investment income (FII) added together (discussed in detail in Learning Outcome 2 of this Study Guide). FII is added only to determine the rate of corporation tax applicable. The rate of tax determined accordingly is then applied to PCTCT.

According to the Finance Act 2009, the rates of corporation tax for the companies for the financial year ended on 31 March 2010 are as follows.

1. **The small companies' rate:** this rate is applicable to companies with profits not exceeding the lower limit (which is £300,000 for FY 2009). **Tax at the small companies' rate is charged at 21% for FY 2009**

2. **Full rate:** this rate applies to companies whose profits are more than the upper limit (i.e. £1,500,000 for FY 2009). **Tax at the full rate is charged at 28% for FY 2009.**

3. **Marginal relief:** this is available to companies whose profits do not exceed the upper limit but are more than the lower limit. The upper limit for FY 2009 is £1,500,000. Hence, for the companies whose **profits lie between £300,000 and £1,500,000**, the tax rate is applicable at the full rate, but the tax liability is reduced by marginal relief. Marginal relief is explained in detail later in this Study Guide.

Let us summarise the **tax rates** for the financial year ended on 31 March 2010.

Diagram 1: Tax rates

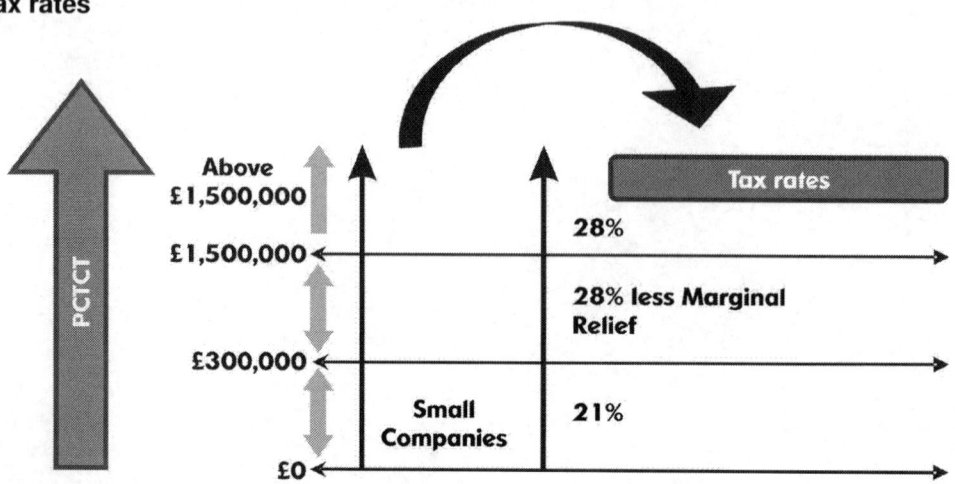

Test Yourself 1

The chargeable profits of three companies for the FY 2009 are given below. The three companies are not associated.

Company	Chargeable profits (£)
Jasmine Ltd	3,562,350
Orchids Ltd	1,242,400
Marigold Ltd	215,900

Required:

State at which rate the corporation tax will be calculated for each of these companies.

1.2 Franked investment income

Dividends received by a company from a UK company are exempt from corporation tax. However, these are added to PCTCT to find out the profits of the company for determining the rate of corporation tax applicable.

Therefore, the term franked investment income (FII) is used to refer to the UK dividends received by a company, together with the notional 10% tax credits. Hence, dividends need to be grossed up by multiplying them by 100/90 for calculation purposes.

Dividends received from other UK companies are paid out of the profits on which the corporation tax has already been paid. Therefore, to avoid double taxation, such dividends are **not included in the chargeable profits of the receiving company.**

The treatment of dividends received from an overseas company has been changed by the Finance Act 2009. Previously, these dividends were not exempt from the UK corporation tax and hence were not included in franked investment income. But from now onwards, according to Finance Act 2009, **the dividends received from an overseas company will be exempt from corporation tax and hence will be included in FII.** However, the overseas dividends received from any company from the same group (group provisions are discussed in detail in Study Guide D4) are not included in the franked investment income.

Hence, the dividends received from associated companies whether a UK company, or an overseas company, is not included in FII.

> **Tip** It is very important to note here that even though franked investment income is not charged to corporation tax, the FII received by a company is taken into account when determining the rate at which the company is liable to pay the tax.

1.3 Marginal relief

A company's corporation tax liability is reduced by an amount known as "marginal relief" if the company's profits fall between the small companies rate's lower and upper limits (i.e. tax liability is calculated at the full rate less marginal relief).

The following formula is applied to calculate marginal relief for the financial year ended 31 March 2010.

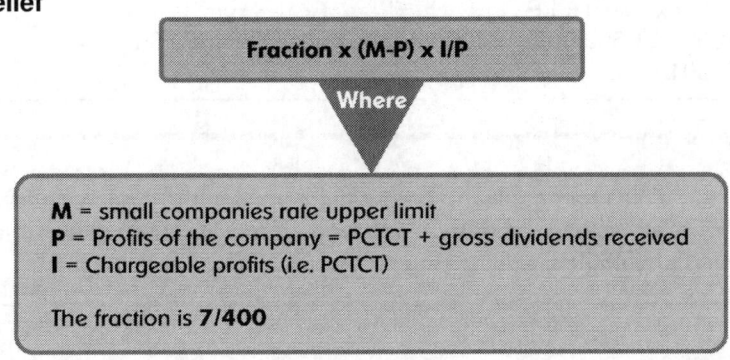

Diagram 2: Marginal relief

$$\text{Fraction} \times (M-P) \times I/P$$

Where

M = small companies rate upper limit
P = Profits of the company = PCTCT + gross dividends received
I = Chargeable profits (i.e. PCTCT)

The fraction is **7/400**

Important

Marginal rate: The rate of tax on each incremental £ of profits

£		£
1,500,000 (upper limit)	@ 28%	420,000
(300,000) (lower limit)	@ 21%	(63,000)
1,200,000		**357,000**

Hence, the effective tax rate at marginal rate is (£357,000/£1,200,000) x 100 = 29.75%

Example

The chargeable profits of Sweet Ltd for the year ended 31 March 2009 are £57,500. As the profits are less than £300,000 (lower limit), the tax is assessable at the small companies rate, which is 21%.
Hence, the corporation tax liability of Sweet Ltd is £57,500 x 21% = £12,075

The chargeable profits of Candy Ltd for the year ended 31 March 2009 are £2,357,500. As the profits are more than £1,500,000 (upper limit), the tax is assessable at the full rate, which is 28%.
Hence, the corporation tax liability of Candy Ltd is £2,357,500 x 28% = £660,100

Example

The chargeable profits of Sun Ltd for the year ended on 31 March 2010 are £450,000. Dividends received from UK companies for the year were £10,000. Sun Ltd has also received overseas dividends of £7,280.

Calculation of profits of Sun Ltd for the year ended 31 March 2010 is as follows.

	£
PCTCT (I)	450,000
FII [(£10,000 + £7,280) x 100/90]	19,200
Profits (P)	**469,200**

As the profits of £469,200 are less than the upper limit of the small companies rate (£1,500,000 for FY 2009-10) and is more than £300,000 (lower limit for small companies rate for FY 2009-10), the tax is assessable at 28% less marginal relief.

Hence, the corporation tax liability for Sun Ltd is calculated as follows.

	£
(£450,000 x 28%)	126,000
Less: Marginal relief (W1)	(17,301)
Corporation tax liability	**108,699**

Note: FII is added only to determine the rate of corporation tax applicable. The rate of tax determined accordingly is then applied to PCTCT.

Working

W1 Marginal relief = Fraction x (M-P) x I/P
= 7/400 x (£1,500,000 – £469,200) x £450,000/£469,200
= £17,301

Test Yourself 2

ABC Ltd has profits of £297,200 chargeable to corporation tax for the year ended 31 March 2010. Total dividends received for the year include dividends received from UK companies amounting to £8,000 and overseas dividend amounting to £5,680. Calculate the corporation tax liability.

1.4 The upper and lower limits are reduced if:

a) the accounting period is **less than 12 months**

Example Jackson Ltd commenced trading on 1 July 2009 and made up its first accounts to 31 March. As the company's accounting period is 9 months (1 July 09 to 31 March 10) i.e. less than 12 months, the small companies rate lower and upper limit will be reduced proportionately (for Jackson Ltd as below).

Small companies rate's lower limit will be £300,000 x 9/12 = £225,000
Small companies rate's upper limit will be £1,500,000 x 9/12 = £1,125,000

b) if the company has associated companies (explained in detail in Learning Outcome 1, Study Guide D4)

Example **Continuing the previous example of Jackson Ltd**

Assume in the above example that Jackson Ltd has two associated companies.
In this case the small companies rate's lower and upper limits are divided among all the three associated companies as follows:

Small companies rate's lower limit will be £225,000/3 = £75,000
Small companies rate's upper limit will be £1,125,000/3 = £375,000

1.5 Long period of accounts

As discussed earlier, an accounting period can never exceed 12 months. Then how should the taxable profits of the company be calculated if it has prepared its accounts for a period exceeding 12 months?

In such cases the company is required to divide its period of accounts into two or more accounting periods and for each such period, the profit chargeable to corporation tax is to be calculated and tax liability has to be assessed. A company's profits for a long period of account are usually allocated between the accounting periods as follows:

a) **Adjusted trading profits** before capital allowances are usually apportioned on a **time basis**. Capital allowances are then allowed for each accounting period separately. **WDAs and AIAs need to be time-apportioned** for the short accounting period.

b) **Property income** is usually apportioned on a **time basis**.

c) A net credit on a **non-trading loan relationship** is generally allocated on an **accrual basis** between the accounting periods.

d) The **chargeable gains** are allocated to the **accounting period** in which the **asset giving rise to such gains** is **disposed of**.

e) **Gift aid donations** are allocated to the period in which they are **actually paid**.

f) **Dividends received from other UK companies** are allocated to the **accounting period** in which they are **received** as this is important while determining the rate at which corporation tax is to be paid by the company.

Tip A long period of account must be split into two accounting periods.
The first accounting period is always twelve months long. The rest of the period of account forms the second accounting period.

1.6 Accounting period straddles 31 March

If the accounting period of the company straddles 31 March, then the accounting period will fall into two financial years. If the corporation tax rates, the marginal relief fraction or the lower limit and the upper limit of the companies are different for the two financial years, then the corporation tax liability has to be calculated for each financial year separately.

Important

The corporation tax information will be given in the exams as follows:

Financial Year	2007	2008	2009
Small Companies rate	20%	21%	21%
Full rate	30%	28%	28%
Lower limit	£300,000	£300,000	£300,000
Upper limit	£1,500,000	£1,500,000	£1,500,000
Marginal relief fraction	1/40	7/400	7/400

Example

Forward Ltd has profits of £540,000 chargeable to corporation tax for the year ended 31 October 2009. Dividends received from UK companies for the year were £36,000.

Profits of Forward Ltd for the year ended 31 October 2009 are as follows:

	£
PCTCT	540,000
FII (£36,000 x 100/90)	40,000
Profits	**580,000**

As the profit of £580,000 is between the upper limit and the lower limit of the small companies, marginal relief will be available.

As the accounting period of the company straddles 31 March 2009, the accounting period is to be divided according to the financial year. The period from 1 November 2008 to 31 March 2009 (5 months) will fall in the financial year 2008 and the period from 1 April 2009 to 31 October 2009 (7 months) will fall in the financial year 2009. The corporation tax rates will be applied accordingly.

Hence, the corporation tax liability for Forward Ltd is calculated as follows

	£	£
Financial Year 2008		
(£540,000 x 5/12) = £225,000 x 28%	63,000	
Less: Marginal relief (W1)	6,246	56,754
Financial Year 2009		
(£540,000 x 7/12) = £315,000 x 28%	88,200	
Less: Marginal relief (W2)	8,744	79,456
Corporation tax liability		**136,210**

Workings

W1 FY 2008
Marginal relief = 7/400 x (£1,500,000 – £580,000) x £540,000/ £580,000 x 5/12 = £6,246

W2 FY 2009
Marginal relief = 7/400 x (£1,500,000 – £580,000) x £540,000/ £580,000 x 7/12 = £8,744

Note:

The accounting period of the company crosses two financial years but as the corporation tax rates and limits are same for both the financial years, the computation can also be done simply as follows

	£
(£540,000 x 28%)	151,200
Less: Marginal relief	
7/400 x (£1500,000 – £580,000) x £540,000/£580,000	(14,990)
Corporation tax liability	**136,210**

Test Yourself 3

Boo Ltd makes up its accounts for 18 months to 31 March 2010. The company's results for this period of account are as follows (all figures are gross):

	£
Adjusted trading profits (before capital allowance)	549,000
Property income	180,000
Non-trade loan interest receivable:	
Received on 31 July 2009	1,800
Received on 31 January 2010	1,800
Accrued to 30th June 2010	1,500
Chargeable gains:	
Disposal on 12 March 2009	1,200
Disposal on 15 September 2009	6,900
Disposal on 2 March 2010	12,200
Gift aid donations	
Paid on 30 June 2009	2,500
Paid on 30 September 2009	2,500
Accrued to 31 March 2010	2,500
Loan interest receivable relates to a £36,000 loan made on 1 November 2008 at 10%	

Required:

Calculate Boo Ltd's profits chargeable to corporation tax (PCTCT) for the above periods.

Test Yourself 4

The accounts of Truth Ltd showed the following results for the year ended 31 March 2010. Calculate the corporation tax liability for this period.

	£
Income from UK trade	243,000
UK trade losses brought forward	102,000
Income from land situated in the UK	100,000
Chargeable gains	158,000
Bank interest income	
(Accrued during the year to 31/03/10)	92,000
Donations to UK charities	10,000

Test Yourself 5

Tough Ltd commenced trading on 1 April 2009 as a manufacturer of tools, preparing its first accounts for the nine-month period ended 31 December 2009. The following information is available:

Trading profit

Trading profit is £212,000. This figure is before taking account of capital allowances and any deduction arising from the premium paid in respect of leasehold property.

Leasehold property

On 1 April 2009, Tough Ltd acquired two leasehold office buildings. In each case, a premium of £60,000 was paid for the grant of a twenty-year lease. The first office building was used for business purposes by Tough Ltd throughout the period ended 31 December 2009. The second office building was empty until 30 September 2009, and was then sub-let to a tenant. On that date, Tough Ltd received a premium of £40,000 for the grant of a five-year lease, and annual rent of £12,400 which was payable in advance.

Continued on next page

D3.8: Corporation Tax Liabilities

Loan interest received

Loan interest of £8,000 was received on 30 September 2009, and £4,000 was accrued at 31 December 2009. The loan was made for non-trading purposes.

Dividends received

During the period ended 31 December 2009, Tough Ltd received dividends of £14,400 from Rough Ltd, an unconnected UK company. This figure is the actual cash amount received.

Gift aid donation

A gift aid donation of £5,000 was made on 31 May 2009.

Other information

Tough Ltd has two associated companies.

Required:

Calculate Tough Ltd's corporation tax liability for the nine-month period ended 31 December 2009. Ignore capital allowances.

Test Yourself 6

Apple Ltd has always made up its accounts to 31 December, but has decided to change its accounting date to 31 March. The company's results for the fifteen-month period ended 31 March 2010 are as follows:

1. Trading profit as adjusted for taxation is £220,000. This figure is before taking account of capital allowances.
2. On 1 January 2009, the written down value of plant and machinery was £32,000. Apple Ltd purchased office equipment for £17,000 on 15 January 2010. Assume that the new rules according to Finance Act 2009 have always applied.
3. There is a property income of £43,000 for the fifteen-month period ended 31 March 2010.
4. On 15 April 2009, the company disposed of some investments, and this resulted in a chargeable gain of £29,300. On 18 February 2010, the company made a further disposal, and this resulted in a capital loss of £4,400.
5. Franked investment income of £20,000 (gross) was received on 10 September 2009.
6. A gift aid donation of £5,000 was made on 31 March 2010.

As at 1 January 2009, Apple Ltd had unused trading losses of £15,300 and unused capital losses of £2,000. Apple Ltd has no associated companies.

Required:

Calculate Apple Ltd's corporation tax liabilities in respect of the fifteen-month period ended 31 March 2010.

> **2. Explain how exemptions and reliefs can defer or minimise corporation tax liabilities.**[2]
> **[Learning outcome c]**

2.1 Timing of capital disposals

If the disposal of a capital asset is expected to realise a gain, care should be taken regarding the date of disposal.

1. Disposal near the end of an accounting period means that profits will be increased by the gain. The company needs to consider if this will increase its profits leading to a higher rate of corporation tax.

2. If the gain is delayed into next accounting period, the company should consider the likely rate of tax. Also, from a timing point of view, tax on gain will be paid 12 months later.

If the asset is expected to realise a loss, then it should be disposed of as soon as possible in order to use the capital loss against any capital gains already realised.

2.2 Choice of loss reliefs

Points to consider:

1. Rate of corporation tax at which relief will be obtained: aim to relieve at 29.75%, then 28% then 21%.

2. Cash flow considerations: s393A will mean a reduction of the current liability and a repayment of the liability of the previous 12 months.
   s393(1) means a reduction in a future liability.

3. Extent to which relief for gift aid will be lost.

Rate of tax saved is the most important consideration.

In addition, a company with losses should consider claiming less than the maximum amount of capital allowances. If a s393(A) claim is to be made, and the current rate of tax is 21%, though it is expected to be 28% in the future, then a reduced claim for CAs means a higher TWDV to carry forward, and higher CAs in future years. This means that CAs will be relieved at a higher rate.

2.3 Rollover relief

If a business asset is disposed of (land and buildings or fixed plant and machinery) and a new asset is to be purchased, care should be taken to ensure the reinvestment is in the period 12 months before the disposal or 36 months after the disposal. This ensures that the gain can be rolled over, providing all the proceeds are reinvested.

Answers to Test Yourself

Answer 1

Jasmine Ltd (Note 1)	28%
Orchids Ltd (Note 2)	28% less Marginal Relief
Marigold Ltd (Note 3)	21%

Note:

1. The profits are more than small companies rate upper limit.
2. The profits lie between small companies rate lower and upper limit.
3. The profits are less than small companies rate lower limit.

Answer 2

	£
Profits chargeable to corporation tax	297,200
Add: Dividend (£8000 + £5,680) x 100/90	15,200
Profit 'P'	**312,400**

Note:

1. As the profits are above £300,000 but below £1,500,000 the tax rate applicable is **28% less marginal relief.**

2. Dividends received (both UK dividends and overseas dividends) are not taxable but are added to total profits to arrive at the 'P' figure and to decide the applicable tax rate.

Calculation of corporation tax liability

	£
Corporation tax (£297,200 x 28%)	83,216
Less: Marginal relief (W1)	(19,772)
Corporation tax liability	**63,444**

D3.10: Corporation Tax Liabilities

Working

W1 Marginal relief = Fraction x (M-P) x I/P
= 7/400 x (£1,500,000 - £312,400) x £297,200/£312,400
= £19,772

Answer 3

A long period of account must be split into two accounting periods. The first accounting period is always twelve months long. The rest of the period of account forms the second accounting period.

Therefore, there are two accounting periods: the year to 30 September 2009 and the six months to 31 March 2010. The chargeable profits of Boo Ltd for each accounting period are as follows:

	12 months to 30/09/09 £	6 months to 31/03/10 £
Trading profits (12:6) (note 1)	366,000	183,000
Property income (12:6)	120,000	60,000
Income from loan relationship (note 2)	3,300	1,800
Chargeable gains (note 3)	8,100	12,200
	497,400	257,000
Less: Gift aid donations (note 4)	(5,000)	-
PCTCT	**492,400**	**257,000**

Notes:

1. Trading profits before capital allowances and property incomes are apportioned on a time basis.

2. The loan interest is allocated on an accrual basis. Interest accruing on £36,000 per month @ 10% is £300 (£36,000/12 x10%).

   Loan interest accrued for 11 months from 1 November 2008 to 30 September 2009 is £3,300 and for 6 months to 31 March 2010 is £1,800.

3. The chargeable gains are allocated to the accounting period in which the asset giving rise to such gains is disposed of.

   Chargeable gains on asset disposed on 12 March 2009 and on 15 September 2009 fall within the 12 months to 30 September 2009.

   Chargeable gains on asset disposed on 2 March 2010 falls within the next accounting period i.e. the 6 months to 31 March 2010.

4. Gift aid donations are allocated to the period in which they are actually paid. The charges accrued on 31 March 2010 are ignored for now but will be taken into consideration when calculating the chargeable profits of the subsequent accounting period in which they are paid.

Answer 4

	£	£
Trading Profits	243,000	
Less: Brought forward trading losses	(102,000)	141,000
Property income		100,000
Income from loan relationship		92,000
Chargeable gains		158,000
		491,000
Less: Gift aid donation		(10,000)
Profits chargeable to corporation tax (PCTCT)		**481,000**
Tax on PCTCT (£481,000 x 28%)		134,680
Less: Marginal Relief		
7/400 x (£1,500,000 - £481,000) x £481,000/£481,000		(17,833)
Corporation Tax Liability for the period		**116,847**

Note:

Donations to UK Charities are deductible as gift aid donations.

Answer 5

	£	£
Trading Profits	212,000	
Less: Deduction for lease premium (W1)	(1,395)	210,605
Property income (W2)		30,600
Income from loan relationship (W3)		12,000
		253,205
Less: Gift aid donation		(5,000)
Profits chargeable to corporation tax (PCTCT)		248,205
Add: Franked investment income (£14,400 x100/90)		16,000
Profit		264,205
Corporation tax liability for the period		
Tax on PCTCT (£248,205 x 28%)		69,497
Less: Marginal relief (W4)		(1,821)
Corporation tax liability for the period		67,676

Workings

W1 Deduction for lease premium

1. The first office building has been used for business purposes, and so a proportion of the lease premium assessed on the landlord can be deducted.

2. The amount assessed on the landlord is £37,200 calculated as follows:

	£
Premium received	60,000
Less: £60,000 x (2% x (20 - 1))	(22,800)
	37,200

3. This is deductible over the life of the lease, so the deduction for the nine-month period ended 31 December 2009 is £1,395 (£37,200/20 = £1,860 x 9/12).

W2 Property income

	£
Premium received for sub-lease	40,000
Less: £40,000 x (2% x (5 - 1))	(3,200)
	36,800
Less: Relief for premium paid for head lease £37,200 (W1) x 5 (duration of sub-lease)/20 (duration of head lease)	(9,300)
Premium treated as rent	27,500
Add: Rent receivable (£12,400 x 3/12)	3,100
Property income	30,600

W3 Loan interest

	£
Interest received on 30 September 2009	8,000
Interest accrued at 31 December 2009	4,000
Income from loan relationship	**12,000**

W4 Marginal relief = Fraction x (M-P) x I/P
= 7/400 (£375,000 – £264,205) x £248,205/£264,205
= £1,821

1. The profit of £264,205 for 9 months falls between the small companies rate's lower and upper limit. These limits are calculated as follows:
   (£300,000 x 9/12) = £225,000
   (£1,500,000 x 9/12) = £1,125,000

   Hence, tax rate applicable is 28% less marginal relief.

2. The small companies rate's upper limit is then further reduced to £375,000 (£1,125,000/3) as Tough Ltd has two associated companies (refer to Study Guide D4).

Note: The franked investment income is considered to determine the applicable tax rate. But actual tax liability is calculated on PCTCT.

Answer 6

	Year ended 31/12/09 £	Period ended 31/3/10 £
Trading profits (W1)	176,000	44,000
Capital allowances (W2)	(6,400)	(15,580)
	169,600	**28,420**
Less: Loss relief s393	(15,300)	
	154,300	28,420
Property income (W3)	34,400	8,600
Capital gains (£29,300 – £2,000)	27,300	
	216,000	37,020
Less: Gift aid donation (Note 2)		(5,000)
PCTCT	216,000	32,020
Add: Franked investment income	20,000	
Profit	236,000	32,020
Corporation tax liability (Note 3)		
Financial Year 2008 (Note 4)		
(£216,000 x 3/12) = £54,000 at 21%)	11,340	
Financial Year 2009		
(£216,000 x 9/12) = £162,000 at 21%	34,020	
(£32,020 at 21%)(Note 5)		6,724
Corporation tax liability	**45,360**	**6,724**

Workings

W1

Trading profits are allocated on a time basis: £176,000 (£220,000 x 12/15) to the year ended 31 December 2009 and £44,000 (£220,000 x 3/15) to the period ended 31 March 2009.

W2

Separate capital allowance calculations are prepared for each accounting period as follows.

	FYA £	General Pool £	Allowances £
Year ended 31 December 2009			
TWDV b/f		32,000	
Less: WDA @ 20%		(6,400)	6,400
TWDV c/f		**25,600**	
Allowances			**6,400**
Period ended 31 March 2010			
TWDV b/f		25,600	
Less: WDA @ 20% for 3 months		(1,280)	1,280
Additions qualifying AIA:			
Office equipment	17,000		
Less: AIA	(12,500)		12,500
	4,500		
Less: FYA 40%	(1,800)	2,700	1,800
TWDV c/f		**42,380**	
Allowances			**15,580**

Expenditure incurred by any business on plant and machinery (with the exception of cars) is eligible for AIA up to £50,000. However, AIA is scaled up or down according to the length of the accounting period.

Hence, AIA for the period ended 31 March 2010 is £12,500 (£50,000 x 3/12)

WDA is also scaled up or down according to the length of the accounting period.

The balance, if any, is eligible for FYA at the rate of 40% for the expenditure incurred during the period from 1 April 2009 to 31 March 2010.

W3

Property incomes are allocated on a time basis: £34,400 (£43,000 x 12/15) to the year ended 31 December 2009 and £8,600 (£43,000 x 3/15) to the period ended 31 March 2010.

Notes:

1. The capital loss of £4,400 for the period ended 31 March 2010 is carried forward.

2. Gift aid donations are allocated to the period in which they are actually paid.

3. In each case, the franked investment income is considered to determine the applicable tax rate. But actual tax liability is calculated on profits without considering franked investment income.

4. As the accounting period of the company for the year ended 31 December 2009 straddles 31 March 2009, the accounting period is to be divided according to the financial year. The period from 1 January 2009 to 31 March 2009 (3 months) will fall in the financial year 2008 and the period from 1 April 2009 to 31 December 2009 (9 months) will fall in the financial year 2009. The corporation tax rates will be applied accordingly.

5. The period ended 31 March 2010 is three months long so the small companies tax rate limit is reduced to £75,000 (£300,000 x 3/12). Profits for the period ended 31 March 2010 are below this limit, so the tax rate applicable is 21%.

D3.14: Corporation Tax Liabilities

Quick Quiz

1. What is franked investment income?

2. What is the treatment for franked investment income in a corporation tax calculation?

3. PQR Ltd's results for the year ended 31 March 2010 are summarised as follows:

	£
Profit chargeable to corporation tax	410,000
Dividend received from a UK company	27,000

Calculate PQR Ltd's corporation tax liability for the year ended 31 March 2010.

Answers to Quick Quiz

1. The UK dividends and overseas dividends received by a company, multiplied by 100/90, are known as franked investment income.

2. FII is not chargeable to corporation tax, however, the amount of FII plus chargeable profit is considered to determine the rate at which the company is liable to pay the tax.

3.

	£
Profit chargeable to corporation tax	410,000
Add: Franked investment income (£27,000 x 100/90) (note 2)	30,000
Profits	**440,000**
Corporation tax (£410,000 x 28%)	114,800
Less: Marginal relief: 7/400 x (£1,500,000 – £440,000) x £410,000/£440,000	(17,285)
Corporation Tax Liability	**97,515**

Notes:

1. Dividend from associated companies is not included in the profit for calculating CT liability.
2. UK dividends received (franked investment income) are grossed up by multiplying by 100/90.

Self Examination Questions

Question 1

The following information is given for four companies:

1. A Ltd has chargeable profits of £165,000 and UK dividends of £9,000.

2. C Ltd has chargeable profits of £5,000 and received UK dividends of £148.50.

3. D Ltd has chargeable profits of £1,800,000 and has received no UK dividends.

4. B Ltd has chargeable profits of £295,000 and overseas dividends of £13,500.

Assume that the companies prepare a set of accounts for the year to 31 March 2010 and that none of them have any associated companies.

Required:

Calculate the rate at which corporation tax is liable to be paid by each of these companies and also calculate the corporation tax liability in each case.

Question 2

Bright Ltd commenced trading on 1 October 2008, and its results for the 15-month period ending 31 December 2009 are summarised as follows.

	£
Trading profits	220,000
Chargeable gain in respect of disposal of shares on 9 November 2009	26,000
Franked investment income received on 16 October 2009	6,000

Calculate Bright Ltd's corporation tax liability in respect of the 15 month period ended 31 December 2009.

Answers to Self Examination Questions

Answer 1

	A Ltd £	C Ltd £	D Ltd £	B Ltd £
Chargeable profits	165,000	5,000	1,800,000	295,000
Franked investment income (Dividends + 10% notional tax credits)	10,000	165	0	15,000
Profits	**175,000**	**5,165**	**1,800,000**	**310,000**
Applicable tax rate	21%	21%	28%	28% less marginal relief

	A Ltd £	C Ltd £	D Ltd £	B Ltd £
Chargeable profits	165,000	5,000	1,800,000	295,000
Corporation tax liability				
£165,000 x 21%	34,650			
£5,000 x 21%		1,050		
£1,800,000 x 28%			504,000	
£295,000 x 28%				82,600
Less: Marginal relief (W1)				(19,817)
Corporation tax liability	**34,650**	**1,050**	**504,000**	**62,783**

Note:

In each case the franked investment income is considered to determine the applicable tax rate. But actual tax liability is calculated on profits without considering franked investment income.

Working

W1 Marginal relief = Fraction x (M-P) x I/P
= 7/400 x (£1,500,000 − £310,000) x £295,000/£310,000
= £19,817

Answer 2

	Year ended on 30 September 2009 £	3 months period ended on 31 December 2009 £
Trading profits (12:3) (Note 1)	176,000	44,000
Capital gain	-	26,000
PCTCT	176,000	70,000
Franked investment income	-	6,000
Profit	176,000	76,000
Corporation tax liability (Note 2)		
Financial Year 2008 (Note 3)		
(£176,000 x 6/12) = £88,000 at 21%	18,480	
Financial Year 2009		
(£176,000 x 6/12) = £88,000 at 21%	18,480	
(£70,000 at 28% less marginal relief) (Note 4)		14,781
Corporation tax liability	36,960	14,781

Notes:

1. Trading profits are allocated on a time basis: £176,000 (£220,000 x 12/15) to the year ended 30 September 2009 and £44,000 (£220,000 x 3/15) to the 3 month period ended on 31 December 2009.

2. Franked investment income is considered to determine the applicable tax rate. But actual tax liability is calculated on profits without considering franked investment income.

3. As the accounting period of the company for the year ended 30 September 2009 straddles 31 March 2009, the accounting period is to be divided according to the financial year. The period from 1 October 2008 to 31 March 2009 (6 months) will fall in the financial year 2008 and the period from 1 April 2009 to 30 September 2009 (6 months) will fall in the financial year 2009. The corporation tax rates will be applied accordingly.

4. The profits for the 3 month period ended 31 December 2009 are above the small companies lower rate limit. Small companies lower and upper rate limits are calculated as follows:

    Small companies rates lower limit for a 3 month period = £300,000 x 3/12 = £75,000
    Small companies rates upper limit for a 3 month period = £1,500,000 x 3/12 = £375,000

    Hence, the tax rate applicable for this 3 month period is 28% less marginal relief.

	£
Corporation tax (£70,000 x 28%)	19,600
Less: Marginal relief (7/400 x (£3,75,000 – £76,000) x £70,000/£76,000	(4,819)
Corporation tax liability	14,781

SECTION D: CORPORATION TAX LIABILITIES

D4

STUDY GUIDE D4: THE EFFECT OF A GROUP CORPORATE STRUCTURE FOR CORPORATION TAX PURPOSES

Get Through Intro

In today's global economy, many companies operate as a **group** where one main entity controls the operations of many other entities. **The financial position of the group as a whole** is relevant for the purpose of **calculating** the **tax liability of the individual companies that form the group.**

The group relief provisions enable the **losses** made by member companies to be **set off** against the **profits** of any other member companies of the group. These losses should be set off in a manner which will **minimise the tax liabilities** of all the individual member companies.

In this Study Guide we shall discuss the effect of a group corporate structure for the purpose of determining corporation tax, and introduce you to the group relief provisions which help in effective tax planning. It also deals with the principles of transfer pricing.

Learning Outcomes

a) Define an associated company and recognise the effect of being an associated company for corporation tax purposes.
b) Define a 75% group, and recognise the reliefs that are available to the members of such a group.
c) Define a 75% capital gains group, and recognise the reliefs that are available to members of such a group.
d) Compare the UK tax treatment of an overseas branch to an overseas subsidiary.
e) Calculate double taxation relief for withholding tax and underlying tax.
f) Explain the basic principles of the transfer pricing rules.

D4.2: Corporation Tax Liabilities

Introduction

Case Study

Merlin Ltd holds 80% of the shares in Marvin Ltd. Marvin Ltd sold one of its major assets during the year and made a large chargeable gain.

Merlin Ltd had excess funds and it wanted to invest those funds in assets to increase the productivity of the company.

The managments of both the companies want to know whether there are any provisions whereby the tax on chargeable gains of Marvin Ltd can be minimised.

In this Study Guide, we will discuss the various provisions relating to groups of companies and try to find out whether there is any solution to this problem.

1. Define an associated company and recognise the effect of being an associated company for corporation tax purposes.[2]

[Learning outcome a]

1.1 What is an associated company?

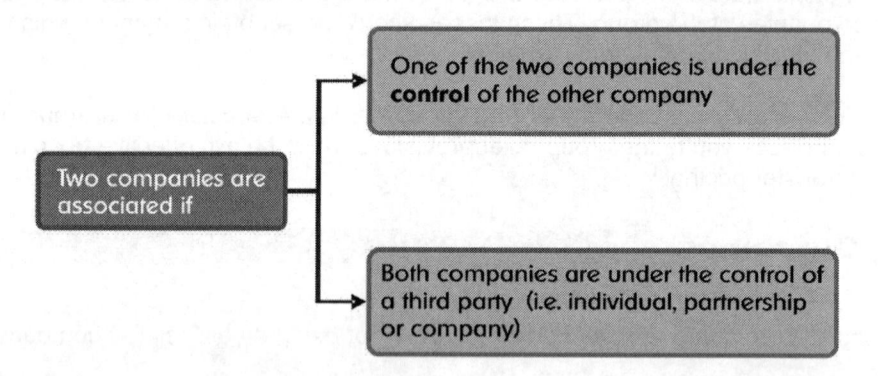

Two companies are associated if:
- One of the two companies is under the **control** of the other company
- Both companies are under the control of a third party (i.e. individual, partnership or company)

In other words, companies are associated when a person or group of persons can control both, either personally, or via their interests in other corporate shareholdings.

1.2 A company is said to be under control if any of the following conditions are fulfilled:

1. Ownership of over **50% of the company's issued share capital**
2. Ownership of over 50% of the company's voting rights
3. Entitlement to over 50% of the company's income, if it were all distributed.
4. Entitlement to over 50% of the company's assets, if the company were wound up.

1.3 Effects of being an associated company for corporation tax purposes

1. The upper and lower limits for the small companies' rate are **divided by the number of associated companies.**
2. Only **one annual investment allowance (AIA)** upto £50,000 is available for a group.
3. For calculating the company's profits, **inter group dividends are not considered as FII**.

These provisions are inserted as an anti-avoidance measure to restrict the separation of a big company into several smaller ones to take advantage.

Example Global Ltd has four associated companies. The small companies rates lower limit, which is £300,000 for FY 2009, will be divided among the five companies (Global Ltd and its four subsidiaries). Therefore each company will have a small companies' rate's lower limit of £60,000.The upper limit also will be equally divided among the five members of the group and it will be 1,500,000/5 = 300,000

Important The chart below makes it clear that the small companies' rate's upper and lower limits are equally divided among all associated companies.

No of companies in group	Small companies' rate's lower limit (for each Co)	Small companies' rate's upper limit (for each Co)
	£	£
1 (for individual company)	300,000	1,500,000
2	150,000	750,000
3	100,000	500,000
4	75,000	375,000
And so on	.	.

1.4 Points to be noted regarding association of the companies

1. An associated company should be considered as such, **even if it is an associated company for only part of an accounting period.**

Example Bigfoot Ltd prepares its accounts to 31 March every year. It held 60% shares of Lillyput Ltd until 31 December 2009 on which date all shares of Lillyput Ltd were sold. In this case, even though Bigfoot Ltd held shares of Lillyput Ltd for only part of the accounting period, Lillyput Ltd will be considered an associated company of Bigfoot Ltd for the whole of the accounting period ended 31 March 2010.

2. An associated company that is not in any trade or business at any time during that accounting period **(a dormant company) is to be ignored.**

3. Companies are considered to be associated even if they are **associated for different parts of the accounting period.**

Example Rose Ltd prepares its accounts to 31 December every year. It owns 90% shares in Orchids Ltd. Orchids Ltd purchased 60% shares in Lily Ltd in January 2009. In April 2009, these shares were sold and 70% of Marigold Ltd's shares were purchased.

Therefore, up to April 2009, Rose Ltd has two associated companies: Orchids Ltd (60% shareholding) and Lily Ltd (90% x 60% = 54% shareholding). From April 2009, Rose Ltd has two associated companies: Orchids Ltd and Marigold Ltd (90% x 70% = 63% shareholding).

However, for the accounting period ended 31 December 2009, Rose Ltd is considered to have three associated companies: Orchids Ltd, Lily Ltd and Marigold Ltd. Hence, the upper limit, lower limit and AIA will be divided equally among these four associated companies.

4. When **calculating 'profits'** for the purposes of determining the rate of corporation tax, **dividends from associated companies are excluded.**

Tip An overseas company (O/S Co) can also be an associated company.

SUMMARY

Associated companies

- **corporation tax purpose**
  - upper & lower limits for small companies' rate are divided by number of associated companies
  - only one AIA upto £50,000 is available for group
  - inter group dividends are not considered FII for calculating profits
- **considered as such even if**
  - associated for only part of an accounting period
  - associated for different parts of accounting period
- **dormant company** is to be ignored

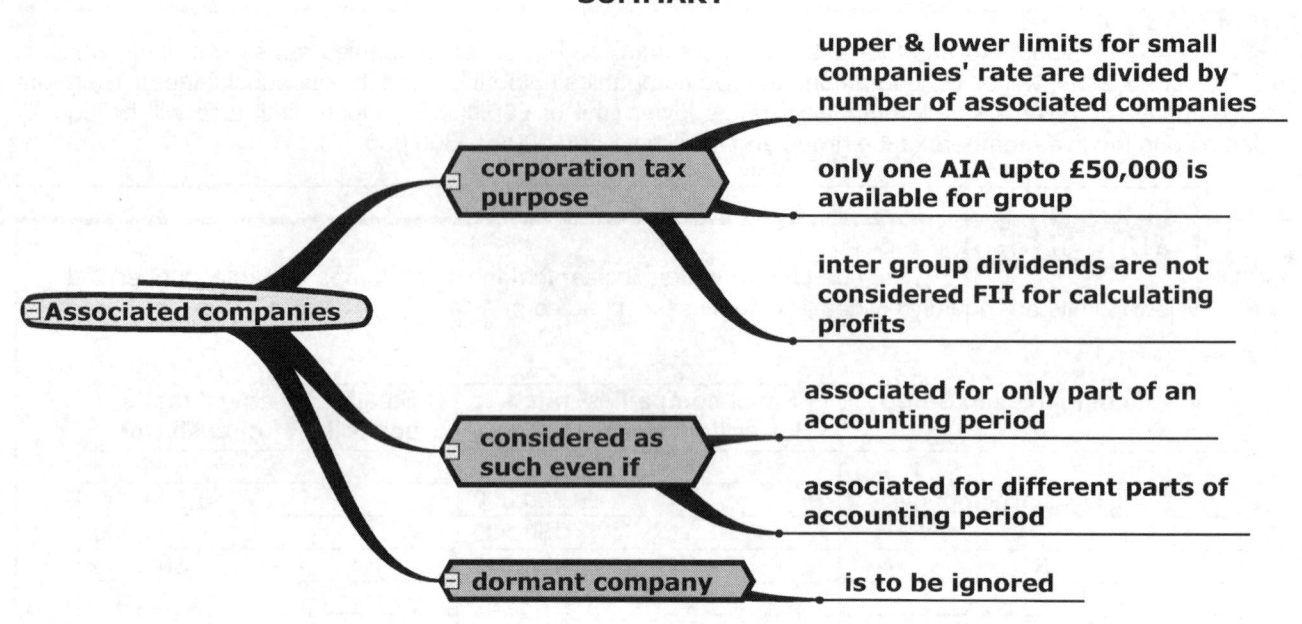

Diagram 1 : Associated companies

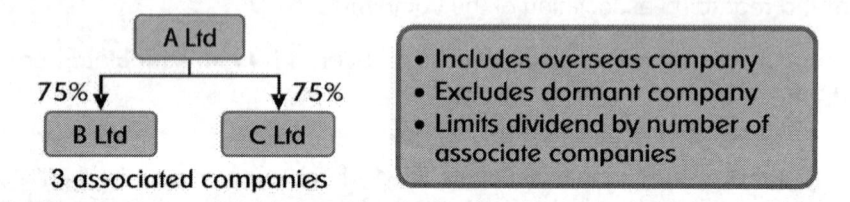

A Ltd
75% → B Ltd
75% → C Ltd

3 associated companies

- Includes overseas company
- Excludes dormant company
- Limits dividend by number of associate companies

Test Yourself 1

Country Ltd owns 70% of the shares of State Ltd and Division Ltd. State Ltd owns 60% of the shares of City Ltd. City Ld is an overseas company and Division Ltd is a dormant company. Country Ltd purchased shares in State Ltd on 31 December 2009. The accounting period of all the companies is the year ended on 31 March 2010.

Required:

Explain which of these companies are associated with one another in the year ended on 31 March 2010.

Test Yourself 2

King Ltd holds 90% shares of two companies: Giant Ltd and Big Ltd. Big Ltd holds 60% shares of two subsidiaries: Medium Ltd and Small Ltd. Small Ltd is dormant. The chargeable profits of King Ltd are £150,000 for the year ended 31 March 2010 and it has no franked investment income.

Required:

Calculate King Ltd's corporation tax liability for the period.

2. Define a 75% group, and recognise the reliefs that are available to the members of such a group.[2]

[Learning outcome b]

2.1 When are the two companies said to be in a group?

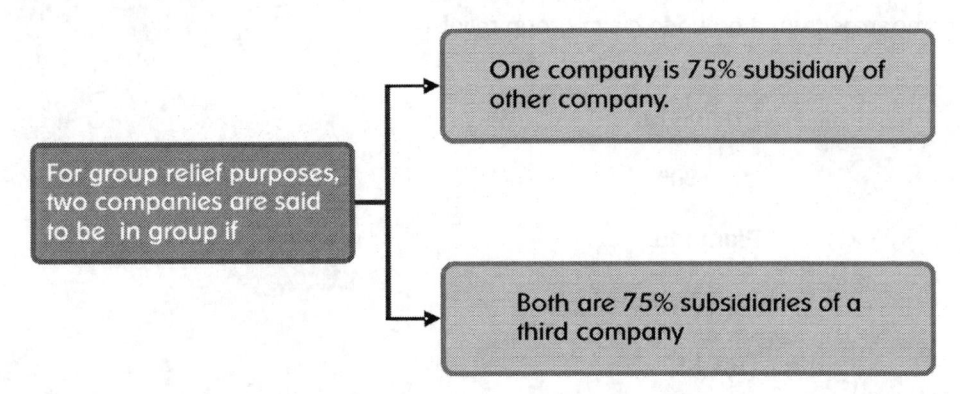

For group relief purposes, two companies are said to be in group if:
- One company is 75% subsidiary of other company.
- Both are 75% subsidiaries of a third company

A company is said to be a 75% subsidiary of another company when **all of** the following conditions are fulfilled:

1. At least 75% of the ordinary share capital of the subsidiary company is owned by the holding company **directly or indirectly**.

Example

Direct holding

Saga Ltd owns 85% of the issued share capital of Jana Ltd. As more than 75% shares of Jana Ltd are held by Saga Ltd, Jana Ltd is a 75% subsidiary of Saga Ltd.

Indirect holding

Saga Ltd owns 85% of the issued share capital of Jana Ltd and Jana Ltd owns 95% of the shares of Raga Ltd. Therefore, Saga Ltd indirectly holds 80.75% (85% x 95%) of the shares of Raga Ltd. Hence Raga Ltd is also a subsidiary of Saga Ltd.

2. The holding company is entitled to 75% of the distributable income of the subsidiary company.

Example

Net Ltd and Set Ltd are two companies. Net Ltd owns 80% of the share capital of Set Ltd. It means Net Ltd is entitled to more than 75% of the profit of Set Ltd. This signifies that Set Ltd is a 75% subsidiary of Net Ltd.

3. The holding company is entitled to at least 75% of the net assets of the subsidiary company on the winding up of the subsidiary.

Example

Mark Ltd has a claim to 80% of the assets of The Fine Art Ltd that has been liquidated recently. The major charge to the assets of The Fine Art Ltd is from Mark Ltd hence Mark Ltd exercises control over The Fine Art Ltd. Hence, The Fine Art Ltd is a 75% subsidiary of Mark Ltd for group relief purposes.

4. For the purpose of F6 examination, all the companies in the 75% group must be resident in the UK.

Important

> The effective interest of the holding company must be atleast 75% in all the companies in the group whether subsidiaries or sub-subsidiaries.
> The companies which form a group are eligible to claim group relief under group relief provisions.

Example

Branch Ltd holds 80% of the ordinary shares of Plant Ltd and Plant Ltd holds 75% of the shares of Tree Ltd.

Required:

Which of these companies form a group to claim group relief ?

Answer

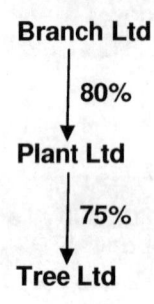

Branch Ltd
↓ 80%
Plant Ltd
↓ 75%
Tree Ltd

Branch Ltd	Holding
Plant Ltd	80%
Tree Ltd	60% (80% x 75%)

Associate companies

Branch Ltd, Plant Ltd and Tree Ltd are all associated companies as Branch Ltd (holding company) holds more than 50% shareholding in Plant Ltd and Tree Ltd. The lower and upper limit will be shared equally among these three members of the group (family).

75% group for loss relief

Group 1 (Branch Ltd and Plant Ltd): Branch Ltd and Plant Ltd are in 75% group but Tree Ltd is not in a group with Branch Ltd as the shareholding of Branch Ltd (holding company) in Tree Ltd is less than 75%. Therefore losses may be surrendered between Branch Ltd and Plant Ltd but it is not possible for Branch Ltd to surrender losses to Tree Ltd.

Group 2 (Plant Ltd and Tree Ltd): Tree Ltd is a 75% subsidiary of Plant Ltd and hence these two companies can also form a group to claim group relief to surrender their losses. However, Plant Ltd cannot claim group relief from Tree Ltd and pass it on to Branch Ltd.

Test Yourself 3

Branch Ltd holds 90% of the shares of Plant Ltd. Plant Ltd holds 90% of the shares of Tree Ltd. Tree Ltd owns 90% of the shares of Farm Ltd.

Required:

Which of these companies form a group to claim group relief?

2.2 Relief Available

1. **Group relief provisions are applicable** to members of a 75% group.

2. By applying group relief provisions, a company which is part of a 75% group can **transfer its trading losses** to other companies within the group. These losses can be set off against the taxable profits of the other companies in the group. Therefore, **the group's overall corporation tax liability reduces.**

3. The company surrendering its trading losses is termed the **"surrendering company"** and the company to whom the losses are surrendered is termed the **"claimant company"**.

The main items which may be surrendered are:
a) Trading losses
b) Property business losses
c) Gift aid payments
d) Non-trading loan interest and loan written off (i.e. non-trading loan deficit)
e) Excess management charges (in case of companies having only dividend income which are not taxable)

Capital losses realised by any company in the group **cannot be surrendered** for claiming group relief. Excess gift aid payments have to be surrendered before excess property business losses.

4. A surrender of losses may be from a holding company to a subsidiary company or vice versa or from a subsidiary company to a fellow subsidiary company.

5. Only the surrendering company's **losses for the current period** are **eligible for group relief**.

6. The losses must be **set off against** the **profits** of a **corresponding accounting period**. If the accounting periods of the claimant and surrendering company do not correspond exactly, then both profits and losses respectively have to be apportioned and the result of the overlapping period can only be set off.

7. The **losses surrendered** to a claimant company **cannot exceed the claimant company's PCTCT** for the **corresponding accounting period (AP)**.

   In other words, the maximum claim is the lower of:
   - the available loss or
   - the available PCTCT

   PCTCT for this purpose is considered after deducting current year and brought forward losses, and gift aid payments, whether they are actually claimed or not.

Diagram 2: Group of companies

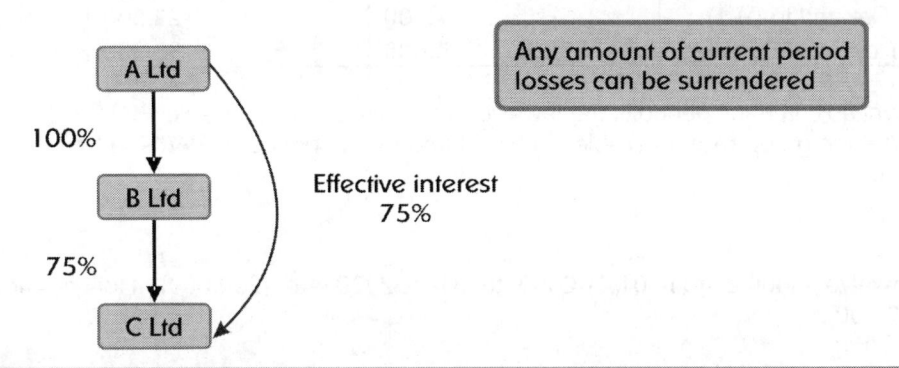

[Diagram: A Ltd owns 100% of B Ltd, which owns 75% of C Ltd. Effective interest of A Ltd in C Ltd is 75%. Note: Any amount of current period losses can be surrendered.]

Example

Fortune Ltd prepares its accounts annually to 31st December. It has trading losses of £80,000 for the year ended 31 December 2009. The company also has brought forward trading losses of £26,000.

Its holding company, Destiny Ltd (holding 80% of the share capital in Fortune Ltd) has trading profits of £95,000 for the year ended 31 December 2009 and brought forward trading losses of £32,000.

Required:

What is the amount of group relief that may be claimed?

Answer

As the accounting periods of Fortune Ltd and Destiny Ltd are same, the maximum group that can be claimed is the lower of:
- the available loss or
- the available PCTCT

Continued on next page

As only the current period losses can be surrendered, the available loss is £80,000 of Fortune Ltd.

The available PCTCT of Destiny Ltd is £63,000 (£95,000 - £32,000) after deducting b/f trading losses.

Hence, the maximum group relief that can be claimed is £63,000, i.e. lower of available loss or available PCTCT.

Fortune Ltd's unrelieved current year trading loss of £17,000 (£80,000 - £63,000) and brought forward trading loss of £26,000 can be carried forward to claim against the first available trading profits of the company.

Example

Cream Ltd prepares its accounts annually to 31st December. Its holding company, Cake Ltd (holding 80% of the share capital in Cream Ltd), prepares its accounts annually to 31st March. Their trading results are:

Cream Ltd
Loss up to 31/12/2009   £30,000

Cake Ltd

Profits up to 31/03/2009   £20,000
Profits up to 31/03/2010   £45,000

Required:

What is the amount of group relief that may be claimed?

As the accounting periods of Cream Ltd and Cake Ltd do not correspond, the profits and losses are required to be apportioned on a time basis:

	01/01/09 to 31/03/09 £	01/04/09 to 31/12/09 £
Available loss of Cream Ltd (W1)	7,500	22,500
Available PCTCT of Cake Ltd (W2)	5,000	33,750

The group relief available in each period is the lower of available loss or available PCTCT. Hence, for the period 01/01/09 to 31/03/09 the group relief available is £5,000 and for the period 01/04/09 to 31/12/09, the group relief available is £22,500.

W1 Cream Ltd

Total profits for twelve months from 01/01/2009 to 31/12/2009 are (£30,000). Hence, monthly profits are (£30,000)/12 = (£2,500).
Therefore, profits from:

01/01/2009 to 31/03/2009 (three months) = £2,500 x 3 = £7,500
01/04/2009 to 31/12/2009 (nine months) = £2,500 x 9 = £22,500

W2 Cake Ltd

Total profits for twelve months from 01/04/2008 to 31/03/2009 are £20,000. Therefore, profits from:

01/01/2009 to 31/03/2009 (three months) = £20,000 x 3/12 = £5,000

Total profits for twelve months from 01/04/2009 to 31/03/2010 are £45,000. Therefore, profits from

01/04/2009 to 31/12/2009 (nine months) = £45,000 x 9/12 = £33,750

8. The surrender of losses **can be in part or in full.** Similarly, losses can be surrendered to other companies in the group even though there are sufficient profits available to set off against the company's own profits for that accounting period.

9. A group relief **claim is normally made on the claimant company's tax return**. However, a notice of acceptance is required to be given by the surrendering company.

10. **Effective use of group relief:** to avail the maximum group relief, it is advisable to claim it in the following order (according to the Finance Act 2009 rates):

a) first surrender **to companies which pay corporation tax at a marginal rate** of 29.75% (in order to bring profits to the small companies' rate's limit)

b) then surrender **to companies paying tax at full rate of 28%**

c) finally surrender to companies paying tax at **21%**

Diagram 3: Order of relief

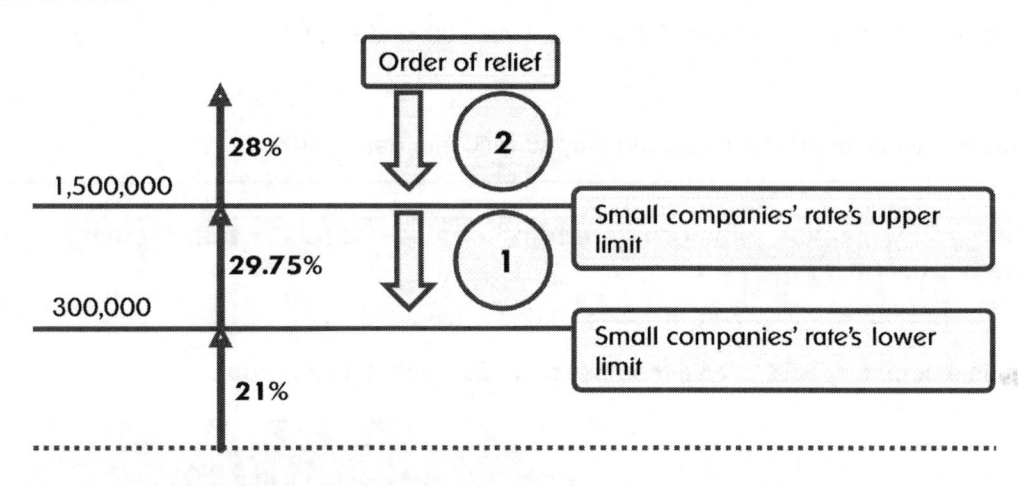

```
                        Order of relief
                 28%          ⇓
     1,500,000 ─────────────  ② ──────────  Small companies' rate's upper
                                            limit
                 29.75%       ⇓
                              ①
       300,000 ─────────────────────────── Small companies' rate's lower
                                            limit
                 21%
     ·············································
```

Profits between £300,000 and £1,500,000
Actual rate of tax is between 21% & 28% but the **marginal rate** (i.e. the rate on every additional £) is 29.75%

SUMMARY

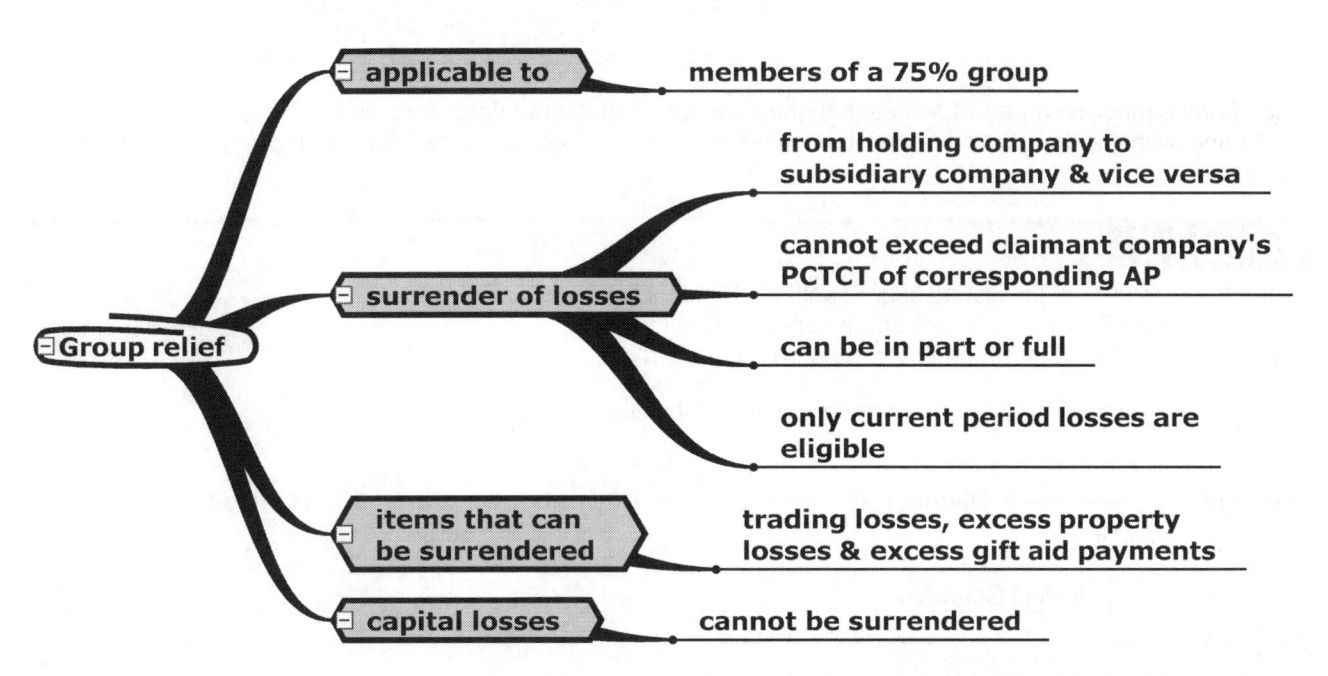

Group relief
- **applicable to** — members of a 75% group
- **surrender of losses**
  - from holding company to subsidiary company & vice versa
  - cannot exceed claimant company's PCTCT of corresponding AP
  - can be in part or full
  - only current period losses are eligible
- **items that can be surrendered** — trading losses, excess property losses & excess gift aid payments
- **capital losses** — cannot be surrendered

Test Yourself 4

Amanda Ltd owns 100% of the ordinary share capital of Baron Ltd. Their results for the year ended 31 March 2010 are as follows:

	£
Amanda Ltd	
Trading loss	(80,000)
Capital loss	(15,000)
Property income	45,000
Baron Ltd	
Trading profits	90,000
Income from loan relationship	35,000

Amanda Ltd has a trading loss brought forward on 1 April 2009 of £12,000.

Required:

What is the amount of loss that Amanda Ltd may surrender to Baron Ltd?

---

3. Define a 75% capital gains group, and recognise the reliefs that are available to members of such a group.[2]

[Learning outcome c]

3.1 When is a company said to be a member of a 75% capital gains group?

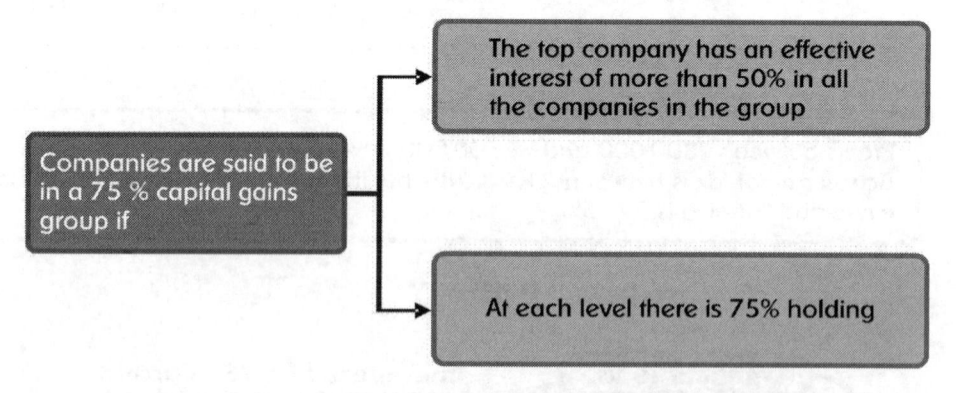

Companies are said to be in a 75% capital gains group if:
- The top company has an effective interest of more than 50% in all the companies in the group
- At each level there is 75% holding

A company cannot be a part of two capital gains groups at the same time. A capital gains group is determined by starting with the top company and then working down according to the two conditions mentioned in the diagram.

Example

State Ltd holds 90% of the issued share capital in District Ltd
District Ltd holds 75% of the issued share capital in City Ltd
City Ltd holds 50% of the issued share capital in Home Ltd

Which of the above companies are members of a 75% capital gains group?

State Ltd →90%→ District Ltd →75%→ City Ltd →50%→ Home Ltd

State Ltd	Holding Company
District Ltd	90%
City Ltd	67.5% (90% x 75%)
Home Ltd	33.75 % (90% x 75% x 50%)

Continued on next page

Associate Companies

State Ltd, District Ltd and City Ltd are associated companies as holding company (State Ltd) owns more than 50% shareholding in other two companies The lower and upper limit will be shared equally among these three members.

75% group for loss relief

Group 1 (State Ltd and District Ltd): State Ltd and District Ltd are in 75% group but City Ltd is not in a 75% group with State Ltd as the shareholding of State Ltd (holding company) in City Ltd is less than 75%. Therefore losses may be surrendered between State Ltd and District Ltd but it is not possible for State Ltd to surrender losses to City Ltd.

Group 2 (District Ltd and City Ltd): City Ltd is a 75% subsidiary of District Ltd and hence these two companies can also form a group to claim group relief to surrender their losses. However, District Ltd cannot claim group relief from City Ltd and pass it on to State Ltd.

75% capital gains group

1. At each level, there is a 75% holding between State Ltd, District Ltd and City Ltd. But City Ltd does not have a 75% holding in Home Ltd, hence Home Ltd is not a member of the 75% capital gains group.
2. The top company i.e, State Ltd. has an effective interest of more than 50% in District Ltd and City Ltd, but not in Home Ltd.

Therefore, State Ltd, District Ltd and City Ltd are in a 75% capital gains group.

3.2 Reliefs available to members of a 75% capital gains group

Special reliefs are available for companies in a capital gains group (75% direct holding, and more than 50% effective holding in all the companies). These are as follows:

1. **Transfer of chargeable assets without any gain / loss**

   ➢ Transfer of chargeable assets between the members of a 75% capital gains group takes place **without giving rise to any chargeable gain or allowable loss**.

   ➢ Deemed proceeds for the transferor company on transfer of chargeable assets is the original cost of the assets plus indexation allowance.

   ➢ On the subsequent disposal by the company acquiring the asset, the same figure is treated as the deemed cost for the acquiring company.

   ➢ The company recieving the asset must remain as a member of the 75% capital gains group for six years. If the holding company sells its controlling interest in the subsidiary company within the period of six years from the date of transfer of the asset, the gain at the time of transfer will arise on the subsidiary company which recieved and is still holding that asset.

   ➢ **This treatment is automatic and there is no need to claim it.**

Example

In February 2001 (RPI 172.0) Rise Ltd purchased an office building for £200,000. In May 2005 (RPI 192.0), Rise Ltd transferred the building to Climb Ltd, its wholly owned subsidiary company, for £325,000. The market value of the office building at the time of disposal was £400,000.

In August 2009 (RPI 214.4), Climb Ltd sold the office building for £527,000.

As Rise Ltd holds more than 75% of the shares in Climb Ltd, they both form a 75% capital gains group. When there is a disposal between members of a 75% capital gains group, neither a chargeable gain nor an allowable loss arises.

Continued on next page

Deemed proceeds for Rise Ltd will be the original cost of the office building plus indexation allowance.

	£
Cost	200,000
Indexation allowance	
$\dfrac{£192.0 - £172.0}{£172.0} = (0.116) \times £200,000$	23,200
Deemed proceeds	**223,200**

Calculation of chargeable gain on the disposal of office building by Climb Ltd is as follows:

	£
Disposal consideration	527,000
Less: Allowable deductions	
Deemed cost	(223,200)
Unindexed gain	303,800
Less: Indexation allowance	
$\dfrac{£214.4 - £192.0}{£192.0} = (0.117) \times £200,000$	(23,400)
Chargeable gain	**280,400**

2. Notional transfer of assets

➢ The capital gain realised by one company cannot be transferred to another company to utilise the capital losses realised by another company in the group. However, the companies in a 75% capital gains group can elect to use the provision of notional transfer of assets to utilise their capital losses.

➢ In a notional transfer, the asset on which the gain is realised can be treated as if it had been transferred to another company in the group (having capital losses) before the asset was sold outside the group.

➢ This election must be made within two years of the end of the accounting period in which the disposal of the asset took place.

➢ This election can help to set off the group's capital losses against the gains of any company in the group and helps to ensure that corporation tax is paid at the lowest rate on gains by the companies in the group.

➢ This election also helps to set off the brought forward capital loss of the group member to whom the asset is being transfered.

Example

Forward Ltd owns 100% of the ordinary share capital of Speed Ltd. In the accounting period ending on 31 December 2009, Forward Ltd sold an asset at a capital gain of £100,000. During the same period, Speed Ltd sold an asset at a capital loss of £70,000.

As both the companies form a 75% capital gains group for group relief purposes, they can utilise the capital losses through the provision of notional transfer of assets. The companies can elect the transfer by Forward Ltd which resulted in a capital gain of £100,000 to be treated as being made by Speed Ltd. This will help to set off the loss of £70,000 made by Speed Ltd and therefore the group will have to pay tax only on the net chargeable gain of £30,000 (£100,000 - £70,000).

Alternatively the companies can also make an election to treat the transfer by Speed Ltd which resulted in a capital loss as being made by Forward Ltd. The overall result will be the same in both the conditions.

However, this election should be made within two years of the end of the accounting period in which the disposal of the asset took place, i.e. before 31 December 2011.

3. Group rollover relief

- All the companies in the 75% capital gains group are treated as one for rollover relief.

- According to the group rollover relief provisions, if one company disposes of an asset eligible for capital gains rollover, and another group member purchases a new qualifying asset within the time limit for reinvestment (i.e., in the period of one year before and three years after the disposal of the old qualifying asset), the gain for the first company can be rolled over into the cost of the new asset purchased by the second company.

Diagram 4: Group rollover relief

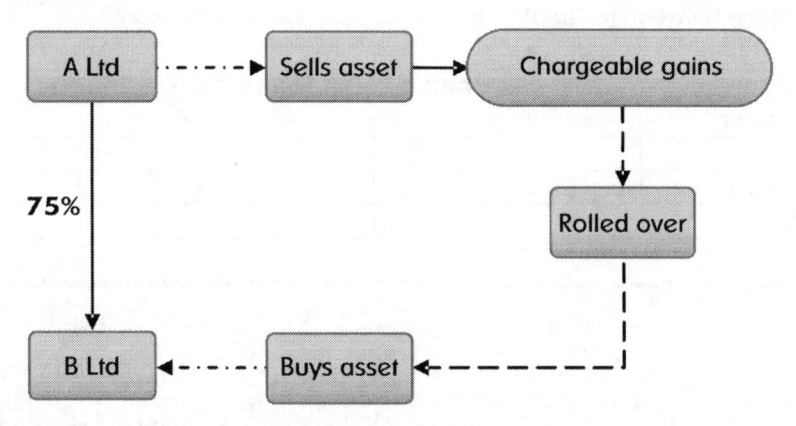

```
  A Ltd  ----> Sells asset ----> Chargeable gains
   |                                    |
  75%                                   |
   |                                    v
   v                               Rolled over
  B Ltd  <---- Buys asset  <-----------|
```

Test Yourself 5

Giant Ltd owns 100% of the ordinary shares of both Big Ltd and Small Ltd. The following information for each company is available for the year ended 31 March 2010:

	Giant Ltd £	Big Ltd £	Small Ltd £
Trading profit (loss)	(135,000)	660,000	140,000
Capital gain (loss)	166,000	(6,000)	-

Giant Ltd's capital gain arose from the sale of property on 1st May 2009 for £396,000. Small Ltd purchases a warehouse for £260,000 on 31st December 2009.

Required:

How should the group relief be allocated between the companies to maximise the benefit from group relief?

Calculate the corporation tax liability of the three companies for the year ended 31 March 2009 assuming reliefs are claimed in the most favourable manner.

---

4. Compare the UK tax treatment of an overseas branch to an overseas subsidiary.[2]
[Learning outcome d]

A company is said to be resident in the UK for tax purposes if it is incorporated in the UK or in the case of a foreign company if its control and management is exercised from within the UK.

The companies which are resident in the UK are liable to corporation tax on all the profits and chargeable gains arising worldwide. A UK resident company can decide to extend its business overseas through either a subsidiary or a branch. Tax treatment of an overseas subsidiary and an overseas branch is different.

Tax treatment of Overseas Branch

A branch is an extension of the structure of the overall company. A UK resident company can extend its business overseas through a branch in which case all the profits from the branch will be assessed to UK corporation tax. Whether the profits are remitted to the UK or not is irrelevant.

Relief is also available to the overseas branches in the UK on any trading loss incurred. Similarly, UK capital allowances are also available to the overseas branch on capital assets.

Tax treatment of Overseas Subsidiary

All profits from the overseas subsidiaries are exempt from UK corporation tax. Previously, the dividends remitted to the UK from overseas subsidiaries were assessed to UK corporation tax as overseas dividend income but from FY2009, overseas dividends are also exempt from corporation tax. Relief is not available to the overseas subsidiary company in the UK for any trading losses incurred. UK capital allowances are also not available to overseas subsidiary companies on its capital assets.

The disadvantage of the overseas subsidiary is that if it is an associate of the UK company, then the small companies' lower and upper limits will be reduced, thus increasing the rate of corporation tax.

A summary of the difference between tax treatment of overseas branch and overseas subsidiary is as follows:

		Overseas Branch	Overseas Subsidiary
1	**C** = Capital allowances	✓	X
2	**L** = Loss relief	✓	X
3	**A** = Associated company	x	✓
4	**P** = Profit taxed in UK	✓	X

Remember **CLAP**

> **Tip**
> According to the Finance Act 2009, overseas dividends which are received on or after 1 July 2009 are exempt from UK corporation tax. However, according to the examiner, the treatment of overseas dividends received before this period will not be examinable.

Example

Nice Ltd has profits of £210,000 chargeable to corporation tax for the year ended 31 March 2010. Dividends received from overseas resident company, Fair Ltd, in December 2009 were £36,000. Nice Ltd holds 52% shares of Fair Ltd. Nice Ltd has no other associated companies.

Required:

Calculate the profits chargeable to corporation tax and the rate of corporation tax applicable to Nice Ltd.

Answer

Fair Ltd will be considered an associated company of Nice Ltd as Nice Ltd holds more than 50% shares of Fair Ltd.

Fair Ltd is an overseas resident company and dividends received from overseas resident companies on or after 1 July 2009 are exempt from UK corporation tax.

Hence, profits chargeable to corporation tax (PCTCT) of Nice Ltd for the year ended 31 March 2010 are £210,000 as dividends are exempt from corporation tax.

Profits of Nice Ltd are also £210,000 as dividends received from associated companies are not included in FII.

Small companies upper limit and lower limit will be divided between both the companies as both are associated companies. Hence,
small companies lower limit will be = £300,000/2 = £150,000
small companies upper limit will be = £1,500,000/2 = £750,000

As profits of £210,000 fall between the small companies rate's upper limit and lower limit, the corporation tax rate applicable for Nice Ltd will be 28% less marginal relief.

5. Calculate double taxation relief for withholding tax.[2]

[Learning outcome e]

The situation may arise where a UK company is taxed both in the UK and overseas on the same profits. The income earned overseas by a UK resident company is taxable in the UK and might also be taxed in the country in which the income arises, depending upon that country's taxation laws.

Double taxation relief is granted in such a situations. This relief is granted by providing **tax credit** to the UK resident company. Hence, it is also referred to as a 'credit relief'. Under this method, the income earned overseas by the UK resident company has to be **grossed up** and included gross while calculating its corporation tax liability. A tax credit is then available equal to the lower of the overseas tax suffered **or** the amount of UK tax payable on the overseas income.

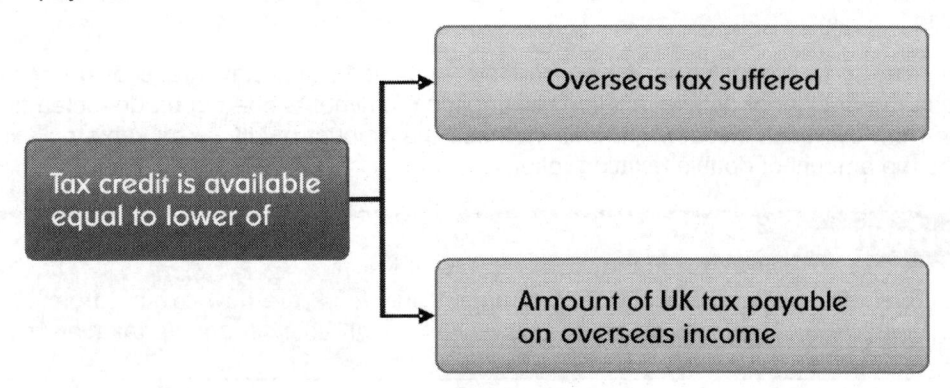

Tax credit is available equal to lower of:
- Overseas tax suffered
- Amount of UK tax payable on overseas income

Pro-forma for calculation of PCTCT in respect of overseas income:

Trading income	X
Overseas income (O/S income) (Gross figure)	X
PCTCT	**X**
Corporation tax liability (on PCTCT)	X
Less: Double taxation relief Lower of – overseas tax on O/S income – UK Corporation tax on O/S income	(X)
Corporation tax payable	**X**

> **Tip**
> Double taxation relief is calculated separately for each type of overseas income.

Example
During the year ended 31 March 2010, a UK resident company had UK trading income of £180,000 and received a remittance on account of overseas profits of £80,000 from its overseas branch. The actual profits earned by the branch for the year ended 31 March 2010 are £100,000. These profits were taxed overseas at the rate of 20%.

Required:

Calculate the corporation tax liability for the year.

Answer

Calculation of corporation tax liability

	UK £	Overseas £	Total £
Trading profits	180,000	100,000	180,000
PCTCT	**180,000**	**100,000**	**280,000**
Corporation tax @ 21%	37,800	21,000	58,800
Less: DTR lower of: (1) Overseas Tax £20,000 (£100,000 x 20%) (2) UK tax on overseas income £21,000		(20,000)	(20,000)
Corporation tax due	**37,800**	**1,000**	**38,800**

Withholding tax

It is the amount of direct tax deducted overseas on any overseas income. Overseas income can be from branch profits, rent and interest. Double taxation relief is always available on withholding tax.

Gift aid payments

Gift aid payments are to be deducted in the appropriate manner to take advantage of double taxation relief. Hence, to increase the amount of double taxation relief, gift aid payments need to be deducted first from the UK income and then from overseas income. This will increase the amount of UK tax payable on overseas income and thus increase the amount of double taxation relief.

> **Important**
>
> As overseas dividends received on or after 1 July 2009 are now exempt from UK corporation tax, they will not be included in the corporation tax and hence, double taxation relief will not be applicable for this income.

Test Yourself 6

Zeta Ltd's taxable UK trading profits for the year to 31 March 2010 were £786,250. Zeta Ltd had received dividends of £40,000 (net of withholding tax of 20%) from Tetra Inc.

Zeta Ltd had rented a building owned in Switzerland to Spectra SA and received a rental income of £48,000 (net of withholding tax of 40%) during the year ended 31 March 2010.

Both Tetra Inc and Spectra SA are overseas resident companies.

Zeta Ltd had also paid gift aid donation of £15,000 during the year. Zeta Ltd paid no dividends during the year and received no UK dividends.

Zeta Ltd owns 90% of the ordinary shares of Tetra Inc. It has no other associated companies.

Required:

Calculate Zeta Ltd's UK corporation tax liability after double taxation relief.

---

6. Explain the basic principles of the transfer pricing rules.[2]
[Learning outcome f]

Transfer Pricing

A UK resident company might attempt to reduce its tax liability by transferring goods at artificially low prices to an overseas subsidiary. This would have the result of decreasing the UK resident company's profits and increasing the foreign subsidiary's profits which are not taxable in the UK. The overseas subsidiary may also have a lower tax rate in its own country of domain.

To avoid this situation, "transfer pricing legislation" was brought into existence.

This applies to the transactions between the two companies if one of the two companies is under the control of the other company or both the companies are under the control of a third party (i.e, individual, partnership or company).

According to the provisions of this legislation, the profits of a UK resident company in such circumstances **are to be calculated as if the transaction had been carried out at arm's length prices i.e. the true market price should be substituted for the transfer price and the UK resident company has to make adjustments to its profits accordingly.**

Therefore, companies must self-assess their tax liability under transfer pricing provisions and pay corporation tax due.

Small and medium-sized companies are generally exempt from the transfer pricing legislation.

Answers to Test yourself

Answer 1

Country Ltd is the holding company. The status of the other companies is as follows:

Company	Whether associated or not
State Ltd	Holds more than 50% of the shareholding hence associated for the whole accounting period even though the shares were not owned for the whole year.
Division Ltd	Not associated as it is a dormant company
City Ltd	Not associated as Country Ltd holds less than 50% of the shareholding in City Ltd. It holds only 42% (70% x 60%) of the shareholding.

Hence, the associated companies are only two companies, Country Ltd and State Ltd. The upper limit, lower limit and AIA must be shared equally between these two companies.

Answer 2

King Ltd is deemed to have three associated companies: Giant Ltd, Big Ltd and Medium Ltd (Small Ltd is dormant, hence ignored). The group is as follows:

King Ltd	Holding Company
Giant Ltd	90%
Big Ltd	90%
Medium Ltd	54% (90% x 60%)
Small Ltd	Excluded as it is dormant

Therefore group (family) consist of four members and the limits will be shared equally among these four companies. Therefore, the small companies' rate's lower and upper limits are reduced to £75,000 and £375,000 respectively (one fourth of their usual values). The profit of £150,000 falls between these limits, hence, marginal relief is available.

	£
£150,000 @ 28%	42,000
Less: Marginal relief:	(3,938)
7/400 (£375,000 - £150,000) x £150,000/£150,000	
Corporation tax liability	**38,062**

Answer 3

Branch Ltd is the holding company and it's effective interest in all the companies should be minimum 75% to claim group relief.
The effective interest of Branch Ltd in each of the companies is as follows:

Company	Effective interest	Member of 75% group
Plant Ltd	90%	Yes
Tree Ltd	81% (90% of 90%)	Yes
Farm Ltd	72.9% (90% of 81%)	No

Hence, Branch Ltd, Plant Ltd and Tree Ltd are in a 75% group and can claim group reliefs. However, as effective interest of Branch Ltd in Farm Ltd was less than 75%, it will not be part of the group.

Answer 4

Only current year trading losses may be surrendered. Moreover, there is no group relief for brought forward trading losses or capital losses. Hence, Amanda Ltd may surrender only a £80,000 loss to Baron Ltd.

Answer 5

1. To maximise the benefits, group relief should be allocated to the company with the highest marginal rate of tax.

   As the three companies i.e. Giant Ltd, Big Ltd and Small Ltd are associated companies, the small companies' lower limit rates will be divided among them. Therefore, the small companies rate's lower limit for each company is £300,000/3 = £100,000.

   Any profit of Giant Ltd and Small Ltd above £100,000 is taxable at the highest marginal rate, which is effectively 29.75%. Hence group relief should be first allocated to these companies to bring their profit to £100,000.

   Big Ltd bears tax @ 28% hence the remainder of the relief should be allocated to Big Ltd.

2. Small Ltd can claim rollover relief for Giant Ltd's gain in respect of investment.
   The excess amount of proceeds over the amount invested by Small Ltd
   i.e. (£396,000 - £260,000) = £136,000 remains chargeable.

3. If the assets disposed of at a loss by Big Ltd are treated as having been disposed of by Giant Ltd, then the capital loss of £6,000 can be set off against gain of £136,000, leaving chargeable gain £130,000.
   Giant Ltd should then make a current year loss relief claim to bring its profits down to £100,000.

4. Small Ltd will also make a claim for group relief of the loss realised by Giant Ltd to bring its profit down to £100,000 (lower limit rate).

   The calculation of capital gains roll over relief and capital losses set off among the companies in the group is as follows:

	Giant Ltd £	Big Ltd £	Small Ltd £
Capital gain / (loss)	166,000	(6,000)	-
Less: Roll over relief	(30,000)	-	-
Chargeable gain (amount not re-invested)	136,000	(6,000)	-
Less: Set off of Big Ltd capital loss	(6,000)	6,000	-
Net Chargeable Gain	**130,000**	**Nil**	-

The corporation tax liability of the three companies for the year to 31st March 2010 is calculated as follows:

Remaining loss = £135,000 – £30,000 – £40,000

	Giant Ltd £	Big Ltd £	Small Ltd £
Trading profits	-	660,000	140,000
Net capital gains	130,000	-	-
	130,000	660,000	140,000
Less: relief for trading loss under s393 (1)	(30,000)	-	-
Group relief	-	(65,000)	(40,000)
PCTCT	**100,000**	**595,000**	**100,000**
Tax @ 21%	21,000	-	21,000
Tax @ 28%	-	166,600	-

Answer 6

	UK Trading Income £	Tetra Inc Overseas Dividend Income £	Spectra SA Overseas Rental Income £	Total £
Trading Profits	786,250			786,250
Overseas income (note 1)		-	80,000	80,000
PCTCT	786,250	-	80,000	866,250
Less: Gift aid payments (note 2)	(15,000)	-	-	(15,000)
	771,250	-	80,000	851,250
Corporation tax (£851,250 × 28%) (note 3)	215,950	-	22,400	238,350
Less: DTR (W1)	-	-	(22,400)	(22,400)
Corporation tax liability	215,950	-	-	215,950

Notes:

1. Overseas income need to be grossed up while calculating corporation tax liability. Hence,
   Gross dividends received from Tetra Ltd are = £40,000 × 100/80 = £50,000
   Gross rent received from Spectra Ltd is = £48,000 × 100/60 = £80,000
   However, overseas dividends are exempt from UK corporation tax, hence dividends received from Tetra Ltd will not be included in the calculation of CT liability.

2. To take better advantage of gift aid payments, they need to be deducted first from the UK income and then from overseas income.

3. Zeta Ltd and Tetra Inc are associated companies as Zeta Ltd (holding company) holds more than 50% shareholding in Tetra Inc. Hence, upper limit and lower limit will be divided between the two companies as follows:
   Small companies rate's lower limit will be £300,000/2 = £150,000
   Small companies rate's upper limit will be £1,500,000/2 = £750,000

   As Zeta Ltd's profits is above the upper limit, the tax rate applicable will be 28%.

Working

W1 Calculation of double taxation relief

	Tetra Ltd £	Spectra Ltd £
DTR: Lower of		
Overseas tax	10,000	32,000
UK tax on overseas income	-	22,400
	-	22,400

Quick Quiz

1. What is an associated company?

2. What is credit relief?

Answers to Quick Quiz

1. In a situation where one company has control over the other company or both the companies are under the control of the same person or persons then the companies are known as associated companies.

2. Tax credit is available equal to the lower of overseas tax suffered or the amount of UK tax payable on overseas income.

Self Examination Questions

Question 1

Briefly explain the following:

a) What is the group relationship that must exist in order to claim group relief?
b) What is the group relationship that must exist to form a group for capital gains purposes?
c) What are the advantages of companies being in a capital gains group?
d) What is an arm's length price?

Question 2

James Ltd owns 80% of the ordinary share capital of Jolly Ltd. Both companies prepare accounts to 31 March. James Ltd incurs a loss in the year ended 31 March 2010. The company also has a trading loss brought forward on 1 April 2009. Determine the loss to be surrendered to Jolly Ltd in the year ended 31 March 2010.

Question 3

What are the losses that may be surrendered in a 75% group?

Question 4

Sweet Ltd owns 80% of the ordinary share capital of Salty Ltd. Their results for the year ended 31st March 2010 are as follows:

	£
Sweet Ltd	
Trading loss	(160,000)
Property income	25,000
Salty Ltd	
Trading profits	90,000
Chargeable gain	40,000
Gift aid payments	(15,000)

What is the maximum amount of loss of Sweet Ltd that can be claimed by Salty Ltd for group relief?

Question 5

Jimmy Ltd owns 100% of the ordinary share capital of Johnny Ltd. The results of the companies for the year ended 31 March 2009 are as follows:

	£
Jimmy Ltd	
Trading profits	140,000
Property income	15,000
Trading loss b/f under S393 (1)	(23,000)
Gift aid donations	17,000
Johnny Ltd	
Trading profits	(134,000)
Property income	19,000
Gift aid donations	21,000
Trading loss b/f under s393(1)	(31,000)

Calculate the maximum group relief that may be claimed for the year by Jimmy Ltd.

Answers to Self Examination Questions

Answer 1

a) The group relationship that must exist to claim group relief needs to meet all of the following conditions:
   i. one company must be a 75% subsidiary of the other, or both companies must be a 75% subsidiary of a third company.
   ii. the holding company must have an effective interest of at least 75% of the subsidiary's ordinary share capital.
   iii. the holding company must have the right to receive at least 75% of the subsidiary's distributable profits and net assets on winding-up.
   iv. The companies must all be resident in UK

b) The group relationship that must exist to form a group for capital gains purposes are as follows:
   i. companies form a capital gains group if at each level in the group structure there is a 75% shareholding.
   ii. the parent company must have an effective interest of at least 50% in each group company.

c) The advantages of companies being in a capital gains group are:
   i. the companies in a group can elect to treat any disposal or part of the disposal of the chargeable assets outside the company as if it had been transferred between the companies in the group before the disposal. This can help to set off the group's capital losses against the gains of any company in the group.
   ii. gains may be taxed at the lowest marginal rate in the group.
   iii. rollover relief is available between group members.

d) An arm's length price is that price which trading stock can fetch if sold to an unconnected buyer.

Answer 2

All of James Ltd's loss in the year ended 31 March 2010 may be surrendered to Jolly Ltd provided Jolly Ltd has the profits to absorb it. The relief is not restricted to the percentage shareholding. Only the current year's losses may be surrendered, not brought forward losses.

Answer 3

The losses which may be surrendered in a 75% group are:
i. Trading losses
ii. Unrelieved property losses
iii. Unrelieved gift aid payments

Answer 4

Salty Ltd has chargeable profit of £115,000 (£90,000 + £40,000 - £15,000). Hence £115,000 of Sweet Ltd's loss may be surrendered to Salty Ltd.

Answer 5

The amount of losses of Johnny Ltd that can be claimed for group relief are calculated as follows:

	£
Trading profits	-
Property income	19,000
Total profits	19,000
Less: Gift aid donations	(21,000)
	(2,000)
Less: Current year losses	(134,000)
Losses for group relief	(136,000)

However, Jimmy Ltd has chargeable profits of only £115,000 (£140,000 + £15,000 - £23,000 - £17,000). So, the maximum group relief that may be claimed for the year by Jimmy Ltd is £115,000.

SECTION E: NATIONAL INSURANCE CONTRIBUTIONS

E1

STUDY GUIDE E1: NATIONAL INSURANCE: SCOPE AND CLASS 1 AND 1A CONTRIBUTIONS FOR EMPLOYED PERSONS

Get Through Intro

Once an employee's earnings exceed a specific threshold, it becomes mandatory for both the employer and the employee to contribute to class 1 NIC (National Insurance contributions).

In this Study Guide we will discuss the various provisions relating to the employer's and employee's contributions to class 1 NIC, and the tax benefits that they both get from these contributions.

This knowledge will be useful when, as a tax consultant, you need to advise your clients about this threshold for mandatory registration with the National Insurance Contributions Office (NICO).

Examiners often test this knowledge in the first compulsory question.

Learning Outcomes

a) The scope of national insurance
   i. Describe the scope of national insurance.
b) Class 1 and Class 1A contributions for employed persons
   i. Compute Class 1 NIC.
   ii. Compute Class 1A NIC.

Introduction

National Insurance Contributions are used to fund the welfare state and to pay state benefits such as state pensions and unemployment allowance. The contributions goes to a common pool and disbursed as social security benefits to those who are in need. Therefore it is another form of taxation by the administrative system.

NICs are payable by self-employed persons and employees.

NICs are collected:

- by the National Insurance Contributions Office (NICO)
- from self-employed persons, employees and their employers

NICs are significant factors for the self-employed and employers.

Main classes of NICs
1. Class 1 primary paid by employees
2. Class 1 secondary and Class 1A paid by employers
3. Class 2 paid by the self-employed
4. Class 4 paid by the self-employed

1. Describe the scope of national insurance.[1]

[Learning outcome a]

1.1 Applicability

Class 1 NICs are payable by all "employed earners" who fulfill the following criteria:

1. the **age** of the employed person is **above 16 years**. He is required to pay for class 1 NIC until he becomes eligible for pension **AND**

2. an employed person **earning more than £110 per week** (£5,715 per annum / 52 weeks) **or £476 per month** (£5,715 per annum / 12 months).

> **Definition**
> An employed earner is a person who is paid either as an employee under a contract or as a holder of office.

1.2 Basis

The amount of class 1 NIC payable by the employee is based on a percentage of the employee's earnings during the tax year.

Where a person has more than one job, that person is liable to pay class 1 NIC contributions in respect of **each job.**

An employee's earnings **include gross pay** in the form of:

1. salary, remuneration, wages, commission, bonus

2. all **non-cash vouchers** except those that are exempt under income tax. Examples of non-cash vouchers which are not included in gross pay (so are exempt from tax) are:

   a) **transport vouchers for lower-paid employees** by passenger transport bodies
   b) vouchers to obtain a **parking space for a car / motorcycle or bicycle** etc
   c) vouchers for meals in the work premises
   d) luncheon vouchers of 15p per day (above this amount is included in gross pay)
   e) vouchers used in connection with sporting or recreational facilities
   f) vouchers for overnight expenses of £5 per night and £10 if the employee is outside the UK

3. amount of employee loan which is written off by the employer (i.e. the employee is not in a position to repay the amount, therefore the employer treats the loan amount as a bad debt, and completes forms P11D and P9D)

4. **employer's contributions to funded unapproved retirement benefit schemes**

5. remuneration in the form of **non-cash assets**, which are readily convertible into cash (examples of non-cash assets are: gold bars, coffee beans, fine wines etc.)

However, an employee's earnings do not include:
a) employee's contribution to approved personal pensions
b) employee's contribution to approved occupational pension schemes
c) employee's contribution to private schemes
d) charitable gifts under the payroll giving scheme
e) tips received directly from customers
f) business expenses paid or reimbursed by the employer

2. Class 1 and class 1A contributions for employed persons
i. Compute Class 1 NIC.[2]
ii. Compute Class 1A NIC.[2]

[Learning outcome b]

As mentioned previously, both **class 1 and class 1A contributions** are payable in relation to employees who are **above 16 years** old.

Class 1 contributions are calculated on emoluments received in cash and/or which are easily converted into cash.

Class 1A contributions are calculated on benefits in kind received.

2.1 Class 1 primary

1. Paid by employees from age 16 to state retirement age (women 60 years, men 65 years).

2. Charged **on earnings**

3. Earnings **means gross pay (salary and bonus) before deduction** of:
   a) payments into an occupational pension scheme
   b) donations under the payroll deduction scheme
   c) expenses incurred by employee

4. **Exempt from class 1**
   a) Business expenses **reimbursed**
   b) **First £55 per week of childcare vouchers**
   c) **Tips** from **third parties**
   d) **Mileage allowances** not exceeding the statutory rates
   e) Exempt benefits

5. Employer deducts NICs from **pay via Pay As You Earn (PAYE)**

6. Payable **monthly under PAYE** with income tax, **14 days after the end of the tax month i.e. 19th of the following month.**

7. **Earnings period**
   a) Employees are paid **weekly or monthly** – known as the 'earnings period'.
   b) Class 1 calculated by reference to the earnings paid in the earnings period.
   c) Lower and upper limits apply but all earnings over the lower limit will be subject to some NICs.
   d) The annual lower and upper limits are given in the exam as follows:

National Insurance Contributions (Not contracted out rates)		
		%
Class 1 Employee	£1 – £5,715 per year	Nil
	£5,716 – £43,875 per year	11.0
	£43,876 and above per year	1.0
Class 1 Employer	£1 – £5,715 per year	Nil
	£5,716 and above per year	12.8
Class 1A		12.8
Class 2	£2.40 per week	
Class 4	£1 – £5,715 per year	Nil
	£5,716 – £43,875 per year	8.0
	£43,876 and above per year	1.0

E1.4: National Insurance Contributions

> **Tip**: Employees are not contracted-out unless they contribute into an occupational pension. In the exam assume none of the employees are contracted out.

Class 1 is calculated as follows:

Employee's earnings	Class 1 primary contributions payable
Not exceeding the primary threshold (£5,715 per annum)	Nil
Exceeds primary threshold but does not exceed the upper earnings limit (£43,875 per annum)	(Earnings – Primary threshold) x 11%
Exceeds the upper earnings limit	(Upper earnings limit – Primary threshold) x 11% + (Earnings – Upper earnings limit) x 1%

If **earnings are even** (i.e. the same amount in each earnings period – no bonus) use the £5,715 figure given in the rates.

If **earnings are not even** (for e.g. because of a bonus) then calculate NIC by reference to the earnings period.

> **Tip**: The weekly and monthly equivalent of **annual primary threshold** is calculated as follows:
>
> Weekly threshold = (£5,715/52 weeks) = £110 per week
> Monthly threshold = (£5,715/12 months) = £476 per month
>
> The weekly and monthly equivalent of the **annual upper earnings limit** is calculated as follows:
>
> Weekly upper earnings limit = (£43,875/52 weeks) = £844 per week
> Monthly thresholds = (£43,875/12 months) = £3,656 per month

Example

The following information is available for three friends:

Name of employee	Earnings	Period
Tom	£1,260	Monthly
Dick	£180	Weekly
Harry	£4,938	Monthly

The NICs will be calculated as follows:

Name of employee	Workings	NICs
Tom	11% x (£1,260 – £476)	86.24
Dick	11% x (£180 – £110)	7.70
Harry	11% x (£3,656 - £476) + 1% x (£4,938 – £3,656)	362.62

Notes:

1. Tom earns more than the monthly primary threshold of £476.
2. Dick earns more than the weekly primary threshold of £110.
3. Harry earns more than the monthly upper earnings limit.

Test Yourself 1

Calculate the class 1 primary NICs payable by the following employees:

Name of employee	Earnings	Period
Alan	£120	Per week
Bob	£1,000	Per month
Cathy	£4,000	Per month

> **Tip**: Dividends paid to employees do not attract NICs.

2.2 Class 1 secondary

1. Paid by **employers**.
2. **For employees aged over 16** (no upper age limit).
3. Lower limit of **£5,715 applies.**
4. Payable on **all earnings over the limit.**
5. Payable **monthly under PAYE** with income tax and Class 1 primary, **14 days after the end of the tax month i.e. 19th of the following month.**
6. Class 1 secondary is **deductible when calculating trading income.**
7. **Class 1 secondary is deductible as an expense by the employer in computing the trading profit of the business**
8. Class 1 secondary is calculated as follows:

Employee's earnings	Class 1 secondary contributions payable
Not exceeding the primary threshold (£5,715 per annum)	Nil
Exceeds primary threshold	(Earnings – Primary threshold) x 12.8%

Tip: If an employee decides to continue to work even after reaching the state pension age (i.e. 60 for women and 65 for men), the employee need not pay his primary contribution but the employer **must continue to pay secondary contributions for these employees.**

Example

The following information is available for three friends:

Name of employee	Earnings (£)	Period
Tom	260	Monthly
Dick	180	Weekly
Harry	2,830	Monthly

Class 1 secondary NICs will be calculated as follows:

Name of employee	Workings	NICs
Tom	-	Nil
Dick	12.8% x (£180 – £110)	8.96
Harry	12.8% x (£2,830 - £476)	301.32

Notes:

1. Tom's earnings do not exceed the monthly primary threshold of £476.
2. Dick earns more than the weekly primary threshold of £110.
3. Harry earns more than the monthly primary threshold of £476.

Test Yourself 2

Calculate the class 1 secondary NICs payable by the following employees:

Name of employee	Earnings (£)	Period
Alan	120	Per week
Bob	1,000	Per month
Cathy	3,000	Per month

2.3 Class 1A NIC

1. **Paid by employers** not employees.
2. **On benefits** e.g. living accommodation, assets loaned to the employee for private use (same figure as calculated for employment income).
3. **Exempt** from Class 1A:
    a) workplace **childcare facilities**
    b) **first £55** of contracted-for childcare
4. Calculated **annually.**
5. **Due on 19 July** following the tax year.

> **Example** During the tax year 2009-10, Tulip Ltd provided a car for private use to one of the senior managers of the company.
>
> The employer (i.e. Tulip Ltd) is liable to contribute for Class 1A NIC on this benefit given to the employee in kind.
> The due date for paying this contribution is 19 July 2010 (i.e. 19 July following the tax year).

6. Class 1A is **deductible when calculating trade profits.**
7. The contribution is calculated at **12.8%** on the amount of benefits.

> **Example** Jack (whose monthly salary is £500) gets the following benefits from his employer:
>
> 1. The chargeable value of living accommodation provided to Jack is £6,000 per annum.
> 2. Jack's employer also pays his private medical insurance premium of £750 per annum.
>
> The employer's class 1A NIC liability = (£6,000 + £750) x 12.8% = £864.

Test Yourself 3

In January, Black Ltd purchased a TV system for £18,000. In the same month, the company gave this TV to John for his private use. John's salary is £750 per month.

Required:

Calculate the employer's class 1A NIC liability for the tax year 2009-10.

Test Yourself 4

Simon, an employee earning £45,000 per annum, is provided with taxable benefits of £12,520 during 2009-10.

Required:

Calculate:

1. Class 1 primary NIC
2. Class 1 secondary NIC
3. Class 1A NIC

Diagram1: Class 1 NIC

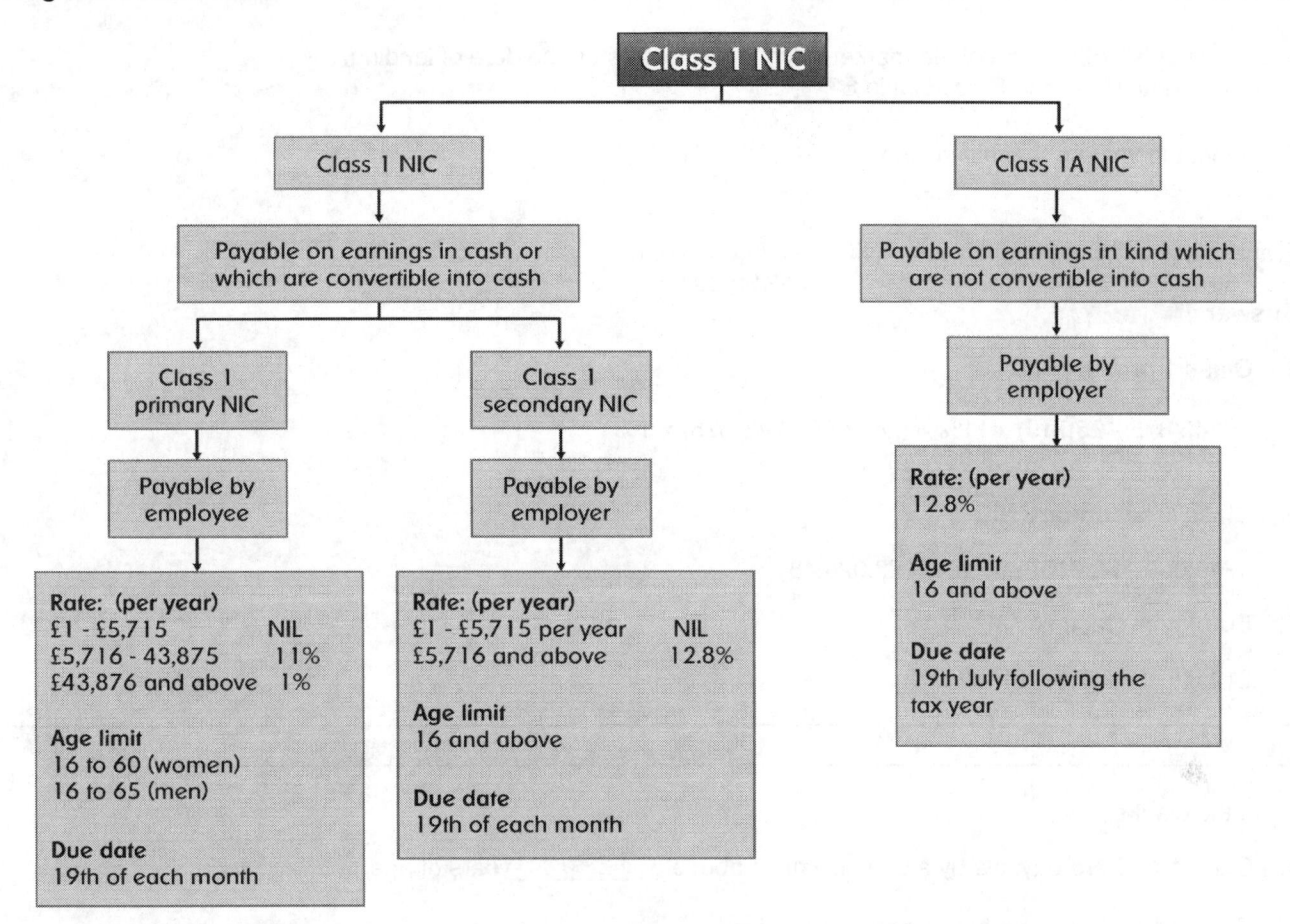

```
                        Class 1 NIC
                       /            \
              Class 1 NIC           Class 1A NIC
                  |                       |
    Payable on earnings in cash or    Payable on earnings in kind which
    which are convertible into cash   are not convertible into cash
         /            \                       |
    Class 1          Class 1             Payable by
    primary NIC      secondary NIC       employer
        |                |
    Payable by       Payable by          Rate: (per year)
    employee         employer            12.8%

                                         Age limit
                                         16 and above
    Rate: (per year)     Rate: (per year)
    £1 - £5,715   NIL    £1 - £5,715 per year  NIL     Due date
    £5,716 - 43,875  11% £5,716 and above     12.8%   19th July following the
    £43,876 and above 1%                              tax year
                         Age limit
    Age limit            16 and above
    16 to 60 (women)
    16 to 65 (men)       Due date
                         19th of each month
    Due date
    19th of each month
```

Answers to Test Yourself

Answer 1

1. Alan earns more than the weekly primary threshold of £110. Therefore, his NIC is
   11% x (£120 - £110) = £1.1

2. Bob earns £1,000 per month i.e. his earnings are more than monthly primary threshold of £476. Hence he should pay 11% x (£1,000 - £476) = £57.64 as class 1 NIC.

3. Cathy earns £4,000 per month i.e. her earnings are more than the monthly upper earnings limit. Therefore, she should pay the following amount as class 1 NIC:
   = 11% x (£3,656 - £476) + 1% x (£4,000 – £3,656)
   = £349.8 + £3.44
   = £353.24

Answer 2

1. Alan earns more than the weekly primary threshold of £110. Therefore, his weekly class 1 secondary NIC is

   12.8% x (£120 - £110) = £1.28

2. Bob earns £1,000 per month i.e. his earnings are more than the monthly primary threshold of £476. Therefore, his class 1 secondary NIC is:

   12.8% x (£1,000 - £476) = £67.07

3. Cathy earns £3,000 per month i.e. her earnings are more than the monthly primary threshold of £476. Therefore, her monthly class 1 secondary NIC is:

   12.8% x (£3,000- £476) = £323.07

Answer 3

The value of benefit = 20% of the market value of the assets on the date of lending.
(For more details refer to Study Guide B2)

For John, the value of benefit in kind   = 20% x £18,000
                                                = £3,600

Employer's contribution for class 1A NIC   = £3,600 x 12.8%
                                                        = £460.80

Answer 4

1. **Class 1 primary NIC**

   = (£43,875 - £5,715) x 11% + (£45,000 - £43,875) x 1%
   = £4,198 + £11 = £4208.85

2. **Class 1 secondary NIC**

   (£45,000 - £5,715) x 12.8% = £5,028.48

3. **Employer class IA NIC**

   £12,520 x 12.8% = £1602.56

Quick Quiz

Fill in the blanks.

1. Class 1 NIC are payable by a person who is above _____ years of age.

2. Class 1A NIC are payable on benefits received in _____ .

3. Class 1 secondary NIC and Class 1A NIC are payable by _____ .

4. Class 1 primary NIC are payable by _____ .

5. Class 1A contributions are due by _____ following the tax year.

Answers to Quick Quiz

1. 16
2. kind
3. employers
4. employees
5. 19th July

Self Examination Questions

Question 1

The remuneration of various employees is given below. Advise them on their contribution to class 1 NIC.

1. Tom Gulliver is employed with Star Co. His remuneration is £2,500 per month.
2. Joydeep is an employee of Tele Ltd. His weekly remuneration is £885.
3. Irma is a waitress at Red Diamond Hotels Pvt. Ltd. Her monthly remuneration is £500. She also receives tips from customers of around £600 per month.
4. Freda works in a small shop as a sales assistant. Her weekly remuneration is £90.

Question 2

Rimy is a manager at Woodland Ltd. The company pays her a monthly salary of £2,500. In addition to this, the company provides her with a house in Krakow. The company has taken this house on a rental basis. The monthly rental charges are £100.

Required:

Advise Woodland Ltd how much it should pay towards secondary Class 1 and Class 1A NIC

Question 3

Linda is a 65 year old lady. She works with a watch-making company as a supervisor. She gets a salary of £100 per week.

Required:

Advise her how much she should pay towards class 1 NIC.

Question 4

Marcus is employed with Venus Ltd, earning a salary of £30,000 per annum. He was provided with a new diesel-powered company car on 6 August 2009 with an official CO_2 emission rate of 132 grams per kilometre. The motor car has a list price of £13,500.

Required:

What is the class 1A NIC payable by Venus Ltd?

Answers to Self Examination Questions

Answer 1

1. Tom Gulliver should pay £223 per month class 1 NIC.
   (£2,500 – £476) x 11%

2. Joydeep's class 1 NIC contribution is £81 per week
   (£844 - £110) x 11% + (£885 - £844) x 1%

3. An employee's earnings for class 1 NIC specifically excludes tips directly received from customers. Hence, Irma's contribution towards class 1 NIC needs to be calculated considering her remuneration of £500.

   She is required to pay £2.64 per month towards class 1 NIC. (£500 – £476) x 11% = 2.64

4. Freda's weekly remuneration is below £110 per week. So, she need not contribute anything towards class 1 NIC.

Answer 2

Secondary class 1 NIC contributions are payable by the employer in relation to the employee, if the employee's earnings in the period exceed the secondary threshold.

Employees total earnings = Earnings in cash + Earnings readily convertible in cash
                         = £2,500 + £100
                         = £2,600

Woodland Ltd pays Rimy a total remuneration of £2,600 (£2,500 + £100).

As Rimy's earnings exceed the primary threshold, Woodland Ltd's total contribution are
Class 1 secondary NIC (£2,500 - £476) x 12.8% = £259.07
Class 1(A) NIC 100 x 12.8%   = £ 12.80
Total   = £ 387.07

Answer 3

Linda does not have to pay any contributions towards class 1 NIC, as she has already reached pension age. If any employee continues to work after reaching the state pension age, he or she does not need to pay Class 1 NIC.

Answer 4

Chargeable value of car = 13,500 x 18% x 8/12
= £1,620.

Class 1A NIC payable by Venus Ltd = £1,620 x 12.8%
= **£207.36**

Notes:

1. The CO_2 emissions are below the base level figure of 135 grams per kilometer, so the percentage is 18% (15% plus a 3% charge for a diesel car).
2. The motor car is only available for eight months, so the benefit is multiplied by 8/12.

SECTION E: NATIONAL INSURANCE CONTRIBUTIONS

STUDY GUIDE E2: CLASS 2 AND CLASS 4 CONTRIBUTIONS FOR SELF-EMPLOYED PERSONS

Get Through Intro

In the previous Study Guide we discussed various provisions relating to Class 1 NICs applicable to the employer and employee.

In this Study Guide we will discuss the various provisions of NIC relating to self-employed individuals. We will also discuss the tax benefits a self-employed person gets by contributing to Class 2 and Class 4 NIC.

Although you cannot expect a full question from this Study Guide, you may expect a question from this part of the Study Guide as part of the first compulsory question.

A sound knowledge of this topic is necessary for you to gain full marks in the first question and also to advise your client when it is necessary to notify the inland revenue.

Learning Outcomes

a) Compute Class 2 NIC.
b) Compute Class 4 NIC.

E2.2: National Insurance Contributions

Introduction

Case Study

Jeremy is an employee of a shop situated in London. He is also a good singer. His major income source is his salary from the shop, but he also performs stage shows. His income from the stage shows is not more than £100 per month. As he is an employee, his Class 1 contribution is collected through the PAYE system.

He is under the impression that, as his major source of income is salary; he doesn't have to pay Class 2 and 4 NIC. Claud Chapperon, Jeremy's friend, is of the opinion that Jeremy is liable to contribute towards Class 2 and Class 4 NIC. Jeremy does not accept this.

In this Study Guide we will discuss the various provisions of Class 2 and 4 NIC and decide who is right: Jeremy or Claud Chapperon.

1. Compute Class 2 NIC.[2]

[Learning outcome a]

1.1 Class 2 NIC

1. Paid by **self-employed**.

2. Aged **between 16 and the state retirement age.**

3. **Flat weekly rate of £2.40 per week** if earning is **above £5,075 for 2009-10.**

4. Payments start when individual turns 16, and cease when they reach the state retirement age.

5. Paid to the National Insurance Contributions Office by monthly direct debit or quarterly billing.

Example

Maurice follows 31 December as his annual accounting date. His profits for 2009 - 10 are £5,610.

His Class 2 NIC liability = £2.40 (per week) x 52 (weeks) = £124.80.

1.2 Registration for Class 2 NIC

1. A self-employed person must register himself for Class 2 NIC with HMRC.

A self-employed person must notify HMRC **within three months** from the date of commencement of self employment. Failure to do so may give rise to a penalty of £100.

Example

On 20 April 2009, Karen started her new business. In this situation, she is liable to notify HMRC within three months from the date of commencement of her employment i.e. before 20 July 2009.

2. In the case of failure to notify HMRC, a person may be liable for a penalty of £100.

2. Calculate Class 4 NIC.[2]

[Learning outcome b]

2.1 Class 4 NIC

1. Paid by **self-employed individuals.**

2. **Start if aged 16** at start of the tax year **and profits exceed the lower earnings limit (£5,715).**

3. No longer payable if individuals **reach the state retirement age at the start of the year.**

4. Class 4 **payable on profits:**

	£
Trading income assessment for the tax year	X
Less: Trading loss relief	(X)
Profits for Class 4 NIC purposes	**X**

2.2 Calculation of Class 4 NIC

1. If profit is between £5,715 and the upper limit of £43,875
   8% x (profits - £5,715)

2. If profit is above £43,875
   8% x (£43,875 - £5,715) plus 1% x (profits - £43,875)

2.3 Important points to remember

1. Class 4 NIC is payable **along with the income tax under self-assessment.**

2. This payment is to be made to **HMRC.** If the person fails to contribute towards Class 4 NIC in time, then he / she is liable for penal interest.

3. If a person is **self-employed** as well as an **employee**, he / she is **liable to Class 1, 2 and 4** contributions.

4. Each active partner in a partnership firm is individually liable to Class 2 and Class 4 contributions.

5. The following is the list of persons who are **exempt** from Class 4 NIC:

   a) Persons **above the pension age** (i.e. male 65, female 60) at the beginning of the tax year.

   b) Individuals who are **not resident** for income tax purposes.

   c) **Trustees and executors** who are chargeable to income tax on the income they receive on behalf of some other persons (e.g. incapacitated person).

   d) **Sleeping partners** i.e. a partner in a partnership firm who supplies capital but is not actively involved in the business activities.

   e) **An individual** who is **below 16** at the beginning of the particular tax year.

   f) **Divers and diving supervisors** who are working on exploration and exploitation activities on the UK Continental Shelf or in UK territorial waters.

E2.4: National Insurance Contributions

> **Tip**
>
> How to remember a person who is exempt from Class 4 NIC?
> Well you need to S P E N D some time!
>
> Just remember the word **"SPEND"** as given below:
>
> **S: S**leeping partners
> **P: P**erson **above** pension age 60 / 65 and **below** 16
> **E: E**xecutors and Trustees
> **N: N**on-Residents of the UK
> **D: D**ivers & Diving supervisors

Test Yourself 1

Calculate the Class 4 NICs payable for 2009-10 in the following cases:

1. Ted has trading income for 2009-10 of £15,820.
2. Mary has trade income for 2009-10 of £51,720.
3. Mark has trading income for 2009-10 of £4,820.

Answer to Test Yourself

Answer 1

1. 8% x (£15,820 - £5,715) = £808.40

2. 8% x (£43,875 - £5,715) + 1% x (£51,720 - £43,875)
   £3,053 + £78 = £3,131.25

3. Mark's Class 4 liability for the year is nil, as his profits are less than the lower profit limit (i.e. £5,715).

Quick Quiz

Fill in the blanks.

1. The rate for contribution for Class 2 NIC for 2009-10 is _____ per week.

2. Men and women over _____ age are exempt from Class 2 NIC.

3. A self-employed person is liable to Class 4 NIC if his income is above _____ for the year 2009-10.

Answers Quick to Quiz

1. £2.40 per week

2. State pension

3. £5,715.

Self Examination Questions

Question 1

Ritu is self-employed. She has elected 31 March as the year-end. For 2009-10 her books of accounts showed a profit of £4,000. Does she need to pay Class 2 NIC?

Question 2

Alana is a 63 year old self-employed person. In 2009-10 she earned £5,000.

Required:

Is she liable for any contribution to Class 2 NIC?

Question 3

Stewart has a wholesale stationery business. He prepares annual accounts to 5 April. His trading income from this business for 2009-10 is £3,900. He also owns a toy shop. His income from this business for the year 2009-10 is £4,200.

Required:

How much should he contribute to Class 2 NIC?

Question 4

Bernard is a carpenter. He is working with a company that manufactures furniture. On holidays he also works independently. In the year 2009-10 his monthly salary was £1,900. His income from self-employment was £300 per month.

Required:

Calculate his Class 2 and 4 NIC liability for the year 2009-10.

Question 5

Matthew has trading profits of £52,150 for the tax year 2009-10.

Required:

Advise him how much he should pay towards Class 2 and 4 NIC.

Answers to Self Examination Questions

Answer 1

For 2009-10, a self-employed person whose earnings from self-employment are less than £5,075 need not contribute anything to Class 2 NIC.

Answer 2

Class 2 NICs are payable by self-employed persons, who are under the pension age. The pension age for females is 60 years. Therefore Alana, being over 60, need not contribute to Class 2 NIC. However, Alana can voluntarily contribute to Class 2 NIC.

Answer 3

Stewart is a self-employed person. Therefore, for the year 2009-10, he is required to contribute £125 (52 weeks x £2.40) towards Class 2 NIC.

Answer 4

Bernard's total earnings are as follows:
Salary income £22,800 (£1,900 x 12)
Trading income £3,600 (£300 x 12)
Therefore total earnings are £26,400.

A self-employed person is liable to Class 2 if his **trading profits** are more than £5,075, and he is liable to Class 4 NIC if his **trading income** is more than £5,715.

However, his earnings from self-employment (i.e. £3,600) are less than the small earning exception limit (i.e. for 2009-10, it is £5,075); Bernard need not pay Class 2 NIC. However, he may contribute voluntarily.

In the same way, his trading income is less than the lower profit limit (i.e. £5,715 for 2009-10,) therefore he need not pay Class 4 NIC.

Answer 5

Matthew should pay:

1. £124.80 (52 weeks x £2.40) towards Class 2 NIC.
2. £3,135.55 towards Class 4 NIC.
   Calculation of contribution to Class 4 NIC is as follows:

	£
Up to first £5715	-
Next £(43,875 – 5,715) x 8%	3,052.80
On remaining amount (£52,150 – £43,875) x 1%	82.75
Total Class 4 NIC contribution	**3,135.55**

SECTION F: VALUE ADDED TAX

F1

STUDY GUIDE F1: THE SCOPE OF VALUE ADDED TAX (VAT)

Get Through Intro

VAT is an indirect tax that you pay when you buy goods and services in the European Union (EU), including the United Kingdom. Where VAT is payable it is normally included in the price of the goods or service you buy. However, some goods do not attract VAT.

'Value added tax' – VAT is an important topic of your syllabus for this paper. It is essential that you devote considerable time to this section as a minimum 10 mark question is normally based on this topic.

As the taxation consultant of a big group of companies, you will have to be armed with complete, up-to-date knowledge of the scope, applicability and requirements of VAT.

In the course of the next four Study Guides, **we will take you through the whole syllabus for VAT.**

You will learn about the concept of VAT, all the formalities of VAT registration, calculation of VAT liabilities and payments, filing of VAT returns, assessments and the effect of special accounting schemes.

Learning Outcomes

a) Describe the scope of VAT.
b) List the principal zero-rated and exempt supplies.

Introduction

Value added tax is an indirect tax which means that it is charged on turnover, not profits.

The basic principle of VAT is that tax should be charged at each stage of manufacturing / production as well as at each stage of the whole distribution chain.

The total tax due is ultimately borne by the final consumer of the product i.e. the manufacturer recovers it from the consumer.

The name itself suggests that it is a tax on the value addition put in to the process. The final consumer does not "add value" but consumes the final goods or service, therefore the consumers absorbs the charge to tax.

1. Describe the scope of VAT.[2]

[Learning outcome a]

The scope of VAT

- VAT is charged on the **taxable supply** of goods and services in the UK by a **taxable person** in the course of a business run by him.

- VAT is an **indirect tax** in that it is charged **on turnover, not profits**.

- VAT is charged on the consumption of goods and services by the **final consumer**.

- **At each stage** of the manufacturing process, a **trader adds VAT onto his sales** (output VAT), and acts as a collector of taxes for HMRC.

- Each **supplier receives credit for any VAT** he pays **on his purchases** (input VAT).

- The **supplier pays HMRC the difference between the VAT charged and the VAT suffered** – so the supplier does **not suffer VAT** himself.

- The **final consumer suffers the total tax**.

Example

Tasty Ltd manufactures chocolates. The selling price of the chocolates is £60 per packet plus VAT. The cost of the raw materials required to make 1 packet of chocolates is £20 plus VAT of 15%. Mega Ltd is a wholesaler of chocolates. It buys chocolates from Tasty Ltd, wraps them in attractive packaging, and thus adds some value to it.

These chocolates are then sold to various retail outlets for £100 per kg plus VAT. The retail outlets sell the chocolates at £120 per kg plus VAT. Let's see how VAT is accounted for to HMRC at each stage of manufacturing. Ultimately, the final customer will bear the VAT.

	Input		Output		
	Cost £	VAT @ 15%	Net Sales £	VAT on sales @ 15%	VAT payable £
Manufacturer	20	3.0	60	9.0	**6.0** (9.0 – 3.0)
Wholesaler	69	10.35	100	15.0	**4.65** (15.0 – 10.35)
Retailer	115	17.25	120	18.0	**0.75** (18.0 – 17.25)

Notice that each of the businesses (manufacturer, wholesaler, and retailer) in the chain only account for VAT on the value they are adding. Remember, in accounting for VAT you will have debited the input VAT on purchases to the VAT account while the purchases account has been debited with the purchase value. Similarly the output VAT on sales is credited to VAT account and the sales account is credited only with the sales value.

The final customers are unable to reclaim the VAT that they have paid (£18.0). They suffer the VAT.

1.1 Taxable supply: a taxable supply is a supply of goods or services made in the UK. A taxable supply can be standard or zero rated.

1. Standard-rated e.g. supplies of stationery or

2. Zero-rated e.g. supplies of books

> **Tip**
> However, some supplies are charged at a reduced rate of 5% (e.g. supplies of fuel and power for domestic use).

a) Standard-rated supplies

i. Standard-rated supplies are **taxable at 15%** (up to 31 December 2009) and at 17.5% (from 1 January 2010 onwards)
ii. A trader who is registered for VAT suffers VAT on the purchases (inputs) which are standard-rated. The VAT suffered on the purchases is set off against the output VAT collected on sales at the standard rate. The excess amount collected is paid to HMRC. If the amount suffered is greater than the amount collected, then a refund for the VAT suffered is received.

b) Zero-rated supplies

i. Zero-rated supplies are **taxable at 0%**
ii. A trader whose supplies (output) are zero-rated but whose purchases (inputs) are standard rated will **receive a refund for the VAT suffered** on them.

c) Exempt supplies

i. Exempt supplies are **not chargeable to VAT.**
ii. A trader whose supplies (output) are exempt will not charge any VAT but will suffer VAT on purchases (inputs). Such a trader will not be able to recover the input VAT.

A person making exempt supplies may not
➢ **register** for VAT
➢ **recover VAT** in purchases (**inputs**)

Example Heden makes standard-rated supplies, Alan makes zero-rated supplies and Acme makes exempt supplies.

The inputs of all the three traders are standard-rated.

	Helen £	VAT (£)	Alan £	VAT (£)	Acme £	VAT (£)
Sales	45,000		45,000		45,000	
Output VAT @ 15%		6,750		Nil		Exempt
Purchases	(35,000)		(35,000)		(35,000)	
Input VAT @ 15%		(5,250)		(5,250)	(5,250)	Exempt
VAT Payable / (Refundable)		1,500		(5,250)		Exempt
Net Profits	10,000		10,000		4,750	

Working

W1

(£51,750 - £1,500) - £40,250 = £10,000
(£45,000 + £5,250) – £40,250 = £10,000
(£45,000 - 0) – £40,250 = £4,750

The example clearly shows that net profit of standard-rated (Heden Ltd) and zero-rated supplies (Alan Ltd) is the same, whereas the net profit of exempt supplies (Acme Ltd) is lower than the other two. This is because it cannot recover input VAT. In the course of accounting for VAT, the standard rated and zero rated traders can open a VAT account and debit and credit the VAT on purchases and sales. The net amount is either payable or recoverable. On the other hand, the exempt trader who is not registered cannot open a VAT account and therefore the VAT suffered on purchases is a cost to the business.

SUMMARY

- **Taxable supply**
  - **standard rated**
    - 15% up to 31 December 2009
    - 17.5% from 1 January 2010 onwards
  - zero rated (0%)
  - exempt supplies are not chargeable to VAT

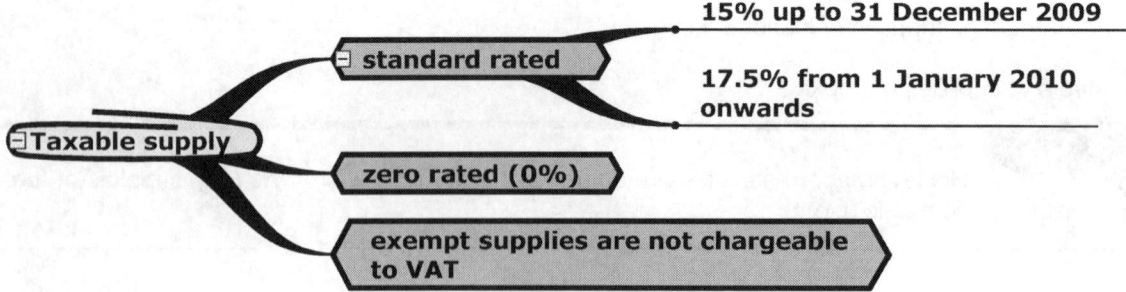

1.2 Taxable persons

A taxable person is a **person making taxable supplies** who **is, or is required** to be, **registered for VAT.**

A person **includes a sole trader, partnerships and limited companies.**

1.3 Supply of goods

Supply of goods occurs when:

1. **Ownership** of goods **passes** from one person to another.

> **Example**
> In the case of the purchase of a car, the dealer of the car registers the car in the name of the purchaser. In short, ownership is transferred from the dealer to the purchaser of the car.

2. **Goods are supplied for some consideration**. Consideration can be in the form of money or any other goods (such as in the barter system) but there should be some consideration.

> **Example**
> James **bought** a suit for the consideration of £100. The shop owner gives James the suit in return for payment of £100. VAT is included in the cost of the suit.

However, if James received a shirt as a **gift** from his grandfather, this does not amount to taxable supply of goods. The grandfather is giving him the suit as a personal gift and hence no VAT is charged.

> **Example**
> Dodson gave his Mercedes Benz (worth £20,000) to Fogg and in return Fogg gave him a factory building for a consideration of £18,200 in Stockholm. This car is considered to have been sold (through a barter system) and VAT is applicable on £18,200.

3. **Goods are sold on a hire purchase (HP) basis.**

Although ownership of the goods is only transferred at the end of the contract, VAT is charged at the time when the HP contract is signed on the cash price of the goods, not on the hire purchase (HP) price.

In general, VAT is charged only when ownership of the goods is transferred. However, in the case of HP contracts, VAT is charged at the time of signing the contract and not when actual ownership is transferred.

> **Example**
> Catherine purchased a home theatre system on an HP basis. The cash price of the home theatre system is £3,000. As she took it on an HP basis, she agreed to pay £3,120 to the shop owner. This amount is payable in equal instalments of £520 per month for six months.

As the home theatre system is a taxable good, as mentioned above, she has to pay VAT on the amount of £3,000 (i.e. the cash price) and not on the £3,120 (HP price). VAT is charged at the time when the HP contract is signed by Catherine.

The following is a list of transactions, which are **deemed to be supplies** for VAT purposes (i.e. on which VAT must be charged):

a) A **gift** of a **business asset**, except gifts costing less than £50.

Example Shine Ltd has a showroom for diamonds. In 2009, the company gave a diamond ring to all its managerial category employees as a New Year gift. Each ring is worth £100.

This gift by the company to its employees is taxable under VAT (diamonds are inventory of the company and the cost of the gift is more than £50).

Gifts include **samples.** Usually **one sample** can be given **VAT free**, but if two or more identical goods are given to the same person as samples, then this is considered to be supply.

Example The samples of newly-marketed chocolates in well-designed boxes are given to retail outlets. Each retailer was given two sample boxes of chocolates; therefore they will be taxable under VAT.

b) Goods on which VAT has been paid and which are removed from the business permanently by the owner or his employee for **private use.**

Example Kitty runs an ice-cream shop. In April 2009, she purchased a computer for invoicing purposes. In December 2009, she took the computer home permanently for her personal use.

In short, Kitty started using the business computer for her personal purposes. This is also considered to be a supply of taxable goods and accordingly VAT is applicable.

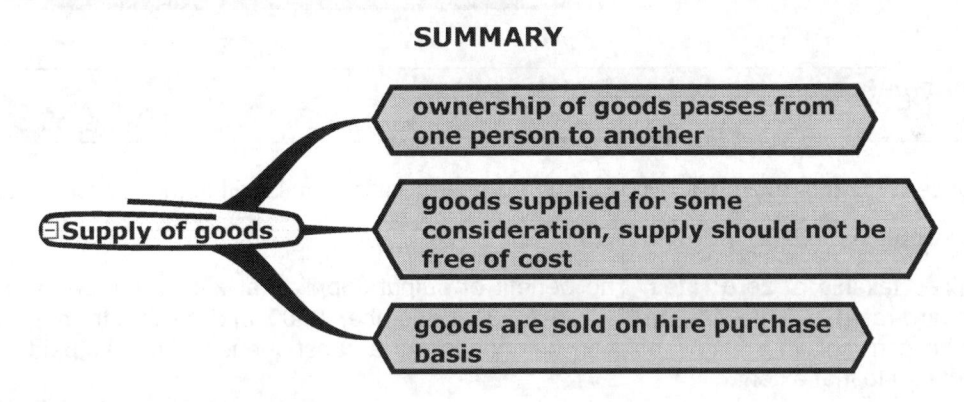

SUMMARY

Supply of goods
- ownership of goods passes from one person to another
- goods supplied for some consideration, supply should not be free of cost
- goods are sold on hire purchase basis

1.4 Supply of services

A supply of services takes place when:

1. Supply is in exchange for **some consideration.**
2. Supply is not a **supply of goods.**
3. **Goods are hired** by customers but ownership is not transferred to the customer.

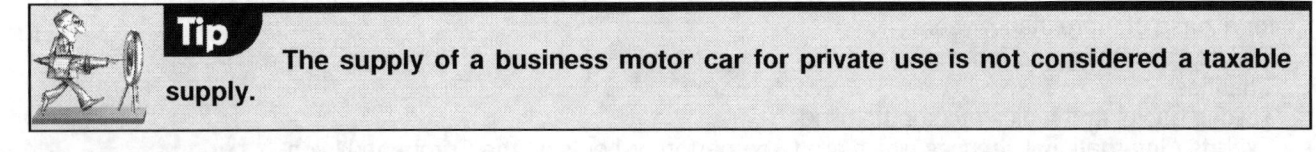

Tip The supply of a business motor car for private use is not considered a taxable supply.

Example Idea Plc, a leading software company, hired a helicopter on a monthly basis to transport the company's executives. By availing the helicopter on a hire basis, the vendor is supplying services to the company.

In this transaction, even though the ownership of the helicopter is not transferred, the services are liable for VAT.

The following transactions are **deemed supplies**, where the owner or his employee:

a) temporarily makes **private use of goods** owned by the business and while purchasing these goods VAT (input tax) has been paid.

Example A director of Sigma Plc used the company warehouse for six months to hold his household furniture while his house was renovated. This temporary usage of the warehouse by the director is considered a supply of services.

b) makes **private use of services**, which are supplied to the business and while hiring those services VAT (i.e. input tax) has been paid.

Example Linda, the CEO of a software company used a helicopter for a weekend with her family, which the company had taken on a hire basis. The company paid £450 (including VAT) for hiring the helicopter.

Here the cost of services for private usage of helicopter over the weekend by Linda is deemed cost of supplies.

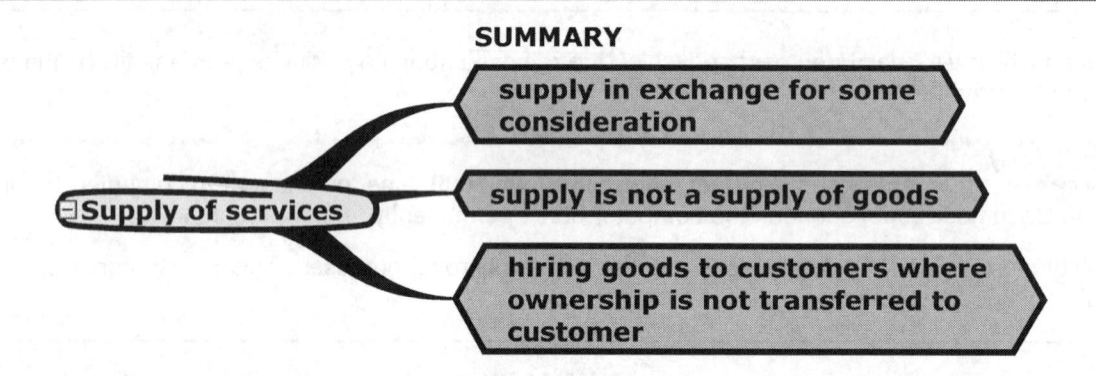

SUMMARY

Supply of services:
- supply in exchange for some consideration
- supply is not a supply of goods
- hiring goods to customers where ownership is not transferred to customer

2. List the principal zero-rated and exempt supplies.[1]

[Learning outcome b]

If a supply is not zero-rated or exempt it will be standard rated (unless it falls within the reduced rate category).

2.1 Zero-rated supplies

These are supplies taxable at **zero rates.** The benefit of output supplied at zero rates is that if a supplier's inputs are standard-rated (i.e. taxable @15% up to 31 December 2009 and 17.5% from 1 January 2010 onwards), then he can reclaim the VAT paid on purchases. As a consequence, the VAT paid on the cost of purchases is reduced to that extent.

Principal categories are

1. Food (for human and animal consumption) except luxury food (e.g. chocolates, ice-cream, alcoholic drinks or food supplied in catering)
2. Drugs and medicines prescribed by a practitioner and certain aids to the handicapped
3. Passenger transport (except taxis and hire cars)
4. Books, newspaper, journals etc. (but not stationery)
5. Sale of new buildings by a builder for residential or charitable purposes or an amount payable by tenant for a lease of more than 4 years
6. Children's clothing and footwear
7. Charities
8. Talking books and radios etc. for the blind
9. Exports / International services which are to be performed outside the European Union
10. Sewerage services and water (except for industrial use)
11. Certain caravans and houseboats
12. Bank notes
13. Gold supplied by one central bank to another central bank or member of the London gold market.

2.2 Exempt supplies

Exempt supplies are business supplies other than taxable supplies **on which VAT is not charged.**

Exempt supplies are at par with supplies of a non-registered person. This means that a person making a **supply of exempt output is not allowed to recover VAT paid on input.**

Principal categories are

1. Betting, lotteries and gaming
2. Burial and cremation services
3. Fund-raising events by charities
4. Cultural services
5. Education provided by schools and universities
6. Financial services (e.g. bank charges, stock broking, underwriting)
7. Health and welfare services
8. Insurance
9. Investment gold
10. Land
11. Non profit-making sports competitions etc
12. Postal services provided by post offices
13. Supplies of goods on which input tax is not recoverable
14. Supplies to members by trade unions and professional bodies
15. Disposal of works of art to approved bodies

Quick Quiz

1. State whether the following statements are true or false:

    a) VAT is charged only on goods.
    b) A 'taxable person' is a person who charges VAT on supplies made by him.
    c) A person who sells exempt goods but whose purchases are liable to VAT actually bears the cost of the VAT.

2. State which case is not applicable for VAT and justify your answer.

    a) Amazon Ltd hired a creative designer as a consultant to design a new product portfolio at a mutually acceptable consideration.

    b) John, a sole trader of computer hardware, gave an assembled computer to his daughter as a gift. This computer was assembled from the VAT paid inventory of computer hardware.

    c) Cleanex Ltd manufactures detergents. The company has introduced a new soap. As a marketing strategy, the company appoints salesmen to distribute the samples of soap across households. The company has decided to give a small soap as sample. Is the company liable for VAT on a sample of soap?

Answers to Quick Quiz

1.
a) **False.** VAT is also charged on supply of services.

b) **False.** A taxable person means a person who is registered (or is required to be registered) for VAT.

c) **True.** A person who sells exempt goods, but whose purchase price includes VAT, cannot register for VAT. Therefore he cannot reclaim the VAT paid on the purchases. In short, he becomes the last person in the distribution chain and therefore bears the VAT.

2.
a) The supply of services is also taxable under VAT. Services for designing products are not specifically exempt from VAT. If a consultant is a taxable person (i.e. registered for VAT), VAT is applicable.

b) If the owner of the business takes out (permanently) VAT paid business goods, then this is considered a supply of taxable goods. In short, the owner is liable for VAT on the supply.

In the case of John, he used VAT paid inventory for his personal use (i.e. to give a gift to his daughter). This is considered deemed supply and is therefore liable for VAT.

c) VAT is also applicable on free samples. If two or three identical goods are given as samples to the same person, the transaction is deemed to be a supply for VAT purposes. However, one sample can be given VAT-free.

As Cleanex Ltd has decided to give one bar of soap to each customer, VAT is not applicable. Hence, Cleanex Ltd need not pay VAT on the free samples distributed.

SECTION F: VALUE ADDED TAX — F2

STUDY GUIDE F2: THE VAT REGISTRATION REQUIREMENTS

Get Through Intro

This Study Guide will discuss **when it becomes essential for a person to register for VAT and the advantages of voluntary registration for VAT**. It will also explain when and how a person can **deregister for VAT.**

This Study Guide also introduces you to the concept of recovery of pre-registration input VAT. A thorough understanding of this concept will help you to advise your client as to how voluntary registration for VAT helps to maintain a competitive selling price.

Proper tax planning requires an in-depth knowledge of all the rules and provisions of income tax as well as the VAT Act (Value Added Tax Act 1994)

A thorough study of this Study Guide will enable you acquire this knowledge which will help in your exams as well as in your professional life as a tax consultant.

Learning Outcomes

a) Recognise the circumstances in which a person must register for VAT.
b) Explain the advantages of voluntary VAT registration.
c) Explain the circumstances in which pre-registration input VAT can be recovered.
d) Explain how and when a person can deregister for VAT.

Introduction

Case Study

Jake and Josh design and manufacture digital flat screen televisions. They are not required to register for VAT as their turnover does not exceed the threshold set by HMRC. They heard from a friend that it may be beneficial to them to register for VAT and are now wondering whether to register. They make taxable supplies of 40 televisions in a year and they retail at £500 each (before VAT). The materials used to produce these taxable supplies cost Jake and Josh £100 each (before VAT).

As Jake and Josh's tax adviser, consider whether they should apply for voluntary registration of VAT?

	If registered £	If not registered £
Sales		
40 x (£500 + 15% VAT)	23,000	
40 x £500		20,000
Less: Output tax		
40 x (£500 x 15%)	(3,000)	-
Sales (excluding VAT)	20,000	20,000
Cost of sales		
40 x (£100 + VAT 15%)	(4,600)	(4,600)
Input tax reclaimed	600	-
Profit	**16,000**	**15,400**

It is advisable to register voluntarily as the profit is more by £600.

The various advantages of voluntary VAT registration are discussed at length in this Study Guide.

1. Recognise the circumstances in which a person must register for VAT.[2]
[Learning outcome a]

A person must register for VAT if his taxable turnover exceeds the registration limit of **£68,000**.

1.1 There are two situations where registration is compulsory:

1. historic test
2. future test

1. Historic test

a) Registration

Registration is **compulsory if,** at the end of any month, the **taxable turnover (excluding VAT) for the last 12 months exceeds £68,000.**

VAT registration is **not required if** taxable supplies in the following 12 months do **not exceed £66,000. A trader may wish to register voluntarily.**

b) Notification to HMRC

Notification to HMRC must be **within 30 days of the end of the month in which the £68,000 limit is exceeded.**

c) Effective registration date

Registration is **effective from the end of the month following the month when the limit was exceeded.**

> **Example**
> Stephen started his new business in April 2009. His taxable turnover during the first six months of trading is as follows (sales figures provided are individual as well as cumulative):
>
> | 2009 | £ | £ (Cumulative) |
> |---|---|---|
> | April | 2,000 | 2,000 |
> | May | 4,100 | 6,100 |
> | June | 10,300 | 16,400 |
> | July | 12,000 | 28,400 |
> | August | 21,300 | 49,700 |
> | September | 18,400 | 68,100 |
>
> Taxable turnover exceeds the registration threshold (£68,000) at the end of September 2009. Stephen must notify HMRC by 30 October 2009. The registration will be effective from 1 November 2009.

Test Yourself 1

Adobe Ltd commenced trading on 1 January 2009. It prepares accounts to year end 31 December every year. Its sales are as follows:

	£		£
January 2009	6,000	September 2009	7,100
February 2009	3,650	October 2009	4,000
March 2009	5,000	November 2009	5,600
April 2009	4,100	December 2009	5,650
May 2009	4,850	January 2010	4,050
June 2009	4,990	February 2010	4,400
July 2009	3,770	March 2010	4,200
August 2009	5,800		

Required:

1. When will Adobe Ltd become liable for compulsory VAT registration?
2. When will it have to notify HMRC?
3. When will the registration be effective?

2. Future test

a) Registration

Registration is **compulsory if** taxable supplies are **expected to exceed £68,000** during the **next 30 days alone.**

This is **not a cumulative test**; the **taxable turnover in the previous months is not relevant.**

b) Notification to HMRC

Notification to HMRC must be by the end of the 30 day period.

c) Effective registration date

Registration is effective from the beginning of the 30 day period.

> **Example**
> Star Ltd commenced trading on 1 September 2009. Sales for the following months are as follows:
>
> | | | £ |
> |---|---|---|
> | 2009 | September | 6,000 |
> | | October | 7,500 |
> | | November | 30,500 |
> | | December | 50,000 |
> | 2010 | January | 74,500 |

Continued on next page

1. Star Ltd realised that its taxable supplies for January 2010 would be at least £70,000. So, the company is liable for registration from 1 January 2010, being the beginning of the 30 day period.
2. Star Ltd has to notify HMRC by 30 January 2010, being the end of the 30 day period.
3. Registration is effective from 1 January 2010, being the beginning of the 30 day period.

Test Yourself 2

Charmie Ltd started trading on 1 October 2009. The details of sales for different months are as follows:

		£
2009	November	5,000
	December	25,000
2010	January	69,500

Required:

1. When will Charmie Ltd become liable for compulsory registration?
2. When will it have to notify HMRC?
3. When will the registration be effective?

> **Tip**
> Standard and zero-rated supplies are taxable supplies, exempt supplies are not.

Example

Moon Ltd intends to start its business in the near future. The company operates a vehicle, and is about to consider three different alternative types of business.

They are as follows:

1. transportation where all the sales will be zero-rated
2. training where all the sales will be standard-rated, and
3. a charitable service, where all the sales will be exempt from VAT.

Sales for each of the above-mentioned alternatives will be £80,000 per month (exclusive of VAT), and standard-rated expenses will be £15,000.

Zero-rated supplies

In this case, as zero rated supplies are also taxable, Moon Ltd will have to register for VAT.

Output VAT will not be due, but input VAT of £1,957 (£15,000 x 3/23) per month will be recoverable.

Standard-rated supplies

Here, Moon Ltd will be required to register for VAT as it will be making taxable supplies.
Output VAT of £12,000 (£80,000 x 15%) per month will be due, and input VAT of £1,957 per month will be recoverable. Net VAT payable will be £10,043 (£12,000 – £1,957).

Exempt supplies

Moon Ltd will not be required to register for VAT; in fact, it will not be permitted to register, as it will not be making taxable supplies.
As it is dealing with exempt supplies, neither will output VAT be due nor will input VAT be recoverable.

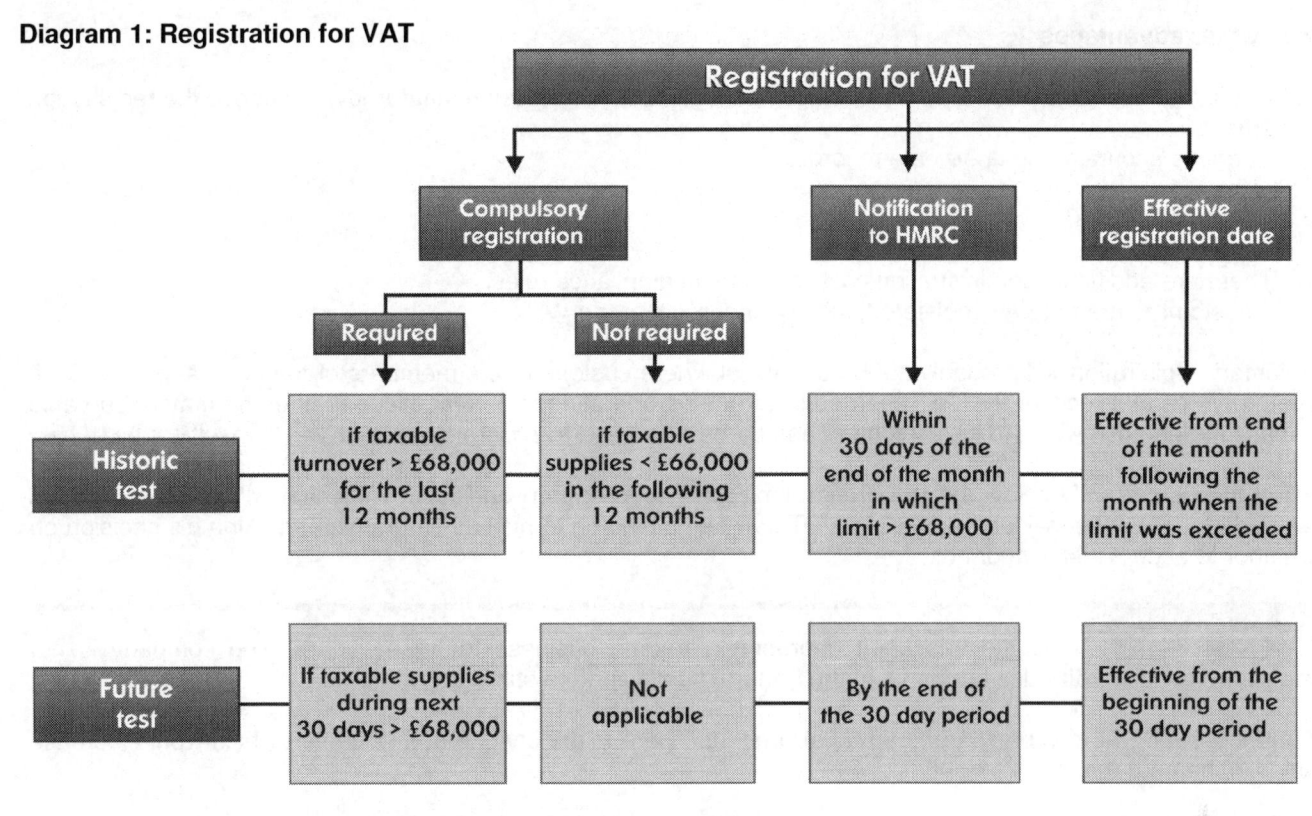

Diagram 1: Registration for VAT

```
                        Registration for VAT
                                │
        ┌───────────────────────┼───────────────────────┐
        ▼                       ▼                       ▼
   Compulsory              Notification            Effective
   registration             to HMRC            registration date
        │
   ┌────┴────┐
   ▼         ▼
Required  Not required
```

	Required	Not required	Notification to HMRC	Effective registration date
Historic test	if taxable turnover > £68,000 for the last 12 months	if taxable supplies < £66,000 in the following 12 months	Within 30 days of the end of the month in which limit > £68,000	Effective from end of the month following the month when the limit was exceeded
Future test	If taxable supplies during next 30 days > £68,000	Not applicable	By the end of the 30 day period	Effective from the beginning of the 30 day period

2. Explain the advantages of voluntary VAT registration.[2]

[Learning outcome b]

A person may become registered for VAT even though his supplies fall below the registration limit.

The individual must then charge output VAT on his supplies and may reclaim input VAT on his purchases.

2.1 Voluntary registration will be beneficial if:

1. The **customers are registered for VAT**. The customers can reclaim the VAT, and the trader should be able to charge VAT on top of the pre-registration selling price.

2. **The supplies are zero-rated**. Output tax is at zero % and input VAT will be recoverable.

> **Example**
>
> Star Ltd commenced trading on 1 September 2009. Sales for the following months were as follows:

		£
2009	September	6,000
	October	7,500
	November	30,500
	December	50,000
2010	January	74,500

The company sales were all standard-rated and were all made to VAT registered businesses.

Assume that input VAT for the period 1 September to 31 January 2010 was £14,500.

The input VAT wouldn't have been recoverable if Star Ltd had registered for VAT on 1 February 2010 (when turnover exceeded £68,000).

If it had registered voluntarily on 1 September 2009 it would have recovered input VAT of £14,500.

Also, all sales were to VAT registered businesses, so output VAT can be passed on to customers.

2.2 Other advantages

1. Registration lends credibility to the business as it gives the impression that turnover is above the registration limit.
2. Requires accurate and up-to-date records.

2.3 Disadvantages

1. There are additional administration costs and strict compliance rules.
2. If customers are not VAT registered, they cannot recover the VAT.

Voluntary registration will probably not be beneficial where customers are members of the general public. Such customers cannot recover the VAT charged. If a trader is operating in a competitive market, he may not be able to pass the output VAT on to his customers and so he may need to absorb the output VAT himself.

If a trader is currently below the registration limit, and he is offered additional work that will mean the limit is exceeded, he must consider if the output VAT can be passed on to his customers when making his decision on whether to accept the work or not.

Example

Acme Ltd has been operating a trading business for many years. The company is not registered for VAT. All sales are made to the general public and are standard-rated.

Annual sales of the company are £59,500 at present. There is the chance of a price rise which would increase sales in the near future to £68,500.

Acme Ltd's standard-rated expenses are £6,000 per annum (inclusive of VAT).
Net profit when sales were £59,500 is (£59,500 - £6,000) = **£53,500**.

When prices go up, sales will increase above the VAT registration limit of £68,000. Therefore the company will have to register for VAT.

As sales are made to the general public, Acme Ltd will have to absorb the output VAT and therefore there won't be any scope for an increase in prices.

Revised annual net profit will be as follows:

	£
Revenue (£68,500 x 20/23)	59,565
Expenses (£6,000 x 20/23)	(5,217)
Net profit	**54,348**

Therefore, we can see that there is an increase in net profit of £848 (£54,348 - £53,500).
It is beneficial for the company to raise its prices.

3. Explain the circumstances in which pre-registration input VAT can be recovered.[2]
[Learning outcome c]

Input VAT relating to pre-registration supplies can be **recovered if** the following **conditions are satisfied:**

Goods
- The goods were supplied for **business purposes.**
- The goods have **not** been **sold or consumed before the date of registration.**
- They were **not** acquired **more than three years before registration.**
- They include inventory and fixed assets.

Services
- The services were supplied for **business purposes.**
- The services were **not** acquired **more than six months before registration.**

Example

Gemini Ltd started trading on 1 August 2009, but registered for VAT on 1 December 2009. For the period 1 August to 30 November 2009, the company had the following inputs:

	August £	September £	October £	November £
Goods purchased	2,500	4,500	15,500	28,500
Services incurred	2,200	3,000	4,500	5,000
Fixed assets	70,000			

On 1 December 2009, there was stock of goods costing £15,000.

All figures are exclusive of VAT. The stock of goods was neither acquired more than three years before registration nor was it sold or consumed before registration.

So, input VAT of **£2,250** (£15,000 x 15%) can be recovered on 1 December 2009 on stock of goods.

In the same way, input VAT on fixed assets **£10,500** (70,000 x 15%) can be recovered.

As the services were not supplied more than six months before registration, input VAT on services **£2,205** (£2,200 + £3,000 + £4,500 + £5,000 = £14,700 x 15%) can be recovered.

Total input VAT that can be recovered = £2,250 + £10,500 + £2,205 = £14,955

Test Yourself 3

Bonsai Ltd commenced business as a manufacturer of children's toys on 1 August 2008. Its output and input for each of the months from January to April 2009 were as follows:

	January £	February £	March £	April £
Output				
Sales	6,000	8,500	31,400	71,510
Input				
Goods purchased	2,500	5,300	21,700	6,400
Services incurred	1,000	2,000	3,000	4,000

The above figures are all exclusive of VAT.
Bonsai Ltd's sales as well as inputs are all standard-rated.
On 1 April 2009 Bonsai Ltd realised that its sales for April 2009 were set to exceed £68,000, and therefore the company immediately registered for VAT. On the date of registration, the company had a stock of goods that had cost £22,000 (exclusive of VAT).

Required:

Calculate the amount of VAT reclaimable relating to goods purchased and services hired prior to the registration of VAT.

Test Yourself 4

On 5 June 2009, Gary began trading. On 10 November 2009, he voluntarily registered himself for VAT. On 10 July 2009 (i.e. before he had registered his business for VAT) he had taken a lorry to carry machinery for business use, on a rental basis and had paid VAT of £300.

Required:

Can he reclaim VAT paid on services hired before registration for VAT?

---

4. **Explain how and when a person can deregister for VAT.**[1]

[Learning outcome d]

4.1 Deregistration from VAT

1. **Compulsory**

a) A registered person must deregister if he **ceases to make taxable supplies.**

b) **Notification** to HMRC should be given **within 30 days** of ceasing to make taxable supplies. Failure to do so may lead to a penalty being charged.

c) **Effective deregistration date** is the day taxable **supplies ceased.**

2. Voluntary

a) A registered person may deregister voluntarily **if taxable supplies in the next twelve months are not expected to exceed £66,000.**

b) Notification to HMRC may be made when it appears that the taxable turnover in the next twelve months will not exceed £66,000.

c) **Effective** deregistration **date** is the **date HMRC are notified.**

On deregistration there is a deemed supply of business assets (plant, equipment and trading stock).

However, the transfer of a business as a going concern (as opposed to piecemeal sale of assets) does not usually give rise to VAT – it is outside the scope of VAT.

Example

Nickle Ltd has been registered for VAT since 2000. It intends to cease trading on 31 March 2010.

It has two options on cessation: option one - to sell its business assets on a piecemeal basis to individual buyers, or, option two - to sell its entire business as a going concern to a single purchaser.

The effects on cessation of trading under these two options will be as follows:

Option one

Business assets sold on piecemeal basis
- Nickle Ltd's VAT registration will be cancelled on 31 March 2010 as it will cease to make taxable supplies.
- Output VAT will be due on fixed assets on which VAT has been claimed.
- Notification to HMRC: the company will have to notify HMRC by 30 April 2010, being 30 days after the date of cessation.

Option two

Business sold as a going concern
- VAT registration will be cancelled, if the purchaser is already registered for VAT.
- If the purchaser is not registered for VAT, then it can take over the VAT registration of Nickle Ltd.
- Output VAT will not be due as sale of a business as a going concern is outside the scope of VAT.

Diagram 2: Deregistration for VAT

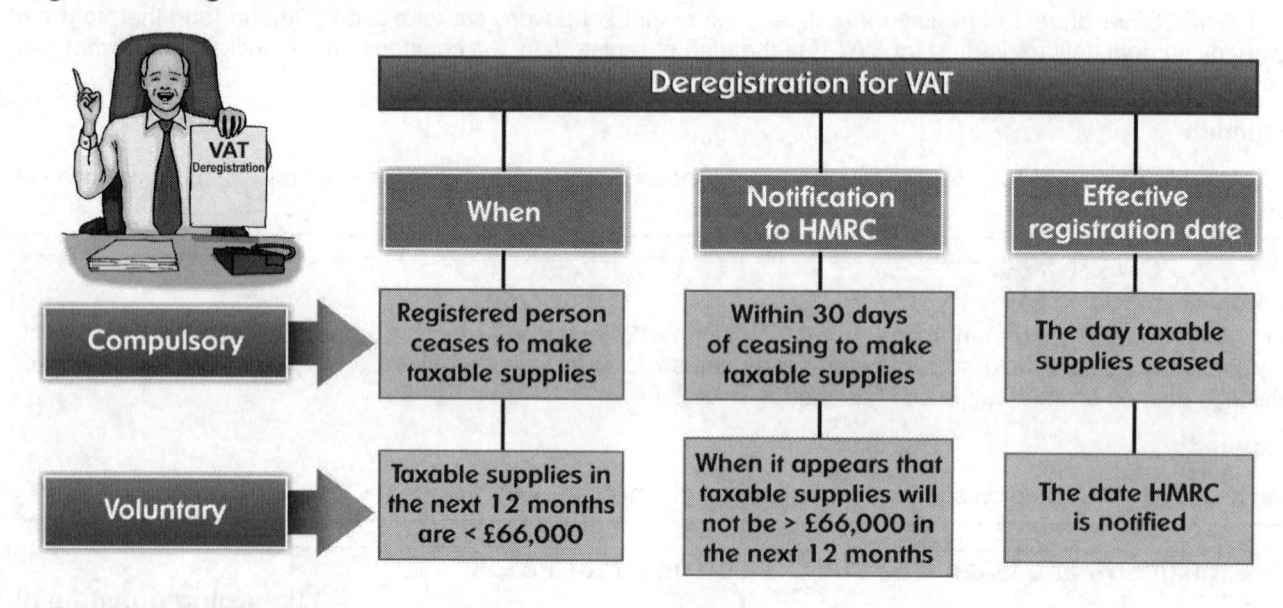

	When	Notification to HMRC	Effective registration date
Compulsory	Registered person ceases to make taxable supplies	Within 30 days of ceasing to make taxable supplies	The day taxable supplies ceased
Voluntary	Taxable supplies in the next 12 months are < £66,000	When it appears that taxable supplies will not be > £66,000 in the next 12 months	The date HMRC is notified

4.2 Other important points

1. When a change in a person's legal status takes place, e.g. a business is taken over by a new owner, the new owner of the business can continue with the existing VAT registration number, provided he agrees to take over all liabilities and rights from the date of transfer of the business. In short, registration under VAT **is in relation to the business and not in relation to the person who owns the business.**

In effect, on the transfer of business from one person to another, the old registration need not be cancelled just because the ownership has changed.

2. When a person ceases to make taxable supplies, VAT becomes chargeable on all remaining inventory after deregistration and all remaining capital goods on which input tax was claimed previously.

Example

For the last twenty years, Stella has been a manufacturer of calculators. It is her practice to purchase the raw material for the whole month on the first day of the month. As usual, on 1 July 2009, she purchased raw material worth £20,000 required for the month of July 2009. She paid input VAT of £3,000 on these purchases.

On 10 July 2009 she supplied calculators worth £30,000. She adjusted the input VAT paid on purchases made in the month of July against the output VAT payable on the sales.

However, due to a sudden major physical disability, she became unable to run her business and, on 20 August 2009, she ceased manufacturing. She deregistered her business from the VAT regime. On the date of deregistration, raw material worth £14,000 was in inventory (out of the raw material purchased on 1 July 2009).

In this situation, Stella needs to pay VAT on £14,000 (i.e. on the raw material held in inventory out of the purchases made on 1 July 2009 and input VAT which is adjusted against output VAT).

Test Yourself 5

In July 2009, Tim expects that in the current year (i.e. 2009-10) his turnover will not be more than £58,000. He informs HMRC that he wants to deregister himself from the month of September 2009.

Required:

Advise him on whether this is possible.

Answers to Test Yourself

Answer 1

1. Adobe Ltd will become liable for compulsory VAT registration when its taxable supplies during any 12 month period exceed £68,000.

    This will happen in February 2010 when taxable supplies will amount to £68,960
    (£6,000 + £3,650 + £5,000 + £4,100 + £4,850 + £4,990 + £3,770 + £5,800 + £7,100 + £4,000 + £5,600 + £5,650 + £4,050 + £4,400)

2. Adobe Ltd will have to notify HMRC by 31 March 2010, i.e. **within 30 days of the end of the month in which the £68,000 limit is exceeded.**

3. Adobe Ltd's registration will be effective from 1 April 2009.

Answer 2

1. Charmie Ltd realised that its taxable supplies for January 2010 would be at least £68,000. So, the company is liable to registration from 1 January 2010, being the start of the 30 day period.
2. Charmie Ltd has to notify HMRC by 30 January 2010, being the end of the 30 day period.
3. Registration is effective from 1 January 2010, being the beginning of the 30 day period.

Answer 3

The calculation of VAT amount that can be recoverable is as follows:

	Goods	Services
Value of input	£22,000 (in inventory)	£6,000 (£1,000 + £2,000 + £3,000)
VAT paid at standard rate	15%	15%
VAT recoverable	**£3,300**	**£900**

Input VAT paid on goods which are purchased not more than three years prior to the date of registration (i.e., in the case of Bonsai Ltd, goods purchased not before 1 April 2006) can be reclaimed provided the goods remain in inventory on the date of registration. Therefore, Bonsai Ltd can reclaim input VAT on the goods remaining **in inventory (i.e. on £22,000).**

The company can also recover VAT incurred on services from 1 October 2008 to 1 April 2009 (i.e. services hired not more than six months prior to the date of registration).

Answer 4

A registered person can reclaim input tax paid on services purchased prior to registration for VAT if and only if:

1. services are supplied for **business purposes**
2. services are supplied **within 6 months prior to date of registration**

Gary satisfies both these conditions:

a) he had hired services four months prior to the date of registration for VAT and
b) the services were hired for business purposes.

He can reclaim the input tax paid on services prior to registration for VAT.

Answer 5

If HMRC is satisfied that taxable turnover will not exceed £66,000 in the next twelve months, HMRC cancels the registration from the date of the taxable person's request.

Tim can request HMRC to deregister him from September 2009.

Quick Quiz

1. Lindsey is a manufacturer. She pays VAT on purchases at the rate of 15%. Her annual turnover is less than 68,000 and, on her output, VAT is chargeable at 'zero' rate. In this situation she considers VAT paid as her expenditure and recovers it from customers. Hence, the price of the product is not competitive. What action should she take to make her prices more competitive?

2. State with reasons whether the following sentences are correct or not?
    a) If a supplier expects his taxable turnover to exceed £68,000 within the next 30 days, by the end of the next 30 days he must notify HMRC.
    b) A person can voluntarily register himself for VAT even if his turnover is below £68,000.
    c) When a person starts dealing in taxable supplies, he must immediately register for VAT.

3. Humpty is a trader. He has run his business for the last four years. His yearly turnover is £100,000 (approximately) so he has registered himself for VAT.

    In April 2009 he admits Dumpty as his partner. Being a registered dealer what are the consequences of changing the legal status of the business (from a sole trader to a partnership firm)?

Answers to Quick Quiz

1. If Lindsey voluntarily registers herself for VAT, she can reclaim the VAT paid on purchases. This will reduce the cost of purchases. By doing so, she can maintain the profit margin and reduce the selling price.

2.
a) **Correct.** If a person believes his taxable turnover during the next 30 days will exceed £68,000, it is his duty to notify HMRC by the end of the 30 day period. The registration will be effective from the beginning of the 30 day period.

b) **Correct.** Even if a person's taxable supply is below the prescribed limit (presently £68,000), he can voluntarily register for VAT.

c) **Incorrect.** From 1 April 2009, a person must register for VAT if his taxable supplies exceed £68,000 or a person expects his taxable turnover to exceed £68,000 during the next 30 days.

    When a person starts dealing in taxable supplies, if his turnover does not exceed £68,000 or his turnover is not likely to exceed £68,000 within next 30 days, registration for VAT is not compulsory.

3. When there is a change in legal status of a person, compulsory deregistration is triggered. Humpty admitted a partner, so his sole trading business became a partnership. As there was a change in the legal status of a person, HMRC will take steps for compulsory deregistration.

Self Examination Questions

Question 1

Tedtot Plc deals in spare parts for computers. The company started its business on 20 September 2008. In the month of May 2009, the company's turnover exceeded £68,000. In the month of June, the company was registered for VAT. A list of the company's purchases since formation is as follows:

Month	£
October	720
November	8,900
December	7,500
January	10,500
February	12,540
March	17,800
April	17,000

At the time of registration the company had inventory of £32,400 in hand.

Required:

Can the company claim input VAT paid on the inventory after it gets registered for VAT?

Question 2

Twinkle Ltd's turnover during the last year was £68,000. The company supplies exempt goods to a reputed retail outlet in London. The company pays VAT on its input at standard rates. The company wants to become registered under VAT so that it can reclaim the input tax paid on purchases. Advise the company when it should become registered.

Question 3

In April 2009, Chempco Ltd started its business. In the same month the company took a car on a rental basis. The total bill included VAT of £2,000. In the month of July 2009, Chempco Ltd's turnover was above £68,000 and the company became registered for VAT.

Due to a slack season, goods produced in the month of April lay in the final inventory until July.

Required:

Can Chempco Ltd claim VAT paid on the services while paying VAT on sales?

Question 4

Sibel Ltd started trading on 1 September 2009, but registered for VAT on 1 December 2009.
For the period 1 September to 30 November 2009, the company had the following inputs:

	September £	October £	November £
Goods purchased	5,600	16,000	30,500
Services incurred	5,000	6,000	7,000
Fixed assets	80,000		

On 1 December 2009, there was inventory of goods costing £25,000.
All figures are exclusive of VAT.

Required:

Calculate the total input VAT that can be recovered.

Answers to Self Examination Questions

Answer 1

VAT incurred on purchases before registration for VAT can be treated as input tax only if:
1. Goods are purchased within three years prior to the date of registration.
2. Goods are used for business purposes.
3. The goods have not been consumed or supplied further, before the date of registration or, if at all consumed, final goods are consumed for production of other goods, and final goods are still held as inventory.

In the case of Tedtot Plc, the inventory that was remaining as on the date of registration for VAT was purchased within three years prior to the date of registration. The company can claim input VAT paid on its purchases.

Answer 2

The company which supplies only exempt goods / services cannot register for VAT. As a result, the company is not a taxable person and it cannot reclaim input VAT.
In short, the company has to treat that input VAT as cost of the input.

Answer 3

A taxable person can reclaim VAT paid on services prior to registration, on fulfilment of the following conditions:
1. The services are supplied for the business.
2. The services are supplied six months before the date of registration.

In the given question, Chempco Ltd had purchased services two months before the date of registration. The company can definitely reclaim the VAT paid on services acquired prior to registration.

Answer 4

The inventory of goods was neither acquired more than three years before registration nor was it sold or consumed before registration.
So, Input VAT of **£3,750** (£25,000 x 15%) can be recovered on 1 December 2009 on inventory of goods.
In the same way, input VAT on fixed assets **£12,000** (£80,000 x 15%) can be recovered.
As the services were not supplied more than six months before registration, input VAT on services **£2,700** (£5,000 + £6,000 + £7,000 = £18,000 x 15%) can be recovered.

Total input VAT that can be recovered = £3,750 + £12,000 + £2,700
= **£18,450**

SECTION F: VALUE ADDED TAX

F3

STUDY GUIDE F3: THE COMPUTATION OF VAT LIABILITIES

Get Through Intro

In this Study Guide we will discuss **how VAT is accounted for and administered and when the tax point emerges**. We will also examine the information that has to be given in an invoice.

This Study Guide also introduces you to the concept of valuation of supplies and the circumstances when input VAT is not deductible. A thorough understanding of this concept will help you to guide your client on how to account for his VAT liabilities.

In addition, this Study Guide explains the various penal provisions relating to VAT.

Proper tax planning requires an in-depth knowledge of all the rules and provisions of income tax as well as the VAT Act.

A thorough study of this Study Guide will enable you to acquire knowledge which will help you in your exams as well as in your professional life as a tax consultant.

Learning Outcomes

a) Explain how VAT is accounted for and administered.
b) Recognise the tax point when goods or services are supplied.
c) List the information that must be given on a VAT invoice.
d) Explain and apply the principles regarding the valuation of supplies.
e) Recognise the circumstances in which input VAT is non-deductible.
f) Compute the relief that is available for impairment losses on trade debts.
g) Explain the circumstances in which the default surcharge, a serious misdeclaration penalty, and default interest will be applied.

Introduction

Case Study

Jones Limited sells luxury products with quarterly sales of £50,000 plus VAT of £7,500 = £57,500.

The cost of making the sales for the quarter is £30,000 plus VAT of £4,500 = £34,500.

The net amount to be paid to HMRC is £7,500 less £4,500 = £3,000. This illustration shows the net amount of VAT to be paid and the simplistic mechanism used to calculate amounts owing or to be repaid.

Case Study

James is the owner of a garden design and landscaping business. On his quarterly VAT return he declares his output tax to be £90,000 and claims input tax of £25,000. With further investigation it was discovered that the output tax was understated by £40,000.

In this case a penalty would not be applied as the amount of understated VAT is less than the determined amount.

The first case study exemplifies the basis of payment of VAT.
The second case study tells us about the penalty provisions and the consequences of non-disclosure to the authorities.

All these concepts are explained in the respective Learning Outcomes.

1. Explain how VAT is accounted for and administered. [2]

[Learning outcome a]

1. Accounting for VAT

a) The VAT period is a period covered by the VAT return.
b) Normally a VAT return is completed **quarterly** (i.e. for a 3 month period).
c) Return is submitted to HMRC **by the end of the month following the end of the return period.**
d) Return shows total output VAT and total input VAT for the quarter.
e) Return shows **amount payable** (or repayable).
f) Payment should be sent with return.

Example

Cellarage Ltd had an output VAT of £15,000 and an input VAT of £8,000, for the quarter ended 31 December 2009.

The company should submit the VAT return for the quarter ended 31 December 2009 by 31 January 2010.

Payment of VAT is (£15,000 - £8,000) = £7,000. This amount is due on 31 January 2010 when the VAT return is submitted.

2. Monthly VAT accounting

a) Taxable person may **request** to submit monthly returns.
b) Good for cash flow if input VAT exceeds output VAT in a repayment situation.

Example

If some or all of the goods we supply are zero-rated, then our input VAT may be greater than our output VAT which means that HMRC will owe us money. If we prepare and submit a return every 3 months, then we receive this money every 3 months. However, if we do a monthly return, then our repayment is monthly which means we receive the money earlier. This is good for cash flow.

A disadvantage of monthly VAT accounting is that it increases administration as 12 VAT returns are to be submitted instead of 4 per year.

3. VAT payments on account

If the annual **VAT liability exceeds £2 million,** the taxable person must make payments on account. This is in respect of each quarter. The payment of 1/24 of the total VAT paid in the previous year will have to be paid at the end of each month in the quarter from the second month end. The taxpayer may elect to pay their actual VAT liability instead.

Example
Quarter ended 31/03/2010

Due 28/02/2010 payment on account of 1/24 of the total VAT liability for previous year.
Due 31/03/2010 payment on account of 1/24 of the total VAT liability for previous year.
Due 30/04/2010 balancing payment of balancing amount for the quarter.

Test Yourself 1

Yaan Ltd is liable to make payments on account calculated at £325,000 each for the quarter ended 31 March 2010.

Required:

Calculate the amount of payment or repayment that is due if Yaan Ltd has the following VAT liabilities:

1. £700,000
2. £500,000.

4. Control visits

a) VAT is self-administered.
b) HMRC make control visits to check the accuracy of VAT returns.

5. Records

A taxable person must keep records for **6 years.**

6. Refund of overpaid VAT

VAT that has been overpaid can be refunded, subject to a **3 year time limit.**

Example
Cuba Ltd has prepared its return for the quarter ended 31 December 2009. The company found that it has not been claiming the input VAT on £545 (inclusive of VAT) that is paid towards the rent of soft-drinks machines for each quarter. The same monthly amount has been paid since 1 January 2004.

A claim for a VAT refund can be made subject to a three-year time limit.

Therefore, Cuba Ltd can claim the input VAT incurred during the quarter ended 31 December 2009 and during the period 1 October 2006 to 30 September 2009.

1.2 Administration of VAT

Her Majesty's Commissioner of Revenue and Customs is responsible for the VAT systems. For the purpose of administration of VAT, the department of HMRC is divided into:

1. Local area office
2. Central unit

1. Local area office

Local area offices deal with local VAT administration. The officers visit the registered person's office in their area. They check the accuracy of the registered person's VAT returns as well as the overall functioning of the VAT system.

2. Central unit

The main functions of the VAT Central Unit are:

a) Maintenance of registration records (every taxable person needs to file a registration form). The registration form is maintained by this department.

b) Collection of VAT returns (i.e. the registered person has to file their returns with this unit) and processing of completed returns.

c) Collection of VAT due from a registered person and its repayment when it is due.

Diagram 1: Functions of central unit and local area officer

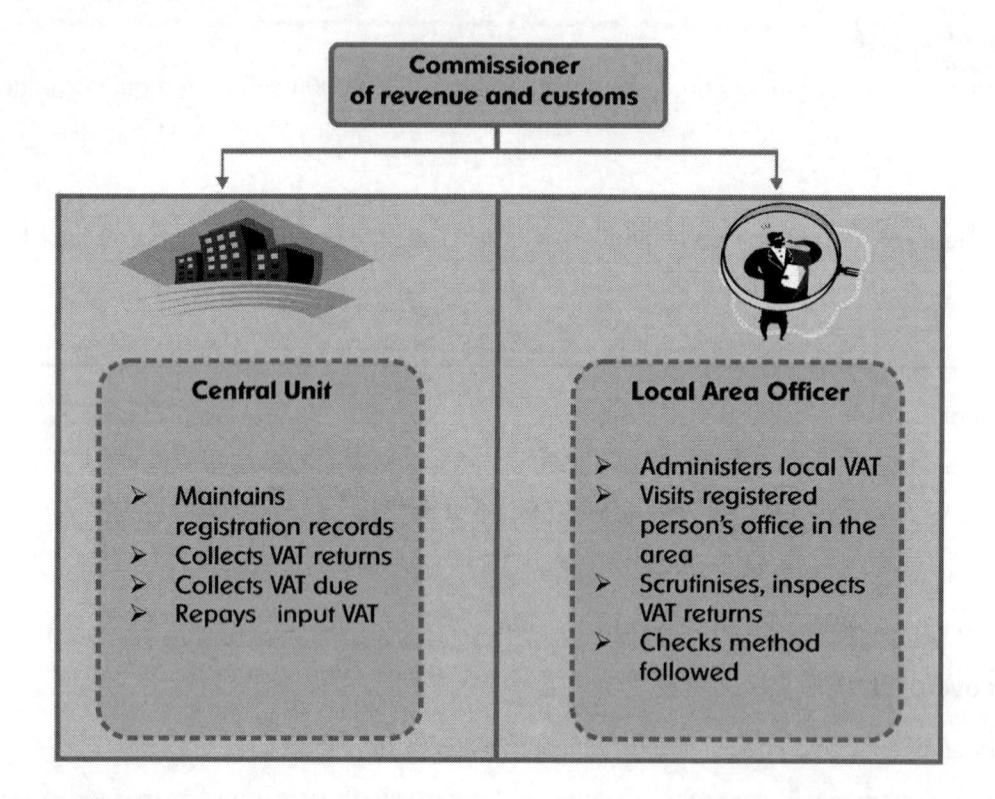

```
                    Commissioner
                of revenue and customs
                    /            \
        Central Unit              Local Area Officer
        
        > Maintains               > Administers local VAT
          registration records    > Visits registered
        > Collects VAT returns      person's office in the
        > Collects VAT due          area
        > Repays input VAT        > Scrutinises, inspects
                                    VAT returns
                                  > Checks method
                                    followed
```

1.3 VAT assessments

VAT is a self-assessed tax, i.e. normally it is not required to make formal tax assessments. However, when any taxable person fails to submit his VAT return or submits a VAT return which is either incomplete or incorrect, HM Revenue and Customs may issue an assessment order.

The normal period for carrying out VAT assessment is three years from the end of the VAT period to which the VAT return relates. However, this period can be extended to 20 years in case of fraud, dishonesty, and unauthorised issue of VAT invoices.

> **Example**
>
> Black Ltd is a wholesaler of shoes. The company's average yearly turnover is £500,000. It was the practice of Black Ltd to issue invoices to registered persons only. During the year 2009-10 Black Ltd raised invoices for only £400,000 and paid output VAT on this amount.
>
> During the year 2009-10, the company also managed not to issue invoices for £90,000 and of course did not pay output tax on this amount.
>
> As Black Ltd has committed fraud, HMRC can extend the assessment period to 2028/29.

1.4 Appeals

If a taxable person disagrees with the decision made by HMRC, within 30 days from the date of the decision by HMRC, the person may:

- ask a local VAT officer to reconsider the decision or
- make an appeal to a VAT tribunal.

The local VAT officer may:

a) confirm the decision or
b) revise the decision.

A taxable person may **file** an **appeal** to a VAT tribunal provided the **VAT returns** and **amount** shown payable thereon, is paid by the taxpayer. The tribunal can waive payment of the VAT shown in the return before the appeal is heard.

A person must file an appeal with a VAT tribunal within:
- **21 days** from confirmation of decision by a **local officer.**
- **30 days** from the date of decision given **by a central unit** or revised decision of a local officer.

A tribunal's hearings are normally held in public and decisions are published. If a taxable person is dissatisfied with the decision of the tribunal, he may refer the case to the High Court and beyond.

Diagram: 2 Appeal procedures for a person aggrieved with a VAT decision

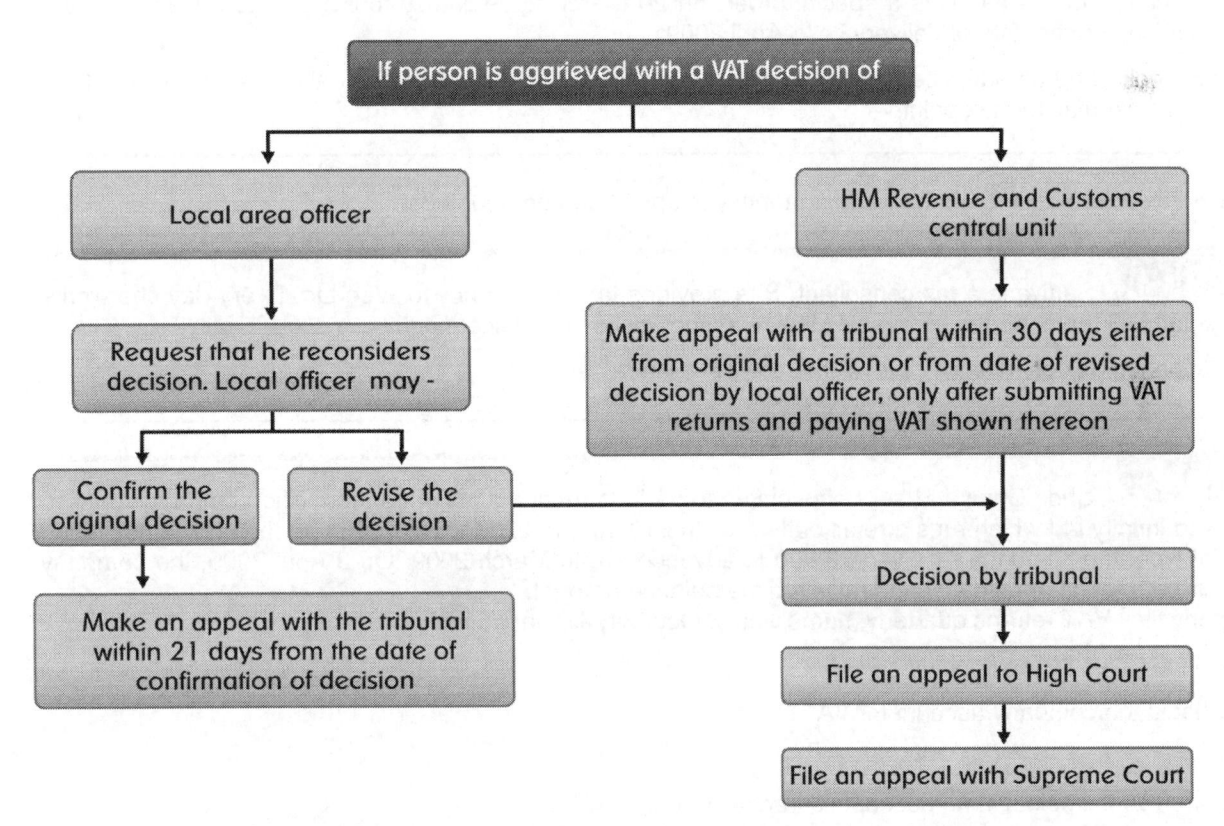

```
                    If person is aggrieved with a VAT decision of
                         │                              │
                         ▼                              ▼
                 Local area officer            HM Revenue and Customs
                         │                         central unit
                         ▼                              │
            Request that he reconsiders                 ▼
            decision. Local officer may -      Make appeal with a tribunal within 30 days either
                         │                     from original decision or from date of revised
              ┌──────────┴──────────┐          decision by local officer, only after submitting VAT
              ▼                     ▼          returns and paying VAT shown thereon
        Confirm the           Revise the                │
     original decision         decision ───────────────▶│
              │                                         ▼
              ▼                                 Decision by tribunal
    Make an appeal with the tribunal                    │
    within 21 days from the date of                     ▼
        confirmation of decision            File an appeal to High Court
                                                        │
                                                        ▼
                                           File an appeal with Supreme Court
```

2. Recognise the tax point when goods or services are supplied. [2]
[Learning outcome b]

VAT is **due at** the **tax point date.** The tax point is the deemed date of supply.

The tax point date determines:
- **the VAT return** in which the VAT must be **accounted** for and
- the **rate of VAT** that applies

2.1 Determination of basic tax points

1. The basic tax point is the point when **goods** are **made available** or **services are performed** irrespective of whether the invoice is raised or not.

Example

Eletronica Ltd is a wholesale dealer of electronics goods. On 5 June 2009, Task Ltd made a delivery of 50 music systems to Electronica Ltd. However, the invoice was raised on 10 July 2009.

In this situation, the tax point is taken as the date of delivery of the music systems i.e. 5 June 2009.

---

2. When an invoice is raised before goods are made available or within 14 days from the date of supply of goods or services, the basic tax point is the **date on which the invoice was raised.**

Example

Shine Ltd is a dealer of gold ornaments. On 1 September 2009, Lucy purchased a diamond ring worth £1,000 from Shine Ltd. As she was a relative of one of the directors of Shine Ltd, the invoice was raised on 10 September 2009.

The invoice was raised within 10 days of the date of delivery of goods. Therefore, the date of invoice (i.e. 10 September 2009) is taken as the basic tax point.

---

3. When **payment is received before the goods or services are supplied or the invoice is raised**, then the **date of receipt of payment** is taken as the **basic tax point.**

Example

Nancy is a manufacturer of pastries and cakes. On 1 April 2009 she supplied 500 pastries to Victory Ltd. As this was a special order, on 29 March 2009 Nancy took £500 as advance. The invoice was raised on the date of delivery i.e. 1 April 2009.

Here, Nancy took £500 as advance before the goods were supplied. Therefore the date of advance (i.e. 29 March 2009) is taken as the tax point.

---

4. When invoices are raised monthly then a monthly tax point can be adopted.

Example

Saniya is a tax consultant. She provides tax consultancy to Web Ltd. Every day she works for approximately 3 hours for the company. However, she raises an invoice monthly.

In this situation, the tax point is the date of (monthly) invoice raised.

Example

Choc Chips Ltd sells chocolates to various retail outlets in London. The company supplied chocolates to Infinity Ltd which runs a retail outlet, worth £10,000 on 22 May 2009. Due to the chocolates being of a special type, the company received £3,000 in advance on 20 March 2009. On 3 April 2009, the company issued an invoice to the retail outlet and received the balance amount.
The company files VAT returns quarterly, namely July, October, January and April every year.

1. State Choc Chips Ltd's tax point.
2. How should the company account for VAT?

Answer

1. There are two tax points in respect of this transaction:
    - Advance of £3,000
    - Balance payment of £7,000
2. Company should account for VAT as follows:
    - Advance received on 20 March 2009.

        Company should account for VAT of **£450** (3,000 x 15%) in April 2009 return.
    - Balance payment of £7,000 received after invoice is raised on 3 April 2009.

Company should account for VAT of **£1,050** (7,000 x 15%) in July 2009 returns.

Test Yourself 2

Sun Ltd sells electronic items to various retail dealers. To produce these items, Sun Ltd requires a high quality machine. The machine is ordered from High-tech Ltd on 5 June 2009. The cost of the machine is £10,000.

The company is in urgent need of the machine so it deposits £1,000 on 10 June 2009 and receives delivery of the machine on 20 June 2009. However, the invoice is issued by High-tech Ltd on 2 July 2009.

The balance of £9,000 is paid on 4 July 2009.

Required:

1. What are the different tax points of this transaction?

2. How will the company account for VAT?

---

3. List the information that must be given on a VAT invoice.[1]

[Learning outcome c]

3.1 VAT invoices

1. When a taxable person supplies taxable goods to another taxable person then he **must issue a tax invoice** to the **buyer** within **30 days**.

1. **No invoice** is required **if the supply is zero-rated**.

2. The **supplier** must **keep one copy** for himself **as documentary evidence**.

3. The tax invoice must show the following details:

    a) identifying serial **number**
    b) **date** of supply
    c) **date of issue** of document
    d) **name, address and registration number** of **supplier**
    e) name and address **of person to whom** the goods or services are **supplied**
    f) a **description** sufficient to identify the goods or services supplied, and for each, the **quantity** of the goods or the extent of the services, the **rate of VAT** and the **amount payable, excluding VAT** expressed **in** any **currency**
    g) the **gross amount payable**, excluding VAT
    h) rate of any **cash discount** offered
    i) the **total amount of VAT charged**, expressed in sterling

4. A taxable person may issue a less detailed invoice where value of supplies including VAT is less than **£250** (e.g. invoice for telephone calls, car park fees). In such situations a taxable person can claim input tax **without VAT invoice**.

    A less-detailed VAT invoice must contain

    a) **name address and registration number** of the **retailer**
    b) the date **of the supply**
    c) a description sufficient to identify the **goods or services supplied**
    d) the total **amount payable including VAT**
    e) the **rate of VAT** in force at the time of the supply

5. Every VAT registered dealer must retain this tax invoice for **6 years**. These may be kept **on paper, computer or microfilm**.

F3.8: Value Added Tax

6. If a customer returns any goods after issuing the tax invoice to him then, a credit note must be issued on a customer. This credit note must contain the number and the date of the original VAT invoice.

A typical example of a VAT invoice

From: Bean Ltd Enterprise House Victoria Road Chesterfield SE1 7RU		**Sales Invoice No. 199** VAT Reg. 938 2583 45
To: Pea Ltd Carbuncle Drive Wither Sea North Yorkshire NY1 8WE		Date of Invoice :05/07/09 Date of Supply :30/06/09 Tax Point :05/07/09

Quantity	Description	Net Amount
10	Desk Teak £30.00	£300.00
	Less:	
	Cash Discount @2%	(£6.00)
	Total	£294.00
	Add:	
	VAT @15%	£44.10
	Total Net	£294.00
	Total VAT	£44.10
	Total to Pay	**£338.10**

This amount is payable in full 30 days from the date of issue of this invoice.
All goods remain the property of Bean Ltd until payment in full is received.
All cheques should be made payable to Bean Ltd.

Test Yourself 3

The following is a sample of the new sales invoice that Tara-rum-Pam Ltd is going to issue to its customers.

SALES INVOICE

Tara-rum-Pam Ltd   Customer   Ding-Dong Plc
121 The West Street   Address: 90, The LS Road
London WC1 2AB
                                            Glasgow G1 2CD

Telephone 0208 100 1234

Invoice Date and Tax Point: 1 March 2009

Item description	Quantity	Price
Music system	5	125
Amplifier	2	75
Total amount payable (Including VAT)		**200**

Directors: Tara & Pam
Company Number: 1234666
Registered Office: 121 The West Street, London WC1 2AB

Several customers have recently defaulted on the payment of their debts. In order to encourage prompt payment, Tara-rum-Pam Ltd is considering offering all of its customers a 5% discount if they pay within one month of the date of the sales invoice.

No discount is currently offered.

Required:

State what alterations Tara-rum-Pam Ltd will have to make to its new sales invoices in order for them to be valid for VAT purposes.

4. Explain and apply the principles regarding the valuation of supplies. [2]

[Learning outcome d]

As we have seen in the previous Study Guide, goods and services which are liable to VAT either at the standard, reduced or zero rate are called 'taxable supplies'. The total value of these supplies is called 'taxable turnover'.

4.1 What is the value of supply?

Output VAT is charged on the value of supply, which is usually the **price charged by the taxable person when the supply is of goods or services**.

The amount of VAT is calculated as follows:

> **VAT = Value of supply x VAT rate**

The tax value of a supply depends on what is received by a supplier in exchange for the supply. This something in exchange is called the **consideration**. The consideration for supply is the total value paid by the buyer to the seller. This also includes VAT.

Example

Twinkle is a wholesaler of cosmetics. On 2 April 2009, she supplied 300 bottles of perfume to Casuals (an exclusive boutique in south London). Each bottle was worth £10. The VAT amount and total consideration is calculated as follows (assume perfumes are liable to VAT at standard rate):

	£
Value of supply (300 x £10)	3,000
Add: VAT (@ 15% (£3,000 x 15%))	450
Total consideration	**3,450**

The VAT portion included in the total consideration can be calculated separately from the total consideration if you know the VAT rate.

The formula below will make it easy to calculate the VAT portion.

> $$\text{VAT} = \frac{\text{Rate of tax}}{100 + \text{Rate of tax}} \times \text{Total consideration}$$

Example

Continuing the above example of Twinkle

The total consideration of £3,450, VAT is calculated as follows:

$$\text{VAT} = \frac{\text{Rate of tax}}{100 + \text{Rate of tax}} \times \text{Total consideration}$$

$$\frac{£15}{£100 + £15} \times £3,450$$

$$= \frac{£3}{£23} \times £3,450$$

$$= £450$$

This 3/**23** is called a **VAT fraction**. The VAT fraction varies according to the rate of tax chargeable.

Test Yourself 4

Vince Ltd supplies goods worth £220. The VAT rate applicable to supplies is the standard rate. Calculate the VAT charged and the total consideration that Vince Ltd receives.

Judo Ltd receives consideration of £17,390 against the supplies of goods. What amount of VAT is included in the consideration? (The VAT rate is standard).

SUMMARY

Valuation of supply
- price charged by taxable person when supply is of goods or service
- VAT = Value of supply x VAT rate

1. Exceptional cases where the value of supply is the deemed price of goods/services

a) Where supply includes the value of a business asset given as a gift

If a business asset is given as a gift, then the taxable person has to pay VAT on the value of the asset. In this situation, the value of supply is the value of identical goods that one can purchase from the open market.

Example

Luxury car Ltd is involved in the production of gear boxes and spares for sports cars. Luxury car Ltd receives a gift of shaft equipment (machine used for shaping gear rolling) from Car-point Plc (both the companies are owned by Jim Bonds). The market value of this equipment at the time of the gift was £10,000.

Car-point Plc gave shaft equipment to Luxury car Ltd as a gift. In this situation, Car-point Plc must include the market value of the equipment on the date of gift (£10,000) as its taxable supply.

b) Temporary use of business asset

If at any time the employee or owner of a company uses a business asset for his personal use, then this results in supply of services. In this situation, the value of the service provided is equal to the amount by which the asset depreciates.

Example

Rosy is an accountant in Red Ltd. With the permission of the company, Rosy used the company's car for private purposes. Rosy used this car for one month. During the tax year the company claimed capital allowances of £3,000 on this car.

In this situation, Red Ltd has to pay VAT assuming that the company has given Rosy the car on a hire basis. The value of services is calculated as follows:

Value of services = Depreciation that Red Ltd would have claimed for one month.
= £3,000/12
= £250.

c) Private use of services

If an employee / owner uses a service provided to the business for his private purposes, then it is considered that the business has provided those services to the employee or the owner. In this situation the value of the resulting services is equal to the **proportionate cost of supplies to the business.**

Example

Octopus is a manager in Sea Ltd. Sea Ltd has hired a small boat to transport goods to the sea shore. For this boat, the company pays a monthly rental of £3,000. During the Christmas vacation, Octopus used the boat (which is hired by the company) for one week.

Here, it is assumed that Sea Ltd gave the boat to Octopus on a rental basis. The value of service is calculated as follows:

Value of service = monthly rental charges/4 weeks (on average, there are 4 weeks in a month)
= £3,000/4
= £750.

2. Special situations of output VAT

a) Discount

If the supplier of the goods offers a trade discount (quantity discounts) or discount for prompt payment to the buyer of the goods then the **VAT** is **calculated** on the **net value of the supply**.

Net value = sales price less discount

> **Tip** Even though the customer does not actually take advantage of the discount, VAT is calculated on the net value of the supply.

Test Yourself 5

Morgan is a wholesaler of plastic goods. She offered a 2% discount to any customer who pays within 20 days of the date of delivery of goods. On 14 June 2009, she supplied goods worth £40,000 to Sargon who runs a retail shop.

Required:

Assuming the VAT rate as 15%, calculate the VAT charged on the supply and value of supply in the following situations:

1. Sargon pays within 20 days.
2. Sargon does not pay within 20 days.

b) Motor expenses

i. Input VAT can be recovered even when the owner of the business or the employee uses the fuel for private mileage. If the business pays for both private and business fuel used in a car, a fixed VAT charge is applicable based on the cubic capacity of the engine and fuel type - this is called the fuel scale charge.

ii. This simplification method allows the business to reclaim VAT on both the business and private elements of the fuel.

> **Tip** For VAT purposes, home to office journeys are not treated as business mileage.

> **Tip** **Student Note**: in the exam, students must take care while reading the problem as the examiner may give scale rates either inclusive or exclusive of VAT.
>
> If the rates are **inclusive** of VAT then calculate output tax as follows:
>
> VAT = Fuel scale charge x 3/23 (i.e. VAT fraction as we have seen previously)
>
> If the fuel rates are **exclusive** of VAT then calculate output tax as follows:
>
> VAT = Fuel scale charge x VAT rate (i.e. 15%)

c) VAT inclusive scale rates

> **Tip** The scale charge will be given to you in the examination.

i. Input VAT can be fully recovered for repairs to a motor car provided the car is put to some business use. However, if a vehicle is used **solely for private motoring**, you cannot recover the VAT on repairs and maintenance.

ii. If a car is used only for business purposes (i.e. for leasing, selling and so on), VAT may be reclaimed. However, a taxable person needs to account for VAT when he sells a car.

iii. Input tax paid on **repairs & maintenance** expenses paid by the business is **fully reclaimable** even though the car is partially used for private purposes.

iv. If a car is purchased in order to give it out on a lease basis, the lessor can claim the VAT paid when the car was purchased. Normally the lessee also can reclaim the VAT paid on the cost of hire charges.

However if the lessor has reclaimed input charges and the lessee makes private use of a car, the lessee can recover only **50%** of the input tax paid on lease charges.

Output VAT must be accounted for, based on the scale charge if input VAT is claimed in respect of fuel provided for private use without the cost of that fuel being fully reimbursed.

Example

Rent-a-car Plc is a company which provides cars on lease. During the year 2009-10, the company purchased two more cars and paid VAT of £2,000. The company has adjusted this VAT while making payment of output VAT on lease charges.

During the year, Fun Ltd took a car from Rent-a-car Plc on lease for business purposes. The total lease charges paid by Fun Ltd during the year were £500 and VAT of £75. However, Fun Ltd's director also used the car for private purposes.

In this situation, Fun Ltd can claim only 50% of the VAT paid on lease charges i.e. £37.50 (£75 x 50%).

Diagram 4: Motor car expenses

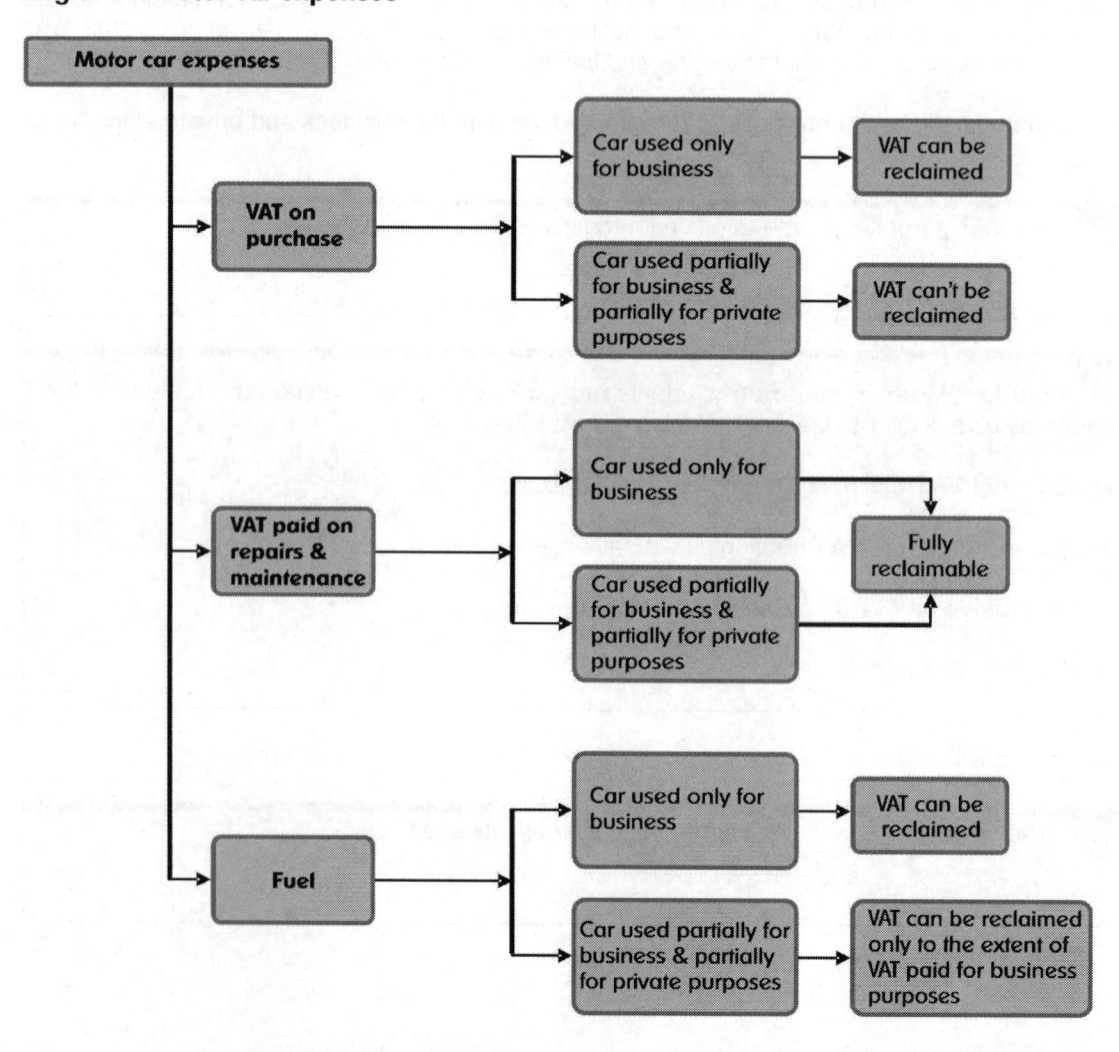

d) Transfer of a business as a going concern

No VAT is due on the sale of a business, provided:

i. all of the business is transferred as a going concern
ii. the purchaser is, or will become, registered for VAT

e) Mixed supplies

Mixed supplies are said to be made, when a supplier charges a single inclusive price for a number of separate supplies of goods or services. In other words, more than two goods or services are invoiced in a single invoice at a single inclusive price.

The VAT rates applicable to all the goods or supplies may be the same or some goods may be chargeable at standard rates; some may be at a zero rate and so on.
In a mixed supply, the supplier of the goods charges VAT **separately** for each element of the supply by applying the appropriate rate of VAT. The supplier can split the total invoice price between the different elements by applying any one of the below-mentioned methods:
i. considering cost to the supplier as a base or
ii. taking open market value as a base

> **Example** A VAT inclusive price of mixed supply is £600. One of the goods, which cost the supplier £200, is standard-rated and the other, which cost the supplier £50, is exempt from VAT.
>
> In this situation, based on the available information, apportionment of the price of the mixed supply across the standard-rated and exempt goods is done on the basis of the cost of the product.
>
> The value of the standard-rated supply is calculated as follows:
>
> Total value of the mixed supply x $\dfrac{\text{Cost of standard - rated goods}}{\text{Total cost of the mixed supply}}$
>
> $= £600 \times \dfrac{£200}{£250}$
>
> $= £480$
>
> The supplier needs to charge VAT on this value. The VAT amount is £72 (480 x15%). The other goods are exempt from VAT. Therefore, VAT on the total mixed supply is £72.
>
> Therefore total price charged should be £672 (£600 + £72).

Test Yourself 6

A price of £490 is charged for a mixed supply of goods which is exclusive of VAT. The goods consist of zero-rated goods of which the market value is £300 and standard-rated goods of which the market value is £400 (excluding VAT). Calculate the VAT due on the mixed supply.

---

e) Composite supplies

Composite supply takes place when goods and / or services are supplied together in such a way that the value of the mixture cannot be segregated into different elements.

Composite supplies are held to be a single supply with ancillary elements being taxed at the same rate as the main supply. In such situations, one VAT rate is applied.

> **Example** Consider a contract for constructing a warehouse where there is a supply of construction material and labour as well as the production of an architectural plan for construction. If the contractor charges £100,000 for constructing the warehouse (with material), we cannot segregate the value of the construction material used, the value of the labour supply and the professional fees of the architect.
>
> In this situation, VAT is charged at one single rate on all the supplies made.

3. Some important points in relation to the valuation of supply

a) When goods are permanently taken out of business for private use, **output VAT** must be paid **on their market value.**

b) When a supplier charges different prices to different customers, depending upon their mode of payment, (through credit card, cash payment, direct debit to bank account etc.) VAT is calculated on the **full value paid** by the customer.

> **Example**
> A trading company is in the business of selling computer spare parts. The charges for a printer are as follows:
>
> 1. £45 if a customer pays in cash.
> 2. £5 extra if customer pays by credit card (the trader needs to pay bank charges)
>
> Hence, calculations of VAT in both cases will be as follows:
>
> a) For cash payment - £45 x 15% = **£6.75**
> b) For card payment – (£45 + £5) x 15% = **£7.50**

c) **Captive consumption i.e. self supply**

If any trading company uses its own services or goods produced or supplied by it which are otherwise liable for VAT, then output tax on these supplies is due.

However, if this final output is not liable to VAT, (i.e. it is exempt from VAT), a trading company cannot reclaim input tax.

> **Example**
> Suppose a company produces two products: X and Z. X is the input for Z and Z is the final product i.e. the company carries out captive consumption of product X. Both X and Z are liable for VAT.
>
> In this situation, output tax on product X is due even though the company produces product X and then uses it in the production of Z (i.e. does not sell it in the open market).
>
> However, if this final output (product Z) is not liable to VAT (i.e. it is exempt), the company cannot reclaim input tax paid on product X.
>
> Then VAT paid on product X will be treated as expenditure.

5. Recognise the circumstances in which input VAT is non-deductible. [2]
[Learning outcome e]

1. **Business entertainment:** input VAT cannot be recovered.

> **Example**
> Fun Ltd decides to give mobile phones as Christmas gifts to all its major buyers. These gifts to customers are not deductible business expenditure while calculating the company's trading profits. Therefore, VAT paid on the purchase of mobile phones cannot be reclaimed.

2. **Purchase of motor car:** input VAT cannot be recovered – unless it is used 100% for business purposes.

A car is not purchased for business purposes if it is purchased for purposes **other than the following:**
a) A car purchased by a car dealer, as **stock in trade**
b) A car purchased for a **driving school**
c) A car acquired totally for business purposes (such as a **leasing** business)

If, after the purchase of a car, accessories (such as a car radio, car A.C.) are purchased & invoiced separately, then **VAT on such accessories is not reclaimable unless the accessories are used for business purposes.**

> **Example**
>
> Allan is a car dealer. He buys cars and then modifies them according to the customers' choice. He bought five cars of which four were bought for business purposes and one for himself. He then modified all five cars. In this case Allan can reclaim input VAT paid on the purchase of accessories for four cars which were bought for business. But he cannot reclaim input VAT on the purchase of accessories for the car which he bought for himself.

3. VAT paid / payable on **second-hand goods** purchased from a dealer operating the **margin scheme**.

> **Example**
>
> Ram Ltd deals in second-hand cars. The company buys used cars from the public, restores them (if required) and then sells them at some margin. Ram is a dealer operating the margin scheme. He has to account for VAT on the difference between the price paid by him for the purchase of the car and the price at which he sells the car i.e. the margin. However, Ram can reclaim input VAT on business expenses such as overheads.

4. **Domestic accommodation for a director:** VAT paid / payable while making provision for **domestic accommodation for a director** of a company cannot be recovered.

5. **Goods or services not used for business purposes:** input VAT cannot be recovered.

6. **Goods and services used partly for business purposes and partly for private purposes:** only input VAT relating to business use can be recovered.

> **Example**
>
> Shiny is a registered dealer of leather products. During the year 2009-10, her total expenditure on telephone was £4,000 (exclusive of VAT). Out of the total usage, 40% was for private purposes and 60% was for business purposes.
>
> Here, Shiny can claim input VAT on £2,400 (£4,000 x 60%). She **cannot claim input VAT** paid on telephone expenses incurred for **private purposes.**

Output tax in relation to element of private use is accounted for.

> **Example**
>
> Continuing the above example of Shiny, she may choose to reclaim input VAT on the total telephone expenditure (i.e. £4,000) and pay output VAT on the telephone expenditure incurred for private purposes (i.e. £1,600 {£4,000 x 40%}).

> **Tip**
>
> Input VAT, which is non-deductible, is included in the cost of purchases as expenditure; whereas deductible input VAT is omitted from the costs. The taxable person may adjust it against output tax payable.

Test Yourself 7

State whether input VAT can be recovered in the following conditions.

1. Bony has taken domestic accommodation on a rental basis. During the year she paid a total of £2,000 as rent (exclusive of VAT).

   Bony sells goods which are liable to VAT at the standard rate. Can she reclaim the VAT paid on domestic accommodation?

2. Comfort Driving is a dealer of 'Sonata cars'. In December 2009, the entity purchased a total of fifty one cars out of which three cars were for office use and forty eight cars were for sale. Can Comfort Driving claim VAT on all the cars purchased?

6. Compute the relief that is available for impairment losses on trade debts. [2]
[Learning outcome f]

Output VAT is accounted for according **to the tax point.**

Output VAT may have been paid to HMRC before the customer has paid his invoice.

Example Suppose Cool Ltd wants to make a claim for VAT bad debt relief. It can do so after fulfilling certain conditions.

The conditions are as follows:

1. In respect of the debt, output VAT must have been accounted for and paid too.
2. In the trader's book, the debt must have been written off as a bad debt.
3. At least six months must have been completed since the time the debt was due for payment.

6.1 Treatment of bad debts

Tip A bad debt is money owed to you that you can't collect.

1. In the case of a cash accounting system

When a taxable person uses the cash accounting system, output tax on supplies made by him during the tax period is accounted for only when payment is received from a debtor. Therefore, a taxable person following the cash accounting system gets automatic bad debt relief.

Example Sharon is a wholesaler of toys. Last year, she voluntarily registered for VAT. She follows the cash accounting system for accounting for VAT. Last year (i.e. 2008/09) she sold toys worth £8,000 to Kids Gallery Ltd. However, Kids Gallery Ltd became insolvent. In the current year (2009-10), Sharon wrote off the amount receivable from Kids Gallery Ltd as bad debt.

In this situation, as Sharon follows a cash accounting system, the supply is not recorded as consideration as it is not actually received from Kids Gallery Ltd and hence she has not accounted for the output tax. In effect, she received automatic bad debt relief.

2. In the case of accrual system of accounting

Unlike the cash accounting system, in the accrual system of accounting, it is likely that a taxable person may account for output tax relating to the supply before receiving the consideration for that supply.

In this situation, if any bad debt occurs, then a taxable person can **claim a refund** of VAT lost on the amount of bad debts, **only** on fulfilment of the following criteria:

a) Goods or services are supplied for a consideration of money.

b) The related **output tax** on those supplies has been **accounted for.**

c) The consideration receivable for the supply is **not more than the value of the product / service in the open market.**

d) A minimum of **six months** have passed from the **date of supply and** from the **due date of payment.**

Claims for bad debt relief can be made within **three years** after the expiry of six months from the date **later** of:
i. the date of the supply and
ii. the date on which payment was due

Example

Passion Suppliers is a partnership firm. The firm uses the accrual system of accounting. On 1 January 2009 the firm made supplies to Fashion Plc. The credit period was ten days from the invoice date. The supply was of £1,150 (inclusive of tax at the rate of 15%)

Five months later, Fashion Plc became insolvent and the amount due from the company could not be recovered.

As Passion Suppliers follows the accrual accounting system, the firm had already accounted for and paid output tax on the supply made to Fashion Plc. However, the firm is unable to recover the amount of VAT from Fashion Plc.

In this situation, Passion Suppliers may reclaim VAT paid on bad debts (i.e. £1,000 (1,150 – 91,150 x 3/230) after six months from the date when the amount became due (i.e. 10 January 2009).

Tip

Summary

Bad debt relief is available provided:
- Debt is written off in financial accounts.
- Output VAT has been paid to HMRC.

Test Yourself 8

Casuals Ltd is a wholesaler of clothes. On 1 April 2008 the company supplied clothes to For Her Ltd for £20,000 (exclusive of VAT). The credit period was 3 months. However, in spite of reminders by the year 2009, For Her Ltd had not made the payment.

In the year 2009-10, Casuals Ltd decided to write off the amount receivable from For Her Ltd.

Required:

Advise Casuals Ltd whether it can do so. (Assume Casuals Ltd follows the cash accounting system).

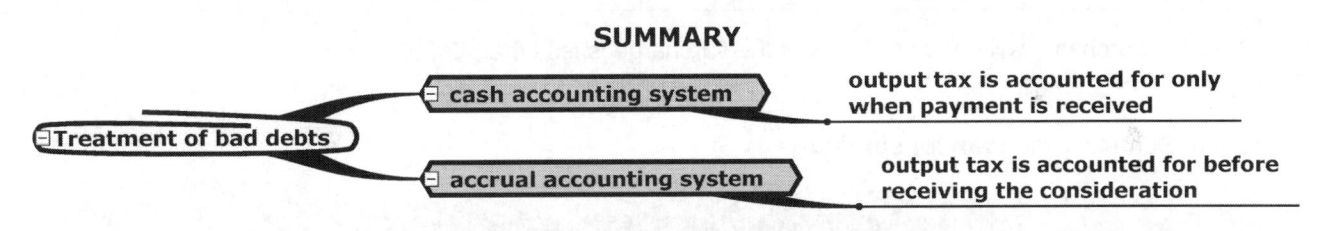

SUMMARY

- Treatment of bad debts
  - cash accounting system — output tax is accounted for only when payment is received
  - accrual accounting system — output tax is accounted for before receiving the consideration

7. **Explain the circumstances in which the default surcharge, a serious misdeclaration penalty, and default interest will be applied.** [1]

[Learning outcome g]

7.1 VAT returns

A return is the summarised information of the transactions for each tax period. This return must be submitted to HMRC in **"Form 100"** for each tax period. A VAT return must show details of VAT payable or repayable and other statistical information.

A VAT return must be filed within **one month** of the end of the tax period. This period of one month automatically gets extended by 7 days if the payment of VAT is made electronically (e.g. bank credit). However, this exception is not available to companies which file returns annually and make payment on account scheme.

A taxable person, by registering for electronic VAT return services, may file his return via the internet.

7.2 Default surcharge

1. Default occurs if the **VAT return is submitted late** or the **VAT is paid late**
2. A surcharge liability notice (SLN) is issued for a period of 12 months from the end of the period for which a taxable person has made default.

> **Example** Sun Shine Co follows quarterly VAT periods as July, October, January and April. During the year 2009-10, Sun Shine Co failed to submit the VAT return for the quarter ended January 2010.
>
> In this situation, HMRC will issue a notice for surcharge liability. The notice period will start from 31 January 2010 (i.e. quarter end for which the return was not filed) and will remain in force for one year (i.e. until 31 January 2011).

If, within this period, a further default occurs, the SLN period is extended to 12 months after the end of the VAT return period.

> **Example** Continuing the above example
> Sun Shine Co failed to submit one more return for the quarter ended April 2010. Because of this failure to file a VAT return, the surcharge period will be extended. Now, the original surcharge period will be extended by **one year** from 30 April 2010.
>
> This period will remain effective until 30 April 2011.

3. During the surcharge period, if a taxable person in addition to failing to file a return **fails to pay VAT or makes a late payment,** surcharge is levied. The rate of surcharge depends on the number of defaults made in payment of VAT during the surcharge period.

Late payment of VAT during surcharge period	Percentage of surcharge
1st default	2%
2nd default	5%
3rd default	10%
4th default	15%

The 2% or 5% surcharge will not be collected if the surcharge is less than £400.
There is a minimum charge of £30.

Diagram 5: Summary diagram for surcharge

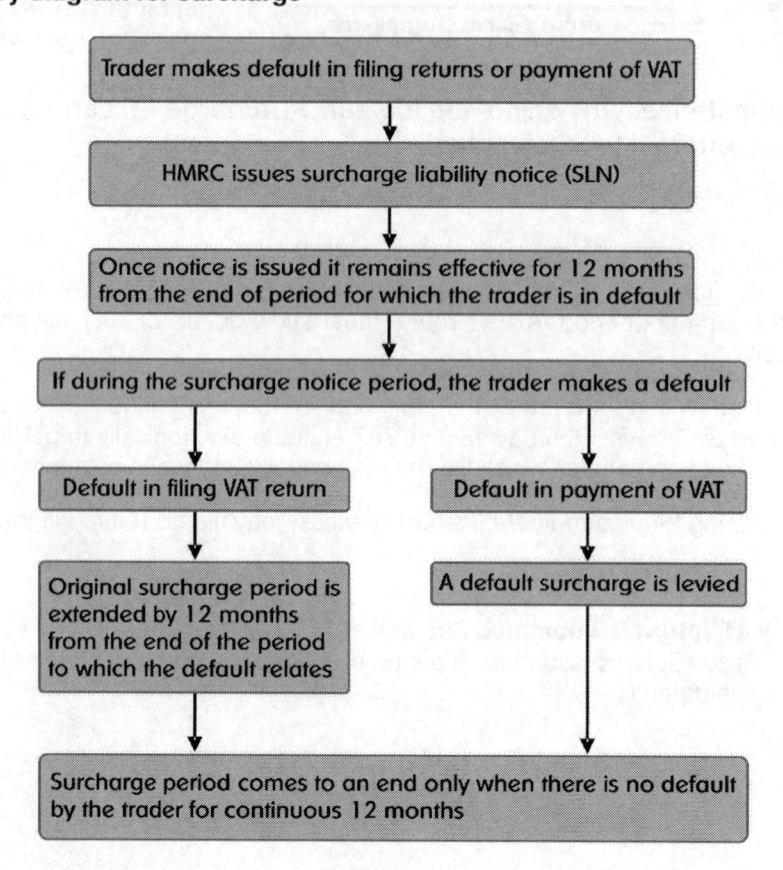

```
Trader makes default in filing returns or payment of VAT
                        ↓
HMRC issues surcharge liability notice (SLN)
                        ↓
Once notice is issued it remains effective for 12 months
from the end of period for which the trader is in default
                        ↓
If during the surcharge notice period, the trader makes a default
               ↓                              ↓
   Default in filing VAT return       Default in payment of VAT
               ↓                              ↓
   Original surcharge period is       A default surcharge is levied
   extended by 12 months
   from the end of the period
   to which the default relates
               ↓                              ↓
Surcharge period comes to an end only when there is no default
by the trader for continuous 12 months
```

> **Example**
>
> Small Ltd has submitted its VAT returns.
> The details of its VAT returns are as follows:

Quarter ended	VAT paid £	Date of submission
30 Jun 2008	3,500	2 Sep 2008
30 Sep 2008	12,000	5 Dec 2008
31 Dec 2008	15,000	24 Feb 2009
31 Mar 2009	8,500	25 Apr 2009
30 Jun 2009	2,000	26 Jul 2009
30 Sep 2009	4,000	26 Oct 2009
31 Dec 2009	7,500	15 Jan 2010
31 Mar 2010	10,000	28 Apr 2010

VAT is paid on the date it is due. The VAT returns were duly submitted by Small Ltd.

The implications of the late submission are as follows:

1. For the quarter ended 30 June 2008, the late submission of the VAT return will result in issuance of surcharge liability notice by HMRC mentioning a surcharge period to 30 June 2009.

2. For the quarter ended 30 September 2008, the late payment of VAT will result in a surcharge of £240 (12,000 x 2%). However as the surcharge is less than £400 it will not be levied. Period of surcharge will have been extended to 30 September 2009.

3. For the quarter ended 31 December 2008, the late payment of return and VAT will result in a surcharge of £750 (15,000 x 5%). This will be liable for surcharge as it is more than £400. Period of surcharge will have been extended to 31 Dec 2009.

4. The company has submitted another four returns on time. These are the returns for the quarters ended 31 Mar 09 and 31 Dec 2009.

5. For the quarter ended 31 March 2010, the late submission of the VAT return will result in issuance of a surcharge liability notice by HMRC applying a surcharge period to 31 March 2011.

> **Test Yourself 9**

Music Ltd fails to submit a VAT return for the first time, for the quarter ended 31 March 2009. Due to financial crisis, during the second quarter ended 30 June 2009, the company was unable to pay VAT of £2,000.

In the third quarter (i.e. the quarter ended 30 September 2009), Music Ltd paid VAT and filed a return two months late. During the third quarter the VAT liability was £7,000. In the fourth quarter (i.e. the quarter ended 31 December 2009) the company again failed to file a return and pay VAT in time. This time the VAT liability was £5,000.

Required:

Show the calculation of the surcharge liability.

7.3 Errors in a VAT return

When an error is made in a VAT return, the consequences are in the form of either misdeclaration penalty or penalty interest or both depending upon the circumstances.

1. Where the net error is less than £10,000 or 1% of turnover for the period (whichever is higher) subject to a maximum of £50,000, one can voluntarily disclose the error on the next VAT return.
   There will not be any serious misdeclaration penalty or penalty interest.

2. Where the net error is more than £10,000 or 1% of turnover for the VAT period (whichever is higher) subject to a maximum of £50,000, one can voluntarily disclose, but the disclosure must be separately made to HMRC.
   There will be penalty interest, but no serious misdeclaration penalty.

3. Where errors are discovered as a result of a control visit, then in such a case, there can be both serious misdeclaration penalty and penalty interest.

7.4 Misdeclaration penalty

The amount of penalty is determined according to the single new penalty regime introduced for incorrect returns. This applies to incorrect self assessment tax returns, self assessment corporation tax returns and where a misdeclaration has been made on a VAT return.

The amount of penalty is based on the amount of tax understated, but the actual penalty payable is linked to the taxpayer's behaviour, as follows:

➢ There will be no penalty where a taxpayer simply makes a mistake
➢ There will be a moderate penalty (up to 30% of the understated tax) where a taxpayer fails to take reasonable care.
➢ There will be a higher penalty (up to 70% of the understated tax) if the error is deliberate, and an even higher penalty (up to 100% of the understated tax) where there is also concealment of the error.

However, the penalty will be substantially reduced where a taxpayer makes disclosure, especially when this is unprompted disclosure of an incorrect return following a failure to take reasonable care, the penalty could be reduced to nil.

Example Venus Ltd has submitted the VAT return for the quarter ended 31 December 2009.

Mac, the tax consultant of Venus Ltd, was appointed by the company after the submission of the December quarter return. While going through the past records, he found some errors in the VAT return already submitted by the company.

In such a situation, Venus Ltd can voluntarily disclose the error in the next quarter ended VAT return i.e. 31 March 2010, if the net error total is less than £10,000 or 1% of the turnover for the period (whichever is higher) subject to a maximum of £50,000.

If the total net error is more than £10,000 or 1% of turnover (whichever is higher) subject to a maximum of £50,000, then the company can voluntarily disclose the error, but the disclosure must be made separately to HMRC.

Moreover, the default interest will be charged only if the net errors total more than the higher of £10,000 or 1% of the turnover for the VAT period, and not if they are less than the higher of £10,000 or 1% of turnover for the VAT period.

Example HMRC makes a control visit to the premises of Mars Ltd.

The **purpose** of such a visit is to give HMRC an opportunity to check the accuracy of the VAT returns of Mars Ltd.

The **circumstances** in which the discovery of the understatement of output VAT results in a serious misdeclaration penalty are as follows:

1. If Mars Ltd's VAT return includes a large misdeclaration
   A misdeclaration is said to be large when it is 30% or more of the total output VAT and input VAT for the relevant VAT return.

2. If Mars Ltd cannot convince HMRC that there was a reasonable excuse for the misdeclaration.

7.5 Penalty for late registration

Where a taxable person makes late notification of his liability to register, he is liable for a penalty. The penalty is calculated on the amount of **tax due between the date** on which a person **becomes liable to get registered under VAT** and the **actual date of VAT registration.** The percentage of penalty is as follows:

If registered	Penalty rate
Less than 9 months late	5%
9 to 18 months late	10%
More than 18 months late	15%

Example

In June 2008, Miranda started her own business manufacturing soft drinks. In a few months time, she captured a market. By the end of December 2008, her total turnover was £60,000 and by the year end i.e. March 2009, her turnover was £90,000. She had paid input tax of £6,850 on purchases.

However, due to lack of knowledge she did not register for VAT. If Miranda had registered for VAT, her output liability would have come to £15,750. In the month of March, Miranda registered herself for VAT.

In this situation, the penalty for late registration for VAT is calculated as follows:

Miranda registered for VAT 3 months late. Therefore the applicable penalty rate is 5%.

Penalty = Total tax due until the actual date of VAT registration x 5%
= (£15,750 - £6,850) x 5%
= £445.

Test Yourself 10

In January 2008, Arnold started a beauty hair salon. As he was very good at his job, his turnover within twelve months exceeded £68,000. He was aware of VAT registration provisions but did not register for VAT as he felt that after VAT registration he may be forced to increase the prices.

During these three months, he paid VAT on purchases. The amount of input VAT was £2,000. Arnold wanted to recover VAT paid on purchases so eventually, on 10 May 2009, he registered for VAT. On the day of registration total turnover was £70,000. The VAT rate applicable to him is 15%.

Can HMRC charge him a penalty? What is the amount of the penalty?

Test Yourself 11

Mango Ltd is a manufacturer of fruit jams. Mango Ltd has submitted a VAT return for the quarter ended 30 June 2009. The turnover in the VAT period is £256,000. The figures disclosed in the return were as follows:

	£
Output tax	100,000
Input tax	(10,000)
Net VAT payable	**90,000**

After the VAT assessment was over, the output VAT liability arose to £150,000. Do you think a misdeclaration penalty will apply? State the amount of penalty if HMRC has discovered that Mango Ltd is liable for moderate penalty.

7.6 Repayment Supplements

Repayment supplement is paid in the case of tax overpaid by the taxpayer. It is paid subject to certain conditions. If these conditions are fulfilled a taxable person will get a supplement of the higher of:

1. £50
2. 5% of the amount due

The conditions to satisfy for repayment supplement are:

a) Taxpayer must have submitted the VAT return within the due date.
b) The return should not show the amount repayable by more than the greater of:
   - £250 and
   - 5% of the amount due
c) HMRC has unnecessarily delayed the repayment.

Example

Butterfly Ltd filed its VAT return for the quarter ended on 30 June 2009. The Company had claimed a VAT refund of £730. However, HMRC wrongly issued a refund of £370.

Here, Butterfly Ltd has filed its quarter end return in time. The amount shown on the return is also correct. However, HMRC wrongly issued a refund cheque for the wrong amount.

As HMRC failed to repay the correct amount of VAT return within 30 days from the receipt of the return, it will pay the repayment supplement. The taxable person is entitled to get a supplement of the higher of the following:

1. £50
2. 5% (£730 - £370) = £18

Bacardi Ltd will get a supplement of £50 (greater of £50 and £18).

Example

Raddle filed his tax return for the quarter ended 31 March 2009, in time. He had claimed a refund of £1,000. HMRC completed the assessment and issued a written instruction for the repayment of a VAT amount of £440. HMRC's instruction was issued 50 days after receipt of the return.

In this situation, Raddle can get repayment supplement if the difference between the refund according to the return and the correct amount according to HMRC's assessment (i.e. £1,000 – £440 = £560) is not more than the higher of the following:

1. £250
2. 5% of (correct refund) (i.e. 5% x £560= £28)

Greater of the above is £250

As the difference is greater than £250, Raddle is not entitled for a supplement refund.

Test Yourself 12

Cluppins filed his VAT return for the quarter ended 30 June 2009 in time. He had made a claim for a refund of £2,450. Within 10 days, HMRC sent him a written instruction for the repayment of £1,200.

He did not get any supplement repayment with this amount.

Required:

Advise Cluppins as to whether he is entitled for supplement repayment.

Answers to Test Yourself

Answer 1

1.

28/2/10	payment of	£325,000
31/3/10	payment of	£325,000
30/4/10	payment of	£50,000 to be made with submission of VAT return for quarter

2.

28/2/10	payment of	£325,000
31/3/10	payment of	£325,000
30/4/10		£150,000 to be repaid by customs on submission of return for quarter

Answer 2

The given transaction provides various dates for various occasions.
To determine the tax points in this particular transaction, we should understand the significance of dates.

There are two tax points in respect of this transaction:

a) When the advance of £1,000 is received on 10 June 2009, is the first tax point.
b) When the invoice was raised (as the invoice was raised after advance was received) i.e. on 2 July 2009 is the second tax point.

The company should account for VAT as follows:

a) Advance received on 10 June 2009: the company should account for VAT of **£150 (£1,000 x 15%)** in the June 2009 return.
b) Delivery was made on 20 June but invoice was raised within 14 days i.e. on 2 July 2009. The payment of £9,000 was received on 4 July 2009 after invoice was raised on 2 July 2009. Although the delivery date is earlier, it will be replaced by the invoice date as the invoice was raised within 14 days. The company should account for VAT of **£1,350 (£9,000 x 15%)** in the quarter ended September (July – September) return. .

Answer 3

The information already given on the invoice is as follows:

1. Name and address of the supplier and the purchaser.
2. Invoice date and tax point
3. Description and the price of the goods
4. Final amount of the invoice

Tara-rum-Pam Ltd is planning to give a discount to its customers. Along with the amount of discount, the company must give following information on the invoice:

1. Invoice number.
2. Tara-rum-Pam Ltd's VAT registration number
3. The rate of VAT for each supply.
4. The VAT-exclusive amount for each supply.
5. The total VAT-exclusive amount.
6. The amount of VAT payable.

Answer 4

1. VAT charge is £220 x 15 % = £33.

    Total consideration = Value of supplies + VAT
    = £220 + £33
    = **£253**

2. Total consideration = £17,390

$$VAT = \frac{Rate\ of\ tax}{100 + Rate\ of\ tax} \times Total\ consideration$$

$$= \frac{£15}{£100 + £15} \times £17,390$$

$$= \frac{£3}{£23} \times £17,390$$

$$= £2,268$$

Answer 5

Once the supplier **offers** a discount to its customers, VAT is calculated on the net value irrespective of whether the customer takes advantage of the discount or not.

Net value = Sales – Discount
= £40,000 - £800 (i.e. £40,000 x 2%)
= £39,200

In both situations (i.e. whether customer pays within the credit terms or not) for the purpose of calculating VAT, value of the supply will be £39,200.

The VAT amount is **£5,880** (£39,200 x 15%)

If the customer pays after twenty days, then the value of supply will be £40,000 (without discount). The total consideration is calculated as follows:

Total consideration = Sales value + VAT amount.

1. If Sargon pays within 20 days:
   = £39,200 + £5,880
   = £45,080

2. If Sargon does not pay within 20 days-
   = £40,000 + £6,000
   = £.46,000

Answer 6

The apportionment of the price of mixed supply across the standard-rated and zero-rated goods is made on the basis of the market value of the product.

The value of the standard-rated supply is calculated as follows:

Total value of the mixed supply x $\frac{\text{Market value of standard - rated goods}}{\text{Total market value of the mixed supply}}$

= £490 x $\frac{400}{700}$

= £280

VAT charged on these standard-rated goods is £42 (£280 x 15%). The other product in the mixed supply is charged to VAT at zero rates. Therefore the total VAT due on the mixed supply is £42.
The total price charged should be £532 (£490 +£42).

Answer 7

1. An individual cannot reclaim VAT on costs incurred in relation to the provision of domestic accommodation.

   Bony, therefore, cannot recover VAT paid on costs incurred for the domestic accommodation.

2. Input VAT can be reclaimed on the purchase of the cars if the following conditions are met.

   i. Cars are used exclusively for business purposes e.g. a pool car
   ii. Cars will be used as taxis
   iii. Cars are stock in trade and will be sold by the dealer / manufacturer within twelve months (except second hand cars).

Comfort driving has bought fifty one cars and out of them, three cars are bought for office use. Therefore input VAT can be reclaimed on them. Any subsequent private use of any those cars will attract a liability i.e. the output tax on the current market value of those cars or similar cars.

The input VAT paid on 48 cars can also be reclaimed as they are held as stock in trade provided they are sold within twelve months from the of purchase and those cars are not second hand cars.

Answer 8

A taxpayer can claim a refund of the VAT lost on the amount of bad debts if the following conditions are fulfilled:

1. Goods or services are supplied for a consideration of money.

2. The related **output tax** on those supplies has been **accounted for.**

3. The consideration receivable for the supply is **not more than the value of the product / service on the open market.**

4. A minimum of **six months** have passed since the **date of supply and** since the **due date for payment**.

Claims for bad debt relief can be made within **three years** after the expiry of six months from the **later** of the following dates:
   a) The date of the supply and
   b) The date on which payment was due.

Here, Casuals Ltd supplied garments to For Her Ltd for the consideration of £20,000. A six months period has passed since the date of supply and the due date of payment (due date was 30 June 2007). The company is applying for bad debt relief within three years of the date of supply.

However, Casuals Ltd had not accounted for VAT on this bill (as the company follows the cash accounting system i.e. records bills on the receipt of the bill amount). Therefore, Casuals Ltd cannot reclaim VAT on the bill raised on For Her Ltd.

Answer 9

1. Music Ltd, for the first time, fails to submit a VAT return for the quarter ended 31 March 2009. This being a default, HMRC will issue a SLN. This notice will be effective from the end of the period to which the default relates i.e. 31 March 2009. This notice will remain effective for 12 months i.e. until 31 March 2010.

2. During the surcharge notice period, Music Ltd failed to pay VAT. This being the second default on 30 June 2009 for payment of VAT during the SLN period, surcharge is due at 2% on £2,000. Therefore surcharge is £40. The original surcharge period will be extended to 30 June 2010.

3. However, HMRC will not charge surcharge as the surcharge is calculate at 2% and the surcharge liability is less than £400.

4. By the end of the third quarter, Music Ltd failed to submit a return and to pay VAT in time. Due to this, the original surcharge period is extended by 12 months from the end of the period to 30 September 2010.

5. Therefore the VAT surcharge period is extended to 30 September 2009. As there is second default in payment of VAT, surcharge is calculated at the rate of 5%. Total surcharge liability is £350 (£7,000 x 5%).

6. Again HMRC will not charge surcharge as the applicable surcharge rate was 5% and the surcharge liability was less than £400.

7. By the end of the fourth quarter, Music Ltd again failed to submit a return and to pay VAT in time. This will extend the surcharge period until 31 December 2010. The surcharge is due at 10% and the surcharge liability is £500 (£5,000 x 10%).

Answer 10

When a taxable person makes late notification of his liability to register for VAT, he is liable for a penalty. The amount of the penalty is calculated as penalty rate multiplied by total tax liability.

Arnold registered for VAT 5 months late. Therefore the applicable penalty rate is 5%. His total output tax if he had registered for VAT would be £10,500. He had already paid input tax of £2,000. Therefore the total tax liability will be £8,500 (£10,500 – £2,000).

Answer 11

There is an underassessment of £60,000 (£90,000 – £150,000). This underassessment of VAT will attract a penalty if it exceeds the higher of the following:

1. £10,000
2. 1% of turnover for the VAT period (1% x £256,000 = £2,560) subject to a maximum of £50,000.

Higher of the above is £10,000.

The tax lost (£150,000 – £90,000 = £60,000) is more than £10,000.

The amount of penalty is based on the amount of tax understated, but the actual penalty payable depends on the taxpayer's behaviour, as follows

i. If the tax payer has made a simple mistake no penalty will be charged
ii. If the taxpayer fails to take reasonable care there will be a moderate penalty up to 30% of the understated tax
iii. If the error is deliberate a higher penalty up to 70% of the understated tax will be charged, if the taxpayer tries to conceal the error a penalty of up to 100% of the understated tax may be charged.

If the taxpayer makes an unprompted disclosure of an incorrect return the penalty may be reduced to zero even though the taxpayer has failed to take reasonable care.

Mango Ltd is liable to a moderate penalty of 30% of the understated tax.

= 30% (£60,000)
= £18,000.

Answer 12

Cluppins was entitled for a VAT refund but there was a difference between the amount of VAT claimed in the return and the correct amount according to the VAT assessment.

HMRC had issued a written instruction for the repayment of VAT amount within 30 days from the receipt of the return.

As a result, Cluppins is not entitled to any repayment supplement.

Quick Quiz

1. Moon Ltd manufactures pens. The company decides on a wholesale price for fountain pens of £5 per pen. The company also decides to give a 2% discount to those who pay within 15 days.
   Advise Moon Ltd on the amount it should charge for VAT and the steps the company should take if a customer does not pay the bill within 15 days.

2. Beauty Ltd sells cosmetics to various retail outlets; its turnover is £28,793,000 for the VAT period. The company declares its output tax liability as £120,000. It claims input tax of £97,000. The company submitted its VAT return for the June 2009 quarter in time. Later it was discovered that input tax was overstated by £50,000. Can HMRC apply a penalty order for misdeclaration?

3. Cow Plc supplies milk to retailers in bottles. A VAT-exclusive price of £10 is charged for a bottle of milk. Each milk bottle consists of standard-rated bottles, which cost the company £2 (inclusive of VAT) per bottle and zero-rated bottles which cost the company £5 per bottle. Show the calculation of the output tax due.

4. Décor Ltd makes wooden furniture. Interior Plc owns a furniture shop. Both companies signed an agreement for supply of furniture for the next two years. Being its first dispatch, Interior Plc gave an advance of £20,000 on 10 May 2009, against which an invoice was raised for £30,000 on 10 July 2009.

    The balance amount of £10,000 was paid on 1 August 2009. State Décor Ltd's tax point.

5. Camel Plc, a newly-incorporated company, has entered into a contract with the government to provide car parking on Dessert Street. The company's rates for parking are as follows:

    For 3 hours - £2
    For 5 hours - £3
    For 10 hours - £5
    For 24 hours - £8

    Camel Plc decides that the contents of the invoice to be issued to its customers will be as follows:

    a) Date and number of invoice.
    b) Car no.
    c) Car park fees and VAT on the same.

    The company also decides not to preserve the invoices for more than two years. Can the company do so?

Answers to Quick Quiz

1. Moon Ltd has offered a cash discount for prompt payment. In this situation, the company should charge VAT on the net amount of sales (i.e. sales price less discount offered). The company has to charge VAT on the net sales price only, irrespective of whether or not the customer actually takes advantage of the discount.

    In effect, the company has to charge VAT on £4.9 (£5 – 2%).

2. Beauty Ltd has overstated the VAT repayable. The company is liable for a misdeclaration penalty if the VAT which would have been lost equals or exceeds the higher of the following:

    a) £10,000

    b) 1% of turnover for the VAT period subject to a maximum of £50,000
       = 1% (£28,793,000)
       = £287,930.

    The error of £50,000 is less than £287,930. As this is not large; the company is not liable for a misdeclaration penalty.

3. Cow Plc supplies a mixture of two goods invoiced together under a single inclusive price. Both the items in the mixture are chargeable to VAT at different rates. Hence, to calculate output tax, it becomes necessary for Cow Plc to apportion the price charged between the various ingredients of the mixture.
    As the cost of each item in the mixture is known, this apportionment needs to be done on the basis of the cost of each item to the supplier. However, these costs are inclusive of VAT.

    The value of the supply represented by the standard-rated goods is £10 x 2/7 = £2.86. (Out of total cost of £7, the cost of bottles is £2)
    VAT at standard rate on these bottles is £2.86 x 15% = £0.429

    Therefore, the output tax due per bottle is £0.429.

4. There are two tax points in respect of these transactions between Décor Ltd and Interior Plc.

    a) In the case of the advance of £20,000, the tax point is the date of advance payment i.e. 10 May 2009. (Being the date of receipt of payment and the date of invoice, whichever is earlier).

F3.28: Value Added Tax

b) In the case of the balance of £10,000, the tax point is the date of invoice i.e. 10 July 2009 (being the date of invoice and the date of receipt of payment, whichever is earlier).

5. In accordance with the standards prescribed for VAT invoices, each VAT invoice must give the following details:

   a) **Date** of issue of invoice and invoice number

   b) **Tax point**

   c) **Name, address** and **VAT registration number** of the person issuing the VAT invoice.

   d) Customer's **name** and **address**

   e) **Descriptions of goods** or **services** supplied for each type of the goods, its quantity, amount and rate of VAT

   f) **Unit prices** of goods / services supplied

   g) **Cash discount** if any offered

   h) **Total VAT** charged

Out of these, Camel Plc gives only three details.

A taxable person who supplies services or goods, of which the value of the supply is less than £250, can issue an invoice with fewer details than prescribed in the standards. Therefore, in the given case, Camel Plc is allowed to issue an invoice with fewer details.

But it is binding on the company to preserve invoices for a minimum of six years.

Self Examination Questions

Question 1

State the VAT rules that determine the tax point in respect of a supply of services.

(June 2005)

Question 2

Tardy Ltd registered for Value Added Tax (VAT) on 1 July 2005. The company's VAT returns have been submitted as follows:

Quarter ended	VAT paid/ £	Submitted
30 Sep 07	18,600	One month late
31 Dec 07	32,200	One month late
31 Mar 08	8,800	On time
30 Jun 08	3,400	Two months late
30 Sep 08	(6,500)	One month late
31 Dec 08	42,100	On time
31 Mar 09	(2,900)	On time
30 Jun 09	3,900	On time
30 Sep 09	18,800	On time
31 Dec 09	57,300	Two months late
31 Mar 10	9,600	On time

Tardy Ltd always pays any VAT that is due at the same time that the related return is submitted.

Required:

State, giving appropriate reasons, the default surcharge consequences arising from Tardy Ltd's submission of its VAT returns for the quarter.

(June 2006)

Question 3

Puzzled Ltd has discovered that a number of errors have been made when preparing its VAT returns for the previous four quarters. As a result of the errors, the company will have to make an additional payment of VAT to **HMRC.**

Required:

Explain how Puzzled Ltd can voluntarily disclose the errors that have been discovered and whether default interest will be due, if the net errors in total are
(i) less than the higher of £10,000 or 1% of turnover for the VAT period or
(ii) more than the higher of £10,000 **or 1% of turnover for the VAT period.**

Question 4

Malcolm has filed his VAT return for the quarter ended 31 December 2009. This return represents output tax of £150,000 and input tax of £85,000. Subsequently it was discovered that the output tax was understated by £30,000. The turnover is £456,000 for the VAT period. Is he liable for a misdeclaration penalty?

Answers to Self Examination Questions

Answer 1

1. The basic tax point for services is the date on which they are completed.

2. If an invoice is issued or payment is received before the basic tax point, then this becomes the actual tax point.

3. If an invoice is issued within 14 days of the basic tax point, the invoice date will usually replace that in (1).

Answer 2

1. If a taxable person fails to file returns in time or to make the payment of VAT in time, HMRC issues a surcharge notice. In the case of Tardy Ltd, the company failed to file two quarter end returns in time.

   This has resulted in HMRC issuing a surcharge liability notice specifying a surcharge period. The surcharge period starts from the end of the period to which the default relates, i.e. 30 September 2007. This notice remains effective until 30 September 2008 (i.e. for 12 months).

2. During a surcharge period, if the taxable person fails to pay VAT or makes late payments, HMRC levies a surcharge. In the case of Tardy Ltd the company has made a late payment of VAT for the quarter ended 31 December 2007.

   This has made Tardy Ltd liable for a surcharge of £644 (£32,200 x 2%) and the surcharge period is extended to 31 December 2008.

3. For the quarter ended 30 June 2008, the company has also failed to pay VAT in time. This has resulted in a surcharge liability of £170 (£3,400 x 5%). However, no surcharge notice will be issued as the surcharge amount is less than £400 and the surcharge period is extended to 30 June 2009.

4. For the quarter ended 31 September 2009 the return is late attracting a surcharge liability of 10% of the tax paid. However in this quarter as there is a refund there will be a surcharge. During the surcharge liability period, if the taxable person fails to file a return in time, this increases the rate of surcharge. Tardy Ltd has failed to file a VAT return in time. Therefore, this will result in a surcharge.

5. During the surcharge liability period, if the taxable person fails to file the return then the original surcharge period will get extended by one year from the date to which the new default relates.

   So, in Tardy Ltd's case, continuous late submission of VAT returns has resulted in the surcharge period being extended to 31 December 2008, then to 30 June 2009 and finally to 30 September 2009.

6. During the period between quarters ended on 31 December 2008 to 30 September 2009, Tardy Ltd has submitted four consecutive VAT returns on time. This has brought the surcharge liability period to an end.

7. Again Tardy Ltd has failed to submit the VAT return for the quarter ended 31 December 2009 in time. Therefore HMRC will again issue a surcharge liability notice specifying a surcharge period running to 31 December 2010.

Answer 3

1. If a taxable person makes net errors of which the total is less than the higher of £10,000 or 1% of turnover for the VAT period, he will not be penalised. He can voluntarily disclose the errors by simply entering them on the next VAT return.

2. If the taxable person makes net errors totalling more than the higher of £10,000 or 1% of turnover for the VAT period then he can voluntarily disclose the errors, but disclosure must be made separately to HMRC.

   In this situation a taxable person is not liable for serious misdeclaration penalty if the net errors total more than the higher of £10,000 or 1% of turnover for the VAT period.

Answer 4

Misdeclaration penalty is based on the amount of tax understated, but the actual penalty payable is linked to the taxpayer's behaviour as follows:

1. There will be no penalty where a taxpayer simply makes a mistake.

2. There will be a moderate penalty (up to 30% of the understated tax) where a taxpayer fails to take reasonable care.

3. There will be a higher penalty (up to 70% of the understated tax) if the error is deliberate.

4. And an even higher penalty (up to 100% of the understated tax) where there is also concealment of the error.

In Malcolm's case, the error is of £30,000.

1% of £1,456,000 = £14,560. Therefore the higher of £10,000 and £14,560 is £14,560. However the error of £30,000 is more than £14,560. Hence, Malcolm is liable for a misdeclaration penalty. The amount of penalty will depend on the behaviour of Malcolm.

If he has made a mistake unintentionally then no penalty would be charged or would be reduced substantially. However if he has not taken reasonable care then a moderate penalty upto 30% of the understated tax is charged. If he has deliberately made a misdeclaration, then a higher penalty up to 70% of the understated tax is charged and an even higher rate of up to 100% of the understated tax is charged on a deliberate error and its concealment.

SECTION F: VALUE ADDED TAX

F4

STUDY GUIDE F4: THE EFFECT OF SPECIAL SCHEMES

Get Through Intro

To make the correct payment of VAT a taxable person needs to maintain proper accounting records. This Study Guide explains various accounting methods such as the cash accounting scheme, the annual accounting scheme and the flat rate accounting scheme.

In this Study Guide we will also discuss the advantages of these schemes. A thorough understanding of these accounting schemes will help you to advice a client on which accounting method he should follow, depending on the turnover of the business.

Learning Outcomes

a) Describe the cash accounting scheme, and recognise when it will be advantageous to use the scheme.
b) Describe the annual accounting scheme, and recognise when it will be advantageous to use the scheme.
c) Describe the flat rate scheme, and recognise when it will be advantageous to use the scheme.

Introduction

Case Study

Jenny Smith Floral Designs Ltd is a small event company, which specialises in providing exotic flowers for corporate clients. It is owned by two sisters and employs a part-time administration assistant. The company has recently registered for VAT and Jenny and her sister are wondering what the differences are between the various VAT schemes available.

After researching the schemes on HMRC's website Jenny concluded that the Cash Accounting Scheme would be beneficial for the company. It recognises VAT only when the cash has been paid or received, thereby providing considerable cash flow benefits.

Let us study this Study Guide and see if Jenny's conclusion is correct.

1. Describe the cash accounting scheme, and recognise when it will be advantageous to use the scheme.[2]

[Learning outcome a]

1.1 The cash accounting system

The cash accounting scheme allows businesses to account for VAT on a cash receipts basis, rather than an accruals basis.

Under the cash accounting scheme a person accounts for VAT on the basis of **payments received and made**, rather than on invoices issued and received. It simply means that, in the books of accounts, VAT is recorded when actual cash is received or paid.

Under this accounting system, a taxable person need not follow tax points. The **actual date of cash receipt or payment** will determine the return under which the transaction should be covered.

Conditions for joining the cash accounting scheme

1. Value of taxable supplies (excluding VAT) in the next 12 months is not expected to exceed **£1,350,000**.

2. The company must be **up to date with its VAT returns and payments.**

3. No convictions for VAT offences or assessment penalties for VAT evasion in the preceding 12 months.

4. Businesses using the scheme must cease doing so once the value of taxable supplies in the previous 12 months exceeds £1,600,000.

Example

Edward follows tax periods ending in July, October, January and April. By the end of September 2009, his turnover for the last twelve months was £1,625,000.

In this situation, Edward must withdraw himself from the cash accounting system by the end of the tax period i.e. October 2009.

1.2 Advantages

1. Where a period of credit is given to customers, VAT is not paid until one month after the return period in which the invoice was paid.
2. Automatic bad debt relief as VAT is only paid to HMRC once the invoice is paid.

Example

On 1 January 2009, Sam sold goods worth £5,000 plus VAT of £250 to Nita. The credit period was 30 days. However, Nita made the payment on 10 February 2009.

In this situation Sam need not pay VAT to HMRC until the actual date of receipt i.e. 10 February 2009.

1.3 Disadvantage

The recovery of input VAT is delayed until the business has paid for its purchases.

Example

Renaldo uses steel rods in manufacturing spare parts for cars. The spare parts are liable for VAT at the rate of 15%. On 10 May 2009, Renaldo purchased steel rods from James Bond worth £1,000 and paid VAT of £150 on the same. The steel rods were purchased on a credit basis. The credit period was one month. Renaldo paid for these goods on 30 September 2009.

In May 2009, Renaldo used the rods in manufacturing the spare parts. However, while paying VAT on output, he cannot set off input VAT until he has paid for the goods. He can therefore set off input VAT only after making the actual payment for the goods (i.e. on or after 30 September 2009).

SUMMARY

Cash accounting system
- **VAT is recorded** — when actual cash is received or paid
- **no need to follow tax points** — actual date of cash receipt / payment determines the return
- **conditions**
  - expected VAT in next 12 month should be <£1,350,000
  - VAT returns & payments must be up to date
  - no VAT offences or assessment penalties in preceding 12 months
  - must be ceased once the taxable supplies in previous 12 months > £1,600,000

---

2. Describe the annual accounting scheme, and recognise when it will be advantageous to use the scheme.[2]

[Learning outcome b]

2.1 Annual accounting scheme

Under the scheme:
1. Only **one VAT return** is submitted each year, due within two months of the end of the year.
2. **Nine monthly payments,** each equal to 1/9th of the previous year's VAT payable, are made on the account, the **first one at the end of the fourth month** of the year.

Example

Peter manufactures furniture. He pays VAT regularly. His year end is March. Last year i.e. in the year ended 31 March 2009, his net VAT liability (output VAT – input VAT) was £9,000. If, in the year ended 31 March 2010 he wants to move to the annual accounting system, he must pay VAT of £8,100 (90% of 9,000) during the current year. The first instalment must start from the 4 month of the year i.e. July 2009.

3. HMRC **estimates the liability for the year** based on the previous year's liability.
4. Any **balancing payment** must be made with the return.

2.2 Conditions for joining the annual accounting scheme:

1. Value of **taxable supplies** (excluding VAT) in the next 12 months is **not expected to exceed £1,350,000**.
2. All eligible businesses can join the annual accounting scheme as soon as they register for VAT.
3. Businesses using the scheme **must cease** doing so once the value of taxable supplies in the previous 12 months **exceeds £1,600,000**.

F4.4: Value Added Tax

2.3 Advantages

1. **Reduced administration.**
2. Only **one VAT return,** so less chance of incurring a default surcharge.
3. **Payments on account are known**, allowing improved budgeting and cash flow if business is expanding.

> **3. Describe the flat rate scheme, and recognise when it will be advantageous to use the scheme.**[2]
>
> [Learning outcome c]

3.1 Flat rate scheme

Under this scheme:

1. The business issues VAT invoices, charging VAT at either standard or zero rate.
2. **No records** need to be kept of input VAT suffered.
3. VAT payable to HMRC is the flat rate percentage multiplied by the **VAT INCLUSIVE turnover** for the period.

> VAT liability = Total turnover x Flat rate percentage

4. **No input VAT is recovered.**
5. There is a reduction of 1% of the normal rate in the first year of registration.

> **Tip**
> The flat rate percentage varies according to the type of trade, it will be given in the examination.

3.2 Conditions for joining the flat rate scheme

1. Value of **annual taxable supplies** (excluding VAT) does **not exceed £150,000.**
2. The **annual total turnover** (excluding VAT) does **not exceed £187,500.**

Example For the year ended 31 March 2009 Robert's turnover was £80,000.

In the next 12 months, Robert does not expect his business turnover to exceed £150,000. During these 12 months i.e. during the year ended 31 March 2009 he had planned to sell one of the machines that he owned and used in the business.

He expects that during the year ended 31 March 2010 his total turnover (including the sale proceeds from the sale of the asset) will not exceed £187,500.

In this situation, Robert can join the flat rate scheme.

Test Yourself 1

Alistair expects that, during the next 12 months, his business turnover will be £130,000. He may dispose of an asset in the business for £60,000. Knowing this, can he join the flat rate scheme?

3.3 Advantages

1. **Simplified** VAT administration
2. Only need to issue VAT invoices to VAT registered customers
3. Business may benefit from paying less VAT to HMRC

3.4 Disadvantages

1. Cannot reclaim input VAT on purchases

> **Example**
>
> Neptune Ltd is registered for VAT on 1 March 2009. The company has annual standard-rated sales of £86,500. These sales are made to the general public. The annual standard rated expenses of the company are £15,000. These amounts are all inclusive of VAT. The relevant flat rate scheme for the company is 10%.
>
> The **conditions** that the company must satisfy before being permitted to use the flat rate scheme are as follows:
>
> 1. The company's expected taxable turnover for the next 12 months does not exceed £150,000.
> 2. The company's expected total income (including exempt supplies) for the next 12 months does not exceed £187,500.
>
> Neptune Ltd also gains the following advantages by using this scheme. The advantages are as follow:
>
> 1. Simplified VAT administration.
> 2. On the basis of normal provisions, the VAT liability is calculated as follows:
>   £86,500 - £15,000 = £71,500 x 3/23 = **£9,326**.
>   If the company uses the flat rate scheme, then, it will have to pay VAT liability amounting **£8,650** (£86,500x10%).
>
> There is therefore an annual saving of £676 (£9,326 - £8,650).

Test Yourself 2

Ping Ltd is a food shop, which sells mainly ice-creams, a variety of chocolates and fruit drinks. In addition to this, Ping Ltd supplies food such as bread, cake, yoghurt, cheese etc.

Ping's turnover from the sale of chocolates, ice-creams and fruit drinks is around £40,000 (excluding VAT). VAT on all these items is collected at 15%. The turnover of the other food supplies is £11,250. These supplies are taxable at zero-rate.

Required:

Calculate the VAT payable by Ping Ltd if it opts for the flat rate scheme. (Flat rate percentage for retailing food is 2%).

Answers to Test Yourself

Answer 1

A person can join the flat rate scheme, provided he fulfils the following conditions for the next 12 months:

1. He does not expect turnover to exceed £150,000, and
2. He does not expect his total turnover (including exempt and non-business income) to exceed £187,500. In Alistair's case he expects his total turnover to exceed £187,500. Hence, even though his expected business turnover is less than £150,000, he cannot join the flat rate scheme.

Answer 2

	Total turnover of Ping Ltd	£
1.	Turnover of ice-creams, chocolates & fruit drinks	40,000
	Add: VAT @ 15%	6,000
	Gross turnover of ice-creams, chocolates and fruit drinks	**46,000**
2.	Turnover of daily required food items	11,250
	Add: VAT – at zero rate	Nil
	Gross turnover of daily required food items	**11,250**
3.	**Total turnover (1 + 2)**	**57,250**

Total VAT payable by Ping Ltd = £57,250 x 2%
= £1,145

Quick Quiz

1. To whom is the cash accounting system advantageous?
2. To whom is the annual accounting system advantageous?
3. To whom is the flat rate system advantageous?
4. Tom has been registered for VAT for the last six years. He expects that, within the next 12 months, his turnover will exceed £800,000. Can he join the cash accounting system?

Answers to Quick Quiz

1. Under the cash accounting system a taxable person doesn't have to pay tax until the business receives payment of its sales invoice. So, when the goods are sold on a credit basis and the customer does not pay for the same, the trader doesn't have to pay VAT on these supplies (i.e. the supplies which have become bad debts).

   In this way, a trader automatically gets bad debt relief. Hence, the cash accounting system is mainly advantageous to traders who mainly sell goods on a credit basis.

2. The annual accounting system is more advantageous to small traders whose taxable annual turnover will not exceed £1,350,000 in the next 12 months, as they don't have to file tax returns very frequently.

3. Flat rate accounting is mainly advantageous to small businesses. Due to the flat rate accounting system, the supplier doesn't have to maintain records for VAT payable on output or VAT paid on purchases. Small businesses with a small turnover find this convenient as it makes record-keeping easier.

4. The cash accounting system can be followed only if a taxable person expects that, during the next 12 months, his taxable turnover will not exceed £1,350,000. As Tom expects his turnover to exceed £800,000 in the next 12 months he can join the cash accounting system.

Self Examination Questions

Question 1

Kinte follows the cash accounting system. In the last two years he was irregular in making his VAT payments. What are the consequences of this?

Question 2

Danesh runs the 'Cook & Food' restaurant and has rented out a flat. His total turnover, for the year ended 2009 - 10 is as follows:

a) VAT inclusive taxable turnover for catering supplies £80,000 at standard rate.
b) VAT inclusive supplies (takeaway food) £5,000 at zero rate.
c) Exempt flat rentals £4,000.

Required:

Calculate the total taxable turnover and VAT liable if the applicable flat rate is 12%.

Answers to Self Examination Questions

Answer 1

When a registered person who follows the cash accounting system fails to make regular VAT payments, he becomes debarred from the scheme.

Answer 2

Under the flat rate scheme, a flat rate percentage is applied on the VAT inclusive of total turnover for the period. Total turnover includes zero rate supplies, low rate supplies and exempt supplies.
Calculation of the total turnover for the year ended 2009 - 10 is as follows:

VAT inclusive turnover	£
Standard-rated catering	80,000
Zero-rated takeaway food	5,000
Exempt flat rentals	4,000
Total	**89,000**

VAT payable by Danesh under flat rate scheme = 12% x £89,000 = **£10,680.**

SECTION G: THE OBLIGATIONS OF TAX PAYERS AND / OR THEIR AGENTS

G1

STUDY GUIDE G1: THE SYSTEMS FOR SELF-ASSESSMENT AND THE MAKING OF RETURNS

Get Through Intro

In this Study Guide, we will see how a taxpayer is required to self-assess his tax liability. Although, the Inland Revenue will send the taxpayer, (whether an individual or a company) a notice and an appropriate tax form, the responsibility is placed on the taxpayer to inform HMRC about their chargeability to tax in the case of non-receipt of the notice.

Understanding the provisions relating to informing HMRC about tax chargeability, the due dates, exceptions to it and consequences of not informing HMRC about tax chargeability, etc. is very important to you as a prospective tax consultant.

Learning Outcomes

a) Explain and apply the features of the self-assessment system as it applies to individuals.
b) Explain and apply the features of the self-assessment system as it applies to companies.

Introduction

What is self-assessment? Does a taxpayer always need to self-assess his tax liability?

Self-assessment is broadly the process by which taxpayers declare:

- Taxable income and gains on tax returns
- Income tax
- Capital gains tax
- Class 4 National Insurance Contributions as appropriate

However, the Inland Revenue can calculate these liabilities for the taxpayer, provided a tax return is sent by the individual well in advance. **If any taxpayer wants HMRC to calculate his tax liability,** he has to file the tax return by 31 October following the end of the tax year. e.g., for the year ended 5 April 2009, the return must be sent to HMRC by 31 October 2009.

Remember, **companies do not have the option of leaving their tax calculations to HMRC.**

1. Explain and apply the features of the self-assessment system as it applies to individuals.[2]
[Learning outcome a]

Most individuals **pay tax** on their earnings or pensions **through PAYE** (**P**ay **A**s **Y**ou **E**arn). Under PAYE, the employer deducts tax on behalf of HMRC. But if a person is **not on PAYE,** and / or is liable to pay additional tax because of other income not taxed through PAYE (e.g. income from property or investments above a certain amount, trading profits etc.), the taxpayer has to **assess himself** for tax liability. Under the self-assessment system, the **amount of tax** due for the year is **calculated by the taxpayer,** and then checked by HMRC.

1.1 Chargeability to tax

Individuals who are chargeable to income tax are sent a notice by HMRC of their chargeability to tax. Those who are chargeable to income tax for any tax year, but have not received any notice from HMRC, are required to inform HMRC about their chargeability to tax by sending a notice. This notice is to be given within **six months** from the end of the tax year in which the liability arises.

Example For the tax year 2009-10, the notice of chargeability by the individual to HMRC should be given before 5 October 2010.

1. **Exception:** an individual generally has to give notice to HMRC about his chargeability to tax, but is not required to do so, if the following conditions are fulfilled:

Diagram: 1 Exception to tax chargeability

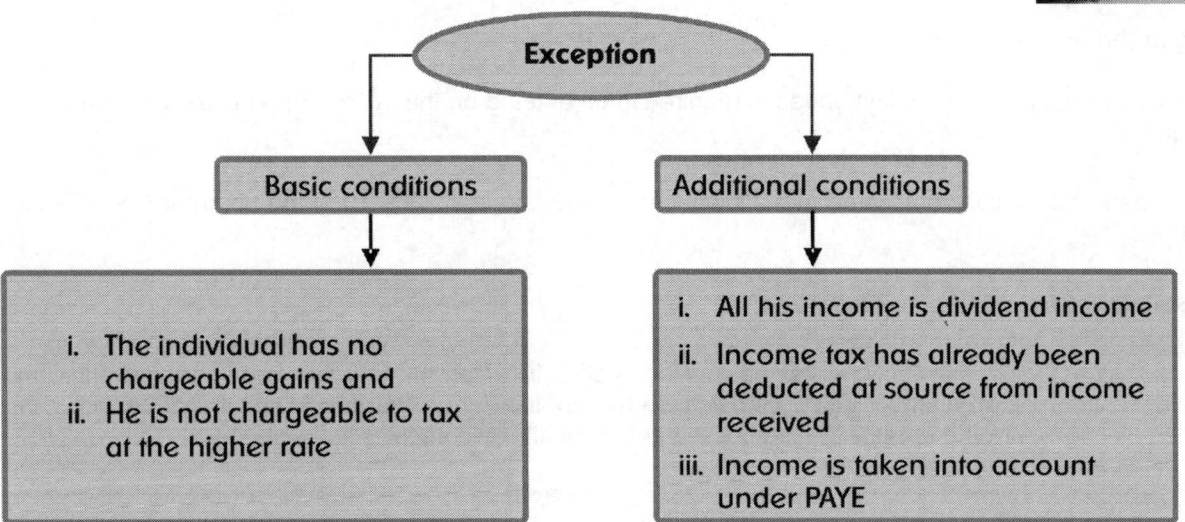

```
                    Exception
                   /         \
          Basic conditions   Additional conditions
```

Basic conditions:
i. The individual has no chargeable gains and
ii. He is not chargeable to tax at the higher rate

Additional conditions:
i. All his income is dividend income
ii. Income tax has already been deducted at source from income received
iii. Income is taken into account under PAYE

2. **Consequences of not giving notice regarding chargeability**

Where an individual is chargeable to income tax, but fails to give notice of chargeability to HMRC, a penalty **to the extent of 100%** of the tax assessed which is not paid on or before 31 January following the tax year, is payable.

Test Yourself 1

In what circumstances, does a taxpayer receive or need to ask for a self-assessment tax return?

1.2 Filing a tax return

HMRC encourages tax payers to file their self-assessment tax returns online by using its website. It has kept two separate filing dates from 2009-10.

The deadline to file a tax return online will remain 31 January following the tax year. For 2009-10 the deadline to file tax returns will be 31 January 2011.

However if a tax payer wants to follow the traditional way of filing his tax return, then the filing date will be 31 October following the tax year. Therefore, for 2009-10 the deadline to file the tax returns will be 31 October 2010.

If a tax payer wants HMRC to prepare a self assessment on his behalf by the traditional method, then the deadline for the return would be 31 October (previously it was 30 September) following the tax year. This means that all the tax payers, who file their returns using the traditional paper based method, by the 31 October, will have the option of HMRC preparing a self-assessment on their behalf. Online tax returns are automatically provided with self assessment as a part of the filing process.

1. **Receiving the tax form**

A ten-page tax form along with various supplementary pages relevant to the sources of income declared by the individual is sent to the individual by HMRC.

a) This tax form is accompanied by a tax guide and various notes relating to the supplementary pages.

b) If the taxpayer has received income from any new source for which supplementary pages are not sent by HMRC, he may have to ask for additional pages.

c) A four-page short tax return is available to taxpayers with simpler tax affairs.

2. Electronic return filing

Taxpayers can also choose to file a return online. Where a taxpayer has filed his income tax return electronically in the previous year, HMRC will send him a notice to file the return, instead of sending him the tax form.

3. Filling in the return

The information related to the year just ended is required to be entered on the tax return. The tax return must be submitted in full.

A taxpayer has to give details of income and allowances for the tax year 2009-10 in the tax return received in April 2010.

4. Assessment of tax

The main tax return includes an optional tax calculation section in which the taxpayer may calculate their tax liability. If this column is left blank, HMRC will calculate the tax liability on the individual's behalf. If the main return is filed electronically, the tax liability is assessed automatically by computer software.

Test Yourself 2

Individuals who are chargeable to income tax for any tax year, but have not received a notice from HMRC, are required to notify HMRC about their chargeability.

Required:

1. What is the time limit for giving this notice?
2. What are the exceptions to this rule?

---

1. Explain and apply the features of the self-assessment system as it applies to companies.[2]
[Learning outcome b]

Self-assessment means that companies are required to **assess themselves** to corporation tax, and to **take full responsibility** for that assessment. **If the self-assessment is wrong** through negligence or recklessness, the company can be liable to **tax-geared penalties**.

1. Chargeability to tax for the first time

Within **three months** of the start of their first accounting period, companies must inform HMRC of their chargeability to tax.

2. Subsequent chargeability to tax

A company, which is chargeable to corporation tax, is sent a notice by HMRC for the filing of a corporation tax return, for the period specified in the notice. However, a company which is chargeable to corporation tax for an accounting period but has not received any notice to that respect from HMRC must notify HMRC about its chargeability to tax within **twelve months** of the end of the accounting period.

Answers to Test Yourself

Answer 1

A taxpayer receives or needs to ask for a self-assessment tax return if:

1. He is self-employed and / or a company director.
2. He gets rent from property that's not accounted for through PAYE.
3. He gets other untaxed income not accounted for through PAYE.
4. He has substantial income from savings and investments.
5. He makes gains (profits) on the sale of shares or other assets above the Capital Gains Tax (CGT) allowance.

Answer 2

1. Those who are chargeable to income tax for any tax year but have not received a notice from HMRC are required to inform HMRC about their chargeability, by sending a notice. This notice is to be given within **six months** from the end of the period.

2. **Exception:** it is not required if the following conditions are fulfilled:

Basic conditions

a) The individual has no chargeable gains.
b) He is not chargeable to tax at the higher rate (40%).

Additional conditions

i. All his income is dividend income.
ii. Income tax has already been deducted at source from income received.
iii. Income is taken into account under PAYE.

Quick Quiz

State true or false.

1. Notice is normally sent by HMRC to individuals who are chargeable to income tax.

2. Information relating to the current year is filled in the tax return.

3. Companies which are chargeable to tax for the first time, must inform HMRC of their chargeability to tax within three months of the **start** of their first accounting period.

Answers to Quick Quiz

1. **True**, however, those who are chargeable to income tax for any tax year, but have not received any notice from HMRC, are required to inform HMRC about their chargeability to tax by sending a notice.

2. **False,** the information related to the **year just ended** is required to be entered on the tax return.

3. **True.**

Self Examination Questions

Question 1

Ambika has been trading for many years, preparing accounts to 31 December. Which accounts will be assessed in 2009-10?

Question 2

Jojoba Ltd prepares its first accounts for a 15 month period ended 31 March 2010. When should notice be sent to HMRC regarding its chargeability to tax?

Answers to Self Examination Questions

Answer 1

The information related to the year just ended is required to be entered on the tax return. Therefore, accounts relating to the year ended 31 December 2009 will be assessed in 2009-10.

Answer 2

The provisions of the Act requires that companies which are chargeable to tax for the first time, must inform HMRC of their chargeability to tax within three months of the start of their first accounting period. As Jojoba Ltd prepared its first accounts for a 15 months period, and the period of 15 months ended on 31st March 2010, it indicates that Jojoba Ltd started business on 1 January 2009 (1/1/2009 to 31/3/2010 = 15 months). Hence Jojoba Ltd must inform HMRC on or before 31 March 2009 i.e. within three months of the start of their first accounting period.

SECTION G: THE OBLIGATIONS OF TAX PAYERS AND / OR THEIR AGENTS

G2

STUDY GUIDE G2: THE TIME LIMITS FOR THE SUBMISSION OF INFORMATION, CLAIMS AND PAYMENT OF TAX, INCLUDING PAYMENTS ON ACCOUNT

Get Through Intro

While dealing with HMRC, following the due dates is very important as any delay in filing returns and paying tax can lead to heavy penalties.

This Study Guide studies in detail the due dates for tax payments, due dates for return filing, interest and penalties applicable. It also explains how HMRC can inquire into a person's self-assessment return.

Students will need this information to advise clients on how to minimise penalties. A thorough understanding of this topic is important for your examination, as well as in your professional life.

Learning Outcomes

a) Recognise the time limits that apply to the filing of returns and the making of claims.
b) Recognise the due dates for the payment of tax under the self-assessment system.
c) Compute payments on account and balancing payments / repayments for individuals.
d) Explain how large companies are required to account for corporation tax on a quarterly basis.
e) List the information and records that taxpayers need to retain for tax purposes.

Introduction

Case Study

Julian was a dealer of electrical goods. He always filed his income tax return well in advance so that HMRC could prepare a self-assessment form on his behalf.

In May 2009, Julian and two of his friends in a similar line of business formed a private limited company. Julian was under the impression that HMRC would also prepare a self-assessment form for this company.

In this Study Guide, the various provisions regarding the filing of returns, what the due dates are, whether HMRC can prepare self-assessment forms on behalf of taxpayers etc. are explored.

1. Recognise the time limits that apply to the filing of returns and the making of the claims.[2]
[Learning outcome a]

1.1 For individuals

1. **Due dates for submitting tax returns are the later of:**

a) **within three months** of the tax return being sent by HMRC

b) **31 January** following the **end of the tax year** covered by the return for filing tax returns online, and 31 October for filing paper based tax returns.

Example

HMRC issued a tax return for the tax year 2009-10 to Trish on 15/11/10. Therefore, the due date for her to submit her tax return (online filing of return) is **the later of**:
- within three months from 15/11/10 i.e. 15/02/2011
- 31/01/ 2011

The due date is 15/02/2011.

Where **an individual requires HMRC to prepare their self-assessment forms on their behalf,** the due date for filing the return is **31 October** following the tax year.

All paper tax returns submitted by 31 October will have the option of HMRC preparing a self assessment on their behalf. Self assessment is automatically provided for online tax returns as a part of the filing process.

1.2 For companies

1. **Filing of return**

On receiving a notice from HMRC, a company must file a corporation tax return for the period **specified in the notice.** The return is in the Form CT600 with the relevant supplementary pages. The supporting accounts and calculations must be attached along with the return.

Tip

Companies do not have the option of leaving the tax calculations to HMRC.

2. Due dates for filing returns with HMRC

The return has to be filed **on or before the due date.** The due date for filing the return is the **latest** of:

a) **twelve months after the end of the period covered** by the return i.e. the period specified in the notice by HMRC.

b) if the **period of accounts is less than eighteen months,** then the due date is twelve months after the end of the period of accounts.

c) if the period of accounts is **more than or equal to eighteen months,** then the **due date is thirty months from the start of the period of accounts.**

d) **three months after** the issue of notice.

Diagram 1: Time limits for filing returns for individuals and companies

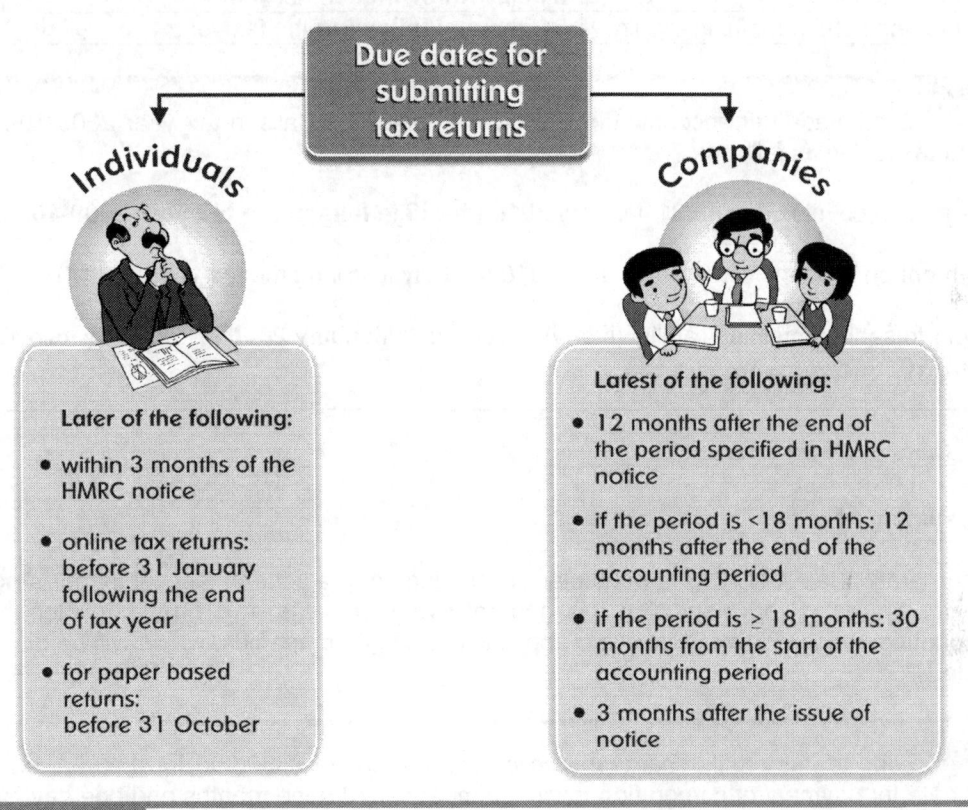

Due dates for submitting tax returns

Individuals

Later of the following:
- within 3 months of the HMRC notice
- online tax returns: before 31 January following the end of tax year
- for paper based returns: before 31 October

Companies

Latest of the following:
- 12 months after the end of the period specified in HMRC notice
- if the period is <18 months: 12 months after the end of the accounting period
- if the period is ≥ 18 months: 30 months from the start of the accounting period
- 3 months after the issue of notice

Test Yourself 1

State the date of filing the return by Turbo Ltd if it prepares its accounts for:

1. 15 months to 31 March 2009. Notice was issued by HMRC on 15 May 2009.
2. 18 months to 31 May 2009. Notice was issued by HMRC on 1 July 2009.
3. 9 months to 31 December 2009. Notice was issued by HMRC on 12 February 2010.

The required filing date is normally **twelve months after** the **end** of the **period of account** since the majority of companies prepare their accounts to the same date each year. Notices are usually issued within a few weeks of the end of each period of account.

Test Yourself 2

State the date that CompuServe Ltd's self-assessment corporation tax return for the year ended 31 December 2009 should be submitted.

The time limit for making claims under income tax and corporation tax is four years from the end of the tax year. For e.g. for the tax year 2009-10, the claim can be made by 5 April 2014.

2. Recognise the due dates for the payment of tax under the self-assessment system.[2]
[Learning outcome b]

2.1 For individuals

Payment of tax: Tax due for self-assessment is payable as follows in three parts:

1. A first payment on account is due on **31 January in the tax year** to which the self-assessment relates.

2. A second payment on account is due on the following **31 July.**

3. A final **balancing payment** is due on **31 January** following the end of the tax year to which it relates.

Payment	Due date
1st payment on account	31 January **in** the tax year
2nd payment on account	31 July **following** the tax year
Final payment to settle the remaining liability	31 January **following** the tax year

Example Simi made her accounts up to 31 December 2009 (falls in tax year 2009-10). Payment of self-assessment tax is due as follows:

1. First payment on account is due on 31 January **2010** (this date **falls in the tax year 2009-10).**

2. Second payment on account is due on 31 July 2010 (31 July following the tax year 2009-10).

3. Final payment to settle remaining liability (if any) is due on 31 January 2011 (31 January following the tax year 2009-10).

2.2 For companies

Due date for payment of tax

A company's corporation tax liability for a particular accounting year is generally payable in a **single payment**. The **due date** for the actual payment of tax is generally **nine months and one day** after the end of the concerned accounting period. Different rules are applicable to large companies, which will be discussed later in this Study Guide.

Example Zen Ltd has profits chargeable to corporation tax of £690,000 for the year ended 31 March 2009. The due date for payment of corporation tax is 1 January 2010 (nine months and one day after the end of the accounting period).

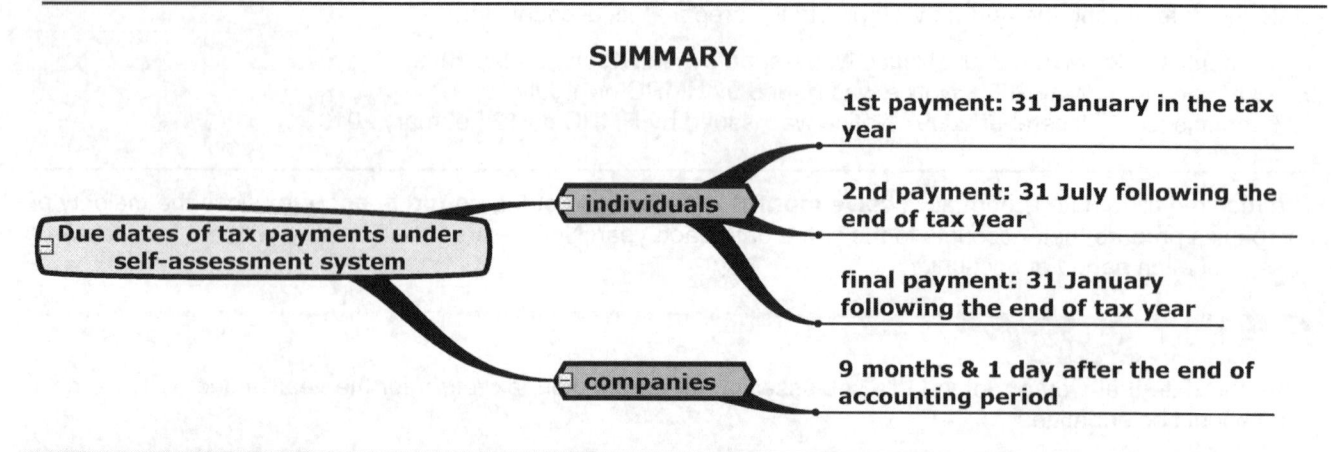

SUMMARY

Due dates of tax payments under self-assessment system

- **individuals**
  - 1st payment: 31 January in the tax year
  - 2nd payment: 31 July following the end of tax year
  - final payment: 31 January following the end of tax year
- **companies**
  - 9 months & 1 day after the end of accounting period

Test Yourself 3

Sasha made her first accounts up to 30 June 2009. When are payments on account due?

3. Compute the payments on account and balancing payments / repayments for individuals.[2]
[Learning outcome c]

3.1 Payment on account

Payments on account are normally fixed by reference to the previous year's tax liability. The payment on account **on each instalment** is equal to **50% of the relevant amount for the previous year.** If the current year's tax and Class 4 NIC liabilities are more than the previous year's tax liability, then the excess portion is paid by way of a **balancing payment** payable on **31 January following the end of the current tax year.**

Example Simi's income tax liability for **2008-09** (previous year) excluding tax deducted at source was £10,000. Her tax liability for the **2009-10** is £14,500.

The payments on account for 2009-10 are as follows:

Date		£
31/01/2010	1st **payment on account** (50% of 2008-09 liability)	5,000
31/07/2010	2nd **payment on account** (50% of 2008-09 liability)	5,000
31/01/2011	**Balancing payment** to settle the remaining liability	4,500
	Total	14,500

Note: There will also be a payment on 31 January 2011 of £7,250, the first instalment of the tax year 2010-11 (50% of the 2009-10 liability).

1. Payment on account on each instalment is 50% of the previous year's tax liability. Hence, a situation may arise where a taxpayer may have paid excess tax over the current year's tax liability, by paying on account. In such a case, the taxpayer is entitled to a **balancing repayment** (i.e. to receive the excess tax paid by him).

Example Roma's income tax liability for **2008-09** (previous year) excluding tax deducted at source was £10,000. Her tax liability for **2009-10** is £8,500.

The payments on account for 2009-10 are as follows:

Date		£
31/01/2010	1st **payment on account** (50% of 2008-09 liability)	5,000
31/07/2010	2nd **payment on account** (50% of 2008-09 liability)	5,000
	Total	10,000

However, Roma's total tax liability for 2009-10 is only £8,500. This means that she paid excess tax on the payment on account.

The **balancing repayment** due is £1,500 i.e. (£10,000 - £8,500).

Test Yourself 4

Ted's tax liability for **2009-10** is £18,300. Calculate payment of account and balancing payment / repayment due, assuming his income tax and class 4 NIC liability for **2008-09** excluding tax deducted at source was:

1. £12,300
2. £21,800

2. Payment on account of Capital Gains Tax liability is done on 31st January following the tax year, i.e. for 2009-10 it will be paid on or before 31st January 2011. The Class 2 NIC is paid on a monthly basis (in the case of direct debit and on a quarterly by billing) and therefore not required to be included in the computation for payment on account.

Example

Julie is a self-employed musician. Her tax liability for 2008-09 and 2009-10 is as follows:

	2008-09 £	2009-10 £
Total amount of income tax charged	12,500	15,000
This included:		
Tax deducted on savings income	6,200	
She also paid: Class 4 NIC	2,800	
Capital gains tax	6,100	2,000

Payments on account for 2009-10 are calculated as follows:

	£
Income tax	
Total income tax charged for 2008-09	12,500
Less: Tax deducted	(6,200)
	6,300
Add: Class 4 NIC	2,800
Self-assessment tax and Class 4 NIC	**9,100**

Payments on account for 2009-10:

Date		£
31/01/2010	1st payment on account (50% of £9,100 i.e. 2008-09 liability)	4,550
31/07/2010	2nd payment on account (50% of £9,100 i.e. 2008-09 liability)	4,550
31/01/2011	Final balancing payment to settle the remaining liability (2009-10 less sums already paid)	= 5,900
	Chargeable gains of 2009-10	2,000
	Total	**17,000**

Notes:
1. Class 2 NIC is not paid through the self-assessment system, but is paid directly to contributing agencies. Therefore no question of payment on account arises.
2. There is **no requirement** to make payments on account of **capital gains tax. It is all paid on balancing payment.**

3. Taxpayers are not required to make payments on account of their income tax (and Class 4 National Insurance) liability if:

a) **more than 80%** of the previous year's liability was covered by PAYE, tax deducted at source and dividend tax credits, or

b) the previous year's tax (and Class 4 National Insurance) liability was **less than £1000.**

Example

Helen's total liability to income tax and Class 4 NIC for 2008-09 was £22,500. Out of this, she had paid £19,900 by deduction at source. Her total liability for 2009-10 is £25,000, of which £22,000 is paid by deduction at source.

Helen's total liability to income tax   £22,500
Tax deducted at source   £19,900

More than 80% of Helen's total **liability for 2008-09** (£22,500) was **paid by deduction at source**. Therefore, **no payments on account are required** for 2009-10.

Her 2009-10 liability of £3,000 i.e. (£25,000 – £22,000) is payable on 31 January 2011.

Example Victor's total liability to income tax and Class 4 NIC for 2008-09 was £750. His total liability for 2009-10 is £5,000 of which £2,800 is paid by deduction at source.

Victor's previous year's tax and Class 4 National Insurance liability was **less than £1000**. Therefore, **no payments on account are required** for **2009-10**.

His 2009-10 liability of £2,200 i.e. (£5,000 – £2,800) is payable on 31 January 2011.

---

4. Those taxpayers who are required to make payments on account, but who believe that the liability for that year will be less than the liability for the previous year, **may make a claim to** reduce or eliminate payments on account by 31 January following the end of the tax year.

A taxpayer can apply to reduce his payments on account if he knows that his income has decreased from the previous year.

Example Alan's liability for tax and Class 4 NIC for the tax year 2008-09 was £15,600. Unfortunately, he had an accident in June 2009 and was in hospital for three months. As he was advised to take full rest, he was not able to run his business until December 2009. Therefore his income decreased by more than 70% from that of the previous year.

Alan can apply to reduce his payments on account, as his income has gone down from the previous year, and therefore his tax liability for 2009-10 will be less than the liability for the previous year (2008-09).

The claim may be made on Inland Revenue form SA303, on the tax return itself, or by letter, giving the reasons for the claim.

A taxpayer needs to be careful about reducing payments on account. If the payments are reduced, and then his income increases so that the tax for the year is as much, or more than the original payments on account, he will have to pay interest from the date the payment on account was due.

Interest is charged if payments on account are too low following the claim, and penalties may be charged for fraudulent or negligent claims.

SUMMARY

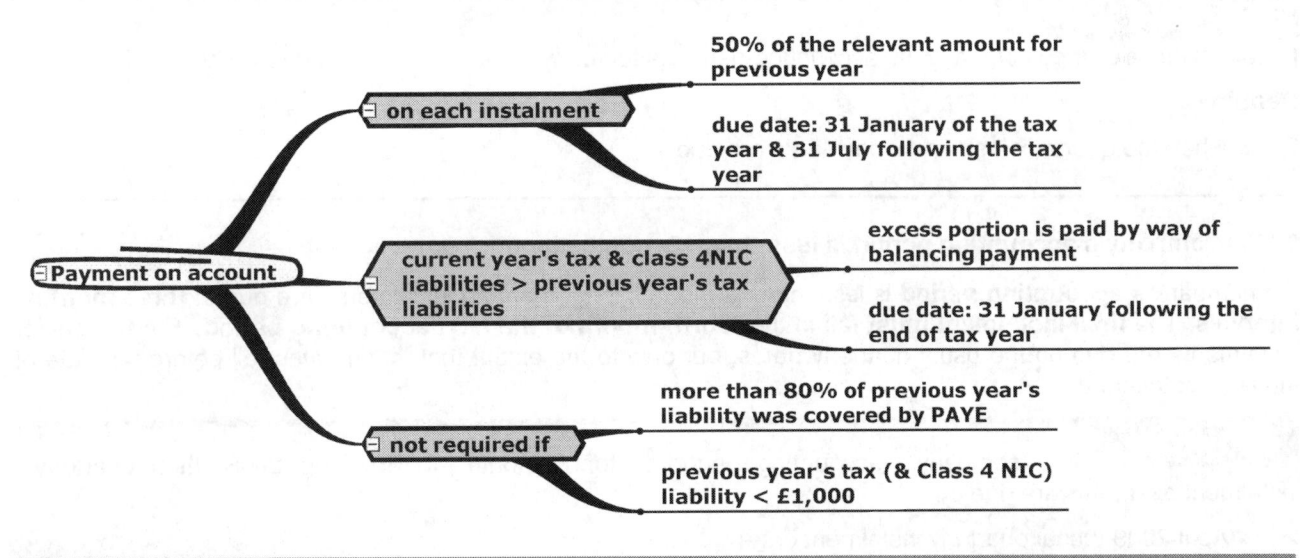

Payment on account

- **on each instalment**
  - 50% of the relevant amount for previous year
  - due date: 31 January of the tax year & 31 July following the tax year
- **current year's tax & class 4NIC liabilities > previous year's tax liabilities**
  - excess portion is paid by way of balancing payment
  - due date: 31 January following the end of tax year
- **not required if**
  - more than 80% of previous year's liability was covered by PAYE
  - previous year's tax (& Class 4 NIC) liability < £1,000

Test Yourself 5

Judy's total liability for income tax and Class 4 NIC for 2008-09 was £20,100. Out of this, she paid £7,500 by deduction at source.

Her total tax and Class 4 NIC liabilities for 2009-10 are £22,800 out of which £2,000 is paid by deduction at source.

Required:

State the dates when Judy needs to pay her income tax and Class 4 NIC for the tax year 2009-10. Also, calculate the amount payable on each date.

4. Explain how large companies are required to account for corporation tax on a quarterly basis.[2]

[Learning outcome d]

4.1 What is a large company?

A company that pays corporation tax at the full rate (28%) without deduction of marginal relief is categorised as a large company.

4.2 Method of payment of corporation tax

Large companies have to pay their corporation tax in **instalments**.

However a large company is **not required to pay** its corporation tax liability by **instalments** for each quarter in the following cases:

1. If the chargeable profits of the company are £10 million or less for the accounting period **and** the company was not a large company in the twelve months preceding that period.

2. The company has a tax liability of less than £10,000 for the period, but still pays tax at a full rate, either because of dividend income, or because it has a number of associated companies.

4.3 When are quarterly instalments due?

1. If a company's accounting period is 12 months long

A large company **with a 12 month accounting period** will pay tax in four equal instalments, **starting with 14th day of seventh month, then 14th day of tenth month, after that 14th day of thirteenth month and lastly 14th day of sixteenth month** from the beginning of the accounting period.

Example

If a company's accounting period is for 12 months starting on 1 January 2009, then quarterly instalment payments are due on 14 July 2009, 14 October 2009, 14 January 2010 and 14 April 2010.

Test Yourself 6

Excellent Ltd is a large company. Its accounting period is for 12 months starting on 1 June 2009.

Required:

Show when the quarterly instalment payments are due.

---

2. If a company's accounting period is less than 12 months long

If a company's **accounting period** is less than 12 months long, then the instalments are due at **three monthly intervals**. The **final instalment must fall** in the **fourth month of the next accounting period.** The two earlier instalments are due on the usual quarterly dates, but only to the extent that those dates fall before the date of the final instalment.

Example

If a company's accounting period is for 8 months to 30 June 2008, then quarterly instalment payments are due on:

- 14 April 2009 (usual quarterly instalment date)
- 14 July 2009 (usual quarterly instalment date)
- 14 October 2009 (final payment must fall in the fourth month of the next accounting period)

Test Yourself 7

Well done Ltd is a large company. Its accounting period is for 10 months to 31 October 2009.

Required:

Show when the corporation tax liability is due for payment.

4.4 Estimation of tax liability by a company

As a company has to pay tax for the current year on an instalment basis, it is required to estimate its corporation tax liability in advance for the current period. Failure on the part of the company to estimate its tax liability correctly can result in heavy penalties. Therefore it is imperative to correctly estimate tax liability.

> **Tip**: Installments of corporation tax are based on the estimated corporation tax liability for the current year and not the previous year as in the case of individuals.

How to calculate the amount of instalments

1. Estimate the tax liability

2. If the accounting period does not equal to 12 month, perform the following calculation, then **perform** the calculation:

$$3 \times \frac{\text{Estimated Corporation Tax}}{\text{No. of months in the period}}$$

3. This procedure is repeated for the next instalments until the amount allocated is equal to the corporation tax liability.

Example

Tempo Ltd has a corporation tax liability of £990,000 for the 9 month period to 31 October 2009. Accounts had previously always been prepared to 31 December.

The amount of each instalment is calculated as follows:

$$\text{The amount of each installment} = 3 \times \frac{\text{Estimated Corporation Tax}}{\text{No. of months in the period}}$$

$$= 3 \times \frac{£990,000}{9 \text{ months}}$$

$$= £330,000$$

The due dates and amount payable on each instalment:
14 September 2009	£330,000
14 December 2009	£330,000
14 February 2010	£330,000

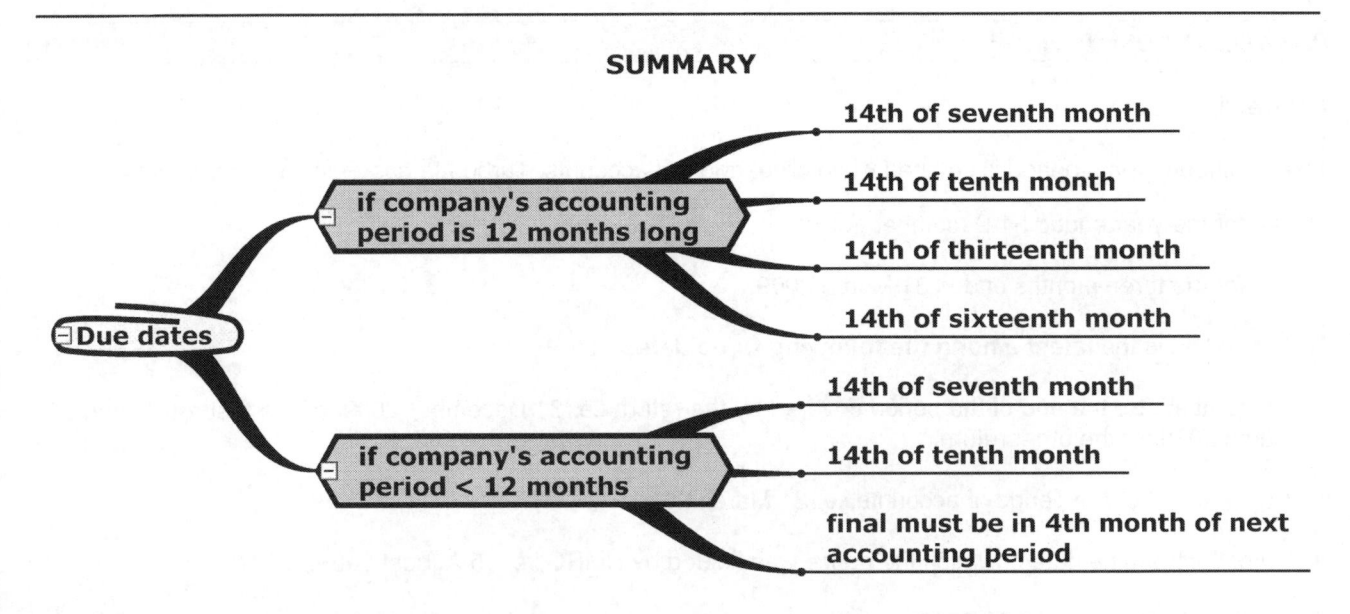

SUMMARY

Due dates

- if company's accounting period is 12 months long
  - 14th of seventh month
  - 14th of tenth month
  - 14th of thirteenth month
  - 14th of sixteenth month

- if company's accounting period < 12 months
  - 14th of seventh month
  - 14th of tenth month
  - final must be in 4th month of next accounting period

Test Yourself 8

Tick-tock Ltd has profits chargeable to corporation tax for the year ended 31 December 2009 of £2,400,000.

Required:

Show how the liability for the year ended 31 December 2009 will be settled.

---

5. List the information and records that taxpayers need to retain for tax purposes.[1]

[Learning outcome e]

Information and records to be kept by employees and directors

- Details of payments made for business expenses (e.g. receipts, credit card statements etc)
- Share options awarded or exercised
- Deductions and relief
- Documents you have signed or which have been provided to you by someone else
- Interest and dividends
- Tax deduction certificates
- Dividend vouchers
- Gift aid payments
- Personal pension plan certificates
- Personal financial records which support any claims based on amounts paid e.g. certificates of interest paid

Information and records to be kept by business

- Invoices, bank statements and paying-in slips
- Invoices for purchases and other expenses
- Details of personal drawings from cash and bank receipts

Important points to remember

1. **All the records** relevant to a taxpayer's return must be kept until 31 January of the sixth year from end of tax year.

2. If the taxpayer has income from a business or from **letting a property**, he has to keep records until 31 January of the sixth year from end of tax year.

3. If a **formal enquiry** into the return is commenced by HMRC before the expiry of the time limit specified for such an enquiry, then the **records must be kept until that enquiry has been completed.**

4. A taxpayer can **keep records on a computerised system,** provided they can be produced in legible form whenever required.

5. **A penalty of up to £3,000** is chargeable **when** the required **records are not kept** in respect of any tax year.

Answers to Test Yourself

Answer 1

1. As a fifteen month period is covered while preparing the accounts, Turbo Ltd has to file two tax returns:

a) one for the year ended 31 December 2008

b) one for the three months ended 31 March 2009.

The filing date is the **latest among the following three dates:**

i. 12 months after the end of the period covered by the return i.e. 31 December 2009 for the first return and 31 March 2010 for the other return.

ii. 12 months after the period of accounts i.e. 31 March 2010.

iii. 3 months from the date on which the notice was issued by HMRC i.e. 15 August 2009.

Hence the filing date is 31/03/2010.

2. As an eighteen month period is covered while preparing the accounts, ABC Ltd has to file two tax returns:
a) one for the year ended 31 November 2008
b) one for the three months ended 31 May 2009.

The filing date is the **latest among the following three dates:**

i. 12 months after the end of the period covered by the return i.e. 31 November 2009 for the first return and 31 May 2010 for the other return.

ii. 12 months after the period of accounts i.e. 31 May 2010.

iii. 3 months from the date on which the notice was issued by HMRC i.e. 1 October 2009.

Hence the filing date is 31/05/2010.

3. The filing date is the **latest among the following three dates:**

i. 12 months after the end of the period covered by the return i.e. 31 December 2010.

ii. 12 months after the period of accounts i.e. 31 December 2010 or

iii. 3 months from the date on which the notice was received from HMRC i.e. 12 May 2010.

Hence the filing date is 31/12/2010.

Answer 2

31 December 2010

Answer 3

The accounting date, 30 June 2009 falls in the tax year 2009-10. Therefore, due dates for the payment of tax are as follows:

1. First payment on account is due on 31 January 2010.
2. Second payment on account is due on 31 July 2010.
3. Final payment to settle remaining liability (if any) is due on 31 January 2011.

Answer 4

1. Assuming Ted's income tax and Class 4 NIC liability for 2008-09 was £12,300

The payments on account for 2009-10 are as follows:

Date		£
31/01/2010	1st **payment on account** (50% of £12,300)	6,150
31/07/2010	2nd **payment on account** (50% of £12,300)	6,150
31/01/2011	**Balancing payment** (£18,300 - £12,300)	6,000
Total		18,300

Note:

There will also be a payment on 31 January 2011 of £9,150, the first instalment of the 2010-11 tax year (50% of the 2009-10 liability of £18,300).

2. Assuming Ted's income tax and Class 4 NIC liability for 2008-09 was £21,800

The payments on account for 2009-10 are as follows:

Date		£
31/01/2010	1st **payment on account** (50% of £21,800)	10,900
31/07/2010	2nd **payment on account** (50% of £21,800)	10,900
Total		21,800

However, Ted's total tax liability for 2009-10 is only £18,300. This means he paid excess tax on payment on account.

Hence the **balancing repayment** due is £3,500 i.e. (£21,800 - £18,300).

Answer 5

The payments on account for 2008-09 are as follows:

Date		£
31/01/2010	1st **payment on account** (50% of (£20,100 - £7,500))	6,300
31/07/2010	2nd **payment on account** (50% of (£20,100 - £7,500))	6,300
31/01/2011	**Balancing payment** (£22,800 - £2,000 - £6,300 - £6,300)	8,200

Note: there will also be a payment on 31 January 2011 of £10,400, the first instalment of the 2010-11 tax year (50% of (£22,800 - £2,000)).

Answer 6

Excellent Ltd is a large company. Therefore, the due dates are as follows:

➢ 14 December 2009 (6 months 13 days from 1 June 2009)

➢ 14 March 2010 (9 months 13 days from 1 June 2009)

➢ 14 June 2010 (12 months 13 days from 1 June 2009)

➢ 14 September 2010 (15 months 13 days from 1 June 2009)

Answer 7

The due dates are:

➢ 14 September 2009
➢ 14 December 2009
➢ 14 February 2010 (final payment must fall in the fourth month of the next accounting period)

Answer 8

The corporation tax liability of Tick-tock Ltd is £672,000 i.e. (£2,400,000 x 28%).

Tick-tock Ltd is a large company (as its profits exceed £1,500,000).

Corporation tax is payable in quarterly instalments of £168,000 i.e. (£672,000/4) on 14 July 2009, 14 October 2009, 14 January 2010 and 14 April 2010.

Quick Quiz

Fill in the blanks.

1. A first payment on account is due on _____ in the tax year to which the self-assessment relates.

2. A final payment made on 31 January following the end of tax year to settle the balance income tax and Class 4 NIC liability is known as _____.

3. Taxpayers are not required to make payments on account of their income tax and Class 4 National Insurance liability if more than _____ of the previous year's liability was covered by tax deducted at source.

4. Payment on account on each instalment is _____ of the previous year's tax liability.

5. When a taxpayer receives an amount of money, due to an excess amount paid in the previous year, it is known as _____ .

Answers to Quick Quiz

1. 31 January

2. balancing payment

3. 80%

4. 50%

5. Balancing repayment

Self Examination Questions

Question 1

What are the normal dates for tax payment by individuals regarding self-assessment?

Question 2

State the date of filing self assessment corporation tax returns for the following period of accounts:

a) YL Ltd prepared its accounts for twenty months to 31 January 2009. It received notice from HMRC on 15 April 2009 for this period.

b) AS Ltd prepared its accounts for the year ended 30 April 2009.

c) TR Ltd made up its accounts for the year ended 31 March 2009. It received notice for this period from the Inland Revenue on 1 July 2009.

d) BK Ltd prepared its accounts for thirteen months to 31 December 2009.

Question 3

A company has an accounting period with a year end of 31/12/2009. Show the due dates for quarterly payment of tax.

Question 4

Jolly Good Ltd has a corporation tax liability of £770,000 for the 7 month period to 30 November 2009.

Required:

Show when the Corporation Tax liability is due for payment. Also, calculate the liability on each due date.

Answers to Self Examination Questions

Answer 1

Tax due in self-assessment is payable as follows:

1. A first payment on account is due on **31 January** in the tax year to which the self-assessment relates.

2. A second payment on account is due on the following **31 July.**

3. A final balancing payment is due on **31 January** following the end of tax year.

Answer 2

a) As the period of account of YL Ltd is twenty months, it has to be divided into two accounting periods. Two tax returns have to be filed:

> One for the year ended 31 May 2008.

➢ One for the eight months ended 31 January 2009.

The filing date is the latest among the following three dates:

i. 12 months after the end of the period specified in the notice i.e. 31 May 2009 for the first return and 31January 2010 for the other return.

ii. 30 months from the start of the period of accounts i.e. 30 November 2009.

iii. 30 months after the issue of the notice i.e. 15 July 2009.

The date of filing the return is 31 January 2010.

b) 30 April 2010

c) The filing date is the **latest** among the following two dates:

1. Twelve months after the end of the period covered by the return i.e. 31 March 2010.

2. Three months after the issue of the notice i.e. 1 October 2009.

The date of filing the return is 31 March 2010.

d) 31 December 2010

Answer 3

The tax will have to be paid as follows:

1st instalment	6 months and 14 days after the **beginning** of the accounting period	14/07/2009
2nd instalment	9 months and 14 days after the **beginning** of the accounting period	14/10/2009
3rd instalment	12 months and 14 days **after the end** of the accounting period	14/01/2010
4th instalment	15 months and 14 days **after the end** of the accounting period	14/04/2010

Answer 4

The amount of each instalment is calculated as follows:

$$\text{The amount of each installment} = 3 \times \frac{\text{Estimated Corporation Tax}}{\text{No. of months in the period}}$$

$$= 3 \times \frac{£770,000}{7 \text{ months}}$$

$$= £330,000$$

The due dates and amount of each instalment:

14 October 2009	£330,000
14 January 2010	£330,000
14 March 2010	£110,000 (balance)

SECTION G: THE OBLIGATIONS OF TAX PAYERS AND / OR THEIR AGENTS

G3

STUDY GUIDE G3: THE PROCEDURES RELATING TO ENQUIRIES, APPEALS AND DISPUTES

Get Through Intro

This Study Guide covers the various enquiries that HMRC can make on self-assessment returns.

When HM Revenue & Customs (HMRC) start an enquiry it doesn't mean that the return is necessarily incorrect. Sometimes, HMRC routinely checks a proportion of tax returns to make sure that they are correct.

However, most enquiries arise with the Revenue because there is something they don't understand or they have some information which makes them think that the tax return or claim might be wrong. Perhaps the return filed is considerably different than those filed in the past or the income may be considerably less than in the past.

Understanding these enquiries is extremely important for tax professionals, who frequently have to deal with HMRC in responding to enquiries, appealing the decisions of HMRC etc.

Understanding these concepts will help you to successfully answer the question.

Learning Outcomes

a) Explain the circumstances in which HM Revenue and Customs can enquire into a self-assessment tax return.
b) Explain the procedures for dealing with appeals and disputes.

Introduction

What can the possible outcomes of a tax enquiry be?

If nothing is wrong

You will receive a letter from HMRC informing you that the enquiry has finished. No changes will be made to the tax return or claim.

If you've paid too much tax

Your return will be changed by HMRC to reflect the lower figures. HMRC will also pay you interest from the date of your incorrect payment until the date you receive a repayment.

If you've paid too little tax

HMRC will agree any changes with you. You will receive a closure notice confirming the changes and will then have 30 days in which to pay the tax due.

If you are unable to pay the full amount immediately, you may be allowed to pay in instalments. If the amount owed is small, you may be able to increase your self-assessment 'payments on account' for the following year.

You may be required to pay interest on underpaid tax, depending on the circumstances. Other surcharges for late or non-payment of tax after issue of a closure notice will also apply.

---

1. Explain the circumstances in which HM Revenue and Customs can enquire into a self-assessment tax return.[2]

[Learning outcome a]

1.1 Revision of returns

Individuals

In all cases the last date for amending a tax return will be 12 months after the 31 January deadline. For example for 2009-10 the deadline for amending a tax return will be 31 January 2012 regardless of whether it is paper-based or filed online.

Example Angelina prepares its accounts for twelve months ended 31/03/2010 and files its return online on 15 August 2010. The **deadline for filing the return in this case is however 31/01/2012.** So Angelina can amend its tax return any time up to 31/01/2012.

If Angelina wants to amend the tax return after twelve months of the required filing date for that return, then she can make an "error or mistake" claim to recover any excess tax paid within six years of the end of the relevant accounting period.

Companies

The last date for amending a tax return will be within 12 months of the return filing date. For example for an accounting year ending on 31 March 2010, the filing date is 31 March 2011 and so the company can amend its return until 31 March 2012.

1.2 Correction of errors or omissions by HMRC

Where any errors or omissions in the return filed by the company are discovered by HMRC, then HMRC has the right to rectify such errors or omissions. HMRC can make such a rectification **within nine months of the date the return was filed** by the company. If the company itself notices an error and makes a rectification by filing an amended return, HMRC has 9 months from this date to make the rectification.

Example Tweety Ltd filed its return on 12 June 2009. Afterwards, it revised the return on 23 August 2009. Within what date can HMRC make any rectification to Tweety Ltd's return?

Continued on next page

HMRC has the right to rectify errors or omissions appearing in the return. It can make such a rectification within nine months of the date the return was filed / amended by the company. The return was amended by the company on 23 August 2009. The time limit for rectification of return by HMRC is **nine months** starting from 23 August 2009 i.e. 22nd May 2010.

1.3 Enquiry by HMRC

HMRC has an explicit right to enquire into the completeness and accuracy of any tax return. This right covers all enquiries, from straightforward requests for further information on individual items through to full reviews of a company's business including examination of the company's records.

For conducting such an enquiry, a written notice must be issued to the concerned company within a period of 12 months from the date that a corporation tax return is received by HMRC.

> **Tip**
> **Only one enquiry can be made in respect of any one return or amendment.**

Example Sun Ltd prepares its accounts to 31/03/2009. Sun Ltd filed its return on 12/01/2010. HMRC can open enquiry in Sun Ltd's return provided a written notice is issued to the company within a period of 12 months from the date that a corporation tax return is received by HMRC i.e. on or before 11/01/2011.

1.4 Time limit for an enquiry by HMRC

After the end of **twelve months** from the required filing date (date of receipt of return, for income tax return), no enquiry can be opened by HMRC. The tax return is usually regarded as finalised after the expiry of this twelve month period.

Example A company has filed its return for the period of twelve months ended 31 March 2009 on 02/10/2009. In this case, if no enquiry is opened by HMRC by 01/10/2010 then it cannot open an enquiry in the case of this return.

However, HMRC can make **Discovery Assessment** even after twelve months from the required filing date. This is discussed in 1.7 below.

1.5 Procedure for the enquiry

The HMRC may amend a self-assessment at any time during an enquiry if it is found that:
1. less tax is paid than required
2. no tax is paid at all
3. revenue of HMRC is lost in any other way

The company may appeal against such an amendment within **thirty days.**

1.6 Result of an enquiry

An enquiry ends when HMRC gives notice that the enquiry is complete. A company has to amend its self-assessment return within thirty days of receiving HMRC's conclusions. If HMRC is not satisfied with the amendments made by the company, it can amend the self-assessment within the next thirty days. The company then has another thirty days in which it may appeal against the HMRC amendments.

> **Example**
>
> Zigzag Ltd received a notice from HMRC of the completion of the enquiry on 12/06/2009. The tax assessed by HMRC as a result of the enquiry was £15,500. Zigzag Ltd has to file the amended return within a period of thirty days of receiving HMRC's conclusions i.e. on or before 12/07/2009 (30 days from 12/06/2009).
>
> If HMRC is not satisfied with the amendments made by the company, it can amend the self-assessment within the next thirty days i.e. on or before 11/08/2009 (30 days from 12/07/2009).
>
> If the company wants to appeal against the amendment made by HMRC in the company's return, such appeal can be made on or before 10/09/2009 (30 days from 11/08/2009).

1.7 Discovery assessment by HMRC

However, if after the expiry of twelve months from the required filing date, HMRC discovers that the company has been assessed to insufficient tax then it can raise a "**discovery assessment**". The time period for a discovery assessment can be raised **up to six** years after the end of the accounting period to which it relates. In other words, **no discovery assessment can be made later than six years after the expiry of accounting period to which it relates.** However, in the case of fraud or negligence on the part of the company or persons representing the company, this period is extended to **twenty years.**

> **Test Yourself 1**
>
> Zatac Ltd prepares its accounts up to 31/03/2009. Zee is the Director of Zatac Ltd. Zatac Ltd purchased a new office and let out the old office to another company for a monthly rent of £700. It was also decided that the tenant company would pay this £700 directly to Zee as directorial remuneration. Zatac Ltd ignored this income of £8,400 as it was given directly to the director, Zee. Zee in his personal return, disclosed this income from Zatac Ltd as director's remuneration.
>
> What actions can be taken by HMRC?

1.8 Determination of the tax amount by HMRC

If a company fails to file a tax return before the required filing date, HMRC may make a determination of the amount of tax due. Such determination can be displaced only if the company delivers the required return. There is no right of appeal against a determination.

1.9 Preservation of records by the company

A company is required to preserve all the records and accounts including contracts and receipts, on the basis of which a tax return is filed and other relevant records until **the latest of:**

1. six years after the end of the concerned accounting period
2. the date enquiries started by HMRC are completed
3. the date after which enquiries may not be commenced

HMRC do not usually insist on keeping original records. However, in the following cases, original records must be kept

a) Qualifying distributions and tax credits
b) Gross and net payments and tax deducted for payments made net of tax
c) Details of foreign tax paid

2. Explain the procedures for dealing with appeals and disputes.[1]

[Learning outcome b]

2.1 Appeals

1. **Appeal against decisions:** If a taxpayer is not satisfied with any of the decisions of HMRC, they can file an appeal against the decision. The main classes of appeals are:
a) Imposition of a penalty
b) Imposition of a surcharge
c) Appeal against the order requiring submission of records and documents.
d) Appeal against the amendment made to self assessment as a result of enquiry
e) Appeal against the existence of relevant grounds for making of discovery assessment
f) Appeal against a discovery assessment

Diagram 1: The order of authorities to whom the appeal can be made

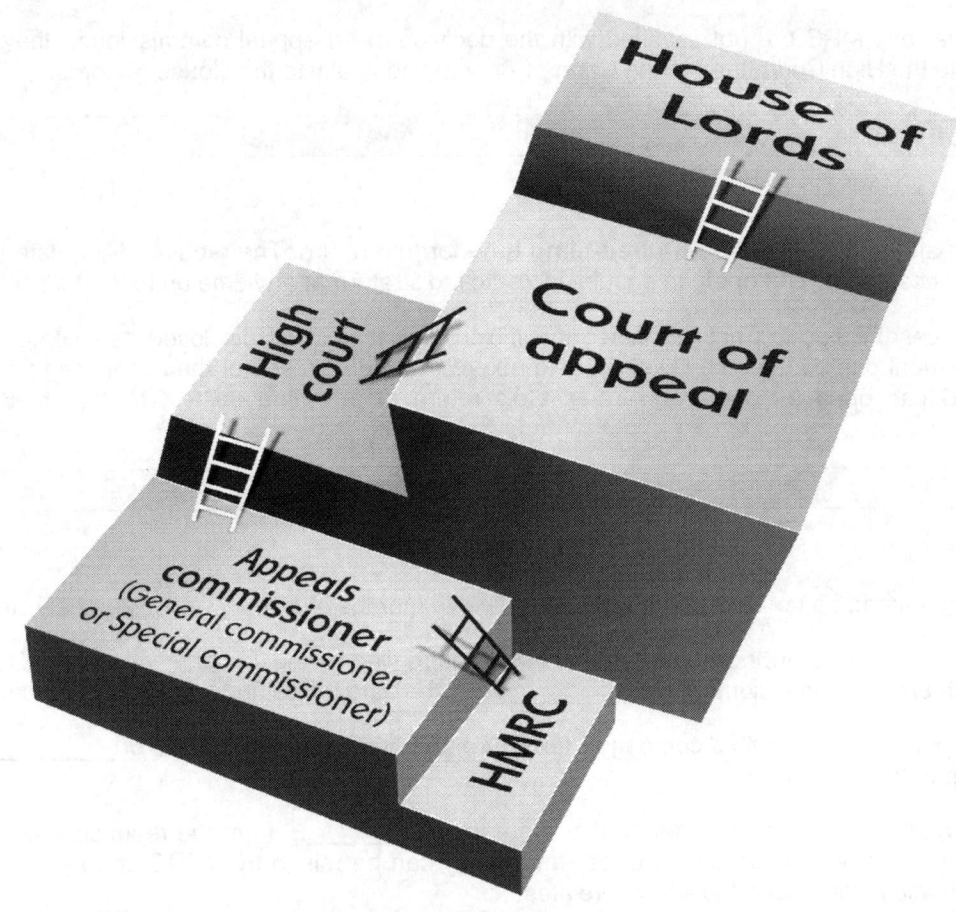

House of Lords
Court of appeal
High court
Appeals commissioner (General commissioner or Special commissioner)
HMRC

2. **Procedure of appeal:** The procedure is summarised below.

a) When any taxpayer wishes to appeal against an order issued by HMRC, he has to make the appeal in **writing** to HMRC within **thirty days** of the relevant HMRC decision.

b) A taxpayer may appeal for postponement of a tax payment, if the appeal is against the amount of tax assessed.

c) A taxpayer can be represented by his agent during the hearing of the appeal.

d) An appeal is settled by means of informal discussions between HMRC and the taxpayer or his agent.

e) If the parties to the appeal i.e. the taxpayer and HMRC cannot come to a settlement, the appeal is referred to an appeal commissioner.

f) Appeal commissioners fall into the following two categories:

Diagram 2: Categories of appeal commissioners

Categories of Appeal Commissioners
- General Commissioners
  - hear appeals locally
  - no formal qualification required
  - assisted by paid accountants or solicitors
- Special Commissioners
  - travel the country to hear appeals
  - similar to circuit judges
  - full-time tax professionals

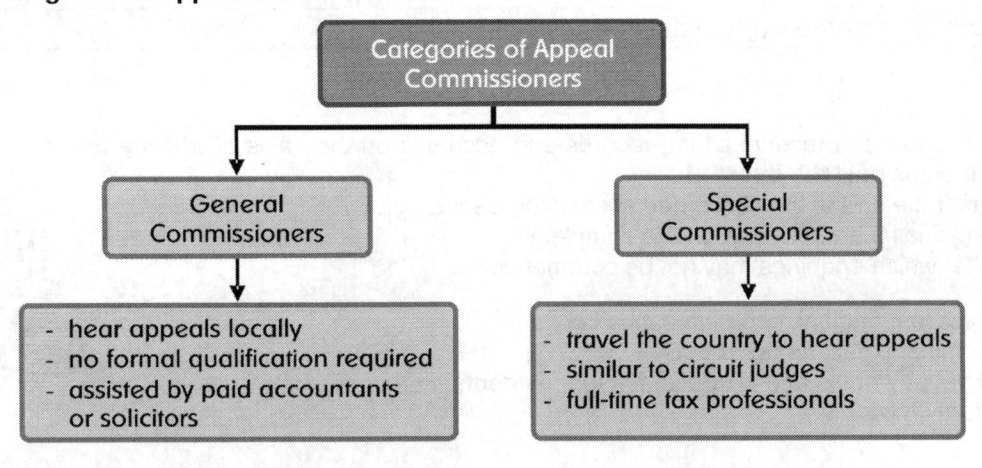

g) The appeal commissioners may **confirm, reduce or increase** a disputed assessment.

h) If the taxpayer or HMRC are not satisfied with the decision of an appeal commissioner, they may appeal further, first to the High Court, then to the Court of Appeal and finally to the House of Lords.

Answer to Test Yourself

Answer 1

HMRC can open an enquiry from the **required filing date** for that return. The required filing date for Zatac Ltd is 31/03/2010. Hence HMRC can open an enquiry in Zatac Ltd's return at any time up to 31/03/2011.

However, in this case, Zatac Ltd has assessed insufficient tax. It has not disclosed its income of £8,400. A discovery assessment can be raised by HMRC up to **six years after** the end of the accounting period to which it relates. HMRC can open an enquiry in Zatac Ltd's return at any time up to 31/03/2015 (6 years from 31/03/2009).

Quick Quiz

Fill in the blanks.

1. A company can amend a tax return filed by it within twelve months of the _____ for that return.

2. If any errors or omissions are noticed by HMRC in the return filed by the company, then HMRC has the right to rectify such errors or omissions within _____ from the date the return was filed by the company.

3. HMRC can open an enquiry into a company's tax return at any time before the end of _____ from the required filing date for that return.

4. No enquiry can be opened by the HMRC after the end of _____ from the required filing date, except in the case of a discovery assessment where an enquiry can be raised by HMRC up to _____ after the end of the accounting period to which it relates.

5. The appeal commissioners may confirm, _____ or increase a disputed assessment.

Answers to Quick Quiz

1. required filing date
2. nine months
3. one year
4. twelve months, six years
5. reduce

Self Examination Question

Question 1

For how long is a company required to preserve its records and accounts?

Answer to Self Examination Question

Answer 1

A company is required to preserve all the records and accounts on the basis of which a tax return is filed and other relevant records until **the latest of:**
1. six years after the end of the concerned accounting period
2. the date enquiries started by HMRC are completed
3. the date after which enquiries may not be commenced

In the following cases, original records must be kept
a) Qualifying distributions and tax credits
b) Gross and net payments and tax deducted for payments made net of tax
c) Details of foreign tax paid.

SECTION G: THE OBLIGATIONS OF TAX PAYERS AND / OR THEIR AGENTS

G4

STUDY GUIDE G4: PENALTIES FOR NON-COMPLIANCE

Get Through Intro

During the tax year (6 April one year to 5 April the next) there are key dates by which taxpayers need to send in their tax returns and/or make certain payments. It's important to be aware of these dates - HM Revenue & Customs (HMRC) imposes penalties and surcharges if they are missed.

In your career as a tax consultant, you will have to be very careful about following the rules. Your clients may suffer penalties if they miss any dates for filing returns or paying taxes or if they pay inadequate taxes.

This Study Guide explains the penalties a tax payer might have to pay for various faults.

Learning Outcomes

a) Calculate interest on overdue tax.
b) State the penalties that can be charged.

G4.2: The Obligations of Tax Payers and / or their Agents © GTG

Introduction

Case Study

Energetic Ltd is an oil refining and marketing company. John, the company tax accountant, assumed profits would remain constant and did not forecast the large increase in turnover due to the launch of a number of new petrol filling stations.

As a result Energetic Ltd's payments on account were grossly understated owing HMRC a considerable amount of tax.

In this Study Guide we shall see the way in which HMRC apply penalties by way of interest and surcharges on overdue payments.

1. Calculate interest on overdraft tax.[2]

[Learning outcome a]

1.1 Underpaid tax

A taxpayer has to pay interest on underpaid corporation tax for the period beginning **on the date** on which the tax **should have been** paid, up to the date on which it is **actually paid.**

> **Tip**
> For the June and December 2010 sitting, the assumed rate of interest on underpaid tax is 2.5%.

1.2 Overpaid tax

If a taxpayer has paid excess tax, HMRC pays interest to the taxpayer on the excess tax amount for the period beginning on the date on which the tax was paid, up to the date on which the excess tax is refunded to the taxpayer.

> **Tip**
> For the June and December 2010 sitting, there is no interest to be paid for overpaid tax any more.

Surcharge

Over and above the interest paid on the delay in payment of tax due, the tax payer is under an obligation to pay a "surcharge".

In other words, a surcharge is payable if tax is paid late.

Various rates at which the surcharge is charged are as follows:

	Rate of surcharge
1. **Balancing payment** remains unpaid **less than** 28 days after the due date	0%
2. **Balancing payment** remains unpaid **more than** 28 days after the due date	5%
3. **Self-assessment** is amended and additional amount becomes payable remains unpaid for **more than** 28 days after due date	5%
4. Amount remains unpaid for more than 6 months after the due date	Additional 5%

It is important to note that the rule relating to surcharge does not apply to late payments on accounts.

Example

The dates of payment made and to be made by McMilan are given. Calculate the amount of surcharge to be imposed wherever applicable.

Actual Date of Payment	Amount	Due Date of Payment	Amount
31/01/2009	15,000 (POA)	31/01/2009	15,000
01/09/2009	15,000 (POA)	31/07/2009	15,000

Answer

1. As first POA is paid in full and on time, no surcharge is imposed.
2. There is an exception to the surcharge rule that POAs do not attract surcharges even though the second POA is paid 32 days late.

Payment of Surcharge

Surcharge is payable within 30 days of the date on which it is imposed.

Test Yourself 1

A taxpayer completes a self-assessment for 2009-10 showing a total tax liability of £11,000. Payments on account are paid on time. The balancing payment due on 31 January 2010 is £3,750.

Required:

State the amount of surcharge if the balancing payment of tax was made on:

1. 28 February 2010
2. 31 August 2010

Tip

- If an **individual receives / pays interest to / from HMRC,** it is **not chargeable / deductible.** However, for companies, interest paid / received on underpaid / overpaid corporation tax is **dealt with under income from loan relationship** as interest paid / received on a **non-trading loan relationship.**
- **Rates** of interest / penalty are **same** for **individuals and companies**.

2. State the penalties that can be charged.[2]

[Learning outcome b]

Penalties are payable in addition to the interest. Penalties are charged if a company does not file its tax return, together with the supporting accounts and calculations, by the required date.

2.1 Penalty for failure to submit the return on time

Diagram 1: Penalty for failure to submit the return on time

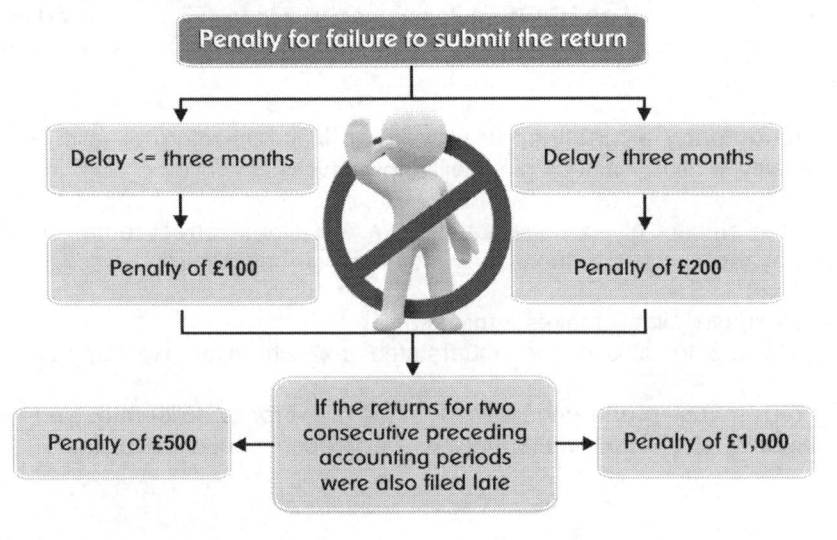

Penalty for failure to submit the return

- Delay <= three months → Penalty of £100
- Delay > three months → Penalty of £200

If the returns for two consecutive preceding accounting periods were also filed late:
- Penalty of £500 (from £100)
- Penalty of £1,000 (from £200)

G4.4: The Obligations of Tax Payers and / or their Agents © GTG

Example

Yoyo Ltd prepares its accounts for twelve months ended 31/03/2009. The due date for filing the tax return was 31/03/2010. Calculate the amount of penalty if Yoyo Ltd:

1. Files the return on 05/05/2010 and during the preceding two years the return was filed on time
2. Files the return on 12/06/2010 but the return was also filed late during the preceding two years
3. Files the return on 28/04/2010 but the return was also filed late during the preceding year
4. Files the return on 05/07/2010 and during the preceding two years, the return was filed on time
5. Files the return on 12/08/2010 but the return was also filed late during the preceding two years
6. Files the return on 28/09/2010 but the return was also filed late during the preceding year

Answer

	Date of filing return	Period of delay	Delay for preceding two years	Penalty £
1	05/05/2010	Less than three months	No	100
2	12/06/2010	Less than three months	Yes	500
3	28/04/2010	Less than three months	No	100
4	05/07/2010	More than three months	No	200
5	12/08/2010	More than three months	Yes	1,000
6	28/09/2010	More than three months	No	200

2.2 Additional penalty

In addition to the above penalty, a further tax-geared penalty is charged if one return is submitted more than six months late. This penalty is charged as a percentage of the amount of tax outstanding at the end of the six months as shown below:

Diagram: 2 Additional penalties for delay in filing returns

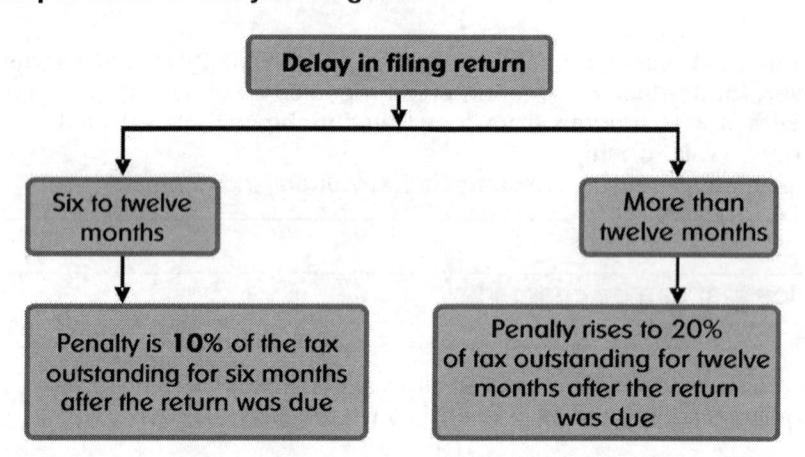

Delay in filing return
- Six to twelve months → Penalty is **10%** of the tax outstanding for six months after the return was due
- More than twelve months → Penalty rises to **20%** of tax outstanding for twelve months after the return was due

2.3 Other penalties

1. If the company **neither files a return, nor notifies HMRC** of its chargeability to tax within a period of twelve months from the end of an accounting period, a penalty of **100%** of the tax which remains unpaid may be charged.

2. If an individual or a company **fraudulently or negligently** submits an incorrect return or fails / delays to notify HMRC of a new taxable activity, a new penalty regime will apply which is as follows:

The amount of penalty is based on the amount of tax understated as a result of incorrect return or failure to notify HMRC, but the actual penalty payable is linked to the taxpayer's behaviour, as follows:

- There will be no penalty where a taxpayer simply makes a mistake.
- There will be a moderate penalty (up to 30% of the understated tax) where a taxpayer fails to take reasonable care.
- There will be a higher penalty (up to 70% of the understated tax) if the error is deliberate, and an even higher penalty (up to 100% of the understated tax) where there is also concealment of the error.

However a penalty will be substantially reduced where a taxpayer makes a disclosure, especially when it is an unprompted disclosure of an incorrect return following a failure to take reasonable care. In such cases, the penalty could be reduced to nil.

3. A failure to **preserve the necessary records** for the required period by the company may lead to a penalty of **£3,000**.

Answer to Test Yourself

Answer 1

1. If the balancing payment is made on 28 February 2010, the amount of surcharge will be:
   = (£3,750 @ 5%) = £187.5

2. If the balancing payment is made on 31 August 2010, a further surcharge of £187.50 is due again (£3,750 @ 5%).

Quick Quiz

Fill in the blanks.

1. Surcharge is payable within _____ days from the date on which it is imposed.

2. If a company **fraudulently or negligently** submits an incorrect return, a penalty amounting to **100%** of the _____ may be charged.

3. A surcharge is payable if tax is paid _____.

Answers to Quick Quiz

1. 30

2. tax lost

3. late

Self Examination Questions

Question 1

What is the penalty charged if the income tax self assessment return is submitted late?

Question 2

The corporation tax liability of Soho Ltd was £65,000 for the year ended 30 September 2009. It paid the tax on 30 September 2010. For what period will interest be due on the corporation tax?

Question 3

State the date from which interest due from HMRC will be incurred in the following cases:

1. Poppins Ltd paid corporation tax of £47,000 for the year ended 31 December 2009 on 1 August 2010. The actual liability came to £37,000.

2. Mangola Ltd paid corporation tax of £54,000 for the year ended 30 September 2009 on 1 August 2010. The liability was finally agreed as £45,000.

Answers to Self Examination Questions

Answer 1

If the delay in filing the return is up to three months, a fixed penalty of £100 is charged. The penalty increases to £200 if the return is more than three months late. In addition to this, a tax-geared penalty is charged at 10% of the tax outstanding if the return is more than six months late, or 20% if more than twelve months late.

Answer 2

Interest will be due for the period from the due date to the date the tax was actually paid i.e. from 1 July 2010 to 30 September 2010.

Answer 3

1. Interest will run from the **later of**:
a) due date: 1 October 2010 (9 months + 1 day after the end of the accounting period)
b) date tax actually paid: 1 August 2010

Hence, interest is due from 1 October 2010.

2. The interest will run from the **later of**:
a) due date: 1 July 2010 (9 months + 1 day after the end of the accounting period)
b) date the tax was actually paid: 1 August 2010.

Hence, interest is due from 1 August 2010.

INDEX

A

Accounting for VAT	F3.2
Accounting Period	D1.2
Accruals Basis	B4.2, D2.11
Acquisition cost	C2.4
Additional loss relief	B3.73
Allowable deductions	C2.4
Allowances on cessation	B3.53
Ancillary services connected with living accommodation	B2.20
Annual accounting scheme	F4.3
Annual allowance	B6.2
Annual exemption	C2.9
Annual investment allowance	B3.34, D4.2
Appeals	G3.4
Approved mileage allowances	B2.26
Asset damaged	C3.6
Asset lost / destroyed	C3.4
Assets loaned to employee for private use	B2.19
Associated company	D4.2
Availability of loss reliefs	B3.83
Average method	B2.18

B

Badges of trade	B3.3
Balancing adjustments	B3.44
Balancing allowances	B3.42
Balancing charges	B3.42
Balancing repayment	G2.5
Basis period	B3.15
Beneficial loans	B2.18
Benefits assessable on P11D employees	B2.21
Bonus issue	C5.8
Building Society interest	B4.8

C

Capital allowance for motor car	B3.41
Capital allowances	B2.24, B3.32, D2.6
Capital expenditure	B3.6
Capital gains	B6.10
Capital gains tax	C1.2, C2.9
Capital losses	C2.12
Car leasing and rental costs	B3.9
Cars provided for private use	B2.13
Cash accounting system	F4.2
Cash ISA	B4.10
Cessation of trade	B3.16
Change of accounting date	B3.18
Chargeability to tax	G1.2
Chargeable asset	C1.3
Chargeable disposal	C1.2
Chargeable person	C1.3
Chattel	C4.2
Choice of loss reliefs	D3.9
Class 1 NIC	E1.2
Class 1 primary	E1.3
Class 1 secondary	E1.5
Class 1A contributions	E1.3
Class 1A NIC	E1.6
Class 2 NIC	E2.2
Class 4 NIC	E2.3
Classic car	B2.14
CO_2 emissions rate	B3.39
Commencement of trade	B3.13
Connected person	C2.3
Continuing partners	B3.99
Corporation tax liability	D3.2
Correction of errors or omissions	G3.2

D

Depreciation	B3.6
Discovery assessment	G3.4
Dispensation	B2.33
Disposal consideration	C2.3
Disposal proceeds	C2.3
Dividend income	B4.9, B5.8
Donations	B3.7
Dormant company	D4.3
Double Tax Treaties	A3.4
Double taxation relief	D4.15
Due dates	G2.2

E

Earned income	B5.2
Earnings period	E1.3
Electronic return filing	G1.4
Employment	B2.2

Index

Employment income	B2.5	**L**	
Enhancement expenditure	C2.4	Large company	G2.8
Enquiry	G3.3	Lease premiums	B4.2
Entrepreneurs' relief	C6.2	Lease premiums	D2.9
Exempt assets	C1.3	Letting out furnished property	B4.3
Exempt chattels	C4.2	Letting relief	C4.11
		Lifetime allowance	B6.5
F		Limited Liability Partnerships	B3.101
Financial year	D1.3	List price	B2.14
First year allowance	B3.35	Living accommodation	B2.10
Flat rate scheme	F4.4	Loan relationship	D2.10
Franked investment income	D3.3	Long period of accounts	D3.5
Fuel provided for private use	B2.17	Long-life assets	B3.49
Full rate	D3.2	Loss relief claims available to partners	B3.101
Furnished holiday letting	B4.5	Low emission cars	B3.39
G		**M**	
General pool	B3.34	Marginal rate	D4.9
Gift aid donations	B5.11, D2.12	Marginal relief	D3.2
Gift aid payments	D4.16	Mark to market basis	D2.11
Gifts	B3.7	Market value	C2.3
Gilt-edged securities	C5.18	Married couple allowance	B6.8
Group relief	D4.6	Mileage allowance	B2.22
Group rollover relief	D4.13	Misdeclaration penalty	F3.20
H		**N**	
Historic test	F2.2	National insurance	E1.2
Holdover relief	C6.12	National Saving Certificates	B4.11
		Net income	B5.2
I		Non-savings income	B5.6
Incidental costs of acquisition	C2.4	Non-wasting chattel	C4.2
Incidental costs of disposal	C2.3	Notional transfer	D4.12
Income exempt from tax	B5.4		
Income taxed at source	B5.3	**O**	
Incorporation relief	C6.15	Operative event	C5.4
Indexation allowance	C2.6	Ordinary residence	C1.4
Indexation factor	C2.6	Overlap profits	B3.15
Individual Savings Account	B4.10	Overlap relief	B3.17
Industrial building	B3.54	Overpaid tax	G4.2
Industrial building allowances	B3.55	Overseas Branch	D4.13
Inheritance Tax	A2.3	Overseas Subsidiary	D4.14
Inter group dividends	D4.2		
Investment income	B5.2	**P**	
		P11D (higher paid) employees	B2.8
J		P9D (lower-paid) employees	B2.8
Jointly owned assets	B6.9	Part disposal	C3.3
		Partners joining	B3.99

Partners leaving	B3.99
Partnership	B3.96
PAYE	B2.28
PAYE Forms	B2.31
Payment of tax	G2.4
Payment on account	G2.5
Payroll deduction scheme	B2.22
Payroll giving scheme	B5.11
Penalties	B2.32
Penalties and fines	B3.8
Penalty	G4.3
Period of Account	D1.2
Personal Age Allowance	B5.4
Personal Allowance	B5.4
Personal pension scheme	B6.2
Plant and machinery	B3.32
PPR relief	C4.7
Pre-trading expenditure	B3.11, D2.5
Principal private residence	C4.7
Private use adjustments	D2.4
Private use assets	B3.45
Profit sharing ratio	B3.97
Profits chargeable to corporation tax	D2.2, 38
Property business loss	B4.7, D2.37
Property business profits	D2.8
Property income	B4.2
Provisions	B3.6

Q

Qualifying business assets	C6.6
Qualifying corporate bonds	C5.18
Qualifying expenditure	B3.54
Qualifying holiday accommodation	B4.5
Quoted shares	C5.2

R

Records	G2.10
Registered occupational pension	B2.22
Relief against capital gains	B3.75
Relief against future trading income	B3.67, D2.26
Relief against TI	B3.69
Relief against total profits	D2.29
Relief under s64	B3.72
Relief under s72	B3.78
Relief under s83	B3.68
Relief under Section 86	B3.84

Renewals basis	B4.3
Rent-a-room relief	B4.6
Residence	C1.4
Resident	B1.2
Revision of returns	G3.2
Rights issue	C5.10
Rollover relief	C6.5
Rollover relief	D3.9

S

Savings income	B4.8
Savings income	B5.6
Self assessment	B5.3
Share identification rules	C5.3
Short Lease	B4.3
Short life assets	B3.45
Short term lease premiums	B3.9
Small companies' rate	D3.2
Special rate pool	B3.49
Statute law	A3.3
Stocks and shares ISA	B4.10
Strict method	B2.18
Subscriptions	B3.7
Surcharge	G4.2

T

Takeovers and reorganisations	C5.14
Tax avoidance	A4.2
Tax code suffixes	B2.30
Tax codes	B2.29
Tax evasion	A4.2
Tax return	G1.3
Tax Tables	B2.30
Taxable gains	C2.9
Taxable income	B5.2
Taxable persons	B5.2, F1.4
Taxable supply	F1.3
Tax-adjusted trading profit	B3.5
Tax-exempt investments	B4.11
Terminal loss relief	B3.81, D2.33
Total Income	B5.2
Transfer Pricing	D4.16
Travel expenses	B2.22

U

UK tax system	A3.2
Underpaid tax	G4.2

Index

V

Vans provided for private use	B2.17
VAT assessments	F3.4
VAT invoices	F3.7
VAT payments on account	F3.3
VAT returns	F3.17
Vouchers exchangeable for goods or services	B2.10

W

Wasting asset	C4.2
Wasting chattel	C4.2
Wear and tear basis	B4.3
Wholly, exclusively and necessarily	B2.22
Withholding tax	D4.16
Writing down allowance	B3.36

Z

Zero-rated supplies	F1.6